The Life of Evelyn Waugh

BLACKWELL CRITICAL BIOGRAPHIES

General Editor: Claude Rawson

The Life of
EVELYN WAUGH

A Critical Biography

Douglas Lane Patey

BLACKWELL
Oxford UK & Cambridge USA

First published 1998

2 4 6 8 10 9 7 5 3 1

Blackwell Publishers Ltd
108 Cowley Road
Oxford OX4 1JF
UK

Blackwell Publishers Inc.
350 Main Street
Malden, Massachusetts 02148
USA

British Library Cataloguing in Publication Data
A CIP catalogue record for this book is available from the British Library.

Library of Congress Cataloging-in-Publication Data
Patey, Douglas Lane.
The life of Evelyn Waugh: a critical biography / Douglas Lane Patey. p.   cm.
(Blackwell critical biographies; 8)
Includes bibliographical references and index.
ISBN 0-631-18933-5 (acid-free paper)
1. Waugh, Evelyn, 1903–1966 — Biography.   2. Authors, English — 20th century–Biography. I. Title. II. Series.
PR6045.A9727494 1998
823'.912–dc21
[B]
97-15469
CIP
Typeset in 10 on 11 pt Baskerville
by Puretech India Limited, Pondicherry
Printed in Great Britain by TJ International, Padstow, Cornwall
This book is printed on acid-free paper

For Edith Patey

Contents

Chronology of Waugh's Works

Illustrations

Abbreviations

Works by Waugh

ALL	*A Little Learning: The First Volume of an Autobiography.* London: Chapman & Hall, 1964.
Apprentice	*Evelyn Waugh, Apprentice: The Early Writings, 1910–1927*, ed. Robert Murray Davis. Norman, OK: Pilgrim Books, 1985.
BM	*Black Mischief.* London: Chapman & Hall, 1932.
BR	*Brideshead Revisited: The Sacred and Profane Memories of Captain Charles Ryder.* London: Chapman & Hall, 1945.
BR2	Revised edn. London: Chapman & Hall, 1960.
BSRA	*Basil Seal Rides Again, or The Rake's Regress.* London: Chapman & Hall, 1963.
Compassion	'Compassion'. *The Month*, August 1949, 79–98.
D	*The Diaries of Evelyn Waugh*, ed. Michael Davies. London: Weidenfeld & Nicolson, 1976.
DC	*Mr. Wu and Mrs. Stitch: The Correspondence of Evelyn Waugh and Diana Cooper*, ed. Artemis Cooper. London: Hoddard & Stoughton, 1991.
DF	*Decline and Fall: An Illustrated Novelette.* London: Chapman & Hall, 1928.
EAR	*The Essays, Articles and Reviews of Evelyn Waugh*, ed. Donat Gallagher. London: Methuen, 1983.
EC	*Edmund Campion: Jesuit and Martyr.* London: Longman's, Green, 1935.
EC2	2nd edn. London: Hollis and Carter, 1947.
EC2a	2nd edn. Boston: Little, Brown, 1946.
GP	*The Ordeal of Gilbert Pinfold: A Conversation Piece.* London: Chapman & Hall, 1957.
H	*Helena.* London: Chapman & Hall, 1950.
HD	*A Handful of Dust.* London: Chapman & Hall, 1934.

HP   *The Holy Places.* London: Queen Anne Press, 1952.
K   *The Life of the Right Reverend Ronald Knox, Fellow of Trinity College, Oxford, and Pronotary Apostolic to His Holiness Pope Pius XII.* London: Chapman & Hall, 1959.
Labels   *Labels: A Mediterranean Journal.* London: Duckworth, 1930.
L   *The Letters of Evelyn Waugh,* ed. Mark Amory. London: Weidenfeld & Nicolson, 1980.
LO   *The Loved One: An Anglo-American Tragedy.* London: Chapman & Hall, 1948.
LAR   *Love Among the Ruins: A Romance of the Near Future.* London: Chapman & Hall, 1953.
MA   *Men At Arms.* London: Chapman & Hall, 1952.
MLLO   *Mr. Loveday's Little Outing and Other Sad Stories.* Boston: Little Brown, 1936.
NM   *The Letters of Nancy Mitford and Evelyn Waugh,* ed. Charlotte Mosley. Boston: Houghton Mifflin, 1997.
NTD   *Ninety-Two Days: The Account of a Tropical Journey Through British Guiana and Part of Brazil.* London: Duckworth, 1934; Harmondsworth: Penguin, 1985.
OG   *Officers and Gentlemen.* London: Chapman & Hall, 1955.
RP   *Remote People.* London: Duckworth, 1931.
POMF   *Put Out More Flags.* London: Chapman & Hall, 1942.
PRB   *P.R.B.: An Essay on the Pre-Raphaelite Brotherhood.* 1926; Westerham, Kent: Dalrymple Press, 1982.
R   *Rossetti: His Life and Works.* London: Duckworth, 1928.
Reynal   Preface to R. H. Benson, *Richard Reynal, Solitary.* Chicago: Regnery, 1956, vii–xvii.
RP   *Remote People.* London: Duckworth, 1931.
RUL   *Robbery Under Law: The Mexican Object-Lesson.* London: Chapman & Hall, 1939.
S   *Scoop: A Novel About Journalists.* London: Chapman & Hall, 1938.
SH   *Sword of Honour.* London: Chapman & Hall, 1966.
SK   *Scott-King's Modern Europe.* London: Chapman & Hall, 1947.
TA   *A Tourist in Africa.* London: Chapman & Hall, 1960.
TE   *Tactical Exercise.* Boston: Little, Brown, 1954.
'Tess'   'Tess, as a "Modern" Sees It'. *Evening Standard,* 17 Jan. 1930, 7.
US   *Unconditional Surrender.* London: Chapman & Hall, 1961.
VB   *Vile Bodies.* London: Chapman & Hall, 1930.
WA   *Waugh in Abyssinia.* London: Longmans, Green, 1936.
WGG   *When the Going Was Good.* Boston: Little, Brown, 1946.
WPW   *Wine in Peace and War.* London: Saccone & Speed, Ltd., 1947.
WS1   *Work Suspended.* London: Chapman & Hall, 1942.
WS   *Work Suspended and Other Stories Written Before the Second World War.* London: Chapman & Hall, 1948.

Other Abbreviations

BL	British Library
CH	*Evelyn Waugh: The Critical Heritage*, ed. Martin Stannard. London: Routledge, 1984.
EWN	*Evelyn Waugh Newsletter and Studies*
Face to Face	Interview with John Freeman, 'Face to Face' series, BBC TV, 26 June 1960.
HRC	Robert Murray Davis, *A Catalogue of the Evelyn Waugh Collection at the Humanities Research Center, The University of Texas at Austin*. Troy, NY: Whitston, 1981.
HRCT	Harry Ransom Humanities Research Center, University of Texas at Austin
HW	*Evelyn Waugh and his World*, ed. Alan Pryce-Jones. Boston: Little, Brown, 1973.
LAF	*The Letters of Ann Fleming*, ed. Mark Amory. London: Collins, 1985.
Lecture	'Waugh Lecture: Noted British Wit Discusses Three Fellow Convert Writers, Chesterton, Knox and Greene'. *Books on Trial*, 7 (April 1949), 277–8.
MGM	Jeffrey Heath, '*Brideshead*: The Critics and the Memorandum', *English Studies*, 56 (1975), 222–30.
ND	*Night and Day*, ed. Christopher Hawtree. London: Chatto & Windus, 1985.
RC	'Evelyn Waugh: Letters (and Post-cards) to Randolph Churchill'. *Encounter*, July 1968, 3–19.
ST1	Martin Stannard, *Evelyn Waugh: The Early Years, 1903–1939*. London: Dent, 1986.
ST2	Martin Stannard, *Evelyn Waugh: No Abiding City, 1939–1966*. London: Dent, 1992.
WM	Christopher Sykes, 'Evelyn Waugh – The Man.' In Derwent May, ed., *Good Talk: An Anthology from BBC Radio*. New York: Taplinger, 1969, 11–34.

Preface

Nearly a hundred years have passed since Evelyn Waugh was born, thirty since his death. A generation is not long enough to produce consensus in the evaluation of any writer, least of all one so celebrated (as the finest satirist, stylist, and historical novelist of his century) and so reviled (mainly for his strong conservative stands and because his gifts permitted him so successfully to savage and deflate the objects of his ridicule). But it is long enough that readers may find themselves strangers in the writer's world. Because they engage actuality in such detail, satire and historical fiction require unusually thorough contextualization in order to be understood. A generation is also long enough that, with the passing of a world, open-minded readers may find themselves concerned to understand even Waugh's famously rebarbative personality historically, in light of the shape of his life and achievement.

Waugh's first biographers, Frederick Stopp (1958) and Christopher Sykes (1975), wrote of a friend – from within a world of social, political and religious attitudes still so familiar as not to require much elaboration. A fine critic, Stopp knew little more of Waugh's life than he learned from the subject himself; Sykes, an older and more jaundiced friend, produced a readable narrative whose errors of fact and emphasis have taken twenty years to correct. Many of these corrections have been the work of Martin Stannard, to whose two-volume life (1986, 1992) all students of Waugh must be indebted. But despite his thoroughness, Stannard's standpoint is often so alien and unsympathetic to Waugh as to render his subject's values and habits of mind nearly opaque.[1] Sykes remains a more reliable guide than Stannard to the ethos of pre-Vatican II Catholicism that underpinned Waugh's politics and spiritual life, and only from Stopp does one learn of his enduring concern with the nature and theology of love – one of Waugh's constant themes, and, in *Brideshead Revisited*, the source of a masterpiece.

Readers will find here few previously unpublished letters, few new identifications of the 'models' for Waugh's characters. What I have attempted instead is to reconstruct mainly from published sources some of the ideological and social matrix in which Waugh's own character was formed, and, within that matrix, his sense of his own life as possessed of a meaningful shape. All Waugh's writing explores the possibility of finding some ground of meaning and value in experience; to an unusual extent, he shaped even his own personality into a provocation and a protest – a provocative advertisement for the coherence of character and principle he thought his contemporaries ignored.

This book owes most to those most thoughtful of Waugh's readers, Donat Gallagher and George McCartney. Selina Hastings's fine biography (1994), the most satisfactory guide to date to the details of Waugh's life, appeared while this book was being written; I have made full use of her new findings, especially about the collapse of his first marriage. John Howard Wilson's Freudian exploration of Waugh's childhood and youth, *Evelyn Waugh: A Literary Biography, 1903–1924* (1996) – the first of three promised volumes – appeared too late for either use or cavil. Unlike these writers, I have given equal attention to Waugh's varied and voluminous non-fiction – his works of biography, travel, and political journalism – and to his novels. I have sought to convey an understanding of both as expressions of a profound and often moving engagement with some of the most important and disturbing developments of his troubled century.

1

Becoming Modern (1903–1930)

I was driven into writing because it was the only way a lazy and ill-educated man could make a decent living.... Of course, in my case, writing happens to be the family business; that takes away some of the glamour.... My brother took to the trade without a moment's reluctance.... I held out until I was 24, swimming manfully against the tide; then I was sucked under. I tried everything I could think of first.

'General Conversation: Myself' (1937)

Of course the contemplative's ideal is what we must all come to before we reach heaven, and of course if one can it is convenient to stop wasting time and get through as much as possible of purgation here. But don't you think most souls are of slow growth? It is not the most precocious child whom the parent loves most. Is there not a slight hint of bustle and salesmanship about the way you want to scoop us all into a higher grade than we are fit for?

Letter to Thomas Merton, 28 August 1949[1]

Though from the time he went up to Oxford Evelyn Waugh learned to prefer faster, smarter, and more worldly company than he knew at home, and so escaped his parents' world as quickly as he could, he never denied or sought to exaggerate his background. Nor despite the myriad accusations of snobbery that would be directed against him – and much posturing on Waugh's part contrived to invite such accusations – did he ever seek to mask that his income derived entirely from what he liked to call the 'family business'. 'I know what you mean about purple patches', he wrote to a much richer novelist friend in 1929. 'My new book is black with them – but then I live by my pen as they say and you don't' (L 37). When in the 1930s he regularized the family coat of arms with the College of Heralds, he had it carved in stone on the front of his house along with the motto *Industria Ditat* (Hard Work Pays).

Yet Waugh also liked to say that he was long in deciding that the family business was for him. Born into an exceptionally literary household, he began writing early, often in conscious competition with his older brother Alec.[2] But as a teenager seeking an identity of his own, different from that of his critic father and novelist brother, Waugh set himself to become an artist. At school he made extra money designing book-jackets; at Oxford he attended the Ruskin School of Art, published drawings in university magazines, and was better known among friends as a draughtsman than a writer. He stayed three years at Oxford only because his father thought this a better course than leaving to study painting in Paris. 'I never imagined myself a Titian or a Velasquez. My ambition was to draw, decorate, design and illuminate' (ALL 190). His first significant publications treated painting and art theory. After Oxford, Waugh became, like many friends uncertain of their careers, a schoolmaster; he began an apprenticeship in printing; he applied for a job as an announcer with the BBC, and tried his hand as a newspaper reporter; for a few months he studied cabinetmaking. (His mother regretted his giving up this last choice. Reminded by his brother of Evelyn's literary accomplishment, she replied 'I know, Alec dear, I know; but furniture is so useful; besides he would have been happier designing furniture.')[3]

Only when these other avenues failed did Waugh commit himself to the business of writing. 'I wanted to be a man of the world and I took to writing as I might have taken to archaeology or diplomacy or any other profession as a means of coming to terms with the world' (EAR 302). At twenty-three, having lost one job (as a schoolteacher) and having been told he was unsuited for another ('being a parson'), he reflected: 'It seems to me the time has arrived to set about being a man of letters' (D 281). The first fruits of this resolution were the pamphlet *P.R.B.* (1926), followed by *Rossetti* and *Decline and Fall* (both 1928); by 1940, he had published a dozen books and established himself among Britain's best known authors. But through the thirties he continued to express uncertainty whether his path lay in writing or some other, more active way of life, and toyed with ideas of entering other professions – politician, spy, scholar.

World War II put an end to such uncertainty. Just before VE Day in 1945, Waugh reflected how the War had changed him:

> It is pleasant to end the war in plain clothes, writing. I remember at the start of it all writing to Frank Pakenham [a friend since the 1920s, later Earl of Longford] that its value for us would be to show us finally that we were not men of action. I took longer than him to learn it. I regard the greatest danger I went through that of becoming one of Churchill's young men, of getting a medal and standing for Parliament; if things had gone, as then seemed right, in the first two years, that is what I should be now.

> (D 627)

The book he was then beginning was *Helena* (1950), a saint's life and story of vocation which was to remain in his own view (if not that of many critics) his best. This novel – rich in its evocation of the Feast of the Epiphany, personally significant to Waugh as the feast of artists and of latecomers to the faith – was important to him partly because it was the first product of a newfound certainty that writing was not only his career, but, in a full religious sense, his vocation. Two decades later he recorded this certainty in the words he chose for his epitaph: 'Evelyn Waugh, Writer'.

Waugh was twenty-four when he published *Decline and Fall* – hardly a late age to 'set about being a man of letters'. His frequent remarks on the lateness of his choice were meant to evoke associations with a religious tradition of latecomers including St Paul, Augustine, and Newman. But he was early in sensing a need to choose, to define his life in terms of its own progression and its place in larger patterns of community and history.

Waugh's early expressions of uncertainty reflect a young man's puzzlement about how to make his way in the world; more than this, they are early instances of a lifelong thirst for pattern. He always needed to find some meaningful shape in the narrative of his life: some intelligible design, rather than simply a series in which each event is (as Margot says in *Decline and Fall*) 'simply something that's going to happen'. From childhood he possessed an acute sense of life's stages, of the kinds of behaviour appropriate to each, and of larger cyclic patterns of return into which such stages fit. In his diaries (which Waugh had elaborately bound and often reread), religious holidays, personal anniversaries, and changes of season spur outpourings of memory, stock-taking, and musings about his own development. The events of his novels characteristically take on meaning from their place within larger patterns of change and return – a cyclic year in *Decline and Fall*, the transition from dry season to rainy in *Black Mischief*, from rainy to dry in *Scoop*, the four seasons in *Put Out More Flags*, and, beginning with *Vile Bodies*, the liturgical calendar, that most shapely of narratives which is the Christian year.

'The Waugh of before *Brideshead Revisited* seldom wrote about himself; the Waugh of after *Brideshead* seldom writes about anything else', complained Conor Cruise O'Brien with characteristic inaccuracy in a sour review of *Gilbert Pinfold* (CH 381). It would be more accurate to say with Stephen Spender that he always wrote 'disguised spiritual autobiography' (*Creative Element* 162). Though Waugh insisted that the artist 'is not the subject of his art' and complained often of that 'universal nuisance among the unimaginative', 'keys to explain who everyone was', a large public enjoyed the game of identifying the real life 'models' on whom he based his characters.[4] Friends recognized both his private jokes and use of fiction as a vehicle for self-exploration, and looked especially to those novels which began with warning-labels to the contrary – *Decline and Fall, Vile Bodies, Put Out More Flags, Brideshead, The Loved One, Officers and Gentlemen* – for more or less oblique reflections on his own experience. Even before the creation of Charles Ryder or Guy Crouchback (both born, like their author, in October 1903), many of Waugh's protagonists are precisely his own age; some share, in precise detail, his own literary background; nearly all confront what he understood as his own choices and struggles. The habit was in place even before *Rossetti*; in *Sword of Honour*, as Waugh said of Anthony Powell's *Dance to the Music of Time*, 'the experiences of half a lifetime have been fully digested and transfigured'.[5]

I

The choice of authorship might have seemed obvious for Evelyn Waugh from the first. Prudent Catherine Raban and Arthur Waugh, though they had known each other since their teens, waited to marry until 1893, when Arthur was twenty-seven and his income seemed secure. Both were gentlefolk, descended of generations of doctors, lawyers, soldiers, and clergy. With the help of his distant cousin Edmund Gosse, Arthur Waugh had launched a career as a 'man of letters' – that professional identity whose demise in later decades his son Evelyn was often to mourn, as the gifted amateur (trained not in 'English' but classics or history) came to be displaced by 'state-trained literary critics'. A life of Tennyson published shortly after the poet's death in 1892 brought Arthur modest reputation; journalistic writing gained on the strength of that book brought a suitable income. An essay entitled 'Reticence in Literature' for the first number of the *Yellow Book* (1894), widely considered an island of health in that otherwise sickly collection, secured his position further, and so in 1898 a first child, Alec, was born. Without giving up writing, in 1896 Arthur Waugh traded dependence on freelance work for a regular income by taking a job with Kegan Paul; in 1902 he became managing director of Chapman and Hall, publishers of Thackeray, Trollope, and Dickens. The firm prospered under his leadership, and a second and last child, Arthur Evelyn St John Waugh, known in the family as Evelyn, was born in the fast-growing suburbs around Hampstead on 28 October 1903. In 1907 a small legacy permitted Arthur to build a house, named Underhill, in the still rural village of North End (shortly to be swallowed up by Golders Green).

If writing was the family trade, it was also (along with cricket, at which only their father's favourite Alec excelled) a valued family recreation. In his autobiography, *A Little Learning* (1964), Waugh gives eloquent testimony to his pleasure as a boy in listening to his father's dramatic readings from Shakespeare and a great range of nineteenth-century literature – experience that informed his precocious stylistic mastery and ability to deploy, seemingly without effort, a remarkable range of literary reference.

> In these recitations of English prose and verse the incomparable variety of English vocabulary, the cadences and rhythms of the language, saturated my young mind, so that I never thought of English Literature as a school subject, as a matter for analysis and historical arrangement, but as a source of natural joy. It was a legacy that has not depreciated.
>
> (ALL 72)

Next to *A Little Learning*, our most substantial record of Waugh's uneventful Edwardian childhood is the diary he began to write at the age of seven and continued, off and on, for the rest of his life. A self-proclaimed 'novel' called 'The Curse of the Horse Race' survives from when he was six. He first appeared in print at the age of twelve, when a pleased father had *The Life to Come*, a laboured poetic vision of purgatory in three cantos, privately printed to give to friends. Two years later, in 1917, the journal *Drawing and Design* published a short essay 'In Defence of Cubism,' the product of visits to galleries with his future sister-in-law Barbara Jacobs, who shared the young Evelyn's admiration for Post-Impressionism and the Futurists, for everything 'modern.' The two studied Filippo Marinetti's *Futurist Manifesto* (knowledge later put to use in *Vile Bodies*) and produced their own versions of cubist paintings on the walls of the Underhill day-nursery, renamed the 'studio'.

'I see before Cubism a glorious future', proclaimed the fourteen-year-old, having competently defended new trends in painting that only a few years later he would deplore as 'tumultuous aesthetic heresies' which has come from the Continent to destroy all that previous generations had 'understood by art'.[6] The essay seems a remarkable effort until it is compared with Clive Bell's modernist manifesto *Art* (1914), from which Waugh borrows his denigration of Victorian narrative painting (later his favourite style), the epigram that 'the resemblance to life does not in the least concern the merits of the picture', and much else. Though he would soon reverse all the evaluative judgments of this early essay, Waugh remained fascinated by its theoretical terms – by the nature of visual form and representation – for the rest of his life. *Rossetti* mounts a sustained argument against Bell and Roger Fry; in *Brideshead Revisited*, Bell's *Art* is quoted and rejected; in *Helena*, the emperor Constantine excoriates the fourth-century Roman equivalent of abstract design.

Waugh lived at home until 1917, going as a day boy to nearby Heath Mount, where he founded *The Cynic*, a rival to the official school magazine, and bullied the young Cecil Beaton (as Waugh recalled with pleasure, and Beaton with pain, to the end of their lives). He would subsequently have followed his father and brother to school at Sherborne. But two years earlier Alec had been made to leave because of a homosexual escapade among the boys, and instead of keeping quiet wrote an autobiographical novel that when it appeared in 1917 became a notorious best-seller. *The Loom of Youth* launched both Alec's career and a new kind of school novel, but hardly commended further Waughs to the authorities at Sherborne. (From *Tom Brown's Schooldays* onward, school novels had celebrated the friendships, sport, and discipline that formed boys into responsible men; with *The Loom of Youth*, 'the age of Almamatricide had begun' (Annan 47), when schoolboy victim-heroes would be deformed by, or at best manage to outwit, hidebound and hypocritical authority.)

Entry to Sherborne barred, Arthur Waugh sent his second son to Lancing College, 'a small public school of ecclesiastical temper on the South Downs' (as Paul Pennyfeather's school is described in *Decline and Fall*), a choice largely determined by the young Evelyn's lively High Anglican piety. 'I was, when I went to Lancing, if not genuinely devout, a particularly church-loving boy. I had aspirations to becoming a parson' (ALL 141). Here Lancing notably failed. The diary for 13 June 1921 records: 'In the last few weeks I have ceased to be a Christian (sensation off!) I have realized that for the last two terms at least I have been an atheist in all except the courage to admit it to myself.' The next sentence adds, 'I am sure it is only a phase' (D 127).

Bespectacled, ungainly, and small (he never grew beyond 5' 5"); ashamed of what he thought his stubby, inartistic hands; only moderate at games; and slow to find the successful public persona of what his friend Dudley Carew called 'the

1 Evelyn Waugh at Lancing College (Private Collection).

licensed, the over-licensed, jester' (*Fragment*, 9–10), Waugh was, predictably, often unhappy at Lancing, especially in his first years. (He had come a term later than most boys, and a rule that boys associate only with those in their 'class' meant that at first he had only one friend.) The diaries are filled with studiously self-pitying gestures: 'I do wish I could get a little taller'; 'I seem to miss everything by just a hair's breadth, first my House colours and now this [library privileges]. I expect when I die, I shall miss getting into heaven by one place and the golden gates will clang in my face'; 'Most depressed as usual'; 'I think a lot about suicide' (D 77, 21, 145, 131).

Such gestures do not of course tell the whole story. Waugh came to see his early diaries as 'replete with affectation' (ALL 141), and was aware of how easily the young can cast themselves as persecuted victims. 'Throughout early adolescence, one is apt to give way to the sort of pessimism which ascribes the incongruities of life to malignancy in some higher power' (*'Tess'*). In addition to boredom and 'black moods', the Lancing diaries tell as well of successes – editor of the *Lancing College Magazine*, president of the Debating Society, a prize essay on Alexander Pope – and of elaborate rags. With friends he founded modestly rebellious new clubs: the Dilettanti, for drawing and discussions of art theory; and the Corpse Club, 'for those who were weary of life' (i.e. bored stiff), whose members wore black insignia and wrote to one another on mourning paper. Waugh held the office of Undertaker, inducting new members with the formula: 'The Undertaker finds a mournful pleasure in announcing the interment of the late...'. The lonely 'I' of the earliest school diaries becomes 'we'. Dudley Carew, schoolboy disciple and would-be Boswell of a young Waugh already sure of his own 'genius' and ambitious for distinction, tells in his gushing memoir of these years of a teenager 'bursting with ideas and enthusiasms', generosity and infectious laughter – someone whose 'rudeness and apparent intolerance were, in reality, invitations to a game' (*Fragment* 7, 22).

The Lancing diaries are most interesting not as records of daily activities but for the drama played out in their pages of an adolescent's efforts at self-fashioning, at crafting a public identity and private sense of self that, given the acute sense of 'period' Waugh inevitably shared with many growing up in the years surrounding World War I, were appropriately 'modern'. At home, Waugh had strongly felt the years that separated him, in temperament as well as age, from his father. 'I never saw him as anything but old, indeed as decrepit' (ALL 63). Cut off also by five years' difference in age from Alec, who confessed to seeing Evelyn when young as 'no more than an encumbrance in a corner', he very early came to generalize family strains into a sometimes rebellious assertion of generational difference.[7]

Then came the War, in which Alec fought and at Passchendaele was taken prisoner, but for which Evelyn, still at school, was too young. Like many of his contemporaries, too young to fight and sharply aware of changes in day-to-day life brought on by the War, he developed very early what in *The Doom of Youth* (1932) Wyndham Lewis called 'youngergenerationconsciousness' (98). 'During the last few years, a new generation has grown up', he declared, aged eighteen, in an editorial for the school newspaper on 'The Youngest Generation'; 'between them and the young men of 1912 lies the great gulf of the war' (EAR 11). The Lancing diaries are full of musings about 'our generation':

> I wonder if we are really going to produce any great men or if we will fizzle into mediocrity. We certainly are precocious if that is at all a good sign.
>
> (D 27)

> What a ridiculous generation we are. In the last generation people never began to think until they were about nineteen, to say nothing of thinking about publishing books and pictures. Time can only show if we are going to be any better for it.
>
> (D 29)

The more I see of Lancing the more convinced I become of the fact that our generation...was a very exceptional one. One day I must try and work out the many influences which contributed to this. I think that if I do I shall find that the war is directly responsible for most of us.

(D 112)

In the late 1920s Waugh would exploit this theme in complex ways; earlier in the decade, he was more concerned to embody as fully as possible his generation's 'modern' character. This effort often took the form of shocking his elders – by advertising a taste for the most avant-garde art and the poetry of T. S. Eliot, or by ragging instructors in the training corps.[8] In 1920, Waugh joined a debate at Lancing, opposing the motion that 'This House deplores the disrespect for age by modern youth' (and was so pleased with his remarks as to transcribe them into his diary (D 102–3). One school report included the warning, 'He must learn to "approve those things that are excellent", not merely those that are ultra-modern' (ALL 117). Much of the 'affectation' in the diaries stems from an effort to construct a voice to capture this modern identity: many of the voices of the subsequent fiction are found germinating here. By turns he practices speaking as fastidious connoisseur, put-upon naïf, unshockable insouciant, sententious conservative, sententious 'bolshevik,' and, especially, bored and world-weary cosmopolitan. His father noticed that the 'distinguishing foible' of Lancing schoolboys was 'a premature assumption of the modern undergraduate pose of boredom'; Waugh himself, reading over these diaries years later, confessed 'I absurdly thought cynicism and malice the marks of maturity.'[9]

In his last years there Waugh encountered the 'two mentors', as he calls them in *A Little Learning*, who were to have the deepest influence on him of any at Lancing: Francis Crease and J. F. Roxburgh. In what became a lifelong habit of mental bifurcation, these two seemed to present alternative choices of life. Starting in January 1920, Waugh studied calligraphy and manuscript illumination with the shy, quiet, 'mystical' Crease, walking each Thursday afternoon across the downs to Crease's rooms at Lychpole Farm, where instead of games he could discuss aesthetics. Soon after, he began to study with Roxburgh, an elegant and forceful teacher of French and classics recently back from the front. Waugh made Roxburgh's fastidious 'precision of grammar and contempt of cliché' (ALL 159) his own; he never forgot a letter of congratulation Roxburgh once sent him: 'If you use what the Gods have given you, you will do as much as anyone I know to shape the course of your generation' (D 144).

A sense of the alternatives presented by Crease and Roxburgh – a quietly retired life devoted to art, or one of energetic public 'panache' – colours the rest of Waugh's life and fiction. In a late interview Waugh said he had 'always wanted to be a man of action – soldiering, exploring, being a carpenter or making things'; meanwhile he also claimed always to have considered himself an 'aesthete', always to 'have sought dark and musty seclusion, like an animal preparing to whelp'.[10] Only after World War II did he find a way to be what he called a 'national figure' yet live in privacy. He would capture (and enact) this composite stance most remarkably in *The Ordeal of Gilbert Pinfold*, at once autobiography and novel, which purports to give the world an intimate portrait of Evelyn Waugh as Gilbert Pinfold, famous but fiercely private author resident at the 'secluded village' of Lychpole (named in memory of Crease).

II

In 1922, having won a scholarship in modern history, Waugh went up to Hertford College, Oxford, where after a quiet first year he collected a celebrated circle of friends and enjoyed the life of colourful dissipation, lovingly recalled in *Brideshead Revisited* and *A Little Learning*, which would make him a legend among undergraduates. In his autobiographical poem *Summoned by Bells*, John Betjeman described this Oxford: 'No wonder, looking back, I never worked'; 'life was luncheons, luncheons all the way' (81). Not rich enough to sponsor many such luncheons himself, Waugh invited friends to meals of beer and cheese, occasions he called 'offal'. He gained notoriety as illustrator and reviewer for student magazines; for his clothes (already something of a dandy at Lancing, at Oxford he sported sea-green plus-fours and tight-fitting blue tweeds); for owning a revolver, supposedly much in demand by suicidal friends; and for raucous and outrageous jokes, especially when drunk. 'Do let me most seriously advise you to take to drink', he wrote to Tom Driberg back at Lancing. 'There is nothing like the aesthetic pleasure of being drunk and if you do it the right way you can avoid being ill the next day. That is the greatest thing Oxford has to teach' (L 10). A willing pupil, Waugh began at Oxford a lifetime of drinking that came to dominate his social life, undermined his health, and contributed to his early death at sixty-two.

Serious study of history was never his plan. 'From the first I regarded Oxford as a place to be enjoyed for itself, not as the preparation for something else' (ALL 171). Such an attitude guaranteed that Waugh would ultimately leave without a degree, and so resoundingly did it cause him to fall out with his tutor, the decorated veteran and distinguished historian C. R. M. F. Cruttwell, that the two came barely to speak. Waugh took revenge by spreading rumors of his tutor's bestiality; with his friends Terence Greenidge and Christopher Hollis, he erected a stuffed dog under Cruttwell's windows, hid, and made barking noises, explaining that he hoped to lure out the don and catch him *in flagrante*. After Waugh left Oxford in 1924, Cruttwell remained an irritant, scotching his candidacy for at least one teaching job and later helping to convince a potential mother-in-law of his unsuitability for her daughter.[11] Waugh got the last word by making 'Cruttwell' an obnoxious minor character in each of his first five novels and the homicidal hero of his story 'Mr. Cruttwell's [later changed to Mr. Loveday's] Little Outing'. (The real Cruttwell ended his life in an insane asylum.)[12]

'The record of my life [at Oxford] is essentially a catalogue of friendships' (ALL 190). In his first term Waugh met Greenidge, who shared his fascination with the new art-form of cinema, and through him the conservative Catholic Douglas Woodruff, scouting for like-minded Union debaters, and a whole 'circle of Chestertonian friends', 'Christopher Hollis and other robust wits already steering for Rome' (Acton, *Memoirs*, 126). Greenidge also introduced Waugh to the Hypocrites Club, described in *A Little Learning*:

The President was Elmley [William Lygon], now Earl Beauchamp. . . . it was, at the
time I joined, in process of invasion and occupation by a group of wanton Etonians
who brought it to speedy dissolution. It then became notorious not only for
drunkenness but for flamboyance of dress and manner which was in some cases
patently homosexual. Elmley ordained that: 'Gentlemen may prance but not
dance', but his rule was not observed. . . . It was the stamping ground of half my
Oxford life, and the source of friendships still warm today.

(ALL 179–81)

Among the Hypocrites were the rich, flamboyantly homosexual, socially ambi-
tious Brian Howard, 'a dazzling young man to my innocent eyes' (L 506); Robert
Byron, future travel-writer, who liked to dress up as Queen Victoria; John Sutro,
founder of the Railway Club; hard-drinking Alfred and Hubert Duggan, sons of
Lady Curzon; the handsome actor Tony Bushell; Peter Rodd, model for the
Basil Seal of *Black Mischief* and *Put Out More Flags*; and Harold Acton, to whom
Decline and Fall would be dedicated.

A year younger than Waugh, Acton brought to Oxford a much more fully
formed knowledge of the arts and commitment to modernism. His father had
been a buyer of furniture and decorations for the American architect Stanford
White until marriage to a cultivated Chicago heiress allowed him to retire to
Italy. Harold was brought up at the villa complex of La Pietra outside Florence,
among the paintings, statuary, and furniture his parents collected (all of which
Acton left upon his death in 1994 to New York University). While growing up
Acton met and became the acolyte of the Sitwells, Gertrude Stein, Ronald
Firbank, Cocteau, Diaghilev, Bakst and Stravinsky At Eton he founded with
Brian Howard a 'Society of the Arts' and in 1922 launched the *Eton Candle*. This
magazine – printed in gold ink on pink paper – lasted for only one issue, but its
editors had become well enough known that it was reviewed in the *Times Literary
Supplement* and led an to offer from Duckworth for Acton's first, assertively
modern book of poems, *Aquarium* (1924), published while he was still an undergraduate.

At Oxford Acton established himself as what he liked to call an 'aesthetic
hearty' – an aesthete, but not in the 1890s manner. 'I painted my rooms lemon
yellow and filled them with Victorian bric-à-brac' (not souvenirs of the decadent
nineties, but early Victorian objects like waxed fruit under glass domes) (*Memoirs*
118). He delivered papers on the Victorian painters Augustus Egg, William
Frith, and William Etty, then at the nadir of their reputation. Acton's knowledge,
proselytizing zeal, and idiosyncratic dress – he invented the broad, brightly
coloured pleated trousers later known as 'Oxford bags' – made him the conspicuously central figure in modernist taste in the university; at his invitation,
Edith Sitwell and Gertrude Stein came to lecture. Waugh first met him at a talk
given by G. K. Chesterton to the Newman Society and the two were soon
'inseparable boon companions'; when Acton again founded a magazine, the
Oxford Broom (printed on tangerine-coloured paper and named for its aim of
sweeping away the out-of-date), Waugh contributed the cover design and a
mannered, macabre story, 'Antony, Who Sought Things that Were Lost'.[13]

THE SEVEN DEADLY SINS
No. 2

The horrid sacrilege of those that
illtreat books

2 From a series on 'The Seven Deadly Sins' in the *Cherwell*, Oxford University (1923) that included: 'The intolerable wickedness of him who drinks alone'; 'The horrid sacrilege of those that ill-treat books'; 'The wanton way of those that corrupt the very young'; 'The hideous habit of marrying negroes'; 'That grim act parricide'; "That dull, old sin, adultery'; and 'The grave discourtesy of such a man as will beat his host's servant' (*The Cherwell*/Bodleian Library, Oxford).

Waugh was enchanted: 'Harold led me far away from Crease to the baroque and the rococo and the *Waste Land*' (ALL 197).

'There is an aesthetic bugger who sometimes turns up in my novels under various names – that was 2/3 Brian and 1/3 Harold Acton', Waugh wrote after

Howard's suicide in 1958, thinking especially of Ambrose Silk in *Put Out More Flags* and Anthony Blanche in *Brideshead Revisited* (L 506). Blanche's mannered speech and dark, perhaps Jewish, features come from Howard, his reading of poems through a megaphone and getting dunked in Mercury fountain from Acton. These portrayals bring with them the mature Waugh's reservations about homosexuality and a life devoted wholly to art and pleasure. But at Oxford he was the eager pupil. Acton introduced him to the novels of Ronald Firbank and deepened his understanding of Eliot and the Victorian artists and designers he would soon write about and collect. Acton fostered Waugh's interest in the baroque, deprecated as 'bad taste' by Bloomsbury theorists but beginning to enjoy a revival, aided by Sacheverell Sitwell's series of studies beginning with *Southern Baroque Art* (1924).[14] For Waugh, the 'organized vitality of the baroque' quickly came to represent the last great international style in art that could bring rich variety of ornament into satisfying artistic wholeness, uniting integrity of design (as opposed to 'disintegration and diffusion') with fullness of representation.[15] His discussions with Acton (and Robert Byron) fostered a sense of period styles in the arts as expressions of each age's fundamental moral and intellectual commitments, which would lead in the novels to a dense symbolic shorthand whereby the style of a building becomes a clue to the mind of its owner, artistic taste an index of moral character.

Waugh also imbibed Acton's dislikes, especially for the earnestness of Bloomsbury. He arrived at Oxford already interested in aesthetic theory, his understanding of modernism shaped by Roger Fry (a family friend) and Clive Bell. A 'Roger Fry screen, rather exotic and startling', was on display at Underhill, a gift from Fry to Arthur Waugh (Greenidge 51): even before reading their works Waugh knew of Bell and Fry's theories of 'aesthetic emotion' and 'significant form', according to which artistic value resides only in the formal qualities of a work, not the artist's skill in representing anything. ('You see this important mass of colour here', Fry is supposed to have said in a lecture, pointing to a representation of Christ's body on the Cross.) Creation of such forms required no academic training and so might appear with stark purity in 'primitive' art, which Bell and Fry loudly championed.[16] 'At Fry's Omega Workshops in Fitzroy Square', Acton recalled, 'there was a painstaking revival of primitive forms. The patterns a Polynesian produced intuitively in the calm of a coral atoll were refurbished in Bloomsbury amid much soul-stirring and high-flown discourse' (*Memoirs* 89–90).

In *Brideshead* Charles Ryder disposes of a screen from Fry's Omega Studios after he is introduced to Sebastian Flyte, whose undergraduate taste for Victorian décor resembles Acton's. From Acton Waugh learned to distrust 'intuition' and the 'primitive', to prefer instead the products of 'civilization'. 'That the primitive negro sculpture satisfies the aesthetic emotion ought to make the healthy Western critic doubt the formula rather than acclaim the barbarian' (R 223).

Waugh learned to distrust not only Bloomsbury's abstract theorizing – what Acton called Roger Fry's 'magic carpet of argument' that sweeps us 'into an abstract realm' having 'nothing to do with beauty' (*Memoirs* 59–60) – but also its portentous way of pronouncing, its posture of high intellectual piety. Learning was to be worn lightly, with the 'high spirit, elegance, impudence, unpredictability', and, above all, the 'sheer enjoyment' personified in Acton and the Sitwells (EAR 423). The Pre-Raphaelite movement, *Rossetti* remarks dismissively, 'began, as it ended, with people talking in Bloomsbury' (R 29–30); the mad, pontificating architectural theorist of *Decline and Fall* Otto Silenus – like Bell and Fry, a believer in the exclusion of 'the human element from the consideration of form' – 'was starving resignedly in a bed-sitting room in Bloomsbury' before being hired to replace Margot's Tudor house with a hideous modernist construction (DF 154).

For all his genuine concern with what *Rossetti* calls 'the urgency of abstract speculation' (222), the distrust of theorizing Waugh learned at Oxford thus contributed to what often seems his anti-intellectualism, better understood as a rejection of the voice and persona of the 'intellectual'. At Oxford Waugh liked to portray himself as a lone 'man in the street' surrounded by 'intellectuals'; Dudley Carew noted of him, 'anybody less of an intellectual I have seldom met'; 'part of his personality, and one of the disguises that went with it, [was] to express himself in unremarkable and elementary terms'. He declared proudly of his well-known attention to the details of dress: 'I once had an intellectual friend who complained that my appearance was noticeable in Bloomsbury.'[17] 'Highbrow' and 'good taste' were favourite denigrations. The posture was shared by many of his Oxford friends – by Robert Byron, of whom Anthony Powell recalled, 'The very words "intellectual" or "good taste" threw him into paroxysms of rage'; when they eventually settled in London, Acton noted approvingly, both Byron and Waugh chose neighbourhoods (Paddington and Islington) which were 'the symbol of all that Bloomsbury is not'. By the thirties, when the labels 'intellectual' and 'intelligentsia' seemed to become the property of the Left, Waugh could say flatly: 'I am not an intellectual. That's a Marxist term . . . . I don't like the word.'[18]

Many of those at the Hypocrites and around Acton were actively homosexual; from 1922 until about 1925–6, this became Waugh's primary orientation as well. (Unlike Alec, he had had no such experiences at school.) Richard Pares, he later told Nancy Mitford, was 'my first homosexual love'; but Pares 'did not enjoy drinking and as a result we drifted apart'.[19] A later, lengthier, more fully sexual affair with Alastair Graham, the 'Hamish Lennox' of *A Little Learning*, outlasted their time at Oxford and would be memorialized in the love of Charles Ryder for Sebastian Flyte in *Brideshead*, which in manuscript occasionally reads 'Alastair' for 'Sebastian'. Waugh destroyed his Oxford diaries, perhaps because of their record of these relationships; what survives from the years immediately following contains coy remarks such as 'did much that could not have been done had Mrs. Graham been here' (D 218) and a few more graphic accounts, such as that of a visit to a Paris brothel over Christmas 1925: 'I arranged a tableau by which my boy should be enjoyed by a large negro who was there but at the last minute, after we had ascended to a squalid divan at the top of the house and he was lying waiting for the negro's advances, the price proved prohibitive and, losing patience . . . , I took a taxi home and to bed in chastity. I do not think I regret it' (D 240).

From his own experience Waugh came to believe that maturation succeeds best when it proceeds slowly – that 'most souls', as he wrote to Thomas Merton, 'are of slow growth'. The point of going to university, he suggested in 1930, is not to train for a career but rather to afford time 'to grow up gradually'; those who miss this opportunity 'often show signs of a kind of arrested development' in later life (EAR 84). Homosexual relationships might be positively useful in this process. In the chapter of *A Little Learning* on his Oxford years (significantly titled 'Never a Palinode'), Waugh quotes Charles Ryder's words from *Brideshead* in application to himself:

> Looking back, now, after twenty years, there is little I would have left undone or done otherwise. I could match my cousin Jasper's game-cock maturity with a sturdier fowl. I could tell him that all the wickedness of that time was like the spirit they mix with the pure grape of the Douro, heady stuff full of dark ingredients; it at once enriched and retarded the whole process of adolescence as the spirit checks the fermentation of the wine, renders it undrinkable, so that it must lie in the dark, year in, year out, until it is brought up at last fit for the table.
>
> (ALL 169, quoting BR 41)

On one visit to London in the summer of 1924 he began a novel, a tale of black magic called *The Temple at Thatch* (later destroyed when Acton sent comments on the manuscript); on another, he wrote and, with Terence and John Greenidge, produced a short comic movie, *The Scarlet Woman*, in which the Pope seeks to convert the Prince of Wales and so bring England back to Catholicism. Filmed at a total cost of £20, partly in Hampstead, partly at Oxford, the cast included Terence Greenidge, Evelyn and Alec Waugh, Lord Elmley, John Sutro, and a new friend met through Alec, the young Elsa Lanchester, then managing a nightclub and willing to act in exchange for lunches. Waugh liked to say that he had 'discovered' her.[20]

By this time Waugh's deferred childhood had accelerated into an expensive round of parties and trips. He lost his scholarship and had to auction off his collection of books and pictures to meet the most pressing debts. He wanted to leave Oxford, but his father refused to finance a move to Paris to study painting. Letters to Carew (almost the only surviving documents from his last term) hint melodramatically at dissipations too disturbing to explain, an emotional crash only barely averted: 'At present I am keeping my balance but I may crash any moment'; 'I have been living very intensely the last three weeks. For the last fortnight I have been nearly insane'; 'St John has been eating wild honey in the wilderness. I do not yet know how things are going to end. They are nearing some sort of finality' (L 12–13).

Avoiding other friends to spend all his time with Alastair in pubs or at Mrs Graham's house at Barford, Waugh predictably emerged in July from his Final Schools with a poor third, which as Alec said 'disqualified him for the recognized professions' (CH 469). He determined thereafter to enjoy what time with Alastair remained before harsher realities intervened. In September 1924, to

3–4 Stills from *The Scarlet Woman: An Ecclesiastical Melodrama* (1924)

(**3**) 'The Dean of Balliol, leading Catholic layman of England' (Waugh) with his instrument, Father Murphy, SJ (Terence Greenidge). The background is Waugh's parents home, Underhill in Hampstead.

(**4**) The 'penniless peer' Lord Borrowington (Waugh) with Beatrice de Carolle (Elsa Lanchester), a down-at-heels cabaret singer of 'Evangelical principles' who foils the papal plot to bring England back into the Catholic fold.

Waugh's dismay, Alastair, long drawn to Roman Catholicism, was received by Father C. C. Martindale into 'the Italian Church' (D 178); a week later he left for a long visit to a sister in Kenya. Waugh, seeing no purpose in staying the final term at Oxford needed to take a degree, returned to Hampstead, dispirited, £200 in debt, and without prospects.

III

The next four years, from 1924 until he turned twenty-five in 1928, were to be what Harold Acton called Waugh's 'Dostoievski period': an aimless round of occasional employment, parties in London, weekend trips back to Oxford (where he made such new friends as Anthony Powell, John Betjeman, and Henry Yorke), afternoons whiled away in the cinema, and, throughout, drunkenness – punctuated by occasional vows to slow down, to dedicate himself to some course of action. To Carew, who thought his drinking suicidal, it seemed 'Evelyn was taking a relish Byron would have appreciated in the wreck he seemed to be making of his life.'[21] Waugh recorded of one week of cumulative futility in 1924:

> I am at the moment just recovering from a very heavy bout of drinking.... I suddenly went to Oxford...and drove to 31 St Aldate's [home of the Hypocrites] where I found an enormous orgy in progress. Billy and I unearthed a strap and whipped Tony. Everyone was hideously drunk except strangely enough myself. Next day I...had a dinner party of Claud [Cockburn, Waugh's cousin], Elmley, Terence, Roger Hollis and a poor drunk called Macgregor. I arrived quite blind after a great number of cocktails at the George with Claud. Eventually the dinner broke up and Claud, Roger Hollis and I went off for a pub-crawl which after sundry indecorous adventures ended up at the Hypocrites where another blind was going on. Poor Mr Macgregor turned up after having lain with a woman but almost immediately fell backwards downstairs. I think he was killed. Next day I drank all the morning from pub to pub and invited to lunch with me at the New Reform John Sutro, Roger Hollis, Claud and Alfred Duggan. I am not sure if there was anyone else. I ate no lunch but drank solidly and was soon in the middle of a bitter quarrel with the president – a preposterous person called Cotts – who expelled me from the club. Alfred and I then drank double brandies until I could not walk. He carried me to Worcester where I fell out of a window and then relapsed into unconsciousness punctuated with severe but well-directed vomitings. I dined four times at various places and went to a drunk party at Worcester in someone's rooms I did not know.

> (D 189–90)

With drink came attacks of depression and insomnia, from which Waugh suffered for the rest of his life. No wonder the diaries register a yearning for what the hero of *Vile Bodies* can describe only vaguely as 'something different' – for the 'permanence' of which in that novel Fr Rothschild speaks. 'On Friday morning I received a letter from Richard Greene telling me that he is become definitely engaged with Elizabeth [Ponsonby]. It makes me sad for them because any sort of happiness or permanence seems so infinitely remote from any one of us' (D 202).

These names represent new friends among the fast set named by the newspapers in 1924 'Bright Young People'. Waugh had 'fallen in love with an entire family', the Plunket Greenes.[22] The brothers David and Richard, handsome and nearly seven feet tall, were friends from Oxford; in London he met their mother Gwen and sister Olivia, a notably Bright Young Person who impressed everyone she met by her peculiar combination of gin-drinking promiscuity and other-worldliness. Usually dressed in black, her face covered in white pancake makeup, Olivia was equally at home dancing the Charleston, debating Bergson and Dostoevsky, and drunkenly bedding fashionable black performers such as Paul Robeson. Soon Waugh, his sexual interest in men waning, was infatuated with her, but Olivia, willing to sleep with so many others, was not attracted to him. (Alec described her as 'the last person equipped to restore' his brother's 'self-confidence and self esteem'; 'She was a profound depressant': *Brother* 177.) Waugh pursued her for two years of frustration and self-doubt.

He met as well the Greene's cousins Elizabeth Ponsonby (a model for Agatha Runcible of *Vile Bodies*), with whom, more briefly but equally fruitlessly, he tried to have an affair, and her brother Matthew, with whom over Easter in 1925 Waugh was jailed for drunk driving (a scene recreated in *Brideshead*). He threw himself into the world of cocktail parties, bottle parties, jazz parties (featuring popular black singers like Florence Mills and the Blackbirds), fancy-dress parties and treasure-hunts. With these fast new friends and Alastair Graham, back from Africa, he took jaunts to the Isle of Wight, Ireland, and Scotland.

But in the autumn of 1924, just down from Oxford, living at home and in debt to his father, there remained the problem of making a living. In September Waugh enrolled at Heatherley's Art School, between classes visiting galleries, drinking with Tony Bushell, and engaging in long conversations with another Oxford friend, the philosophically minded art historian Adrian Stokes, then fashionably in the grip of Bergson and at work on his first book, *The Thread of Ariadne* (1925).[23] A month at Heatherley's convinced him that he lacked skill or interest in figure-drawing. 'I had neither the talent nor the application – I didn't have the moral qualities' (Jebb 108). There seemed no other course but school-teaching, the fate of so many Oxford contemporaries. From January to July 1925, at an annual salary of £160, he taught History, Latin, and Greek at Arnold House, Llanddulas, Wales; from September 1925 until he was sacked in February 1927, he worked closer to friends, teaching English, History, and Art (at the same salary) at Aston Clinton in Buckinghamshire. The second job came through Richard Greene, already teaching music there; when Greene left he gave Waugh in consolation – and much to his students' admiration – a motor-cycle named Queensberry on which to racket over to Oxford and London on weekends. Dismissed from Aston Clinton, he was reduced from March until April 1927 to teaching for £5 a week in a state school at Notting Hill: 'quite awful. All the masters drop their aitches and spit in the fire and scratch their genitals. The boys...pick their noses and scream at each other in a cockney accent' (D 282).

5 Waugh's postcard of himself on 'Queensberry,' Magdalen Bridge, Oxford (1925) (Private Collection).

Memories of all these schools would fill the first half of *Decline and Fall*, especially Arnold House, a drab establishment Waugh transfigured into Lla-nabba Castle. Like Paul Pennyfeather, the wholly unmusical Waugh (his pupil Derek Verschoyle recalled) gave lessons 'on the organ, an instrument with which he was not familiar', and 'in the matter of academic studies' adopted 'a policy of live-and-let-live'. Here he met Dick Young, model for Captain Grimes, a tireless pederast 'expelled from Wellington, sent down from Oxford, forced to resign his commission in the army,' now in his sixth teaching job.[24]

Waugh was a popular master and later often said that schoolteaching 'was very jolly and I enjoyed it very much'.[25] But at the time teaching seemed to offer few pleasures, small pay, and no prospect of distinction. Exiled from Olivia Greene in Wales, he indulged in self-pity:

> I arrived here yesterday in immeasurable gloom...I think that my finances have never been so desperate or my spirits so depressed....In school I find a certain perverse pleasure in making all I teach as dreary to the boys as it is to myself...I debate the simple paradoxes of suicide and achievement, work out the scheme for a new book, and negotiate with the man Young to buy a revolver from him.
>
> (D 210–11)

How deeply Waugh felt all this we cannot say. An entry of the following week retails an anecdote then reflects, 'This story is not really quite true but I have recounted it in so many letters that I have begun to believe it' (D 211). *A Little Learning* famously concludes with another moment of despair in Wales. The date is July 1925; Waugh has given notice, thinking himself sure of a new position – secretary to C. K. Scott Moncrieff, the translator of Proust, in Italy. Then comes news that the job has fallen through:

> One night, soon after I got the news from Pisa, I went down alone to the beach with my thoughts full of death. I took off my clothes and began swimming out to sea. Did I really intend to drown myself? That certainly was in my mind and I left a note with my clothes, the quotation from Euripides about the sea which washes away all human ills. . . . It was a beautiful night of a gibbous moon. I swam slowly out but, long before I reached the point of no return, the Shropshire Lad was disturbed by a smart on the shoulder. I had run into a jelly-fish. A few more strokes, a second more painful sting. The placid waters were full of the creatures. . . .
>
> I turned about, swam back through the track of the moon to the sands which that morning had swarmed under Grimes's discerning eye with naked urchins. . . . Then I climbed the sharp hill that led to all the years ahead.
>
> (ALL 229–30)

The story makes a fine ending for a book; perhaps something like it actually occurred. The diary contains no echo either of the event or of the feelings one might expect to have surrounded it. The whole of *A Little Learning*'s last chapter was in fact a late and hurried addition, added because the manuscript (which Waugh had planned to conclude with his coming down from Oxford) seemed too short.[26]

Meanwhile something that in retrospect would look like a career in writing was beginning. *The Temple at Thatch* had been a failure, but during his last months in Wales, Waugh began an avant-garde novel, finished in August as a short story called 'The Balance: A Yarn of the Good Old Days of Broad Trousers and High Necked Jumpers'. Its hero is Adam Doure, student at a London art school like Heatherley's, too poor to capture the affections of the fashionable Imogen Quest. Frustrated in love, Adam returns to Oxford and the solace of old friends, then poisons himself. Succeeding only in making himself sick, he recovers and resolves upon 'detachment'. Finally, 'by the grace of God', Adam falls asleep, and on waking decides that pursuit of his craft is better than suicide, since art is one with 'the appetite to live – to preserve in the shape of things the personality whose dissolution you see eventually'.[27] Amidst Bergsonian musings on the nature of identity probably inspired by Stokes (whose philosophy of 'balance' seems also to have supplied its title), the tale constitutes Waugh's first sustained use of fiction as the vehicle for exploring the shape of his own life.

Architecturally, as *Scoop* says of the Pension Dressler, 'The Balance' was a mess. But its experiment with extreme objectivity of stance in presenting Adam and Imogen's conversations as if in a film script looks forward to the cinematic techniques of *Decline and Fall* and *Vile Bodies*. The story was rejected by three publishers (including Leonard Woolf) before Alec – by now a well-known novelist, essayist, and autobiographer – paid Waugh £2 to include it in a collection of

Georgian Stories (1926) he was editing for Chapman and Hall, where it appeared alongside tales by A. E. Coppard, William Gerhardie, Huxley, Maugham and Gertrude Stein.

The chain of events that led to Waugh's first book began soon after he finished 'The Balance'. At Lancing he had planned a talk on 'The Failure of the Pre-Raphaelites' (D 35); laid up in Hampstead in November 1925 – on leave from Aston Clinton to recover from an ankle twisted by falling, drunk, from a window at Oxford – he took up the subject again, noting in his diary 'I want to write a book about them' (D 233). He was in fact reviving an old interest rooted in Waugh family history. Holman Hunt, always for Waugh the central figure of the group, was an ancestor by marriage: the Pre-Raphaelite sculptor Thomas Woolner had 'married one of three handsome sisters called Waugh; Holman-Hunt married both the others' (R 35). He wrote nothing until July 1926, when Alastair, as an apprentice at the Shakespeare Head Press, asked for something he might print. In 'four and a half days, in between correcting exam papers' (D 257), Waugh completed *P.R.B.: An Essay on the Pre-Raphaelite Brotherhood* (1926), a twenty-five-page pamphlet mainly on Millais and Hunt.

While *P.R.B.* was in proof, Waugh proposed a short book called *Noah, or the Future of Intoxication* for Kegan Paul's series *Today and Tomorrow*, which had already printed Robert Graves's *Lars Porsena, or the Future of Swearing*. Kegan Paul agreed; Waugh wrote *Noah* at Aston Clinton over the last three months of 1926, sending off the manuscript just before leaving to spend Christmas in Athens with Alastair, who had abandoned publishing for the diplomatic service. On returning via Corfu in January he found that Kegan Paul had rejected *Noah*, which he destroyed, but February brought an offer of £10 for another short story.[28] That month, too, he was fired from Aston Clinton for making a drunken pass at a matron. Back home in Hampstead, Waugh noted ruefully in his diary, 'the time has arrived to set about being a man of letters' (D 281).

P.R.B. received little notice – the student at Aston Clinton who had been assigned the task neglected to send out review copies – and so Waugh was able to recycle its most striking passages two years later in *Rossetti*, a project born when Anthony Powell passed on a copy of *P.R.B.* to his employers at Duckworth. The result was an advance of £20 ('spent in a week') for a biography of the most colourful of the Pre-Raphaelites, to appear in time for the centenary of Rossetti's birth in May 1928. Waugh began, then procrastinated. The diary records for April 1927: 'I am in doubt at the moment whether to go on the *Express*' – Lord Beaverbrook's *Daily Express*, to which he was recommended by Osbert Sitwell – 'or write a biography that Duckworth show some interest in' (284). He chose reporting, which paid £5 a week, at least until his internship was up in May (he never had a by-line). In June he went on holiday with his family for a month in the south of France (a trip with Alec to the tough streets of Marseilles provided material for *Decline and Fall*). Work on the biography, under the title *The Last Born of Eve*, began in earnest in July; in August, he moved to the Abingdon Arms at Beckley, near Oxford, close to the Bodleian and to Mrs Graham, who took him to William Morris's Kelmscott. (He also renewed contact with Francis Crease, living nearby, and wrote a preface for a collection of Crease's designs.)[29] Renamed *Rossetti: His Life and Works*, the biography was done by Christmas and published the following April.

IV

Though Waugh later dismissed it as 'hurried and bad' (Jebb 108), *Rossetti* was the first book to mark the centenary, and so received wide publicity. Reviewers spoke mainly of the occasion, but found space for favourable notice of the new author as well. The TLS gave it a front-page review, provoking an angry letter from the author it misidentified as 'Miss Waugh' and a lively letter of praise from Rebecca West (CH 79).

West especially admired the book's arresting voice, its ability to teach through compressed wit. The author of *Rossetti* was already master of the neatly surprising verbal formulation ('Mrs. Rossetti was by birth half Italian and wholly pedagogical'; 'Millais, engaged to be married to Ruskin's wife'); of the inverted cliché (of Rossetti's sensuous *Beloved*: it portrays 'a royal wedding, pure and elaborate'); and of the blandly impertinent generalization ('The burying of manuscript poems' – as Rossetti buried his with the body of Elizabeth Siddall – 'has never been a European funeral custom'). Carefully planted phrases (or single-sentence paragraphs inserted between longer ones) shift levels of diction, usually for purposes of satiric deflation:

> The [critics'] attack was mainly upon three counts. The Pre-Raphaelites were presumptuous. They were very young men, daring to set themselves up as superior to the artistic standards of their age. They thought themselves cleverer than Raphael. They wanted to teach their grandmothers to suck eggs.
>
> (R 44)

All these passages instance Waugh's lifelong habit of formal mixture, his gift for putting elements from different rhetorical registers and generic kinds side by side.

Such mixture also characterizes *Rossetti* as a whole. The book opens with a self-conscious discussion of contrasting methods of biography: the old-fashioned Victorian 'Life and Letters', and the 'new method' made popular by Lytton Strachey's *Eminent Victorians* (1918). In the older form we 'assist with our fathers' decorum at the lying-in-state of our great men', 'their faces serenely composed and cleansed of all the stains of inhumanity'; in the new,

> We have discovered a jollier way of honouring our dead. The corpse has become the marionette. With bells on its fingers and wires on its toes it is jigged about to a 'period dance' of our own piping; and who is not amused? Unfortunately, there is singularly little fun to be got out of Rossetti.
>
> (R 12)

As the last sentence suggests, *Rossetti* presents not some third kind of life-writing but a volatile mixture of old and new. (In a single sentence, for instance, we learn, in Stracheyan fashion, that most of the great Victorians – 'the fabulous paladins of the last century' – were 'humbugs', but also that Rossetti himself escaped this fate.) From this volatility comes much of the book's energy.

Waugh's mixture of approaches and styles is partly strategic: it permits him to celebrate a painter then in disrepute. Deflationary gestures allow Waugh to celebrate Rossetti's emotional power without appearing sentimental himself.

> Rossetti's art reached the highest pinnacle of pure visual splendour in the two great pictures that flame and sparkle upon the walls of the Tate Gallery, *Monna Vanna* and *The Beloved....* [I]n these two superb paintings he had enriched his fellow-men with the most sumptuous visions of barbaric glory that had ever burst into the grey city of his exile. All these adjectives are used deliberately and for what they are worth. It is the moment when the real Rossetti enthusiast, if such a one survives, holds his breath and strains his imagination for words of adequate luxury. We who are less single hearted can echo his phrases word for word, but with a slight and significant shifting of implication.[30]

Stylistic mixture establishes a critic who can at once appreciate Rossetti's 'single hearted' appeal yet also distance himself, the more complex and unsentimental modern, from it.

It was *Rossetti*'s final, theoretical chapter on which Waugh laboured hardest. Here he makes explicit an argument hinted throughout: that the example of the Pre-Raphaelites undermines 'the modern ... critical standpoint'. The doctrine of significant form, invented to explain Cézanne, Post-Impressionism, and 'the pellucid excellencies of Picasso', cannot account for the pleasure we take in Rossetti, who sought to express ideas 'in colour', not 'about colour', and whose 'impure' painting (like that of Frith and Landseer) is literary and anecdotal rather than concerned simply with the 'relation of forms'.

Only two reviewers, C. S. Lewis and Richard Murray, noted that throughout *Rossetti*, Roger Fry represents 'the modern movement' in criticism.[31] Waugh's diagrams of the two-dimensional 'rhythms' of Rossetti's paintings recall Fry's similar diagrams in *Flemish Art* (1916) while subverting the point Fry used them to illustrate: his doctrine ('which is now taught in Art Schools as the primary impulse of art') of form as merely a matter of coloured volumes in space.

But it is really once again Clive Bell's more logical presentation in *Art* from which Waugh draws his terms. Bell had proceeded in the time-honoured fashion of philosophers of beauty since the eighteenth century. All art arouses a distinctive emotion, named by Bell 'aesthetic emotion'; objects arousing this emotion have something in common, named by Bell 'significant form'. Pictures that depend for their effect on 'representation' or 'imitation' of the visible world are thus 'impure' – mere 'illustration', not 'art'. To this kind of argument from stipulative definition Waugh responded as had Dr Johnson to similar claims that Alexander Pope did not really write 'poetry' ('If Pope be not a poet, where is poetry to be found?'): 'Well, if these paintings are not works of art, what are they?' Waugh denies that the 'entirely new thing which they called the "aesthetic emotion"' really exists, and even suggests that Post-Impressionism was a mistake that could have been avoided: 'If the robust influence of Madox Brown and Rossetti had been given full scope, English art might easily have escaped from the 'greenery-yallery' fever which has...made the progress of post-impressionism so inevitable.'[32]

Rossetti contains as well remarkable discussions of the role of patronage in shaping the artist's career, and of the ways photography had changed both artistic practice and the nature of visual response – a subject on which in 1928 Waugh proposed to Robert Byron writing a separate 'treatise' and to which he eventually returned in 1956, in an essay on 'The Death of Painting' (EAR 503–7).

Much of Waugh's insight in *Rossetti*, both theoretical and psychological, stems from the extent to which he identifies with his subject. Rossetti, as Waugh often admitted of himself, had no ear for music, regarding it 'as an invention of his enemies devised expressly for his own discomfort' (119) ; 'Mathematics and science were abhorrent to him' (18). His mother – a practical, devoted, upright woman (common characteristics in 'the mothers of important people') (19) resembles Waugh's view of his own mother. Rossetti drank too much, was often depressed and sometimes suicidal, and suffered from 'restless insomnia': 'Others afflicted by this terrible disease have contrived in some measure to adapt themselves to it, to reserve their waning vitality, manage with what sleep they can get, and when not sleeping to take adequate rest' (148). (In later life Waugh found further parallels in Rossetti's aural hallucinations and addiction to sleeping drugs [L 418].) Most strikingly, Rossetti was 'born into an age devoid of artistic standards; a man of the South, sensual, indolent, and richly versatile, exiled in the narrow, scrambling, specialised life of a Northern city; a mystic without a creed; a Catholic without the discipline or consolation of the Church' (13–14). Here already is Waugh's distinction, learnt from works like Norman Douglas's *Siren Land* (1912) and *South Wind* (1917), between North and South, Anglo-Saxon phlegm and the freer world of Italy and the Mediterranean; here is his view of his own age as one that has abandoned 'qualitative value', an age urgently in need of spiritual discipline. Waugh passes a final judgment on Rossetti much like those he had made of Adam Doure at the end of 'The Balance,' and of his own youthful self at Heatherley's:

there was fatally lacking in him that *essential rectitude* that underlies the serenity of all really great art. The sort of unhappiness that beset him was not the sort of unhappiness that does beset a great artist; all his brooding about magic [one thinks here of *The Temple at Thatch*] and suicide are symptomatic not so much of genius as of mediocrity. There is a spiritual inadequacy, a sense of ill-organization about all that he did.

(R 226–7)

No wonder that Waugh's mind returned to the topics raised in this early book when he came to write the story of an artist's conversion to Catholicism in *Brideshead*. In 1928 Holman Hunt stands as a counter-example to Clive Bell in knowing 'no valid distinction between beauty of picture and beauty of subject'; two decades later, quoting Bell, Sebastian Flyte makes the same point to Charles Ryder.[33]

6 Waugh and Evelyn Gardner dressed for safari at Vyvyan Holland's Tropical Party (July 1929), during the weeks when they tried to repair their marriage. 'The author of *Decline and Fall* looks somewhat scared, although there were no fierce Zulus on board', noted the *Bystander* (Private Collection).

V

The first edition of *Rossetti* appeared with a dedication to Evelyn Gardner, a distant cousin of Olivia Greene's whom Waugh had met twelve months before. Lively, stylish, and shallow, with the boyish figure popular in the twenties, 'She-Evelyn', as she would be known, was a daughter of the dowager Baroness Burghclere and niece of the Earl of Carnarvon who discovered Tutankhamen's tomb. In the spring of 1927, following a series of engagements rejected as unsuitable by her domineering mother, she escaped home by moving into a flat with her friend Pansy Pakenham (sister of Waugh's Oxford friend Frank), who had left home to see more of the painter Henry Lamb. Each girl's mother thought, wrongly, the other's daughter would discipline her own. Pansy liked Waugh and did what she could to further his attachment to her flat-mate.

That summer Waugh travelled and researched *Rossetti*; in September he returned home to write and look again for paying work. His father agreed to give him an allowance of £4 a week and arranged occasional reviewing; Waugh supplemented his income with part-time teaching and later in the autumn began a course in carpentry at the Central School of Arts and Crafts. Meanwhile he saw as much as he could of Evelyn Gardner, now installed with Pansy Pakenham in a tiny flat above a tobacconist's shop. (Under their doorbell She-Evelyn printed 'Blondes'.) With Pansy and Henry Lamb, the two Evelyns formed the centre of a circle that included Nancy Mitford, Anthony Powell (later to marry Pansy's sister Violet), Robert Byron, Harold Acton, Henry Yorke, Peter Quennell, Cyril Connolly, and Sacheverell Sitwell – 'the nucleus of an alternative Bloomsbury' (ST1 146).

To friends the two Evelyns seemed playmates rather than lovers. Waugh was still smarting from Olivia Greene's rejection; Evelyn Gardner, doubtless aware of his recent affairs with men, wrote of him in November 1927: 'Lately we have become such terribly good friends, and it's such a good plan, because I know he would never make love to me, & everyone else does, & it's such a bore' (Hastings 163). But one evening over dinner at the Ritz Grill in December 1927, when he was planning a woodworking apprenticeship in Bournemouth and she considering emigration to Canada, Waugh proposed that they marry and 'see how it goes' (D 305). She-Evelyn accepted by phone the next day. Both were twenty-four; neither had any financial prospects.

Lady Burghclere reasonably opposed any connection between her daughter and an impecunious, pushful failed schoolmaster. 'It never occurred to me to think I wasn't a gentleman until Lady Burghclere pointed it out', he wrote later (L 363). Investigations of Waugh's character, including an interview with Cruttwell at Oxford, provided Lady Burghclere with a full brief against what she called 'ses moeurs atroces'. Hoping to prevent a marriage, she enlisted the help of relatives to keep Waugh poor. She persuaded her millionaire son-in-law Geoffrey Fry to prevent him from receiving a job at the BBC (Beaty 188–9), and may even have succeeded in holding up publication of *Decline and Fall*.

In September 1927, with *Rossetti* nearly done, Waugh had also found time to begin a 'comic novel' (D 289). In late nights at Hampstead he read sections to Anthony Powell and Dudley Carew, laughing uproariously at his own jokes; hearers were sure the book would be a success, though Waugh, mindful of past failures, wrote Acton, 'I should so much value your opinion on whether I am to finish it' (L 25). 'Do you like "Untoward Incidents" as a title', he asked Powell; 'The phrase, you remember, was used by the Duke of Wellington in commenting on the destruction of the Turkish Fleet in time of peace at Navarino. It seems to set the right tone of mildly censorious detachment' (L 27). Other working titles included *Facing Facts: A Study in Discouragement* and *Picaresque, or the Making of an Englishman*. The novel was finished as *Decline and Fall: An Illustrated Novelette* in April 1928, the same month *Rossetti* appeared, its final title meant to recall Gibbon's

Decline and Fall and Oswald Spengler's popular work of oracular historiography *The Decline of the West*, both of which Waugh had recently been reading.

He submitted the novel first to Gerald Duckworth, publisher of *Rossetti* – and a cousin of Lady Burghclere. Duckworth insisted on sweeping changes. In 1928, the Obscene Publications Act was in full force: copies of *Ulysses* had to be smuggled from France; both *Lady Chatterley* and Radclyffe Hall's *Well of Loneliness* had been suppressed. Even 'obscene' paintings could be confiscated, as happened when D. H. Lawrence mounted an exhibition in 1929. Duckworth reasonably didn't want to risk references to Welshmen 'mat[ing] freely with sheep'; even the word 'lavatory' was dangerous. He insisted especially that all mention of homosexuality be excised. In manuscript, Grimes's connexion with young Clutterbuck is explicitly sexual; Peter Pastmaster appears on the morning of Paul's wedding 'looking absurdly like a male impersonator'; his mother complains, 'It's terrible having a pretty son in these days...no one looks at one when Peter's in the room.'[34]

Many of Duckworth's changes were reasonable, but his manner of demanding them, perhaps the result of knowing Lady Burghclere's feelings about her prospective son-in-law, drove Waugh down the street to his father's firm, whose insistence on nearly all the same changes he soon accepted. In the next few years Waugh would denounce censorship and craft the fine moment in *Vile Bodies* when a customs official confiscates Dante's *Purgatorio*, saying 'Particularly against books the Home Secretary is. If we can't stamp out literature in the country, we can at least stop its being brought in from outside.'[35] But the changes his editors demanded were nearly all for the better. Some forms of literature may thrive best under conditions of complete freedom, but satire is not one of them. Under censorship, satirists resort to artful obliquity and innuendo to express what they cannot say directly. In the published novel, Grimes' relation with Clutterbuck emerges from a series of coyly teasing hints, and his dull admission 'I've never really been attracted to women' becomes the splendid illeism, ' "Women are an enigma," said Grimes, "as far as Grimes is concerned" ' – a formula Waugh would often use again when lost or despairing souls among his characters reflect on themselves.[36]

After his proposal of marriage there is a six-month gap in Waugh's diary. (At this time Henry Lamb began his famous portrait of Waugh, paid for by their rich friend Bryan Guinness, husband of Nancy Mitford's younger sister Diana, in whose honour Waugh appears holding a glass of Guinness.) The next entry, for 22 June 1928, records in his most insouciant voice:

> Evelyn and I began to go to Dulwich to see the pictures there but got bored waiting for the right bus so went instead to the vicar-general's office and bought a marriage licence. Lunched at Taglioni. Went to Warwick Square to see Harold and show him our licence. With him to Alec where we drank champagne.

> (D 294–5)

Without informing Lady Burghclere, they married the next week at a ceremony to which only Acton, Byron, Pansy Pakenham, and Alec Waugh were invited.

'The happy pair will not be poorer than they were before', wrote Pansy Paken-ham (who had done her best to persuade Evelyn Gardner to accept what she thought Waugh's good influence), 'as long as they don't start a family. To prevent this they have invoked all the magic of Marie Stopes' (Hastings 178–9). After a week's honeymoon at Beckley they moved in with Waugh's parents in Hampstead and set about trying to reconcile Lady Burghclere to a connexion by which, she said, she felt 'quite inexpressibly pained' (D 295).

At the end of August they moved with their possessions – so few, a wheel-barrow could carry them – to a five-room flat in Canonbury Square, Islington, subleased for a pound a week from Waugh's old friend Joyce Fagan. Waugh decorated it on the cheap, producing what Acton described as a 'sparkling nursery' (*Memoirs* 204). There was enough to entertain on (invitations for one party gave directions to the flat from Buckingham Palace); an especially frequent guest was their new friend John Heygate, a good-looking, hard-drinking news-writer for the BBC with whom the Evelyns formed 'a happy trio'.[37] Waugh met the bills by writing; She-Evelyn also tried to launch herself in journalism.

It was *Decline and Fall*, published in September by Chapman and Hall (the imprint of all his subsequent fiction), that made this life possible. Judicious editing, always one of Waugh's greatest gifts, had produced a first novel that won universal praise. Arnold Bennett, to whom Arthur Waugh had sent a copy, produced a generous review in his influential 'Books and Persons' column in the *Evening Standard*; Winston Churchill made it his Christmas present of the year. On the strength of the book Duckworth commissioned a life of John Wesley (never written), and A. D. Peters, already agent to C. S. Forester, V. S. Pritchett, Rebecca West, Hugh Walpole, and Alec Waugh, offered his services, beginning a relationship – as literary agent, accountant, financial adviser, and friend – that would last until Waugh's death.[38]

By December *Decline and Fall* had sold 2000 copies and Doubleday, Doran paid $500 for American rights. The novel achieved what Waugh knew was crucial to any writer's success: 'the important thing is to make people talk' (EAR 50). It allowed him to launch a campaign of advancement through self-advertisement that he disarmingly described two years later:

> Now, one of the arts of successful authorship is preventing the reading public from forgetting one's name in between the times they are reading one's books.... so you spend half your leisure in writing articles for the papers; the editors buy these because people read your books, and people read your books because they see your articles in the papers. (This is called a vicious circle by those who have not got into the running.) The rest of your leisure you have to spend in doing things which you think other people will think interesting.
>
> (*Labels* 9–10)

From 1928 onward Waugh made sure that he was news, especially in the society gossip-columns written by his friends Tom Driberg, Patrick Kinross, and Elea-nor Smith. He later called the twenties a time when 'The test of a young man's worth was the insolence which he could carry off without mishap'; by 1930 his campaign was so successful that reviewers knew him as 'the second most impertinent young man in London.'[39]

Later, too, Waugh would distinguish serious 'essays' from 'beastly little articles' written wholly for money; but in 1928 he asked Peters, 'Please fix up anything that will earn me anything – even cricket criticism or mothers welfare notes' (L 30). When he suggested an essay on 'manners' but was misunderstood to have written 'mothers', he promptly turned out 'Matter-of-Fact Mothers of The New Age'. He wrote on 'Careers for Our Sons', interior decoration, hats, the night-clubs of London and Paris, 'Old Fashioned Drinks', and men's clothing (how to dress well on £60 a year), and proposed myriad other topics, including 'a detective serial about the murder of an author rather like Alec Waugh' (HRC E90). He began a second novel and, toward the end of January 1929, suggested a series of illustrated articles about a trip by cargo boat around the Black Sea (HRC E96). Peters arranged instead a proper honeymoon for the couple: a four-month Mediterranean cruise aboard the *Stella Polaris*, to be paid for by favourable publicity about the shipping line.

The trip was in nearly every way (except for producing the travel book *Labels*) a disaster. She-Evelyn had fallen ill with German measles the previous October; by February she seemed well, but as they travelled by train through a winter of record cold to meet their ship in Monaco, she fell sick again. They nonetheless boarded the *Stella*, bound for Haifa and Port Said; in Egypt, her life clearly in danger, she was hospitalized for pleurisy and double pneumonia. Amidst efforts to turn out the light-hearted articles for which he had contracted, Waugh wrote anxious postcards home reporting his wife's illness and begging for money to cover unexpected on-shore expenses. 'A pathetic SOS from the Evelyns' brought a loan from Alastair Graham, who visited from Athens for a few days.[40] At the end of March She-Evelyn was well enough to move to the expensive comfort of a hotel outside Cairo, where she regained strength and he admired the treasures of Tutankhamen; by early April – with more loans – they went to Malta, where by good fortune the *Stella* was docked. She-Evelyn now fully recovered, they proceeded to Constantinople (where they dined with the Sitwells) and Athens (where they visited Alastair and Mark Ogilvie-Grant, both freed from 'the burden of keeping up appearances' and having 'terrific affairs' with local boys) (L 34). After brief stops at Venice, the Dalmatian coast, Algiers, Barcelona, and Gibraltar, they reached home by the end of May. 'We found bills of over £200 waiting for us and each overdrawn at our banks so I must write a lot quickly' (L 35–6).

VI

Whatever the assignment, nearly all Waugh's journalism in the years following *Decline and Fall* explores the topic that had occupied him since his Lancing editorial on 'The Youngest Generation.' A shrewd judge of the market, Waugh wrote Peters early in their relationship: 'Could you get the *Express* to take an article on the Youngest Generation's view of Religion? – very serious & Churchy. I see they are doing a series of the sort. It seems to me that it would be so nice if we could persuade them that I personify the English youth movement' (L 30).

As the press cuttings collected by Wyndham Lewis in *The Doom of Youth* attest, 'modern youth' obsessed the twenties. Newspapers ran debates between youth and age on the merits, or mere waywardness, of the young, and most of the popular writers of the decade joined in. On 21, 22 and 24 January 1929 the *Evening Standard* printed a retired schoolteacher's 'Greedy, Rebellious, Anarchic Youth: Whither are they Tending?'; Waugh's 'Too Young at 40: Youth Calls to the Peter Pans of Middle-Age who Block the Way' (precipitating, he claimed, a sheaf of letters threatening 'kickings and whippings'); and Arnold Bennett on 'Idleness and Dawdling: The Sins of an Age which Exults in Cocktails and Bed at 2 a.m'. Waugh followed up with a series of pieces written 'to qualify for the trade label of "challenging"' (EAR 125), including 'Matter-of-Fact Mothers', 'What I Think of My Elders', and one of his most searching early essays, 'The War and the Younger Generation'.[41]

'A violent sincerity is totally modern', the *Oxford Broom* had declared in its opening 'Credo'. Unsentimental and unillusioned, quick to scent euphemism and the 'bogus', Waugh's essays on youth speak in the voice that his Lancing editorial had argued would be characteristic of 'The Youngest Generation'.

> They will be, above all things, clear-sighted, they will have no use for phrases or shadows. In the nineteenth century the old men saw visions and the young men dreamed dreams. The youngest generation are going to be very hard and analytical and unsympathetic, but they are going to aim at things as they are.... The young men of the nineties subsisted upon emotion...middle-aged observers will find it hard to see the soul in the youngest generation.
>
>   But they will have – and this is their justification – a very full sense of humour...a greater egotism than did the young men of the nineties, but it will be with a cynical smile and often with a laugh.
>
> (EAR 11)

'Too Young at 40' cites five writers – Acton, Byron, Hollis, Quennell and Stokes – 'all known already to a considerable public' (and all Waugh's friends), who 'sum up the aspirations and prejudices of my generation'.

> I see certain common tendencies which may be called the Spirit of the Age. One is a tendency to be bored with the problems of Sex and Socialism, which so vexed our seniors; another is the horror of the 'ye olde' picturesque, folk-dancing, art-and-crafty relaxations of our seniors; another is a disposition to regard very seriously mystical experience and the more disciplined forms of religion; another is a complete freedom from any kind of prudery.
>
> (EAR 47)

The strategy of setting up as spokesman for youth worked, and it was in this light that most readers approached Waugh's first novels and travel books. Already in 1928, Cyril Connolly praised *Decline and Fall* for its 'subtle metallic' humour, 'which, more than anything else, seems a product of this generation'; by 1930, reviewers greeted *Labels*: 'no writer quite so representative of his own day has appeared as Evelyn Waugh'; 'If I were asked who best represents the post-war spirit I should reply unhesitatingly, "Evelyn Waugh"' (CH 86, 118, 116).

But the essays on youth were also deliberately misleading. Even Wyndham Lewis was taken in: *The Doom of Youth* classes Waugh with the lightweight Godfrey Winn as founders of the 'Youth Racket', proponents of mere lawlessness; Lewis suspected him of Marxism (99, 106). True, Waugh chaffs both 'the phalanx of the Indestructible Forties' (the generation who had fought in World War I and now blocked youth's advancement) and the generation of the fathers, who only think they are 'modern':

> In the Church we see tough old clergymen expounding the exploded heresies of the Dark Ages under the name of 'Modern' Churchmen. Cézanne died long before we were born and still his imitators proclaim their paintings as 'Modern' Art.... There are the Peter Pans of Bloomsbury, the skittish old critics who will not grow up, who must always be in the movement.
>
> (EAR 46)

But such examples suggest a commitment to very traditional standards. For all Waugh's ultra-modern pose, his essays 'defend' the young by arguing that they could scarcely have turned out better, given the failure of their elders to discipline them, to inculcate those standards. 'The War and the Younger Generation' (1929) makes the case most clearly:

> Every accident of environment contributed to make of this latter generation the undiscriminating and ineffectual people we lament today.... Darkened streets, food rations, the impending dread of the War Office telegram, hysterical outbursts of hate and sentiment... these were the circumstances which war-time children observed as universal... the real and lasting injury was caused, not by danger, but by the pervading sense of inadequacy. Everything was a 'substitute' for something else, and there was barely enough of that. The consequence is a generation of whom 950 in every thousand are totally lacking in any sense of qualitative value...
>
> The only thing which could have saved these unfortunate children was the imposition by rigid discipline, as soon as it became possible, of the standards of civilization. This was still possible in 1918 when the young schoolmasters came back to their work. Unfortunately, a great number... came with their own faith sadly shaken in those very standards which, avowedly, they had fought to preserve. They returned with a jolly tolerance of everything 'modern'. Every effort was made to encourage the children at the public schools to 'think for themselves'. When they should have been whipped and taught Greek paradigms, they were set arguing about birth control and nationalization. Their crude little opinions were treated with respect.... It is hardly surprising that they were Bolshevik at 18 and bored at 20.
>
> (EAR 62)

Thus it is 'absurd to blame' the young if 'they turn instinctively to the second-rate in art and life'. Behind such half-flippant argument is a belief that would run through all Waugh's fiction: 'The muscles which encounter the most resistance in daily routine are those which become most highly developed and adapted. It is thus that the restraint of a traditional culture tempers and directs creative impulses. Freedom produces sterility.' As he wrote ten years later, 'One of the good effects of discipline should be to provoke a healthy resistance' (RUL 203). *Decline and Fall* and *Vile Bodies* mount the same case.

By 1932 Waugh admitted what had all along been his double game. 'The Youth boom has been very convenient for young men like myself who have made a living by it, but it seems to me time that criticism adopted some more significant standard' (EAR 128). 'Matter-of-Fact Mothers' had grazingly attacked the young's 'intolerable tolerance'; in 1932, a contribution on 'Tolerance' to a series on 'The Seven Deadly Sins of Today' offers the forthright statement,

> It is better to be narrow-minded than to have no mind, to hold limited and rigid principles than none at all.
> That is the danger which faces so many people today – to have no considered opinions on any subject, to put up with what is wasteful and harmful with the excuse that there is 'good in everything' – which in most cases means an inability to distinguish between good and bad.
> There are still things which are worth fighting *against*.[42]

But by this time Waugh's marriage had ended in divorce.

VII

The collapse of Waugh's first marriage during the summer of 1929 has occasioned speculation and debate. Christopher Sykes, who met Waugh only in 1930 and never knew Evelyn Gardner, loyally told a story in which 'Evelyn's friends were shocked by the betrayal of which he had been the victim' (Sykes 140); Martin Stannard veered to an opposite extreme. The most balanced account emerges from new research by Selina Hastings.

In June, while She-Evelyn remained in London to enjoy a busy social season, Waugh – who always required seclusion 'to maintain the fervent preoccupation which is absolutely necessary to composition' (L 176) – went to Beckley to continue his new novel, *Vile Bodies*, returning on weekends. Nancy Mitford moved into their flat to keep She-Evelyn company, and Acton, Heygate, and Tony Bushell escorted her to the many parties of a season that Mitford thought the most extravagant of the interwar years: a White Party, a Circus Party, a Baby Party, Heygate's own Party Without End, Bryan and Diana Guinness's 1860s Party.[43] On 9 July Waugh received a letter from his wife saying she had fallen in love with Heygate. He rushed home, offering reconciliation if she would give up her infatuation. She-Evelyn at first agreed, but was soon photographed at yet another party, on Heygate's arm. Over two tense weeks, according to Pansy Pakenham, She-Evelyn 'so obviously was determined to make it impossible for Waugh to take her back that while promising to return to him if he wished, she took care that he shouldn't' (Hastings 195). Alec Waugh recalled a conversation with her at this time:

> 'How is Evelyn taking it?' I asked.
> 'It's terrible. He's drinking much too much. It makes him feel ill. And he thinks I'm trying to poison him.'

Poor, poor Evelyn, racked by a 'Belladonna' hallucination.

'You always seemed so happy together,' I said.

'Yes, I suppose I was,' then after a pause, 'but never as happy as I've been with my sisters.'

That seemed an extraordinary thing for a wife to say about a husband.

(*Brother* 191)

After two weeks Waugh lost patience and wired to Munich, where Heygate had gone to stay with Anthony Powell: 'Instruct Heygate return immediately Waugh.'

Both Evelyns' parents counselled further consideration. Waugh agreed to delay any decision while She-Evelyn, sent to an aunt in Venice, also thought matters through. She soon ended all hope of reconciliation by returning to London to live with Heygate. Waugh sued for divorce on 3 September, after only fourteen months of marriage. She-Evelyn said on hearing the news: 'Well, you can't call life dull!' (Hastings 199). Unlike Tony Last in *A Handful of Dust*, Waugh did not act the gentleman by taking the blame; his wife agreed to appear as respondent.

'I did not know it was possible to be so miserable and live', Waugh wrote during the strained month of August 1929 (L 39). Friends and critics reading his novels of the 1930s – especially *A Handful of Dust*, described by Acton as 'written in blood' (*More* 318) – have all too readily found in that succession of tales of men betrayed by women evidence of a deep and enduring psychological wound. But all Waugh's important stories written before his divorce – 'Antony,' 'The Balance,' *Decline and Fall* – had also told of men betrayed by women. His pain in the autumn of 1929 seems to have been more humiliation than heartbreak. 'There is practically no part of one that is not injured when a thing like this happens,' he wrote to Henry Yorke, 'but vanity is one of the things one is most generally conscious of' (L 40). John Sutro thought his friend felt 'intense humiliation', as if 'he had been held up to ridicule'; Diana Guinness diagnosed 'wounded pride' mixed with a certain 'relief' and in their many weeks together found him 'the best company imaginable. Never was there a more agreeable man'; 'we laughed all the time'. Dudley Carew, the friend who knew Waugh best at this time, said later 'I have never been able to convince myself that' his wife's defection 'had such traumatic consequences for Evelyn as those who knew him afterwards seem incline to believe'.[44]

Nor was Waugh too distraught to return to *Vile Bodies*, finished by the end of September. He had left off in July halfway through, just before the introduction in chapter 7 of Ginger Littlejohn, whom Nina marries and betrays. ('The reader may, perhaps, notice the transition from gaiety to bitterness', he explained in a 1964 preface.) By December he could write to Henry Yorke, 'I have decided that I have gone on for too long in that fog of sentimentality & I am going to stop hiding away from everyone. I was getting into a sort of Charlie Chaplinish Pagliacci attitude to myself as the man with a tragedy in his life and a tender smile for children. So all that must stop' (L 41).

The marriage had been undertaken too young and too lightly. Perhaps, as his mother thought, Waugh had left his wife too much alone; perhaps he was still too much the homosexual. Mrs Nightingale (as She-Evelyn became) confided to Martin Stannard, 'my marriage wasn't exactly warm. Evelyn was not an affectionate person. I was' (ST1 185), leading Stannard to speculate about a sexual failure on Waugh's side – a failure perhaps also reflected in an article Waugh wrote in the summer of 1930, 'Tell the Truth About Marriage':

> Responsible people – doctors, psychologists, novelists – write in the papers and say, 'You cannot lead a happy life unless your sex life is happy.' That seems to me just about as sensible as saying, 'You cannot lead a happy life unless your golf life is happy.' It is not only nonsense, it is mischievous nonsense. It means that the moment a wife begins to detect imperfections in her husband she thinks her whole life is ruined.... Then they get into the divorce courts.
>
> (EAR 94–6)

Both *Gilbert Pinfold* and *Men at Arms* tell of honeymoons marred by young couples' 'not knowing how to set about what needs to be done'; perhaps the two Evelyns, like Adam and Nina in *Vile Bodies*, 'suffer[ed] from being sophisticated about sex before they were at all widely experienced'.[45]

By 1932, Waugh speaks of the mistake of thinking of marriage as 'a temporary emotional relationship instead of a permanent social one', a mistake that denies to each party 'moral development within the unit of home and family'.[46] With the break-up of his marriage he moved out of the flat in Islington, and for the next eight years remained rootless, with no regular home or fixed address. He kept constantly on the move between the houses of his friends, trips abroad, country inns (for writing), his London club, and – sometimes only to pick up letters, books, and a change of clothes – Underhill. The affection for stable country-house life in Waugh's novels of the 1930s stems in part from his own lack of such stability.

To escape London in August 1929 he visited Richard and Elizabeth Plunket Greene, then went to Belfast with their brother David, an amateur driver, to watch what *The Times* called 'the greatest motor road race in history' – material soon to find its way into *Vile Bodies*.[47] Next he stayed with Bryan and Diana Guinness at their house outside Dublin. (Here he wrote the article 'Let the Marriage Ceremony Mean Something', arguing that 'The real value of marriage to any two people is not so much the opportunity for each other's society which it provides as the illusion of permanence.')[48] He then moved on to Pansy Pakenham and Henry Lamb, now married, while Henry completed his portrait; to his Oxford friends, the Byzantinist David Talbot Rice and his wife Tamara (with whom he stayed up discussing religion); and the Guinnesses again, this time at their apartment in Paris. (Waugh dedicated *Vile Bodies* to the Guinnesses, and later made them a gift of the manuscript.)[49] After Christmas he was off to Ireland with Frank Pakenham, now a frequent companion, to Pakenham Hall, the Gothic Revival house of Frank's elder brother, the Earl of Longford.

It was the immediate success of *Vile Bodies*, published on 14 January 1930 – three days before Waugh's divorce was granted – that brought him national fame and wealth sufficient, as Cyril Connolly said, 'to form himself into an ideal of the tough, rather rakish English gentleman of the early Thirties' (WM 17). The strategies of public insolence and speaking for the young had paid off. Reviewers were lavish with words like 'outrageous', 'audacious', 'impertinent' and 'smart':

> Mr. Waugh is very clever and amusing, but, above all, he is smart. The only book which could be read immediately after this one without giving the impression of dowdiness is 'Decline and Fall', last year's model by the same artist. One feels the same awe-stricken admiration for it as one feels for 'the last word' in a car or a hat or any other triumphant expression of the spirit, not of the age, but of the moment.
> (*Nation and Athenaeum*, 15 Feb. 1930, 682)

Like *Decline and Fall*, *Vile Bodies* brims with the stage-properties of modernity, from cocktails and car-racing to aeroplanes, films, telephone chatter and the vogue of professionalized interior decoration. Rebecca West wrote: 'This young man, I fancy, is destined to be the dazzling figure of his age as Max Beerbohm was of his'; V. S. Pritchett framed his response more simply: 'I laughed until I was driven out of the room.'[50]

Vile Bodies was twice adapted for the stage (first in a version that had the good fortune to be censored); it helped spread a craze for the language of the Bright Young People, terms like 'shy-making' and 'too, too sick-making'. In imitation of the novel's Miss Mouse, Ramsay Macdonald's daughter Isabel held a (nonalcoholic) bottle party at 10 Downing Street. Its success launched Waugh in society, bringing him to the tables of the Mayfair hostesses Sybil Colefax and Emerald Cunard. And on the strength of its commentary on contemporary fashions, Peters found Waugh more journalistic work than he could handle, even as he began sharply raising his prices. The *Daily Mail* paid thirty guineas a week for thirteen articles, of only a few paragraphs each, on any topic he chose; the *Graphic*, ten guineas each for weekly book reviews (in eighteen weeks Waugh reviewed 84 books). Editors sought him for the glossy pages of *Harper's Bazaar* and *Town and Country*. 'That brings my regular income temporarily up to about £2,500 a year. I feel rather elated about it' (D 309). (Throughout the thirties editors complained of Waugh's prices, but paid them; his annual income through the decade, spent as soon as earned, averaged £2000, of which about a third came from journalism.)[51]

Shortly after *Vile Bodies* appeared (and while also producing about ten essays a month), Waugh began *Labels*. He wrote it mainly while visiting Diana and Bryan Guinness; he grew deeply attached to Diana, then radiantly pregnant and hungry for companionship. Their relationship, later explored in *Work Suspended* (as Waugh himself admitted (L 639)) in the love of John Plant for the pregnant wife of a friend in *Work Suspended*, was the first of many passionate attachments to worldly and highly cultivated women (the Lygon sisters, Diana Cooper, Nancy Mitford, Ann Fleming), all safe relationships because a sexual connection was impossible. *Labels* was finished in April 1930 and again dedicated to the Guinnesses. The American title was *A Bachelor Abroad*: Waugh solved the problem of writing about his honeymoon after being divorced by converting himself and

Evelyn Gardner into the newlyweds Gregory and Juliet, whom the narrator befriends (and whose saccharine endearments he lampoons).

That summer he engaged in a tepid affair with Audrey, unhappily married daughter of E. V. Lucas; now Waugh had the pleasure of being the pursued rather than the pursuer. (When it briefly appeared that Audrey might be pregnant, he recorded only, 'I don't care either way really so long as it is a boy', and a few days later, 'She says she is not going to have a baby so all that is bogus': D 312, 316.) *Labels* appeared in September 1930, completing Waugh's *annus mirabilis*. It was prefaced by the Author's Note: 'So far as this book contains any serious opinions, they are those of the dates with which it deals, eighteen months ago. Since then my views on several subjects, particularly on Roman Catholicism, have developed and changed in many ways.' In July he had asked Olivia Greene to find him a religious instructor, and on 29 September 1930, a week after *Labels* appeared, was received into the Roman Catholic Church. Waugh's conversion, so much longer in the making than his first travel book, needs to be considered first.

VIII

Though it came as painful news to his family – Arthur Waugh liked to speak of his son's 'perversion' to Rome (Greenidge 11) – and surprised even Catholic friends like Christopher Hollis, no one following the London gossip-columns in September 1930 could have been unaware that the author of *Vile Bodies* had converted. Waugh invited Tom Driberg, whose 'Talk of the Town' column appeared in the *Daily Express*, to the ceremony. Like 'modern youth', 'the condition of the Church' was what editors in the popular press called a 'talking point' (K 232), and celebrity defections to Rome always made good copy: Waugh joined Alfred Noyes, G. K. Chesterton, Eric Gill, Compton Mackenzie, Maurice Baring, Arnold Lunn, Ronald Knox, Graham Greene and Wyndham Lewis. The *Express*, for which he had worked and in which he now published, served as 'a kind of journalistic sponsor at Waugh's conversion', both newspaper and author profiting from the publicity (Linck 26). On 30 September it ran the headline: 'Another Author Turns to Rome, Mr. Evelyn Waugh Leaves Church of England, Young Satirist of Mayfair'. (An accompanying editorial, in which Waugh may have had a hand, cites a 'longing for permanency' and escape from the 'cocktail world' as reasons why a young man with 'an almost passionate adherence to the ultra-modern' might turn 'to the Church that does not alter with the years'.) Such coverage generated correspondence, and by the end of October, in a show of correcting misconceptions, the paper announced on its front page: 'My Conversion to Rome, by Evelyn Waugh, the Young Novelist, A Striking Article, See Page 10 Today'. Inside was 'Converted To Rome: Why It Has Happened To Me' (EAR 103–5).

Nowhere do Waugh's diaries or his carefully impersonal public statements probe his feelings about the event or its preparation. For all his self-advertisement, he did not regard such personal information as 'included in the price of my book[s]' (EAR 301); as he wrote in concluding *Ninety-Two Days*, 'The journey was over and here the book might well come to an end.... It makes no claim to being a spiritual odyssey. Whatever interior changes there were – and all experience makes some change – are the writer's own property and not a marketable commodity' (167). Underpinning such reticence was a deep belief that psychology itself, especially psychoanalysis, is a sham: 'Voodoo, Bog-magic, the wise woman's cabin.' 'Psychology – there isn't such a thing as psychology', he told an interviewer in 1949; 'Like the word *slenderizing*. There isn't such a word. The whole thing's a fraud.'[52] When another interviewer asked too closely about his characters' thoughts, Waugh replied: 'But look, I think that your questions are dealing too much with the creation of character and not enough with the technique of writing. I regard writing not as investigation of character, but as an exercise in the use of language. . . . I have no technical psychological interest' (Jebb 110).

Such hostility to 'psychology' was widely shared among the devout, especially Catholics suspicious of all speculative systems that undermined belief in the soul, will and divine purpose. 'Then there is the enormous progress of psychology – all clean against us for at least a century' declares an old Catholic in the grim futuristic world of Robert Hugh Benson's *Lord of the World* (1907), a novel that made a lasting impression on Waugh. (Benson's atheist anti-hero Oliver Brand 'had wondered once or twice in his life how human beings could believe such rubbish' as Catholicism, 'but psychology had helped him'.) For Baron Friedrich von Hügel, only religion 'makes straight for' realities; 'psychology' merely 'potter[s] over those other, lesser things.'[53] During World War II, Waugh once had to undergo a psychological examination. After a barrage of questions about his childhood and parents, he counterattacked: 'Why have you not questioned me about the most important thing in a man's life – his religion?' 'People are going mad & talking balls to psychiatrists,' he wrote to John Betjeman in 1946, 'not because of accidents to the chamber-pot in the nursery, but because there is no logical structure to their beliefs.'[54] He was always quick to deny, on principle, the relevance of psychology to religious phenomena such as vocation and especially conversion. In a 1949 exchange with V. S. Pritchett and others in the *New Statesman* on Thomas Merton's monastic vocation, he stressed that Merton had not simply found 'a manner of life that suited his psychological state', but was 'guided by a power *outside himself*', and so ranked among the 'men and women who were called personally by God for special services – not those who *felt* called, but who were so in fact'.[55] A deliberate reticence shrouds the conversions of the central characters of *Brideshead* and *Helena*: both events pointedly occur offstage, implying that as works of grace, comings-to-faith are not finally explicable in psychological terms (i.e., through narrative) at all.

Waugh's accounts of his conversion – 'Converted to Rome', 'Come Inside' (written in 1949 for a collection of conversion stories) and the 'Brief History of My Religious Opinions' in *A Little Learning* – are thus uncompromisingly general: a youthful period of shallow ritualistic piety is followed by adolescent 'atheism' or 'agnosticism' (triggered by exposure to the most rudimentary bits of sceptical argument and Higher Criticism); the ensuing period of dissipated young manhood then yields to the only persuasive offer of meaning and hope. 'Those who have read my works will perhaps understand the character of the world into which I exuberantly launched myself [after Lancing]. Ten years of that world sufficed to show me that life there, or anywhere, was unintelligible and unendurable without God' (EAR 367). These narratives make Waugh's conversion seem both sudden, and as simple and straightforward as the solution to a problem in geometry – a change of mind as easy as that of the newly converted Virginia Troy, who says in *Unconditional Surrender*: 'I mean it's all quite obvious really, isn't it, when you come to think of it?' (US 206). If Christianity, then its original institution, Catholicism; 'It only remained to examine the historical and philosophic grounds for supposing the Christian revelation to be genuine. I was fortunate enough to be introduced to a brilliant and holy priest [Martin D'Arcy] who undertook to prove this to me, and so on firm intellectual conviction but with little emotion I was admitted into the Church' (EAR 368). Father D'Arcy described his catechumen: 'talking with him [was] an interesting discussion based primarily on reason. I have never myself met a convert who so strongly based his assent on truth. It was a special pleasure to make contact with so able a brain' (HW 64).

But in 1930 as now, the willingness of so worldly, irreverent, and self-indulgent a spirit to submit to the most dogmatic of churches seemed to call for further explanation. Waugh's enemies would charge that he had succumbed to Rome's aesthetic appeal, or to a snobbish taste for England's old Catholic nobility, or that he had simply asserted an ornery contrarianism in the face of an increasingly secular modernity. (The last was always among Waugh's favourite amusements. 'If he was accused of some quality usually regarded as contemptible ... he studied it, polished up his performance, and treating it as both normal and admirable, made it his own' (Donaldson 21); he doubtless relished championing a faith that 'progressive' intellectuals deplored.) Many suspected that he fled to Rome to escape the hurt of Evelyn Gardner's desertion.

Waugh was aware of all these explanations and was at pains to rebut them. When a reviewer of *Brideshead* charged that his faith stemmed from 'love of money' and a preference for 'the company of the European upper classes,' he replied:

> I can assure you it had no influence on my conversion. In England Catholicism is predominantly a religion of the poor. There is a handful of Catholic aristocratic families but I knew none of them in 1930 when I was received into the Church. My friends were fashionable agnostics and the Faith I then accepted had none of the extraneous glamour which your reviewer imputes to it.[56]

Waugh knew in 1930 that most Englishmen associated Catholicism with smug piety, superstitious cult practices, and lower-class, largely Irish membership. (There had been no protest during World War I when Lord Kitchener decreed that Roman Catholics should not serve under Catholic officers, lest Irish soldiers thereby become ungovernable.) Nor was his choice aesthetic, like that of the sentimental converts of the *fin de siècle*: 'in this country, where all the finest ecclesiastical buildings are in the hands of the Anglican Church, and where the liturgy is written in prose of unexampled beauty, the purely aesthetic appeal is, on the whole, rather against the Roman Church' (EAR 103). Waugh surely had his own experience in mind when he wrote in 1959 of his friend and fellow-convert Ronald Knox: 'when he was canvassing the advice of his Anglican friends and relations about his change of obedience, they all warned him that whatever the historical grandeurs of the Church of Rome, he would find himself in twentieth-century England associating with men who were notoriously deficient in taste and manners' (K 292–3). Conversion meant giving up (Waugh thought) the chance to remarry; it ended valued friendships, such as that with the vehemently anti-papist Robert Byron. 'Nothing in the Church attracted him save her divine authority' (K 156).

Waugh's accounts of his turn from 'atheism' to faith – a kind of narrative in which sudden conversion is conventional – in fact mask a gradual process: as he would also say of Gilbert Pinfold, the word '"conversion" suggests an event much more sudden' (GP 6) than really occurred. He was on the way to Rome from the mid-twenties, long before the failure of his first marriage, even before the publication of his first novel. In 1927 he had considered becoming a clergyman (D 281). The collapse of his marriage only speeded events already under way. Announcing his divorce to Alec in 1929, he complained: 'The trouble about the world today is that there's not enough religion in it. There's nothing to stop young people doing whatever they feel like doing at the moment.'[57]

Many of Waugh's closest friends during the period of his 'agnosticism' were markedly devout, either as Anglo-Catholics (Betjeman, Tom Driberg, Billy Clonmore – the last soon also to convert), Catholics (Acton, Woodruff), or Catholic converts (Hollis, Graham, Gwen and Olivia Greene). He was close to Hollis and especially Graham at the time of their conversions, and his diaries of the twenties record frequent religious discussions and attendance at 'Mass with Alastair'. Many of these references are of course of the baiting variety, like the letter he wrote pious Tom Driberg soon after going up to Oxford: 'I do no work and never go to Chapel' (L 7). *The Scarlet Woman* was in part a way of chaffing friends like Graham and Hollis, who kept thrusting their views at him. He had become a peculiarly energetic doubter. Once, after several weeks spent with Alastair, Waugh 'went out to read Gibbon in the church' (D 170). The man who would take such trouble wants both to read Gibbon and to be in church.

Starting in 1925 the tone of these references changes. There are late-night discussions of the kind dear to youth: 'We [Graham, Hollis, and Waugh] got drunk in the evening and argued about foreigners and absolution' (D 257). On at least one occasion, given what we know of his interlocutors, Waugh seems to have taken the role of faith's defender: 'Claud and I took Audrey to supper and sat up until 7 in the morning arguing about the Roman Church' (D 237). By 1928, he records fairly frequent church-going on his own, treating such occasions as routine.

His earliest publications reveal the same preoccupations. *P.R.B* (1926) repeatedly recurs to the religious views of its subjects; *Rossetti* berates 'crude Liberal atheism' and comments of Gabriele Rossetti, Dante's father: 'A Catholic who had never recovered his faith from the raw free-thinking of his youth, he . . . left his children very little but a mild and muddled awe with which to confront a very difficult world' (R 126, 14–15). The book ends with its diagnosis of Rossetti's artistic 'failure' as rooted in 'spiritual inadequacy'. A later essay makes the diagnosis clearer: 'Certainly [his father] did a huge injury to Gabriel in depriving him of his faith. . . . If he had been schooled in the habit, once firmly attached to that invisible thread of Chesterton's, his moral failure, which at every point frustrated his genius, would have been saved' (EAR 376–7).

Finally, there were Gwen and Olivia Greene, who had converted in 1925. Even while employed far from London, Waugh saw as much of both as he could; in January 1926 he had 'Tea with Gwen who has lent me von Hugel's letters to her to read' (D 243). The famous Catholic historian and theological busybody had married Gwen's aunt Mary Herbert; Gwen's selection of *Letters from Baron Friedrich von Hügel to a Niece*, published in 1928, became a popular work of apologetics. (We find Paul Pennyfeather reading the book at the end of *Decline and Fall*.) Much in the *Letters* is congruent with what we know soon to be Waugh's own beliefs, often expressed in language close to his.

Asked 'what kind of spiritual reading came his way in the earlier period of indecision', Waugh also singled out Mrs Greene's *Mt. Zion* (1929), a powerfully personal work that purports to answer questions mailed by readers of the *Letters*. She wrote for instance of the Church of England, expressing sentiments soon to become Waugh's own:

> Man, who loves romance, beauty, poetry, was given a religion without any expression for these elements in himself[;] his faith became thin and empty and he no longer ran into his church as his natural home; it was always locked up except on Sundays. . . . Yet religion is not social service. . . . The Englishman has a heart the same as anyone else, and it is not so long ago that the English Church was Catholic, and not only national, and meant a home for everyone.[58]

A similar spirit infused Mrs Greene's conversations, full of what in *Brideshead* Lady Marchmain calls 'the poetry, the Alice-in-Wonderland side, of religion' (BR 113). Olivia's was an even more passionate and mystical piety. On conversion she renounced life as a flapper for a vow of chastity (later years would bring religious mania); she became an energetic proselytizer (as Waugh himself would later seek to convert all those he cared for). It was Olivia who, Waugh recalled gratefully, 'bullied me into the Church' (Sykes 156), directing him in 1930 to Farm Street and Fr D'Arcy.

Waugh's 'firm intellectual conviction but little emotion' reflects both his own temperament in 1930 and the public character of the institutional, teaching Church he joined, then enjoying a Scholastic revival and triumphantly sure in its possession of a finished, complete, systematic account of matters of faith and morals.[59] Waugh's stance was also that of Fr D'Arcy, a distinguished neo-Thomist who argued in his treatise on *The Nature of Belief* (1931) that not 'intuition' or 'sentiment' but 'reasoned assent' must be the criterion of religious truth; to believe otherwise was to fall into 'subjectivism'. 'The Faith', Waugh wrote in 1935, was a 'logical system', 'absolutely satisfactory to the mind, enlisting all knowledge and reason in its cause', 'completely compelling to any who give it an "indifferent and quiet audience"' (EC126).

While the Church emphasized its supreme deposit of truth, English Catholics in the wake of World War I also mounted a case (learnt from their Continental co-religionists) for its cultural mission. Popular and articulate apologists such as G. K. Chesterton and Hilaire Belloc – both of whom Waugh read and admired – vigorously asserted the centrality of Catholicism to the very idea of European 'civilization', and exemplified the connection in prose of high artistic merit. Belloc wrote in 1920 of the possibilities for evangelizing his countrymen:

> It is essential for us to impress it upon our contemporaries that the Catholic is intellectually the superior of everyone except the sceptic.... Four powers govern man, avarice, lust, fear and snobbishness. One can use the latter. One cannot use the first three. Blackmail ... would cut little ice. Pay we cannot, because we are not rich enough.... Threaten we cannot, because we are nobody, and all the temporal power is on the other side. But we *can* spread the mood that we are the bosses and the *chic* and that a man who does not accept the faith writes himself down as suburban.
>
> (Wilson, *Belloc*, 242–3)

Such 'snobbery' is based not on class or income but possession of a cosmopolitan, historic culture such as T. S. Eliot would soon also celebrate. Two of Belloc's best-known slogans were 'The Faith is Europe, and Europe is the Faith' and 'A European people or individual is, other things being equal, more civilized as it or he is more Catholic'. 'Before the coming of Christianity there was no Europe' argued Waugh's friend, the Catholic historian Christopher Dawson in such works as *The Making of Europe* (1932). Even Fr D'Arcy pauses from his Scholastic rigours to put forward similar views in *The Nature of Belief*.[60] Waugh's *Campion* can be read as an attempt to demonstrate these propositions for England through a Catholic reading of the English Reformation. That already in 1930 he accepted such arguments about the Catholic basis of European civilization is clear from a passage in 'Converted to Rome' that is also crucial for understanding the framework of historical allusion that informs his novels.

> It seems to me that in the present phase of European history the essential issue is no longer between Catholicism, on one side, and Protestantism, on the other, but between Christianity and Chaos. It is much the same situation as existed in the early Middle Ages. In the sixteenth and seventeenth centuries conflicting social and political forces rendered irreconcilable the division between two great groups of Christian thought. In the eighteenth and nineteenth centuries the choice before any educated European was between Christianity, in whatever form it was presented to him in the circumstances of his upbringing, and, on the other side, a polite and highly attractive scepticism. So great, indeed, was the inherited subconscious power of Christianity that it was nearly two centuries before the real nature of this loss of faith became apparent.
>
> Today we can see it on all sides as the active negation of all that western culture has stood for. Civilization – and by this I do not mean talking cinemas and tinned

food, nor even surgery and hygienic houses, but the whole moral and artistic organization of Europe – has not in itself the power of survival. It came into being through Christianity, and without it has no significance or power to command allegiance. The loss of faith in Christianity and the consequential lack of confidence in moral and social standards have become embodied in the ideal of a materialistic, mechanized state, already existent in Russia and rapidly spreading south and west. It is no longer possible, as it was in the time of Gibbon, to accept the benefits of civilization and at the same time deny the supernatural basis upon which it rests.

(EAR 103–4)

But it is important to recognize as well how the nature of Waugh's faith changed as he grew older, more secure and mature in his Church. He wrote Fr D'Arcy during his instruction:

> As I said when we first met, I realize that the Roman Catholic Church is the only genuine form of Christianity. Also that Christianity is the essential and formative constituent of western culture. In our conversations and in what I have read or heard since, I have been able to understand a great deal of the dogma and discipline which seemed odd to me before. But the trouble is that I don't feel Christian in the absolute sense. The question seems to be must I wait until I do feel this – which I suppose is a gift from God which no amount of instruction can give one, or can I become a Catholic when I am in such an incomplete state – and so get the benefit of the sacraments and receive faith afterward?

(Phillips 54)

A more thoroughgoing identification with his faith would come, especially in the form of a very personal idea of vocation that emerges in the 1940s. Though he never stopped thinking of himself as what he called a 'logical rule-of-thumb Catholic' (EAR 364), Waugh's faith matured from an early emphasis on 'logic' to greater concern with the historical and the personal. While many Catholics moved in the opposite direction, he increasingly emphasized what Charles Ryder calls the Church's 'intransigeant historical claims' (BR 77) and ritual practices that he had once thought 'superstitious'.

The new convert of 1930 delighted in affronting popular secular opinion by celebrating the 'delicate and interesting refinements of logic' to be found in such knotty theologians as the seventeenth-century Spanish Jesuit Francisco Suárez. Against the 'old theory' of the Renaissance 'as a vindication of human reason against authority', he argued 'the more tenable view that it was a superstitious, sensual and romantic movement against the restrictions of Thomist logic' (EAR 225). Systematic theology – in the popular mind a source of learned obscurities – he insisted (in good neoscholastic fashion) on calling a 'science' – indeed, a 'science of simplification'. In a famous passage redolent of Catholic contempt for the Reformation churches' efforts to revive a 'pure' primitive Christianity, he reflected of a visit to the dark, disorderly Abyssinian monastery of Debra Lebanos in 1930:

> I had sometimes thought it an odd thing that Western Christianity, alone of all the religions of the world, exposes its mysteries to every observer, but I was so

accustomed to this openness that I had never before questioned whether it was an essential and natural feature of the Christian system. Indeed, so saturated are we in this spirit that many people regard the growth of the Church as a process of elaboration – even of obfuscation; they visualize the Church of the first century as a little cluster of pious people reading the Gospels together, praying and admonishing each other with a simplicity to which the higher ceremonies and subtle theology of later years would have been bewildering and unrecognisable. At Debra Lebanos I suddenly saw the classic basilica and open altar as a great positive achievement, a triumph of light over darkness consciously accomplished, and I saw theology as the science of simplification by which nebulous and elusive ideas are formalised and made intelligible and exact.... I began to see how these obscure sanctuaries had grown, with the clarity of the Western reason, into the great open altars of Catholic Europe, where Mass is said in a flood of light, high in the sight of all, while tourists can clatter round with their Baedekers, incurious of the mystery.

(RP 88–9)

Individual ritual practices meant little to Waugh in these years. As if to prove the hard-headedness of his new faith, *Labels* (1930) consistently laughs at 'superstitions', especially veneration of relics. 'We went to Cana of Galilee, where a little girl was offering wine jars for sale. They were the authentic ones used in the miracle. If they were too big she had a small size indoors; yes, the smaller ones were authentic, too' (64). In the Church of Sansevero in Naples, a girl takes him downstairs to see what at first look like statues, but turn out to be 'exhumed corpses':

There were man and woman. The man's body was slit open, revealing a tangle of dry lungs and digestive organs. The little girl thrust her face into the aperture and inhaled deeply and greedily. She called on me to do the same.
'Smell good,' she said. 'Nice.'
We went up into the church.
I asked her about the corpses. 'They are the work of the priest,' she said.

(*Labels* 57–8)

The young Waugh thus treated 'superstitions' in the manner of the as-yet-unconverted Charles Ryder: 'You think you can kneel down in front of a statue and say a few words, not even out loud, just in your mind, and change the weather?' (BR 77–8). In later years Waugh offered just such prayers:

I went to London by train for Teresa's ball [his daughter's coming-out party]. It was dark with some drizzle after a stormy night, but I had sent £2 to the Poor Clares at Looe asking them to arrange good weather from 7 pm onwards and at 7 it cleared and remained fine throughout the night; a remarkable performance by these excellent women to whom I have sent another £3.

(D 764)

Harold Acton recalled a visit in 1952 with a hobbling, rheumatoid Waugh to a church in Palermo where 8000 corpses of the faithful were on open display:

The monk who showed us round rattled off a facetious commentary in slangy English like a Shakespearean clown. Evelyn ordered him sharply to shut up. He spent a full hour examining the grisly relics with an expression akin to rapture. According to my guide book, 'the atmosphere of the catacombs is impregnated with a smell so offensive that it cannot be wholesome,' but Evelyn differed. He announced that his knee was cured and left his stick in the taxi. Whether it was due to the dryness of the air or the emanations of the mummies, he felt so much better that he would recommend it in future to sufferers from rheumatism. Turning to take a last sniff, he muttered 'Delicious!' as if it had been jasmine.

(More Memoirs 316)

Men at Arms (1952) attributes efficacy to a religious medal; *Helena* (1950) details the life of a saint whose achievement was to find a relic, the True Cross. Waugh never lost his belief that, because Catholicism's 'intransigeant historical claims' extended beyond the life of Christ to the long tradition of the Church, 'in the economy of revelation dogma develops from the vague to the definite'.[61] But he could write in 1962 that though 'Sharp minds may explore the subtlest verbal problems', 'I know of no [lay theologian] whose judgment I would prefer to that of the simplest parish priest' (EAR 606).

Further travel, more adventurous than the voyage described in *Labels*, was crucial in precipitating this change. He told Penelope Betjeman in 1948: 'It took me years to begin to glimpse what the Church was like. I was constantly travelling in those days and it was chiefly missionaries who taught me' (L 267). Waugh was deeply moved while travelling by the brotherhood he found among fellow believers of distant nations and different races; such experience convinced him that 'Western reason' mattered less than the individual's relation to God. Exposure in 1938 to Mexican churches in which believers of all classes jostled and 'the limitless variety of the Church seemed to be represented' led him to reflect on Catholicism as 'a faith which, within its structure, allows of measureless diversity' (RUL 234, 208). In such contexts he felt the force of Ronald Knox's point in *The Belief of Catholics* (1927) – 'a text-book for countless catechumens', Waugh noted, and perhaps one he had used himself – that the Church is 'the analogue of a nation or country', but transcending 'the clan, the tribe, the nation'. After visiting a convent in Goa in 1952 he wrote, 'Belloc "Europe and the Faith" my foot.'[62]

These religious experiences were especially important in altering Waugh's early, little-England views on race. *Remote People* (1930) suggests – albeit in a context so wry, one cannot really judge its seriousness – that 'It is just worth considering the possibility that there may be something valuable behind the indefensible and inexplicable assumption of superiority by the Anglo-Saxon race' (RP 191). But by the end of the thirties, he was sure that 'Christianity and the race myth cannot long work together' (RUL 271). The account Waugh wrote in 1956 of R. H. Benson describes his own faith as well: 'Superficially he was an aesthete, but the Catholic church made little aesthetic appeal to him'; 'What he sought and found in the church was authority and catholicity. A national church, however wide the empire . . ., could never speak with universal authority and, because it was provincial, [was] forever incapable of enclosing the vast variety of humanity' (Reynal ix–x).

IX

'The book that interests me most this week' said the *Graphic*'s reviewer in October 1930, 'is a new travel book issued by Duckworth's under the title of "Labels". My interest in it comes less from any outstanding merits it may possess, than from the fact that I wrote it myself.' Though another reviewer called it nothing more than a 'farrago of longitude and platitude', *Labels* contains some of Waugh's finest comic writing.[63] 'Farrago' is just the right word for the genre he had chosen: the most mixed of forms, travel-writing permits the writer to assemble, within the loosest of narrative frames, passages of autobiography, reflective essays, scenes of dialogue, 'discursions' (Osbert Sitwell's word) on art history or the state of society, jokes. (In one long discursion, *Labels* introduces English speakers to the architect Antonio Gaudí, then little known outside Spain.)[64] For an author whose primary ways of generating humor and meaning are clever generic juxtapositions and shifts of tone, it is a perfect choice. Travel-books could be serialized in advance of hardback publication, thereby advertising their author (and usually earning more than the hardback publication). Waugh would eventually write seven travel books and an anthology drawn from the first four, *When the Going Was Good* (1946).

Before leaving on the cruise that led to *Labels*, he made sure his plans were aired in the gossip-columns. Friends in the trade such as Patrick Balfour (son of the prime minister) and Eleanor Smith gladly provided publicity; Lady Eleanor, soon herself to become Catholic, reported in her *Sunday Dispatch* column, under the appropriate title 'Determined – to Impress':

> Mr. Evelyn Waugh, the young author who has written a very funny satirical novelette called *Decline and Fall*, has this idiosyncrasy:
>   That he considers that only two good travel books have ever been written.
>   1. Mr. Robert Byron's Europe in the Looking-Glass.
>   2. The Acts of the Apostles.
>   The third he proposes to write himself.
>   In order to do so he is going to 'do', in prose and picture, the Mediterranean, the Black Sea, and Soviet Russia.
>   He is starting shortly from Monte Carlo in extreme luxury in the Stella Polaris, preparatory to real squalor in a Turkish cargo boat.[65]

From all points of view Waugh's false claim of a Russian destination was useful. It gave him, besides publicity, a way to begin his book: by admitting the ruse in a splendid piece of self-advertisement (including a plug for a previous book).

> My hope was that, when someone saw in the gossip page that I was going to Russia, she would say, what a very interesting young man, and, I must get his life of Dante Gabriel Rossetti out of the circulating library. Well, even this did not happen to any appreciable extent, so I must begin this book, which is going to aim at what the reviewers call the uncompromising sincerity and frankness of youth, by admitting that the whole lie was a flop.
>
> (*Labels* 10)

Meanwhile, the amenities of the *Stella Polaris*, whose owners had made the trip possible, could await graceful insertion in chapter 3.

In announcing Russia as his destination, Waugh sought to profit from growing public interest in the 'Soviet experiment'. Few Westerners visited Soviet Russia before Lenin's death in 1924; those who did, like Bertrand Russell and H. G. Wells, returned with chilling reports. But in the late twenties, as Europe and America experienced economic depression, political thinking began the sharp Leftward swing that would characterize the thirties and lead to enthusiastic curiosity about the one nation that advertised itself as free of unemployment and class division. John Dewey and Theodore Dreiser returned delighted at what they had seen; Alexander Wicksteed marvelled in *Life Under the Soviets* (1928) at 'the complete equality that one finds in Russia'; in *The Challenge of Bolshevism: A New Social Ideal* (1928), D. F. Buxton found 'The Communist view of human nature ... far more inspired by Faith, Hope and Charity than our own'. These opinions were soon echoed by G. B. Shaw, Lady Astor, and Hewlett Johnson (the Dean of Canterbury who found in Russia the 'perfection of Christianity') (Hollander 112–15). Waugh meant to raise expectations of a dissenting view, the kind of witty dissent Robert Byron soon also provided, following a trip with Christopher Sykes, in *First Russia, Then Tibet* (1933).

The author of *Labels* in fact felt himself in competition with Byron, 'the first and best of angry young men', with whom he was often compared but whose career in writing had begun so much earlier than his own.[66] 'I hear Robert has beaten us all by going to India in an aeroplane', he wrote to Henry Yorke in June 1929, 'which is the sort of success which I call tangible' (L 35). By this time Byron had already published three books to Waugh's one – *Europe in the Looking-Glass* (1926), a book on Greece called *The Station* (1928) and *The Byzantine Achievement* (1929); an *Essay on India* would follow in 1931. *Europe*, one of the first of a new generation of ultra-sophisticated travel books to which *Labels* also belongs, had been the fruit of a motor-trip through familiar Continental sites in 1925. To justify a book 'whose interest, if any, ... must depend largely on the angles adopted towards places already familiar,' Byron declared his purpose to be that of measuring at each stop how far 'American influence' had eroded 'European Consciousness' (*Europe* 4, 7). Waugh announces, 'I have called this book *Labels* for the reason that all the places I visited on this trip are already fully labelled', and his purpose 'that of investigating with a mind as open as the English system of pseudo-education allows, the basis for the reputations these famous places have acquired' (16).

Their competition is visible in *Labels* itself. The friendship had already been strained (and would later be destroyed) by Byron's noisy anti-Catholicism. All Byron's books of the twenties pause to attack Rome, the papacy and Catholic art, favouring instead Byzantine and Islamic styles. 'Byzantine is to Mr. Byron what Baroque is to the Sitwells', D. H. Lawrence said in reviewing *The Byzantine Achievement*. In that book Byron had celebrated the mosaic of Christ Pantocrator at Daphne as 'the most absolutely spectacular example of Byzantine representative art extant.'[67] *Labels* coyly replies:

We did, however, ... drive out to the church at Daphne. I think I should be trespassing too dangerously upon Mr. Robert Byron's ground if I were to venture upon any eulogy of these superb mosaics. They have had a disturbed history, what with the arrows of the Crusaders – who were moved by the theological differences of the Western and Eastern patriarchates to shoot away the eyes from the vast head of Christ in the dome – the Turks, who lit log fires in the nave, and, in quite recent times, the missiles of lunatics, who used to resort there from a neighbouring institution, and employed the time between their devotions in throwing stones and old bottles at the glittering ceiling; large parts of them, however, have survived intact.

(Labels 150–1)

Waugh also meant to irritate Byron by consistently mocking 'the glamour of the East,' by running down the Orthodox churches he visited (always unfavourably compared to Catholic), and by his wholesale, deliberately Blimpish condemnations of Islamic art and culture, whose 'stultifying', 'kindergarten' quality moves him 'to something of the Crusader's zeal for cross against crescent'. 'Living as we are under the impact of the collective inferiority of the whole West, ... we can still hold up our heads in the Mohammedan world.... there is no single aspect of Mohammedan art, history, scholarship, or social, religious, or political organization, to which we, as Christians, cannot look with unshaken pride.'[68]

In all this Waugh (like Byron) differs sharply from the travel writers of the generation before his own. 'In the early years of the twentieth century a new breed of literary travellers emerged eager for experience of other cultures to place in a wider context what they saw as the ferocious egotism, and chauvinism, of their forebears. D. H. Lawrence, Norman Douglas, and Aldous Huxley all paid serious attention to "primitive" cultures and disavowed their allegiance to the "mechanist", Christian civilisation of their homeland.'[69] But like Byron, Waugh conceals a deep affection for English life and institutions beneath his mask of flip criticism. Like the essays on youth written at the same time, *Labels* adopts the modern, debunking style, and directs it especially at 'Ye Olde Merrie Englande' (12), but does so in order to insinuate a defence of tradition and home.

The voice of *Labels* is that of a Bright Young worldling, someone who has grown up with such amenities as butlers and is pained by hearing 'intolerable French', but now – like the socialite shopkeepers of his generation – writes books, because 'You see, I couldn't get any other sort of job.'[70] He has friends in Paris; he cannot take 'business' seriously. Most of all, like the speaker in his essays on youth, he is 'modern': in Paris he finds the couture industry, 'because it is modern and commercialized', 'by far the most interesting' aspect of the city. From what Paul Fussell calls the 'I Hate it Here' opening explaining why he leaves England, Waugh portrays himself as beset by 'the hatred and weariness which the modern megalopolitan feels toward his own civilization', 'the world-weariness we all feel at the dead weight of European culture'.[71]

This persona delights in clear-sighted spotting of humbug: the pyramids of Egypt 'are less impressive when seen close'; 'The sphinx is an ill-proportioned composition of inconsiderable aesthetic appeal'. Gibraltar may to the sentimental Thackeray have resembled Britain's imperial lion, but 'to me it appeared like a great slab of green cheese'. Best of all in this vein is Waugh's description of Mt Etna, in a passage perhaps aimed at Byron's lush celebration of Stromboli in *Europe in the Looking-Glass*:

> I do not think I shall ever forget the sight of Etna at sunset; the mountain almost invisible in a blur of pastel grey, glowing on the top and then repeating its shape, as though reflected, in a wisp of grey smoke, with the whole horizon behind radiant with pink light, fading gently into a grey pastel sky. Nothing I have ever seen in Art or Nature was quite so revolting.
>
> (*Labels* 169)

The speaker is detached, fastidious, sophisticated; prostitutes sitting on his knee 'embarrass him rather' – the 'rather' making clear that he is too worldly for real embarrassment or shock, or anything more than mild bemusement. Of a lesbian bar: 'We went to a café called *Le Fétiche*, where the waitresses wore dinner-jackets and asked the ladies in the party to dance. I was interested to see the fine, manly girl in charge of the cloakroom very deftly stealing a scarf from an elderly German' (23). This is Waugh's 'dandy' style, a pose of 'insolent composure' which 'refuse[s] to be shocked, disoriented, embarrassed or involved', one that substitutes aesthetic evaluation where we might expect moral, lest moral judgment reveal the speaker as provincial (Littlewood 14–15). With the 'freedom from any kind of prudery' he had identified as characteristic of his generation, this language finds sexual (like other) oddity 'amusing' or 'interesting'.

Or so it seems at first. In its failure to offer a moral judgment, Waugh's blandly amused account of the 'deft' act of thievery draws attention to the judgment that is withheld. Amidst all his insouciant appreciation of exotic sexual practices, Waugh inserts a coy defence of the most conventional sexual attitudes, including even the Catholic position on birth control – a lively issue in 1930.[72]

> What a lot of nonsense people will talk about sex repression. In many cases an enforced and unrationalised celibacy does give rise to those morbid conditions which supply material for the jollier passages in the Sunday newspapers. But in healthier psychological organisms, a sublimated sex motive may account for a vast proportion of the beneficial activities of man; copulation is not the only laudable expression of the procreative urge – certainly not copulation in which the procreative motive has been laboriously frustrated. The Christian virtues of charity and chastity have from old time an indissoluble alliance.
>
> (*Labels* 50)

Many readers have supposed *Labels* a pre-Catholic work, but passages such as this – along with the book's evaluations of religious architecture and slighting references to 'sectarian religious beliefs', as opposed to the Universal Church (206) – surely prove otherwise. The very mockery of superstition and ignorant priests that has made *Labels* seem pre-Catholic are themselves the fruit of Waugh's way of believing in the 1930s.[73]

What is truly valuable in modernity, *Labels* everywhere suggests, is clear-sightedness in isolating oddity and fakery – the better to appreciate what is and validly traditional. The 'still small voice of the debutante' whispers that Paris itself, the capital of modernism, is 'bogus'; Jean Cocteau, the great entrepreneur of modernism, is 'the apotheosis of bogosity'. Though Waugh unsparingly derides English 'ye oldeness', even such false historicism is better than the 'sham modernity' of Paris:

> The French, through the defects rather than the qualities of their taste, are saved from the peculiarly English horrors of folk dancing, arts and crafts, and the collection of cottage antiquities, only to fall victim, one false thing driving out another, to the worst sort of sham modernity. If the choice is inevitable between pewter-*cum*-warming-pan-*cum*-timbered-gables and the glass of M. Lalique, it is surely better to be imposed upon by a past which one has not seen than by a present of which one is oneself a part?
>
> (*Labels* 19)

As Fussell has argued, *Labels* comprises a delightful tour of oddities and anomalies – like the Frenchman whose umbrella unaccountably catches fire – which allow the traveller better to appreciate the norm from which they deviate. In this way (and like most satire), *Labels*, for all its modishness of tone, turns out to celebrate commonplace, familiar virtues. For all the book's air of aristocratic worldliness, Waugh's account of the luxury and convenience of the *Stella* – its cleanliness, efficiency, and even its guided tours – constitute a celebration of that most unfashionable of classes, the middle one, the class with which he always identified himself. Waugh's procedure can usefully be compared to that of a work such as Stella Gibbons' *Cold Comfort Farm* (1932), whose emancipated, clear-eyed, 'modern' heroine seems at first a sexual and social radical, but emerges the champion of such middle-class values as soap and hot water, tidy house-keeping, hearty regular meals (even for the heroine of a romance), and avoidance of casual sex with scruffy intellectuals.

In *Labels'* comparisons between England and France, England always, if subtly, emerges victorious, once we peel away the modish qualifiers Waugh uses to distract us from his final judgments. 'Paris is bogus in its lack of genuine nationality', whereas though 'London is squalid and coarse', 'Englishmen can feel at ease there, as . . . in revisiting their homes' (17). At the end Waugh returns gladly to a nation where despite the depredations of modernity there remains a traditional culture with which he can identify:

> I had left in the depth of winter and was coming back to late spring; then, if ever, England is still a lovely country. . . . I do not know on quite what terms we now deal with the emotions that were once called patriotism. . . . And yet, although everything one most loves in one's own country seems only to be the survival of an age one has not oneself seen, and though all that one finds sympathetic and praiseworthy in one's own age seems barely represented at all in one's own country, there still remains a certain uncontaminated glory in the fact of race, in the very limits and circumscription of language and territorial boundary; so that one does not feel lost and isolated and self- sufficient. It seems to me that there is this fatal deficiency about all those exiles . . . who . . . have made their home outside the country of their

birth; it is the same deficiency one finds in those who indulge their consciences with sectarian religious beliefs, or adopt eccentrically hygienic habits of life, or practise curious, newly classified vices: a deficiency in that whole cycle of rich experience which lies outside personal peculiarities and individual emotion.

(*Labels* 205–6)

Like such earlier travel books as *The Man of Feeling* (1771) – Henry Mackenzie's reply to Laurence Sterne's account of how 'they order things better in France' – *Labels* is finally a work of anti-travel, an argument for the virtues of home.[74] Modernist style in the service of endangered tradition is also the method of Waugh's first novels.

Like all Waugh's writing, *Labels* consistently celebrates 'individuality', 'variety', 'diversity', 'integrity' and 'vividness' (a word used with a strong etymological sense of *life*) – that which has grown organically from the distinctive character of its nation and surroundings rather than being incongruously imported from outside.

In England, the craze for cottages and all that goes with them only began as soon as they had ceased to represent a significant part of English life. In Naples no such craze exists because the streets are still in perfect harmony with their inhabitants. With his unfailing discernment Baedeker points firmly and unobtrusively to the essential – 'the diverse scenes of popular life'.

(56)

But it was not local colour or picturesque bits...which drew me [to Port Said's Arab Town] day after day, but the intoxicating sense of vitality and actuality.

(85)

Dubrovnik [was].... one of the free city states of the west which, generation after generation, by courage and guile and good fortune, was enabled to maintain its integrity against barbarian influence.

(160)

[Lisbon pleases for its] unique style of architecture, and inhabitants of marked racial peculiarities.

(201)

Celebration of the uniquely individual and characteristic, a 'delight in the foreignness of foreigners' and in 'how intensely different places can be', will characterize all Waugh's writing; it is typical that his favourite way of praising a book was to say that 'no one but' its author could have written it.[75] Such views were closely allied to Waugh's conservative politics and so intensified as he grew older. In 1936 he celebrates the 'unique', 'complete', 'individual', 'characteristic and beautiful' forms of life that 'progressive parties' in Abyssinia and around the globe seek to render 'uniform and utterly drab' (WA 65–6); in 1959, he predicts of the new decade of the sixties:

The most dismal tendency I see is that with our class system we are fast losing all national character. It was thought absurd by many and detestable by some, but it was unique and it depended for its strength and humour and achievements on variety: variety between one town and another, one county and another; one man different from another in the same village in knowledge, habits, and opinions. There were different vocabularies and intonations of speech; different styles of dress. Now all those things that gave the salt to English life and were the raw materials of our Arts are being dissolved.

(EAR 359)

2

The Doom of Youth: *Decline and Fall* and *Vile Bodies*

Modernism consists essentially in affirming that the religious soul must draw from itself, from nothing but itself, the object and motive of its faith. It rejects all revelation imposed upon the conscience, and thus, as a necessary consequence, becomes the negation of the doctrinal authority of the Church established by Jesus Christ, and it denies, moreover, to the divinely constituted hierarchy the right to govern Christian society.

Cardinal Mercier, *Modernism* (1910)

Anti-religious rationalism and orthodox intellectualism...both start from the same idea of the absolute. Modernism moves on a very different plane – the plane of reality, of life, of experience.... The Modernists have introduced into philosophy and dogmatics the idea of relativity.

Paul Sabatier, *Modernism* (1908)

...human nature requires an absolute. The exquisite chaos of modern thought offers this one incomparable opportunity – the creation of new absolute values. Recent intellectual sap has yet to vitalize any adequate forms of existence, and an imaginative apathy is still in vogue. But what sporadic imagination has survived is inevitably God-seeking.

'A Modern Credo', *Oxford Broom*, 1: 1 (1923)

Writing of Rossetti's masterpiece *Beata Beatrix* in 1927, three years before his formal conversion, Waugh suggested that modern critics missed what was most important about the painting: its 'sanctity'.

It is, perhaps, the most purely spiritual and devotional work of European Art since the fall of the Byzantine Empire. This statement is offered as a considered judgment and not as an ecstatic outburst. Anyone who, confronted with its sublime and pervasive sanctity, can speak of it coldly in terms of saturation, and planes and plastic values (as many people, hatless and dishevelled, may be heard declaiming daily in the Tate Gallery) has constricted his artistic perceptions to an antlike narrowness.

(R 130)

Observing the painting's central figure only in itself, not in relation to the larger system of representation of which it forms part and from which it takes its meaning, the critic fails to understand Rossetti's creation.

Yet such a critic at least avoids what Waugh thought an opposite but equally mistaken approach to what in a popular phrase of the twenties was called 'the aesthetic problem'.[1] Early in 1929 he praised Ronald Firbank for having solved 'the aesthetic problem of representation in fiction' without adopting a merely 'subjective attitude to his material' (EAR 57–9). Portraying his characters 'object-ively', from the outside, Firbank avoided what Waugh later called the 'pre-sumption and exorbitance' of examining character only in terms of individual psychology, not in relation to the larger systems that give it meaning (EAR 302). Such 'exorbitant' subjectivism was for instance what Virginia Woolf had called for in a famous essay on 'Modern Fiction' (1919):

> The mind receives a myriad of impressions – trivial, fantastic, evanescent, or engraved with the sharpness of steel.... Life is not a series of gig lamps symmet-rically arranged; life is a luminous halo, a semi-transparent envelope surrounding us from the beginning of consciousness to the end. Is it not the task of the novelist to convey this varying, this unknown and uncircumscribed spirit, whatever aberra-tion or complexity it may display, with as little mixture of the alien and external as possible?
>
> (Woolf 212–13)

'For moderns', according to Woolf, 'the point of interest lies . . . in the dark places of psychology'; but to Waugh as to von Hügel, such a focus engages only 'lesser things', not 'reality'.

Waugh did not use the word 'modernism' to characterize Rossetti's critics or the 'subjective' method in fiction. Only in the 1960s did that word become a commonplace name for the artistic movements of the first part of this century (Faulkner viii–ix). In the 1920s and 1930s, the word referred primarily to developments in theology born the century before and still controversial. Even when used in a literary or cultural context, Waugh's language of 'modernism' and the 'modern' – along with a related vocabulary, including 'subjectivism' and 'humanism' – bears the marks of these theological origins.

'Modernism' might be said to have been first defined in 1864, when Pope Pius IX published with his encyclical *Quanta cura* a 'Syllabus of Errors' condemning 80 propositions in fields ranging from theology and science to 'modern political liberalism'. Section 80 summed up the Syllabus, condemning the assertion that 'the Roman pontiff can and should reconcile and harmonise himself with progress, with liberalism, and with recent civilisation'. To combat such tenden-cies, Pius called for a revival of scholastic philosophy, a call memorably repeated by his successor Leo XIII in *Aeterni Patris* (1879). Leo further sought to limit the corrosive effects of the new 'higher criticism' of the Bible in *Providentissimus Deus*

(1893). Finally, in July 1907, Leo's successor St Pius X published a further syllabus of sixty-five errors of criticism and dogma in the decree *Lamentabili sane exitu*, and two months later condemned modernism root and branch in his great encyclical *Pascendi Domini gregis* (1908), which also called for diocesan 'committees of vigilance' to monitor all publications for modernist content, and required seminaries to make Thomism the basis of their teaching.

The acknowledged leaders of Catholic modernism, such as the French Biblical exegete Alfred Loisy and the Irish Jesuit George Tyrrell (who criticized *Pascendi* in *The Times*), were first silenced, then excommunicated. But most made their submission. In 1910 Pius required all clerics and seminary teachers to take an 'Oath against Modernism', affirming that God's existence can be known with certainty by reason, that the Church was founded by Christ on earth, and that faith is an intellectual assent to truth (rather than a mere impulse of the heart or of a 'will trained to morality').[2] Those who took the Oath abjured any belief that the dogmas which comprise the Church's deposit of faith change in meaning from age to age. It is easy to forget, from a late twentieth-century, post-Conciliar perspective – which often sees Pius's campaign as a kind of terror, creating secret files like the one marked 'Suspected of Modernism' that John XXIII, on becoming pope, found had been kept on himself – that in the years of Waugh's youth, most Catholics, lay and clerical, wholeheartedly supported Pius's condemnations.

To Pius, the intellectual core of modernism was a kind of immanent evolutionism, a belief that the divine is available not to abstract reason but only in the concrete flow of direct personal experience. Though each age may seek to capture its intuitions of the divine in the rigid categories of dogma, such formulations must change as experience itself changes; no rational theology can be wholly true or true for all time, but part only of a continuous becoming. *Lamentabili* thus condemns the propositions 'Christian society like human society is subject to perpetual evolution' and 'Truth is not any more immutable than man himself, since it is evolved with him, in him, and through him'; *Pascendi* condemns the view that faith rests 'in the personal experience of the individual'.[3]

Modernism so understood resembles arguments such as Matthew Arnold's in 'The Study of Poetry' (1880) that criticism should not seek to define its vocabulary with precision, because such formulations merely dress the profound truths resident in great literature – Arnold's substitute for revelation – in the transient theoretical terminology of the critic's own age. It had roots as various as Kantian idealism, Biblical criticism and the evolutionary doctrines of Schleiermacher and David's Strauss's *Leben Jesus* (1835) (Pius called it 'the synthesis of all the heresies'). In his teens Waugh was attracted to the version of such notions he found in Bergson, whom he read with enthusiasm. The enthusiasm soon passed. Both *Decline and Fall* and *Vile Bodies* make slighting reference to Bergsonian 'dynamism' and 'becoming'.[4]

Though Benedict XV relaxed Pius's harshest strictures, the Oath effectively ended the modernist movement within the Catholic Church. But the impulses that had fuelled the movement survived, while meanwhile the same issues, discussed in the same language, remained very much alive among other confessions. In 1911 Ronald Knox, soon to convert to Rome, thought modernism 'the prime danger' to the Anglican Church (K 112); a decade later one of Waugh's teachers at Lancing 'introduced Dr Schweitzer's teaching to his Divinity class', thus unwittingly 'making an agnostic of at least one impressionable boy' (K 143). By this time the term had come for both Catholics and conservative Anglicans to denote a wide range of ideas and tendencies all associated with a 'subjectivist' spirit loosed by the Reformation and so 'the outcome of Protestantism'. The 'root principle' of modernism, explained Wilfrid Ward in 1893, 'is subjectivism'; 'According to the Modernist', wrote Fr D'Arcy in 1931, 'subjective experience is the foundation of religious belief'.[5] He has 'no standards of judgment but his personal reactions', Waugh said in 1937 of Robert Byron: 'It is a grave handicap' (EAR 198).

If modernism was born with the Reformation, its final fruit was 'humanism', another term equally the target of Catholics and conservative Anglicans (especially those who took inspiration from Charles Maurras and his *Action française*). In *Speculations: Essays on Humanism and the Philosophy of Art* (1924), T. E. Hulme attacked attempts to ground value merely in the human realm, arguing that like 'modernism' in general, 'humanism' – a sentimental 'inability to realise the meaning of the dogma of Original Sin' – 'entirely misunderstands the nature of religion', and indeed constitutes an 'alternative to religion' leading inevitably to 'relativism'. Using Hulme as a starting point, T. S. Eliot added in 1927 that humanism represented the 'last agonies' of 'the liberal Protestant theology of the nineteenth century'; as a merely sentimental 'derivative of religion', a set of half-remembered habits derivative from a lost faith, humanism was a 'parasite' that would 'work only for a short time in history'. 'The humanist has suppressed the divine, and is left with a human element which may quickly descend again to the animal'. (Waugh himself put this last point: 'Man without God is less than Man'.)[6]

Catholic writers made especially clear the notion that the modern humanist lives on spiritual capital accumulated in earlier ages of faith, faith that was now a wasting asset. For Fr D'Arcy, Christianity, 'affected at the Reformation', was kept alive among Protestants only 'by sentiment, habit, and good will' – especially in the nineteenth century, when religion became a matter of 'feeling, sentiment, and experience' rather than of 'reason resting in a metaphysic' (*Belief* 27, 32). Waugh's friend and admirer Christopher Dawson put the point sharply in 1935: 'To the modern Protestant the essence of the Gospel is to be found in its moral teaching'; having lost its doctrinal moorings, 'There is a real danger that English religion, at least English Protestantism, may allow itself to be identified with an enthusiasm for social justice and reform which is hardly distinguishable from the creed of secular humanitarianism' (Dawson 76, 109).

Robert Hugh Benson's popular *Lord of the World*, published in the months after *Pascendi*, provides a fine composite picture of what all these tendencies meant to Catholics in the first part of this century. A favourite of Waugh's, the novel is a fantasy of a future in which modernism is globally triumphant. In the 'new order' of 'unimpeded subjectivity', God has been redefined as 'the developing sum of created life'; 'the State Church [has] melted into the Free Church, and the Free Church was, after all, nothing more than a little sentiment'. Benson's dystopia makes especially clear what were understood to be modernism's political implications. By making 'opinion' the arbiter in matters of right, modernism fostered long-condemned levelling tendencies in both the Church and secular politics – the 'mistaken idea', in Cardinal Mercier's formulation, that 'the directing authority of the country is made up of the collective wills of the people'. In Benson's future of 'absolute Materialism and Socialism' (the result of an imagined Labour victory in 1917, when 'Communism really began'), there survive 'no patriotism, no class distinctions'; only a tiny underground of Catholics remains to denounce, as the papacy had once done freely, 'democratic ideas of every kind', and to propound instead the traditional doctrine that the power and authority of rulers 'comes from above', 'not from their subjects but from the Supreme Ruler of all'.[7]

Waugh soon made all these views his own. His Helena muses: 'I have a terrible dream of the future. Not now, but presently, people may forget their loyalty to their kings and emperors and take power for themselves. Instead of letting one victim bear the frightful curse they will take it all on themselves, each one of them. Think of the misery of a whole world possessed of Power without Grace'. Here as throughout his life, those of Waugh's political views most unnerving to secular intellectuals comprised little more than restatements (albeit provocatively formulated) of quite ordinary Catholic social teaching.[8]

All Waugh's fiction of the thirties explores the implications of modernism – his sense, as he put it in 1931, that 'the enlightened people of Northern Europe', 'having lost their belief in revealed religion', are now 'falling back helplessly for moral guidance on their own tenderer feelings' (RP 181). Infused with a convert's zeal, he argues especially the Church of England's disarray in the face of the modernist challenge. That disarray is most searchingly explored in *A Handful of Dust* (which he said 'contained all I had to say about humanism': EAR 304) and *Edmund Campion*. But Waugh's response to modernism is already visible in *Decline and Fall*, in which the unbelieving Prendergast reassumes Anglican orders upon learning (from magazine articles by a 'popular bishop') of 'a species of person called a "Modern Churchman" who draws the full salary of a beneficed clergyman and need not commit himself to any religious belief'.[9] From the start of his career Waugh devoted his fiction to exploring – and giving a historical account of – the cultural circumstances that led him to Rome.

I

What was at stake in the debates around modernism must have been clear to Waugh at least since his reading in 1926 of von Hügel. 'More and more', von Hügel wrote to Gwen Greene, 'I am coming to see the errors of subjectivism'; 'what, especially nowadays, we want again very badly' is 'a system of objective ethics':

> 'modern' movements have been very largely dominated by a most ruinous, excessive, or even exclusive emphasis upon the subject – your own (or at least humanity's) apprehending power, feelings, etc. These subjective powers get, here, more or less taken as alone certain . . . [but in fact] we know ourselves, at all adequately, least of all.

'How poor a thing is all purely personal religion!' his niece reflected; man 'needs, he yearns, to give himself to something beyond himself'.[10] Feeling the same need, Waugh began in the mid-twenties to elaborate what he liked to call a 'mystical' view of the objective connexion of individuals to a larger normative whole. He wrote in his diary during the General Strike of 1926:

> I suppose that the desire to merge one's individual destiny in forces outside oneself, which seems to me deeply rooted in most people and shows itself in social service and mysticism and in some manner in debauchery, is really only a consciousness that this is already the real mechanism of life which requires so much concentration to perceive that one wishes to objectify it in more immediate (and themselves subordinate) forces. How badly I write when there is no audience to arrange my thoughts for.
>
> (D 250–1)

With more fluency, *Rossetti* distinguished this 'mystical' viewpoint from the merely 'romantic':

> Among the Victorians, and, for that matter, among most modern people too, there were two main attitudes towards the rest of the universe. There was the breezy, common-sense attitude to life, typified by Millais as 'one damned thing after another', and there was the solemn perception of process, typified by Holman-Hunt, an attitude which saw the earth as part of a vast astronomical system, and... any individual life as small and unimportant except as an inseparable part of the whole....
>
> The romantic outlook sees life as a series of glowing and unrelated systems, in which the component parts are explicable and true only in terms of themselves; in which the stars are just as big and as near as they look and '*rien n'est vrai que le pittoresque*'.
>
> It is this insistence on the picturesque that divides... the mystical from the romantic habit of mind.
>
> (R 52)

The debate over modernism concerned not only the need for a secure and unchanging ground of ethics, but larger questions about the individual's place in the world, and so about the nature of human personality itself. According to von Hügel, the modern, subjectivist self – cut off from the larger systems of which it is part, from the traditions which inform, and inform us of, our nature – remains always in a state of 'wayward childishness', condemned to be a mere 'type' of humanity, not one of 'God's individuals'. Without the shaping discipline of tradition, the individual is left at every moment to reinvent himself, with no guide but his own wayward appetites; but 'you can't have growth if you do what you like as we ordinarily mean it' (*Letters* 72, 114–16, 29). *Decline and Fall* and *Vile Bodies* are populated by just such maimed modern selves, characters whose lives comprise (in the name of a popular stage revue of the late twenties) 'one damned thing after another' (D 88), and who readily shift identities because they lack the tools with which to achieve any coherent, stable self.

That modern folk no longer possess such tools was for Waugh the result of historical processes of a sort that would always fascinate him: processes of cultural rupture.[11] *Decline and Fall* and *Vile Bodies*, like the essays on youth, focus on the rupture in tradition created by World War I, which broke families and revealed the hollowness – the 'bogosity' – of inherited (Victorian and Edwardian) institutions, leaving both old and young adrift. As is often remarked, fiction after the Great War, a war prosecuted by 'the fathers', contains few examples of responsible parents; in Waugh's first novels, parents are invariably mad, silly, corrupt, or dead. ('He who comes into life from a broken or incomplete family comes into life to that extent an incomplete man, and modern society, as Mr Waugh sees it ... is essentially a society of incomplete men and women': Hollis, *Waugh*, 295.) His heroes Paul Pennyfeather and Adam Fenwick-Symes are orphans, young men thrown into the world on their own, without guidance, while all around them the visible symbols of the passing order suffer change and decay, demolition and collapse.

Distrust of the merely 'subjective' was thus as congenial to Waugh in his novelistic practice as in his religion: the two are connected. By the late 1920s he had come to believe that human lives and selves take their meaning from their place in a larger system – a household, a family, a civilized order supported by grace. But no such informing tradition sustains 'all those exiles' who by a 'fatal deficiency' have cut themselves off from the 'whole cycle of rich experience which lies outside personal peculiarities and individual emotion' (*Labels* 205–6). Outside the whole of which he is properly part, the individual can be only a meaningless, unfulfilled (though perhaps colourful) fragment.

The point comes clearest in Waugh's treatment of what would always be a central theme in his fiction (and his theology): love, the inbuilt hunger for connection with others beyond ourselves. The early novels are full of maimed moderns like Adam and Nina in *Vile Bodies* who hunger for 'something more' but cannot articulate what. Johnnie Hoop's party-invitations contain 'two columns of close print; in one was a list of all the things Johnnie hated, and in the other all the things he *thought* he liked'; *A Handful of Dust*'s Jock Grant-Menzies responds to an invitation from Tony Last: 'I *think* I'd love to'.[12] In stark ironic contrast to his name, *Vile Bodies*'s Prufrockian Mr Outrage, in doubt of his immortal soul, can achieve no connection with the Baroness Yoshiwara. Later novels such as *The Loved One* and *Love Among the Ruins* diagnose yet more grimly the impossibility of love in a spiritually dead world. 'To know and love one other human being', says Charles Ryder, 'is the root of all wisdom' (BR 41); but such wisdom, Waugh suggested from the outset of his career, is denied those whose spiritual house is not in order. Cut off from saving tradition, unable to realize themselves fully, these characters never grow up or grow whole. Characters in Waugh's first novels seem empty, without psychological depth, because they have no depths to probe; an 'external', un-subjective presentation accurately captures their modern selves.

The literary form in which such limited 'characters' are most at home is satire. As Wyndham Lewis observed in a book that Waugh said 'no novelist and very few intelligent novel readers can afford to neglect', *Satire and Fiction* (1930):

'To let the reader "into the minds of the characters," to "see the play of their thoughts" – that is precisely the method least suited to satire. That it must deal with the outside...is one of the capital advantages of this form of literary art'. Satiric characters, Waugh agreed in 1937, tend to be 'mere dialectical abstractions'.[13] (Much later Waugh denied that he had ever written 'satire', but only to score the debating point that the world was too far gone for satire to reform it.)[14] *Satire and Fiction* accurately describes the method of Waugh's first novels: eschewing what Lewis called the 'auriferous mud' of 'internal monologue' ('the romantic snapshotting of the wandering stream of the Unconscious', a 'phenomenon of decadence' and 'inveterate *humanism*'), satire evokes its 'tragic laughter' by portraying people as mere 'shells, or pelts'. It is the apt form, Waugh would add, in which to portray people whose spiritual incapacity renders them no more than 'pelts'. 'Mr Waugh has a missionary ambition', said one reviewer of *Vile Bodies*: 'less, perhaps, to save souls than to expose what pass for souls'.[15]

But from *Decline and Fall* onward, only a minority of readers grasped Waugh's method or purposes. Arnold Bennett and an anonymous reviewer in *Life and Letters* recognized *Decline and Fall* as 'satire', a work that 'implies a latent philosophy of life, which is not the less genuine because it is wittily or fantastically expressed'. But the majority, especially among the young, welcomed a new 'humourist', the author of 'comedy' or 'farce'. Thomas Matthews found *Decline and Fall* a 'nonsense novel' that 'take[s] nothing seriously'; J. B. Priestley, a 'good light-weight fiction' whose story was 'a frank absurdity'; Cyril Connolly, 'not a satire, but a farce', a work that 'sets out purely to amuse'.[16]

Disagreement over genre – satire, comedy, or farce – intensified with *Vile Bodies*. L. P. Hartley and V. S Pritchett were in a minority in arguing that 'Mr Waugh is not the happy humorist he seems'; 'He is a satirist' (CH 97–8). Once again, most found instead 'a masterpiece of inconsequence' whose events are 'utterly fantastic'; the *New York Times* explicitly rejected the novel's claim to be 'satire'. *Vile Bodies*'s episodic form led one reviewer to comparisons with Petronius' *Satyricon*, but it was more often characterized as an 'extravaganza' or 'revue between covers', the novelistic equivalent of the theatrical form pioneered by C. B. Cochran and Noël Coward. This comparison still guided Rose Macaulay in her 1946 survey of Waugh's novels, where *Decline and Fall* and *Vile Bodies* are said to be amiable 'nonsense', 'revue shows' which move 'in a sphere where morality does not apply'.[17]

Thus was born the tenacious myth of Waugh's wholly playful 'early novels' which, as Alan Pryce-Jones claimed in 1964, 'do not assert any values at all, except those of the Lord of Misrule'.[18] Especially useful to those who had enjoyed his fiction from *Decline and Fall* to *Put Out More Flags* but recoiled from *Brideshead* and Waugh's later outspoken Catholic conservatism, the myth found fullest expression in the 1950s and 1960s, as reviewing passed into academic criticism. According to Malcolm Bradbury in 1964, Waugh's 'early novels', written 'from a position of moral uninterest', offer 'no secure centres of value and no real substantiation of any interpretive statements'; to Sean O'Faolain, Waugh was 'a purely brainless genius'; to Brigid Brophy, 'Waugh writes a prose as fluent, lovely, and lacking in intellectual content as a weeping willow'.[19] These analyses predictably generated opposed readings such as Jeffrey Heath's argument in *The Picturesque Prison* (1982) that Waugh was a Catholic moralist from the time of *Rossetti*. But the view persists that, in the words of a study of the novels *From Grimes to Brideshead* (1990), 'whenever Waugh allowed ideas to invade his fiction, his fiction suffered' (Garnett 21).

The nature of satire itself fosters such critical confusion. As Waugh often said, 'Scorn is the essence of satire' (EAR 461). The satirist's energies are occupied mainly in his elaborately crafted negations; his positive values – generally conventional, even dull – are usually only implied, by negation of their contraries. Absence of explicitly positive models is easily confused with absence of positive values. Moreover, though satirists in the tradition of Juvenal might provide interpretive guideposts in the form of comparisons to a morally superior 'good old days', Waugh's sense of history prevented him from aiding readers in this way. He often drew adverse comparisons from the 'ample days preceding the War' (DF 126), but he was equally aware of the 'natural' but misguided inclination 'to regard all periods but one's own as a conservative Utopia, where everything was tranquilly rooted in tradition, the rich respected, the poor contented, and everyone slept well and ate with a hearty appetite' (EAR 166).

Waugh characteristically understood historical change as a process running not from good to bad, but from already bad to worse. ('With us', as Newman said, 'Earth and sky are ever failing'.) *Decline and Fall*'s Otto Silenus razes King's Thursday to make way for a hideous modernist structure, but the old house (built in the Tudor style Waugh detested) was already culturally otiose.[20] Wilfred Lucas-Dockery practices a mad and dangerous modern penology, but we are not asked simply to admire the opposed policies of his thoughtlessly repressive predecessor. Such representatives of the old order as we meet in *Decline and Fall* and *Vile Bodies* – Grimes, Fagan, the old rakes Kitty Blackwater and Lady Throbbing, the political leaders Maltravers and Outrage, and all those who drink of the fetid 'well of Edwardian certainty' (VB 32) still available at Lottie Crump's Shepheard's Hotel – conform to Waugh's judgment in a late review that nearly 'everything which came after 1914 was a degradation from its [already] degraded antecedent' (EAR 510).

Waugh was thus never the kind of reactionary who valued tradition for tradition's sake; as *A Handful of Dust* argues most powerfully, a healthy society requires a tradition both vital and true. *Decline and Fall* mocks modern architecture, modern penology, modern education, modern churchmanship – even modern photography – not merely to discredit the new, but to point up the need for a proper ground of value in all these areas, an 'objective ethics' without which man's fallen nature cannot be restrained and his energies fruitfully channelled.

The novels from *Decline and Fall* onward develop a symbolic shorthand designed at once to convey a sense of modern disorder and explain its causes. Comparisons of people to animals (soon extended to parallels between England and the jungle) point by negation to the meaning of properly human nature; fad cults and religions point by negation to the true faith such alternatives ignore or deny. ('Deprived of the sacraments imaginative minds invent all kinds of fetishes for themselves': EAR 377.) Childish speech and behaviour betoken deeper spiritual immaturity; unrestrained eating becomes the sign of a more general unrestrained appetite.[21] Historic buildings (especially houses) – described in precise architectural detail, usually with attribution to period and architect – suffer demolition and decay, mapping the most recent stages in the degradation of the already degraded antecedents for which, in Waugh's view of history, those periods stand. Where love is thwarted, cruelty emerges; where men deny the faith without which civilization lacks 'the power of survival' (EAR 104), chaos ensues.

II

In 1937, four successful novels to his credit and a fifth begun, Waugh outlined what he knew to be a sure-fire novelistic plot:

> a prosaic hero ... falls accidentally into strange company and finds himself trans-ported far beyond his normal horizons and translated into a new character; finally he returns to his humdrum habits. It is one of the basic stories of the world ... it has been treated romantically, farcically, sentimentally, satirically, melodramatically; it never fails if it is well treated.

(ND 52)

The formula fits *Decline and Fall* and *Scoop*; do not allow the hero to return, leave him in jungle or battlefield, and the result is the tragic shape of *Vile Bodies* and *A Handful of Dust*. Each of these stories follows the fortunes of a relatively 'empty' central character, a naïf who meets in dizzy succession that 'parade' of char-acter-types which Alvin Kernan has identified as central to *The Plot of Satire*. Each ends with a brief account of events occurring after a lapse of time, an epilogue that completes a circle (either of return or intensification) and draws attention to its meaning.

Midway through *Decline and Fall* Waugh interrupts the narrative to assure us in his own voice that the colourless, ever-victimized Paul Pennyfeather is in fact 'an intelligent, well-educated, well-conducted young man, a man who could be trusted to use his vote at a general election with discretion and proper detach-ment' and 'acquit himself with decision and decorum in all the emergencies of civilized life' (DF 159–60). That in the course of the novel Paul displays few of these virtues testifies that the world which sweeps him up is *not* civilized, not one his education has prepared him for. Unfairly sent down from Oxford, cheated of his inheritance, reduced to schoolteaching ('That's what most of the gentlemen does, sir, that gets sent down for indecent behaviour'); engaged to a society beauty (the mother of a pupil), imprisoned for unwittingly assisting in her white-slaving business, made to escape by feigning death; Paul finally returns, disguised as his own cousin, to the quiet collegiate life 'reading for the Church' from which he began. Events in the novel follow one another so fast, characters disappear and reappear so hilariously, amidst so many topical references and historical allusions, that it is easy to overlook what Claud Cockburn called his cousin's habit of seeing 'the details of life and human behavior exemplifying the clash of general beliefs and tendencies, virtues and vices, as in a morality play' (Cockburn 55).

The Prelude sets the novel's tone. Of moderate and regular habits himself, diffident, middle-class Pennyfeather has recently read a 'daring' paper on drunkenness to the Thomas More Society, displaying, in Frederick Stopp's words, 'that combination of personal innocence and theoretically progressive views which is the blessed patrimony of nine-tenths of English undergraduates' (*Portrait* 65). He comes to grief while bicycling home from 'a most interesting paper about plebiscites in Poland' at the League of Nations Union, when he collides with the aristocratic Bollinger Club, enjoying its rowdy annual dinner (first of the novel's many scenes of drunken self-indulgence). At this 'difficult time for those in authority', most of the College's administrators have prudently absented themselves; two remain to look on as Paul is 'debagged' (in the same manner as Waugh's friends Tom Driberg and Patrick Balfour had had their pants removed by the Bullingdon Club). Fearing the Bollers 'might not prove amenable to discipline', the Junior Dean and Bursar do nothing to help; instead, hoping to garner large fines from the evening's destruction, they pray in tremulous excitement: 'Oh, please God, make them attack the Chapel'.

These authorities watch as the Bollers destroy a Matisse, a grand piano, the manuscript of a prize poem – embodiments of the cultural traditions it is the university's job to foster and protect. The rampaging Bollers include representatives of the highest social classes (properly, Waugh said elsewhere, 'the custodians of tradition, morality, and grace' (EAR 583)): 'epileptic royalty from their villas of exile; uncouth peers from crumbling country seats; smooth young men of uncertain tastes from embassies and legations; illiterate lairds from wet granite hovels in the Highlands; ambitious young barristers and Conservative candidates torn from the London season and the indelicate advances of debutantes' (DF 2). 'There is tradition behind the Bollinger', Waugh's narrator gaily remarks – a tradition of decay, of failed stewardship and discipline matched in the Bursar and Junior Dean.

Paul's fate is sealed when an illiterate laird, Lumsden of Strathdrummond, sways across his path 'like a druidical rocking stone', too drunk to distinguish Paul's old school tie from the Bollers' own. ('The whole of thought and taste', Waugh wrote in 1937, 'consists in distinguishing between similars'.)[22] With deadpan irony, saying the opposite of what Waugh means, the narrator remarks: 'It is not for nothing that since pre-Christian times his family has exercised chieftainship over uncharted miles of barren moorland'. Embodying ancient, aboriginal, barbarous human nature, the natural man which civilization should train and Christianity redeem, the drunken laird – who as social leader should instill such civilization in others – precipitates Paul's debagging and consequent expulsion.

The Prelude thus establishes Waugh's simplest satiric procedure in *Decline and Fall*: indecorum, a gap between characters' roles and their behaviour. In the later scene of Margot's house-party, the names of her guests embody the principle starkly: Sir Humphrey Maltravers, Minister of Transportation; the Honourable Miles Malpractice, who appears on the arm of the society photographer Davy Lennox; deep-voiced Pamela Popham, 'square-jawed and resolute as a big-game huntress', and chirpy, 'emasculate' Lord Parakeet.[23] In the course of the novel Paul meets guardians who don't guard, teachers who don't teach, servants who don't serve, and parents who don't parent ('He wants beatin' and hittin' and knockin' about generally', says Lady Circumference of her 'toad of a son', 'and then he'll be no good'). There are priests without faith, unjust judges, a physician who kills, mannish women and womanish men, childlike adults and children such as Peter Pastmaster (at the age of fifteen an expert mixer of cocktails) prematurely catapulted into adult knowingness. The same indecorum governs Margot's new house, designed, as Waugh says of the 'promiscuous' decor of Jenny Abdul-Akbar's flat in *A Handful of Dust*, in wild 'disregard for the right properties of things' (HD 179). Appropriately, it is the bigamist pederast Grimes who alone expresses admiration for this 'new-born monster to whose birth ageless and forgotten cultures had been in travail': 'His eye travelled appreciatively over the glass floor, the pneumatic rubber furniture, and the porcelain ceiling, and the leather-hung walls. "It's not to every one's taste," he said, "but I think you'll be comfortable"' (180, 182).

The novel's finest exercise in indecorum is Margot Beste-Chetwynde (pro-nounced 'beast-cheating') herself. White-slaving was in the news as Waugh wrote *Decline and Fall*: in 1927, the League of Nations released a much-publicized *Report of the Special Body of Experts on Traffic in Women and Children*, largely about the brothels of Buenos Aires (Guy, ch. 4). Handsome, clever, and rich, the sister-in-law of an earl – and the sexually omnivorous head of a South American prostitution ring who is rumoured to have murdered her first husband – Margot appears after her 'little bout of veronal, fresh and exquisite as a seventeenth-century lyric' (doubtless of the 'come live with me and be my love' variety) (174). Based partly on society gossip about Nancy Cunard and the young Edwina Mountbatten (both notorious for their affairs with American blacks), she is the first of what will become a familiar Waugh character-type: the fascinating, rootless goddess of modernity, wholly at home in and therefore mistress of a world that has lost its moorings. Her ancestors include Aldous Huxley's Mrs Viveash and Michael Arlen's Iris Storm (who, like Margot, drives a Hispano-Suiza); her progeny include, in their different ways, *A Handful of Dust*'s Mrs Rattery and Brenda Last, *Scoop*'s Mrs Stitch and Kätchen, Angela Lyne of *Black Mischief* and *Put Out More Flags*, and most searchingly, the war trilogy's Virginia Troy. Waugh commented in a review in 1937: 'The heroine is straight from the 1920s – elusive, irresponsible, promiscuous, a little wistful, avaricious, delectable, ruthless – how often we have all read or written about such people. Well, the type wears well' (ND 160).

Satire typically defines characters through their roles (teacher, lawyer, doctor); behavioural rules follow from roles, but characters do not live up to them. Through such structural irony the satirist is able to teach without preaching – without making his standards of judgment tediously explicit; no commentary beyond the assignment of role is necessary to point up indecorum, leaving the narrator free to pretend neutrality or even admiration. ('It was a lovely evening', we hear of the Boller party.) As Waugh often said, such irony depends on a fund of unspoken agreement between writer and reader about how characters inhabit-ing various roles *should* act. Calling on antecedently shared values, satire is thus a fundamentally conservative literary form, one that usually ratifies existing moral and social norms. Like Austen's or Pope's, Waugh's mockery of the rich and titled (such as the deliciously named Alastair Digby-Vaine-Trumpington) constitutes not an attack on hierarchy but on individuals' failure to live up to their rank. This conservatism makes satiric irony irritatingly manipulative to those who do not share the writer's values. If we laugh at the spectacle of Prendy setting up as a 'Modern Churchman', we implicitly accept Waugh's assumptions about how a priest ought to believe and behave; if we find humour in the exchange between the horsey, tyrannical Lady Circumference and her submissive husband – 'It takes a man to bring up a man'; '"Yes", said Lord Circumference meekly' – to that extent we have accepted his views about proper gender roles.[24]

Armed with such satiric procedures, *Decline and Fall* surveys through their debased representatives the major cultural institutions whose task is to teach, moralize, and discipline us: guardians, teachers, priests, judges, prison governors, leaders of the state and of 'society'. In this conspectus of the institutions central to any civilization's effort to preserve, cultivate, and transmit its traditions of value, all are in decay. The novel begins where education itself begins, with parents and teachers. After leaving Oxford the orphaned Paul first visits his guardian, who blithely blows cigar-smoke in his face while paraphrasing Matthew Arnold on seeing life steadily and whole, and who proceeds to cheat Paul of his inheritance. Next, acting on the maxim that 'It doesn't do to be too modest. It's wonderful what one can teach when one tries', the incompetent Paul himself turns school-teacher at Llanabba Castle, Wales, a fantasticated version of Arnold House, Denbighshire.

Llanabba occupies so large a place in *Decline and Fall* not merely because Waugh's own experience provided him with material, but because the institution of school is so central in the transmission of culture. A Victorian country house dressed up on one side with a fake-medieval façade, Llanabba demonstrates how Victorian values, dubious to start with, have become further corrupted in the world after 1914. Its headmaster 'Dr' Fagan (named for Dickens's misleader of youth) professes Thomas Arnold's educational philosophy: 'You will find that my school is built upon an ideal – an ideal of service and fellowship' (14). In practice the ideal amounts to no more than concern with social 'tone' and a love of parties at which, according to Fagan's own prescription, 'taste and dignity shall go unhampered' (57). Two chapters about 'school sports' recall the playing-fields on which, according to the Duke of Wellington, citizen-soldiers are trained. But at Llanabba the great Duke's maxim dwindles into Paul's halfhearted commendation, 'So useful in case of a war or anything' (84). Grimes – with delightful appropriateness, the school's French master – has decided all the winners in advance (though even so, young Clutterbuck cheats); one young citizen-soldier is shot by the drunken Prendy. 'There's no discipline in the place', says Grimes (who should know); falling in with local mores, Paul establishes order among his pupils by assigning 'an essay on "Self-indulgence". There will be a prize of half a crown for the longest essay, irrespective of any possible merit' (19, 43).

Scene after scene evokes indulgence in the form of drinking, drug-taking, theft, promiscuous sex, and simple self-serving hypocrisy. Meanwhile, carefully placed parallels suggest that all these varying manifestations of indulgence are at root the same. The 'bottle-green' of the Bollers's evening coats reappears in the 'bottle-green glass floor' at the new King's Thursday; King's Thursday's architectural indecorums recur in Blackstone Gaol, where Sir Wilfred Lucas-Dockery indulges the fad for 'artificial sunlight'.[25] Llanabba's failures of discipline reappear here as well: now prison chaplain, Prendy stumbles over 'discipline, my old trouble' and finds that 'criminals are just as bad as boys' (218). Grimes's complaint in prison of becoming a mere 'machine' (259) recalls the mechanisms celebrated by Otto Silenus. As in Swift's *Tale of a Tub*, 'modern' follies blend into one another, uniting as instances of divergence from a single unstated norm. As in *Gulliver's Travels*, references to people as animals – the Bollers 'baying for broken glass', Clutterbuck the 'little beast', Grimes seeking to outperform a 'trained sea-lion' – suggest willful renunciation of proper human nature.

Parallels among practices seemingly different, designed to invite readers to make comparisons and exercise discriminating judgment, have long been a staple of satire – as has been their use to lay bare a definition of human nature itself. The example of Waugh's admired 'master' Swift (DC 320) helps explain another of his procedures in *Decline and Fall*: the creation of paired characters whose equal and opposite errors stem from opposed, equally mistaken conceptions of human nature. *Gulliver's Travels* placed its representative European man between pygmies and giants, angelically rational Houyhnhnms and bestial Yahoos, in order to elucidate the human nature that, properly understood, partakes of both extremes. Waugh's bifurcating imagination produces Flossie and Dingy Fagan, Pamela Popham and Lord Parakeet, willful Grimes and timid Prendy, 'optimistic' Sir Wilfred Lucas-Dockery and despairing Otto Silenus.[26]

'It doesn't do to rely on one's own feelings, does it, not in anything?' asks Prendy, the ex-Anglican priest plagued by religious 'Doubts' (50). By contrast, Grimes's optimistic, Browningesque faith – a vestige of Victorian belief in 'progress' – licenses a career of unrestrained appetite:

> 'When you've been in the soup as often as I have, it gives you a sort of feeling that everything's for the best, really. You know, God's in His heaven; all's right with the world. I can't quite explain it, but I don't believe one can ever be unhappy for long provided one does just exactly what one wants to and when one wants to'.[27]

Grimes cheerfully confesses what his name also tells us, that he is 'singularly in harmony with the primitive promptings of humanity', with the lower or animal component of mixed human nature. Prendy by contrast has never come to terms with this side of himself. At the hotel supper when Grimes imitates a sea lion (thereby unconsciously establishing his kinship with the beast), Prendy is surprised to discover that 'animals fall in love': 'Do they? I didn't know that'. To Grimes's agonized questions – 'How do we come into being? What is birth?' – Prendy replies with bemusement extraordinary in one who has been a priest: 'I've often wondered'.[28] The two characters embody alternate misconstructions of human nature, traceable finally, Waugh implies, to mistaken spiritual premisses.

Prendy's confessions to Paul provide a first instance of what will become a commonplace of Waugh's fiction: jibes at Anglican concern with externals rather than a traditional, living, sacramental faith.

> 'Ten years ago I was a clergyman of the Church of England. I had just been presented to a living in Worthing. It was such an attractive church, not old, but very beautifully decorated, six candles on the altar, Reservation in the Lady Chapel, and an excellent heating apparatus which burned coke in a little shed by the sacristy door; no graveyard, just a hedge of golden privet between the church and the rectory.... the dentist's wife, gave me a set of the *Encyclopædia Britannica* for my study. It was all very pleasant until my *Doubts* began'.
>
> (DF 34–5)

The absent graveyard signals the disconnexion of such a church from the lives of its parishioners, the encyclopedia its reliance on merely human wisdom. No wonder Prendy is attacked by 'Doubts' – by a sense of meaninglessness – rooted in his inability to answer the simplest question in the Catechism:

> 'You see, it wasn't the ordinary sort of Doubt about Cain's wife or the Old Testament miracles or the consecration of Archbishop Parker. I'd been taught how to explain all those while I was at college. No, it was something deeper than all that. *I couldn't understand why God had made the world at all* .... I asked my bishop; he didn't know. He said that he didn't think the point really arose as far as my practical duties as a parish priest were concerned'.
>
> (DF 36–7)

On re-entering orders as a Modern Churchman, Prendy is brutally dismembered by a fanatical Calvinist who notices, rightly, that 'He's no Christian'. Waugh delighted in putting unexpected wisdom into the mouths of children, drunkards, and madmen; he coyly implies that there is divine justice in the murder of a Modern Churchman by a yet more degraded – but at least believing – exemplar of his Protestantism: 'From all points of view it was lucky that the madman had chosen Mr. Prendergast for attack. Some people even suggested that the choice had been made in a more responsible quarter'.[29]

Grimes by contrast survives the novel; the gods themselves seem to connive at his success. Condemned to hard labour at Egdon Heath prison, he tells Paul, 'just you watch Grimes next time there's a fog!'; 'As luck would have it, there was a fog the next day, a heavy, impenetrable white mist' in which Grimes makes his escape (260). Like his fellow-survivors Margot, Fagan, and the mysterious Philbrick, Grimes embodies what Waugh elsewhere calls the 'anarchy' and 'barbarism' in fallen human nature that is 'never fully defeated' (RUL 279).

> Grimes, Paul at last realized, was one of the immortals. He was a life force. Sentenced to death in Flanders, he popped up in Wales; drowned in Wales, he emerged in South America; engulfed in the dark mystery of Egdon Mire, he would rise again somewhere at sometime, shaking from his limbs the musty integuments of the tomb. Surely he had followed in the Bacchic train of distant Arcady, and

played on the reeds of myth by forgotten streams, and taught the childish satyrs the art of love? Had he not suffered unscathed the fearful dooms of all the offended gods of all the histories, fire, brimstone, and yawning earthquakes, plagues and pestilence? Had he not stood, like the Pompeian sentry, while the Citadels of the Plain fell to ruin about his ears? Had he not, like some grease-caked Channel swimmer, breasted the waves of the Deluge? Had he not moved unseen when darkness covered the waters?

(DF 262–5)

In one of many allusions whereby the novel extends its meaning beyond the present, Paul's eulogy parodies Pater's famous description of the *Mona Lisa*. Pater had read all history in Mona Lisa's face, the survival of the past into the present; reversing Pater's time-sequence, Waugh traces in Grimes's wilfulness the whole history of human perversity, working backward through Greece, the Flood sent to punish human wickedness, to the brute, unformed material of Creation itself.

The contrast between Prendy and the vastly more attractive Grimes makes clear that in protesting undisciplined indulgence, Waugh does not merely recommend its bloodless opposite. 'A conservative is not merely an obstructionist'; 'He has positive work to do' (RUL 278). Sober, Prendy is a bore; drunk, he canes twenty-three boys and shoots Lord Tangent. The animal will always be with us; utopian attempts to deny our mixed nature always result in explosions of cruelty. Our task is not to deny our animal energies but to channel them fruitfully. 'It is thus that the restraint of a traditional culture tempers and directs creative impulses' (EAR 62). T. E. Hulme put the point in his attack on humanism: man 'can only accomplish anything of value by discipline – ethical and political. Order is thus not merely negative, but creative and liberating' (*Speculations* 47). The same point, more philosophically elaborated, governs Waugh's contrast between two other characters, both modelled on well-known public figures: the architect Otto Silenus and Wilfred Lucas-Dockery, governor of Blackstone Gaol.

Not having 'yet been sent to prison' (as he assured readers in a note to the first edition of *Decline and Fall*), Waugh must have done some rudimentary research in order to portray such penal practices as numbered diets and 'progressive stages' of punishment from cellular confinement to communal activity.[30] Tried over the years in various localities, these methods were made national practice in the Penal Servitude Bill of 1898; the man who oversaw their administration – and ultimately Waugh's original for Sir Wilfred Lucas-Dockery – was Sir Evelyn Ruggles-Brise, from 1895 until his retirement in 1921 Chairman of the Prison Commission. Sir Evelyn was the first university man to hold such a post (before his appointment to Blackstone, Sir Wilfred was 'Chair of Sociology at a Midland University'); like Sir Wilfred, he had stood for Parliament. Ruggles-Brise replaced Sir Edmund Du Cane, an ex-soldier and plain-spoken believer in fierce punitive deterrence; Lucas-Dockery replaces old Colonel MacAdder, 'veteran of numberless campaigns on the Afghan frontier' whose maxim is 'If you make prison bad enough, people'll take jolly good care to keep out of it' (220).

Widely celebrated as a reformer, Ruggles-Brise also celebrated himself, fulsomely, in a book on *The English Prison System* (1921); Sir Wilfred, already the subject of a 'flattering article' in the *New Nation* (the first of Waugh's many swipes at the Leftist *New Statesman and Nation*), dreams of the day when historians will write that 'no single man occupies so high a place in this history of the social reform of his century' as that 'intrepid and far-seeing official' – himself – whose appointment to Blackstone will be seen as 'One of the few important events of this Labour Government's brief tenure of power' (226).

An experimentalist like Sir Wilfred – in 1901 he pioneered the Borstal system of rehabilitation – Ruggles-Brise was a consultant to the Gladstone Commission on Prisons whose 1895 Report, a milestone in 'progressive', 'optimistic' penology, the 1898 Bill was designed to effect. The Report called for sweeping changes to create a rehabilitative

> system of training such as will fit the prisoner to re-enter the world as a citizen. To this end the first requisite is greater activity in mind and body, and the creation of habits of sustained industry.... Next comes the removal of any features of unnecessary degradation in prison life, and the promotion of self-respect; and education on broad lines calculated to arouse some intelligent interests, and to raise the mind out of a sordid circle of selfish broodings.
>
> (Watson 152)

Under Ruggles-Brise, handicrafts proliferated in prisons, including one much-publicized experiment with a printing and book-binding shop. (At Blackstone Sir Wilfred institutes an 'Arts and Crafts Workshop'; hungry inmates prefer paste from the 'Bookbinding Shop' to their porridge.) Sir Wilfred, too, seeks to promote self-respect, telling Paul, 'I want you to take a pride in your prison and in your work here'; he believes that knowledge of their role in his 'Experiments' will give the prisoners 'corporate pride'. (No 'unnecessary degradation' at Blackstone, where 'far from being a mere nameless slave', each inmate becomes 'part of a great revolution in statistics'.) The enemy of selfish brooding, Wilfred determines whether each prisoner is, in the fashionable new jargon, an 'introvert' or an 'extrovert', and consigns 'narcissists' to a socializing regime of 'conversation'. 'We don't want you to feel your personality is being stamped out', he tells Paul with delicious irony; 'Have you any experience of art leather work?' (220–1).

Proud that his treatment of prisoners has 'the human touch' (though in fact he is cruel and impersonal), Sir Wilfred is Waugh's first exemplar of a type increasingly common in his novels: the modern secular humanist, ludicrously at sea in a world he can neither understand nor control. Possessing 'genuine optimism in a degree rarely found in his office' (226), he embodies what in 1960, perhaps with Bell and Fry again in mind, Waugh called 'the illusions of the recent past, that every man is a natural artist' (TA 134): Sir Wilfred bases his 'experiments' in a fundamental faith that 'All crime is a form of insanity', brought on by a 'repressed desire for aesthetic expression' (DF 236, 221). His 'experiments' are thus exercises less in punishment than psychotherapy; he yearns for a staff psychiatrist while resting content with a Modern Churchman as chaplain. The religious maniac who murders Prendy is right in saying that Sir

"I Do Not Think It Possible for Domestic Architecture to Be Beautiful, but I Am Doing My Best"

7 Waugh's drawing of Otto Silenus for *Decline and Fall* (1928).

Wilfred also is 'no Christian'; Wilfred and Prendy recognize their kinship (Prendy praises the governor as 'very modern', Wilfred the chaplain as 'a very broad-minded man': (218, 220)). The 'progressive' Sir Wilfred thus embodies a distinct view of human nature: one that denies the reality of evil and original sin, of moral responsibility and free choice. (Even Otto knows – though he doesn't like it – that it is the human capacity for choice which distinguishes us from 'machines'.) And the fruit of his utopian theorizing is explosive cruelty: by giving a madman (and convicted murderer) the tools with which to 'express' his 'creative urges', Lucas-Dockery causes Prendy's beheading.

No passage better captures Waugh's purposes in creating Sir Wilfred than that in which we see him meting out justice. Having abjured the traditional Christian account of human nature, Wilfred possesses no standards of judgment, and so falls into the form of relativism since named 'situation ethics'.

Sir Wilfred Lucas-Dockery felt very much like Solomon at ten o'clock every morning of the week except Sunday. It was then that he sat in judgment upon

8 The Swiss architect Le Corbusier in his trademark double-breasted suit and glasses.

the cases of misconduct among the prisoners that were brought to his notice. From this chair Colonel MacAdder had delivered sentence in undeviating accordance with the spirit and the letter of the Standing Orders Concerning the Government of His Majesty's Prisons, dispensing automatic justice like a slot machine: in went the offence; out came the punishment. Not so Sir Wilfred Lucas-Dockery. Never, he felt, was his mind more alert or resourceful or his vast accumulation of know-ledge more available that at his little court of summary justice. 'No one knows what to expect', complained warders and prisoners alike.

'Justice', said Sir Wilfred, 'is the capacity for regarding each case as an entirely new problem'. After a few months of his administration, Sir Wilfred was able to point with some pride to a marked diminution in the number of cases brought before him.

(DF 237–8)

Legal precedents not only provide standards of uniformity, but are the vehicle by which the accumulated wisdom of past generations is transmitted to the present. In his vanity, Sir Wilfred abjures all such inherited wisdom, supposing that he can instead 'start from zero', that he can rebuild the whole edifice of human morality out of himself.[31]

If Sir Wilfred optimistically supposes human nature fundamentally good, Otto Silenus argues that 'All ill comes from man'. The view comes appropriately from an architect who (like those other modernists, Bell and Fry) sees 'the problem of all art' as 'the elimination of the human element from the consideration of form' (154–5). Otto's German first name signals the Bauhaus origins of the architectural style that came to Britain in the mid–1920s and had already produced such celebrated 'machines for living' as Professor Bernard Ashmole's ferro-concrete country house, High and Over (1927); his last name comes paradoxically from the satyr Silenus, teacher of Bacchus. (One of the few characters in *Decline and Fall* never to appear drunk, Otto's is an inebriation of the spirit.) When Margot, who thinks timbered Tudor architecture 'bourgeois and awful', seeks to replace the old King's Thursday with 'something clean and square', she engages 'Professor' Silenus, veteran of 'Moscow' and 'the Bauhaus' (152–3). In Waugh's own illustration, Otto strikingly resembles Le Corbusier, whose *City of Tomorrow* Waugh would soon review – and who at just the time *Decline and Fall* appeared embarked on a celebrated trip to Moscow, hoping in Stalin's Russia to win the commissions that had so far eluded him in the West.[32]

The age-old name for Sir Wilfred's overestimation of human nature (and a word often on his lips) is pride; Otto by contrast despairs of humanity. Otto's doctrine that 'The only perfect building must be the factory, because that is built to house machines, not men' (154) stems from a view of human nature presented in a parody of Hamlet's speech celebrating 'What a piece of work is man':

> 'What an immature, self-destructive, antiquated mischief is man! How obscure and gross his prancing and chattering on his little stage of evolution! How loathsome and beyond words boring all the thoughts and self-approval of this biological by-product! this half-formed, ill-conditioned body! this erratic, maladjusted mechanism of his soul: on one side the harmonious instincts and balanced responses of the animal, on the other the inflexible purpose of the engine, and between them man, equally alien from the *being* of Nature and the *doing* of the machine, the vile *becoming*!'
> (DF 157–8)

Otto's is not the pessimism of the satirist. He is of course right that 'all ill comes from man'. But this for any Christian is only half the story; only through embracing our messy state of 'becoming' – through its proper use – can humanity realize itself. The pairing of pride and despair – equal, seemingly opposite, in fact related misreadings of human nature – has a long history in both theology and literature.[33] Perhaps no other feature of *Decline and Fall* so clearly demonstrates that Waugh was a Christian moralist even in this, his first novel.

The question that has most divided readers of *Decline and Fall* is what we are to make of its ending. As Alvin Kernan notes, 'It is the arrangement of incidents and the overall pattern of events – plot – which ultimately establish the "meaning" in Waugh's novels' ('Wall' 87). At the very least, a story in which, over and over, outrageous and unpredictable events 'just happen' conveys a certain sense of life. After a year of such buffetings Paul Pennyfeather returns in the novel's Epilogue to what seems precisely his condition in the Prelude. Once again he is 'in his third year of uneventful residence at Scone'; again he hears 'an interesting paper about

the Polish plebiscites' (4, 284). His earlier friend Potts is replaced by the similar-
sounding Stubbs; the Bollers again drunkenly carouse. Critics divide evenly over
whether the novel traces a circle of meaningless change and repetition (leaving
Paul as naive as ever), or whether Waugh means to hint a pattern of development
– to hint that, like his literary forebear Candide, Paul indeed learns something –
and so to turn a novel that seems a parody of a *Bildungsroman* (especially in early
chapters such as 'Vocation') into a real tale of vocation after all.

Proponents of the first reading point especially to Otto Silenus's final speech
comparing life to the Big Wheel at Luna Park. Some people, Otto tells Paul,
scramble on the wheel, are thrown off, and scramble on again; others like
Margot 'sit as far out as they can and hold on for dear life and enjoy that';
yet others (like Otto himself) crawl toward its still centre, where 'generally some
one . . . stands up and sometimes does a sort of dance' (272). The image recalls
Fortune and her wheel, the 'much-maligned lady' to whom twice in the novel
characters offer a drunken toast. It seems an apt emblem for the world of *Decline
and Fall*, seemingly governed by chance, where reward is disconnected from
desert, effects cannot be predicted from causes, and undeserving gamblers
always win.[34] Characters in this world disappear and reappear as if by accident
– as on the morning of his wedding to Margot, Paul refills his glass of brandy,
offers a toast to Fortune, and is immediately arrested by the police.

But Paul's sudden arrest is an event from an older novelistic world, one where
seeming accidents – providentially sudden and seasonable turns of events –
signal underlying order and purpose. To novelists from Defoe and Fielding to
Austen and beyond, Providence guarantees the educative order that makes
human development possible (and so also crucially underwrites novelistic
plots).[35] Like Fielding, Waugh distinguishes the pagan notion of Fortune from
Christian Providence, God's ordering of events into a meaningful design of cause
and effect, desert and reward. Only such as Fagan can suppose the 'amazing
cohesiveness of [life's] events' as merely a collection of fortuitous 'accidents'.

In his speech on the Big Wheel as in that about 'becoming', Otto is the first of
a long line of would-be truth-tellers in Waugh's fiction, figures who grasp a
partial truth but not the whole, and so become partial spokesmen for their
author. (Later instances include Father Rothschild, Ambrose Silk, and Anthony
Blanche.) Sensing the appropriateness of Paul's clerical vocation, Otto rightly
tells Paul he 'needn't get on [the wheel] at all', but the final meaning of his own
comparison escapes him. Just as Prendy 'couldn't understand why God made
the world at all', Otto ends his long speech: 'And when we do get to the middle
it's just as if we never started. It's so odd' (278).

In his downward progress after expulsion from Oxford Paul becomes part of
the chaotic world around him, but there always remain saving possibilities about
him, signalled especially by his capacity, unique among the novel's characters,
for love. This capacity gives him from the start the glimmering of a higher
wisdom than Otto's. 'Why can't the creatures stay in one place?' asks Otto,
despairing of human possibility; 'Up and down, in and out, round and round!
Why can't they sit still and work?' A few pages later Waugh recalls Otto's
phrasing, describing Paul's growing attachment to Margot: 'Up and down the

shining lift shafts, in and out of the rooms and along the labyrinthine corridors of the great house he moved in a golden mist' (157, 175). When Philbrick tells his various life stories, skillfully adapting each to the proclivities of his listener, he tells Prendy a tale of religious guilt, Grimes one of educational and class guilt; to Paul he recounts a tale of love. As in all Waugh's fiction, the capacity for love, however misguided its initial objects, signals larger possibilities of spirit, supplying the necessary first step in a process of growth which Waugh traces to its completion only in *Brideshead.*

From the start, characters pour out their life stories to Paul in confessions that hint the appropriateness of his clerical vocation. 'It doesn't do to let that out to everyone. Funny thing, but I feel I can trust you', says Grimes; 'I don't know why I'm telling you all this; nobody else knows. I somehow feel you'll understand', says Prendy. ('Why was it, Paul wondered, that every one he met seemed to specialize in this kind of autobiography?') Paul's regeneration begins in prison, where he befriends the chaplain (Prendy's more devout successor) and where by a Pauline paradox, he feels free. Here he recognizes that in the face of enormities like Margot, 'there was something radically inapplicable' about the 'whole code of ready-made honour' in which he has been educated and on which he has relied (247). In effect, he approaches the knowledge all Waugh's early heroes need to gain: that the modern world is living on dwindling cultural capital, on inherited institutions deformed by having been cut off from the living faith that was the source of their authority. Without authoritative institutions, anarchy takes over; by the novel's end, no longer the naive progressive, Paul is clear on what is needed to restore order.

Paul's second stay in Oxford does not exactly parallel his first: once again creating contexts for comparative judgment, Waugh carefully plants divergences within a larger pattern of similarity. Unlike Potts, Paul's new friend Stubbs is a fellow 'theological student'; Paul now finds the Junior Dean's reference to the College chaplain 'rather supercilious'.[36] The previously meek Paul displays a new decisiveness. 'He liked the ugly, subdued little College, and he liked Stubbs' (281); he forthrightly counsels Peter Pastmaster, now a Boller, 'You drink too much' (287). The inspiration and direction of this new firmness come clear in two striking passages condemning religious heresy which Waugh added to the novel after the manuscript was completed, presumably to clarify what Paul has learned (and to frame Paul's initial 'meek' curse of the university authorities in the Prelude). The first reads like an oblique catalogue of all that has happened to him in the course of the story: 'There was a bishop in Bithynia, Paul learned, who had denied the Divinity of Christ, the immortality of the soul, the existence of good, the legality of marriage, and the validity of the Sacrament of Extreme Unction. How right they had been to condemn him!' (283).

Decline and Fall's final paragraphs make the same point through the series of *double entendres* that fill Paul's last conversation with the drunken Peter. 'I'm going to be ordained soon', he tells Peter, who replies with unconscious irony: 'Damned funny, that'; 'Wish I didn't feel so damned ill' (286–7). Peter tries to persuade Paul once more to offer the toast to 'Fortune, a much-maligned lady', but now Paul refuses. After a year learning about indulgence, indiscipline, and infidelity, the Paul who once habitually read the Forsyte saga before going to bed – and in the heady atmosphere of King's Thursday, Frazer's *Golden Bough* – now calls on stronger medicine:

> So Peter went out, and Paul settled down in his chair. So the ascetic Ebionites used to turn towards Jerusalem when they prayed. Paul made a note of it. Quite right to suppress them. Then he turned out the light and went into his bedroom to sleep.[37]

Otto has confessed to Paul that he never sleeps; Margot takes drugs to do so; Grimes, Prendy, and Philbrick all confess to guilt that keeps them awake. Paul's final sleep implies not an escape from 'real life' but clearness of conscience.

Waugh was not yet a Catholic when he wrote *Decline and Fall*. But he was already capable of appreciating the sketch of religious history (later to be dramatized in *A Handful of Dust* and made explicit in *Campion*) Fagan inserts into his delightful slur on the Welsh: 'we can trace almost all the disasters of English history to the influence of Wales... the Tudors and the dissolution of the Church, then Lloyd George... Non-conformity' (81). It is tempting to read personal significance into Pennyfeather's final exchange with Stubbs:

> 'D'you want to take Von Hugel?' Paul asked.
> 'No, not to-night. May I leave it til to-morrow?'
>
> (DF 284)

III

Waugh announced *Vile Bodies* on its dust-jacket as a 'tragedy in which comic relief overwhelmingly predominates'. It was also, he admitted later, 'a totally unplanned book'.[38] Short of money and so needing to 'write a lot quickly', he chose for the victim-hero of his second novel the young writer Adam Fenwick-Symes, short of money and under contract to produce twelve books in a year. Trying to rush the novel to a conclusion in July 1929, Waugh boasted to Henry Yorke of writing 25,000 words 'in ten days', 'rather like P. G. Wodehouse all about bright young people'; 'I hope it will be finished by the end of the month & then I shall just have time to write another book before your party'. He told Harold Acton: 'It is a welter of sex and snobbery written hastily in the hope of selling some copies. Then if it is [at] all a success I want to try and write something more serious' (L 36–7).

Written in two short bursts, *Vile Bodies* achieved popularity in part simply as a 'scrapbook of popular culture' (Garnett 63). The 'female evangelist' Mrs Ape is Aimée Semple McPherson, whose 'illustrated sermons' (elaborate, operatic stage-shows, complete with troupe of vocalists and her own famously 'magnetic' presence) filled Albert Hall in 1926 and 1928; Lottie Crump's Shepheard's Hotel is 'a pretty accurate description of Mrs. Rosa Lewis and her Cavendish Hotel, just on the brink of their decline but still famous' (at which, after the novel's publication, Waugh was no longer welcome).[39] Most of all Waugh memorializes the generation Noël Coward sang about in *I Went to a Marvellous Party*: the Bright Young People. Parties fill nearly every scene of the novel – 'Masked parties,

Savage parties, Victorian parties, Greek parties', as the narrator wearily (and accurately) lists them – along with their late-twenties appendages, gate-crashers and gossip-columnists. Patrick Balfour proudly claimed in 1933 that his own, Tom Driberg's and Eleanor Smith's gossip-columns inspired the novel's 'Mr Chatterbox'.[40] More than once the intrusive narrator of *Vile Bodies* likens his own role as novelist to that of gossip-columnist.

Returning to the novel in the weeks after Evelyn Gardner's defection, Waugh wrote to Henry Yorke, 'I am relying on a sort of cumulative futility for any effect it may have' (L 39). But from the outset *Vile Bodies* describes a darker world than had *Decline and Fall*. The action is punctuated by scenes of nausea and vomiting (culminating in Nina Blount's sickness on peering down from an aeroplane at the wasteland of modern England); comically gruesome deaths like little Lord Tangent's have become commonplace. Flossie Ducane (née Fagan?) dies falling drunk from a chandelier; Simon Balcairn puts his head in a gas oven; crying 'Faster, Faster', Agatha Runcible, brightest of the Bright Young People, dies in hospital after crashing a racing-car.[41] Like racing-cars speeding round a track (a central image in the novel), events move faster and faster until a whole world crashes.

'How much confidence can we have', Waugh asked in 1929, 'in the stability of an economic system that has so far directed itself almost unconcernedly towards chaos?' (EAR 63). In a brief conversation between Lord Circumference and Paul Pennyfeather, *Decline and Fall* had already predicted what many thought the inevitable result of the botched peace of 1919 and its aftermath: 'Do you really and truly think…there's going to be another war?'; 'Yes, I'm sure of it' (DF 86). *Vile Bodies*, having opened with Adam's return from France, ends by depositing him there once again, lost and alone, sitting on 'a splintered tree stump in the biggest battlefield in the history of the world'; 'presently, like a circling typhoon, the sounds of battle began to return' (VB 247, 252). All Waugh's novels traverse some version of a circle, recalling their first pages in their last and ending with an abruptness that points a blunt symbolism. *Vile Bodies*'s abrupt 'Happy Ending' embodies a characteristic double irony: the onset of Armageddon is obviously not happy; but like all 'happy endings', it embodies poetic justice. A global explosion of cruelty, Waugh implies, is the natural, even merited outcome of what has come before.

What has come before is a synoptic survey of late-twenties England that gives dramatic form to the arguments of Waugh's journalism about the 'perverse and aimless dissipation' of the younger generation, 'chronicled daily by the gossip-writers of the press' (EAR 62). 'I don't understand them', says Mr. Outrage, last week's prime minister:

> They had a chance after the war that no generation has ever had. There was a whole civilisation to be saved and remade – and all they seem to do is to play the fool. Mind you, I'm all in favour of them having a fling. I dare say that Victorian ideas were a bit-strait-laced…. But there's something wanton about these young people today.
>
> (VB 142)

The novel's youth are everywhere at sea because age – once again represented by a parade of failed parents, heads of government and of society – has left them rudderless. We can hardly be surprised if an older generation comprising Kitty Blackwater (the name means a tropical disease) and Lady Throbbing yields such perverse fruit as Miles Malpractice. 'All my cousins are in lunatic asylums or else they live in the country and do indelicate things with animals', Simon Balcairn remarks off-handedly; 'except my mamma' – Mrs Panrast, her name a compendious summary of unruly impulse – 'and that's worse' (89). The novel's final battlefield is simply a magnified rendering of all that has come before: 'Damn difficult country to find one's way about in', says another lost soldier; 'No landmarks...' (249).

Waugh realizes the rudderlessness of youth most poignantly in Adam and Nina, whose on-again, off-again engagement (narrated in clipped conversations inspired, he admitted, by Hemingway) perfectly captures the ethos of a generation stunted by an absence of landmarks. In Waugh's best dandy style, their conversations mix childishness and a hyper-sophisticated suspicion of their forebears' unguarded sentimentality: 'don't let's get intense'; 'I say, Nina, you are getting sentimental'; 'Do be amusing, Adam. I can't bear it when you're not amusing' (54, 41, 94). Most of all they betray a yearning unable to articulate itself, desire unable to compass its own proper end:

> 'Nina', said Adam, 'let's get married soon, don't you think?'
> 'Yes, it's a bore not being married'....
> '...I don't know if it sounds absurd', said Adam, 'but I do feel that a marriage ought to *go on* – for quite a long time, I mean. D'you feel that too, at all?'
> 'Yes, it's one of the things about a marriage!'
> 'I'm glad you feel that. I didn't quite know if you did. Otherwise it's all rather bogus, isn't it?'
>
> (VB 132)

Adam and Nina are in love – as much as two spiritual cripples can be; prematurely sophisticated, they are quick to recognize the 'bogus', but lack the tools (and the vocabulary) for articulating value.[42] Meanwhile, frustrated humanity expresses itself in what forms it can – most commonly, in cruelty.

> There were Adam and Nina getting rather sentimental.
> 'Do you know', she said, pulling out a lump, 'I'd quite made up my mind that your hair was dark'. Archie Schwert, pausing with a bottle of champagne, said, 'Don't be so sadistic, Nina'.
>
> (VB 52–3)

A search of the novel for instances of thoughtless violence and cruelty yields an extraordinary catalogue, from Ginger's childhood torturing of cats and Adam's stabbing a dressmaker's dummy to the adult blood-hunger of spectators at the motor-race, crowding for a sight of the most dangerous turns. It is equally remarkable how many such instances are perverse manifestations of friendship and love, from the easy cruelty to one another of the young – Adam 'amuses'

Nina by telling of their friend Simon's being horsewhipped, and studies the dying Agatha's medical chart 'with pleasure' – to the Duchess of Stayle's delicate forcing of her daughter into a marriage she does not want. Once again the novel's final battlefield is a magnified realization of what has come before. World war is the complete negation of love, not only in its weaponry – 'liquid-fire projectors' and 'Huxley Haldane bombs (for the dissemination of leprosy germs)' – but also in the haunting obscenity of Waugh's final image: the drunken major (now a general) having sex with Chastity in the back seat of a stranded car as Adam falls asleep in front.

Adam and Nina's condition is diagnosed by Father Rothschild, who after some gentle satire – and praise for the Jesuit's possession of what Waugh celebrated in his own 'clearsighted' generation, 'penetrating acumen in the detection of falsehood and exaggeration' (42) – becomes in a central passage Waugh's own spokesman.

> 'Don't you think', said Father Rothschild gently, 'that perhaps it is all in some way historical? I don't think people ever *want* to lose their faith either in religion or anything else. I know very few young people, but it seems to me that they are all possessed with an almost fatal hunger for permanence. I think all these divorces show that.... And this word "bogus" they all use...'.[43]

Another truth-teller, Rothschild sees clearly but not to the end. 'I think they're connected, you know', he tells Outrage and Metroland, trying to explain the link between particulars such as Peter Pastmaster's drinking and the 'radical instability in the whole world order' that presages war; 'But it's all very difficult'. Rothschild grasps obscurely what the novel as a whole demonstrates: if the sleep of reason produces monsters, so does the frustration of that inbuilt *conatus* for love which, seeking 'permanence', draws souls to something higher.

The basis of Rothschild's judgment (and of the novel as a whole), then, is the same as Waugh's complaint to Alec: 'The trouble about the world today is that there's not enough religion in it'. When in his gossip-column Simon Balcairn accuses the guests at Margot's party of piety, the result is an orgy of libel suits; no wonder the Bright Young People regularly misapply such words as 'divine', 'angel', 'awful', and 'damned'. So relentlessly does Waugh hammer the point home that but for its riotous pace and inventiveness, *Vile Bodies* would seem a tract. The story opens with passengers on boardship who, 'to avert the terrors of seasickness' (a condition like Peter Pastmaster's feeling 'damned ill'), 'indulge in every kind of civilised witchcraft' – efforts that fail because 'they were lacking in faith'.[44] It culminates on Christmas, when Nina and Adam adulterously conceive a child: the day accordingly brings tidings not of comfort and joy, but news that 'War has been declared'. Under the pretext of clarifying the novel's chronology, an Author's Note (dropped from later editions) blandly reminds readers that 'Christmas is observed by the Western Church on December 25th' – a slap like that administered at the end of *Helena*, where Waugh remarks off-handedly that in the centuries after the saint's death, 'Britain for a time became Christian' (H 265).

Though *Vile Bodies*'s plot was unplanned, Waugh had its title in mind from the first: an echo of Philippians (the passage also formed part of the Anglican burial service).

> Brethren, be followers together of me, and mark them which walk so as ye have us for an ensample.
>   (For many walk, of whom I have told you often, and now tell you even weeping, that they are enemies of the cross of Christ:
>   Whose end is destruction, whose God is their belly, and whose glory is in their shame, who mind earthly things.)
>   For our conversation is in heaven; from whence also we look for the Saviour, the Lord Jesus Christ:
>   Who shall change our vile body, that it may be fashioned like unto his glorious body, according to the working whereby he is able even to subdue all things unto himself.
>
>   (3: 17–21, Authorized Version)

The allusion signals a hope everywhere missing in the world of the novel. As the story opens, Mrs Ape (whose name suggests both bestiality and mere imitation of a truer faith) calls the roll of her angels: Faith and Charity, Fortitude and Temperance and Chastity, Creative Endeavour and Divine Discontent. Conspicuously absent from this (skewed) catalogue of the seven virtues is any angel named for the virtue Mrs Ape tries to instil in her queasy fellow-passengers:

> You'll feel better for [singing] body *and* soul. It's a song of Hope. You don't hear much about Hope these days, do you? Plenty about Faith, plenty about Charity. They've forgotten all about Hope. There's only one great evil in the world today. Despair.[45]

That 'great evil' suffuses a novel in which the loveless Mr Outrage, considering whether he is 'an immortal soul...born for eternity', 'resign[s] himself to the dust' (141), and Adam says of Nina's marriage to Ginger: 'I'm desperate about it. I'm thinking of committing suicide like Simon' (208).

Early in the story Nina directs Adam to her father's country house: 'It's a house called Doubting and it's all falling down really' (64). Later this child of Doubting says of the consummation of love in marriage: 'I don't believe that really divine things like that ever do happen' (82). Lest we miss the echo of Doubting Castle from Waugh's youthful favourite, *Pilgrim's Progress*, the name appears again:

> At Aylesbury Adam got into a Ford taxi and asked to be taken to a house called Doubting.
>   'Doubting 'All?'
>   'Well I suppose so. Is it all falling down?'
>   'Could do with a lick of paint', said the driver.
>
>   (VB 67)

Bunyan's Doubting Castle is the home of Giant Despair, reached by leaving the straight path for 'By-Pass Meadow'; Agatha Runcible comes to grief by driving her 'Omega' off the stated racecourse onto a 'bye-road', 'turning left instead of right at Church Corner', and smashing directly into a 'market cross' (195, 200). 'They shouldn't put up symbols like that in the middle of the road, should they, or should they?' she asks in truth-telling delirium, to which a nurse replies more truly than she knows: 'There's nothing to worry about, dear... *nothing at all... nothing*' (224).

A place where (in Wodehouse fashion) only the servants keep order, not the master, Doubting is 'all falling down'; Waugh predicts the same fate for Anchorage House, that 'last survivor of the noble town houses of London' (135). Like many contemporaries, he mourned the decay of hundreds of country houses in the interwar years (chronicled in the pages of *Country Life*) and the even more spectacular levelling of London's historic buildings to make way for characterless hotels and blocks of flats. (With 'the disappearance or the conversion into other uses of London's private palaces', wrote E. B. Chancellor after the demolition of Dorchester House in 1926, 'something of the grace of life seems to be departing'.)[46] The buildings of *Vile Bodies* are not only in decay, but indicate the source of that decay, initiating a symbolic procedure found throughout Waugh's early novels. A 'lofty Palladian' structure set in a park complete with 'equestrian statue' dominating its central avenue (a military figure more commanding than its owner Colonel Blount), Doubting descends from the same architectural period that produced the 'broad Adam staircase' of Margot's town house and the 'pillared façade' of Anchorage House (which inspires in Mrs Hoop a 'glorious dream of eighteenth century elegance'). All are artifacts of the period Waugh identified in 'Converted to Rome' as an age of 'polite and highly attractive scepticism', the period when the erosion of Christian faith really began.[47]

Doubting is the appropriate site for a film biography of John Wesley, the eighteenth-century founder of Methodism – a movement that took England yet further from its Catholic roots. The novel's emphasis on film and use of cinematic technique capture what Waugh understood as a further stage in the same historical progression. From youth he was fascinated by what *Labels* calls 'the one vital art of the century' (11); while still at Lancing he advised Dudley Carew, working on a novel:

> Try and bring home thoughts by actions and incidents. Don't make everything said. This is the inestimable value of the Cinema to novelists (don't scoff at this as a cheap epigram it is really very true). Make things happen.... GO TO THE CINEMA and risk the headache.
>
> (L 2)

Film provided the model for suitably modern, non-subjective storytelling, what in 1930 Waugh prophesied would become 'the manner for fiction of the next twenty years':

> There are practically no descriptive passages except purely technical ones. The character, narrative and atmosphere are all built up and implicit in the dialogue, which is written in a vivid slang, with numerous recurring phrases running through

as a refrain. Ronald Firbank began to discover this technique, but his eccentricity and a certain dead, 'ninetyish' fatuity frustrated him. I made some experiments in this direction in the telephone conversations in *Vile Bodies*. Mr Ernest Hemingway used it brilliantly in *The Sun Also Rises*. It has not yet been perfected but I think it is going to develop into an important method.[48]

In a later review of Graham Greene's *The Heart of the Matter* (1948), Waugh catalogued the cinematic devices useful to novelists: montage and cross-cutting; close-ups of 'significant details'; an impersonal narrative stance, wherein by imitating the 'camera eye', 'the writer has become the director and producer'. 'It is the modern way of telling a story': filmic devices yield a narrative formally imitative of disjointed modern life.[49] Even *Vile Bodies*'s authorial intrusions into the narrative, usually marked off with parentheses, serve like the captions in silent films.

Late in life Waugh declared *Vile Bodies* 'a bad book', 'not so carefully constructed' as *Decline and Fall*; 'separate scenes tended to go on for too long – the conversation in the train between those two women, the film shows of the dotty father' (Jebb 108–9). Its cataclysmic ending was something he would have to ignore as later novels continued to follow the fortunes of Margot and Peter, Alastair and Sonia. But Waugh never lost what Claud Cockburn called his vision of life as a 'morality play', or its corollary that 'it is with [characters'] final destiny that their creator is primarily, if unobtrusively, concerned'. He freely admitted his 'wish to see justice done' in novels – his belief that in order to be truthful, authors must present 'the moral welfare or exemplary punishment of [their] characters'.[50] 'The trouble about the pessimism of [Hardy's] *Tess*', he argued (not quite consistently) in 1930, 'is that it is bogus':

> If the constitution of the universe is malignant, then malignant ceases to have any meaning. True tragedy consists in taking some theme in daily life, suffering, waste, decay, cruelty, death, separation, that seems in conflict with the benevolent organisation of the universe, and by making an artistic and significant form out of the chaos to reconcile it with the universe.
>
> ('*Tess*')

3

Political Decade – I (1930–1935)

For myself and many better than me, there is a fascination in distant and barbarous places, and particularly in the borderlands of conflicting cultures and states of development, where ideas, uprooted from their traditions, become oddly changed in transplantation. It is there that I find the experiences vivid enough to demand translation into literary form.

Ninety-Two Days (1934)

Politics, everywhere destructive, have here dried up the place, frozen it, cracked and powdered it to dust. Is civilization, like a leper, beginning to rot at its extremities? In the Sixteenth Century human life was disordered and talent stultified by the obsession with theology; today we are plague-stricken by politics.

Robbery Under Law (1939)

In his 1975 biography, Christopher Sykes claimed of Waugh, 'He was without any serious political or sociological interests'. Many have since agreed; the view seems to have much to recommend it.[1] In the partisan thirties, Waugh himself began to speak dismissively of all 'politics' as a pernicious diversion from more important concerns. For writers so infected (as he complained in a lecture in 1937), all literature becomes 'Ideological Writing'.[2] In later life he called politics 'the cocaine of the people' and could tell a visiting stranger: 'I loathe politics. Please change the subject'. Auberon Waugh reports that he 'never once' heard his father 'discuss politics seriously'.[3]

Waugh was bored by the details of day-to-day party manoeuvering, which he liked to argue in Bellocian fashion 'are a game played by the rich to oppress the poor' (Donaldson 103). But the pose of eschewing 'politics' altogether is a familiar, usually conservative political stance. Sykes meant to defend his old friend by minimizing Waugh's commitment to widely unpopular views. His comment must astonish any reader of Waugh's non-fiction (nearly as voluminous as the fiction), which demonstrates that Waugh not only kept abreast of politics but prided himself on probing in any debate to the principles at stake in it. He always sought what T. S. Eliot called 'the stratum down to which any sound political thinking must push its roots, and from which it must derive its nourishment' – its answers to the questions 'no political philosophy can escape': 'What is Man? what are his limitations?... what, finally, his destiny?' ('Literature of Politics', 144).

As a boy Waugh had inherited his father's generally Conservative loyalties, though Arthur recalled as well his son's experiments with more modern notions.[4] At Lancing he confided to his diary, 'The more I see of politics the more dishonest and fascinating they appear' (D 41). Oxford, where his friends ran the gamut from socialists to romantic Jacobites, brought the predictable reaction to such adolescent earnestness. There he adopted a colourful Tory diehard pose, advising socialist friends to do the same because, the 'best brains' having chosen Labour, budding Leftists 'would find the competition too hot'. In later years he liked to say that in his Oxford days he 'could not have defined Tory policy on any current topic' (ALL 182–3), but friends such as Christopher Hollis remembered him as already attracting 'attention [as] an intelligent Conservative' (HW 13).

The maturation of Waugh's political views occurred amidst what Aldous Huxley called a general late-twenties reaction 'away from the easy-going philosophy of general meaninglessness towards the hard, ferocious theologies of nationalistic and revolutionary ideology' (*Ends* 274). 'Just as the sturdy assurance of the average Englishman thirty years ago... is yielding rapidly to a fear of economic collapse', wrote Fr D'Arcy in 1931, diagnosing 'the Crisis of the West', 'so in the realms of politics, morality and religion, beliefs have been shaken and are no longer trusted. We are face to face, as a result, with a dangerous condition of mind, one which some would regard as a herald or symptom of defeat, others as a warning that we must recover some lost faith or set about making another' (*Belief* 17).

While Waugh took D'Arcy's first route, recovering his faith, a younger generation of writers energetically announced its quest for meaning along the second. In 1927 a young W. H. Auden argued that 'no universalized system – political, religious or metaphysical – has been bequeathed to us', making a 'new synthesis' necessary. The first important anthology of this new generation, *New Signatures* (1932) – including works by Auden, Day Lewis, William Empson, Louis MacNeice, William Plomer and Stephen Spender – announced in its preface the need for a 'new harmonisation', a 'social communism' achieved 'without recourse to any external system of religious belief'. For Spender in 1935, 'The question is whether this despairing stage is now over, whether it is now possible for the artist to discover a system of values that are not purely subjective and individualistic, but objective and social'.[5] As such language suggests, much of this new generation's faith would be grounded in collectivist political ideology. The Depression had made 'individualism' suspect; even Pius XI's *Quadragesimo anno* (1931) attempted to steer a middle course between an 'evil individualism' and socialism, 'a remedy far worse than the evil' it meant to cure (§10).

Day Lewis wrote in 1935, the year he joined the Communist Party: 'It is already becoming more evident to serious writers that the prevailing "consciousness" of the times is a political consciousness, and this is increasingly manifest in their work.'[6] In the decade of the Depression, Italy's invasion of Abyssinia and the Spanish Civil War, political views polarized and hardened. Spain especially divided British intellectuals more bitterly than had any conflict since the 1790s. Just as in the wake of the French Revolution Englishmen could only be 'conservative' or 'radical', there seemed by 1936 (in the words of the surrealist poet Roger Roughton) 'no longer a fence for intellectuals to sit on'. The *Left Review* agreed: 'It is impossible any longer to take no side' between socialism (or Communism) and Fascism. By 1938 Cyril Connolly could declare simply, 'Most creative writing to-day is Left in sentiment.'[7]

That capitalism was in crisis was the faith that guided the Labour Party manifesto of 1920:

> We of the Labour Party... recognize, in the present world catastrophe, if not the death, in Europe, of civilization itself, at any rate the culmination and collapse of a distinctive industrial civilization, which the workers will not seek to reconstruct....
> The industrial system of capitalist production, with the monstrous inequality of circumstances which it produces and the degradation and brutalization, both moral and spiritual, resulting therefrom, may, we hope, indeed have received a death-blow.
>
> (Graves 151)

In 1926, H. G. Wells calmly added 'A Forecast of the Next War' to a new edition of his *Outline of History*; by the early thirties many believed that all Europe, in the title of a widely distributed Communist pamphlet of 1929, was *Heading for War*. Novels appeared such as Fowler Wright's *A Prelude in Prague: A Story of the War of 1938* (1935) and Aldous Huxley's *Eyeless in Gaza* (1936), whose Anthony Beavis predicts 'another war quite soon – about 1940'. Even so seemingly disengaged a text as Fr D'Arcy's *Nature of Belief* (1931) presented its philosophical theology as an alternative to 'Fascism and Bolshevism'. The literary journal *Scrutiny*, founded the next year, took as its task the support of 'standards' at a time when 'the end of Western civilization is in sight'.[8]

The general election of 1931 brought in the coalition National Government, still led by Ramsay Macdonald but mainly Conservative. Labour's defeat radicalized the Left, leading some to join new splinter parties (such as the Independent Labour Party to which *Vile Bodies*'s Agatha Runcible complains she has not been invited); others grew convinced that 'radical measures of Marxism' were 'necessary to defeat reaction and stop the drift towards a new war'.[9] The flow of socialist writing became a flood. In 1930 the *Daily Worker* began publication, and in 1934 the *Left Review*, official organ of the British Writers International. In 1936 Victor Gollancz – who had already established himself with his New Soviet Library – inaugurated the decade's most successful venture in political publishing, the Left Book Club. A year later the Club had 57,000 members, who for 2s 6d each month received a new book selected by its three judges, Gollancz, John Strachey and Harold Laski, Professor at the London School of Economics and author of *Communism* (1927). By 1940 it had circulated over a million volumes.

A year after the elections the young aesthete-turned-Liberal-turned-Fascist-turned-Communist John Strachey published one of the most influential texts of the decade: *The Coming Struggle for Power* (1932). Following Lenin's analysis in *Imperialism: The Highest Stage of Capitalism* (1916), Strachey argued that capitalism was in its final, violent, imperialist phase. Left to itself, it would inevitably devolve into Fascism.

> Menaced from within and from without, [capitalism] must become incomparably more violent.... Direct, open terror against the workers, violent aggression against its rivals, can alone enable a modern empire to maintain itself. A name for such a policy has been found: it is fascism.... The whole capitalist world is on the way to barbarism.
>
> (8)

> The capitalist system is dying and cannot be revived.... [it] was adapted to an age of individualism and 'freedom' alone. And the age of individualistic freedom is very nearly over.... It is undoubtedly true that the cause of individualistic freedom is to-day the cause of everything that is reactionary, stupid, barbaric and repressive in the world, and that it can only triumph by destroying civilization and pulling us back into an age of darkness.
>
> (156)

Strachey paused in a footnote to place Evelyn Waugh in the new ideological landscape:

> quite the best – and in many ways actually the most accurate – account of present-day English society, written by an author with something of Mr. Faulkner's capacity for still being appalled by his surroundings, is contained in Mr. Evelyn Waugh's two humorous books, *Decline and Fall* and *Vile Bodies*. After writing these books, Mr. Waugh had clearly only three alternatives open to him. He could either commit suicide, become a communist, or immure himself within the Catholic Church. He chose this last (and easiest) alternative.
>
> (228n)

This political background is crucial for understanding Waugh's career in the thirties. His continuing playfulness and much-reported Mayfair social life were now necessarily fraught with political meaning. Rising to the occasion, he made them a form of provocation – assertions, often deliberately outrageous, of his opposition to the Left. As poverty and the condition of the working classes came to dominate 'serious' literature – in works from J. B. Priestley's *English Journey* (1933) and Walter Greenwood's *Love on the Dole* (1933) to Orwell's *Road to Wigan Pier* (1937) – Waugh continued unabashedly to focus his novels on the well-to-do. As Leftist critics began to deprecate as 'escapist' texts that did not engage economic 'reality' as, Waugh wrote celebrations of Wodehouse, Lewis Carroll, the 'Victorian Escapist' Edward Lear and the 'delectable unreality' of Max

Beerbohm.[10] As the same critics came to argue that only a style of unadorned, objective reportage was appropriate to proletarian ideals, Waugh turned to what he called 'jewelled prose' and the subjectivity of first-person narrative. Against 'the lurking puritanism...which is ever ready to condemn pleasure even in its purest form', he proclaimed literature's value as 'pure enjoyment' (EAR 478, 424). As intellectuals espoused collectivist ideologies, his anti-intellectual pose hardened. 'Those of us who can afford to think without proclaiming ourselves "intellectuals", do not want or expect a Fascist regime', he wrote in 1938 (EAR 223). Against champions of a classless society, he defended stratification and hierarchy; when most on the Left wished to free themselves of the burden of the imperialist, capitalist, repressive nineteenth century, Waugh celebrated 'pre-1914 sweetness of life', England's 'free and fecund' Victorian age.

By the middle of the decade Waugh had been goaded to articulate a self-declared conservative individualism deeply informed by his religious view of human nature. In a stream of essays and books, he argued against the Left that liberty and equality are not finally compatible; that the measure of any system of rule is the quality of private life it permits and fosters; and that utopian notions of 'progress', either in their nineteenth-century Liberal form or in more modern Marxian guise, rest on a 'sentimental belief in the basic sweetness of human nature' (EAR 135) which, reduced to practice, ends in cruelty.

Waugh entered the maelstrom of public political debate hesitantly with *Remote People* (1931), a travel book that began as the record of a trip to Abyssinia but grew into a meditation on what Strachey identified as 'the key question of our day, the question of imperialism' (*Struggle*, 189–90). In the years to follow, though not initially in his novels, Waugh made his political and religious views increasingly explicit, sometimes in reasoned argument, sometimes with hilarious vitriol and deliberately provocative public posturing. For his support of the Italian invasion of Abyssinia he was – wrongly – called a Fascist, and the label stuck. *Robbery Under Law* (1939) contains as if in reply Waugh's most sustained straightforward elaboration of his political views. In 1931 *Remote People* apologised for straying into politics: 'It is very surprising to discover the importance which politics assume the moment one begins to travel' (159). *Robbery Under Law* begins bluntly: 'This is a political book' (5).

Such strong commitments might have led Waugh to follow those of his friends who actually entered government service. An article of 1937 confessed: 'somewhere, deep in the English mentality, is a feeling that no one has led a really complete life unless he has at one time or another, in one party or another, sat [in the Commons] as a member'.[11] The year before, he had toyed with the idea of doing in real life what Basil Seal does in fiction: 'Grand about Duff in the cabinet', he wrote to Diana Cooper just after her husband became Secretary of War; 'Will he get me into the Secret Service?' (DC 58). As late as 1945 he seriously considered seeking a seat in Parliament.

This continuing desire to shape events needs to be understood in light of the extraordinary pressure that thirties politics exerted on writers to re-evaluate a whole range of relationships: the relations of author to audience, of public to private life and of art to propaganda, questions that engaged Waugh with

increasing intensity. The twenties 'idea of futility', Cyril Connolly argued, had
arisen 'from a disbelief in action and in the putting of moral slogans into action,
engendered by the Great War' (*Enemies* 41); but some form of action now seemed
necessary. In literature the problem was one of creating heroes, in recent writing
a species to whose 'death' Ralph Fox, the Communist literary critic killed in
Spain, devoted the central chapter of his study of *The Novel and the People* (1937).
While younger writers sought what they variously called the 'great leader' (Rex
Warner), the 'healer' (Day Lewis) and 'The Truly Great Man' who could 'Make
action urgent and its nature clear' (Auden),[12] Waugh created in 1935 his first
unalloyed activist hero: not a political leader but *Edmund Campion: Jesuit and
Martyr*, in whom human action takes on heroic meaning through its submission
not to temporary exigencies but to the divine plan.

I

By the end of 1930, Waugh was the celebrated author of four books. Lionized at
literary luncheons and cocktail parties, he moved in grander social circles than
ever before. He thoroughly enjoyed his success. Douglas Woodruff recalled: 'one
would meet him at the luncheon parties of society hostesses, arriving in a large
limousine and offering to take any of the guests anywhere they wished, saying "I
have a large car at my disposal because I am *nouveau riche*"' (HW 104). Sometimes the sheer number of these affairs tired even Waugh. He joked that his next
book should be called 'Tax Dodging in Central Africa or Six Months out of
Reach of Lady Cunard'.[13]

To secure his income Waugh would need to perpetuate this success, but how
to follow up *Vile Bodies*? And how without dwindling into a novelist who wrote
only, and repetitively, about Mayfair? The vogue of the Bright Young People
had passed. Waugh considered a return to history and biography, going so far as
to contract for a life of Jonathan Swift, perhaps following the lead of Edith
Sitwell's *Alexander Pope* (1930). (He dropped the project on learning that two
other lives of Swift, one by Carl Van Doren, had already been commissioned for
publication in 1931.) But as *Vile Bodies* had already predicted, politics, not art
and fashion, would be the focus of the new decade.

For the next six years, travel provided an answer, providing adventures to fill
travel books and, later, novels. *Labels* had demonstrated that travel writing could
be a vehicle for social (if not yet fully political) commentary as well as discussions
of art. Robert Byron made a living by writing up his journeys; other friends
(Peter Fleming, Peter Quennell, and Christopher Sykes) soon followed. 'It
seemed an ordeal', Waugh wrote in 1946 of the rough journeying of all these
men who had been too young to fight in the Great War, 'an initiation into
manhood'. (Many writers of about Waugh's age discussed what Christopher
Isherwood called the 'feeling of shame that we hadn't been old enough to take
part in the European War', a sense that war 'meant The Test. The test of your
courage, your maturity, of your sexual prowess'. 'You felt yourself a little less
than a man, because you had missed it', recalled Orwell, and as a result
pretended uninterest in all things military, such as Waugh also displayed in his
schoolboy rags.)[14]

The modern traveller would of course have to strike out for exotic places. To remain, like the writer of *Labels*, in the Mediterranean was to remain in Europe. 'The Mediterranean is the human norm', says Fielding in Forster's *A Passage to India* (1924); 'When men leave that exquisite lake...they approach the monstrous and extraordinary'. Byron stalked instructive monsters from Persia to Tibet; D. H. Lawrence had gone to Mexico and the South Seas; Fleming, Quennell and Acton would choose China. Waugh, like Ernest Hemingway, selected Africa – guided in part by the current interest back home in everything black. Fashionable England was reading Carl van Vechten's *Nigger Heaven* and listening to Florence Mills and the Blackbirds; soon would come Nancy Cunard's 900-page *Negro: An Anthology* (1934) and Geoffrey Gorer's anti-imperialist *Africa Dances* (1935). Given their sense of European crisis, many writers (including Waugh) entertained the possibility that, as Shaw predicted in *The Adventures of a Black Girl in Her Search for God* (1932), the next great civilization would be a black one.

From 1930 to 1935 – to cite only those journeys that issued in books – Waugh escaped winters in England by travelling to Africa and South America. Diaries that would later serve as the writer's *aides-mémoire* survive from all these trips. From the start his plan was to collect material for a travel book, then transform his experiences into a novel. A few weeks after arriving in Africa for the first time he wrote home, 'I have the plot of a first rate novel'; during his second visit, 'all this will make a funny novel' (L 51, 101). The first African trip issued in *Remote People* (1931) and, more loosely related to experience, *Black Mischief* (1932). Two more visits occasioned *Waugh in Abyssinia* (1936) and *Scoop* (1938). Meanwhile a journey to South America in the winter of 1932–3 produced *Ninety-Two Days* and the final sections of *A Handful of Dust* (both 1934). There was a hastily undertaken expedition to the Arctic in the summer of 1934, and in 1938 a short trip to Mexico to gather material for *Robbery Under Law* – journeys that did not produce novels but contributed to later works, particularly *Brideshead*.

As his non-fiction grew more explicitly political, Waugh continued to keep partisan politics in the background of his novels, implying general principles rather than explicitly taking sides. So successful was the procedure that few grasped what these novels were about. Most reviewers, while still very favourable, were as uncertain about their genre and meaning as they had been about *Decline and Fall* and *Vile Bodies*.

II

The idea of visiting Africa may have arisen by chance. In September 1930, at a house party at Pakenham Hall that included Waugh, Frank Pakenham, Alastair Graham and John Betjeman, the subject of travel came up, and with it the coronation later that year of Ras Tafari as Haile Selassie ('The Power of the Trinity'), King of Kings, Lion of Judah and Emperor of Ethiopia. *Remote People* tells the story:

Six weeks before, I had barely heard Ras Tafari's name. I was in Ireland, staying in a house where chinoiserie and Victorian gothic contend for a mastery over a Georgian structure. We were in the library, discussing over the atlas a journey I proposed to make to China and Japan. We began talking of other journeys, and so of Abyssinia. One of the party [Graham] was on leave from Cairo; he knew something of Abyssinian politics and the coming coronation. Further information was contributed from less reliable sources; that the Abyssinian Church had canonised Pontius Pilate, and consecrated their bishops by spitting on their heads; that the real heir was hidden in the mountains, fettered with chains of solid gold; that people lived on raw meat and mead; ... an obsolete encyclopædia informed us that, 'though nominally Christian, the Abyssinians are deplorably lax in their morals...'. Everything I heard added to the glamour of this astonishing country. A fortnight later I was back in London and had booked my passage to Djibouti.

(RP 13–14)

The account is charming, and deliberately misleading. Waugh hardly needed Graham to tell him about Abyssinia. For months the newspapers had been full of stories of the coming coronation, of the 175-pound cake Tafari had ordered from England and his purchase of the ex-Kaiser's ceremonial coach. Britain was sending a royal duke and a gift of jewelled swords. *Decline and Fall* had already adverted to the questionable 'Apostolic Claims of the Church of Abyssinia' (DF89); from Dean Stanley's *Eastern Church* (that favourite survey of heresies), Waugh learnt that

'there is a daughter of the Coptic Church, yet farther south.... The Church of Abyssinia, founded in the fourth century by the Church of Alexandria, furnishes the one example of a nation savage yet Christian; showing us ... the utmost amount of superstition with which a Christian Church can be overlaid without perishing altogether.... The endless controversies respecting the natures of Christ, which have expired elsewhere, still rage in that barbarous country. Abyssinia, as she now is, presents the most singular compound of vanity, meekness, and ferocity; of devotion, superstition and ignorance.... There is, perhaps, no portion of the whole continent to which European civilization might be applied with better ultimate results.

(Stanley 96–9)

Placed at the start of *Remote People*, the house-party story helps to establish Waugh's persona in the book as an apolitical *ingénu* – a pose that soon crumbles as the book becomes an extended meditation on European colonial policy.

Still in Ireland, he sent a postcard to Peters:

I want very much to go to Abyssinia for the coronation of the emperor. Could you get a paper to send me as a special correspondent. If needs be I could pay 1/2 my expenses. I think I am going anyway.
P.S. This is a serious suggestion.

(L 49–50)

Appointment as a correspondent would not only pay expenses but guarantee entry to the ceremony. Soon Waugh was the accredited representative of three papers, the *Daily Express*, the *Graphic*, and, with Douglas Woodruff's help, *The*

Times, which together would print seventeen of his cabled news despatches, three 'colour' stories and a long background essay, the politically astute and well informed 'Ethiopia Today: Romance and Reality'.[15]

On 10 October, a few days after being received into the Catholic Church, Waugh boarded a train for Marseilles, where he met a steamer for Djibouti (in French Somaliland). From the coast it was a 36-hour train-ride upcountry to Addis Ababa, where he arrived on 26 October, in good time for the coronation on 2 November. The 'whole town seemed still in a rudimentary stage of construction', barely ready to entertain the hundreds of dignitaries and reporters assembling from all over the world. Tafari meant the event to demonstrate how far, under his enlightened leadership, his young nation had progressed; Waugh found 'a tangle of modernism and barbarity, European, African, and American', yet 'of definite, individual character' (RP 53). Belgian-trained soldiers appeared in elaborate new khaki uniforms with shining buttons and medals, barefoot; invitations to parties, elaborately engraved on heavy paper with the imperial crest, were delivered by illiterate couriers hours or days after events had already passed. The ex-Kaiser's coach, driven by 'a Hungarian coachman in fantastic livery', proved a failure when its horses bridled at the unfamiliar sound of guns firing a salute. The diaries reveal occasional irritations, but *Remote People* records only Waugh's delighted sense of 'an atmosphere utterly unique, elusive, unforgettable', where reality was transfigured into fantasy:

> The preposterous *Alice in Wonderland* fortnight has begun. It is to *Alice in Wonderland* that my thoughts recur in seeking some historical parallel for life in Addis Ababa.... it is in *Alice* only that one finds the peculiar flavour of galvanised and translated reality.... How to recapture, how retail the crazy enchantment of these Ethiopian days?
>
> (RP 29)

Addis also afforded a close-up look at the workings of modern journalism. 'I found the Press reports shocking and depressing' (RP 53). The coronation itself, five long hours of Coptic liturgy relieved only by mis-timed aerial salutes, took place on a Sunday, when cable offices were closed. Journalists' 'only hope of getting their reports back in time for Monday's papers was to write and despatch them well before the event' (48). That Monday most European and American papers indeed printed stories of the coronation's 'barbaric splendour', complete with an 'imperial chariot' drawn by 'six snow-white horses' amidst 'scores of natives' being 'trampled in the dust'. All were fabrications. Responsible papers simply noted that the event had occurred, supplying truthful reports (marked 'Delayed in Transmission') on Tuesday.[16] *Remote People* includes a long discursion on modern journalism, corrupted by the incompatible demands of 'getting in first with the news' and 'giving the public what it wants' (RP 39–42). Over the next few years, further experience as a reporter would convince Waugh that modern journalistic practices seriously undermined international stability.

In his own cables Waugh deliberately veered from truth only once. Tafari's coronation was actually a week-long party (on which he spent $3,000,000 of his

impoverished nation's money). On the day after the coronation proper came the
Emperor's *gebbur* (feast) for native chiefs. That day, as the diary records, irritated
by the Press Minister's unhelpfulness, 'I said all right, will report spectacle
disgusting barbarity' (D 332). On Wednesday the ordinarily soft-spoken *Times*
carried his report:

> The Chiefs came in full dress and were all armed to the teeth. Altogether about
> 30,000 guests were served, in three relays.... The guests were first served with
> small squares of cooked mutton and bread covered with a peculiarly pungent red
> pepper sauce. After immense quantities of this had been consumed, and also a
> liberal supply of the local beer, the party settled down to serious eating.
>   Large joints of raw, freshly slaughtered beef were borne down the ranks. Each
> man carved for himself with his own dagger. Strict etiquette was observed. The
> meat was raised to the mouth with the left hand, and the piece taken between the
> teeth was then severed by an upward slash with the dagger. Dexterity was needed
> to avoid amputation of the guest's nose....
>   Three hours later, when the tent was cleared for the second service, the guests
> walked with difficulty, more overcome by food than by drink. Many required a
> surfeit of support, and the somnolent were forcibly moved out by the police.[17]

Other papers carried similar accounts. But in fact foreigners had been barred
from the ceremony. Waugh's diary reports the truth: 'Lunched. Wrote description barbarous *gebbur*. Went out to see what I could barbarous *gebbur*. 3.30 no
signs barbarity. Changed, went to garden party American Legation' (D 332).
This lapse into invention aside, Waugh was a diligent and responsible reporter;
his despatches were second in accuracy and detail to those of only one other
correspondent on the scene: Sir Percival Phillips, who, because his paper (the
Daily Mail) prominently supported Tafari, attended the coronation as the
Emperor's particular guest.

The *ingénu* narrator of *Remote People* remarks off-handedly, 'One need not
explore any deep political causes for a plausible explanation' of foreign interest
in Tafari's coronation (RP 17). 'Ethiopia Today' aimed, Waugh wrote, 'to restore
a correct balance of opinion' (EAR 122); it makes explicit what the travel book
only implies.

Tafari's rise to power had been spectacularly bloody: only two years before, he
had murdered the Empress regent and put down an ensuing uprising by sending
his air force, armed with machine guns, against natives armed only with spears.
But through skilled publicity during many visits to Europe, he had also secured
Abyssinia's membership in the League of Nations and persuaded many in the
press that he was a visionary reformer, the native leader on an otherwise
colonialized continent of a unified, independent nation soon to take its place
beside the Western democracies. From such pieties Waugh demurred, telling
readers of *The Times*: 'It would be absurd to pretend that Ethiopia is a civilized
nation in any western sense of the word'. To anti-imperialists he pointed out that
Ethiopia was itself an empire, a feudal agglomeration of diverse, mutually
antagonistic races and tribes forced together in 1895 by a 'conquering minority'
of northern Amharic nobles. Tafari himself had come to power only after 'a

campaign marked by the most severe barbarities'; in 1930, despite promises of reform, slavery was 'still universal' and there continued 'intertribal raids and crimes of atrocious violence'. (Both were in fact matters of continuing concern to neighbouring British territories.) The 'pageantry and hospitality' of the coronation was an elaborate propaganda effort to shore up his power at home (by showing potential rebels 'that he was accepted by the royal families in Europe') and abroad (by convincing foreigners, both investors and members of the League, 'that Ethiopia was an up-to-date, civilized nation'). Nearly all this information also finds its way into *Remote People*, but with such graceful irony, in so many historical asides interspersed among comic passages, so many offhand references to raw meat, slave-boys, khat-chewing, and (in one bland footnote) the continued practice of 'infibulation', that one may not notice the formation of a concerted point of view.[18]

Waugh stayed in Addis until 15 November collecting material that would surface again both in *Remote People* and *Black Mischief*. On the trip up he had shared a carriage with the brother of Sir Sidney Barton, Britain's 'Envoy Extraordinary' to Abyssinia, a richly ironic title when given in the novel to Sir Samson Courteney. He met the originals of Dame Mildred Porch and Miss Tin: 'two formidable ladies . . . square-jawed, tight-lipped, with hard discordant eyes', concerned not about cruelty to animals but 'Vice'. 'Prostitution and drug traffic comprised their modest interests, and they were too dense to find evidence of either' (RP 44). (The comment is typical of the book's bitter celebration of bachelordom and its recurrent hostility to women, marriage and domestic life.) An exhausting drive from Addis to the shrine of Debra Lebanos, whose squalid, ignorant monks Waugh found funny and disgusting, inspired *Black Mischief*'s Monastery of St Mark the Evangelist. He even saw the disused lorry, abandoned in the centre of a road, that becomes in *Black Mischief* an emblem of recalcitrant human nature.

On the return journey to the coast, a detour to the decaying Arab city of Harar allowed Waugh to interview an aging priest who had known Rimbaud in the poet's days of trading in guns and slaves for Menelik, founder of the Empire. Here too he befriended the Armenian merchant Mr Bergebedgian, model (along with a Cairo taxi driver from *Labels* who gleefully tried to run down small children) for *Black Mischief*'s Mr Youkoumian.

> I found great delight in all [Bergebedgian's] opinions; I do not think I have ever met a more tolerant man; he had no prejudice or scruples of race, creed, or morals of any kind whatever; there were in his mind none of those opaque patches of inconsidered principles, it was a single translucent pool of placid doubt. . . . Everywhere he went he seemed to be welcome; everywhere he not only adapted, but completely transformed, his manners to the environment. A race [Armenians] of rare competence and the most delicate sensibility. They seem to me the only genuine 'men of the world'.[19]

After a 'First Nightmare' of frustration and boredom getting out of Abyssinia, Waugh proceeded (now at his own expense) to Aden, Zanzibar, Kenya and Uganda – further and further into British imperial Africa. In the process he found increasing stability, prosperity and 'civilization'. Everywhere he scouted political questions, and complained when there was nothing to discuss. At the height of equatorial summer, under 'benevolent' British administration, 'more than the climate, it is the absence of any kind of political issue which makes Zanzibar so depressing' (165). Meanwhile Abyssinia hovers over the rest of the narrative, providing a standard of comparison against which to measure what follows. An attractive aerial photograph of the *gebbi* (palace) at Lahej, Aden – 'European in conception, smaller than the Gebbi at Addis, but much better planned and better kept' (148) – recalls an earlier photograph of Tafari's dingy, ramshackle palace; Abyssinian farming was a primitive affair, whereas Aden's farmers, in 'a complete parallel to the enlightened landed gentlemen of eighteenth-century England', experiment with 'new methods of irrigation, new tractors and fertilisers, new kinds of crops' (153).

In Aden, where his cousin Sir Stewart Symes was Resident, Waugh 'made a serious attempt to grasp some of the intricacies of Arabian politics; an attempt which more often than not took the form of my spreading a table with maps, reports, and notebooks, and then falling into a gentle and prolonged stupor' (138). In fact he studied hard to understand Symes's upcoming conference on tribal reorganization, and analysed it in detail both in *Remote People* and in a feature for *The Times*.[20] Here too he met the eccentric millionaire 'M. Leblanc', in reality Antonin Besse, representative of Shell Oil (and at his death donor of £2,000,000 to found St Anthony's Hall, Oxford), who would later contribute his fastidious tastes in food and clothing to the ultra-cosmopolitan Mr Baldwin of *Scoop*.[21]

In Zanzibar, abandoning *Labels'* feigned hostility to all things Islamic, Waugh found that 'Arabs are by nature a hospitable and generous race and are "gentlemen" in what seems to me the only definable sense, that they set a high value on leisure'. But because of well-intentioned British interference in suppression of the slave trade, the business of the protectorate now belonged to East Indian immigrants 'without roots or piety', to the detriment of traditional Arab culture. 'No doubt the process was inevitable', he concludes; 'but it is a matter for regret' (167–8).

Finally Kenya, whose 'tremendous' scenery, 'finer than anything I saw in Abyssinia', elicits the most alluring descriptive prose in the book:

> Amber sunlight in Europe; diamond sunlight in Africa...In the evening we go down to the lakeside to shoot duck; thousands of flamingo lie on the water; at the first shot they rise in a cloud, like dust from a beaten carpet; they are the colour of pink alabaster; they wheel round and settle further out. The head of a hippopotamus emerges a hundred yards from shore and yawns at us. When it is dark the hippo comes out for his evening walk.
>
> (RP 192, 196)

Waugh was enchanted by the spacious life of the Kenyan settlers, trying to revive 'the traditional life of the English squirearchy' by recreating 'Barsetshire on the equator' (182–3). Here, at the heart of the British empire, he sets out from behind a mask of flippancy to adjudicate the case for European presence in Africa.

His discussion is guided by a pragmatic, Burkean notion of politics ('not an exact science but, by their nature, a series of makeshift, rule-of-thumb, practical devices for getting out of scrapes') and a modish contempt for 'the old-fashioned ideal of representative institutions' – 'the wretched old principle of head-counting', a discredited relic of nineteenth-century Liberalism particularly out of place in a land of perpetually warring tribal factions (180, 189). Seeking deliberately to irritate 'progressives' (especially those who thought there could be a unified 'theory' of imperialism), Waugh asserts that colonies emerge in too many ways, and take too many forms, for economists and politicians to generalize about them. Colonialism's proponents may often be cruel racialists – a besetting sin of 'Northern Europeans', among whom 'Anglo-Saxons are perhaps worse than any' (190) – but its enemies are inconsistent socialists: those whose motto is 'Africa for the Africans' are 'quite ready to hasten the eviction of traditional landowners in their own country' (180). Waugh concludes his anti-theoretical account with the reflection that populations are always moving into what was others' territory: 'Conquest, colonisation, commercial penetration, religious pro-selytising, topographical changes, land becoming worked out, pastures disap-pearing, harbours silting up . . . . The process will go on, because it is an organic process in human life'; 'it is quite certain that, in the expansive optimism of the last century, Africa would not have been left alone. Whether it wanted it or not, it was going to be heaped with all the rubbish of our own continent' (180–1).

Waugh sees the colonial project as both inevitable and doomed, romantically appealing but a lost cause. (As even *Black Mischief*'s foolish Sir Samson Courteney knows, 'You couldn't expect the calm of *Barchester Towers* in a place like Azania': BM 269.) If nothing else, the European crisis already predicted in *Decline and Fall* and *Vile Bodies* will bring it to an end. In a striking prediction of what a second world war and the hasty *dégringolade* of the 1950s would bring, Waugh muses that 'it is uncertain whether the kind of life which the Kenya settlers are attempting to re-establish, is capable of survival; whether indeed the European colonisation of Africa will survive in any form; whether there may not be in the next twenty-five years a general Withdrawal of the Legions to defend Western civilisation at its sources' (RP 191). Thus his final word on colonialism comes not in Kenya but Uganda, among Catholic missions and convents that provide 'little island[s] of order and sweetness in an ocean of rank barbarity' (and serve as pendant to the book's earlier description of Debra Lebanos, as Britain's African colonies bal-ance its initial account of Abyssinia). Despite the 'anti-imperialist interpretation of history' which views missionaries as 'the vanguard of commercial penetra-tion', 'Europe has only one positive thing which it can offer to anyone, and that is what the missionaries brought' (204–5).

After Kenya and Uganda Waugh made his way west into the Belgian Congo in hope of finding quick air transport across the continent and home. But the air service he had been told of did not exist. Frustrated, bored, and dangerously short of money, he was reduced to the 'Second Nightmare' of backtracking to Elizabethville, boarding a train for the long ride to Cape Town, and returning by mail-boat to England, where he arrived on 10 March 1931. As a final frame to the book, his first night home in London supplies a 'Third Nightmare': a crowded restaurant 'hotter than Zanzibar, noisier than the market at Harrar, more reckless of the decencies of hospitality than the taverns of Kabalo'. The scene prompts a final ironic judgment prophetic of all Waugh's writing of the 1930s on faraway, 'barbaric' places:

> Why go abroad?
> See England first.
> Just watch London knock spots off the Dark Continent.
> I paid the bill in yellow African gold. It seemed just tribute from the weaker races to their mentors.

(RP 240)

III

Five hundred pounds poorer for his travels beyond Abyssinia, Waugh needed once again to 'write a lot quickly'. *Remote People*, begun in the Congo and hastily finished during his family's regular June holiday in France, appeared in November 1931, to reviews full of praise for its prose but some hostility to its politics and, for the first time, to Waugh's religion.[22] He also began a novel based on his travels under the working titles *Further South* (an echo of the passage quoted above from Stanley's *Eastern Church*) and *Accession* (abandoned when his American publisher suggested that this word would mean little to readers in the United States). *Black Mischief* occupied him from late 1931 until the following May; Waugh knew the novel was good and wanted to take his time with it. He wanted also to pursue new friendships formed since his divorce.

Remote People was dedicated to Hazel, beautiful wife of the society portrait-painter Sir John Lavery, who after meeting him at Emerald Cunard's had drawn Waugh into a flattering, but soon tiresome, affair. Once again Waugh was pursued by women he did not care for while unsuccessfully pursuing one he did. Before leaving for Africa he had met Teresa ('Baby') Jungman, high-spirited, rich daughter of Mrs Richard Guinness and the painter Nico Jungman, who with her sister Zita and their friends Eleanor Smith and Elizabeth Ponsonby had personified the twenties craze for masquerade parties and treasure hunts. Soon Waugh was deeply in love with 'the Dutch girl' (nicknamed for her father's Dutch extraction). But like Olivia Greene, Teresa enjoyed Waugh's company but wasn't sexually attracted; she was also a devout Catholic, and so regarded him as still a married man. His demoralizing attachment dragged on for four years, until 1933.

Meanwhile Waugh had also once again 'fallen in love with a family', the Lygons. He had known the brothers William and Hugh at Oxford, and with them visited their sisters Lettice, Sibell, Mary and Dorothy at the family's sprawling Victorian house outside Malvern, Madresfield Court. Their father, the Earl of Beauchamp, had been hounded into exile in Venice by Bendor, Duke of Westminster, who waged a campaign against the man he called his 'bugger-in-law'; Lady Beauchamp moved away as well, leaving Madresfield for the children. The house became Waugh's favourite refuge, a place of youth, laughter, fantasy and frequent parties for mutual friends: Robert Byron, Hubert Duggan, Richard Greene, and Robert Laycock (later Waugh's superior officer in the Commandos). The family provided hints for the Flytes in *Brideshead*, as did Madresfield's chapel, built in 1865 and redecorated in 1902 by Lady Beauchamp in the *art nouveau* style as a wedding present for her husband.

Mary and Dorothy Lygon, twenty-one and nineteen years old in 1931, became admiring playmates with whom Waugh delighted to act the worldly, rakish uncle. All had nicknames (Waugh's, from masonic lore, was Boaz), and when away he wrote them teasing letters full of private, often smutty jokes.

> Well I am living with the bright young Yorkes.
> Last night I saw a terribly drunk man with a prostitute.
> WOTS A POSTATUTE PLESE?
> Ask your little playfellow——, she will show you....
>
> (L 66)

> Now I will tell you about the sermon I heard on Sunday. First the priest said that it was soon the feast of the Blessed Margaret Clitheroe and the English Martyrs and he told us how they had their arses cut off with red-hot scissors & things like that. Then he said But they are not the only good Catholics who are persecuted. WHAT ABOUT ME he said very loud, why only yesterday I received a blackmailing letter from one of this very congregation accusing me of UNCHASTITY. Goodness we all felt embarrassed.
>
> (L 63)

Waugh wrote most of *Black Mischief* at Madresfield, sometimes calling on Mary and Dorothy to model for illustrations; he dedicated the novel to them.

To perfect his skills of country-house visiting, he enrolled nearby at the riding academy of John ('Jack') Hance, a striking character who 'owed his success with [the *jeunesse dorée*] to the fact that he cursed them like a sergeant-major' (and who later recalled Waugh as one of his most 'serious' pupils). In another gleeful transfiguration of reality into fantasy, Lady Dorothy recalled, 'Evelyn transposed the Captain and his family to an Olympian level at which he invented lives for them which, like the gods in ancient Greece, were still linked with the mortals below; their least pronouncement was debated and scrutinised for omens and auguries. The Captain's name was scarcely mentioned without the mystic initials GBH – which stood for God Bless Him – being added to it and his health was frequently drunk'.[23] It was by retailing the Saga of Captain Hance that Waugh first captured the affections of Diana Cooper.

An illegitimate daughter of the Duke of Rutland, the arrestingly beautiful Diana Manners was born at Belvoir Castle in 1894 (when at night a watchman still walked the ramparts calling each hour 'All is well') and lived to captivate John Kennedy at state dinners in Washington in the 1960s. Like many women of her class she was 'educated' at home, memorizing long stretches of Shakespeare and Keats but never learning long division. At the start of World War I she had been part of the precursor generation to the Bright Young People, shocking her elders by drinking vodka and absinthe, and loudly asking what was the sleeping drug of choice for the night. Waugh had incorporated gossip about her in *Decline and Fall*; her wedding in 1919 to the diplomat Duff Cooper, like Margot Beste-Chetwynde's 'unparalleled success among the lower orders' (DF 195), had been one of the last society weddings 'that crowds and crowds of factory girls talked about and turned out to see'.[24]

In the 1920s Lady Diana took to the stage, acting the role of the Virgin in Max Rheinhardt's production of *The Miracle*. The play was revived in London in the summer of 1932 and that autumn went on tour; Waugh took the train up to Scotland to keep her company between performances, reading to her from *The Wind in the Willows* and joining in visits to country houses – Chatsworth, Belvoir, Hardwick and Lord Brownlow's Belton. Soon he was trying to convert her, always for Waugh part of any intimate friendship. 'Wish I could persuade you to be a Catholic. You have the real mens catholica (Latin for Catholic mind) and all that isn't happy in your nature would be made straight. But I won't go on – at least I will, but not in writing but when I see you' (DC 19). Later memorialized in *Scoop* as Mrs Stitch, she remained for the rest of his life the correspondent with whom he was most ready to open his heart.

Work on *Black Mischief* was slowed not only by these recreations but also the occasional writing necessary to support them before the novel appeared. Stories generally paid better than essays; Waugh now wrote several, (including one, 'Too Much Tolerance', about a man whose wife 'suddenly fell in love and went off', 'I to this day can't think why').[25] Once established as a novelist, Waugh never took the writing of stories seriously, freely telling editors that he considered his work in the form 'pretty thin stuff', money-makers written to buy time for the novels on which he knew he would be judged. He often sold bits of novels-in-progress as stories, or incorporated stories into novels; sometimes material from very early stories surfaces decades later in another context.[26] The best of them are collected in *Mr Loveday's Little Outing* (1936). Just before *Mr Loveday* appeared Waugh wrote to Lady Diana: 'A book of stories of mine is to come out soon but don't read them as all except two are very common' (DC 61). He does not specify which two, but it is tempting to suppose he had in mind 'Excursion in Reality' and the Christmas story 'Out of Depth: An Experiment Begun in Shaftesbury Avenue and Ended in Time' (1933), which tells of a lapsed Catholic sent by a magician to the twenty-fifth century. The passage of 500 years has not brought progress. London is now 'Lunnon', a barbaric cluster of wattle huts where primitive whites are ruled by only slightly less primitive blacks. But amidst the general wreck, the time-traveller finds one cultural survival: a mission church in which a black priest says Mass. Awaking in 1933, he returns to the Faith, confessing to a priest: 'Father, . . . I have experimented in black art'. Waugh borrowed the plot partly from John Gray's eccentric novel *Park* (1932), itself inspired by Waugh's reporting of Haile Selassie's coronation, whose hero dreams of a future in which Roman Catholic blacks have become the dominant race.[27]

IV

Black Mischief appeared in October 1932, published as would be nearly all Waugh's subsequent novels both in a trade edition and a signed, large-paper

9 Waugh's drawing of the Emperor Seth for *Black Mischief* (1930).

edition de luxe (generally of 250 copies, of which Waugh reserved fifty for friends).
It chronicles in parallel the careers of Seth, black emperor of Azania (an island
off the Somali coast), and Basil Seal, a young adventurer the same age as Waugh
who flees the boredom of Depression-era England to become Seth's chief
adviser.[28] In the course of a single year, Seth graduates from Oxford, usurps
the Azanian throne by defeating the armies of his father Seyid, and sets about to
modernize his barbarous country by imposing a hash of progressive European
notions from civil-service examinations to coeducation, community singing, and
compulsory Esperanto.[29] His efforts succeed only in organizing an opposition
which overthrows and murders him. Basil escapes the chaos of Seth's fall only
after suborning a murder of his own and unwittingly joining a cannibal feast;

he returns finally to a London whose parties seem 'a bit flat after the real thing'.

Waugh's manuscripts reflect a new ambition and care in the vastly more extensive revision given this novel than either *Decline and Fall* or *Vile Bodies*. The experienced travel writer now provides detailed historical backgrounds and lingers over natural scenery. In *Remote People* Waugh had learnt to develop devices of montage beyond their use in the earlier novels, crafting descriptive transitions from telegraphic sentence fragments that give the feel of a travel film. *Black Mischief*'s 'cutting – if one may borrow a Hollywood term', said one reviewer, 'is masterly' (CH 130).

> Noon in Matodi. The harbour lay still as a photograph, empty save for a few fishing boats moored motionless against the sea wall.
>
> (BM 24)

> Evening and a small stir of life. Muezzin in the minaret. Allah is great. There is no Allah but Allah and Mohammed is his prophet.
>
> (BM 27–8)

> Night and the fear of darkness. In his room at the top of the old fort Seth lay awake and alone...
>
> (BM 38)

Gone are characters like Otto Silenus and Father Rothschild, speakers (in part) for their author; gone are *Vile Bodies*'s authorial intrusions into the narrative; readers must construe *Black Mischief* for themselves. The result was a book with which many reviewers, while amused, were uneasy. Clearly Waugh had translated his experience of Africa into fiction: Abyssinia becomes Azania (a name Renaissance map-makers such as Ortelius gave to the Horn of Africa); Menelik, who first patched together the Abyssinian empire, becomes Seth's grandfather Amurath the Great; Lej Yesu, true heir to the throne, becomes Seth's aged uncle Achon. (Seth himself resembles less the shrewd and worldly Ras Tafari than Amanullah of Afghanistan, also crowned in 1930, who had ordered that his tribesmen shave their beards and wear bowler hats.) But there was little agreement about Waugh's purposes in what seemed to most simply another 'extravaganza'.

American editors were nervous of a novel that speaks of 'niggers' and 'darkies' 'wagging their tufted rumps', and contains the outrageous passage in which Seth suggests to his leading general the inappropriateness of calling his wife 'Black Bitch':

> 'Don't you think that when she is a Duchess, it might be more suitable if you were to try and call your wife by another name. You see, there will probably be a great influx of distinguished Europeans for my coronation. We wish to break down colour barriers as far as possible. Your name for Mrs. Connolly, though suitable as a term of endearment in the home, seems to emphasise the racial distinction between you in a way that might prove disconcerting'.
>
> (BM 62)

In fact Connolly turns out to have genuine affection for his wife; in a novel full of casual sex, theirs is the only loving relationship.[30] And it is too little noticed how often Waugh personates a non-white perspective, and that when he does, comparisons of Europeans to animals – most often pigs – are not far behind. The ordinarily soft-spoken Baroness Yoshiwara of *Vile Bodies*, exhausted by invitation, explodes at Mr Outrage: 'Ten thousand damns to your pig-face!'; in *Black Mischief*, Seth's coronation party prompts a survey of racial types, all equally unlovely:

> Paper caps were resumed . . . over faces of every complexion, brown as boots, chalk white, dun and the fresh boiled pink of Northern Europe. False noses again; brilliant sheaths of pigmented cardboard attached to noses of every anthropological type, the high arch of the Semite, freckled Nordic snouts, broad black nostrils from swamp villages of the mainland, the pulpy inflamed flesh of the alcoholic, and unlovely syphilitic voids.
>
> (BM 151–2)

From the security of his religious sense that all souls are equal before God, Waugh felt free to generalize about racial groups (Black, East Indian, or Welsh) – and about sentimental attitudes toward them – in ways he hoped would prove offensive to liberal sensibilities. The best approach to Waugh's racialism (and *Black Mischief* as a whole) is through the novel's parallels between the island kingdoms of Azania and Britain. Waugh invites laughter at the spectacle of black natives in top hat and tails, at barefoot savages given the titles earl and viscount; but he insists even more on European barbarity.

Black Mischief in effect invites readers to a thought-experiment. How are white European imperialists typically supposed to view natives? One might assemble some such list: natives are dirty, shiftless, lazy, dishonest and thieving, godless or superstitious, cruel, sexually promiscuous, disorderly and inefficient, bestial, childish. Waugh's Azanians are all this. But even more spectacularly so are his 'civilized' barbarians. Basil is a liar and a thief, someone of whom young Englishwomen say 'It's nice his being so dirty' (97). Azanian cruelty finds its parallel in the two 'humane ladies' who care more for the welfare of 'doggies' than starving children, and in Youkoumian, who wins Basil's esteem by relegating his wife to the baggage car with General Connolly's mules: 'Very savage stinking animals. All day they will stamp at her. No air in the truck. Orrible, unhealthy place. Very like she die or is kicked' (134). Azania's primitive feasts and 'making whoopee' parallel Basil's drunken 'rackets' and Margot's parties; Azanian culinary taste passes modern European muster when Basil renames the local favourite, dripping raw beef, 'steak tartare'. Life amidst the cannibals seems like hell, but, as Basil twice remarks, 'London is hell, isn't it?' (93, 107). Seth's efforts at modernization are foolish *both* because they are out of place in his primitive nation *and* because the 'progressive' ideas on which they are based – all European, and heavily Leftist, in origin – are foolish in themselves. Once again European barbarism, a polished variant on fallen human nature, 'knocks spots off the dark continent'. Europe, Waugh explained, supplies the novel's only 'wholly contemptible' as well as 'wholly admirable' characters, the French legate Ballon and a Catholic priest (L 74).

Waugh is especially careful that we hear much more of European superstition (and atheism) than native. Lord Monomark has his fad diets; European ladies recommend a Hindu fortune-teller to Black Bitch; Ballon, a doctrinaire Mason and atheist, nonetheless keeps 'a small carved nut' under his bolster 'in the belief that it would bring him good luck' (85). Britain's envoy Sir Samson Courteney, fascinated with chain letters and the dimensions of the Great Pyramid, cannot be bothered to protest when Seth orders the Anglican Cathedral demolished. When Seth offers in its place to name a street for him, Sir Samson expresses his delight:

> 'I like to think of all the black johnnies in a hundred years' time driving up and down in their motor cars and going to the shops and saying "Number a hundred Samson Courteney" and wondering who I was. Like, like ...'
> 'Like the Avenue Victor Hugo, Envoy'.
> '*Exactly*, or St. James's Square'.
>
> (BM 180)

Azania is in fact an asparagus-bed of *imported* heresies, superstitions and faiths. From the roof of their hotel Dame Mildred and Miss Tin survey 'Catholic, Orthodox, Armenian, Anglican, Nestorian, American Baptist and Mormon places of worship, the minaret of the mosque, the Synagogue, and the flat white roof of the Hindu snake temple' (254). Such a jumbled list seems to put all faiths on a level. But Waugh begins and ends the novel with references to two whose unchanging observances survive political upheaval.

> Muezzin in the minaret. Allah is great. There is no Allah but Allah and Mohammed is his prophet. Angelus from the mission church. Ecce ancilla Domini: fiat mihi secundum verbum tuum.
>
> (BM 27–8)

> The muezzin in the tower turned north towards Mekka and called azan over the city.... God is great...There is no God but God...Angelus from the mission church...gratia plena: dominus tecum; Benedicta tu in mulieribus.
>
> (BM 316)[31]

In childishness, too, Waugh's Europeans spectacularly outdo the natives. There is Sonia Trumpington's baby-talk to her dog; Prudence's 'large, childlike' hand-writing (and endearments such as 'Lovey-dovey cat's eyes');[32] Lady Seal's 'fire-lit nursery game of "let's pretend"' planning Basil's future. Basil's characteristic expression is 'insolent, sulky, and curiously childish'; Azania's Anglican bishop is named 'Goodchild'. Studiously ignoring the demands of the Foreign Office, the British legation occupies itself wholly with games: we hear of croquet, clock-golf, tennis, poker, picquet, bagatelle, halma, bridge, backgammon, consequences, animal-snap, peggoty, crosswords, chess and craps; the Envoy himself prefers knitting. (For Ballon, diplomacy itself is a game: 'the game is not over yet.... There is still a trick or two to be won.')

In the symbolic economy of the novel, references to childhood and games suggest atavism: reversion to the primitive, to a realm barely human. Escape into immaturity may temporarily seem charming, but the fact of our properly human nature, with all its moral responsibilities, guarantees that it must fail. Sir Samson's escape from adult responsibility in the privacy of his bath collapses in a moment of disappointment of a sort that recurs throughout Waugh's fiction:

> Prudence and William had left an inflated india-rubber sea- serpent behind them in the bath-room. Sir Samson sat in the warm water engrossed with it. He swished it down the water and caught it in his toes; he made waves for it; he blew it along; he sat on it and let it shoot up suddenly to the surface between his thighs.... Soon he was rapt in daydream about the Pleistocene age, where among mists and vast, unpeopled crags, schools of deep-sea monsters splashed and sported; oh, happy fifth day of creation, thought the Envoy Extraordinary, oh, radiant infant sun, newly weaned from the breasts of darkness, oh, rich steam of the soggy continents, oh, jolly whales and sea-serpents frisking in the new brine ... Knocks at the door. William's voice outside.
>
> 'Walker's just ridden over, sir. Can you see him?'
>
> Crude disillusionment.
>
> Sir Samson returned abruptly to the twentieth century, to a stale and crowded world; to a bath grown tepid and an india-rubber toy.
>
> (BM 86–7)

Atavism here seems innocent (if foolish), but it is of course the same irresponsibility in the ironically named Sir Samson that makes him a failed diplomat and parent – that keeps his daughter Prudence a child and brings about her death. Similarly, something 'atavistic' (182) in Basil causes him to break with Connolly, an early step in the process that leads to Seth's murder.

Elsewhere Waugh's montage connects childish games and barbarism:

> 'More tea, Bishop. I'm sure you must be tired after your ride'.
>
> Sixty miles southward in the Ukaka pass bloody bands of Sakuyu warriors played hide and seek among the rocks, chivying the last fugitives of the army of Seyid, while behind them down the gorge, from cave villages of incalculable antiquity, the women crept out to rob the dead.
>
> After tea the Consul looked in and invited Prudence and William over to play tennis. (79)

Abroad or at home, movement backward or inward constitutes a journey to the heart of darkness, to the realm of brute, anarchic nature unillumined by grace that comes to the fore when Basil joins the cannibals in eating Prudence. There is no evidence Waugh knew Conrad's novel. But the perspective of both is that of Europeans who observe Africa with the fear that the barbarians are *not* inhuman. The barbarism of *Black Mischief* as of *Remote People* stems from unregenerate human nature itself, something civilization must always combat.

In that fight, Seth uses all the wrong tools. He boasts during the war with his father:

> 'Defeat is impossible. I have been to Europe. I know. We have the Tank. This is not a war of Seth against Seyid but of Progress against Barbarism. And Progress

must prevail. I have seen the great tattoo of Aldershot, the Paris Exhibition, the Oxford Union. I have read modern books – Shaw, Arlen, Priestley. What do the gossips in the bazaars know of all this? The whole might of Evolution rides behind him; at my stirrups run woman's suffrage, vaccination, and vivisection. I am the New Age. I am the Future.'

(BM 26)

Seth draws his ideas from the whole range of recent European and American follies – especially from the Soviet Union, symbol for Waugh of the most misguided of all utopian humanist experiments to refashion and perfect fallen human nature. His chief engineer is a Mr Marx; Basil's Ministry of Modernization (housed in what was previously the Empress's Oratory) initiates a One Year Plan, outdoing the Five Year Plan announced by Stalin in 1928. ' "Progress",' said T. E. Hulme in his *Essays on Humanism*, 'is the modern substitute for religion' (Hulme 35.)

Seth's innovations fail for the same reasons as Wilfred Lucas-Dockery's. Learning that cannibals have eaten his father, Seth dreamily supposes that education is the answer: 'I am afraid the Wanda are totally out of touch with modern thought. They need education. We must start some schools and a university for them when we get things straight.... We might start them on Montessori methods' (61–2). Seth plans to rebuild his capital on an axial plan, with long straight avenues, but the city streets (like human nature itself) remain incorrigibly crooked. Even the European protectorate which takes over after his fall cannot move the broken-down lorry blocking one major thoroughfare, a recurrent symbol in the novel of recalcitrant human nature. As in *Decline and Fall* and *Vile Bodies*, the chaos of what Youkoumian calls 'every damn modern thing' (196) stands once again in contrast to an unstated principle of traditional truth and order, an implied Catholicism which alone can provide a realistic and trustworthy guide to moral action.

Thus Waugh chooses Seth's campaign for birth-control – an issue that by 1932 clearly distinguished Catholicism from other confessions – to climax and summarize Seth's programme of modernization. Just as Basil's high-handed modernizing loses Seth the support of the army, the birth-control campaign loses him the national (Nestorian) church, whose Patriarch (though we generally see him on the arm of his 'favourite deacon') retains on this topic a 'sturdy orthodoxy'. First in his campaign Seth orders demolition of the Anglican cathedral to make way for a new 'Place Marie Stopes'.[33] Then, to secure public support, Seth issues a 'Soviet-style' poster designed to illustrate the benignant effects of contraception but which his illiterate people misinterpret as advertising 'juju' to increase fertility. Finally comes the Birth Control Gala, a parade complete with a float of prostitutes:

The first car, drawn by oxen, represented the place of women in the modern world. Enthroned under a canopy of coloured cotton, sat Mlle. 'Fifi' Fatim Bey; in one hand a hunting crop to symbolise learning; round her were grouped a court of Azanian beauties with typewriters, tennis rackets, motor bicycling goggles, telephones, hitch-hiking outfits and other patents of modernity inspired by the

European illustrated papers. An orange and green appliquéd standard bore the challenging motto THROUGH STERILITY TO CULTURE.

(BM 258)

After the ensuing riot in which Seth is deposed, only one word from the banner – STERILITY – remains visible. Sterility is all Seth's innovations amount to, all that the 'rubbish of our own continent' (in the words of *Remote People*) has to offer when the shards of European culture are detached from its 'one positive thing'.

Just as in *Decline and Fall* when once King's Thursday is razed and rebuilt, it is soon rebuilt yet again, once a culture loses its moorings it begins an accelerating round of futile change. Seth imposes ever more and crazier innovations until, as the nation plunges into anarchy, he finally goes mad. 'The earnest and rather puzzled young man became suddenly capricious and volatile'; we last see him at night, alone, pick-axe in hand, obsessively chipping away at the granite of the Anglican cathedral.

Black Mischief's most elaborate parallel between Europe and Africa is that between Basil and Seth themselves, civilized barbarian and barbarian civiliser. A kind of anti-providence brings them to the same place at the same time: Basil's ship sails for Azania 'at midnight'; Seth arrives at the coronation party where he first notices Basil 'soon after midnight' (122, 147). 'Basil Seal's arrival in Matodi coincided with the date fixed for Seth's triumphal return to Debra-Dowa'; at just the moment Seth sits alone thinking to himself 'I must find a man of culture, a modern man . . . a representative of Progress and the New Age', 'Basil again passed the window' (130–1, 139). By the end Basil has displaced and excelled Seth as savage chieftain. Basil hastens Prudence's death by proclaiming a *gebbur* in honour of the slain emperor: 'Assemble your people, kill your best meat and prepare a feast in the manner of your people' (305). Among the framing devices which give symmetry to the novel are shrill cries in the night as men are murdered: at the start, Joab (a minor character perhaps named for the assassin in 2 Samuel) murders Seth's secretary Ali without royal approval; at the end, he murders Viscount Boaz on Basil's order. Even the weather changes as if to mark Seth's fall and Basil's ascendancy. Through most of the novel Azania has been parched under a hot tropical sun; at the end, as the nation dissolves in chaos, the rains come – fittingly, 'at midnight' – not, as in *The Waste Land*, with promise of regeneration, but simply turning the land to muck, external equivalent for its internal state.

The novel concludes with paired scenes of Azania after Seth's fall and England on Basil's return. In Azania sterility reigns in the form of a dully bureaucratic European protectorate whose only accomplishment seems to be extermination of the island's stray dogs: 'The dogs had been rounded up and painlessly put away. The streets were empty.... The blank walls of the Arab tenements gave no sign of life' (322). The new regime destroys life without producing any but the most superficial improvement. The broken-down lorry still blocks traffic; 'British justice' triumphs not in moving it – human nature is not changed so easily – but by building a new road around it. In their 'identical bungalows' reminiscent of an English garden suburb, civil servants reproduce in a new key the worst of the old regime: the sensible Connolly is deported; Youkoumian, a survivor like Grimes, remains to become a respected citizen. Over the harbour float melodies from Gilbert and Sullivan: 'Three little maids from school' (suggestive of the childish naïveté of the new imperialists) and 'Tit-willow' (its 'rather tough worm' suggestive of a human nature no more change-able by the new regime than by Seth's progressivism). An ominous final sentence – 'The song rang clear over the dark city and the soft, barely perceptible lapping of the water along the sea-wall' – quietly foretells that the dead and deadening new regime too will be washed away, eroded by the realities it ignores.

Meanwhile Basil has returned to an England deep in the Depression: 'Every-one's got very poor and it makes them duller', says Sonia; 'people have gone serious lately'. By mid-1932 British unemployment exceeded 2.5 millions; Waugh meant his novel to embody a new seriousness as well. Catching him up on local news, Sonia tells Basil, 'There was a general election and a crisis.... Can't think what you see in revolutions. They said there was going to be one here, only nothing came of it' (313). In fact the whole of *Black Mischief*, in describing the havoc worked by European ideas in Azania, suggests what the same ideas could do in Europe – especially were England to adopt the 'pro-gressive' new faiths of Russia or Germany. There is thus a profound irony in Basil's plans for the future: 'I think I've had enough of barbarism for a bit. I might stay in London or Berlin or somewhere like that' (314).

All Waugh's forebodings surface as well in his first talk for the BBC, broadcast on 28 November, 1932, in its series 'To an Unnamed Listener'. Taking the part of a Young Man speaking to an Old one (his father replied for Age the next week), Waugh argued that the older generation had enjoyed the luxury of growing up with a 'belief in Progress'. 'You were told that man was a perfectible being already well set on the last phase of his ascent from ape to angel, that he would yearly become healthier, wealthier and wiser'. But to the author of *Vile Bodies* and *Black Mischief*, 'Progress' is 'a word that must be dismissed from our conversation before anything of real interest can be said'.[34] Not only does 'man's capacity for suffering keep pretty regular pace with the discoveries that amelior-ate it'; current unemployment threatens even the achievements of the past. Waugh singles out its effects on his own class, the middle class of university graduates – 'that part of the community which is normally the guardian of its thought and culture' – unable now to find meaningful work and so succumbing to 'psychological symptoms of futility, inferiority and a revolt from culture'. 'Uncertain of his economic future', the young man is also reluctant to marry, to enter into the 'permanent social relationship' Waugh so deeply wanted for himself. The result is 'sterility': whereas Seth wanted to take Azania 'THROUGH STERILITY TO CULTURE', Waugh argues that 'Physical sterility, whether artificial or organic, results from sterility of spirit'. He sums up with an echo of *Remote People*'s prediction of international crisis:

> I am perfectly confident that in my life-time, if I live as long as you, sir, that I shall see the beginning of a vast recession of the white races from all over the world – a

withdrawal of the legions to defend what remains of European standards on European grounds. I am less confident of how much will remain to be defended.

(HRC C9)

V

On 2 December, 1932, four days after these grim predictions were aired, Waugh boarded a slow cargo ship heading for Georgetown, British Guiana (present-day Guyana). 'It should be an interesting trip & give me material for writing', he told his parents (L69). As in 1930, he had much to escape besides English winter. Despite *Black Mischief*'s recent publication, money was short; since he was not travelling as a reporter on an expense account, Waugh had to beg advances on future work and loans from the always enerous Peters. His friendship with Diana Cooper was flourishing, but little else in his personal or professional life was satisfactory. He was still pursued, and bored, by Hazel Lavery; he was still pursuing Teresa Jungman, whose unresponsiveness he bemoans in many letters to the Lygon sisters and Lady Diana – letters that tell as well, with the predictable mix of bravura and guilt, about the prostitutes he frequented both abroad and at the 43, 'Ma' Meyrick's London night-club-cum-brothel, where his favorite girl was 'Winnie'.[35]

Waugh felt unappreciated professionally in something of the same way he did personally. Just as Teresa found him an amusing companion but nothing more, *Black Mischief*, of whose new depth and quality Waugh was sure, was greeted by praise for its humour joined with blank incomprehension. The book sold, but most reviewers failed to detect even that it was satire, commenting instead (like J. B. Priestley in the *Evening Standard*) on Waugh's invention once again of an 'odd little world' of 'comic inconsequentiality'. The TLS found in it nothing more than another 'extravaganza written largely about, and presumably for, the bright young people', 'insubstantial for its length'; the *Daily Express*, an 'extravaganza' that 'doesn't make much sense'. The *Daily Telegraph* and *Manchester Guardian* could make nothing of its 'air of uncertainty' and 'baffled incompleteness'; to the American Malcolm Cowley – first of many critics to wish for the 'old Waugh' back, for more novels like *Decline and Fall* and *Vile Bodies* – *Black Mischief* 'is fairly amusing to read, if you don't read too carefully, but it is the sort of book a gifted author shouldn't have written'.[36] Worse was to come on his return from South America.

Friends often said that Waugh was untroubled by adverse or uncomprehending reviews. But it is in the context of *Black Mischief*'s reception that we should understand his efforts in 'To an Unnamed Listener' to make explicit what had all along been the burden of his fiction. By December 1932 he recorded in his diary a 'certain inclination to take up being highbrow again' (D 357); soon after, he wrote to Lady Diana from Georgetown, 'I think I shall try to be an intellectual for a bit' (DC 7). Only a profound desire to be understood, for readers to grasp the fundamental point of his entertainments, could lead Waugh to attach such labels to himself. The reading matter he took along to Guiana – Jacques Maritain's *Introduction to Philosophy*, a volume of Aquinas – attests a desire not only to educate himself in his faith but also to clarify his stance as writer; back in

England, he would even toy with the idea of returning to university. He planned the South American trip to issue in a more obviously serious book than heretofore, telling reporters that he hoped especially 'to visit the Catholic missions' among the Indians (ST1 312).

Both the trip and the book that emerged from it (*Ninety-Two Days*) proved disappointments. Many readers of the travel diary and book (whose name suggests a prison sentence) have described Waugh's trip as 'penitential', as if he were actually seeking to punish himself in the jungle, but there is no real evidence to support such a view. Waugh fixed on South America as he had Abyssinia: the interior was alluringly uncharted; more important, it was in the news. Earlier in 1932 he had considered going as a reporter to cover the Japanese invasion of Manchuria. But in June *The Times* sent Peter Fleming to Brazil to learn the fate of Colonel Fawcett, the explorer who mysteriously disappeared in the Matto Grosso searching for a lost city. That autumn Waugh wrote to Peters: 'Will you please take any orders for travel articles – far flung stuff impenetrable Guiana forests, toughs in Diamond Mines, Devils Island' (L 65). A few days before sailing he had tea with Fleming 'to talk of equipment for forests'. Only after shipping out did he begin seriously to read about Guiana itself, suffering 'alternating panics that the journey to the interior will prove impossibly wild or impossibly tame' (D 355–6).

The diaries make clear that Waugh was looking for 'excitement', real and reportable danger and difficulty. Four weeks after arrival he is still writing to Lady Diana: 'The Indians are no good – timid and drab – but I am hoping for some rough stuff on the way back' (DC 25). He found difficulties enough, but primarily in the forms of acute physical discomfort (from thirst, bad food and clouds of biting insects) and boredom. He had no particular plan, travelling in whatever direction chance acquaintances suggested; over and over, alluring destinations proved empty of interest, or for lack of transport could not be reached at all. In February, halfway through the trip, temporarily stuck at the site of his greatest disappointment, the romantically named but in fact dismal Boa Vista (his farthest point inland and only stop in Brazil itself) – among people with whom he could not communicate, with nothing to see, and nothing to read but Bossuet's sermons and some French saints' lives – he confessed to Lady Diana: 'I don't think there will be a book in my experiences up to date' (DC 26).

Ninety-Two Days ends with the disclaimer quoted above (35–6) that the book is not a 'spiritual odyssey'. Probably there was nothing to tell even if Waugh had wished. The most he could say was, 'I had added to my treasure of eccentrics the fantastic figure of Mr Christie' (167–8). This religious fanatic, whose remote cabin Waugh reached three weeks after setting out from the capital, provided the trip's only instance of the kind of fantasy he relished and could translate into fiction. The travel book account closely matches the diary:

> He smiled in a dreamy, absent-minded manner and said, 'I was expecting you. I was warned in a vision of your approach'.... 'I always know the character of any visitors by the visions I have of them. Sometimes I see a pig or a jackal; often a ravaging tiger'.

I could not resist asking, 'And how did you see me?'
'As a sweetly toned harmonium', said Mr Christie politely.

(NTD 63)

He told me that he was at work on a translation of the scriptures into Macushi, 'but I have to change and omit a great deal. There is so much I do not agree with...but I am not worried. I expect the end of the world shortly'....
Lately he had been privileged to see the total assembly of the elect in heaven.
'Were there many of them?'
'It was hard to count because you see they had no bodies but my impression is that there were very few'.
I asked if he believed in the Trinity. 'Believe in it? I could not live without it. But the mistake the Catholics make is to call it a mystery. It is all quite simple to me'.

(NTD 65)

A few days later Waugh was delighted to find the record of another traveller's meeting with Christie. This traveller had given the old man a medal of Our Lady which Christie studied for a moment, then returned, saying 'Why should I require an image of someone I see so frequently? Besides, it is an exceedingly poor likeness' (NTD 73).

Neither diary nor travel book suggests any fear that Christie might keep Waugh prisoner at his remote cabin. This idea emerged three weeks later in Boa Vista, where Waugh passed the empty days by writing 'The Man Who Liked Dickens', in which the fanatical Christian becomes a fanatical Dickensian. On 15 February, trusting the local postal service, he sent this 'grade A short story' (along with '3 grade B articles') to Peters; thereafter he did no more writing during the trip.[37] His plan to proceed further into Brazil foiled by lack of transport, he made his way back to Georgetown – skin raw from scratching the bites of cabouri flies, feet lamed from digging out the djiggas that burrowed in to lay their eggs – where he arrived on 5 April. 'Out of the wild wood at last', he wrote to Lady Diana; 'Longing to see you and everyone and to eat a lot and to see architecture and art and things like that' (DC 27). He arrived at Underhill in May bearing stuffed baby crocodiles as presents, then proceeded immediately to a hotel in Bath to 'get rid of some of the horrors of life in the forest' (L 71), read his post and consider how to write enough to pay for his travels. After the rigours of South America, Bath, 'with its propriety and uncompromised grandeur', 'seemed to offer everything that was most valuable in English life' (NTD 170).

VI

Paying for the trip soon took second place to a new problem – what Waugh called 'heavy Catholic trouble' (DC 28; L 72). The accumulated post of six months revealed that in his absence *Black Mischief* had received its most damning review yet, and this not in the secular press but an influential Catholic weekly. Given Waugh's efforts of the past months to enter more fully into his faith and his fears that the South American trip had been a failure, the news could not have come at a worse time. After a week in Bath he hurried to London to enter a controversy that would last three years.

In January 1933, *The Tablet*'s editor Ernest Oldmeadow, a respected writer of poetry, popular novels and appreciations of Chopin and Schumann, had attacked both *Black Mischief* and its author:

> A year or two ago, paragraphs appeared in various newspapers announcing that Mr. Evelyn Waugh, a novelist, had been received into the Church. Whether Mr. Waugh still considers himself a Catholic, *The Tablet* does not know; but, in case he is so regarded by booksellers, librarians and novel-readers in general, we hereby state that his latest novel would be a disgrace to anybody professing the Catholic name.
>
> (7 Jan. 1933, 10)

In his recent encyclical *Rappresentanti in terra* (1929), Pius XI had called on Catholics to renew their vigilance against 'impious and immoral' books and films; *The Tablet* was owned by, and thought to reflect the opinions of, Francis Bourne, Cardinal Archbishop of Westminster and Primate of Great Britain. Oldmeadow seemed to condemn Waugh with authority.

In Waugh's absence his publisher friend Tom Burns organized a defence in the form of a letter to *The Tablet* signed by twelve prominent Catholics, both clerical (Frs D'Arcy, Martindale, Steuart and Jarrett) and lay (including Woodruff, Hollis, Clonmore, Eric Gill and Wyndham Lewis). The twelve subscribed that 'We think these sentences exceed the bounds of legitimate criticism and are in fact an imputation of bad faith. In writing, we wish only to express our great regret at their being published and our regard for Mr. Waugh'. Undeterred, Oldmeadow printed the letter along with a yet longer editorial particularizing the ways in which *Black Mischief* 'gave scandal' to the Church and was 'a disgrace to a professing Catholic':

> Prudence, daughter of the British Minister at the Emperor's court, goes up to the unsavoury room (the soapy water unemptied) of Basil, a man she hardly knows, and, after saying 'You might have shaved' and 'Please help with my boots', stays till there is 'a banging on the door'. In the end, Basil, at a cannibal feast, unwittingly helps to eat the body of Prudence 'stewed to a pulp amid peppers and aromatic roots'. In working out this foul invention, Mr. Waugh gives us disgusting passages. We are introduced to a young couple dining in bed, with 'a bull terrier and a chow flirting at their feet'. The young wife suddenly calls out 'Oh God, he's made a mess again'; and Basil exclaims 'How dirty the bed is'. These nasty details are not necessary to the story. A dozen silly pages are devoted to a Birth Control Pageant, announced by posters which flaunt all over the island 'a detailed drawing of some up-to-date contraceptive apparatus'. The Emperor 're-names the site of the Anglican Cathedral "Place Marie Stopes"'. Two humane ladies are ridiculed; in one place so indelicately that the passage cannot be described by us. [The reference is to the young members of the British legation who say to each other 'I dare say they've been raped' and 'I hope so'.] There is a comic description of a Nestorian monastery with a venerated cross 'which had fallen from heaven quite unexpectedly during Good Friday luncheon, some years back'. If the twelve signatories of the above protest find nothing wrong with 'during Good Friday luncheon' we cannot help them.
>
> (*The Tablet*, 21 Jan. 1933, 85)

Oldmeadow ended with an implicit claim to speak not only for himself but also for Cardinal Bourne: 'we respectfully and sincerely obey our Cardinal Archbishop's wish that, during this month of January, Catholics shall pray that authors be clearly on the side of the angels'.

There followed a month of controversy pro and con in *The Tablet*'s letters column, including a letter from Marie Stopes professing 'disgust' that her name had 'quite needlessly' been dragged through Waugh's 'unsavoury tale' and praising the editor: 'I am glad that a Roman Catholic should be dealt with by Roman Catholics in the trenchant fashion you have done' (4 Feb. 1933, 149). Finally in February Oldmeadow put an end to the debate with the longest defence of his own position yet. He repeated all his charges, accused Waugh's defenders of a 'feminine terror of being behind the latest fashions in Literature' tantamount to 'Modernism (in Aesthetics, not Faith)', and for good measure threw into the same issue a translation of Cardinal Merry del Val's 'Instruction of the Holy Office concerning Sensual Literature' from the *Index of Prohibited Books*.[38]

Here the controversy rested until May 1933, when Waugh returned to London to plead his case in an *Open Letter to His Eminence the Cardinal Archbishop of Westminster*. The letter was printed but Father Knox counselled against publication (L 342); few copies survive. Oldmeadow's tone had been offensively pontifical, but Waugh's response is insolent, accusing Oldmeadow of stupidity, literal-mindedness, puerility and a barely disguised prurience of his own.[39] The *Open Letter* ends by telling Bourne that 'Your Eminence's patronage alone renders this base man considerable' and petitioning that such 'scandalous misuse of your patronage may be corrected' – i.e., that Oldmeadow be fired.

That Oldmeadow's attacks deeply troubled Waugh is clear from his use of the *Open Letter* to reply to criticism with a detailed interpretation of one of his own works. Identifying his novel specifically as 'satire' – something Oldmeadow, like many others, had missed – Waugh rebuts the accusations of blasphemy and obscenity point for point, arguing that while *Black Mischief* is not an 'actively propagandist work', it is consistent with faith. He rises to a crescendo on the issue of cannibalism, paraphrasing Swift's *Modest Proposal*:

> There remains the climax of the story, when Prudence is eaten at a cannibal feast. Several critics whose opinion I respect more than the Editor of *The Tablet* have told me that they regard this as a disagreeable incident. It was meant to be. *The Tablet* quotes the fact that she was stewed with pepper, as being in some way a particularly lubricious process. But this is a peculiar prejudice of the Editor's, attributable perhaps, like much of his criticism, to defective digestion. It cannot matter whether she was roasted, grilled, braised or pickled, cut into sandwiches or devoured hot on toast as a savoury: the fact is that the wretched girl was cooked and eaten, and that is obviously and admittedly a disagreeable end.[40]

But the *Open Letter* is less successful in arguing that Oldmeadow had no right to question 'my moral conduct in the exercise of my trade', nor does it address what seems the root of Oldmeadow's objections: that 'Nowhere in its three hundred pages is the reader's mind lifted to anything noble'; 'On [Waugh's] dunghill no lily blooms'.[41] In such complaints one can hear not only a desire for explicitly positive models, but also discomfort at a work that invites readers to uncharity, to take pleasure in the distresses of fools and sinners, as we do for instance in the cruelly funny discomforts of Dame Mildred Porch and Miss Tin. Waugh answers Oldmeadow's complaint about flippant references to rape with little more than an assertion of social superiority to his critic, claiming to have used no expressions that 'well-bred person[s] to-day would feel the smallest embarrassment in mentioning'. Knox was right to counsel the pamphlet's suppression.

Despite his indignation, Waugh took Oldmeadow's criticisms to heart. *Ninety-Two Days* takes an explicitly Catholic viewpoint, and to the Lygon sisters he confessed plans that his next novel would be a 'good taste book' (L 85). *A Handful of Dust* is in fact markedly more in line with conventional canons of 'modesty' than *Black Mischief*, as even Oldmeadow himself noted: 'His 1934 novel... is free from the gross indecency and irreverence which made its forerunner abominable'.[42] More revealing of Waugh's effort to establish himself as a believer in good standing is the actively propagandist 'Out of Depth', written two months after the *Open Letter*. And while Waugh did not yet contemplate making his faith an explicit part of his novels, while working on *A Handful of Dust* he also planned a book-length work of apologetic, telling Peters early in 1934: 'Want to write a "Great Life" of Gregory the Great when novel is done' (L 87).

It was thus especially galling that Oldmeadow renewed his attack when *A Handful of Dust* appeared. *The Tablet* ran a full-page editorial titled 'The Pity of It':

> Last year, a novel from the same pen evoked a sequel which gave pain to Catholics. A reproof to the author from our unimportant selves was amplified from a quarter so authoritative that his co-religionists reasonably hoped to find Mr. Waugh turning over a completely new leaf. He has not done so....
>
> The pity of it is that Mr. Waugh is misusing his indubitable talent.... If he wants to taste true happiness, he will make a clean Franciscan break with the past. He will stop the reprinting of every ignoble book of which he controls the copyright, and will show the world that a writer of genuine talent is not dependent upon malodorousness for his drawing-power. So acting, he may lose the recommendations of the Book Society [which had chosen both *Black Mischief* and *A Handful of Dust* as Books of the Month]; but he will some day hear a 'Well done!' from a Voice of more consequence.
>
> (8 Sept. 1934, 300)

Again Oldmeadow missed the point of Waugh's satire. He found Tony Last's fate 'vile' (needlessly cruel), and protested that 'Throughout the book English Society is viewed as godless, while Religion, as the great Anglican Bishop Butler said, is treated as if it is no longer even matter for inquiry' – all of which is exactly Waugh's point. Misreading the novel in this way, Oldmeadow adds a new complaint to the familiar list: that Waugh is snobbish. 'We are sorry to say that any contempt he may have for the cadgers and gluttons and adulteresses is obscured by snobbery – this harsh word is the only word for it – with which he fondly contemplates them'. It was thus the Catholic press which first levelled charges of snobbery against Waugh, charges that would dog him the rest of his life.

This time Waugh answered only the attack on his character. Stung by the charge of snobbery, he responded in his usual manner by acting the part to an extreme. He sent Tom Driberg, gossip- columnist for the *Daily Express*, a letter that ignored Oldmeadow's critical arguments and instead simply and high-handedly denied his right to speak. 'Dragoman' duly reported among 'The Talk of London':

> *Mail, from Evelyn Waugh*, re *Tablet* attack (see this column yesterday):
> Two aspects of *Tablet* article:
> (a) an unfavourable criticism,
> (b) a moral lecture.
> The first is completely justifiable. A copy of my novel was sent to the *Tablet* for review, and the editor is therefore entitled to give his opinion of its literary quality in any terms he thinks suitable.
> In the second aspect he is in the position of a valet masquerading in his master's clothes. Long employment by a Prince of the Church has tempted him to ape his superiors, and, naturally enough, he gives an uncouth and impudent performance.
> (*Daily Express*, 11 Sept. 1934, 6)

No controversy ensued in *The Tablet*'s pages, but the feud continued. In 1935 Oldmeadow – having pointedly ignored the publication of *Edmund Campion* – twice protested that the *Daily Mail* had chosen the author of *Black Mischief* as its special correspondent to Abyssinia.[43] Sparring ended only in 1936, when Cardinal Bourne died and the *Tablet* came under new management. Tom Burns and Douglas Woodruff took over as publisher and editor; their aim, splendidly realized, was to turn the magazine into an up-to-date journal of Catholic intellectual opinion like the American *Commonweal*. Thereafter Waugh became a regular reader and frequent contributor. He took his revenge much later, in *Ronald Knox* (1957), which calls Cardinal Bourne a man devoid of 'scholarship, taste or humour', and Oldmeadow one 'of meagre attainments and deplorable manners, under whom [*The Tablet*] became petty in its interests and low in tone' (K 166, 243).

VII

Once Waugh had written (and suppressed) the *Open Letter*, there remained paying work to be done. Over the summer of 1933 he wrote six travel articles in a series titled 'I Step Off the Map' for the magazine *Passing Show*; before beginning his travel book he had already written nine articles about South America and was bored with the whole subject. To make matters worse Peter Fleming's immensely successful *Brazilian Adventure* appeared in August, recording with brilliant humour a far more eventful trip through the jungle than his own. Reviewing *Brazilian Adventure* in the *Spectator*, Waugh noted: 'It is an intensely self-conscious book. The trouble about all forms of writing is that one is working against a background of predecessors and contemporaries' (EAR 137). He was in the same position when he eventually sat down to write the very self-conscious first chapter of *Ninety-Two Days*.

Meanwhile none of his writing was going well. Editors complained and sometimes refused material previously contracted for; Peters found himself apologizing for the low quality of his client's work. Just when Waugh needed money he seemed least able to earn it. The solution was to defer *Ninety-Two Days* yet further. In August he left England again, on a Hellenic Cruise organized by Arnold Lunn. In the language of *Labels*, this was not travel but simple tourism. The pretext for the trip was to care for his old friend Alfred Duggan, who had lapsed from Catholicism and into alcoholism; Waugh believed that if Duggan could be helped to stop drinking, faith would return as well. The effort did not succeed at the time – Duggan became a project of many years. But Waugh thoroughly enjoyed both sightseeing and his fellow passengers, who included Father D'Arcy and Christopher Hollis and a peppering of British peeresses and foreign princesses, among them Diana Cooper's friend Katherine Asquith, daughter-in-law of the prime minister. Lady Katherine was nearly twenty years Waugh's senior; she had converted to Catholicism after her husband's death in the First World War. Waugh began a correspondence with her immediately after they parted and was soon a visitor at Mells Manor, her house in Somerset, the centre of a small Catholic community where Hollis lived and Knox often visited.

Also on board was Gabriel Herbert, a cousin of Evelyn Gardner, who invited Duggan and Waugh to join a house party at her mother's villa, Altachiara, in Portofino (outside Genoa). This family, too, was Catholic. Their father Aubrey Herbert was an able linguist, scholar, poet and Conservative MP who had fought at Gallipoli, worked with T. E. Lawrence, and travelled widely in the bandit-infested back-country of the eastern Mediterranean; twice offered the throne of Albania (which he refused on the ground that the was too poor to accept), he had become a kind of legend by the time he died young in 1923. (John Buchan based the novel *Greenmantle* (1915) on him.) Influenced by his old friend Hilaire Belloc, Herbert had been considering conversion at the time of his death; his widow Mary and daughters Gabriel and Bridget took the step soon after, followed eventually by the more independent-minded youngest daughter Laura. They too lived in Somerset, near Mells, in a large establishment filled with horses and dogs called Pixton Park. It was at Altachiara in September 1933 that Waugh first met Laura Herbert, then seventeen. He described her at the time only as a 'white mouse' (L 80); four years later she would become his second wife.

Back in England in October, there was nothing for it but to grind out *Ninety-Two Days*. Diana Cooper lent her country house at Bognor; Waugh dedicated the book to her. Without enthusiasm, he expanded his travel diary, turning abbreviated hints such as 't.v.' (short for 'tropical vegetation') into longer passages of description and dialogue. 'It is getting longer', he wrote to Lady Diana, 'and if I go on even like this it will be done some time' (DC 39).

'Half the polite letters of the world', Waugh wrote later, 'take the form of contrasting expectation with realization' (RUL 4). Initially he tried to give order to his meagre materials by turning drab experiences of expectation and disappointment into parables (reminiscent of Johnson's *Rasselas*) of expectation and disappointment. The process begins as soon as he lands in the capital – 'Perhaps it was the name Georgetown, so like that of an Irish country house, that made me expect something different' – and recurs with numbing regularity thereafter. 'I had little idea, however, what to expect [of Kurupukari] and vaguely imagined something like the lake stations at Victoria Nyzna or Lake Tanganyika'; 'What I found' – a single wooden house – 'was a surprise'. 'Through the influence of the cinema, "ranch" had taken on a rather glorious connotation in my mind'; finding only 'three sheds and a wire corral', 'I did feel that the word "ranch" had taken a fall' (NTD 21, 43–4, 39).

Disillusion climaxes in Brazil. Waugh plans to travel overland from Guiana to Boa Vista, then downriver to Manaos and home. He has heard of Boa Vista as

> a place of peculiar glamour – dissipated and violent; a place where revolutions were plotted and political assassinations committed; from there regular paddle steamers plied to Manaos – a city of inexpressible grandeur, of palaces and opera houses, boulevards and fountains, swaggering military in spurs and white gloves, cardinals and millionaires; and from there great liners went direct to Lisbon.
>
> (NTD 48)

> Boa Vista had come to assume greater and greater importance to me.... Everybody...had spoken of it as a town of dazzling attraction. Whatever I had looked for in vain at Figuiredo's store was, he told me, procurable at 'Boa Vist'; Mr Daguar had extolled its modernity and luxury – electric lights, cafés, fine buildings, women, politics, murders.
>
> (NTD 84)

But there is no transport southward, and Boa Vista itself, the city of dreams, turns out a seedy, fever-infested backwater, the lowest point of the trip; Waugh's only choice is to retrace the dismal route by which he came. This climactic disappointment is rendered in language used again in *A Handful of Dust* for the collapse of Tony Last's dreams of 'the City':

> Already, in the few hours of my sojourn there, the Boa Vista of my imagination had come to grief. Gone; engulfed in an earthquake, uprooted by a tornado and tossed sky-high like chaff in the wind; scorched up with brimstone like Gomorrah, toppled over with trumpets like Jericho, ploughed like Carthage, bought, demolished and transported brick by brick to another continent as though it had taken the fancy of Mr Hearst; tall Troy was down.
>
> (NTD 87)

Having begun in tragicomedy, the visit to Boa Vista ends in farce, as Waugh tries to leave, but must three times return (and repeat his goodbyes to his Benedictine hosts) when servants and pack-animals fail to materialize. In between there is only boredom recalling the 'Nightmares' of *Remote People*.

> In a previous book I once remarked that I was bored for some days on a Congo river steamer. Not only did the reviewers take hold of this as a suitable text for their

criticism, but I received a handful of cross letters from strangers saying, no doubt
with good sense, that if travelling bored me I had far better stay at home.... So I
will not repeat my mistake. I will not say I was bored in Boa Vista but merely
remark that I found very little to occupy my time.... I could study the bottled
worms in the laboratory; I could watch the carpenter, in his rare moments of
industry, sawing up lengths of plank. There was really quite a number of things for
me to do, but, in spite of them all, the days seemed to pass slowly.

(NTD 98–9)

Such comedy is pleasant but slender foundation for a book; *Ninety-Two Days* is his
shortest travel book of the thirties. Waugh's active mind thrived not on simple
description of places or events, but on connecting such bare facts to larger
systems of belief: on analysis of their meaning. So far he had found no useful
way to think about his material; he was proceeding by a kind of literary bluff.
Only in November, writing the second half of the book, could he report to Lady
Diana, 'So stimulated that I broke all records with a 4,000 word day yesterday'
(DC 40). His narrative now shifts from a dutiful record of days and places to a
series of more coherent essays reminiscent of the best parts of *Remote People*.
There is a discursion debunking the mystique of 'rough travelling', another on
'pork knocking' (panning for diamonds and gold). But Waugh's imagination
really took fire when memories of primitive Indians led to reflections about
the science of anthropology. He compares his own observations of the *couvade*
among the Wapishiana with Bronislaw Malinowski's discussion of the Trobriand
islanders in *The Sexual Life of Savages* (1929), and generalizes about how the anti-
Christian bias of anthropologists (sponsored by 'the agnosticism of the provincial
universities') colours their interpretation of evidence. So excited was he by this
line of thinking that he asked Lady Diana: 'What do you think of the idea of my
going to a University – which – and studying anthropology?' (DC 40).

Ninety-Two Days was finished too late for the autumn publishing season and so
appeared the following spring. Waugh characteristically thought it 'unreadable'
(DC 44), but reviewers were ready with praise before taking the occasion to
comment once more on his novels. The anonymous TLS reviewer coined the
word 'disgusto' for his response to the asperities of South American travel and
wondered 'why Mr. Waugh, whose spiritual home is, he infers, Bath, should
have betaken himself to Guiana'. More penetratingly, Peter Fleming traced the
book's weaknesses to lack of matter: 'The Brazilian savannah is a monotonous
desolation', and so 'there was very little to report'. Fleming fairly sums up:
'Though the book is far from being dull – the digressions especially are often
brilliant – it is as nearly dull as anything Mr. Waugh can write'. Only the *New
Statesman* noted (with distaste) Waugh's 'discreetly veiled religious preoccupations', including a defence of Catholic missionary work.[44]

The last theme in fact pervades the book, to the point that in its final pages
Waugh excuses himself from a description of an Easter festival in Port of Spain
on the ground that 'this book has too much ecclesiastical flavour already'. From
the first, Waugh identifies himself as a Catholic and praises the valiant, intensely
practical Jesuits and Benedictines at work in the outback. In one remarkable
episode, lost in a bleak district, he prays to St Christopher for 'supernatural

assistance. And it came'. There providentially appears an Indian who happens to speak English, has spare food and drink and is about to set off for the same destination as Waugh, who playfully calculates the odds of such succour as less than '1:54,750,000' (111). Such emphatic piety cannot be attributed simply to the lingering effects of Oldmeadow's attacks. Waugh had planned his focus from the first; even before Oldmeadow, he was on his way to explicit apologetic.

Another religious reference – to native reporters who 'took down all I said laboriously as though I were a witness at an archbishop's court' (20) – was the product not of Guiana but much more recent experience. The writing of *Ninety-Two Days* was interrupted by trips to such a court in London. It is not clear when Waugh first learned that the circumstances of his first marriage might justify a petition for annulment. Like all such cases, Waugh's annulment had first to be heard locally, then again in its entirety in Rome. In October and November 1933, he saw Evelyn Gardner for the last time, as both Evelyns, Pansy Lamb, Alec Waugh and Evelyn Gardner's sister and brother-in-law Geoffrey and Althea Fry gave testimony in five hearings at the diocesan court of Westminster.

Much gossip and unclarity has grown up around Waugh's annulment, recently swept away by Donat Gallagher through a careful reading of the published records of the Roman Rota. It is not true that Waugh tried to coach his ex-wife and friends to lie that the couple had never intended to have children. Waugh contended simply that he and his fiancée agreed temporarily to defer having children, and that they married with the explicit understanding that if things did not work out, they would divorce. The first point was not grounds for annulment; the second, corroborated by others, was sufficient in canon law to constitute defective consent in marriage (Gallagher, 'Vatican Divorce').

Confident of a speedy and successful outcome, Waugh proposed marriage to Teresa Jungman. He reported to Mary Lygon: 'popped question to Dutch girl and got raspberry. So that is that, eh. Stiff upper lip and dropped cock. Now I must go. How sad, how sad' (L 81). The disappointment informed his portrayal of another Teresa, the young Thérèse de Vitré of *A Handful of Dust* (who is looking for a husband but loses interest in Tony Last on learning he is divorced). Nor was the annulment speedily settled. The cleric whose task it was to send Waugh's case on to Rome, a certain Bishop Myers, neglected to do so; the records were sent only two years later, and the annulment became final only in July 1936.[45]

VIII

While sailing for South America in December 1932, Waugh noted in his diary, 'Wrote first page of novel' (D 357). Whether this was the beginning of *A Handful of Dust* we cannot know. The novel began in earnest a year later, when on finishing *Ninety-Two Days* he again escaped England, this time to Morocco. Waugh spent January and February 1934 in Fez, whose architecture, spring flowers and prostitutes he described in letters home and later in *Work Suspended*. The letters also make clear that he considered his new 'good taste book' better and more ambitious than his previous work. In a characteristic act of stock-taking, he reread *Decline and Fall* and *Vile Bodies*, 'much cheered up to find how I have improved at writing' (DC 42); 'I peg away at the novel', he told Katherine Asquith, 'which seems to me faultless of its kind' (L 84).

By the end of January he reported to Diana Cooper having finished over half the novel as we have it:

> As for the book, well it is at a crisis at the moment. I have finished the first section which was to have been 20,000 words and it is nearly 50,000 so there is the alternative of making it 150,000 words long (*Black Mischief* is about 70,000) or else finding a new ending and finishing it off in 2 weeks.... What I have done is excellent. I don't think it could be better. Very gruesome. Rather like Webster in modern idiom. Very fine scene where bereaved and heartbroken father plays animal snap while his little boy lies dead upstairs.... There is also a brilliant scene at the '43' and a divorce expedition to Brighton with a tart – all excellent. And there is a woman called Mrs Beaver who runs a decorating shop, not so good, and a groom who ought to be better. But the general architecture is *masterly.*
>
> (DC 43–4)

Waugh had evidently finished the manuscript to the end of chapter 4 ('English Gothic – II'), to the point when, after the collapse of his marriage, Tony Last suddenly strikes off for Brazil. So far composition had been rapid; there seems no truth to the speculation that painful memories of Evelyn Gardner made it difficult for him to describe Brenda's betrayal of Tony. Tony's staged infidelity at Brighton owes less to Waugh's own experience than to that of the Guinnesses, about whom he read with sorrow in the London papers in June 1933, just after returning from Guiana: 'In an undefended suit Mrs Diana Guinness of Eaton Square prayed for the dissolution of her marriage with Mr. Bryan Walter Guinness on the grounds of his adultery with Isolde Field at an hotel at Brighton in March last'.[46]

By early March a draft was done and Waugh wrote Peters: 'The name of the novel' – long in coming, since earlier drafts read only 'Novel (as yet unnamed)' – 'is A HANDFUL OF ASHES' (L 87, a reference to the dirt or ashes thrown on a coffin during burial). Another working title was *Fourth Decade* (Tony Last turns thirty in the course of the novel, as Waugh himself had recently done). By April Waugh was reading proofs, under the final title (drawn from T. S. Eliot's *The Waste Land*) *A Handful of Dust*. Under the yet different title *A Flat in London*, a serial version of the story began to appear in *Harper's Bazaar* in June. The novel as a whole appeared for the autumn season in September 1934.

Much later Waugh explained that he had all along planned the novel to end with Tony in the circumstances described in his short story 'The Man Who Liked Dickens'. In that tale, Paul Henty leaves his adulterous wife (whose affair does not much trouble him) to travel in South America, where he is trapped by the insane Mr McMaster and condemned to read aloud from Dickens for the rest of his life.

> *A Handful of Dust*... began at the end. I had written a short story about a man trapped in the jungle, ending his days reading Dickens aloud.... Then, after the

short story was written and published, the idea kept working in my mind. I wanted to discover how the prisoner got there, and eventually the thing grew into a study of other sorts of savage at home and the civilized man's helpless plight among them.

('Fan-Fare', EAR 303)

Much in the novel's ending follows the short story word for word. But letters to Peters in January and February 1934 reveal Waugh as being 'not sure' how the novel would end; reuse of the short story was only one of several possibilities (HRC E234–5). The correspondence with Lady Diana suggests that, finding the novel growing too long, Waugh dropped his other ideas and abruptly packed Tony off to search (like Colonel Fawcett) for a lost city – thereby creating a break in genre and tone that has troubled readers ever since. Henry Yorke was the first of many to complain that the novel moves from 'a real picture of real people' in England to a world of 'fantasy' in Brazil: 'Aren't you mixing two things together?'[47] Waugh responded:

I think I agree that the Todd episode is fantastic. It is a 'conceit' in the Webster manner – wishing to bring Tony to a sad end I made it an elaborate & improbable one.... But the Amazon stuff had to be there. The scheme was a Gothic man in the hands of savages – first Mrs Beaver etc. then the real ones, finally the silver foxes at Hetton. All that quest for a city seems to me justifiable symbolism.

(L 88)

As usual in Waugh's fiction, generic mixture signals a shift to a wider perspective which puts events in a new, unfavourable light, showing what had all along been the truth behind them.

The issue does not arise in *A Flat in London*, where Tony's search for 'the City' and imprisonment by Mr Todd do not appear. Not from any desire for a happy ending, but because 'The Man Who Liked Dickens' was already under copyright (having appeared in *Cosmopolitan*), *Harper's* demanded an alternative ending for the serial. In this ending (reprinted in *Mr Loveday's Little Outing* under the title 'By Special Request'), Tony spends several 'lazy months' 'potter[ing] from island to island in the West Indies', then returns to a loveless reunion with Brenda (now pregnant, and abandoned, by John Beaver). Brenda gives up the London flat, but Tony – after some smooth blackmail by Mrs Beaver – secretly keeps it, presumably to pursue affairs of his own. The serial thus remains on the plane of a novel of manners in which Tony, wholly the victim, is betrayed, but finally joins in the corruption around him.

What distinguishes even the serial version of *A Handful of Dust* from Waugh's earlier fiction is its emotional range. Tony's victimization is an altogether more painful affair to contemplate than that of Paul Pennyfeather or Adam Fenwick-Symes because, as Waugh wrote Katherine Asquith, 'for the first time I am trying to deal with normal people instead of eccentrics' (L 84). For the first time Waugh provides his hero with sufficient interior life to render him capable of love, and so to make the pain of Brenda's betrayal credible and sympathetic. George Meredith once defined laughter as 'the temporary amnesia of the heart', but it is Waugh's genius in *A Handful of Dust* consistently to sustain a double perspective in which, as Peter Quennell noted, 'tragedy and comedy are inter-dependent'; the reader 'smiles and is subtly horrified at the same instant'. From its ominous opening sentence – 'Was anyone hurt?' – to the exquisitely painful moment – 'one of the miracles of modern fiction' – when Brenda, told that 'John' is dead, thanks God that death has claimed her son rather than her lover, Waugh presses farther than he had ever done before what J. B. Priestley called 'the funny-grotesque-horrible'.[48]

Early in the novel occurs what seems a parable of Waugh's comedy of cruelty and pain: the story of the mule Peppermint who, unable to vomit, died of rum. 'How very sad' says Tony on hearing the story, to which his 6-year-old son John Andrew (often the innocent mouthpiece of painful truths) replies: 'Well, *I* thought it was sad too, but it isn't. Ben said it made him laugh fit to bust his pants' (HD 53). The story itself and the different responses it evokes – a foretaste of the much more searching analysis of literature and its effects conducted through Tony's readings to Mr Todd in the final scenes of the novel – suggest the double perspective Waugh labours throughout to achieve: a mixture of pity for suffering, and a larger vision which understands the banality of evil and knows that sentimental compassion may sometimes be the sign not of an acute but a dulled moral sense. Waugh's earlier novels had of course depended on something of the same doubling: behind their deadpan narrations lay hints of another order of meaning. *A Handful of Dust* overlays points of view so different as to produce what the reader experiences almost as two different novels: a main tale of domestic infidelity in which Tony is the sympathetic victim; and another tale – really another perspective on the same events – hinted at throughout but kept in the background until, like the world war which concludes *Vile Bodies*, it bursts forth in the final, near-allegorical sequence in Brazil. The second view-point supervenes upon the first, explaining Tony's predicament and making clear that his fate in Brazil is appropriate, even just – horrifying, but also funny. In overlaying these two orders of fiction (and reality), *A Handful of Dust* looks ahead to Waugh's explorations, beginning in *Brideshead*, of the interrelated orders of nature and grace.

The viewpoint that bursts forth at the end of the novel is hinted at the start, in delicately interwoven descriptions of Tony Last's beloved house and 'weekly routine' of churchgoing and estate-management. These early passages give us our first clues for understanding Waugh's explanation in 1946 that *A Handful of Dust* 'was humanist and contained all I had to say about humanism' (EAR 304). Humanism in its modern, secular form, with its denial of sin and utopian belief in a satisfying human order achievable by purely human means, had been a central target of his satire since *Decline and Fall*. Now Waugh deepens his critique by placing his representative humanists within a sharply defined Catholic view of history, the same history sketched in 'Come Inside': 'England was Catholic for nine hundred years, then Protestant for three hundred, then agnostic for a century' (EAR 367). As Richard Wasson notes, 'the Catholic position is central' to *A Handful of Dust*, and the 'chief cultural villains of the piece are the Victorians' (Wasson 124).

The novel's frontispiece (omitted from American editions) shows Tony's Hetton, a place of 'tender memory and proud possession' whose 'every glazed brick or encaustic tile' is dear to him. 'I instructed the architect to design the worst possible eighteen-sixty', Waugh told Tom Driberg, 'and I think he has done well' (L 88). Once an abbey, Hetton became with the Reformation 'one of the notable houses of the country'; it 'stood until [Tony's] great-grandfather demolished it' and, in the words of the Guide Book, 'was entirely rebuilt in 1864 in the Gothic style and is now devoid of interest'.[49] With its theatrical pinnacles, plaster shaped to look like coffered wood, and bedrooms named from characters in Tennyson's *Idylls of the King*, Hetton is not real Gothic but, like Llanabba School, a Victorian imitation: in a description that appeared only in American editions, 'a huge building conceived in the late generation of the Gothic revival, when the movement had lost its fantasy and become structurally logical and stodgy'. Tony's aunt Frances thinks 'the plans of the house must have been adapted by Mr. Pecksniff from one of his pupils' designs for an orphanage' (27). Allusively present from the start of the novel, both Tennyson and Dickens return at the end for searching examination and dismissal.

Frank Kermode and others have argued that in Waugh's fiction, 'great houses' become 'by an easy transition types of the Catholic City, and in this book the threatened City is Hetton'.[50] Nearly the opposite is true; such readings ignore Waugh's view of history. Just as Tony's weekly churchgoing is only vestigial, the formal descendant of an earlier, living faith, Hetton's Arthurian friezes and *trompe-l'oeil* plasterwork – already starting to 'tarnish' and 'decay' – embody Victorian efforts to mask cultural rupture through a merely picturesque assertion of continuity. Mrs Beaver's efforts to install chromium plating and sheepskin carpet in Tony's morning-room – to decorate Hetton in the modernist style to which, as a reaction, Victorian clutter gave birth – constitute but another degradation of an already degraded antecedent. Hetton is, as Kermode says, Tony's 'church', but it is the 'type' not of the Catholic but the modern Anglican City: of what T. S. Eliot called Victorian liberal Protestantism now 'in its last agonies', against which *A Handful of Dust* mounts the most sustained attack of Waugh's career. Modern Anglicanism, with its picturesque churches, vaguely ethical outlook and fuzziness over doctrine represents in this view the final phase of the Victorians' substitution of sentiment for faith.

The novel's first chapter cuts between Hetton and Tony's visits, part of the 'mildly ceremonious order of his Sunday morning', to the local parish church, in whose 'agreeable, slightly musty atmosphere' he 'performed the familiar motions of sitting, standing, and leaning forward' (rather than 'kneeling') and, on holidays, 'read the lesson from the back of the brass eagle'. Here, where once his father rattled a poker 'when any point in the sermon attracted his disapproval', Tony's 'thoughts drifted from subject to subject' – the first time we see him, to 'the question of lavatories and bathrooms' at Hetton – until 'occasionally some arresting phrase in the liturgy would recall him' (53, 50). 'I only go because I more or less have to', Tony tells the visiting John Beaver, an attitude he has passed along to his son: 'We'll go to church in the morning because I have to' (52, 145). 'Do you believe in God?' asks Mr Todd at the end of the novel, to which Tony replies, 'I suppose so. I've never really thought about it much' (328).

What Tony does believe in is Hetton. In what Brenda calls his 'madly feudal' moods, he defines what the estate means to him: 'We've always lived here and I hope John will be able to keep it on after me. One has a duty towards one's employees, and towards the place too. It's a definite part of English life' (33). But since such traditional language now lacks any proper foundation, even Tony can't take it wholly seriously: 'Brenda teased him whenever she caught him posing as an upright, God-fearing gentleman of the old school and Tony saw the joke' (51).

Nor can he take what happens in church more seriously; it too has become a stage property. Waugh brilliantly suggests the irrelevance in modern England of atrophied, unsacramental Anglicanism in the Christmas sermon delivered by Reverend Tendril (whose name captures the same picturesque effort to mask cultural rupture that characterizes Hetton). Written in the previous century for colonial troops stationed in the tropics and now performed, incongruously, in the depth of English winter, Tendril's sermon on the birth of Our Lord is 'an integral part' of the Last family's 'Christmas games'.

> 'How difficult it is for us', [Rev. Tendril] began, blandly surveying his congregation, who coughed into their mufflers and chafed their chilblains under their woollen gloves, 'to realise that this is indeed Christmas. Instead of the glowing log fire and windows tight shuttered against the drifting snow, we have only the harsh glare of the alien sun; instead of the happy circle of loved faces, of home and family, we have the uncomprehending stares of the subjugated, though no doubt grateful heathen. Instead of the placid ox and ass of Bethlehem' said the vicar, slightly losing the thread of his comparisons, 'we have for companions the ravening tiger and the exotic camel, the furtive jackal and the ponderous elephant...' And so on, through the pages of faded manuscript.[51]

No wonder that for Tony as for the rest of the parish, 'Few of the things said in church seemed to have any particular reference to themselves' (54). Without doctrine or efficacious sacraments, modern Anglicanism is incapable of giving guidance or consolation. Many readers have pointed to Tony's remarks about the Reverend Tendril's consolatory visit on the occasion of John Andrew's death: 'He tried to be comforting. It was very painful... after all the last thing one wants to talk about at a time like this is religion'. Even more revealing is the ultra-modern Mrs Rattery's response: 'Some like it'.[52]

Like Prendy's 'modern Churchmanship' in *Decline and Fall*, such a faith is also incapable of providing discipline – of channelling human appetite and disciplining fallen human nature. 'When the practice of religion becomes a matter of social conformity, it is powerless to change the world' (Dawson 126). Brenda's friends and family judge her affair with John Beaver only in social, not moral or religious terms: it is an 'adventure'; she has 'disgraced herself' not by committing adultery but by doing so with a socially unsuitable partner. ('I am sure there was never anything *wrong*' says Brenda's mother of the affair, quickly adding, 'I haven't met Mr Beaver and I do not wish to. I understand he is unsuitable in every way' (200–1).) That Tony himself possesses no deeper resources comes clear in the many scenes in which he signally fails to discipline his not only his wife but his son. When John Andrew calls his nanny a 'tart', Tony can do no better than invoke sentimental platitudes – the same social code that failed Paul Pennyfeather: 'It was very wrong of you to call nanny a silly old tart. First, because it was unkind to her.... And secondly because you were using a word which people of your age and class do not use. Poor people use certain expressions which gentlemen do not' (40).

Waugh later wrote of the Church of England as 'an improvisation which fortuitously assumed an aspect of permanence and then speedily came to nothing', and predicted that 'in a hundred years' time the only Englishmen who know their Bibles will be Catholic' (EAR 353, 355). *A Handful of Dust* already contains fully formed the view of history Waugh shared with his friend Christopher Dawson (whom he often visited in the thirties, stopping at Dawson's home in Yorkshire en route to Stonyhurst). Dawson explained in 1935:

> European culture had already ceased to be Christian in the eighteenth century, but it still retained the inherited moral standards and values of a Christian civilization. And so it attempted to erect these standards into an independent system by providing a rational philosophic justification for them. This was the Liberal idealism that was the faith of the nineteenth century – not a religious faith, but a quasi-religious substitute for one.
>
> But as Liberalism did not create these moral ideals, so, too, it cannot preserve them. It lives on the spiritual capital that it has inherited from Christian civilization, and as this is exhausted something else must come to take its place.
>
> (Dawson 64)

'Big houses are a thing of the past in England I'm afraid', says Brenda's awful brother Reggie, explaining how easy he found it to 'get rid of' his family's house: 'There's a lot in what those Labour fellows say' (234). Humanism, as T. S. Eliot noted nervously in 1930, 'must be subject to criticism while there is still time' ('Second Thoughts', 429).

Thus the emptiness of Tony's suddenly conceived quest for a lost South American Eldorado. Waugh's Brazilian sequences reveal the truth behind Hetton (and Mayfair) first of all by redeploying a device familiar since *Remote People*: parallelling England with the jungle. If in modern England Tony feels the 'world suddenly bereft of order', an 'all-embracing chaos that shrieked about his ears', in Brazil he is surrounded by 'howler monkeys' (216, 233); in both locales, people are persistently likened to animals, mostly pigs. In a sequence of brilliant filmic cross- cuttings between London and the Amazon (actually a development of what has been the novel's procedure all along), Waugh shows both Tony and Brenda hungry, weeping and alone; both revert to childhood; both are let down by faithless and predatory natives. Tony's fevered visions merging England with Brazil, Brenda with the Macushi Indians, are all ironically true. London's savages in fact suffer by comparison with those of the Amazon, who in abandoning Tony at least take away 'nothing with them that was not theirs' (299).

In moving the scene to Brazil, Waugh also moves the novel to a new literary register: Tony steps off the map into an allegorical realm outside ordinary time and space. 'From now onwards the map is valueless to us' says Dr Messinger

(278); Tony loses track of time, and finally loses his watch. Messinger's name means 'angel', but like Mrs Rattery he cannot read God's world:

> [Dr Messinger] watched keenly to right and left for the column of smoke, the thatched domes... that would disclose the village he sought. But there was no sign. In the open water he took up his field glasses and studied the whole wooded margin. But there was no sign.
>
> (HD 273)

Tony ends the prisoner of Mr Todd, whose name suggests 'death' – the living death which, Waugh means to suggest, is all that humanism amounts to.[53]

In language reminiscent of St Augustine, Tony calls the 'radiant sanctuary' of beauty and order which is the object of his quest 'the City'; Waugh casts his imaginings also in the medievalizing language and imagery of the Grail Quest from Tennyson's *Idylls* (Wasson 137–40). But where Arthur had warned that the Grail Castle was not a thing of this world, Tony imagines an earthly city, in fact a 'transfigured Hetton' (HD 253). Even before leaving he hears what should have taught him that the fabled City is merely the embodiment of each quester's appetites and desires:

> 'But what do you suppose this city will be like?'
> 'Impossible to say. Every tribe has a different word for it. The Pie-wies call it the "Shining" or "Glittering", the Arekuna the "Many Watered", the Patamonas the "Bright Feathered", the Warau oddly enough, use the same word for it that they use of a kind of aromatic jam they make'.
>
> (HD 251)

'The City is served' Tony hears when, delirious with fever, he thinks he has finally reached it (317); in another delirium he announces, 'I will tell you what I have learned in the forest, where time is different. There is no City' (325). Both fevered visions are true. There is no earthly paradise of perfected human nature and satisfied desire. But in another sense, what Tony has found – Mr Todd's encampment, the most starkly shocking of Waugh's jungle analogues for England – *is* the city of human desire, the 'transfigured Hetton' of his feudal imaginings.

A bastard born of bastards, the half-caste son of a bigamous Barbadian missionary and a Pie-wie Indian, Todd is the feudal lord of his small society: 'Most of the men and women living in this savannah are my children'. Singularly in touch with the primitive promptings of humanity (as Waugh said of Captain Grimes), he is an expert herbalist, the master of unredeemed nature. And with his precise, old-fashioned speech, he is also an aged survivor of the Victorian age. From his Last ancestors Tony inherited the Victorianized Hetton; from his Protestant preacher-father, Todd has inherited not a Bible, but the novels of Dickens.

There is profound irony in condemning Tony, betrayed by Brenda and imprisoned by Mr Todd, forever to read Dickens's interminable tales of Victorian domesticity, in whose happy endings villainy is defeated and justice finally done. ('I enjoyed that *very* much', says Todd after one reading from *Bleak House*;

'It was an extremely distressing chapter. But, if I remember rightly, it will all turn out well' (331).) Just as in 'Wordsworth in the Tropics' (1929) Aldous Huxley found Wordsworth's Romantic vision of nature untenable in Borneo and Malaya, Waugh tests Dickens's sentimental gospel against the jungles of Brazil and modern England and finds it wanting (Meckier 172).

Part of the generic shift Waugh creates in leaving Tony in the hands of Mr Todd is a metaliterary turn, a shift of attention from Tony's fate to the nature of literature itself. The novel's final pages pause to explain in elaborate detail how good a 'reader' the illiterate Todd is. On every reading, he takes more pleasure and finds new meaning in Dickens's novels ('there is always more to be learned and noticed'); he eagerly analyses character and motive ('Now why does she say that? Does she really mean it?'); he 'laughed loudly' at all Dickens's jokes; 'tears ran down his cheeks' during the 'distressing' passages (329–31). Todd is, in short, the ideal humanist reader, one whose emotional receptivity and sympathetic understanding (and emphasis on character rather than plot) are exactly what Dickens trusted would foster in his audience a moral amelioration akin to the saving change of heart experienced by so many of his characters. Critics from Shelley to Matthew Arnold and beyond preached that our experience of literature might provide a workable substitute for (outdated) revelation in moralizing mankind – that, as I. A. Richards claimed in *Science and Poetry* (1926), poetry 'is capable of saving us; it is a perfectly possible means of overcoming chaos'. Todd responds to literature just as such humanist critics prescribed – but continues to hold Tony prisoner. Once again, sentiment alone cannot substitute for absolute values grounded elsewhere. As T. S. Eliot commented in a review of *Science and Poetry*: 'Poetry "is capable of saving us", he says; it is like saying the wall-paper will save us when the walls have crumbled'.[54]

Waugh wrote in the preface to a new edition of *A Handful of Dust* in 1964: 'This book found favour with the critics who date my decline from it'. By the sixties there was indeed widespread agreement that *A Handful of Dust* was, in Frank Kermode's words, 'Mr Waugh's best book, and one of the most distinguished novels of the century' (CH 283) (though this evaluation was usually accompanied, as in Kermode's case, with resistance to Waugh's religious and historical intent). Initial response was far more mixed. Those like Edwin Muir in the *Listener* who thought it his best novel to date were a small minority. J. B. Priestley wrote to Waugh, 'I do not think it a better book than the others, though I can imagine why you should think so'; Rose Macaulay judged it a 'more ordinary' book than *Black Mischief*.[55] Once again arose the old questions whether Waugh wrote 'satire', and what, if any, were his moral and religious commitments. Both Peter Quennell (in the *New Statesman*) and Michael de la Bedoyère (in the *Catholic Herald*) defended the novel from Ernest Oldmeadow's complaints of its 'vileness' and 'cruelty', but for opposite reasons: Bedoyère found the novel 'one hundred per cent. pure' but also 'laboured' and 'rather dull', merely a 'pious tale'; Quennell expressed relief that Waugh had at last *abandoned* the pose of 'Catholic moralist' which had marred *Vile Bodies* and *Black Mischief*. Others made the usual comments on Waugh's 'amoral comedy', 'insubstantial' and 'fundamentally empty'.[56]

IX

In April 1934, as soon as *A Handful of Dust* was done, Waugh wrote to Mary Lygon:

> I have finished the G[ood] T[aste] book god it is G. T...I am going to live in Oxford all the summer and write a life of Gregory the Great.
> WHO WAS GREGRY THE GRATE?
> He was a famous Pope, Tommy.
> POPE GOES THE WEEZIL?
> No, be quiet and rub your cock like a good boy.
>
> (Hastings 301)

That spring and summer he neither went to Oxford nor wrote on St Gregory, but kept up instead a busy round of country-house visiting. In April, he visited Cyril Connolly and his wife in France. 'Evelyn very crusty and charming' noted Connolly in his diary; 'He is our valued friend – so mature and pithy, and religion apart, so frivolous. Made most of the people we see seem dowdy' (Pryce-Jones, *Connolly*, 242–3).

In July, at loose ends in London, Waugh chanced on Hugh Lygon, who was about to accompany Alexander Glen, an Oxford undergraduate writing a thesis, on a reconnoitre of Spitzbergen in preparation for the University Arctic Expedition the following year. Waugh asked to come along. Two days later, after hastily assembling a kit, he shipped out for seven weeks of rough travel among the glaciers of Norway. The journey ended with Waugh and Hugh falling into an icy river and losing their equipment, and all three trekking for three days (without food, maps, or even a tent) to their base seventy miles away. 'Just back from Spitzbergen, which was hell – a fiasco very narrowly retrieved from disaster', he told Tom Driberg at the end of August (L 88). Two years earlier he had written:

> Those for whom the attraction of travel is primarily anthropological will always be puzzled at the zeal which again and again has driven men to the hideous privations and dangers of the Arctic Circle. Here there is no lost culture to be discovered; no clues to be picked up that hint at the origins of our own social structure or creeds.
>
> ('The Cold North', *Spectator*, 18 June 1932, 869)

As he had predicted, Waugh gained from the experience of ice and snow material only for an article, 'The First Time I Went to the North: Fiasco in the Arctic'.[57]

Over the summer, too, Waugh changed the subject of his projected work of apologetic from St Gregory to Edmund Campion. According to Douglas Woodruff, Waugh grew interested in Campion while examining the manuscript collection at Stonyhurst, and through Woodruff's acquisition of the country house in which Campion was taken prisoner (HW 121–2). At the same time, Campion Hall, the Jesuit house at Oxford, was being rebuilt to plans by Edwin Lutyens and needed funds. 'I wished to do something to bear testimony to my delight in that occasion and to my gratitude to the then Master of the Hall, now the provincial of the English Province of the Society of Jesus, Father Martin d'Arcy' – *Campion's* dedicatee – 'to whom, under God, I owe my faith' (EC2a, Preface).

Christopher Hollis claimed that before 1935 Waugh's faith was not *'engagé'*; 'It was his study of Campion, his discovery of a man who thought that all must be sacrificed for religion, which was the great turning point in his life' (St John viii). In fact the book represented a stage in the increasing religious engagement begun at the time of his trip to South America. A historical work on the Reformation permitted Waugh to explore how the world of *A Handful of Dust*, eaten away by humanism and polite scepticism, came into being.

He explained to Peters that the project's whole proceeds would go to charity and that he would refuse other commitments until it was well along. (To no one else did Waugh advertise his generosity, in this or his many future charities: like the *hypocrite renversé* Jonathan Swift, Waugh enjoyed flaunting his acerbities while keeping his generosity and kindnesses private.) He worked on the 'pious book' (as its colophon makes clear) during stays at the Easton Court Hotel at Chagford, Mells, Belton and Newton Ferrers (the elegant establishment of his new friends Sir Robert and Lady Diana Abdy).

Composition took nine months, from September 1934 to May 1935, the most labour Waugh had yet invested in any book. It thus constituted a real sacrifice. He was used to living on the profits from a book published each year, along with essays and reviews. Not only did he sign away *Campion's* profits; researching and writing it left little time for other projects. No wonder he wrote often to Peters making sure that editors paid up for previous commitments. In that remarkably happy juncture of agent and client, Waugh felt free to write for infusions of 'dash, dough, tin, spondulicks, ready, off, doings or whatever it is', and to give his famous response to an offer of fifteen guineas from the BBC to write some dialogue for its series *Among the British Islanders* 'in which the chief character would be a Martian anthropologist collecting notes on Great Britain': 'B.B.C. L.S.D. N.B.G'.[58]

Graham Greene called *Edmund Campion: Jesuit and Martyr* 'a model of what a short biography should be' (CH 165). The form was well established in the early thirties, when 'several publishers brought out series of short, lively critical biographies of famous men and women, commissioned from noted authors. At least two hundred such appeared, and sold well' (Graves 298). Waugh did not claim to be an original historian, only to have synthesized known materials.

> There is great need for a complete scholar's book on the subject. This is not it. All I have sought to do is to select the incidents which strike a novelist as important and put them into a narrative which I hope may prove readable. The facts are not in dispute and I have, therefore, left the text unencumbered by notes or bibliography. It should be read as a simple, perfectly true story of heroism and holiness.[59]

The result is a powerful tale of the sort of heroism Waugh always found most moving: as he later wrote of Ronald Knox, 'The acts of heroism which he admired were acts of self-sacrifice' and submission (K 132). Unlike his novels to date, it presents an intensely optimistic vision of the moral possibilities of individual action: here the hero is at once victim and wholly successful man of action. Waugh takes Campion from his youth at Oxford, when he wanted nothing more than to be a man of letters but found his intellect unsatisfied by the new church of Elizabeth and Cecil; to Douai, where he resigned that church for Catholicism; to Rome, where he became a Jesuit, and Bohemia, where the army of the Counter-Reformation first sent him; and finally to England, where after a year of travelling in disguise from household to recusant household, he was caught, imprisoned, tortured, and executed – all without recanting, indeed without losing the gay and gallant spirit he possessed from the first. The story is told in Waugh's most finely controlled writing to date, in prose that though it modulates sometimes into restrained irony, sometimes into brief passages of aureate grandeur, keeps generally to a middle style of almost flamboyant purity, precision, and restraint – a style meant to reflect and convey Campion's 'accurate piety' and purity of purpose.

'I am very excited about the reception of Campion', he wrote to Katherine Asquith when the book appeared in September 1935, 'Just as a spinster with a first novel' (ST1 410). Given its celebration of a Jesuit executed for treason, he might well have expected critical response to be sharply divided. Predictably favourable reviews appeared in the Catholic press (with the exception of Old-meadow's *The Tablet*). *Campion* was the first of Waugh's books to be noticed by England's most prestigious Catholic journal, the Jesuit *Month*, which also took the opportunity to print a belated review of *A Handful of Dust*.[60] Yet non-Catholic reviewers were almost equally appreciative. Peter Quennell regretted Waugh's once again 'turn[ing] Catholic apologist', but found the book 'so well written and so full of life that we accept the bias as an incidental part of the author's narrative'; the TLS also professed alarm at Waugh's Catholic 'bias', but found him 'well read in the proper authorities' and 'better versed than most writers on the period in its religious dialectic'; the *Quarterly Review* praised Waugh's 'excellent spirit of fair-mindedness'. In 1936 *Campion* won the Hawthornden Prize, a prestigious annual award of £100 for the best work of imaginative literature by a British author under forty-one.[61]

Campion did engender one noisy, if inconsequential, public scuffle. When Waugh's friend Desmond MacCarthy reviewed it favourably on BBC radio, a hard-bitten controversialist named John Kensit, speaking for the United Protestant Council, wrote in protest both to the Director General of the BBC and to the BBC's new magazine, the *Listener*. To the Director Kensit wrote that the Corporation had chosen 'an unfit person to review historical or biographical books'; to the *Listener*, that had Waugh troubled to consult 'recently recovered Vatican documents at the Public Record Office', he would have known better than to portray Campion as an 'injured innocent who was not righteously executed under the laws of the Realm' (CH 166–71). MacCarthy ably replied, pointing out that even the *Cambridge Modern History* thought it a settled matter that Campion had visited England for pastoral rather than political reasons, and so that he was 'manifestly innocent' of the treasonable plot Elizabeth's government laid at his door. When Kensit did not let the matter rest, Waugh himself wrote to the *Listener*, pointing out that he indeed knew the documents in question (discovered not 'recently' but in 1886), and citing the chief authority on the

10 Receiving the Hawthornden Prize for *Edmund Campion*, June 1936 (Keystone Press).

subject, the Lutheran scholar Arnold Meyer's *England and the Catholic Church under Queen Elizabeth* (1916), to the effect that 'The attempt to prove conspiracy [against Campion] had failed entirely, and was bound to fail because the conspiracy had no existence'. Waugh ends, in a tone not unjustified by Kensit's:

> I am forced to the conclusion that Mr. Kensit has not read [my book] and that his rage is aroused, not that an inaccurate work should be unjustly commended, but that any book by a Catholic about a Catholic should be mentioned at all by anyone anywhere.
> What a funny man he must be.
>
> (EAR 185)

After *Campion* won the Hawthornden, the *Listener* having refused all further correspondence on the subject, Kensit hurried out under the imprint of the

Protestant Truth Society a 56-page pamphlet called *The Campion-Parsons Invasion Plot, 1580: The Jesuit Edmund Campion Martyr or Traitor? Queen Elizabeth's Secret Service Vindicated after 350 Years by the Recently Discovered Vatican Archives* (1937). The whole episode doubtless confirmed Waugh in his view that 'Religious controversy seems the occupation of the lowest minds nowadays' (D 345).

What is perhaps most surprising in the responses to *Campion* is that while attending so closely to Waugh's portrayal of his title character, non-Catholic reviewers missed the book's real polemical nerve. In the largest sense, as *The Month* recognized, *Campion* defends a specifically Catholic view of the English Reformation, rebutting the Protestant 'myth' of the period (enshrined in such texts as Charles Kingsley's virulently anti-papist *Westward Ho!*) 'that has so shamefully possessed our text-books and distorted the average perspective of the British schoolboy' (Oct. 1935, 377–8). Waugh begins his case in the book's opening pages, with their brilliant Stracheyan evocation of the last days of Queen Elizabeth, an 'old perjured woman, dying without comfort' (EC 6).

'What was in Elizabeth's mind as she lay there through the silent hours, sane and despairing?' Waugh does not answer directly. But he has shaped the scene to follow the tradition of the edifying deathbed, the tradition that at death, virtuous souls are vouchsafed a foretaste of heaven, reprobates of hell. Elizabeth suffers nightmare visions and alternating moods of self-pity and rage. When priests are brought 'their appearance roused her to fury'; like all souls in despair, she cannot pray. 'The Archbishop returned to her at the end, and a movement of her hand was interpreted by her ladies-in-waiting as her consent to his presence', but there is no final repentance and absolution. Elizabeth's miserable death, beautifully elaborated, contrasts with Campion's triumphant death at the end of the book. (It also reads like a dress-rehearsal for Lord Marchmain's dying bed in *Brideshead* – though with an opposite outcome – and reminds us that the later scene needs to be interpreted in light of Waugh's knowledge of the traditional *ars moriendi*, the art of dying well.)

Elizabeth's death leads to historical reflections on her age and its aftermath:

> In these circumstances the Tudor dynasty came to an end, which in three generations had changed the aspect and temper of England. They left a new aristocracy, a new religion, a new system of government; the generation was already in its childhood that was to send King Charles to the scaffold: the new, rich families who were to introduce the House of Hanover were already in the second stage of their metamorphosis from the freebooters of Edward VI's reign to the conspirators of 1688 and the sceptical, cultured oligarchs of the eighteenth century. The vast exuberance of the Renaissance had been canalised. England was secure, independent, insular; the course of her history lay plain ahead: competitive nationalism, competitive industrialism, competitive imperialism, the looms and coal mines and counting houses, the joint-stock companies and the cantonments; the power and the weakness of great possessions.

(EC 5–6)

Succeeding pages suggest even more clearly that Elizabeth dies despairing because she has presided over a tragic mistake. Her 'perjury' consists in having 'deposed her bishops, issued a heretical Prayer Book' – in short, 'violated her coronation oath' to defend the faith (42). Even the word 'insular', seemingly innocent in this first usage ('secure, independent, insular') takes on tragic meaning later. 'The official Anglican Church had cut itself off from the great surge of vitality that flowed from the Council [of Trent]; it was, by its own choice, insular and national' (26), deprived of contact with 'the spacious, luminous world of Catholic humanism' (13).

The opening vignette of Elizabeth thus begins to outline a position wholly at odds with familiar treatments of the Reformation as the time when England freed itself from the tyranny and benighted medievalism of Rome and so ensured its glorious future. Those early paragraphs also point to one of the main sources for Waugh's thinking about the period: Hilaire Belloc's popular *How the Reformation Happened* (1928), which also set out to show that the history 'taught in our schools and universities is an official story and a thoroughly false one' (Belloc 170). Waugh's reference to the energies of the Renaissance being 'canalised' echoes Belloc's judgment that 'The Reformation was essentially a diversion of the main stream of the Renaissance into narrower, incongruous channels, flowing in a different direction from that which the mighty stream of rediscovered culture would have followed, had it been left undisturbed'; his sketch of the future parallels Belloc's survey of the Reformation's fruit: 'the principle of competition', 'Industrial Capitalism', 'Subjectivism' and 'Nationalism' (Belloc 266–70).

In a chapter called 'The English Accident', Belloc argued that England's rupture with Rome was imposed from above on a largely 'unwilling people':

> There was no national movement against the Catholic Church in England: the little that happened at first was a government movement, and not even a doctrinal movement. What followed it was not a normal process generally desired by the people. It was an artificial process managed by a very few interested men, and these acting not on a religious fad, but for money.
>
> (Belloc 89)

'At the head of this vested interest', mainly 'new millionaires' profiting from the 'looting' of Church property, was William Cecil, an able manager in whose hands Elizabeth herself was merely a 'figurehead'. In the process of enriching themselves, the new men unwittingly created a 'class, which in a century, destroyed the monarchy' and ushered in those modern diseases, secularism and scepticism. Thus the Reformation 'deflected and warped the main development of our civilization'; Trent came too late to undo the damage, and 'the tardiness of the reaction is perhaps the main cause of our still increasing chaos' (Belloc 268, 209).

The English Reformation, Belloc stresses, 'was indeed what I have called it, a revolution' (115); Waugh carefully adopts the same term, speaking of 'the Tudor revolution' (EC 132). He follows Belloc in portraying Cecil as chief artificer of the destruction of English Catholicism and leader of the 'new, rich families' who would ultimately undermine the throne. Most important, Waugh too argues that 'the new Church attracted little enthusiasm' among common folk, who in the main preferred 'the traditional faith of their country'. In this way he can portray Catholicism in Campion's time as 'still national', 'something historically and continuously English' taken from the people 'by theft'.[62]

Reforming Protestant iconoclasts become in Waugh's account a race of Bollers, smashing sculptures and burning books, wrecking monasteries and churches to build their own new houses. As Campion pursues his ministry in the countryside, he sees everywhere around him 'the desolate monuments of the old orders', 'their memory still sweet with the gentleness and dignity of a lost age'. Belloc had argued that the Reformation initiated a process of secularization whereby, over time, 'the awful figure of a God Apparent faded into that of a mild young man at a loss' (12); as Campion surveys 'the scars of the Tudor revolution', Waugh points to the same development:

> The ruins were not yet picturesque; moss and ivy had barely begun their work, and age had not softened the stark lines of change. Many generations of orderly living, much gentle association, were needed before, under another queen, the State Church should assume the venerable style of *Barchester Towers*.
>
> (EC 132–3)

It is a short step to Tony Last's Hetton and the Anglicanism of Reverend Tendril.

Into this ruined landscape Campion brings 'the chivalry of Lepanto and the poetry of La Mancha, light, tender, generous and ardent' (113–14), a 'gallantry' and 'gaiety' Waugh identifies specifically – and provocatively – as the spirit of the Counter-Reformation. Not even Belloc had managed such romantic enthusiasm for Trent. To most Protestants (and liberal Catholics), the movement symbolized by Trent was an attempt to reinstate, often by force, a rigid, backward-looking faith. Waugh thought it 'a great source of vitality', something both necessary and stirringly heroic. 'For me Christianity begins with the Counter-Reformation', he wrote to Katherine Asquith (L 102). A remarkable passage celebrates St Pius V, whose bull *Regnans in Excelsis* excommunicated Elizabeth and released Britons from their obedience to her:

> His contemporaries and the vast majority of subsequent historians regarded the Pope's action as ill-judged. It has been represented as a gesture of mediaevalism, futile in an age of new, vigorous nationalism . . . and yet . . . a doubt rises, and a hope; had he, perhaps, in those withdrawn, exalted hours before his crucifix, learned something that was hidden from the statesmen of his time and the succeeding generations of historians; seen through and beyond the present and the immediate future; understood that there was to be no easy way of reconciliation, but that it was only through blood and hatred and derision that the faith was one day to return to England?
>
> (EC 44)

The passage drew many criticisms, the harshest from Rose Macaulay, who protested in 1946 that while *Campion* is 'a very readable and often moving book, and its brave and touching story beautifully told', Waugh goes too far in describing 'Pius V, with his notorious record as Grand Inquisitor, his incitement to murder and with his rejoicing over the massacre of the Huguenots', as 'a saint; this is surely to debase the currency of words'. But in 1935, when the news was full of the persecution of priests in Mexico, the Soviet Union, and Germany and when many felt, in Julian Symons's words, that 'the rebirth of Britain must come through chaos and catastrophe', Pius's vision of healing bloodshed must have seemed disturbingly topical.[63] Belloc had argued that if the Counter-Reformation had succeeded 'there would have been no Great War in 1914'; the Reformation fracturing of Europe, ushering in an era of virulently competing nationalisms, 'is perhaps the main cause of our still increasing chaos' (199, 209). By the mid-thirties, Waugh too had come to believe that not only the world of *A Handful of Dust* but the century's savagely divisive political ideologies were, as Roy Campbell put it in *Flowering Rifle* (1939), 'but the Reformation come to roost / Four hundred years after its rage was loosed'.

Waugh never lost the sense of himself as Tridentine counter-revolutionary, issuing repeated calls to order to defend the roots of his endangered culture. In 1955, locked in controversy with the vehemently anti-Catholic Professor Hugh Trevor-Roper (who had called Trent 'mumbo-jumbo' and likened Cardinal Bellarmine to Himmler), he tried to shock readers into considering what the Reformation had cost by putting forward the deliberately outrageous assertion that England would have been better off had the Spanish Armada triumphed: 'that for the fullest development of our national genius we required a third conquest' – presumably following those by Rome and the Normans – 'by Philip II of Spain' (EAR 467). Waugh did, however, outgrow Belloc's oversimple historical analysis (as well as his belief in the unique connection of 'Europe and the Faith'). Though *Campion* always remained one of his favourite books, he confessed two years after it appeared that it had been unbalanced. In 1937 he wrote in a review of Thomas Platter's *Travels* through Tudor England:

> In natural revulsion from the exuberant and unscrupulous liberal historians of the last century, it has lately become fashionable to see the age of Elizabeth as a sombre and threatening time in English history: the old queen, obscene, unprincipled and superstitious; a cutthroat court, extravagant and avaricious; an intelligentsia shrouded in the black despairs of Webster; a cranky and jealous bourgeoisie preparing the overthrow of the monarchy; a dispossessed and oppressed peasantry helpless under the upstart landowners – such in broad outlines has been the impression of the average Englishman educated during the last twenty years; such dissimilar impresarios as Lytton Strachey, Mr. Hilaire Belloc and the 'Left Book' boys have conspired to fix this picture in our minds. No doubt there is more truth in it than in that of the Kingsley–Froude school. It needed emphasizing; now the time has come for more sober reflection and a book like Thomas Platter's travels provides many surprises which make one question the bases of one's assumptions.
>
> (EAR 206)

In later years Waugh would make gentle fun of old Gervase Crouchback's attachment to a Bellocian reading of Anglicanism's founding in a power-grab by 'new rich men' (OG 20) and speak genially of R. H. Benson's efforts 'to rewrite in popular form the history of the English reformation' in novels 'as robustly tendentious as Charles Kingsley had shown himself on the Protestant side' (Reynal xiii). But these reconsiderations did not come until after Waugh unequivocally entered the maelstrom of thirties politics with an exercise in Bellocian rhetoric that won him more enemies than ever before, and from which his reputation never fully recovered: his defence of Italy's invasion of Abyssinia.

4

Political Decade – II (1935–1939)

During the past ten years literature has involved itself more and more deeply in politics.... As early as 1934 or 1935 it was considered eccentric in literary circles not to be more or less 'left', and in another year or two there had grown up a left-wing orthodoxy that made a certain set of opinions absolutely *de rigueur* on certain subjects. The idea had begun to gain ground...that a writer must either be actively 'left' or write badly. Between 1935 and 1939 the Communist Party had an almost irresistible fascination for any writer under forty. It became as normal to hear that so-and-so had 'joined' as it had been a few years earlier, when Roman Catholicism was fashionable, to hear that so-and-so had 'been received'. For about three years, in fact, the central stream of English literature was more or less directly under Communist control.

George Orwell, 'Inside the Whale' (1940)

I

In September 1934, when *A Handful of Dust* was about to be published and *Campion* just begun, Waugh announced through 'William Hickey' (Tom Driberg) that because of Peter Fleming's superior talent, he meant to give up travel writing.[1] Over the next months he contemplated such projects as a life of Mary Stuart and work as a Hollywood screenwriter. But meanwhile public interest in Ethiopia rekindled. Italian invasion seemed increasingly likely, especially after a confrontation between Ethiopian and Italian troops at Wal-Wal in December 1934. Haile Selassie had no need to call on his genius for publicity to persuade the British press once again to represent him as a hero, leader of an underdog nation threatened by a Fascist imperial power. As a member of the League of Nations, Ethiopia was entitled to protection of its borders according to the League's Covenant.

In February 1935 Waugh interrupted work on *Campion* to reiterate his views on Ethiopia in an article for Beaverbrook's *Evening Standard* called 'Abyssinian Realities: We Can Applaud Italy'. (The *Standard*'s line on the crisis was that 'the

whole of Abyssinia will sooner or later be acquired by Italy, but that Lord
Beaverbrook sees no reason why England should worry about it'.)[2] Waugh
had – and long kept – grave doubts about the likelihood of an Italian victory
against native guerrilla forces, but he applauded what he saw as Rome's civilizing mission. Against patronizing Europeans who 'like to imagine a medieval,
independent race living according to their own immemorial customs, just as they
like to find villages where the people still dance round maypoles in their national
costume', he once again stressed that 'Abyssinia is still a barbarous country',
citing especially the institution of slavery and the 'slave raids to which the natives
of all Abyssinia's neighbours are liable'. Once again he stressed that Ethiopia
was itself an imperialist state:

> 'But', the sentimentalists will complain, 'what *right* have Europeans to interfere? If
> people prefer to be badly governed by themselves, rather than well governed by
> foreigners, that is their business'. The answer is that throughout the greater part of
> the country the Abyssinians are just as much foreigners as the Italians. The proper
> title of Abyssinia is the Ethiopian Empire. It was taken by conquest a generation
> ago. The Emperor Menelik succeeded to a small hill kingdom and made himself
> master of a vast population differing absolutely from himself and his own people in
> race, religion and history. It was taken bloodily and is held, so far as it is held at all,
> by force of arms. In the matter of abstract justice, the Italians have as much right
> to govern; in the matter of practical politics, it is certain that their government
> would be for the benefit of the Ethiopian Empire and for the rest of Africa.
>
>   (EAR 163–4)

After explaining how difficult conquest would be – air power would not suffice,
while the terrain would render a land war precarious – he concluded: 'It will be
the supreme trial of Mussolini's regime. We can, with clear conscience, fold our
hands and await the news on the wireless'.

It was not, as enemies often claimed, Waugh's Catholicism that led him to
support the Italians.[3] English Catholics were divided on Italy's role in Africa,
and when fighting did begin, the *Tablet, Month,* and *Dublin Review* all came out in
favour of the Ethiopians. Nor as we shall see was Waugh led by his conservative
politics to any generalized support of Fascism: his distaste for Hitler and what he
called 'the clap-trap of Nazi patriotism' (NTD 95) was clear well before 1935.
Rather, he saw himself once again as the champion of civilization against
barbarism.

From the first Waugh knew that events in Ethiopia were tied to larger issues,
indeed that conflict there could spark another world war.[4] As Italian invasion
drew closer, he sought appointment as a foreign correspondent. This time he
had hopes not merely of producing a travel book but something bigger, 'a
serious war book' (L 100). In 1935 'anyone who had actually spent a few
weeks in Abyssinia itself, and had read the dozen or so books which constituted
the entire English bibliography of the subject, might claim to be an expert' (WA
40). But given overwhelming popular sympathy for the Ethiopians, Peters had
difficulty finding a paper willing to take on a professed supporter of Italy. Finally
Diana Cooper – the Mrs Stitch of *Scoop,* who in that novel persuades Lord

Copper to hire Boot – was able to persuade her friend Lord Rothermere to hire Waugh for the *Daily Mail*, one of the few newspapers to side with the Italians and so take what Waugh thought a 'realistic view' of Abyssinia.[5] Meanwhile rights to the war book were put out to bid; Tom Burns at Longmans came in highest, offering the large advance of £950 – testimony to both Waugh's stature and public interest in the conflict.

Once again high hopes were to issue in disappointment. He left on the familiar route to East Africa on 6 August 1935 and arrived in Addis Ababa two weeks later, delighted to discover his old friend Patrick Balfour representing the *Evening Standard*. On the 24th the *Mail* gave two columns to 'Evelyn Waugh's Vivid Addis Ababa Cable', 'War Certain in Few Weeks', the first of some sixty by-lined articles the paper would run. But relations between Waugh and his employer soon turned to disgust on both sides; his despatches received less and less prominence, until finally at the end of November, by mutual consent, the *Mail* replaced him and he decided to return home.

The story of what went wrong is told in *Waugh in Abyssinia*, the war book into which his great plans finally dwindled, and again in only slightly fantasticated form in *Scoop*. Waugh was *persona non grata* in the capital: the Ethiopians knew of his support for Italy and so considered him an Italian spy; there was no hope of information from the British legation, where the Bartons were still smarting from their transformation into the Courteneys of *Black Mischief*. (On one evening in town the envoy's daughter Esmé threw a glass of champagne in Waugh's face.) And there was too much competition. Foreign media invested heavily in Ethiopia, and by the time war broke out in October more than 120 reporters had arrived, crowding three and four to a room in the city's few ramshackle hotels.

Worst of all, as Waugh wrote home, 'There is no news and no possibility of getting any' (L 97). Editors were ready to pay the nearly five shillings per word in gold demanded by the Ethiopian Press Ministry for cables – one of the highest rates in the world, and source of the lingo of abbreviations called 'cablese'. (This special language, including terms such as 'slongs' for 'so long as' and 'exyou' for 'from you', sometimes produced despatches so cryptic that reporters did not recognize their own stories once editors had unscrambled and expanded them.) Waugh was not alone in receiving frantic wires from his employers demanding news, or, short of that, 'colour' pieces. But before October there was no war. The government confined reporters to Addis, providing only sporadic, carefully prepared press releases calculated to give the outside world the picture of a united nation ready to rise at any time to repel the invader. 'The commands of Fleet Street became more and more fantastically inappropriate to the situation' (WA 74).

Reporters hired native spies in a vain attempt to find something, anything worth cabling home. As a practical joke, the *Daily Express* correspondent O. D. Gallagher faked a cable to George Steer of *The Times*, purporting to be from the *Times*'s proprietor: 'WE NATION PROUD YOUR WORK STOP CARRY ON IN NAME YOUR KING AND COUNTRY – ASTOR'. Gallagher knew how incoming cables were delivered: illiterate runners waited until a pile had accumulated, then carried the lot from hotel to hotel, asking each foreigner they met to pick out any that might be for him. By the time Steer got his cable, the whole city, even Haile Selassie, knew of it; Steer told London: 'The Emperor has given me the longest interview on record – eighty minutes'. Gallagher ruefully considered faking another cable, this time to himself (Knightley 174–5).

Eventually, as Waugh had seen before in 1930, reporters simply began inventing news. But now he encountered fraud on a new scale, of the sort George Orwell later found in Spain, where news reports 'did not bear any relation to the facts, not even the relationship which is implied in an ordinary lie. I saw great battles reported where there had been no fighting, and complete silence where hundreds of men had been killed'.[6] Though more sympathetic than Waugh to Haile Selassie, Balfour's delightful account of his experiences reporting the war, 'Fiasco in Addis Ababa', fully corroborates Waugh's picture of journalistic practices there. This side of the war has been well chronicled by Phillip Knightley, and an understanding of it is crucial to any effort to evaluate Waugh's reporting and comments like the one he made to Diana Cooper as early as 13 September 1935: 'all lying like hell & my job to sit here contradicting the lies they write' (DC 52).

Gallagher's experiences in Addis reporting for the *Daily Express* were not unusual. In September he received a series of cables from his editor demanding material comparable to the stirring (and wholly imaginary) stories being sent to the *Telegraph* by Percival Phillips:

> This sort of wild romancing I was now witnessing actually shocked me, but...I was not going to let Phillips get away with it – especially when I found out that some of his best passages had been paraphrased from an old book called *In the Country of the Blue Nile*, by Colonel C. F. Rey. So with help from Noel Monks [an Australian colleague] I wrote a piece based on Colonel Rey's travels, up-dating it and using it in the terms and situations of the Abyssinian War, and sent it off. The *Express* liked it, so, pleased with my success in this new style of journalism, I did some descriptive stuff about the country, the tribes and their customs, the wild life that the Italians would encounter when they advanced into Abyssinia. I got congratulations each day for a week and the final one came on a Saturday. It said, 'PHILLIPS BRILLIANT IN TELEGRAPH BUT YOU EXCEL HIM STOP KEEP IT UP'.

Gallagher and Monks were astounded. 'Well, now we know', said Monks; 'It's entertainment they want' (Knightley 177).

Matters only got worse when fighting actually began and still the government refused to allow reporters to leave the capital. Mussolini had allowed a few correspondents into Eritrea to cover events from the Italian side, though they were initially allowed to transmit only laconic releases prepared by the Italians. So editors in London and New York naturally preferred to print the more colourful inventions coming from Addis Ababa, full of stirring quotations from the Emperor and tales of Ethiopian victories won against great odds. (One widely publicized Ethiopian victory, in which 700 Italian casualties were reported, turned out to have been an Italian victory won at the cost of six men.) These stories served in turn to cement public sympathy for the Ethiopians, and so editors continued to print the inventions from Addis even after reporters in Eritrea were given freedom of movement and began to paint a quite different picture. The *New York Times* correspondent on the Italian side, Herbert Matthews, found that whenever he and his counterpart in Addis cabled about the same battles, editors in New York ignored Matthews's eyewitness accounts, preferring to print instead the rosier news distributed by Selassie's Press Ministry.

Of course, not all reporting from Eritrea was truthful either. Joe Caneva of the Associated Press later revealed that some of his most widely published combat photographs had depicted elaborately staged mock-battles, for which the Italians were only too willing to loan him soldiers and tanks. Matthews estimated that 'of all the photographs published of the war, ninety-nine out of a hundred had been faked' (Knightley 186). It wasn't until March 1936 that most newspapers 'began to give preference to the Italian bulletins' (WA 214) and so to admit what had long been clear from that front: that the Italians were winning. To explain this seemingly sudden turn of events, editors gave wide play to stories about Italian use of mustard gas and bombing of Red Cross outposts (meanwhile ignoring the same reporters' mention of Ethiopian dum-dum bullets and decapitation of Italian prisoners).

By this time Addis Ababa had emptied of reporters. They had begun to leave the previous November, in despair of ever getting to the front. Many waited, hoping for the day they could report the Emperor's departure to lead his troops in person; when this happened in early December, the cable office was forbidden to transmit the information.[7] By Christmas, when Waugh left, only a dozen of the original 120 journalists remained. Laurence Stallings of Movietone News – who had sent home miles of 'battle' footage, using firecrackers in place of bombs – left complaining: 'I've spent one hundred thousand dollars US and I haven't got one shot of the war' (Knightley 181–2).

In letters home Waugh not only criticized his colleagues but (more often) mourned his own failings as a reporter. 'All the others beat me on all news'; 'I am a very bad journalist' (DC 55; L102). The *Daily Mail* agreed. But considering how the war was reported, one might well conclude that if Waugh was a journalistic failure it was because he was a poor liar. Even those of his despatches most favourable to the Italian side were just that; he didn't fabricate mobilizations, battles, or casualty lists, or participate in what he called the 'inverted time lag' whereby others cabled their stories home days or weeks before the events described actually occurred (WA 164).

In fact Waugh had four 'scoops', though all were overshadowed by other events or went unrecognized at the time. On 26 August his newly hired spy Wazir Ali Beg passed on information about Italian troop movements in Eritrea; the story appeared in London the next week, followed by Italian denials. (A month later Waugh's facts were verified, resulting in Ethiopian mobilization.) In early September, Waugh and Patrick Balfour managed where many other reporters had failed, getting official permission to travel briefly outside the capital. Like most observers in Addis, they supposed that any Italian invasion would come from the south; they received permission to travel to Harar, of which Waugh had fond memories from his earlier trip, and then to proceed further south to Jijiga. At the second town Balfour's spy, nicknamed Mata Hari, unearthed a second scoop: the information that the French Consul there, a Count Drogafoi, had been thrown in prison for spying. The information turned out to be true; Waugh and Balfour had an exclusive; they sent their reports to British Somalialand to be cabled back to London. The next day they chanced on a Turk named Wehib Pasha who was known recently to have 'left Addis in the greatest secrecy': 'His disgust at seeing us was highly gratifying' (WA 107). Mata Hari turned up the information that he had come south to supervise the digging of a defensive line of lion pits, later to be much commented on in other news reports: another exclusive.

On returning to Harar, Waugh and Balfour found telegrams from their editors – not the congratulations they expected, but impatient demands for news of a yet bigger story that had broken in the capital during their absence. Waugh had travelled up from Djibouti to Addis in the company of a mysterious Englishman named F. W. Rickett; the two stayed in the same hotel; Rickett promised some important news, but so often deferred announcing it that Waugh assumed a few days travelling would do no harm. Waugh and Balfour rushed back to Addis to discover that in their absence Rickett had completed his mission and given Phillips his story. The representative of an American 'African Exploration and Development Corporation', Rickett had successfully negotiated with the Emperor for mineral rights to a vast area of Ethiopia – including the territory separating the Addis from Italy's troops. (Selassie hoped to secure American interest in his country, so that if Italy invaded, the United States would come to his aid; but the US State Department immediately repudiated the agreement.) Waugh and Balfour's stories from Jijiga were printed only after the Rickett affair blew over, by which time other reporters had got wind of them too.

The loss of Waugh's last and greatest scoop has become legend. Though he could hope for little information from the Ethiopians or the English, Waugh's political allegiances put him on good terms with the Italian consul in Addis, Count Vinci, whose cool-headedness in the delicate position of hostile national in Ethiopia's capital Waugh admired. At the end of September, Vinci told Waugh that he meant to leave Addis as soon as the rainy season ended. Waugh knew what such a decision meant: that Vinci had orders from Rome to leave, and that the long-awaited Italian invasion would soon follow. To protect his exclusive Waugh cabled to London in Latin. His editors at the *Mail* knew no Latin, thought the transmission gibberish, and complained of his joke. By the time matters were clarified the story was once again not Waugh's alone.

On 2 October, with the Italian bombing of Adowa (the city where they had been defeated in 1895), the war officially began. Still reporters were not allowed to leave the capital. Waugh settled into boring weeks of drinking and gambling with his colleagues, lightened only by a telegram from Alec's wife letting him know that his old enemy Cruttwell had failed to win a parliamentary election. ('It was delightful of you and Alec to cable the news of Cruttwell's ignominy. It has made my week' (ST1 412).) For one briefly interesting moment, the government tried to capitalize on reports of Italian bombings of a Red Cross hospital;

Waugh and his colleagues checked the story, found it a fake, and cabled home 'Nurse Unupblown'. In mid-November reporters were allowed to travel to Dessye, where a week later the Emperor came to set up headquarters. Still there was no news. By the end of the month Waugh heard from London that the *Mail*, frustrated at the little their correspondent had sent them, no longer wanted his services. The official letter of dismissal explained, 'From the beginning this has been a disappointing war to us'.

Still convinced that Ethiopia's terrain and guerrilla fighters would thwart Italian victory,[8] Waugh stayed on in Addis till-mid-December, when at last he boarded the familiar train down to Djibouti. Here he once again met Percival Phillips, still generating imaginary news for the *Telegraph*. (An editor says of 'Hitchcock' (Phillips) in *Scoop*: 'You'll be surprised to find how far war correspondents keep from the fighting. Why, Hitchcock reported the whole Abyssinia campaign from Asmara and gave us some of the most colourful eye-witness stuff we ever printed' (S41).) He then proceeded to Jerusalem, fulfilling a longstanding desire to spend Christmas in the Holy Land. It was here in 1935 that Waugh first recorded his intention to write about St Helena (L 103). In January he returned to England via Rome, where Diana Cooper was serving as informal British emissary to Mussolini. Perhaps with her help he was able to have a brief audience with Il Duce at the Palazzo Venezia. Expecting to meet the preposterous figure familiar from the press, Waugh was favourably impressed (Sykes 226). He was home by the end of the month, just in time for the *Listener* controversy over *Campion* in February.

For six weeks in April and May 1936, Waugh secluded himself in a house lent by the Brownlows trying to turn the previous autumn's disappointments into a book that could justify Longmans' advance. As usual when he worked on a non-fiction project, his interest kindled slowly. 'If the book bores its readers half as much as it is boring me to write', he wrote in April to Daphne Acton, sister of Douglas Woodruff's wife Mia, 'it will create a record in low sales for poor Mr Burns' (ST1 418). In June he told Diana Cooper, 'The Abyssinian book is quite honourable and readable but no one will want to read it by the time it comes out' (DC 61). His anxiety over the book's timeliness was justified. Public attention was already shifting away from Africa. In March Hitler's troops had occupied the Rhineland; in July would come news of war in Spain. But when haste was most needed, further events in Africa conspired to defer the book's completion.

In March and April 1936, though it became clear that the Italians were winning, Waugh like most others thought no great changes would come soon – that the war would 'drag on without incident until the big rains; peace terms disappointing to both sides and heavy with future changes would be devised and accepted' (WA 210). But suddenly Ethiopian resistance collapsed. On 2 May Hailie Selassie fled the country, and by 5 May the Italians reached Addis Ababa, having attacked not from the south but the north. The whole story thus took a shape no one had foreseen; Waugh had first-hand material only about its beginnings. Another trip to Africa would be necessary so that his book could have an ending. And he needed that ending fast.

Travel in occupied Ethiopia required Italian permission, for which Waugh applied at the beginning of June; approval came seven weeks later, on 22 July. While waiting he stayed with his parents at their new house in Highgate, where they had moved when Underhill became too large to manage. He oversaw publication of the first chapters of the new book, under the title 'The Disappointing War', in Douglas Jerrold's ultra-conservative *English Review* (no other magazine had accepted them). In June he received the Hawthornden prize and attended as a guest of honour at the dedication of the new Campion Hall; in July, while he reviewed a French traveller's exaggerated tales of Abyssinian atrocities (EAR 174–6), *Mr Loveday's Little Outing* appeared.

Finally, on 29 July, Waugh left for his third and last visit to Abyssinia. A stop in Rome was necessary to secure a visa; here he also succeeded in badgering an official into agreeing that the Italian government pay his fare to Africa. He was to be the first foreign journalist allowed into the new colony. The more he saw of the victors the less he liked them. Even before leaving Italy, he wrote to Katherine Asquith: 'It was fun being pro-Italian when it was an unpopular and (I thought) losing cause. I have little sympathy with these exultant fascists now' (L 109).

Arriving in Djibouti on 18 August, he found an old acquaintance who retailed hair-raising tales of native guerrillas making the occupation far more precarious than Rome had let on. 'Truth appears to be Wops in jam' (D 398). Italian troops in Addis, too, were anxious: 'Wops gave me guard with machine gun to go to dinner. Pensione Germanica full of apprehension attack and rising in town' (D 401). Coming days convinced him that Italian control was more secure than these initial impressions suggested, but did not reconcile him to the victors. 'When taxed with filth of town Italians say, "We are in Africa." Bad omen if they regard tropics as excuse for inferior hygiene. Reminded that they are race who have inhabited and created the slums of the world' (D 402). On another occasion he was repelled by a 'Fascist meeting in honour of German consul' with its 'Speeches in praise of Hitler': 'thought last night that I had never been in a city so full of unhappy people' (D 401).

His opinion of the Italians began to improve only after meeting the military governor, Marshall Graziani ('Very fresh and businesslike. No Fascist speeches'). Graziani offered to show him whatever he wished. Waugh turned down the chance to visit the southern front, where fighting was still heavy; instead he went north to inspect areas where the occupation had had most time to take effect. On 30 August he flew to Eritrea, where he was met by the Signor Franchi so memorably described in *Waugh in Abyssinia*, all politeness because he expected his visitor to be a woman. For a week Franchi drove Waugh hundreds of miles back into Abyssinia over the 'magnificent' new system of roads the Italians had built. At last content that he had seen evidence of new civilization taking root in Abyssinia, he left on 7 September by Italian military aircraft, convinced 'The new regime is going to succeed' (WA 241).

Longmans was by now impatient for a completed manuscript. Waugh proceeded to Mells to finish, though even here there were distractions: other books on Abyssinia appeared that he needed to read, and so also reviewed; news came from Germany that Hugh Lygon had died in an accidental fall.[9] Two final chapters on the Italian occupation were done on 2 October; in only three weeks, Longmans rushed the book into print. Waugh wanted to call it *The Disappointing War*, but Longmans refused, naming it instead – to his disgust – *Waugh in Abyssinia*. To his further disappointment – not merely financial, but because he meant the book as a serious political treatise, one that would rebut the charges of political naïveté made against *Remote People* – no publisher could be found to bring out an American edition.

Written in short bursts over a long period, *Waugh in Abyssinia* is a patchwork of three parts. It begins with a long chapter of historical background, an expansion of earlier essays such as 'Abyssinian Realities' coyly titled 'The Intelligent Woman's Guide to the Ethiopian Question'. (Even hostile reviewers agreed that this chapter provides 'a very fine piece of lucid condensation'.)[10] There follow four central chapters narrating his experiences as a reporter in Addis; these provide much of the comic material later to animate *Scoop*, and here serve to demonstrate the untrustworthiness of nearly all Western reporting of the war. (Reviewers found these middle sections funny or tendentious, according to political taste.) Finally come the two new chapters, 'Addis Ababa during the First Days of the Italian Empire' and 'The Road'. It was these chapters' full-throated celebration of the Italian occupation, symbolized by its new roads, that provoked profound anger from the Left, both in 1936 and later. 'The Road' concludes:

> And from Dessye new roads will be radiating to all points of the compass, and along the roads will pass the eagles of ancient Rome, as they came to our savage ancestors in France and Britain and Germany, bringing some rubbish and some mischief; a good deal of vulgar talk and some sharp misfortunes for individual opponents; but above and beyond and entirely predominating, the inestimable gifts of fine workmanship and clear judgment – the two determining qualities of the human spirit, by which alone, under God, man grows and flourishes.
>
> (WA 253)

On the basis of passages such as this Rose Macaulay, looking back in 1946, called *Waugh in Abyssinia* a 'blast of triumph over the Italian conquest' and a 'Fascist tract'. Similar attacks were mounted at the time by reviewers such as David Garnett.[11]

What the rhetoric of these final chapters was meant to achieve has not been sufficiently attended to. The reference to 'fine workmanship' is a framing device like those in the novels. From the first Waugh had argued a preference for Italian imperialism over Amharic, on the ground that the latter was 'imperialism devoid of a single redeeming element':

> The Abyssinians had nothing to give their subject peoples, nothing to teach them. They brought no crafts or knowledge, no new system of agriculture, drainage or roadmaking, no medicine or hygiene, no higher political organization, no superiority except in their magazine rifles and belts of cartridges. They built nothing.
>
> (WA 25–6)

There was no Abyssinian middle class. The lowest manual labour and the highest administrative posts were reserved for them; bullying and being bullied. They had no crafts. It was extraordinary to find a people with an ancient and continuous habit of life who had produced so little. They built nothing.

(WA 64)

(As always in Waugh, a nation is judged by the quality of private life it fosters, especially as exemplified in the arts produced by its 'middle class'.)

'The Road' is thus meant to function like the final chapters of Walter Scott's historical novels. Scott established the pattern in *Waverley*: a dangerously violent, if picturesque, old order gives way to a peaceful and productive new one; once the old order has successfully been quelled, what had before seemed its defects can be appreciated in the way we appreciate museum pieces, as 'art'. Whereas earlier in the book Waugh had stressed that Abyssinian peoples 'built nothing', in 'The Road' he pauses to survey works of native architecture. There is a 'finely built sixth-century mausoleum' outside Adowa; Makale 'seemed to be a place of castles'. Adowa itself is an 'imposing city' whose builders 'retain[ed] a sense of architecture from their ancient civilization' (250–1). Waugh meant his ending (which follows immediately after these descriptions of native architecture) to suggest that the Italian engineers were reviving and bringing to fruition native traditions too long left by inept governors (such as Haile Selassie) to decay.

But there remains the question whether Waugh's conservatism ever veered to Fascism.

II

In an essay on Belloc written after the Second World War, Waugh returned to the subject of his early support for Mussolini. Belloc 'saw Mussolini, as did many lesser men (the present reviewer among them) as a hopeful portent.' So, for differing reasons, had figures as diverse as Lady Astor, Neville Chamberlain, Winston Churchill, Harold Nicolson and H. G. Wells. 'No one could then foresee that Italy would be jerked into alliance with Germany' (EAR 474). Waugh's position was both simple and easily misunderstood: 'I am not a Fascist nor shall I become one unless it were the only alternative to Marxism', he wrote in 1937. 'It is mischievous to suggest that such a choice is imminent'.

Name-calling was rife in the thirties. Just as a Conservative or Liberal might call his opponents Bolshevist, any opponent of socialism was liable to be labelled Fascist. In a letter of March 1938 to the *New Statesman* Waugh protested this loose language:

There was a time in the early twenties when the word 'Bolshie' was current. It was used indiscriminately of refractory schoolchildren, employees who asked for a rise in wages, impertinent domestic servants, those who advocated an extension of the rights of property to the poor, and anything or anyone of whom the speaker disapproved....

I believe we are now in danger of a similar, stultifying use of the word 'Fascist'.... When rioters are imprisoned it is described as a 'Fascist sentence'; the Means Test is Fascist; colonization is Fascist; Buchmanism is Fascist; the ancient Japanese cult of their Emperor is Fascist; the Galla tribes' ancient detestation of theirs is Fascist; fox-hunting is Fascist.... Is it too late to call for order?

(EAR 223)

Such protests grew increasingly necessary as Britain entered the 'war against Fascism'.[12]

After Mussolini made accommodation with the Vatican in the Lateran Treaty of 1929, it became possible for British Catholics to support him, if only *faute de mieux*. Some developed real enthusiasm for his rebuilding of Italy. Chesterton saw in Mussolini's successes nothing less than *The Resurrection of Rome* (1930), the return to Italy of 'civilization'. Chesterton made much of the renewed 'flight of the Roman eagles', and described a Fascist meeting in Rome:

> I have seen men climbing the steep stones of the Capitol carrying the eagles and the *labellum* that were carried before Marius and Pompey.... I have seen a forest of human hands lifted in a salute that is three thousand years older than all the military salutes of modern armies... the very faces of the crowd carrying the eagles or the Fasces are not the shifty obliterated faces of a modern mob, but those faces of the old Roman busts.
>
> (*Rome* 194–5)

Waugh's description in 'The Road' of modern Italians carrying 'the eagles of ancient Rome' into a barbaric land owed less to Fascist rhetoric itself (which he despised) than to Chesterton and Belloc. Nor were such views of Abyssinian barbarism and Italy's civilizing mission confined to Catholics. In October 1935, after the war in Abyssinia had begun, George Bernard Shaw wrote to *The Times* celebrating the 'well engineered and policed' roads ('the first material necessity' in any developed society) whereby the Italians, like the legions of 'ancient Rome', were spreading 'European civilization' among 'primitive tribesmen'. 'As between the Danakil warrior and the Italian engineer', Shaw wrote, 'I am on the side of the engineers'.[13]

Despite a few influential sympathizers such as Lords Nuffield (owner of Morris Motors) and Rothermere (the *Mail*), Fascism in any sense more profound than this never made headway in England. So far was it 'from enjoying any measure of popularity in England', explains Alastair Hamilton in his study of *The Appeal of Fascism*, 'that it seems absurd to ask why it failed' (127). 'Mosley and his pimpled followers' in the British Union of Fascists were 'a joke to the majority of English people' said Orwell in 1937, when the BUF was at its height (but still had only a quarter the membership of the CPB) (*Wigan* 186). Waugh was never drawn to Mosley's Blackshirts or plans for industrial reorganization, much less to Nazism. But to him and many others, Italy seemed a different case. 'There appeared to be nothing particularly aggressive about Italian Fascism until the invasion of Ethiopia in 1935, and nothing truly unjust about the régime' until Mussolini shifted his allegiance to Germany and, in 1938, began to enact racialist legislation of his own (Hamilton 257–8).

Most important, until the end of 1936 Mussolini was Britain's ally against Germany. From the start Mussolini had regarded Hitler as a dangerous gangster;

in a speech of 1934 he called the Nazi regime 'drunk with bellicosity' and 'one hundred per cent racism. Against everything and everyone: yesterday against Christian civilization, today against Latin civilization, tomorrow, who knows, against the civilization of the whole world' (Johnson 319). Catholics were especially aware, as Waugh said, that Italy's 'interests in Austria were directly opposed to Hitler's' (EAR 184); given the Nazi record of religious persecution, 'Mussolini appeared not so much the embodiment of Fascism, but Hitler's rival' and 'the only barrier preventing Nazi Germany's annexing Catholic Austria' (Gallagher, EAR 158). The major purpose of *Waugh in Abyssinia* was to persuade British readers not to sacrifice an ally against both Nazism and Communism merely over the war in Africa.

When Hitler formally repudiated the Treaty of Versailles in March 1935, Mussolini initiated meetings at Stresa inviting Britain and France to join in a 'front' against Germany. He expected in return that his allies would not interfere whilst Italy sought to recapture the colony it had lost in 1895. Even before Stresa he had visibly been moving troops to Africa. True, Abyssinia was a member of the League of Nations, but just a few years earlier the League had stood passively by as Japan conquered Manchuria and broke the London Naval Treaty; it could do so again now, as Italy (in its own view) simply reclaimed property guaranteed it at Versailles.

Instead, when Abyssinia protested the bombing of Adowa in October 1935, the League, pressed by Anthony Eden, declared Italy the aggressor and voted to impose sanctions. Shaw called Eden either 'stark mad' or 'blinded by imperialist jealousy'; Churchill too opposed the sanctions, fearing they would alienate a crucial ally: 'Those of us who saw in Hitler's Germany a danger, not only to peace but to survival, dreaded [the] movement of a first-class Power, as Italy was then rated, from our side to the other'.[14] Application of the sanctions was halfhearted at best – France continued to sell oil to the Italians; England did not even close the Suez Canal. Chamberlain correctly called the whole policy 'the very midsummer of madness'. The ineffectual sanctions were finally scrapped – but not before they had stiffened the resolve for war both of the Italians, who felt betrayed, and the Abyssinians, who drew the false hope that members of the League would take action on their behalf. Thus, as Waugh wrote to *The Times* in May 1936, the League and Britain ensured 'the maximum of immediate suffering and future bitterness' (EAR 187). 'The misfortunes that have fallen upon both peoples – the slaughter and terror on one side, the crippling expenditure on the other – are primarily due to the policy pursued by the British government' (WA 46).

And as a direct result of the sanctions, Mussolini also began to shift allegiances in Europe. In mid-1936 he started accepting emissaries from Hitler in Rome; on 1 November, he declared a 'Rome-Berlin Axis'. Waugh noted a few months later: 'The results of English diplomacy are already apparent. Italy and Germany who in 1934 seemed irreconcilable opponents are now in close and formidable alliance' (EAR 194).

The problem with *Waugh in Abyssinia* really was, as he told Lady Diana, that events so quickly outran it. Not only did the war in Spain eclipse Abyssinia. The book appeared just as the developments it sought to avert were irretrievably in motion. In 1946 Waugh omitted its 'many pages of historical summary and political argument' from *When the Going Was Good*, but also said that in rereading them he 'found little to retract'.[15]

The key to Waugh's politics in the thirties is his rejection of the conventional oppositions of Right and Left, Fascist and Communist, which he viewed simply as alternative totalitarianisms equally opposed to what he called 'individualism'. Refusing 'to be misled by the preposterous distinctions of Left and Right that make nonsense of contemporary politics' ('as meaningless and mischievous as the circus colours of the Byzantine Empire'), Waugh argued that there was 'a single proletarian movement aimed at the destruction of traditional culture'; 'remove the sentimental obsessions – the schoolgirl "crush" on the leader, the chivalrous concern for the under-dog – and there is basic agreement' (EAR 227, 246). Though the kinship of Communism and Fascism has become a common-place among historians, it was relatively rare in the partisan thirties for observers to step back and note, in the words of an editorial in the *Month*, that 'The Fascist, the Nazi, the Bolshevik all spring from the same diabolical root – the deification of the civil power'. 'Fascism as a reaction from Communism has its attractions', the journal added, 'but Catholics, at any rate, should be alive to the evil at its heart' (Sept. 1935, 195).

Fascism had its attractions because Communism, with its longer record of religious persecution and its totalist world-view, appeared the greater evil. Fascism, as Waugh put the case, was a 'rough improvisation', its policies merely 'opportunist' (MA 5). In Italy in the 1920s 'The party came to power without any very clear ideas about its policy. Signor Mussolini believed that the first thing was to establish a government, restore order, get the nation back to work and then see what was to be done with it' (EAR 194). So too in the next decade 'Hitler's acts were irrational dooms' (EAR 467). But Communism was based on a philosophy: on an explicitly atheist creed, a utopian 'faith, like a Christian's' (WS 214) that claimed to encompass all of life, to explain the *telos* of human life and history. In all this Waugh followed the influential analysis of Christopher Dawson, who, following Georges Sorel's *Reflections on Violence* (1908), argued in *Religion and the Modern State* (1935) – a work Waugh seems to have read with care – that 'Communism challenges Christianity on its own ground by offering mankind a rival way of salvation', standing 'over against the Christian Church as a *counter-church* with its own dogmas and its own moral standards, ruled by a centralized hierarchy and inspired by an intense will to world conquest' (58).

Thus Waugh's position on the most publicized conflict of the decade, the war in Spain, which divided contemporaries far more deeply than had Abyssinia. The great majority of writers and intellectuals sided passionately with the 'Republicans'. An equally great majority of Catholics, seeing the conflict (in Thomas Merton's words) as 'essentially a religious war ... of modern godlessness against God and the Catholic Church', supported Franco's 'Nationalists' (*Siloe* 211). Waugh's Catholic friends varied in opinion from Arnold Lunn, who argued in *Spanish Rehearsal* (1937) that Franco's alliance with Fascism was distasteful but necessary to combat the Communist Republicans and their atrocities against the Church, to the historian Douglas Jerrold, a genuine Fascist sympathizer who thought Franco's 'the first battle for Christianity in the West since the defeat of the Ottoman Turks in 1683' and who told proudly how he had helped arrange Franco's airline flight from the Canary Islands to Morocco on the eve of the rising.[16] Waugh himself briefly considered travelling as a reporter alongside his sister-in-law Gabriel, who went like Cordelia in *Brideshead* to work among the doctors and ambulances on Franco's side. But at a time when thousands of other writers made their sympathies known (and many went to fight), Waugh – who might have been expected to speak out, to join his fellow Catholics, and to oppose liberal intellectuals – kept remarkably quiet.

Waugh understood Spain from the first as a proxy war, between forces armed on one side by Stalin, on the other by Hitler and Mussolini – what Arthur Koestler, reflecting on his years as a Comintern agent, called 'a battle in the mist' where 'those who suffered and died were pawns in a complicated game between the two totalitarian pretenders for world domination' (*Invisible Writing* 325). Waugh gave public support to neither side, but instead called for a cooling of tempers. Reviewing Billy Clonmore's discussion in *Pius XI and World Peace* (1937) of 'the issue that most distracts Christendom – the civil war in Spain', he wrote: 'Here, where so many Catholics are more papal than the Pope, Lord Clonmore writes with laudable temperance'.[17] But his was a position difficult to make understood when others were 'hysterically disposed to one political extreme or the other' (ND 116) – when, as Roy Campbell (who converted to Catholicism in Spain) said, 'anyone who was not pro-Red in the Spanish War automatically became a "fascist"' (Hoskins 56).

In December 1937 a group at the *Left Review* led by Nancy Cunard and Brian Howard sent out a questionnaire, a broadsheet over a foot in length, strikingly printed in red and black, asking British authors to state in six lines or less their views on the war, the results to be printed in a pamphlet called *Authors Take Sides*. The questioners were confident how the survey would turn out, but to be safe posed the issue in a form that ensured the proper answers – 'Are you for, or against, the legal government and the people of Republican Spain? Are you for, or against, Franco and Fascism?' – and omitted querying more than a handful of writers known to disagree.[18] Of 148 responses, 126 were 'For' the Republicans; Sixteen (including those by T. S. Eliot, Ezra Pound and Alec Waugh) were classed as 'Neutral'; one (Shaw) was 'Unclassifiable'; and five were counted 'Against' the Republicans, including Waugh's:

> I know Spain only as a tourist and a reader of the newspapers. I am no more impressed by the 'legality' of the Valencia government than are English Communists by the legality of the Crown, Lords and Commons. I believe it was a bad government, rapidly deteriorating. If I were a Spaniard I should be fighting for General Franco. As an Englishman I am not in the predicament of choosing between two evils. I am not a Fascist nor shall I become one unless it were the only alternative to Marxism. It is mischievous to suggest that such a choice is imminent.
>
> (EAR 187)

The response scarcely differs from Sean O'Faolain's 'Neutral' reply: 'If you want to know, I do think Fascism is lousy. So is Communism, only more so. But there are other ideas in the world besides either of them – thank God (whom neither of you believe in)' (Hoskins 20). But after *Waugh in Abyssinia*, everyone 'knew' where Waugh stood.

Later he would speak of the 'heroes of the Alcazar siege' (EAR 236); after the fall of Madrid in March 1939, when Nationalist victory was assured, he declared himself 'a partisan of Franco' (meanwhile condemning the violent racialism and nationalism of the Falange and *Hispanidad*, and predicting that Franco's forces might become a danger to the 'individualistic states') (RUL 54). But his reply to the *Left Review* in 1937 was his only public statement on the Spanish war when it was at its height. 'It would be reasonable to suppose that he was restrained by prudent consideration for his sales, for, having made himself unpopular over Abyssinia, he had taken care, when promoting the forthcoming *Scoop* in 1937, to promise "No more Fascist propaganda". But the truth is that he genuinely disliked Franco and Fascism', as *Scoop* and, later, *Scott-King's Modern Europe* (1947) make clear (Gallagher, EAR 159).

Waugh thus believed that, whatever conflicts might be rending the Continent, the Left was wrong in trying to force a choice at home between twin evils. Compared with other states England possessed a tradition of individualism in fairly good working order. He took every opportunity to throw cold water on claims from the Left of a crisis at home, and particularly on those who feared that Britain's upper classes were simply waiting to impose their own version of a Fascist regime.[19] When Cyril Connolly prophesied in *Enemies of Promise* (1938) that because of Fascists at home, Britons might 'at any moment' find their 'libraries burnt, the teachers exterminated, the language suppressed' (87), Waugh responded with ridicule and an alternative theory of how Fascist movements actually start:

> it is into the cold claws of this latter bogy that Mr Connolly finally surrenders himself; the cold, dank pit of politics into which all his young friends have gone tobogganing; the fear of Fascism, that is the new fear of Hell to the new Quakers.... But it is reasonable to hope that... one day he will escape from the café chatter, meet some of the people, whom he now fears as traitors, who are engaged in the practical work of government and think out for himself what Fascism means. It is a growth of certain peculiar soils; principally it needs two things – a frightened middle class who see themselves in danger of extinction in a proletarian state, and some indignant patriots who believe that their country, through internal dissension, is becoming bullied by the rest of the world. In England we had something like a Fascist movement in 1926, when the middle classes broke the General Strike. We have a middle class that is uniquely apt for strenuous physical adventures, amenable to discipline, bursting with *esprit de corps*, and a great fund of patriotism.... It is quite certain that England would become Fascist before it became Communist; it is quite unlikely to become either; but if anything is calculated to provoke the development which none desire, and Mr Connolly dreads almost neurotically, it is the behaviour of his hysterical young friends of the Communist Party.
>
> (EAR 241)

'A queer trade, anti-fascism', wrote Orwell the next year, coming to the same position as Waugh from an opposite direction; 'So terrified of the future that we're jumping straight into it like a rabbit diving down a boa-constrictor's throat' (*Air* 172, 177).

Visitors to England, Waugh said, would find 'that the country, *as a whole*, was coming through its difficulties; that there was strength and resistance in traditional English life that could survive while other countries were turning themselves topsy-turvy in order to meet the same problems'. 'We have a system that has grown up unsystematically through an enormous variety of public and private enterprises. It is a system which suits us, and if properly worked, can provide most of the things that are needed'.[20] Once again Waugh's position may be compared with Christopher Dawson's:

> Hitherto English political institutions have stood the strain of the [first World] War and the crisis better than those of any other country.... Obviously we need not conclude that because parliamentarism has broken down in Italy and Central Europe, it is also fated to be swept away here, for representative institutions in England are not an artificial creation that has been imposed in deference to abstract liberal democratic principles nor are they an alien import that has no roots in our national traditions. They have grown up from the soil and are part of our historic inheritance.
>
> (Dawson 25).

III

Between finishing *Waugh in Abyssinia* in October 1936 and the outbreak of world war three years later, Waugh published over ninety essays and reviews, in the *Spectator* (where his old student Derek Verschoyle was literary editor), *Harper's*, *Nash's*, and, as an act of piety for which he asked little or no pay, in Catholic magazines such as *The Tablet* and Belloc's *G. K.'s Weekly*. Through its editor and film reviewer Graham Greene, he got a weekly book page in *Night and Day*, a glossy new imitation (down to type-face and page-layout) of *The New Yorker* that also regularly carried Osbert Lancaster, Herbert Read, Elizabeth Bowen, Anthony Powell, V. S. Pritchett, and Christopher Isherwood. (Sponsored by Chatto and Windus and launched with a cocktail party for 800 at the Dorchester Hotel, the magazine ran for six months, until driven out of business in December 1937, partly by Shirley Temple. When Greene analysed her pubescent coquetry in *Wee Willie Winkie*, she won a libel judgment of £3500.)[21] From Alexander Korda, trying vainly to recapture the success of his *Private Life of Henry VIII* (1935), Waugh accepted £250 for five months of desultory work on a 'vulgar film about cabaret girls' (D 413) to be called *Lovelies from America* (never released). Meanwhile he reported in October 1936: 'made a very good start with the first page of novel describing Diana [Cooper]'s early morning' (D 409). (*Scoop* would not be finished until 1938.)

The reason for all this activity was simple: 'I am getting spliced', he told Greene, 'and need as much money as I can get' (ST1 439). He had first met the Herberts in Portofino in September 1933; the next year, during a stint of

11 Laura Herbert at the time of her engagement to Waugh (Private Collection).

country-house visiting between the publications of *Ninety-Two Days* and *A Handful of Dust*, he twice visited Pixton from Mells and was soon captivated by Laura, nearly thirteen years his junior, so different from her gregarious and horsey older sisters. In January 1935 he wrote to Mary Lygon: 'I have taken a *great* fancy to a young lady named Laura. What is she like? Well fair, very pretty, plays peggoty beautifully.... she is only 18 years old, virgin, Catholic, quiet & astute. So it is difficult. I have not made much progress yet' (L 92).

'Quiet & astute' is a judgment echoed by everyone who knew Laura Herbert. Her sister Gabriel described her at the time of her first meeting with Waugh as a woman who, though young, had 'a quality of self-containedness and irony', who 'steered a determined course of non-involvement'; 'detached' and 'intensely private' are the terms in which Auberon Waugh has characteristically discussed his mother.[22] She relished Waugh's humour and fantasy, and shared his love of games (especially word games such as crosswords); but at the same time she retained something of the otherworldliness that had attracted him to Olivia Greene – a detachment triply rooted in her unswerving religious faith, the secure sense of self that came of being born with the ancient name of Herbert, and her own natural vein of satire, all of which led her to prefer her own farm and family to the cosmopolitan world in which Waugh travelled. In after years he would complain wryly of her 'tribal torpor', an aristocratic disdain for the matters of social form he so enjoyed, and joke to the children, 'Your dear mother is the kindest and the most hospitable of women, but she has no sense of style'.[23] But the same fierce independence and loyalty quickly impressed Waugh as exactly what he wanted in a wife.

Sure by December 1934 that he wished to marry, Waugh visited often at the Herberts' London house in Bruton Street, where Laura moved in order to pursue desultory study at the Royal Academy of Dramatic Art. But two impediments seemed to render his suit hopeless: his annulment dragged on, leaving him still married to Laura's cousin Evelyn Gardner (one Herbert aunt is supposed to have said 'I thought we had heard the last of that young man'); and Mary Herbert saw little to commend a divorced parvenu novelist as son-in-law. For a time Lady Mary positively forbade the relationship; on the eve of his trip to Abyssinia in the autumn of 1935 – even as he wrote to Bruton Street, 'Darling darling Laura please dont find that you are just as happy without me' (L 95) – Waugh in frustration invited another woman to leave her husband and come with him to Africa.[24]

According to Selina Hastings, 'It was not until Mary Herbert put her foot down and forbade her daughter to continue the unsuitable friendship with Evelyn Waugh that Laura's interest was properly aroused. She enjoyed conducting a forbidden correspondence and the meetings in secret, and by the time her mother began to relent she found herself falling in love' (Hastings 324). By the spring of 1936, while busy writing about Abyssinia, Waugh was confident enough to write her a starkly honest proposal of marriage:

Tell you what you might do while you are alone at Pixton. You might think about me a bit & whether, if those wop priests ever come to a decent decision, you could bear the idea of marrying me. Of course you haven't got to decide but think about it. I can't advise you in my favour because I think it would be beastly for you, but think how nice it would be for me. I am restless & moody & misanthropic & lazy & have no money except what I can earn and if I got ill you would starve. In fact it is a lousy proposition. On the other hand I think I could... reform & become quite strict about not getting drunk and I am pretty sure I should be faithful. Also there is always a fair chance that there will be another bigger economic crash in which case if you had married a nobleman with a great house you might find yourself starving, while I am very clever and could probably earn a living of some sort somewhere. Also though you would be taking on an elderly buffer [Waugh was not yet 33], I am one without fixed habits. You wouldn't find yourself confined to any particular place or group.... All these are very small advantages compared with the awfulness of my character. I have always tried to be nice to you and you may have got it into your head that I am nice really, but that is all rot. It is only to you & for you. I am jealous & impatient – but there is no point in going into a whole list of my vices. You are a critical girl and I've no doubt that you know them all and a great many I don't know myself.... My only tie of any kind is my work. That means that for several months each year we shall have to separate or you would have to share some very lonely place with me. But apart from that we could do what we liked & go where we liked.... When I tell my friends that I am in love with a girl of 19 they looked shocked and say 'wretched child' but I dont look on you as very young even in your beauty and I dont think there is any sense in the line that you cannot possibly commit yourself to a decision that affects your whole life for years yet. But anyway there is no point in your deciding or even answering. I may never get free of your cousin Evelyn. Above all things, darling, dont fret at all. But just turn the matter over in your dear head.

(L 103–4)

Laura agreed, pending his annulment. That decision came in July 1936, while he was waiting for permission to re-enter Abyssinia; Waugh rushed with the news to Mount Street, where Laura and her mother were hearing Mass. Lady Mary at last agreed, though still demanding a frustrating series of postponements.

In October Waugh began house-hunting. He had never saved, and so would have to borrow the money for any purchase. Like John Plant in *Work Suspended*, what he wanted was 'a *house*, no matter how dingy, rather than a cottage, however luxurious' (WS 216). Staying at Pixton over Christmas he found Piers Court, 'a house of startling beauty' (DC 62) in the nearby village of Stinch-combe, Gloucestershire, a mostly Elizabethan structure with a pleasing eighteenth-century façade, on forty-one acres. In the event, no loan was necessary: Laura's grandmother, the Viscountess de Vesci, gave them £4000 as a wedding present. With Laura's approval he offered £3550 for the house, accepted in January. 'Stinkers', as it was soon nicknamed, would be the Waughs' home for eighteen years.

In January 1937 the engagement was announced in *The Times*. Waugh had moved to the Easton Court Hotel to finish work on Korda's 'vulgar film' and write as much as possible before the wedding in April. He made trips back to London to see Laura, inventory wedding presents, oversee repairs to Piers Court, and attend meetings at Chapman and Hall, which in February had made him a director. With so much else going on, *Scoop* made predictably little progress. '[Laura] has bought me a lovely house in Gloucestershire and my head is spinning with plans for its decoration', he told Lady Diana. 'The main objection is the lack of water, light and gas.... Also the snow gets in through holes in the roof' (DC 62). Over Holy Week he attended a retreat at the Benedictine monastery of Ampleforth in Yorkshire, from which he made his first visit to Castle Howard, later to serve as architectural inspiration for Brides-head Castle. Laura oversaw wedding arrangements and travelled to Paris for her trousseau. The wedding took place on 17 April, followed by a month's honeymoon in Italy, a gift from Alec Waugh's rich new Australian wife Joan Chirnside. Their first stop was the Herbert villa at Portofino, where they had first met; Waugh wrote in his diary the next day: 'Lovely day, lovely house, lovely wife, great happiness' (D 422).

Piers Court, still being repaired when the couple returned at the end of May, was habitable by August. For the rest of the year Waugh wrote essays, failed to

12 Piers Court, near Stinchcombe, Gloucestershire (1955) (Hulton Getty).

make progress on his novel, and indulged his taste for landscaping and decorating. Inside, the house needed to be electrified and a great chandelier – a wedding present from the Coopers – repaired and installed in the centre hall; there was his library to be panelled and shelved. Outside began an ambitious programme of new plantings, levelling of lawns and laying out a tennis court and circular drive. Waugh quickly discovered in such activities an escape from writing, and for the next three years, afternoons at home often found him outdoors with a shovel. He was determined to make of Piers Court one of the 'solid and spacious houses of the bourgeoisie' such as he described in an essay on British architecture published in 1938: 'the gentleman's house, "standing", as the house-agents say, "in twenty acres of park-like grounds"' (EAR 215). On the

13 The Abyssinian lavatory at Piers Court (*Country Life*).

stone pediment outside he removed the coat of arms of the Pinfold family, the house's seventeenth-century owners, and erected his own.

Both Waugh and Laura began to collect antique furnishings (and he to write very knowledgeable reviews on the subject) – Georgian pieces when they could afford them, the Victorian objects he had favoured since Oxford days when they could not. The 'market ouvert' in Portobello Road turned up treasures, as did local house- and demolition-sales.[25] Paintings and silver had mainly to be Victorian, but these blended well in what many visitors to the house recalled as Waugh's taste for 'dark surfaces and patterns, heavy furniture, silver and glass' (Donaldson 9). Elsewhere he indulged his fantasy. In the first-floor lavatory, he upholstered the armchair toilet with leopard-skin and decorated the walls with paintings collected in Abyssinia that, as Maurice Bowra noted, 'depicted with a combination of early Christian formality and observant realism the defeat of the Italians by Menelik and did not shrink from showing how the Abyssinians mutilated the enemy [by castration] and hung the trophies so obtained round their necks' (Bowra 176). For £10 Waugh bought Rossetti's *Spirit of the Rainbow*, the start of a fine collection of Victorian story-pictures shrewdly acquired before their prices soared; an agent found 'an enormous pair of portraits, George III and wife, which are disconcerting,' soon installed in the library. 'I think of putting "scribble, scribble" on a ribbon across the top' (D 435, 438).

An establishment like Piers Court was what the Herberts might expect for their daughter; for Waugh, it was the visible symbol of success in his trade, a reward for exchanging youthful freedom for the restrictions of family life, and the fulfillment of deep aesthetic longings. Like Charles Ryder, he had 'nursed a love of architecture' since childhood (BR 81), when with his mother he had toured the countryside visiting old churches; he thought 'the greatest work of art in the world' not a book or a painting but the city of Venice (EAR 545). With like-minded friends such as Betjeman, Connolly and Diana Cooper, he mourned the architectural 'sack of London' and became a discerning visitor of country houses, in person and through the newly popular *Architectural Review* and *Country Life*. A 'specialized enthusiasm for domestic architecture', explains the hero of *Work Suspended*, was 'one of the peculiarities of my generation': 'When the poetic mood was on us, we turned to buildings, and gave them the place which our fathers accorded to Nature – to almost any buildings, but particularly those in the classical tradition'; 'There was never a time when so many landless men could talk at length about landscape gardening' (WS 184).

Piers Court also provided a way to enact long-held aesthetic (and political) principles. From the start of his career Waugh had chosen to write on architecture and design; his essays provide a kind of ideological explanation and justification for Piers Court. As early as 1929, 'Take Your Home into Your Own Hands!' made a plea for individual freedom against 'the plague of "good taste" ' as represented by 'experts' – the magazines, the new professional interior decorators, even one's neighbours.

> Look around your own drawing-room. Where is the fire-screen with the family coat-of-arms worked in coloured wools by your Aunt Agatha?... Have you made all these changes because you really like them or because someone has been at you about 'good taste'?...
>
> If by some odd coincidence you really do heartily agree with your neighbour's taste in house decoration, well and good; but if she likes to fill her window with arts-and-crafts pottery bowls of crocuses, and you like aspidistras better, just fill your house with aspidistras till it looks like a conservatory, and if you like Benares brass pots, put them in those, and if you like bamboo stands, put them on them.
>
> (EAR 44–5)

In his best anti-intellectual fashion, Waugh advised: 'just you say very decisively, "I don't know much about art, but I do know what I like" ': 'then they will see that they are beaten, and Mrs Brown will say to the vicar's wife that it is so sad that you have no taste, and the vicar's wife will say to the doctor's wife that it only shows what sort of people you are, but all three will envy you at heart and even perhaps, one by one, bring out from the attics a few of the things they really like' (EAR 45).

By the thirties, the streamlined modernist functionalism he had satirized in *Decline and Fall* was the 'good taste' that needed opposing. He complained when *Harper's Bazaar* rejected an essay on older styles:

> Miss Reynolds returned an article I had written her about architecture on the grounds that her paper stood for 'contemporary' design. I could have told her all about Corbusier fifteen years ago when she would not have known the name. Now that at last we are recovering from that swine-fever, the fashionable magazines take it up.
>
> (D 428)

Like Tom Wolfe in our time (and for the same reasons), Waugh opposed the rage for 'clean' lines and sparse decor:

> It must not, however, be thought that the plain man had – or to this day has – any natural taste for plainness. Poor fellow, it has been drummed into him by a hundred experts, writing on what are ironically termed the 'home pages', that ornament is vulgar, and today he endures blank slabs of concrete and bakelite, prisonlike bars of steel and aluminum; his only protest is to spend longer hours among the aspidistras of the bar parlour.
>
> (EAR 220)

Decline and Fall had already associated such studied neglect of 'the human element' in design with the political Left; in the thirties Waugh took every opportunity to decry 'the Nazi-factory manner (concrete and steel), which – heaven knows why – is thought to be...Marxist' (RUL 34). Instead he championed the 'bourgeois' values of 'luxury', 'ornament', 'variety', and 'magnificence'. The article rejected by *Harper's Bazaar*, later printed in *Country Life*, was 'A Call to the Orders' (1938), another attack on the 'post-war Corbusier plague' of 'machines for living': 'Villas like sewage farms', 'the style of the arterial highroads, the cinema studios, the face-cream factories'. In rich and archaic diction to match his theme, he proclaimed – more in hope than certainty – a return to Georgian construction, native substitute for his beloved baroque:

> We are again thinking of stone and brick and timber that will mellow and richen with age, and we have instinctively turned to the school in which our fathers excelled. The baroque has never had a place in England...[but] fashion has returned for more austere models – that superb succession of masterpieces from Vanbrugh to Soane which are grouped, far too vaguely, under the absurdly insular title of 'Georgian'.
>
> (EAR 216)

Meanwhile, in a series of articles from 'The Philistine Age of English Decoration' (1938) to 'Those Happy Homes' (1954), he preached (to a public that still considered all things Victorian dowdy, repressive, and dull) the interiors of 'the period between the Great Exhibition and the fall of the Second Empire', whose fine craftsmanship, eclectic variety and attention to 'privacy' remained 'a monument to what the plain Briton can do to his home when he is not badgered by his daughters into buying what he does not like'. To Waugh, Victorian décor, product of a Britain at the height of its liberty, power and respect for 'private life', meant freedom: a way to shun convention and develop individual taste. 'The huge euphoria of the Victorian home may be attributed directly to the abundance of ornament' (EAR 219, 466).

Like Alexander Pope's villa at Twickenham, Piers Court thus became the concrete embodiment of the same aesthetic and political ideals that its owner celebrated in his writing. Like Pope, he often likened literary construction to landscape design; he preferred to characterize writing not as 'creative' but 'architectural': '"Creative" is an invidious term too often used at the expense of the critic. A better word, except that it would always involve explanation, would be "architectural". I believe that what makes a writer, as distinct from a clever and cultured man who can write, is an added energy and breadth of vision which enables him to conceive and complete a structure' (EAR 238). Until World War II (when a deepened sense of vocation led him to superadd the higher language of 'art' and 'inspiration'), Waugh's central critical terms were 'design', 'craft', and 'technique'.

Also like Pope, Waugh considered all the arts, from writing and building to bookbinding and cookery, indices of the civilization than produced them. His views on decoration and design are of a piece with his well-known connoisseurship of food and wine, in which he also championed elaboration and luxury against newer trends toward the hurried and simple. 'Food can & should be a source of delight. As for "nutrition" – that is all balls' (L 352). The diaries often recall menus in careful detail; when in 1954 he was asked to nominate a 'book of the year', he chose not a work of fiction or poetry but Elizabeth David's *Italian Food*.[26] He liked, as he said, to dine in 'marble halls'; *Ninety-Two Days* finds it 'significant that marble, the most grand and delicate of all building material, has today become the symbol of the vulgar and garish'; 'it is part of the flight from magnificence to which both the "ye-olde"-pewter-and-sampler aesthetic and its more recent counterpart, the "modern"-concrete-and-steel-tube, have given impetus' (NTD 15). In both food and design, his argument was not merely for luxury but against the politics that bred its modern opposite. In a decade when it seemed, as T. S. Eliot said, 'high-brows must be socialists', Piers Court was Waugh's protest, a place where he could ostentatiously turn his back on modern politics and live 'like a gentleman', pursuing 'pre-1914 sweetness of life'.[27]

IV

'No one is allowed to leave Addis so all those adventures I came for will not happen', Waugh had written to Laura in the autumn of 1935. 'Sad. Still all this will make a funny novel so it isn't wasted' (L 100). He began *Scoop: A Novel about Journalists* just after finishing *Waugh in Abyssinia*, and by the end of October 1936 completed two 'light & excellent' chapters (HRC E298). But his wedding,

Korda's film, and regular journalistic work meant that by the middle of 1937, the novel was only half done, and needed to be entirely rewritten for coherence and continuity. 'Work on *Scoop* going slowly, with infinite interruptions and distractions' (D 430). The novel was finished in February 1938, sixteen months after it was begun. It was his fourth book about Abyssinia, here called 'Ishmaelia' (nation of outcasts).

When *Scoop* was published in May, reviewers were unanimous in praise of what nearly all thought Waugh's best book since *Decline and Fall* – and relieved to note a return to Waugh's 'early manner'. 'With it Mr Waugh re-entered his peculiar world; it was a relief to those of us who had begun to fear that we were losing him, that the wit was being slain by the propagandist and the partisan' (Macaulay 370–1). His reputation as a comic writer would never be higher. But as so often before, praise for his humour was based on a near-universal failure of understanding, of which John Brophy's review in the *Daily Telegraph* is typical: 'Mr Waugh is not a satirist, for indignation founded on some belief is necessary to satire, and I have never been able from his books to discover what Mr Waugh believes in' (CH 199).

The novel tells of the misadventures of three men named Boot. Framing the main story are appearances by the London writer John Courteney Boot, whose career closely parallels Waugh's own up to 1936.[28] The book's central figure is John's naive young cousin William, author of a weekly nature column called 'Lush Places', a countryman who hates London and wants nothing more than to remain among his eccentric aging relatives and servants on the family's crumbling estate, Boot Magna. Through a series of mistakes, William Boot finds himself a reporter in Ishmaelia for Lord Copper's *Daily Beast*; with the help of a beautiful adventuress and a mysterious financier, he gets the scoop his fellow reporters miss and returns home in triumph. Finally there is William's Uncle Theodore, an old rake who wants to escape Boot Magna for the life of a man-about-town in London. The three Boots capture strands Waugh recognized in himself: the successful author-adventurer; the seeker of privacy quietly making a home in the country with Laura (their first child, Teresa, was born in March 1938); and the raffish weekend visitor to his London club. Never before had Waugh turned so directly to autobiography in constructing a novel, or so filled one with private jokes, recognizable only to family and friends.[29]

The story of a naïf hero who returns from his buffetings in the world to the place where he began, *Scoop* has most often been compared to *Decline and Fall*, though as Waugh said in 1937 of this 'familiar' plot, 'the inspired simpleton' is now 'able to baffle and disconcert the humbugs' (ND 211). A new gentleness intervenes: here are no suicides or dismemberments, none of the comically violent deaths which in earlier novels pushed humour as far as it could go. The men's trouble in *Scoop* is caused mainly by women, but through these same women something like justice is done: William gets his scoop, John a knighthood, and Theodore the London life he has long desired. As Waugh himself noted, the happy domesticity which slowed *Scoop*'s writing also contributed to its sunny outlook: 'This light-hearted tale was the fruit of a time of general anxiety and distress but, for its author, one of peculiar personal happiness' (1964

Preface). Reviewers also noted in the brilliant elaboration of *Scoop*'s plot the influence of Wodehouse, a favourite writer Waugh was at this time also reviewing. Boot Magna recalled Blandings Castle (though as Herbert relatives noted, it owed as much to another country house, also 'near Taunton': Pixton, filled with Herberts and their many housekeepers, maids, and retired nannies).[30]

Scoop's subtitle was dropped in later editions, but Waugh always maintained that its 'main theme', as he said while negotiating film rights in 1957, was 'to expose the pretensions of foreign correspondents, popularised in countless novels, plays, autobiographies and films, to be heroes, statesmen and diplomats' (HRC C50). The names of its reporters – Corker, Pappenhacker, Shumble, Whelper, Pigge, Jakes – suggest (like their newspapers, the *Beast* and *Brute*) a sewer of subhuman behaviour. ('Only a shit could be good on this particular job', Waugh had written from Addis Abbaba in 1935 (L 102); the Ishmaelian Press Bureau appropriately issues cards of identity to foreign reporters 'originally printed for the registration of prostitutes'.) Asked by a cub reporter recently graduated from the Aircastle School (a correspondence school of the sort that had sprung up in the 1920s, the first of them Sir Max Pemberton's London School of Journalism), 'But you do think it's a good way of training oneself – inventing imaginary news?', William replies with the voice of experience, 'None better' (S 261).

Scoop so accurately transposes experiences already described in *Waugh in Abyssinia* that one historian of journalism describes it as 'straight reportage, thinly disguised as a novel to protect the author from libel actions'.[31] Excelsior Movie-Sound News of America was in real life Fox Movietone; Wenlock Jakes was the famous American reporter H. R. Knickerbocker (with whom Waugh had a fist-fight), in Abyssinia for the Hearst organization, which itself was legendary for its journalistic creativity.[32] The *Brute*'s Sir Jocelyn Hitchcock, who concocts news set in the (non-existent) town of 'Laku', was so transparently the *Telegraph*'s Sir Percival Phillips that his newspaper protested.[33] (In 1930, Hitchcock had beaten Waugh to the Rickett story in Abyssinia; as a kind of retrospective wish-fulfillment, *Scoop*'s Rickett, Mr Baldwin, gives his story not to Hitchcock but William Boot.)

As usual Waugh not only diagnoses wrongdoing but analyses its causes and effects. Many in the heyday of the 'corporation press' were troubled by what seemed a newly powerful force manipulating and volatilizing public opinion. Waugh's reviews of the late thirties comment often on the power of mass-circulation newspapers, dominated by the 'ideological preconceptions' of great proprietors such as Lord Beaverbrook (original of Lord Copper) and all too willing to make the public 'crisis-minded', creating 'a state of neurotic apprehension in which crises may very well occur' (ND 116). Copper explains 'the *Beast* Policy for the war': 'The *Beast* stands for strong mutually antagonistic governments everywhere. Self-sufficiency at home, self-assertion abroad'; his news editor is left to explain the specifics:

> 'I think it's the Patriots and the Traitors'.
> 'Yes, but which is which?'

'Oh, I don't know *that*. *That's* Policy, you see. It's nothing to do with me. You should have asked Lord Copper'.

(S 55)

As world war drew closer in 1939, Waugh returned to these themes in *Robbery Under Law*, going so far as to speak of ideologically motivated reporting as part of a 'universal, deliberately fostered anarchy of public relations... rapidly making the world uninhabitable' (RUL 3).

In later editions Waugh also admitted that in creating Ishmaelia, *Scoop* combined Abyssinia with the more timely conflict in Spain. Like Spain (and unlike Abyssinia), Ishmaelia is threatened not with foreign invasion but civil war: its ruling family of Jacksons (based on Liberia's Does) is under attack by Fascist and Communist factions supported from abroad. True to his rejection of 'the idiotic dichotomy of Left and Right', Waugh names Ishmaelia's head Communist 'Dr Benito' and makes the slogans of both sides sound equally foolish. Ishmaelia's (black) Fascists claim theirs is really 'a white race' endangered by 'international Negro finance and secret subversive Negro Bolshevism'; its Communists, supported from 'Moscow, Harlem, Bloomsbury, and Liberia', spout familiar defences of 'the dictatorship of the proletariat' against 'international finance, the subjugation of the worker, sacerdotalism' (S 106–7). In a sly passage Waugh combines the inflated claims being made in the thirties for the cultural achievements of Stalin's regime with similar arguments about blacks advanced by writers such as Nancy Cunard, to form a rhetoric that anticipates modern Afro-Centrism: '"Who built the Pyramids?" cried [Ishmaelia's Communist legate in London]. "A Negro. Who invented the circulation of the blood? A Negro. Ladies and gentlemen, I ask you as impartial members of the great British public, who discovered America?"' (62).

Here as in his response to the *Left Review* questionnaire on Spain, though both sides are deplorable, the Communists pose the more serious threat. Mr Baldwin (the novel's F. W. Rickett) explains:

The Germans, with a minimum of discernment, chose to set up a native of low character named Smiles as prospective dictator. I never had any serious fears of him. The Russians, more astutely, purchased the Young Ishmaelite party and are, as you see, momentarily in the ascendant.

(S 236)

But in the comic world of *Scoop*, neither ideology wins. The 'Soviet State of Ishmaelia' collapses, the recently deposed President is found (in a final, outrageous pun) 'locked in the woodshed' and restored to power, and the nation returns to the control of his merely venal, non-ideological family – 'a pack of rogues, but they suited the country and they suited H.M.G'. (211).

Reviewers were quick to scent a return to Waugh's 'earlier manner' because in subject, theme, and technique, *Scoop* does again, brilliantly, what he had already done before. Once again, England parallels the jungle. Boot Magna houses its motley of Boots, Ishmaelia its prolific Jacksons. Cut off by 'desert, forest and swamp', Ishmaelia 'cannot conveniently be approached from any part of the world' (101); in turn, the trip from London to Boot Magna makes William's editor feel 'like a Roman legionary... tramping through forests beyond the Roman pale, harassed by silent, illusive savages' (291–2). Fakery and bad taste unite Africa, where Corker collects 'synthetic ivory' carvings, and England, where Lord Copper's electric bells are rung by 'synthetic ivory' keys; immaturity – suggested in Waugh's usual manner, through games and mementos of childhood – pervades both. Boot Magna is in a state of advanced decay, Ishmaelia of chaotic, meaningless circular change. Gazing out the window at Boot Magna, Uncle Theodore sings 'Change and decay in all around I see'; looking out on the morning of 'Year One of the Soviet State of Ishmaelia', William intones the same hymn.

In one of Waugh's favourite devices, there preside over the faithless worlds both at home and abroad figures described as if they were earthly gods. As the novel opens, there comes to John Boot from 'high overhead' the 'preternaturally' resonant voice of Mrs Stitch (4), named for the Greek fates who wove men's destinies; at Copper House (Beaverbrook's new Fleet Street offices, opened in 1931) stands a 'chryselephantine effigy of Lord Copper in coronation robes' (30). (The robes hint at his unfortunate closeness to the seats of power, the material – sculpture adorned with ivory and gold, most famously used in Phidias' Olympian Zeus – quasi-divine status.) When, shipping out to Africa, William becomes homesick for England, Corker suddenly appears 'as though conjured there by William's unexpressed wish; as though conjured, indeed, by a djinn who had imperfectly understood his instructions' (81). Finally there is Waugh's finest *deus ex machina*, Mr Baldwin. Urbane and rootless, sexually and nationally ambiguous, master of every language (including Ishmaelian and Swedish) and every situation (from international finance to ping-pong), a survivor – Baldwin is the complete 'man of the world'. Like Philbrick in *Decline and Fall*, he is all things to all men; we never learn his real name. (England's ineffectual, nature-loving Prime Minister Stanley Baldwin provides a convenient – and zanily inapt – alias.)[34] Waugh had worked up all these elements of character before; Baldwin is his finest concatenation of them.

When things look most hopeless – after Kätchen has left him and the Communist coup has seemingly succeeded – William prays 'without hope' to the bird which, like some Ancient Mariner, he has unintentionally wronged: 'O great crested grebe, maligned fowl, have I not expiated the wrong my sister did you; am I still to be an exile from the green places of my heart? Was there not, even in the remorseless dooms of antiquity, a god in the machine?' (227). As if by special providence a machine immediately appears, an aeroplane like Mrs Rattery's from which – 'on pointed, snakeskin shoes' like Margot Metroland's on first descending from her Hispano-Suiza – parachutes William's saviour. 'The milch-goat' which a few pages before triumphantly butted one of Dr Benito's operatives into the rubbish 'reverently mak[es] way for him': brute beast meets nature's god.[35] And this deity conjures yet further miracles with his uncreating word:

'I possess a little influence in political quarters but it will strain it severely to provoke a war on my account.... I should greatly prefer it, if the thing could be settled neatly and finally, here and now'.

   As he spoke there arose from the vestibule a huge and confused tumult; the roar of an engine.... It was the Swede.

(S 236–7)

The gentle and pious Swede, now homicidally drunk, appears on his motorcycle, is 'tolerantly' given more absinthe by Baldwin, and proceeds to topple (literally) Benito and the new Communist regime. Such is the presiding spirit who gives William his greatest scoop, who in fact writes it for him, since in his effortless mastery of all things crooked, Baldwin naturally commands the language of the *Beast* and the *Brute* – even of its instrument, the typewriter, which he manages 'with immense speed'.[36]

Just as *Black Mischief*'s undertone of native drums and allusions to the cannibal Wanda kept 'the darker aspects of barbarism continually and unobtrusively present' as 'a black and mischievous background against which the civilized and semi-civilized characters performed their parts' (L 77), *Scoop* invokes wild beasts and the rubbish-heaps they inhabit. When William and Kätchen consummate their affair, 'The three-legged dog awoke and all over the town, in yards and refuse-heaps, the pariahs took up his cries of protest' (196). Among *Scoop*'s many framing devices – more, and more elaborate, than in any previous novel – is an owl, which first appears in a picturesque mural being painted on Mrs Stitch's bedroom ceiling. ('You're putting too much ivy on the turret, Arthur; the owl won't show up unless you have him on the bare stone and I'm particularly attached to the owl'.) Soon after, we learn that in his nature column William is 'particularly attached' to 'rodents'. Three hundred pages later, as William, back home, composes a column in which 'maternal rodents pilot their furry brood through the stubble', the owl reappears, a clawed predator swooping down into the peaceful scene: 'Outside the owls hunted maternal rodents and their furry broods'.[37] Like the water lapping against the sea wall that frames *Black Mischief*, this startling final image hints that even at the retreat of Boot Magna, conditions cannot last.

What is the owl, the predator that threatens 'change and decay' in England as in Ishmaelia? Waugh could depend on contemporaries' supplying one answer: coming war. His parallels of civilization with the jungle imply that the ideological oppositions dividing Ishmaelia (and Spain) threaten to invade private life everywhere, to turn all Europe into a battlefield. But fear of coming war cannot account for the already crumbling condition of Boot Magna or the ongoing destruction of London's 'once-decent' architecture. Like Waugh's earlier novels, *Scoop* suggests that current instability is deeply rooted in European history and fallen human nature. But to see this, readers need to be alert to patterns of explanation developed in earlier novels and here deployed in a kind of telegraphic shorthand.

The genealogy of Ishmaelia's ruling family insinuates the view of history underpinning *Scoop*. Ishmaelia's first president, Samuel Smiles Jackson, was succeeded by Pankhurst and Rathbone Jackson. The founder of the line recalls the mid-Victorian progressivist author of *Self-Help* (1859), his immediate successors the next generation of liberals: the militant Fabian suffragette Emmeline Pankhurst (1858–1928), and Eleanor Rathbone (1872–1946), vocal supporter of the Abyssinians and Spanish Republicans. The family's modern progeny – Gollancz Jackson, Mander Jackson, Huxley Jackson, Mrs Athol (née Jackson), Mrs Earl Russell Jackson, and Garnett Jackson – recall contemporary socialists, Spanish Republicans, and Left-leaning pacifists.[38] The family's history thus takes one step further the historical devolution of Anglican Protestantism into an empty liberal humanism already dramatized in *Vile Bodies*. In Christopher Dawson's formulation, 'Protestantism, Liberalism and Communism are the three successive stages by which our civilization has passed from Catholicism to complete secularism. The first eliminated the Church, the second eliminated Christianity, and the third eliminates the human soul'.[39]

Like Tony Last, the gentle William Boot, last son of Boot Magna, does not possess the tools to combat this natural downward direction taken by unassisted human nature. The point is hinted early in the novel, when 'Josephine, the eight-year-old Stitch prodigy' murders a line from Virgil. '"*Floribus Austrum*," Josephine chanted, "*perditus et liquidis immisi fontibus apros*; having been lost with flowers in the South and sent into the liquid fountains; *apros* is wild boars but I couldn't quite make sense of that bit"' (7). The line (which also serves as epigraph to Milton's *Comus*) comes from *Eclogues* 2.1; Corydon explains how his love for Alexis has brought disordering passion into his pastoral world: 'I have let the south wind into my flowers, and boars into my crystal springs'. The beast *will* intervene. (Even William's school nickname, we learn, was 'Beastly'.) It has already begun to do so at Boot Magna, whose fine house and landscape garden ('tastefully' laid out by some 'provincial predecessor of Repton') are already in decay. In this ruined garden the springs are no longer crystal; its liquid fountain – on the 'south' terrace – no longer plays:

> The lake was moved by strange tides. Sometimes, as at the present moment, it sank to a single, opaque pool in a wilderness of mud and rushes; sometimes it rose and inundated five acres of pasture. There had once been an old man in one of the lodges who understood the workings of the water system; there were sluice- gates hidden among the reeds, and manholes, dotted about in places known only to him, furnished with taps and cocks; that man had been able to control an ornamental cascade and draw a lofty jet of water from the mouth of the dolphin on the south terrace. But he had been in his grave fifteen years and the secret had died with him. (S 19–20)

In our fallen world, a work of art like a landscape garden – or any tradition of civilization – requires disciplined labour, what Waugh called 'moral stamina' (EAR 321), to keep the beast at bay: to prevent, as he wrote the following year, 'the jungle closing in'. 'It is only by unremitting, concerted defence and counter-attack that man retains his place on the earth' (RUL 247, 93).

And what can alone assist human nature in this 'counter-attack' against decay is once again the anchor of religious faith. The hymn that includes the line 'Change and decay in all around I see' (H. F. Lyte's 'Eventide') begins with the prayer: 'Abide with me'. *Scoop* like all Waugh's previous novels ultimately preaches, through satiric exposure of a series of false faiths, the need for the absolute standards of a true one, a universal faith that does not change. Like *Black Mischief* and *A Handful of Dust*, *Scoop* is full of sly references to false churches and gods, especially Anglican. The valet in William's London hotel inclines 'gracefully towards the bed in a High Anglican compromise between nod and genuflection' (47); at that false church Copper House, specially muffled typewriter keys make 'no more sound than the drumming of a bishop's finger tips on an upholstered *prie-dieu*' (52). In this world of lost and disordered values, Uncle Theodore sings (in an inversion of the hymn 'Where Thou Reignest'), 'In Thy courts no more are needed, moon by day nor sun by night' (279).

Even readers attuned to Waugh's methods of implication might protest that in *Scoop* these hints of the historical and religious roots of current disorders have become an easy, all-too-familiar shorthand: that in this genial comedy, such darker reflexions are unearned. Kätchen's casual leaving of William is a pale shadow of Brenda Last's painful betrayal of Tony; the farcical politics of Ishmaelia, so easily set in order by Mr Baldwin, lack the tragic implications of Seth's Azania. Waugh himself knew he was playing to the crowd – and that except in its superb construction, his fifth novel represented little advance from his earlier work. '*Scoop* is not a book I like particularly', he confessed later.[40]

Two events in particular led him while writing *Scoop* to reflect on his work so far and its future directions. In 1937 the new firm of Penguin began reissuing his earlier novels in inexpensive paperbacks, establishing his popularity with a wider audience than ever before; at the same time, Chapman and Hall launched a hardbound Collected Works, explaining in its advertising, 'We have had collected editions of most of the contemporary bores from Lawrence downwards: here . . . is an author we can read for amusement and not for exercise'.[41] Painfully aware how little his earlier novels had been understood, increasingly eager to attempt a different (and more ambitious) kind of fiction, Waugh chafed at the simple label 'entertainer'. He complained that July:

> The vast bulk of the reading public treat books as they do films. They want something to amuse them on a wet evening – they want a readable book of a certain character – love, travel, detection – according to their mood. They don't care a hoot about individual experiments and technical adventures of the author. Why should they? But they come to associate certain authors' names with a certain mood of entertainment – and woe betide the writer who disappoints them by exhibiting a change of interest.
> ('Barabbas, Publisher', *Nash's Pall Mall Magazine*, July 1937, 10)

The novelist-hero of Waugh's next story, the autobiographical *Work Suspended*, complains to his editor: 'I am in danger of becoming a purely technical expert'; 'I am in danger of becoming mechanical, turning out year after year the kind of book I know I can write well. I feel I have got as good as I ever can be at this particular sort of writing. I need new worlds to conquer'. The alarmed editor is relieved to hear that his best-selling author's current novel – in what can only be a reference to *Scoop* – makes only a few 'new technical experiments. I don't suppose the average reader will notice them at all' (WS 168).

Among *Scoop*'s unobtrusive innovations is an increased psychological range. Unlike earlier characters (drawn almost wholly externally), William Boot has a subconscious, established through dreams and daytime musings – devices that will grow increasingly important in *Work Suspended* and *Put Out More Flags*. Appropriately for 'A Novel about Journalists', *Scoop* also differs from the earlier fiction in the self-consciousness of its meditations on what Waugh soon announced would be a 'preoccupation' in all his writing: style (EAR 302). Waugh always had a good ear for voices, and measured the defects of his characters by the extent to which their speech diverged from his narrator's elegant clarity. *Scoop* not only explores a wider range of voices than ever before – from Algernon Stitch's clipped, upper-class Blimpishness and his wife's endearing public-school slang to the varied verbal offences of the novel's journalists (most delightfully, the colossal vulgarity of Wenlock Jakes) – but pauses to reflect on style as such. 'He has the most remarkable style', 'a very nice little style indeed', says Lord Copper, explaining why he wants to hire John Boot and so setting his underlings to look for a Boot with 'a particularly high-class style'. They light on William, author in his nature column of such sentences as 'Feather-footed through the plashy fen passes the questing vole'. 'That must be good style', say the editors to one another; 'At least it doesn't sound like anything else to me'.[42]

Thoughts of changing direction as a writer always led Waugh to reflect not only on style but the whole shape of his career – indeed, of his life. The marked autobiographical turn that begins in *Scoop* continues in *Work Suspended*, which also begins with what is in effect a capsule summary of Waugh's career to date and proceeds to portray a series of characters who capture what he thought were the contrasting strands in his own psyche. Both works explore his ambivalences about leaving London for life in the country, the topic also of essays such as 'The New Rustics' (1939, EAR 256–9). In part of his mind Waugh now professed, like William Boot, to hate London, its noise and dirt, its little remaining good architecture under constant attack; but London was also the cultural centre to which he returned, on binges like Uncle Theodore's, to shop, eat and meet friends.

Waugh would have done well to pay more attention to Uncle Theodore. Already in 1937, when he was only thirty-four, his health showed alarming signs. Along with references to gardening and a new habit of extremely long walks, the diary records with ominous frequency evenings spent 'tipsy' or simply 'drunk'; many entries conclude with some variation on 'to bed with dope'. Such evenings brought memory lapses – 'I have been surprised again and again lately by blanks and blurs in my memory, being reminded by Laura of quite recent events which delighted me and which I have now completely forgotten' (D 424) – and bouts of what he and Laura came familiarly to call 'p.m.' (persecution mania). Only the War (and a remarkably strong constitution) prevented the events of *Gilbert Pinfold* from happening sooner.

V

In late May 1938, soon after *Scoop* appeared, Waugh travelled to Budapest for the *Catholic Herald* to cover a Eucharistic Congress called in celebration of the ninth centenary of Hungary's patron, St Stephen. He found it a joyous event marred only by the absence of German and Austrian pilgrims, banned by the Nazis from attending. Waugh usually loathed crowds, but surrounded by fellow Catholics – rich and poor, old and young, European and African and Asian – he delighted in the 'diverse life' of a universal faith. 'One longed for [the crowds] to be greater, to include all one's friends and relations and acquaintances and strangers' (EAR 237). His fictionalized St Helena would enjoy the same experience at Rome, as Waugh himself would again in Mexico and Goa. His last book completed before the War, *Robbery Under Law*, describes the mingling of races and classes in the Cathedral at Guadaloupe: 'All the limitless variety of the Church seemed to be represented there' (RUL 234).

Just before leaving for Hungary, he wrote to Peters: 'A very rich chap wants me to write a book about Mexico. I gather he is willing to subsidize it. I am seeing him on Wednesday & will turn him onto you for thumb-screwing' (Sykes 252). The 'rich chap' was Clive Pearson, son of the engineer Weetman Pearson, first Lord Cowdray, who built New York's East River Tunnel and drained Mexico City. In 1908 Cowdray founded the Mexican Eagle oil company, the nation's most successful driller; by 1920 Mexico was the world's second largest producer and supplied nearly half England's oil.

In 1934 General Lazaro Cardenas had taken power in Mexico and, under a banner of Marxism, began a series of radical reforms for which he was hailed by journalists on the Left (most noisily by Kingsley Martin, editor of the *New Statesman*) as a hero of progress and democracy. In March 1938 Cardenas abruptly nationalized the oil industry. Such expropriations were not yet so common as they have since become; Clive Pearson wanted a book written in protest. His interest was not merely personal. Having served in World War I supervising military fuel supplies, he was aware that in another war, the Mediterranean might be closed, and Britain thus made all the more dependent on Mexican oil.

Waugh in turn leapt at the chance for a lavish holiday, expenses paid, for himself and Laura. He had wanted to visit Mexico at least since 1932 (NTD 14), to see for himself the persecution of Catholics that had long drawn international attention and been the subject of numerous complaints from Pius XI, beginning with the encyclical *Inquis afflictis* (1926). In 1931, Cardenas's predecessor General Calles had initiated a brutal and systematic policy of murdering priests (including the famous Jesuit Father Pro), closing churches, and punishing those caught practising their religion. The issue was still very much alive in 1938. That spring, Graham Greene – who had learnt from Waugh the practice of writing travel books, then novels – left to observe religious conditions in Mexico's roughest, least penetrated country on the trip that would issue in *The Lawless Roads* (1939) and *The Power and the Glory* (1940).

Waugh's was a shorter and easier stay: two months in the Mexico City Ritz. He probably thought conditions in Mexico so similar to those he had written about elsewhere that a short stay, along with appropriate background reading, would suffice for the book. Once again, as in Abyssinia, there was a military dictator, ruler of heterogeneous peoples, celebrated in Europe for his progressivism;

once again, as in *Campion*, a government seeking to uproot long-established Catholicism. He and Laura left for New York in August 1938 – their first visit to America – then took a steamer to Vera Cruz, where introductions from Henry Yorke (whose father was a director of the British-owned Mexican Railway) ensured solicitous treatment through to Mexico City. They met officials from business and government, drove to nearby sights, and were back in England by the end of October.

Pearson's conditions were that his association with the book be kept secret and that he be allowed to edit its discussion of the oil industry. In turn, he or his agents probably provided Waugh with background materials (it is hard to believe that Waugh himself unearthed such sources as the *Houston Post*). Waugh wanted to call the book *Pickpocket Government*, but Pearson vetoed the title; it eventually appeared as *Robbery Under Law: The Mexican Object Lesson* (in the United States, *Mexico: An Object Lesson*). Waugh knew there was no novel in his Mexican experiences. He had hoped at least to mine the travel book for articles, but Peters could find no journals interested in serialization. (Four short pieces did appear in the *Tablet*, for which Waugh took his usual minimal fee.)

Greene's *Lawless Roads* appeared in March 1939, while Waugh was still writing *Robbery Under Law*. Waugh confessed in a review to the 'anxiety' 'with which I began to read the report of so immediate a predecessor'; 'Here was a formidable rival'. But he found one important way of distinguishing his own book from Greene's: *Lawless Roads* made 'little attempt, except by occasional implication, to give the historical background of the tragedy' (EAR 249). If Pearson meant to subsidize only a criticism of Mexico's oil confiscations he got a far different book than he bargained for. Waugh took his commission as the opportunity not only to write a long meditative overview of Mexican history and religion, but also to present a straightforward exposition of his own political philosophy, the most extensive he ever wrote. 'This is Evelyn Waugh's fullest, soundest book', he announced on the dust-jacket.

Though the order of topics was later changed to give Church matters climactic rhetorical position, Waugh's outline of the book for Peters accurately summarizes its varied contents.

Pickpocket Government: The Mexican Object Lesson

is primarily an analysis of the danger which Mexico represents to the rest of the world, and in particular to the U.S.A., in its present unhappy condition. It opens with a description of the country as seen by the tourist; its beauties and inconsistencies and the hints which even the most obtuse tripper gets that there is something radically wrong. The government of the country is then examined; its historical origins and the steps by which the present regime has evolved. The regime is an odd mixture of Nazism and communism representing most of the worst features of both systems. In the next few years, perhaps months, it is likely to throw in its lot definitely with one or another of the two extremes. The choice either way, will be of world significance. The next chapter deals at length with the question of oil expropriations. The next with U. S. diplomacy showing the mistakes made by various statesmen who have been deluded into supporting the wrong sides again and again. The behaviour of the U. S. delegates at the recent Latin Congress is examined showing that General Cardenas has been led to believe that he has the full support of the New Deal policy. The Church is next dealt into; it is shown that there has been a savage persecution which still persists. The general public have never been fully informed about this; they were first told that it never existed, now that it is over. The next chapter deals with finance and commerce; the Six Year Plan Exhibition is used as the opportunity to examine Cardenas's disastrous policy. Final chapter deals with independence. Can Mexico survive? Will she be absorbed into U.S.A. or become leader of an anti-democratic Latin-American bloc in alliance with European Axis powers? A post-script gives the warning that Mexico may land us all in the soup; also the moral lesson that we may follow in her retrograde path if we aren't careful.

(HRC C17)

Waugh's chapter on religious persecution, entitled (in an echo of Christopher Dawson) 'The Straight Fight', is the most powerful in the book.[43] But for all its attention to the details of Mexican history both under Spain and since independence, *Robbery Under Law* is not, or not simply, a book about Mexico: it is a more general 'object lesson' about the modern state, a state riven by discordant ideologies, without religious moorings and heading for anarchy and war.

More even than *Scoop*, *Robbery Under Law* was 'Evelyn's Spanish War Book' (Sykes 255). Nowhere else did Waugh argue so fully his belief that the thirties presented three models of government – 'individualist, Fascist, or communist' – and that biased intellectuals and an irresponsible press had failed to recognize the kinship of last two, both 'forms of proletarian rule' (RUL 172, 274). Throughout appear discussions of political philosophy: of private property ('The ills of modern society rise, not from the presence of private property, but from its absence'); the destabilizing political effects that follow from erosion of belief in natural law as the basis of positive law; popular election (neither necessary nor sufficient for an 'individualist' state); the ordinary man's understandable search for an 'oppressor' of which he can be the 'victim'; the middle-class (not upper-class) origins of Fascism; and the folly of a politics like Woodrow Wilson's of ethnic self-determination, which produces not stability but a host of dissatisfied minorities.[44]

Two personal credos frame the book. These are philosophically unoriginal (as Waugh would have wished): they contain little that cannot be found in 'Bolingbroke, Burke, Coleridge and Disraeli' – to cite T. S. Eliot's canon of English conservative writers – or in the social encyclicals *Rerum novarum* (1891) and *Quadragesimo anno* (1931), to both of which Waugh refers.[45] These statements of belief so eloquently summarize habits of mind governing both Waugh's novels and his non-fictional writing as to deserve quotation in full. The first, framed in language that recalls the Creed (and sometimes reprinted under the title 'Conservative Manifesto'), is a straightforward warning to readers of what sort of book *Robbery Under Law* will be.

Let me, then, warn the reader that I was a Conservative when I went to Mexico and that everything I saw there strengthened my opinions. I believe that man is, by nature, an exile and will never be self-sufficient or complete on this earth; that his chances of happiness and virtue, here, remain more or less constant through the centuries and, generally speaking, are not much affected by the political and economic conditions in which he lives; that the balance of good and ill tends to revert to a norm; that sudden changes of physical condition are usually ill, and are advocated by the wrong people for the wrong reasons; that the intellectual communists of today have personal, irrelevant grounds for their antagonism to society, which they are trying to exploit. I believe in government; that men cannot live together without rules but that these should be kept at the bare minimum of safety; that there is no form of government ordained from God as being better than any other; that the anarchic elements in society are so strong that it is a whole-time task to keep the peace. I believe that inequalities of wealth and position are inevitable and that it is therefore meaningless to discuss the advantages of their elimination; that men naturally arrange themselves in a system of classes; that such a system is necessary for any form of co-operative work, more particularly the work of keeping a nation together. I believe in nationality; not in terms of race or of divine commissions for world conquest, but simply thus: mankind inevitably organises itself in communities according to its geographical distribution; these communities by sharing a common history develop common characteristics and inspire a local loyalty; the individual family develops most happily and fully when it accepts these natural limits. I do not think that British prosperity must necessarily be inimical to anyone else, but if, on occasions, it is, I want Britain to prosper and not her rivals. I believe that war and conquest are inevitable; that it is how history has been made and that is how it will develop. I believe that Art is a natural function of man; it so happens that most of the greatest art has appeared under systems of political tyranny, but I do not think it has a connection with any particular system, least of all with representative government, as nowadays in England, America and France it seems popular to believe; artists have always spent some of their spare time in flattering the governments under whom they live, so it is natural that, at the moment, English, American and French artists should be volubly democratic.

(RUL 16–17)

The second credo concludes the book, summarizing its lessons.

A conservative is not merely an obstructionist who wishes to resist the introduction of novelties; nor is he, as was assumed by most nineteenth century parliamentarians, a brake to frivolous experiment. He has positive work to do, whose value is particularly emphasized by the plight of Mexico. Civilization has no force of its own beyond what is given it from within. It is under constant assault, and it takes most of the energies of civilized man to keep going at all. There are criminal ideas and a criminal class in every nation, and the first action of every revolution, figuratively and literally, is to open the prisons. Barbarism is never finally defeated; given propitious circumstances, men and women who seem quite orderly will commit every conceivable atrocity. The danger does not come merely from habitual hooligans; we are all potential recruits for anarchy. Unremitting effort is needed to keep men living together at peace; there is only a margin of energy left over for experiment, however beneficent. Once the prisons of the mind have been opened, the orgy is on. There is no more agreeable position than that of dissident from a stable society. Theirs are all the solid advantages of other people's creation and preservation, and all the fun of detecting hypocrisies and inconsistencies. There are times when dissidents are not only enviable but valuable. The work of preserving society is sometimes onerous, sometimes almost effortless. The more elaborate the society, the more vulnerable it is to attack, and the more complete its collapse in the case of defeat. At a time like the present it is notably precarious. If it falls we shall see the dissolution not merely of a few joint-stock corporations, but of the spiritual and material achievements of our history. There is nothing, except ourselves, to stop our own countries from becoming like Mexico. That is the moral, for us, of her decay.

(RUL 278–9)

Response to a book which argued that Mexico had been better off under Spanish rule and insisted that active religious faith must underpin any stable and worthwhile civilization was perhaps more generous than Waugh could have expected. In Britain, the dependable *Spectator* was alone in unqualified praise ('very brilliant, sad story though it is'); most other journals took the line that, in the formulation of the *Manchester Guardian*, *Robbery* was 'admirably written, and few could have set out more ably this view of Mexico, a view which is open to argument but deserves to be understood'.[46] On the Left, the *New Statesman* ignored the book; Arthur Calder-Marshall (whose fiction Waugh had praised in spite of his Marxist politics) suggested that Waugh's own example proved the Mexican Church to be in league with 'Big Business'; Cyril Connolly planned a trip to Mexico with the object of production a picture-book rebutting Waugh's account.[47] In the United States, where Latin American affairs were better understood, Robert Martin – one of the few reviewers who was also an expert on Mexico – wrote a long tribute in the *New York Times* not only to Waugh's writing ('passages which rank as first-rate literature') but also to his 'persuasive' and 'calm logic', wise 'strictures on United States policy', and 'liberal public service in helping to redress the balance between Right-Wing and Left-Wing opinions on Mexico'.[48] In both countries Catholic response was guarded, though once again Americans found Waugh's case more persuasive.[49]

Though no reviewer seems to have made the comparison, *Robbery Under Law* was a more creditable effort to understand the world crisis from the point of view of a country outside Europe than another such book published earlier the same year, Auden and Isherwood's *Journey to a War*. This was another commissioned work, for which the authors travelled in late 1937 to observe the recently declared Sino-Japanese War; Auden contributed some poems on the nature of war in general, Isherwood a prose account of their journey. Neither knew China to start with, did any historical homework, or advanced any account of what was at stake in the conflict; their book is filled with bemused references to the 'inscrutable East'. (In a review Waugh praised Isherwood's reportorial style and dismissed Auden as 'a public bore': EAR 252.)

Sykes claimed that Waugh came to regard *Robbery Under Law* 'with displeasure and even shame' (Sykes 254), but on no other evidence than that Waugh excluded it from *When the Going Was Good*. Waugh himself explained the omission on the ground that *Robbery* 'dealt little with travel and much with political questions' (WGG 7). There was certainly much that Waugh overlooked. Had he investigated more thoroughly, he would have learnt that religious persecution was waning even as he wrote; he also failed to learn that F. W. Rickett had recently visited Mexico City, seeking an agreement like the one he had negotiated in Abyssinia (Kluckhorn 135–8). But if Waugh indeed grew ashamed of *Robbery Under Law*, it was probably because his timing was once again bad, and, more embarrassing, his predictions that Mexico might enlist with the Axis (and the United States be forced to intervene) turned out to be totally wrong.

He had deferred sitting down to write the book until December 1938, two months after returning home; the manuscript was finished only in April 1939. By the time it was published in July (November in the United States), public attention was firmly fixed on Germany. The book sold little and was never reprinted; in her omnibus survey of Waugh's work published in *Horizon* in 1946, Rose Macaulay seems not to have known of its existence.

With hindsight it seems surprising that Waugh could not guess, given the Roosevelt administration's extraordinary generosity to Cardenas, that if Mexico entered the War it would align itself not with the Axis but the United States. Cardenas's successor Avila Comacho did just that: in May 1942, Mexico declared war on Germany, with the result that, revived by American aid, Mexican manufacturing expanded by fully a third during the War and even more afterwards. In the prosperity of the 1940s and 1950s, Mexican Communism quietly died (Fagg 544–6). But in 1939 well-informed observers such as Robert Martin and Frank Kluckhorn (whose *Mexican Challenge* of the same year seems an American version of *Robbery Under Law*) could share Waugh's fears. Nonetheless, the critic of others' alarmism probably came to regret his own.

VI

In September 1938, while Waugh was still in Mexico, Chamberlain signed the Munich Pact. Well into 1939 the popular press continued to hold out prospects for peace. *The Times* and BBC radio were more pessimistic, drawing letters of complaint about their 'sensationalism'. In March and April 1939, as Germany completed its invasion of Czechoslovakia and Italy overran Albania, air-raid preparations were ordered throughout the country. Busy in his library and garden, Waugh preferred not to discuss what was coming. As the last summer of peace ended he wrote in his diary:

> As in September of last year, it is difficult to concentrate on work at the moment. I spent a restless day, but am maintaining our record as being the only English family to eschew the radio throughout the crisis. I have purchased for £10 16s the thirty-foot run of Gothic balustrade from Box and have inserted Miss Bruce's distillation into the weed-heap.
>
> Working in the afternoon in the garden, clearing the alley, I thought: what is the good of this? In a few months I shall be growing swedes and potatoes here and on the tennis court; or perhaps I shall be away and then another two or three years of weeds will feed here until the place looks as it did when we came here two years ago.
>
> (D 437)

By December he was in uniform, Laura and the children packed off to Pixton and Piers Court rented for the duration.

The work on which he had difficulty concentrating was a new novel, different from any he had written: not another objective, fast-moving satire crowded with characters and events but a slow, ruminative first-person narrative, introspective and emotional, composed in prose of new luxuriance and complexity. He had been planning it even while finishing *Robbery Under Law*, as he told Lady Diana in April: 'I finished a book today. About Mexico. Like an interminable *Times* leader of 1880. People will say well Waugh is done for; it is marriage and living in the country has done it. But I have a spiffing novel in mind and they must think again' (DC 66–7).

Progress was slow. By July he had done no more than rewrite the first chapter 'about six times'; when he left to join the Marines, only about '1/4 of a novel' was finished: two chapters called 'My Father's House' and 'Lucy Simmonds'. Though convinced that 'So far as it went', the new story contained his 'best writing' to date, Waugh told Peters: 'It is clear to me that I shall not resume my novel for the duration. Is there a chance of selling the two chapters under the title "Work not in Progress" or "Work Suspended" to a high-brow paper[?]'[50] *Work Suspended* would not be published for another two years, by which time he had already completed another novel, *Put Out More Flags*; but it is so much a product of the thirties – indeed, a valediction to the decade – that we may consider it here.

An abridgement of 'My Father's House' appeared in the November 1941 issue of *Horizon*, a new monthly founded by Connolly and Spender. Peters suggested that Waugh should not seek to publish such unfinished work elsewhere, or that at best he reprint it only as part of an anthology of stories. (Anthologies sold unusually well in wartime, and were more likely than slender novels to tempt publishers to commit their scarce allotments of rationed paper to.) But Waugh, convinced of its merit, wanted the traditional format of a book. The whole appeared in December 1942, in an expensive edition of 500 copies, the most paper Chapman and Hall were willing to devote to such an unremunerative project.[51] A larger public did not see the story until a revised text, its chapters retitled 'A Death' and 'A Birth', appeared in Britain in *Work Suspended and Other Stories Written Before the Second World War* (1949), and in the United States in the collection *Tactical Exercise* (1954). Originally the fragment had been set in the early thirties; the later versions end just as World War II is declared, when, its hero says in a postscript, 'an epoch, my epoch, came to an end' (WS 238).

The edition of 1942 bore a dedication to the American Alexander Woollcott in thanks for his 'encouragement', itself a hint that Waugh was attempting something new. Previous books had been inscribed to contemporaries – to lovers or friends in whose houses he worked. Woollcott was a journalist and critic of an older generation, an acquaintance of Waugh's father, whose praises had boosted American sales of *Decline and Fall* and *A Handful of Dust* ('the finest novel in a century'); he was well known for his humorous attacks on Marxism and the Soviet Union. (Woollcott may have met Waugh while visiting England in 1941; he recorded his delight on receiving the dedication in a letter to Thornton Wilder.)[52] To this figure Waugh turned as he published his declaration of independence from both current critical trends and his own previous practice.

As Rose Macaulay noted, *Work Suspended* is a 'an experiment, a study, abandoned, in a new *genre*' (Macaulay 371). It is also a demonstration of Waugh's objections to the factual, realistic, Leftward march of prose books in the thirties, whose theoretical premisses he had long attacked in rumbustious essays and reviews.

Samuel Hynes takes 1934 as 'the year in which British communism formally addressed itself to the arts', when the British Section of the Writers' International was founded (along with its official organ, the *Left Review*), and when even the *Daily Worker* began reviewing novels and books of poems. Both journals kept a close watch on Soviet developments. The First Soviet Writers' Congress declared that year, 'Yes, Soviet literature is tendentious, for in an epoch of class struggle there is not and cannot be a literature which is not class literature, not tendentious, allegedly non-political'; many on the British Left, as Julian Bell complained in 1936, soon agreed 'that all art is propaganda'. 'We are . . . in a period in which it is taken for granted that books ought always to be positive, serious, and "constructive,"' wrote Orwell in 1940; 'A dozen years ago this idea would have been greeted with titters'. Any other approach was 'escapism'. The Communist Edward Upward explained in Day Lewis's influential anthology, *The Mind in Chains* (1937): 'a modern fantasy cannot tell the truth, cannot give a picture of life which will survive the test of experience; since fantasy implies in practice a retreat from the real world into the world of imagination, and though such a retreat may have been practicable and desirable in a more leisured and less profoundly disturbed age than our own, it is increasingly impracticable today'.[53]

Waugh liked to say that what other critics called 'the Auden gang' – Auden, Isherwood, Spender, Day Lewis, Calder-Marshall, Upward – had 'ganged up and captured the decade' (EAR 394).

> A school of critics who see no reality except in the raw materials of civilization have popularized the jargon-word 'escapism' as a term to condemn all imaginative work; they hold that the only proper concern of man is buying, selling and manufacturing and the management of these activities in an equitable way; that anyone who interests himself in other things is trying to escape his obligations and destiny.
>
> (EAR 231)

> People now use the phrase 'without contemporary significance' to express just those works which are of most immediate importance, works which eschew barbaric extremes and attempt to right the balance of civilization.
>
> (EAR 200)

Waugh's objections to the literary Left may be considered under three headings: its notions of proper literary stance, style, and the political commitment that underlies both.

The stance of objectivity and 'fact' (associated also with 'documentary' writing) implied, as Orwell noted, that 'Preoccupation with sex and truthfulness about the inner life' – exactly Waugh's concerns in *Work Suspended* – 'are out of fashion'. In the extreme formulation of Storm Jameson (who had criticized *The Road to Wigan Pier* for Orwell's habit of telling readers 'what he felt'), 'As the photographer does, so must the writer keep himself out of the picture while working ceaselessly to present the *fact*'.[54]

The documentary stance enacted a rejection of the 'individualism' so often denounced by theorists on the Left. The premier issue of the *Left Review* called 'individualism' (pervasive in 'the most "advanced" literature immediately before and just after the 1914–18 war') nothing less than 'the licensed relaxation of a prosperous economic dictatorship', and thus an 'antecedent to Fascism'. 'Artists are to abandon individualism' proclaimed Spender in 1935, repeating a slogan from the Kharkov Writers Congress.[55] Factuality of a distinctly Marxian kind was also sought through such experiments in representing the 'collective mind' as literary collaborations, collectively written poems and the anthology of 'people's poetry' Auden and John Garrett presented in *The People's Tongue* (1935), a collection of verses printed without authors or titles, merely numbers. Waugh repeatedly ridiculed literary collaborators, the Parsnips and Pimpernels – 'it always seems to take two people to make a book nowadays, how do they manage it?' – and insisted that the artists and intellectuals are 'people with individual work to do'. (So many on the Left denounced literary 'individualism' that in 1935 André Gide was moved to protest, delivering a speech in its defence at the Paris Writers Conference.)[56]

In a parallel development, the argument became commonplace that – in the words of the decade's most cogent defence of socialist realism, Ralph Fox's *The Novel and the People* – 'the romantic thought will demand a romantic style and the realist thought, the plain "prose" thought, a simple, realistic style' (138). The very word *style*, Cyril Connolly noted, began 'to sound horrible': 'something artificial, a kind of ranting or preening', 'something no good writer should possess' (*Enemies* 9). Under such slogans as 'LITERARY ENGLISH FROM CAXTON TO US IS AN ARTIFICIAL JARGON OF THE RULING CLASS', contributors to the *Left Review* called for 'the proletarianisation of our actual language' and produced essays like Allen Hutt's 'The Revolutionist's Handbook: Flint and Steel English', a formulary of the 'short', 'plain' and 'homely' expressions that alone could rescue the English language from 'the ruling class which has so bastardized it'. 'Flat, cautious statements and snack-bar dialects are now in fashion', complained Orwell.[57] (One measure of the effectiveness of Waugh's ridicule of these ideas in his essays – and of his novels as examples of how to keep an alternative aesthetic alive – is the frequency with which works like Ralph Fox's *Novel and the People* pause to attack him.)

The inconsistent allegiance to Left aesthetics of Cyril Connolly, whose literary intelligence Waugh deeply admired, drew some of his most effective ridicule. Connolly was both a professed socialist and the pupil (and longtime employee) of that vigorous defender of 'fine writing' against the 'Puritanism' and 'economic materialism' of 'Communism and Cambridge', Logan Pearsall Smith. (Waugh called Smith 'that splendid American' and cheerfully borrowed his terminology.)[58] In *Enemies of Promise* (1938), dedicated to Smith, Connolly tried with tortuous illogic both to assert his political correctness and to argue that literature should return to 'the long sentence and the splendour and subtlety of the composed phrase'. Connolly argues:

If culture is to survive it must survive through the masses.... The old world is a sinking ship, to get a place in the boats that are pushing off from it not money nor leisure, the essayist's elegance nor the pedant's erudition will avail; the sailors are not impressed.... Nothing will admit us but realism and sincerity, an honest appeal in downright English.... For this reason left-wing writers have tended to write in the colloquial style while the Mandarins, the wizards and prose charmers remain as supporters of the existing dispensation.

(69)

Yet at the same time, Connolly calls not only for a return to that very 'Mandarin style' but also for a revival of the patronage of writers by the fashionable and wealthy ('warmhearted people of delicate sensibility who form permanent friendships with artists which afford them ease and encouragement for the rest of their lives and provide them with sanctuary'). As Waugh – an unashamed defender of the role of an upper class in nurturing art and middle-class artists – said in one of his shrewdest reviews, Connolly was 'divided in his mind'. 'He seems to have two peevish spirits whispering into either ear: one complaining that the bedroom in which he awakes is an ugly contrast to the splendid dining-room where he was entertained the previous evening; the other saying that the names have been made up for the firing squads; he must shoot first if he does not want to be shot' (EAR 199).

Underlying Left aesthetics, Waugh believed, was the political doctrine 'that the class struggle is the only topic worth a writer's attention' (which as a corollary 'means relegating to insignificance almost the whole of the world's literature') (EAR 199). In response he concerned himself all the more resolutely with gentlefolk. If what Geoffrey Grigson called 'this period of the victory of the masses' demanded that the writer express solidarity with the proletariat, Waugh created Whelper, Shumble and Pigge, and in *Work Suspended* the grotesque Atwater, aptly described by Sykes as a 'lost soul of the aspirant lower middle class, lower public school, lower intelligentsia, lower human being', the antecedent of such even less appetising proletarians as Hooper and Trimmer.[59] In a thoughtful negative review of *Work Suspended*, Nigel Dennis used Spender's line 'It is too late now to stay in those houses your fathers have built' to distinguish Waugh's politics from those of the Auden group. 'What appeared in their writings as a new faith in the proletariat and an enthusiasm for the urban under-privileged was ... an effort to purge the author's own personality of its upper-class preferences and trained acceptance of the old, rural order'; 'The intellectual pledged his new fidelity to the city'. In reaction, Dennis noted, *Work Suspended* elegiacally evokes 'My Father's House' and celebrates the great country house (CH 229).

In was in this political context that Waugh mounted his case, also embodied in the decoration and furniture of Piers Court, for 'ornament, "elegance', and 'magnificence.'

There was a shrinking [after World War I] from the rare and lovely and elaborate, and a welcome for the commonplace.... Vocabularies were purged of all but their drabbest epithets. A decade later all this bilge was canalized by the Marxists. Then it had half London and Paris awash.

(EAR 424)

Elegance is the quality in a work of art which imparts direct pleasure; again, not a universal pleasure. There is a huge, envious world to whom elegance is positively offensive.... and it is, perhaps, in ignoble deference to their susceptibilities that there has been a notable flight from magnificence in English writing. Sixty years ago, when 'jewelled prose' was all the rage, there were some pretentious efforts at fine writing which excited great ridicule. There was an inevitable reaction, but surveying the bleak prospect today, one can recognize that those absurdities are a small price to pay for the magnificence of the preceding masters.

(EAR 478–9)

Such 'fine writing' would notoriously find expression in *Brideshead*, but as Donat Gallagher suggests, several articles of the thirties (such as the full-throated, even pretentious 'Laying Down a Wine Cellar' (1937)) already point in this direction (EAR 154). It is already audible in *Campion*, where – as often in Waugh – the workings of memory elicit 'the long sentence' and 'the composed phrase'.

Or did she contrast her present state, an old perjured woman, dying without comfort, with those early years when the future had been compact of hope and adventure; see the light on the river and hear again the splash of oars as Leicester's barge rode between green banks and pollarded willows, and the flowered damask trailed out in the water behind them; the torchlight at Kenilworth and Rycote, the extravagant, irresponsible dances before the royal suitors, the bonfires kindling from crest to crest as the news travelled across country of the Armada's failure?

(EC 6).

Much later Waugh would say that 1935, the year *Campion* appeared, was a turning point in his literary life, when, after he had 'struck lucky with three or four light novels', he began 'to look about for a suitable "life's work"' and so to plan a new kind of writing, which he could then only describe as 'semi-historic, semi-poetic fiction' (HP 2). The project then initiated began to be realized in earnest only with *Work Suspended*, which engages his Left opponents on all three fronts: style, politics and especially the writer's stance.

The fragment tells of a successful young writer of detective stories named John Plant, who as the story opens returns to London from Fez when his father, a painter, is killed – run down, not quite accidentally, by the travelling salesman Atwater. In the first chapter Plant oversees the closing of his father's house (soon to be demolished to make way for a block of flats), confesses to his editor that he has reached a 'climacteric' as a writer and cannot continue producing the same sort of novels as before, and meets Atwater. In the second, he falls in love with Lucy, pregnant wife of his novelist friend Roger Simmonds, and with her visits the zoo and searches for a country house. At the end Lucy turns her attention from Plant to her new baby, and he again meets Atwater. The narrative is unlike Waugh's previous novels not only in its first-person presentation but also its 'virtual absence of plot' (Sykes 306). *Work Suspended* moves slowly through Plant's memories, meditations on art and efforts to understand his own emotions. It is not satire but something much closer to autobiography. More even than in *Scoop*, all the men in the story are versions of Waugh himself.

Plant seems at first quite unlike his creator: an atheist, thrifty, a writer who after choosing his 'career deliberately at the age of twenty-one' now writes novels which have 'absolutely nothing of [him]self' in them (WS 140). But these differences mask more striking similarities, hinted at in Waugh's usual way through parallel birth dates and allusions to what he saw as the stages of his own career. Plant returns from Fez, where he had been working on his eighth book; in 1934 Waugh returned from Fez, where he had been working on his eighth book, *A Handful of Dust*. References to the Spanish Civil War and dock strikes in Madras place the action a little later, in 1936–7. At the start of the novel Plant tells his editor he has 'been writing for over eight years', again suggesting 1936 – eight years after the publication of *Rossetti*, when Waugh was preparing to marry Laura, hunting for a house in the country and working on another novel that hesitated formal innovation and autobiographical self-exploration: *Scoop*. In chapter two Plant turns thirty-four, as Waugh did in 1937.

But Waugh meant not so much to recreate a particular moment in his life as to assemble a collage of his experience in the thirties.[60] Roger Simmonds, like Waugh, has made a successful career of 'funny novels' and 'jobs with newspapers and film companies', but is now turning to a new style. Old Mr Plant, the subject of long meditations by his son, captures other features of his author. A man for whom it was enough 'to learn that an opinion of his had popular support for him to question and abandon it', he shares Waugh's 'persecution mania', disgust for the 'great, uninhabitable barracks' replacing London's more gracious old buildings and 'repugnance to paying direct taxes, or, as he preferred it, to subscribing to "the support of the politicians" '. He believed that 'public life had become an open conspiracy for the destruction of himself and his class', the upper middle class or 'educated gentry', and that 'There are only three classes in England now', 'politicians, tradesmen, and slaves' – as Waugh would soon argue that the Left was reducing Britain to a nation comprised only of bureaucrats and workers (WS 145–6). Most of all, old Mr Plant, a painter in the manner of Frith (Waugh's touchstone Victorian story-painter since his early essay on Cubism), shares Waugh's views about art. A 'conservative, but [not] where his art was concerned', he abjured Clive Bell and 'never doubted that the function of painting was representational' (148). Like Waugh in *Rossetti*, he thought the tradition of nineteenth-century narrative painting had never 'come to maturity' as it might have done 'had there not been any Aesthetic Movement' and consequent reaction in the form of Cézanne's Post-Impressionism (165).

That his hero John Plant is a writer of detective novels is crucial for understanding Waugh's own sense, at once frustrating and liberating, of having reached a 'climacteric' (a description he soon also used of himself (EAR 302)). Detective fiction is a popular form, elaborate in contrivance and designed to give widespread pleasure. Waugh stresses that Plant is proud of his sales, of the extent to which his writing pleases. In the same way Waugh himself always championed both artistic 'enjoyment' and what he called 'communicativeness', of which one test is 'lucidity'. Campion was a man for whom ideas 'demanded communication, and it was his particular genius to give the expression in lucid and memorable phrases'; in 1937 Waugh praised the painter David Jones for writing a memoir free of the 'obscure' and 'esoteric', one that possessed 'a painter's *communicativeness*'; in 1954, he protested the emergence of a new literary context in which 'readability is a quality to be eschewed in an aspirant for critical attention'.[61] 'It cannot be said too often or too loud that all Art is the art of pleasing', he told Nancy Mitford in 1954 (NM 340); he wrote of James Joyce:

> His later work lost almost all faculty of communication, so intimate, allusive and idiosyncratic did it become.... because he was obscure and can only be read with intense intellectual effort – and therefore without easy pleasure – he is admitted into the academic canon. But it is just in this task of communication that Joyce's style fails, for the necessary elements of style are lucidity, elegance, individuality; these three qualities combine to form a preservative which ensures the nearest approximation to permanence in the fugitive art of letters.
>
> (EAR 478)

Work Suspended asks us to agree with Lucy's remark that 'two private soldiers construing [one of Plant Sr's battle pictures] together, point by point', is 'worth a dozen columns of praise in the weekly papers' (WS 196).

But such an anti-elitist aesthetic has its drawbacks: its practitioner may not be considered a serious artist. In part because of its very popularity, detective fiction is generally thought a lesser form. To old Mr Plant's 'naturally hierarchic mind, and in his scheme of things, detective stories stood slightly above the librettos of musical comedy and well below political journalism'.[62] The same might be said of the 'funny novels' Roger Simmonds writes so successfully – and of the 'light novels' Waugh himself spoke of abandoning for more ambitious work. Plant like Waugh considers himself a 'serious writer' (139); he is proud when a Professor of Poetry calls one of his novels a 'work of art' (146). He says of Simmonds, and by extension himself (and Waugh):

> Roger was a very good novelist – every bit as good in his own way as I in mine; when one came to think of it, it was impossible to name anyone else, alive, who could do what he did, there was no good reason why his books should not be compared with those of prominent writers of the past, nor why we should not speculate about their ultimate fame.
>
> (WS 188–9)

No 'professor of poetry' had spoken this way of Waugh; few noted his artistry or even succeeded in construing his meaning. Most critics, whatever their praise for his stylistic mastery, had consigned him to the rank of 'light novelists'; highbrow journals such as Eliot's *Criterion* and Leavis's *Scrutiny* ignored him. *Work Suspended* attests not only Waugh's desire to adopt a new and more ambitious literary mode, but also his sense of not having achieved the recognition he deserved.

Waugh knew that he was himself partly to blame for this lack of recognition – that his own attitudes to the 'highbrow', especially the highbrow Left, prevented his receiving the comprehension and praise from intellectuals he at once craved and despised. John Plant has nothing but contempt for the newfound Communism of Roger Simmonds, who with Lucy's money can 'sit back in comfort to await the World Revolution' (189); he laughs at the 'ideological' works Roger starts to write, and at the Communist author's need to sink his individuality in toeing to the party line. (Roger tells Plant of his new play *Internal Combustion*, whose 'characters' are not people but parts of an car engine: 'I mean the characters are economic types, not individuals, and as long as they look and speak like individuals it's bad art.... The Finsbury International Theatre are sitting on it now, and if it's orthodox – and I *think* it is – they may put it on this summer if Lucy finds the money' (170).) But even as he scoffs, Plant is aware that Roger, not he, is in the vanguard, as a young woman reminds him over dinner:

> 'I don't take those political opinions of [Roger's] seriously', she said, 'and anyhow, it's all right to be a Communist nowadays. Everyone is'.
>   'I'm not', [Plant] said.
>   'Well, I mean all the clever young people'.

(WS 201)

The 1930s seemed to leave the non-Leftist, non-highbrow who also wished to be a serious writer no workable identity. The only alternatives to going the way of *Internal Combustion* seemed to be either remaining in the lesser realm of 'funny novels' – perhaps, as Plant tells his editor, adding a few 'technical experiments' most readers won't notice – or adopting an ambitious manner that the intellectual Left would think out of date. Perhaps Waugh abandoned the fragment because he as yet saw no better than John Plant how to alter his literary identity.

Work Suspended is of course not merely a meditation on novel writing, though the book if completed would doubtless have supplied by example some answer to John Plant's dilemma about what kind of writing – and self – to turn to next. It might thus have resembled Waugh's later metafictions *The Loved One* and *Gilbert Pinfold*, whose artist-heroes end by writing the book we have just read. Perhaps the novel would have become a murder-mystery with Plant as Atwater's killer; perhaps the atheist Plant would have converted. Young 'Plant' might have struck roots in the country and grown up. Had Waugh completed it, he would doubtless have clarified the portentous but vague symbols that litter the fragment, such as Humboldt's Gibbon and the use of doubles. (Sykes claimed that before abandoning it Waugh had planned 'in detail how the story would develop', and that he himself had been told – but forgotten – Waugh's plans (Sykes 307).)

Since Sykes's biography the view has become common that *Work Suspended* would if completed 'almost certainly have been a great novel, possibly [Waugh's] best' (272). The claim is not justified by the chapters we have – structureless, overwritten and populated by characters who for the most part remain disembodied voices. These failings are interrelated. Waugh was beginning again, seeking a new kind of fiction, one that could present his views positively rather than by negative implication. It is a common vice of first novels that all their characters are projections of their author's moods or mouthpieces for his opinions. This state of affairs had begun to intrude in *Scoop*; it infects the whole of *Work Suspended*, and would mar *Put Out More Flags*. It is corrected only in *Brideshead*, when once again Waugh is able to realize distinctly individual characters within a coherent structure.

That solution entailed solving another problem, an age-old literary problem that took on new urgency in the political world of the late thirties and early forties. Like that of his Marxist opponents, Waugh's criticism in these years is haunted by the language of 'individuals' and 'types'. He recognized that 'satire', including his own first novels, demands characters who are 'mere dialectical abstractions' (ND 211). He knew that as he sought to move beyond satire into a new kind of fiction, he would have to draw characters differently. His reviews of the late thirties repeatedly single out for praise stories in which a character '*is* a character, three-dimensional and fully coloured, never once degenerating into a type' (ND 52). But equally often he expresses doubt whether such characterization is possible, whether such phenomena as sexual attractiveness, love, or any profoundly dislocating psychological experience can ever be realized in fiction.[63] *Work Suspended* returns to the problem; in a muddled passage deleted after 1942, Waugh translated his own failure to create 'individuals' rather than 'types' into a general theory about the limits of fiction: 'The algebra of fiction must reduce its problems to symbols if they are to be soluble at all. There is no place in literature for a live man, solid and active. At best the author may... take the whole man and reduce him to a manageable abstraction' (WS1 82–3).

The issue was philosophic as well as literary, as the Marxists made clear. 'Man is no longer the individual will' declared Ralph Fox in *The Novel and the People* before proceeding to the 'question of questions', how a novelist can portray 'the full life of the individual man, woman, or child' (96, 160, 8). His Marxist solution is that to give a 'complete picture of man', the novelist must demonstrate how his 'individual will' is the expression of the socio-economic forces that have shaped it; writers concerned primarily with psychology have necessarily 'failed to see the individual as a whole' (23, 105, 97). In response to such views Waugh consistently denounced Marxism as a 'denial of individuality to individuals', a failure to observe 'the basic assumption of all traditional Christian art and philosophy that every human being is possessed of free will, reason and personal desires' (ND 52, 171).

> I do not think that any artist, certainly no writer, can be a genuine Marxist, for a writer's material must be the individual soul..., while the Marxist can only think in classes and categories, and even in classes abhors variety.
>
> (EAR 206)

> Men and women are only types – economic, psychological, what you will – until one knows them.
>
> (EAR 214)

> A novelist has no business with types; they are the property of economists and politicians and advertisers and other professional bores of our period. The artist is interested only in individuals.
>
> (EAR 302)

But as we have seen, Waugh shared Fox's suspicion of 'psychology'. What then did it mean for an individual to be an individual, and how portray such a creature in fiction? *Put Out More Flags* repeatedly raises questions about 'individuals' and 'types', but never achieves clarity on what it means to be either. Only with *Brideshead* does Waugh achieve such clarity. Where Fox's solution was economic, Waugh's is theological: what finally individuates us, and what must be at the ground of literary characterization, is the unique purpose given each of us by God.

In one respect the two solutions, the Marxist and the Catholic, are similar. Both, as T. S. Eliot recognized as early as 1930 (in his essay 'Poetry and Propaganda'), lead to writing that is 'ideological'. By the end of the thirties, Waugh had come in effect to accept the Left view that 'all art is propaganda'. *Robbery Under Law* speaks of 'the humbug of being "unbiased"' (15); where earlier he had celebrated the literature of 'escape', *Put Out More Flags* definitively rejects notions of art for art's sake, and satirizes Ambrose Silk for supposing that art can avoid being propaganda. With *Brideshead*, Waugh transparently offers propaganda of his own.

5

A People's War (1939–1945)

Just seven days earlier [Guy Crouchback] had opened his morning newspaper on the headlines announcing the Russian-German alliance. News that shook the politicians and young poets of a dozen capital cities brought deep peace to one English heart....He lived too close to Fascism in Italy to share the opposing enthusiasms of his countrymen. He saw it neither as a calamity nor as a rebirth; as a rough improvisation merely. He disliked the men who were edging themselves into power around him, but English denunciations sounded fatuous and dishonest and for the past three years he had given up his English newspapers. The German Nazis he knew to be mad and bad. Their participation dishonoured the cause of Spain, but the troubles of Bohemia, the year before, left him quite indifferent. But now, splendidly, everything had become clear. The enemy at last was plain in view, huge and hateful, all disguise cast off. It was the Modern Age in arms. Whatever the outcome there was a place for him in that battle.

Men at Arms (1952)

On 3 September, 1939, as evacuees began streaming into the neighbouring town of Dursley, the Waughs broke their 'record as being the only English family to eschew the radio throughout the crisis' to hear Chamberlain announce Britain's entry into the Second World War (D 437). Though he was nearly thirty-six and Laura pregnant with their second child (Auberon, born that November), Waugh had already started looking for war work and advertised the rental of Piers Court. In August he mused:

My inclinations are all to join the army as a private. Laura is better placed than most wives, and if I could let the house for the duration very well placed financially. I have to consider thirty years of novel-writing ahead of me. Nothing would be more likely than work in a government office to finish me as a writer; nothing more likely to stimulate me than a complete change of habit.

(D 438)

At the end of September, having let the house for £600 a year to a small school run by Dominican nuns, the family moved to Pixton. Through the good offices of Bridget Herbert, the local billeting officer, Pixton was itself now also home to some thirty 'slum children': evacuees who spent their days spitting from the landings of the great hall onto passersby below, and during their homesick nights joined what historians record as 'a countrywide outbreak of bedwetting'.[1] Waugh quickly sensed 'Evacuation as a theme for a major work' of fiction (L127), though by the time he unveiled the horrible Connolly children of *Put Out More Flags* (1942) many others had already made use of the idea.[2]

At Laura's request he first sought a desk job at the newly founded Ministry of Information, in whose offices at London University his agent Peters would soon find him work. But what he hungered for was combat: the chance after three sedentary years to become again a man of action, in an honourable public cause. In March 1939 Britain had pledged to defend Catholic Poland. When news arrived in August that Stalin had joined Hitler in a non-aggression pact, demonstrating the kinship of totalitarianisms Waugh had long preached, Britain's duty was clear. 'There seems no reason why war should be delayed' (D 437). That the odds were against a potentially lone Britain made the cause the more unambiguously noble – a sentiment that would become widespread only later, after the fall of France.[3]

> The war seems likely to develop into an attack on Great Britain by an alliance of Russia, Germany, Japan, and perhaps Italy, with France bought out and USA as sympathetic onlooker. Had I no garden to dig in I should be in despair with lack of occupation.
>
> (D 441)

For three frustrating months after Chamberlain's speech Waugh (like many contemporaries) approached well-placed friends, visited government offices, filled out forms and entered his name on lists, but found 'no demand for cannon fodder' (D 440). Meanwhile he continued writing what was to become *Work Suspended* and even negotiated with Chapman and Hall to produce a monthly magazine to be called *Duration* (a project parallel with Cyril Connolly's *Horizon*, whose first issue appeared in January 1940). Finally help came from the highest level. Among those he had approached was Brendan Bracken, whom he had met at Belton and who was now secretary to Winston Churchill, an admirer of Waugh's novels since 1928. With the backing of the First Lord of the Admiralty, Waugh was called up to begin training in December at Chatham, in Kent, as a temporary officer in the Royal Marines.

Thus began six years of soldiering that comprise a remarkable war record for a man well over usual military age. As his friend the Earl of Birkenhead wrote, Waugh always 'deliberately chose the branches of the service most likely to be exposed to extreme hazard' (HW 139). He initially chose Marine infantry over artillery – 'a force being raised for raiding parties' rather than coastal defence (D 451); he transferred from the Marines to the newly formed Special Services Brigade (the 'Commandos') when Marine work seemed to promise only the 'safe and boring': 'I want to be back in Europe fighting Germans' (L 141). Though he never rose in rank above captain or achieved his ambition to become a troop commander, he saw action three times, in raids on Dakar and Bardia, and in the Battle of Crete, where he displayed what one military historian calls a 'degree of courage, astonishing to others yet matter-of-fact to himself' (Beevor, *Crete*, 221). Later he survived a plane crash in Croatia in which half those aboard were killed. The diaries still record him in 1943 'yearning to get to the front' (547), to which end – at the age of forty – he elected a course of parachute training. This dangerous activity he thoroughly enjoyed.

These were immensely productive years for the writer as well as the soldier. Waugh knew from the first that he would convert military experience into fiction: he instructed Laura to keep his letters; against regulations, he kept a detailed diary. While in uniform he continued *Work Suspended*, completed *Put Out More Flags* (1942) and *Brideshead Revisited* (1945), and began *Helena*; afterward he reworked the whole of his wartime experiences in *Men at Arms*, *Officers and Gentlemen* and *Unconditional Surrender*, the three novels that comprise *Sword of Honour*. He continued proselytizing, unsuccessfully with fellow-Marines such as John St John, successfully with the conversion of his soldier-servant Hall in 1943 and, in a deeply moving sequence of events later reworked into the story Lord Marchmain's final days in *Brideshead*, at the deathbed of his old friend Hubert Duggan. And the war brought him three more children, conceived on his various leaves. Laura preferred sons, he daughters; she bore him Mary, born in December 1940 (who lived only a day); Margaret, born June 1942; and Harriet, born May 1944.

Yet for all this, the war commenced for both Waugh and Laura a period of increasing, finally permanent despondence. Not for them the bracing comradeship of a nation pulling together at a time of national peril such as led many afterwards to say that the Blitz had been the most meaningful time in their lives. To Laura as to many other women, the war brought six grim civilian years of rationing, homelessness, sudden calls to join her husband's leaves, resulting pregnancies and attendant illnesses. Always introverted, she turned more inward than ever, so that Waugh could comment in 1945, 'like you I have learned to shut off 2/3 of my mind from what is being said'. 'She retreated from any more demanding social contact into her own private meditations whose direction was not easily to be distinguished from simple misanthropy.'[4]

For him the war years seemed a prolonged national and personal humiliation. Already by 1942 England had so changed, a new kind of modernity taken root so at odds with his most deeply held values, that Waugh could call the war (through the persona of John Plant) the time when 'an epoch, my epoch, came to an end'. Having ardently embraced the opportunity for public service in a cause that seemed at the outset heroic and just, all too soon Waugh came to think of the war instead – in a description that must have seemed blasphemous when it was published in 1947 – as having 'cast its heroic and chivalrous disguise and bec[o]me a sweaty tug-of-war between teams of indistinguishable louts' (SK 5). It left him prematurely aged and permanently embittered. He would live twenty more years after demobilisation and write some of his greatest prose, but in important ways Waugh's emotional and intellectual development – like that of many who outlived the great drama – ended in 1945. The war was the crucible in which his mature pessimism was fully formed; with a few striking exceptions, his writing from *Put Out More Flags* onward is retrospective, sorting through the causes of a modernity from which the author, all disillusions laid, was profoundly estranged.

Waugh's most revealing commentaries on the war were published mainly after 1945 – after wartime censorship regulations making it a chargeable offence to cause 'alarm and despondency' by circulating 'depressing rumours or defeatist opinions' had lapsed. So it is often necessary to look ahead to the 1950s and the completed *Sword of Honour* to understand his views and the war's cumulative effect on him. Christopher Sykes was perhaps right to warn that Waugh initially experienced no such wholesale 'love affair with the army' as Charles Ryder and Guy Crouchback enjoy (Sykes 295). But the letters and diaries do record a deep initial pleasure in soldiering, not only at Chatham, where in historic quarters reminiscent of a gentleman's club the Marines (like the Halberdiers in *Men at Arms*) maintained their long tradition of highly civilized ritual, but also at subsequent, less comfortable postings, where his chief complaint was often 'We have had too little work' (D 462). In later, bleaker periods of the war he could write, 'I wish I could recapture some of that adventurous spirit with which I joined at Chatham' (L 157).

I

The day-to-day excitements, boredoms, and frustrations of Waugh's military service, well summarized by Sykes, make tedious and uninstructive reading. Until the Normandy landings most of the army remained in training camps in Britain; like many another soldier Waugh was shifted suddenly and, it often seemed, pointlessly from camp to camp, expecting shortly to be sent into action and as often disappointed. To alleviate boredom he turned, as so often, to fantasy. John St John, his fellow officer from their first training exercises at Chatham through to Dakar, recalled, 'Evelyn could seldom resist the temptation to poke fun: for example, I once heard him innocently enquire, to the perplexity of a pompous visiting brass-hat, if it were true that "in the Roumanian army no one beneath the rank of major is permitted to use lipstick"'. St John's *To the War with Waugh* (1975) concludes that *Put Out More Flags* and *Sword of Honour* 'provide the truest as well as the funniest guide to what it was really like' (26, 56).

They were moved seven times before their first real action in September 1940, a raid on Dakar intended to assist De Gaulle's Free French forces to secure West Africa. Ruined at the outset by inept communications, failure of British troops in Gibraltar to prevent Vichy from sending reinforcements, and a sudden dense fog off the African coast, the operation was cancelled for fear of excessive casualties before any Marines even landed. During the return voyage Waugh wrote to Laura, 'Bloodshed has been avoided at the cost of honour', and two days later, 'I have written again to London asking for a transfer ... because it seems clear to me that we are never going to be employed in a way I can be proud of' (L 141).

14 Captain Waugh of the Royal Marines (National Portrait Gallery/Howard Coster).

'Most of war seems to consist of hanging about' says Peter Pastmaster while organizing a special commando force in *Put Out More Flags*; 'Let's at least hang about with our own friends' (254). Again with Bracken's help, Waugh secured his transfer and in November 1940 travelled to Scotland to begin training under his old friend Robert Laycock in the Commandos, a secret *corps d'élite* also intended for raiding parties. A 'corps of Buck's toughs' he called them, 'doomed no doubt to ignominy like the marines, but at the moment promising'. Commandos observed a daily routine far less strict than the Marines: 'All the officers have very long hair & lap dogs & cigars & they wear whatever they like'; 'The officers are divided more or less equally into dandies and highly efficient professional soldiers' (L 145–6). In the Marines Waugh had been starved of sophisticated companionship: 'I am friends with all', he told Laura, 'but I do wish sometimes I could meet an adult. They are all little boys' (L 142). Now he was among the sort of worldly, self-assured individualists whose company he relished: old friends such as Harry, Lord Stavordale, Peter Milton (later Earl Fitzwilliam), Philip Dunne and especially Randolph Churchill, who kept a pekinese and spent nights drunkenly losing hundreds of pounds at cards. 'They had a gaiety and independence which I thought would prove valuable in action', he later reflected ruefully; 'I saw few symptoms of their later decay' (D 491).

In the new year Laycock's Commandos sailed not for assignment in Europe but to Egypt, taking the long route around the Cape. After a stop in Cape Town, whose freedom from wartime austerities *Officers and Gentlemen* memorably recalls, they reached Suez in March 1941, too late to help stem the German invasion of North Africa. So often had Layforce, too, been moved from place to place, so often operations planned and cancelled, that the unit came to be known as 'Belayforce'; on ship appeared the graffito, 'Never in the history of human endeavour have so few been buggered about by so many' (D 495). In April, frustrated with inaction, they were allowed a raid on the Libyan coastal town of Bardia, where intelligence reported a German garrison 2000 strong. But this raid proved no more successful than the operation at Dakar: the Germans had already abandoned the town; a lone German patrol escaped by motorcycle when the landing parties, one of whom shot their own officer by mistake, made too much noise; one party lost their way and had to be left behind, later to be captured. Here Waugh first met Colonel F. B. Colvin, the 'Fido Hound' of *Officers and Gentlemen*, whose ineptness he regretted not reporting upward.

Waugh made light of all these difficulties in 'Commando Raid on Bardia', a propaganda article commissioned by *Life* and published that November. But his diary records embarrassment and frustration at the raid, which only increased as the Commandos returned to further weeks of inaction in Egypt. One day during this time of waiting, a superior officer asked Waugh to conduct what seemed yet one more pointless exercise; he responded with a rag reminiscent of his Lancing days.

> The Colonel had had a late night in Alexandria and had returned in the early hours of the morning, no doubt all in the course of duty, but Evelyn chose this particular moment, as dawn broke, to drill his Intelligence section of three men within a few yards of the Commander's hut. One was a very long piece of asparagus with thick spectacles. Number two was fairly square, and very stupid. Number three was a midget. And there they were, out to be drilled. And I remember that Evelyn's first command was: 'Form fours!' So it continued until the Commander put his head out the window and said: 'That's enough, I won't ask you to train your section again'.[5]

He was losing faith in the efficacy of the military, an attitude confirmed the next month during the disastrous Battle of Crete, first of a series of events that eroded Waugh's military pride and ability to commit himself to life in uniform.

In April 1941 German troops overran Greece and Yugoslavia, leaving only British-held Crete between them and Egypt; in May, German paratroopers began a twelve-day battle for the island. Allied troops far outnumbered their attackers. We now know that the battle was lost in its first hours, when the British command, convinced (by a misread Ultra signal) that the main invasion would come by sea, failed to meet the paratroops with sufficient force. But at the time, Allied numbers and positions seemed so superior that soldiers were astounded when the order to retreat came through. Waugh and 800 other Commandos arrived from Egypt on the seventh day, to serve, they thought, as reinforcements. Only on landing did they learn the truth:

> The first indication which we received of conditions on Crete was the arrival in the captain's cabin, where HQ were waiting, of a stocky, bald, terrified naval commander. He was wearing shorts and a greatcoat and could not speak intelligibly on account of weariness and panic. 'My God, it's hell', he said. 'We're pulling out. Look at me, no gear. O My God, it's hell. Bombs all the time. Left all my gear behind, etc., etc'. We took this to be an exceptionally cowardly fellow, but in a few hours realized that he was typical of British forces in the island.[6]

From the harbour, clogged with sunken vessels and wounded men, Layforce proceeded upcountry in their new task as rearguard to the general retreat. Their orders were to oversee the evacuation: 'to embark after other fighting forces but before stragglers', who were to remain and surrender. The last to come, Layforce was to be last to go.[7]

For five exhausting and increasingly hungry days (later brilliantly recreated in *Officers and Gentlemen*) Layforce bravely struggled in the opposite direction from the masses of troops, support personnel, and evacuees from Greece who were retreating, amid German sniper-, tank-, and air-fire, down to the sea. On the third day Colvin cracked, leaving Waugh to proceed on his own in search of Laycock and orders ('It was always exhilarating as soon as one was alone'); they returned to find the shell-shocked Colvin crouching in a drain, where 'Bob as politely as possible relieved him of command' (D 503–4). Having returned to Sphakia harbor on 31 May and learnt that evacuations would end that night, 'Bob took the responsibility of ordering Layforce to fight their way through the rabble [of unformed men on shore] and embark' on the last ships leaving the island (D 509).

Once safely back in Egypt, Waugh wrote to Laura, observing the usual self-censorship of wartime correspondents:

> Since I wrote last to you I have been in a serious battle and have decided I abominate military life. It was tedious & futile & fatiguing. I found I was not at all frightened; only very bored & very weary.... I shall have a great deal to tell you when we meet which I cannot write now. Meanwhile be profoundly grateful to God & his saints for my preservation during the days May 28 – June 1st.
>
> (L 153)

Like Guy Crouchback, he was briefly ill:

I long to shake off the sand of Egypt. Moses cannot have felt more impatient.... I
have been...ill...with what is called a septic throat...not able to eat at all or
sleep much & very, very depressed & homesick & hopeless.

(ST2 39–40)

Meanwhile Waugh's frustration at the disaster also took the form of enraged
speeches about the ineptness and 'defeatism' of the British and their 'unnecessary'
surrender. He told any who would listen 'that he had taken part in a military
disgrace, a fact that he would remember with shame for the rest of his life'. Sykes,
with Waugh at the time, was convinced that these indiscreet speeches 'got back to
the ears of authority, and that this accounts in part for the difficulties he encountered soon afterwards' in trying to find his way back into combat (Sykes 295).

Waugh's explosions of anger at failures of communications and morale on
Crete masked a more personal distress, one he could not discuss. Another letter
to Laura from Egypt speaks of 'my tale of shame', a shame that still rankled
twenty years later in references to 'Laycock's & my ignominious flight' and 'my
bunk from Crete'.[8] Laycock had dictated for Waugh's signature an entry in the
official war diary explaining that he had ordered his men to evacuate 'in view of
the fact that all fighting forces were now in position for embarkation and that
there was no enemy contact'. But even as they left, armed engagements could
still be heard in the hills; in fact hundreds of Commandos, other British troops,
New Zealanders and Australians were left behind to become prisoners of war.
Laycock, a gifted leader whom Waugh deeply admired, had disregarded orders
rather than be captured, and Waugh (albeit under orders) had been complicitous
in concealing the fact. 'As if in sympathy with Evelyn's feelings, a rumour went
round that a special evacuation medal would be presented to all survivors of the
Crete campaign, to be inscribed simply, EX CRETA'.[9]

Waugh's feeling that his one real battle had been tainted, and that he shared
the guilt, surfaces years later in *Officers and Gentlemen*, where 31 May 1941, his last
on Crete, is described as the 'fatal' day on which Guy Crouchback was 'to resign
an immeasurable piece of his manhood' (296). Nothing in the narrative justifies
or even explains this extraordinary sentence, later omitted from the one-volume
Sword of Honour. Nor does any guilt attach to Guy's commanding officer Tommy
Blackhouse (obviously based on Laycock), who breaks a leg on ship and so never
lands. Instead Waugh redirects his own and Laycock's guilt onto Ivor Claire, the
seemingly gallant upper-class officer whose dishonourable flight from the island
profoundly undermines Guy Crouchback's illusions of military heroism. 'While
Waugh, the keeper of the Layforce war diary, made false statements in it to bury
the truth, in the novel Guy Crouchback conceals, then burns the Hookforce war
diary because it alone contains the proof of Ivor Claire's dishonour in abandoning his soldiers' (Beevor, 'Casualty', 26).

In public Waugh always maintained his friendship and admiration for the
hero to whom he dedicated *Officers and Gentlemen* in 1955, echoing Wordsworth:
'To Major General Sir Robert Laycock KCMG CG DSO, that every man in
arms should wish to be'.[10] Yet on reading the book his meddlesome friend Ann
Fleming telegrammed: 'Presume Ivor Claire based Laycock dedication ironical'.

Waugh replied vehemently: 'Your telegram horrifies me. Of course there is no possible connexion between Bob and Claire. If you suggest such a thing anywhere it will be the end of our beautiful friendship.... For Christ's sake lay off the idea of Bob=Claire....Just shut up about Laycock, Fuck You, E Waugh' (LAF 155). In his diary he wrote, 'I replied that if she breathes a suspicion of this cruel fact it will be the end of our friendship' (D 728).

The events of 1941 – Crete, followed soon after by Britain's alliance with Russia – were for Waugh as for Guy Crouchback the lowest point of the war. In June, his posting with the Commandos expired; he returned from Egypt to England, a Marine once more, and was soon writing to Diana Cooper, in response to some protest from her against his bleak view of Britain's present and future:

> Perhaps in the future when Senator Cooper is representing the State of Free England in Washington and I am teaching English syntax to a convent school in Quebec, we may meet at Niagara. Meanwhile I live in the past.
>
> (DC 76)

> Do you understand now why I would have no wireless or talk of Central Europe at Stinchcombe? I have to lie and keep a jaunty front to a hundred men.... The English are a very base people. I did not know this, living as I did. Now I know them through and through and they disgust me.
>
> (DC 77)

Such bitterness was the product not only of Crete and its aftermath, but also of a new problem Waugh had brought upon himself, one that permanently damaged him with the Marines. In September 1941 he was approached by *Life* for an essay on the (previously secret) Commandos. Peters negotiated a fee of £250 for 3000 words, telling Waugh that what *Life*'s editors wanted was something 'colourful, dramatic': 'in fact, it seems that you are being asked for a piece of fiction rather than an article'.[11] 'Commando Raid on Bardia' appeared in *Life* on 17 November along with a suitably inflated portrait of its author: 'A good commando fighter, known jokingly as a "Churchill Marine", should have the imagination of a mystery writer, the cunning of a burglar, the endurance of an Olympic athlete and the patriotism of a hero'.[12] Peters had secured permission from *Life* for simultaneous publication in the *Evening Standard*, which again generated flattering publicity. 'Here is the Story of a "Bright Young Man" Who is One of the Toughest of Our Commandos', gushed Beverley Nichols in the *Sunday Chronicle*; 'Evelyn at this moment is a hard-bitten, sun-scorched Commando, with the dust of the desert in his eyes, and a rifle in his hand'; 'The ex-dilettante, writing exquisite froth between cocktails, has proved one of the toughest of the lot' (23 Nov. 1941).

But the publication also had much more serious repercussions, as Waugh noted morosely in his dairy:

> On my first leave home I was asked by American *Life* to write an article on the Commandos. I said I must get leave first and the editor arranged it with Brendan

Bracken [then Minister of Information]. I wrote about the Bardia raid and got
£200 for it. Then, without my knowledge, Peters sold it to the *Evening Standard*. It
was announced; the other papers complained; the War Office then issued my
article as a news bulletin. The Marine Office became agitated, Brendan backed out
of his responsibility, and I got reprimanded.

                                                                    (D 517)

Waugh had not cleared the essay with his own superiors. 'Yes, the Marine Office
made a fuss this end about that article', he wrote to a worried Peters when the
trouble started; 'I simply replied "special permission Rt. Hon. B. Bracken" that
has held them off for the present' (L 158). In future Peters would instruct Waugh
carefully of his duty as a serving soldier: 'You must bring written permission of
your commanding officer then contact Brigadier Simpson at the War office on
arrival London then contact Admiralty before broadcast', he telegrammed the
following April, the day before Waugh appeared on the BBC's 'Brains Trust'.
But the damage was done: after the reprimand, Waugh never advanced in the
Marines.[13]

As if to ensure he would have no military future, in late 1942 Duff Cooper
took vindictive revenge after an argument by spreading the rumour that Waugh
was crypto-Nazi – no small matter to a man already known for suspicious views
about Abyssinia and Spain.[14] For three years, from the flap over his article on
Bardia until his Yugoslavian mission in 1944, Waugh shifted between services in
a failed effort to find someone willing to send him into combat. In May 1942
Laycock invited him once again to leave the Marines for the Commandos, but
even as a Commando he remained stationed mostly in London and was reduced
to menial tasks. Frustrated and bored, Waugh turned to drink. 'It is not unfair to
say I never draw a sober breath', he confessed to Dorothy Lygon (L 180) –
especially not while in White's Club, to which he and Randolph Churchill had
been elected while abroad. He bruised himself in drunken falls, crashed at least
two army cars and suffered frequent alcoholic blackouts (lapses of memory,
'which for a man who lives entirely in the past, is to lose life itself'). 'Dreams
of unendurable boredom' led once again to heavy use of sleeping drugs (D 532).
Protestations of sobriety to Laura suggest that even she, at long distance, had
grown worried enough to upbraid him.

Like Charles Ryder, Waugh could say 'Here at the age of thirty-nine I began
to be old' (BR 9). Depression and drink combined to make him age very quickly
in these years, a fact of which his letters and diaries demonstrate repeated
awareness. 'If you see me again you will find a man of middle-aged, uncertain
temper & failing powers' (L 152). After a night of particularly hard drinking in
October 1942, he wrote: 'I saw myself in a mirror afterwards, like a red lacquer
Chinese dragon, and saw how I shall look when I die' (D 529). For the first time
in his life, he wrote a will.

He began to fail in his military duties and was increasingly a thorn to his
superiors. On first entering the Marines in 1940 Waugh had won promotion to
captain and the commendation of his senior officer as possessing 'any amount of
moral courage'; 'he will make a first class Company Commander'. He was

equally well liked by those serving under him.[15] But by 1943 even Waugh's friends tried to dissuade Laycock from taking him into combat:

> 'Evelyn's appointment will only introduce discord and weaken the Brigade. . . . And apart from everything else, Evelyn will probably get shot'.
> 'That's a chance we'll have to take'.
> 'Oh, I don't mean by the enemy'.
>
> (Sykes 312)

Laycock was forced in March 1943 to tell Waugh that he was 'so unpopular as to be unemployable' (D 532), and on 24 July, the same day Arthur Waugh died at seventy-six, Laycock sailed for North Africa (in advance of the invasion of Italy) without taking Waugh. A degrading series of protests followed, culminating in fruitless complaints to Lord Mountbatten himself. Finally Waugh resigned and returned again to the Marines. As Allied victory finally came in sight, and while the largest invasion force in history was assembling, Captain Waugh remained in 'Depot in Windsor, unwanted'.[16]

At a particularly low moment that August, while confessing himself still 'yearning to get to the front', Waugh wrote:

> I have got so bored with everything military that I can no longer remember the simplest details. I dislike the Army. I want to get to work again. I do not want any more experiences in life. I have quite enough bottled and carefully laid in the cellar, some still ripening, most ready for drinking, a little beginning to lose its body. I wrote to Frank [Pakenham] very early in the war to say that its chief use would be to cure artists of the illusion that they were men of action. It has worked its cure with me. I have succeeded, too, in dissociating myself very largely with the rest of the world. I am not impatient of its manifest follies and don't want to influence opinions or events, or expose humbug or anything of that kind. I don't want to be of service to anyone or anything. I simply want to do my work as an artist.
>
> (D 547–8)

He would of course return to trying 'to influence opinions or events', and from his disillusion with public service emerged an enriched commitment to his religious faith, including a new belief in his vocation as an writer. *Put Out More Flags* was Waugh's first, fascinating, somewhat confused effort to come to terms in fiction with his responses to the war; only in *Brideshead* and *Sword of Honour* did he achieve coherent synthesis.

II

In Waugh's view 'a minor work dashed off to occupy a tedious voyage', *Put Out More Flags* was the product of the weeks immediately following the disaster of Crete.[17] In June 1941 he boarded a troopship bound for home by the only safe route – a 20,000-mile voyage down the east coast of Africa, past Mombassa and Cape Town, across the south Atlantic to Trinidad, the American coast, and Iceland, reaching Liverpool in September. It was the longest he ever spent at sea; in about a month he completed a new novel, the most hastily written of his career.

He needed a success. He had not published a novel since *Scoop,* three years before; *Robbery Under Law* had not sold. Despite Waugh's confidence in the autumn of 1939, money soon ran short. Soon after war began, the Inland Revenue demanded £200 in back taxes, for which in 1940 he compounded to pay at the rate of £10 a month (later reduced to £5), while also trying to send £15 a month to Laura – a substantial burden. In March he discovered they were £500 overdrawn: '[I] see no possibility of getting my finances square except by prodigious national inflation' (D 465). Military service, he knew, would largely preclude writing, paper-rationing the profitability of any writing he might do; he feared having to sell Piers Court. The success of *Put Out More Flags* from its appearance in March 1942 ended his financial worries for the rest of the war. In England it sold 18,000 hardback copies as a Book Society selection, was soon reprinted, and brought lucrative film rights; in America, it sold better than any of his previous works and was the occasion for Little, Brown, his American publisher since 1935, to buy all his previous copyrights and issue his six novels in a uniform edition.

Put Out More Flags looks back to happier times before Crete: to the 'Phoney War', 'that strangely cosy interlude between peace and war, when there was leave every week-end and plenty to eat and drink and plenty to smoke' (POMF 128). Waugh wrote in his dedication to Randolph Churchill:

> I am afraid that these pages... deal, mostly, with a race of ghosts, the survivors of the world we both knew ten years ago, which you have outflown in the empyrean of strenuous politics, but where my imagination still fondly lingers.... like everyone else, they have been disturbed in their habits by the rough intrusion of current history. Here they are in that odd, dead period before the Churchillian renaissance which people called at the time 'the Great Bore War'.[18]

These were the months between Chamberlain's declaration and the disastrous Norwegian campaign the following spring (which resulted in Chamberlain's replacement by Churchill); the novel ends with Dunkirk and the fall of France, when 'in the space of a few days England had lost both the entire stores and equipment of her regular Army, and her only ally' (246). It tells how the advent of war crystallizes the lives of a group of familiar characters: Basil Seal (now thirty-six, Waugh's own age in 1939); Basil's mother; his mistress Angela Lyne (who had appeared fleetingly in *Black Mischief*); Alastair and Sonia Trumpington; Peter Pastmaster and Margot.

Eager to turn his mind from recent events, Waugh wrote *Put Out More Flags* without any sense of the shape the whole would take. 'I was anxious to know how [the characters] had been doing since I last heard of them, and I followed them with no preconceived plan, not knowing where I should find them from one page to the next' (1966 Preface). Basil seems at first to provide the story's connecting thread, but he is soon upstaged by other characters, more interesting because explored in greater psychological depth: Angela Lyne, Ambrose Silk and Angela's estranged husband Cedric. The last two are a type new to Waugh's fiction, the aesthete. (Ambrose, an insightful portrait of the homosexual no longer young, is based partly on Brian Howard and Harold Acton, partly on Cyril Connolly.)[19] Though the omniscient narrator of this novel eavesdrops on nearly all his characters' thoughts, these three are also given long interior monologues. The device, also new in Waugh's fiction (developed from his experiments with first-person narrative in the as yet unpublished *Work Suspended*), yields characters – including for the first time in Waugh's fiction a woman – whose interiority generates not only intimacy but sympathy.

Reviewers, inattentive to such stylistic innovations, fixed mainly on the novel's evocation of official ineptness in the war's first months: its bitterly funny accounts of ill-run evacuations and of the huge new bureaucracies at the War Office and Ministry of Information in Bloomsbury, run in early 1941 by Duff Cooper. (Already dubbed by the BBC's Tommy Handley the 'Ministry of Misinformation and Twerpery', M.I. actually staffed a religious department complete with representative atheist, Ambrose Silk's position there; its informers, sent to sniff out disaffection and defeatism, were known as 'Cooper's Snoopers'.) Some reviewers found it ill-timed or even 'mischievous' during the dark days of 1942 to recall past mistakes or satirize 'those to whom the nation has to look for orders and guidance'; others, in relief from the general run of sentimental propaganda typified by J. B. Priestley's *Blackout in Gretley* (1942), praised Waugh's 'mature', 'adult' humor (CH 212–18). But all read in the novel's denouement a (more or less convincing) parable of a nation uniting to do its duty in a time of crisis. Previously irresponsible types like Peter Pastmaster, Alastair Trumpington and Basil Seal embrace public service as soldiers; the uncommitted or ineffectual – Ambrose, Cedric, old Mr Rampole, Jo Mainwaring – emigrate, die, go to prison for the duration, or are otherwise shunted off where they can do no harm.

In four sections named for the seasons, the novel seems to enact a comedic pattern of personal and national rebirth. War is declared in 'Autumn'; in 'Winter' Peter and Alastair don uniforms, and in 'Spring' Peter settles down to marriage for the purpose of producing an heir; in the brief concluding 'Summer', Basil and Angela agree to marry, Sonia learns that she is to give birth, and Basil himself gives up playing at spying to join the fighting. '[T]hat racket was all very well in the winter, when there wasn't any real war', he tells Angela. 'It won't do now. There's only one serious occupation for a chap now, that's killing Germans. I have an idea I shall rather enjoy it' (255). 'There's a new spirit abroad' intones Jo Mainwaring at the end, on hearing that Basil has done 'his duty where he found it'; 'The war has entered a new and more glorious phase'. The narrator seems to second these Churchillian pronouncements: 'perhaps for the first time in his long and loquacious life, Sir Joseph approximated to reality... he was bang right' (246, 256).

But Waugh's own recent experiences ensured that even as he thought himself back to the first months of the war, such optimism would be heavily qualified. While seeming to endorse Mainwaring's patriotic optimism, the narrator also reminds us that Sir Jo is an 'old booby', easily taken in by official propaganda.[20] From the start the novel undermines simple enthusiasm for the war, for instance in Lady Seal's schoolroom patriotism, her belief that this would be one more in a heroic series of battles 'England had fought... with many and various allies [now including Russia], often on quite recondite pretexts, but always justly, chivalrously, and with ultimate success' (25). Her sanguine comment at the end that Basil has 'joined a special *corps d'élite*' setting off 'to do great things' (256) must surely be read in the light of Waugh's all-too-fresh memories of his own frustrated ambitions in the Commandos.

The novel exhibits similar ambivalence in treating Alastair, Peter and Basil's motives for joining the army. 'Much later' (seemingly, after he has died in battle), Sonia reports that Alastair refused promotion, choosing instead to go 'into the ranks' as 'a kind of penance or whatever it's called, that religious people are always supposed to do'.[21] But what we see of Alastair and Peter's soldiering seems (like Guy Crouchback's in *Men at Arms*) mainly a matter of boyish games, not a real passage to maturity:

> [Alastair] studied Peter, with the rapt attention of a small boy, taking in every detail of his uniform, the riding boots, Sam Browne belt, the enamelled stars of rank, and felt disappointed but, in a way, relieved that there was no sword; he could not have borne it if Peter had had a sword.... He was excited, turning a page in his life, as, more than twenty years ago lying on his stomach before the fire, with a bound volume of *Chums*, he used to turn over to the next instalment of the serial.
>
> (55, 250)

Nor does Basil's enlistment signal any real change of character, but simply a redirection of his lifelong 'system of push, appeasement, agitation and blackmail, which, except that it had no more distinct aim than his own immediate amusement, ran parallel to Nazi diplomacy' (59). In saying he will 'rather enjoy' killing Germans, Basil looks forward to one more 'racket', just as earlier he told his sister he would 'enjoy' taking over as billeting officer (103). His previous rackets (billeting and spying) depended on 'a world of otiose civilians' (59), vanished with the onset of a real fighting war; not Basil but the world around him has changed.

Between Mainwaring's two optimistic outbursts intrudes a speech by Angela Lyne offering a quite different picture of the 'new spirit abroad'. She replies to Basil's (doubtless correct) admission that he will be 'a terrible husband': 'Yes darling, don't I know it? But you see one can't expect anything to be perfect now. In the old days if there was one thing wrong it spoiled everything; from now on for all our lives, if there's one thing right the day is made' (252). That Angela's outlook was Waugh's own is suggested by his adoption of the same bleak vein in several letters to Diana Cooper written just as *Put Out More Flags* was being published:

> Are there corners where old friends can still talk as though they were free? If there are, they must say in those corners that there is nothing left – not a bottle of wine nor a gallant death nor anything well made that is a pleasure to handle – and never will be again.
>
> (DC 77)

A war so described is at best a necessary evil, not a rebirth.

Angela's forebodings are borne out in what seems, given its recurrence, the novel's central concern: that 'In war time', as Lady Seal says more truly than she knows, 'individuality doesn't matter any more' (29). The book's most sympathetic characters embody an individualism, love of privacy and cultivated taste Waugh also cherished, but which the machinery of war frustrates and destroys. Ambrose in particular shares attitudes with his author, for instance about the pleasures of cultivated conversation.[22] But at the same time Waugh is at pains to suggest that Angela, Ambrose and Cedric's is a decadent individualism: not something whose disappearance in wartime is to be mourned, but the unhappy by-product of their frustrated prewar lives.

'I alone bear the weight of my singularity' complains the genuinely cultivated and talented Silk; 'I don't want to be fitted in' (73, 78). Considering himself 'a single, sane individual' rather than 'part of a herd', Ambrose tries to opt out of the war, to think it a 'nonsense' that 'has nothing to do with me' (86). To him the war embodies a group-mentality whose main accomplishments have so far been to create bureaucratic 'hives' like the Ministry of Information and to separate him from his German lover Hans. In opposition to the new world created by the war, a corporatist 'modern world' into which he does not feel himself 'baptized' (72), Ambrose celebrates the radical individualism of ancient China: 'Invasions swept over China; the Empire split up into warring kingdoms. The scholars lived their frugal and idyllic lives undisturbed, occasionally making exquisitely private jokes which they wrote on leaves and floated downstream'; 'European culture has become conventual; we must make it coenobitic' (204–5).

The last phrase – one Waugh later revised, realizing he had misunderstood the meaning of 'coenobitic' (altered in 1966 to 'hermetic') – serves in the novel as a manifesto of individualism, recurring in passages about both Cedric and Angela. Cedric, who like Ambrose thinks the 'crazy world' of war has 'nothing to do with him' (243), discovers during a solo mission in Norway what Waugh himself had felt in Crete:

> As he walked alone he was exhilarated with the sense of being one man, one pair of legs, one pair of eyes, one brain, sent on a single intelligible task . . . multiply him, put him in a drove and by each addition of his fellows you subtract something that is of value, make him so much less a man; this was the crazy mathematics of war. . . . there's danger in numbers; divided we stand, united we fall, thought Cedric, striding happily towards the enemy, shaking from his boots all the frustration of corporate life. He did not know it but he was thinking exactly what Ambrose had thought when he announced that culture must cease to be conventual and become coenobitic.
>
> (240–1)

To Angela's final, bleak speech about the future, Basil replies: 'That sounds like Ambrose in his Chinese mood' (252).

Cedric's individualism seems admirable, a sane response to the bureaucratic machinery of war. But as so often in this hastily constructed novel, Waugh's divided mind frustrates easy generalizations. Cedric's death immediately after the passage quoted suggests that in wartime, corporate effort, however destructive of civilized life, is necessary. Meanwhile, another strand in the novel suggests that the parallel individualisms of Angela, Ambrose and Cedric are nothing less than a kind of spiritual disease. As the war begins, all three feel trapped by the course their lives have taken and suffer something like despair, of which their individualism is the expression.

To those who do not know her, Angela seems a fully realized version of *Vile Bodies*'s Imogen Quest. 'Her smartness was individual': 'the temperate, cynical, aloof, impeccably dressed, sharply dignified Mrs. Lyne – Mrs. Lyne who never "went out" in a general sense but lived in a rarefied and enviable coterie'; 'who for fifteen years had set a high and wholly individual standard of all that Americans meant by "poise"' (31, 186). But Angela's individual smartness is not a stance of her own choosing; it is the miserable result of a life that has 'foundered on passion'. 'For seven years, ever since she was twenty-five and two years married' to Cedric, she 'had been in love with Basil Seal' (33). Her long adulterous affair has brought nothing but sterility: no home, no children, no family life, no fruitful outlet for her manifest taste and intelligence.

> For seven years she had been on a desert island; her appearance had become a hobby and a distraction, a pursuit entirely self-regarding and self-rewarding; she watched herself moving in the mirrors of the civilized world as a prisoner will watch the antics of a rat which he has domesticated to the dungeon. . . . Nothing, she felt in despair, would ever part [her from Basil] but death.[23]

Angela's 'empty, uncommunicative' service flat, 'as smart and non-committal as herself', is the external realization of her inner sterility: 'There were no ashes to stir in the grate; illuminated glass coals glowed eternally in an elegant steel basket' (139, 141). Here on his rare visits Angela strikes out, 'hard and fierce', at Basil, directing at him an anger born of her own frustration; here, because 'the will to live was gone', she turns to drink.[24]

Ambrose's spiritual condition parallels Angela's. In the self-frustrating prison of her affair, Angela's sharp mind finds release in 'talk[ing] like a highly intelligent man'; Ambrose, who feels as trapped as she ('What was he doing, he asked himself, in this galley'), muses: 'why can I not speak like a man?'[25] Ambrose's self-regarding individualism and cult of style stem, like hers, from the frustration of his own nature – specifically, Waugh suggests, from his homosexuality. Though he alone among the novel's characters has actually been touched by the war (through the internment of Hans), and though he has the clearest understanding of any of what war means, Ambrose cannot bring himself to admit that fighting Nazism has 'anything to do with' him.

> But if, thought Ambrose, I were one of these people, if I were not a cosmopolitan, Jewish pansy, if I were not all that the Nazis mean when they talk about 'degenerates', if I were not a single, sane individual, if I were part of a herd, one of these people, normal and responsible for the welfare of my herd, Gawd strike me pink, thought Ambrose, I wouldn't sit around discussing what kind of war it was going to be. I'd make it *my* kind of war. I'd set about killing and stampeding the other herd as fast and as hard as I could.
>
> (POMF 86)

'*Nature I loved, and next to Nature, Art*' Ambrose muses to himself, in a self-flattering reversal of the truth.[26] At the Café Royal – with its 'distant associations of Oscar and Aubrey', sole public place where he feels free to 'spread his feathers' – Ambrose borrows a leaf from Wilde's *Decay of Lying* to discourse on the London fogs of the previous century, whose great advantage was to hide reality, to prevent us from 'see[ing] ourselves as we are' (203). As *Brideshead* will argue more fully through the character of Anthony Blanche, Ambrose's frustration of the ends of his own nature – embodied also in his nineties notion of art for art's sake, a misunderstanding of the proper ends of art – constitutes a sometimes engaging but ultimately doomed effort to escape ordinary life and its obligations. At best a retreat into fantasy, at worst an expression of pride, art for art's sake embodies a vision perhaps beautiful but finally empty, not really human. Ambrose daydreams:

> There was no foundation here [at the Ministry of Information] for an ivory tower,... no cloud to garland its summit, and his thoughts began to soar larklike into a tempera, fourteenth-century sky; into a heaven of flat, blank blue with white clouds, a vast altitude painted with shaving soap on a panel of lapis lazuli; he stood on a high, sugary pinnacle, on a new Tower of Babel; like a muezzin calling his message to a world of domes and clouds; beneath him, between him and the absurd little figures bobbing and bending on their striped praying mats, lay fathoms of clear air where doves sported with the butterflies.
>
> (POMF 132–3)

Nor finally can a life lived according to such ideals satisfy the inbuilt needs of the human spirit. Early on, Ambrose daydreams (in an aesthete's version of despair) that not heaven or hell but 'Limbo is the place ... for anyone of civilized taste' (72); at the end he gets the condition for which he has rashly wished, a lonely life in neutralist Eire, land of 'mists' (like the London fogs he has celebrated) and of 'escapists' who have turned 'their backs on the world of effort and action'. Appropriately for the representative of what Waugh will soon castigate as 'the mysticism of art', Ambrose travels to Ireland disguised as a priest; but once there he finds himself unable to write. A final comparison to the Wandering Jew makes clear his still unsatisfied spiritual state:

> But he knew it was not for him; the dark, nomadic strain in his blood, the long heritage of wandering and speculation, allowed him no rest. Instead of Atlantic breakers he saw the camels swaying their heads resentfully against the lightening sky, as the caravan woke to another day's stage in the pilgrimage.
>
> (POMF 253)

Waugh's satire is at its subtlest when he draws Ambrose into the company of Poppet Green and her artistic Communist friends. For all his criticism of the homosexual aesthete, Waugh leaves us in no doubt of his preference for Ambrose over 'the rest of the Left Wing writers', many of whom have gone so far as to change their names, adopting 'plebian monosyllables'.[27] Ambrose does not associate with these 'dour young proletarians of the new decade' because he shares their politics. (Appropriately, 'one of his many reasons for shunning communism' is 'that its manifesto had been written for it, once and for all, by somebody else' (215)) Rather, he wants to be 'in the movement' – and he finds their desire to avoid military service congenial.[28]

One renegade in Poppet's circle, a 'red-headed girl' from the London School of Economics who believes in 'People's Total War', supports enlistment even for artists, arguing that the poets Parsnip and Pimpernell's (Auden and Isherwood's) emigration to America – that much-canvassed topic which Cyril Connolly called 'the most important literary event since the Spanish Civil War' – is 'just sheer escapism': 'What I don't see is how these two can claim to be *Contemporary* if they run away from the biggest event in contemporary history'. Waugh here gives his own views to the young Communist, thereby making the Left condemn itself from its own mouth.[29] Ambrose in turn tries but is unable to articulate any defence of the poets' flight (implying the untenability of his aestheticism). He considers parroting the standard Communist line of the time that 'the present conflict, since Russia had declared herself neutral, was merely a phase in capitalist disintegration', merely a 'class war'. But Ambrose knows 'that was not really the answer': even he, for all his vanity and evasions, and for all that such an argument would serve his cause of the moment, is too honest to accept the evasions of the Left.[30]

Despite its many brilliant inventions, Waugh was right in calling *Put Out More Flags* a 'minor' work. In its ambivalences, its incompletely and inconsistently developed themes, this is his only finished novel that can be said to fail architecturally. Such failure is clearest when the novel treats what are plainly elements of its author's own experience and psyche; he had still only begun the task of self-analysis initiated in *Work Suspended*. That Waugh was himself aware of a lack of clarity and resolution is testified by his reuse soon after of many of the novel's materials. Memories of Oxford in the twenties, the homosexual aesthete, the nature of individuality and consideration of art and its purposes return in *Brideshead*. Cedric's seven 'lonely and humiliating' years recur in Charles Ryder's 'dead years' and Guy Crouchback's eight years in Italy after Virginia's defection. (All of these hiatuses obliquely reflect how Waugh had come to think of the period between his marriages.) The military experiences here distributed among Alistair, Cedric and Peter are all rendered again, briefly in *Brideshead*, at length in *Sword of Honour*.

III

The disillusioned pessimism already audible in *Put Out More Flags* grew as much from Waugh's dismay at Allied conduct of the war (and how the war was changing England) as from his personal disappointments as a soldier. No phrase echoes more often through British wartime books, films and radio broadcasts – and Waugh's diaries and novels – than 'what we are we fighting for'. In *Put Out More Flags*, Sonia brightly asks Basil to 'Tell us all about the war':

> 'Well – ' Basil began.
> 'No darling, I didn't mean that. Not all. Not about who's going to win or why we are fighting'.

(46)

Later at the Ministry of Information Mr Bentley tries to enlist Ambrose (of all people) to contribute to 'a very nice little series on "What We Are Fighting For"' (76). The phrase resounds insistently through *Sword of Honour* as Guy grows increasingly convinced that Britain has betrayed its war aims both abroad and at home. Guy's progress reflects Waugh's own.

The problem as Waugh saw it stemmed from British failure to grasp the equivalence between the 'common enemies of Europe', Stalin and Hitler.[31] In this Waugh knew his to be the views of a minority, a minority perhaps even of Conservatives – but not of Catholics, who had watched with growing alarm the fate of Christianity in what as early as 1930 Waugh identified as the 'materialistic, mechanized state, already existent in Russia and rapidly spreading south and west' (EAR 194). 'Let there be no mistake about where Soviet Russia stands', *The Tablet* argued repeatedly after Stalin made his pact with Hitler; 'The Soviet desire is that, through this war, Europe may be prepared for revolutionary destruction. If there is to be a decision, the Soviets are determined that the war shall not be allowed to end in a victory for the West, but in a victory for that German revolution which they believe might be adapted and assimilated to their own' (13 Apr. 1940, 343).

On this view, British failure to carry out its war aims began with and was long symbolized by the fate of Poland. Just after the war occurred a scene Waugh would have relished:

> On 10 January 1946 the Tory MP and diarist 'Chips' Channon attended a society wedding in London and remarked to another guest, Lady ('Emerald') Cunard, 'how quickly normal life had been resumed. After all', [Cannon] said, pointing to the crowded room, 'this is what we have been fighting for'. 'What', said Emerald, 'are they all Poles?'
>
> (Johnson 432)

From Poland, 'the first great test of Allied sincerity',[32] British loss of purpose spread to Finland and culminated on 22 June 1941 – 'a day of apocalypse for all the world for numberless generations' (OG 324) – when Germany invaded the Soviet Union, leading Britain to embrace Stalin as an ally. 'There can be no question of an alliance', *The Tablet* had maintained until the very last moment; 'Stalin's outlook and policy are quite irreconcilable with the ideals of liberty and civilized order for which we are fighting' (28 June 1941, 496). To Waugh, that alliance – the event that leads Scott-King to declare Allies and Axis 'indistinguishable louts' and shatters Guy Crouchback's faith in the justice of his cause – culminated during the war's final months in the sacrifice of half Europe to a totalitarianism the equal of Nazism, a process he watched first hand in Yugoslavia.

After only a few weeks in the army, Guy Crouchback meditates, not for the first time, on the 'quintessential' question, 'What are we fighting for?':

> Guy believed he knew something of the matter that was hidden from the mighty. England had declared war to defend the independence of Poland. Now that

country had quite disappeared and the two strongest states in the world guaranteed her extinction.

(MA 219–20)

Only twenty-five years before, in 1918, Poland had after years of conflict been reunited as an independent Catholic state in whose welfare British Catholics took a lively interest. Britain's pledge to defend it – like the League of Nations' pledge to Abyssinia five years before – had encouraged Poland to fight. But British failure to act on that pledge spelt her bloody defeat, her abandonment not only to Germany but also to equally brutal enemies from the East: 'The papers are all smugly jubilant at Russian conquests in Poland as though this were not a more terrible fate for the allies we are pledged to defend than conquest by Germany. The Italian argument, that we have forfeited our narrow position by not declaring war on Russia, seems unanswerable' (D 443). Guy Crouchback agrees:

> Russia invaded Poland. Guy found no sympathy among these old soldiers for his own hot indignation.
>   'My dear fellow, we've quite enough on our hands as it is. We can't go to war with the whole world'.
>   'Then why go to war at all? If all we want is prosperity, the hardest bargain Hitler made would be preferable to victory. If we are concerned with justice the Russians are as guilty as the Germans'.
>   'Justice?' said the old soldiers. 'Justice?'
>   'Besides', said Box-Bender when Guy spoke to him of the matter which seemed in no one's mind but his, 'the country would never stand for it. The socialists have been crying blue murder against the Nazis for five years but they are all pacifists at heart. So far as they have any feeling of patriotism it's for Russia. You'd have a general strike and the whole country in collapse if you set up to be just'.
>   'Then what are we fighting for?'[33]

In succeeding months Britain stood by as the Soviet Union conquered Finland (quickening in Guy 'the sickening suspicion he had tried to ignore ... that he was engaged in a war in which courage and a just cause were irrelevant to the issue' (MA 175)). But it was the plight of Poland that preyed on Waugh's mind, to be recalled passingly in 1941 as he wrote *Put Out More Flags*: 'Winter set in hard. Poland was defeated; east and west the prisoners rolled away to slavery' (POMF 88). Much more pointed references to the tragedy of Poland punctuate *Men at Arms*, the more effective for appearing as brief asides – and as asides, intended to suggest the ease with which most Britons were content to ignore that tragedy even as its enormous dimensions became clear.

In 1943 news reached England of the massacre at Katyn Forest, near Smolensk, where in 1940 over 3000 Poles had been murdered and dumped in mass graves, and thousands more had disappeared. Berlin radio (correctly, it turned out) blamed the Soviet Union, citing other instances of Poles deported to Soviet prison camps. The British press treated Polish complaints against the Soviet Union as slander of a valued ally; government down-played the affair.[34]

Waugh remarked bitterly: 'The Poles are generally blamed for minding about the murder of 8,000-odd officers by the Russians' (D 537). *Men at Arms* chillingly recalls those 'forests' amidst the festivities of a Halberdier guest night:

> At length when the cloth was drawn for dessert, the brass departed and the strings came down from the minstrels' gallery and stationed themselves in the window embrasure. Now there was silence all over the diners while the musicians softly bowed and plucked. It all seemed a long way from Tony's excursions in no-man's-land; farther still, immeasurably far, from the frontier of Christendom where the great battle had been fought and lost; from those secret forests where the trains were, even then, while the Halberdiers and their guests sat bemused by wine and harmony, rolling east and west with their doomed loads.
>
> (MA 87–8)

Shortly afterward, on St Valentine's day, Guy reads of the British prisoners recovered from the *Altmark*: 'There were long accounts of the indignities and discomforts of the prisoners, officially designed to rouse indignation among a public quite indifferent to those trains of locked vans still rolling East and West from Poland and the Baltic, that were to roll on year after year bearing their innocent loads to ghastly unknown destinations' (MA 155).

As the war ended the trains still rolled. On 7 March 1945, the news was of 'two sealed trains, each with two thousand Polish priests, intellectuals and teachers on board,... sent to Soviet labour camps on the Volga'. By then the Poles deported to the Soviet Union in fact numbered over a million (Gilbert 830). Though Waugh soon came to agree with what he called Ronald Knox's 'profound and neglected pamphlet' *God and the Atom* (1945) that the bombing of Hiroshima had been unjustified – that, as he told Randolph Churchill, 'War as waged by airmen & physicists against civil populations is absolutely wrong in morals' – his first thoughts on learning of the bomb were of Poland: 'News published by 6 o'clock wireless that an 'atomic' bomb had been dropped on Japan. . . . I asked, if we knew early this year that we had this power, why did we betray Poland to Russia?'[35]

So deep was Waugh's horror of the Soviet regime and the 'chaos and tyranny and famine and sheer wickedness' it had brought to 'two-thirds of Europe' (D566) that, as the epigraph to this chapter makes clear, he makes Guy Crouchback enlist less to fight Germany than Russia (while softening the suggestion a bit by allowing that 'for the past three years [Guy] had given up his English newspapers'). And just as *Officers and Gentlemen* connects, through the character of Ivor Claire, Waugh's alter ego Guy with his own sense of dishonourable flight from Crete, so it uses Claire to suggest that the Russian alliance is a national disgrace. Recovering from days in an open boat, Guy discovers both Ivor's desertion and the determination of Julia Stitch and Tommy Blackhouse to keep it quiet, and reflects: 'Why was he here in Mrs. Stitch's basement, why were Eddie and Bertie [fellow Commandos who stayed behind on Crete to be captured] in prison... if it was not for Justice?' (OG 320). Immediately comes news of the Soviet alliance, shattering Guy's sense of the justice of his crusade against 'the Modern Age in arms':

It was on just such a sunny, breezy Mediterranean day two years before when he read of the Russo-German alliance, when a decade of shame seemed to be ending in light and reason.... Now that hallucination was dissolved, like the whales and turtles on the voyage from Crete, and he was back after less than two years' pilgrimage in a Holy Land of illusion in the old ambiguous world, where priests were spies and gallant friends proved traitors and his country was led blundering into dishonour.

(OG 321–2)

In the face of such huge national delinquency, one man's desertion or another's lies hardly matter; Guy responds to the news by destroying the evidence of Claire's guilt:

That afternoon he took his pocket-book to the incinerator.... It was a symbolic act; he stood like the man at Sphakia who dismembered his Bren and threw its parts one by one out into the harbour, splash, splash, splash, into the scum.

(OG 322)

Guy had recognized that man's earlier action as a 'symbolic farewell to arms' (301); Guy's parallel act of burning the evidence against Ivor Claire is a symbolic farewell to justice and honour, both 'forfeited in the Russian alliance'.

IV

'Besides, you know, this is a war for democracy', says Basil Seal as he billets the horrible Connollies on an unsuspecting couple (POMF 113). The war seemed to Waugh to end a world because of the corruption of British war aims not only abroad but also at home. 'Military success kept close company with political disaster', he wrote later (K 302). He watched with growing dismay as his enemies of the 1930s seemed to succeed in the 1940s in capturing the terms of national political debate, turning the war against Germany into a 'people's war', a crusade for socialism at home. Soldiering left little time for any but occasional salvos, but Waugh managed in wartime essays, whether writing on drama criticism, the relation of Marxism to Christianity, prose style, or Victorian design, to protest what in 1943 he diagnosed as a growing 'socialist ascendancy' bent not only on Germany's defeat but on ensuring that 'we shall not see again' a 'world of prosperity, freedom, inequality and moral uprightness' (EAR 274). In the thirties, when his enemies seemed a small if vocal minority, he had often been flippant in rejecting Left myths such as that the Right had been the main appeasers, or that Britain's upper classes were Fascist at heart; a changed political climate required new seriousness and fervour.

With the Soviet alliance, socialism and even Communism became respectable in a new way; in December 1942 the CPB registered its highest membership ever, 56,000 (Porter 247). Prominent Britons celebrated the Soviet itself; Waugh never forgot how as Minister of Supply Lord Beaverbrook praised Stalin over the BBC, or Beaverbrook's notorious speech of April 1942 from the Waldorf Towers in New York, broadcast across the United States and Europe, which was intended to press Churchill into agreeing to open a second front:

Communism under Stalin has produced the most valiant fighting army in Europe. Communism under Stalin has provided us with examples of patriotism equal to the finest annals in history. Communism under Stalin has won the applause and admiration of all the western nations....

Persecution of Christianity? Not so. There is no religious persecution. The church doors are open. And there is complete freedom to practise religion, just as there is complete freedom to reject it.

Racial persecution? Not at all. Jews live like other men....

Political purges? Of course. But it is now clear that the men who were shot down would have betrayed Russia to her German enemy.

(Chisolm and Davie 410)

'Great idea of Max's' say the members of Bellamy's Club, explaining Tanks for Russia Week to Guy Crouchback; 'Naturally the workers are keen to help Russia. It's how they've been educated' (OG 330). (On reading Tom Driberg's 1956 biography of Beaverbrook – advertised as hostile, but in fact financed and corrected by the subject himself – Waugh complained of finding 'a honeyed eulogy'; 'you fail to give the full villainy of the man': L (467))

As George Orwell noted, the ideology of the 'people's war' in fact began to spread well before the alliance with Stalin and attendant heyday of Tanks for Russia Week, Mrs Churchill's Aid to Russia Fund (which raised £8,000,000), Anglo-Soviet Committees, and the London Exhibition of Soviet Progress (complete with symphonic celebration of the twenty-fifth anniversary of the Russian Revolution in an Albert Hall draped for the occasion with Soviet flags).

For the two years following Dunkirk British morale depended largely upon the feeling that this was not only a war for democracy but a war which the common people had to win by their own efforts. The upper classes were discredited by their appeasement policy and by the disasters of 1940, and a social-levelling process appeared to be taking place. Patriotism and left-wing sentiments were associated in the popular mind, and numerous able journalists were at work to tie the association tighter. Priestley's 1940 broadcasts and 'Cassandra's' [William Casson's] articles in the *Daily Mirror* were good examples of the demagogic propaganda flourishing at that time.

(Orwell, *Essays*, 3: 353–4)

J. B. Priestley's 1940 'Postscript' broadcasts following the nine o'clock Home Service news on Sunday nights, followed in 1941 by his series 'Make it Monday', brought the ideology of the 'people's war' into millions of homes. According to Priestley:

We have to get rid of these intolerable nuisances [the Fascists], but not so that we can go back to anything. There's nothing that really worked that we can go back to.... But we cannot go forward and build up this new world order, and this is our real war aim, unless we begin to think differently, and my own personal view, for what it's worth, is that we must stop thinking in terms of property and power and begin thinking in terms of community and creation.

[Britain before the war was] a world of cold narrow minds, of greed, privilege and love of power. And we're fighting not merely to keep the German jack-boot off our necks but also to put an end once and for all to that world, and to bring into existence an order of society in which nobody will have far too many rooms in a house and nobody have far too few.[36]

To Waugh such propaganda constituted an effort by the Left 'to direct the struggle for national survival into proletarian revolution and identify the enemy with their own upper classes' (EAR 562). In this his views were far more widely shared than were his criticisms of war aims abroad. In 1940 Maynard Keynes protested the 'attempts to exploit the war in favour of something you want anyhow' of Kingsley Martin's *New Statesman* (a magazine whose 'peevish socialism' Waugh too lost no opportunity to attack); in 1941 the *Tablet* consistently attacked Priestley as one of many 'who want to use the war as an occasion for social transformation'.[37] Britons of many political outlooks agreed that it was not only 'war socialism' itself but the popularization over several years of the ideology of the 'people's war', for instance in the weekly group discussions of social issues mandated for soldiers by the Army Bureau of Current Affairs, that made possible the victory of the Labour Party over Churchill's coalition in 1945, giving socialists for the first time a majority in the House of Commons. Kingsley Martin recalled (with characteristic self-importance),

> I published many articles, particularly by Harold Laski, who urged that the Government, in which Attlee, Morrison and Bevin all held important offices, should introduce such Socialism as was possible during the war. Churchill opposed social changes, but pressure was brought to bear on the Government to obtain such a reform as the Beveridge Plan. Churchill was defeated in his opposition to any army education which involved discussion on social questions.... The troops, most of the time in England, were insupportably bored, read [the *New Statesman*] with avidity and wrote to me with a gratitude which they finally expressed by voting Labour in 1945.[38]

After parliamentary pressure led Churchill to take him off the air, Priestley made his case even more starkly in *Blackout in Gretley* (1942), whose hard-boiled detective hero, employed like Basil Seal in detecting Fascist sympathizers at home, argues that 'the real fight is between those who still have some belief in and affection for ordinary people and those who only believe in the Fascist idea' – between 'ordinary people' and 'a social system that's diseased in every part of it'. 'Joe Stalin may be as tough as hell, but in the long run he's plotting and planning to give the folk who believe in him the best life possible' (102, 212). It's thus only 'idiotic old noodles who...ask the people to fight and sweat for "our traditional way of life"', for the 'idiotic genteel tradition' (28, 93). In a famous passage that Waugh would remember and quote against him fifteen years later, Priestley suggested that 'The country has the choice, during the next two years, of coming fully to life and beginning all over again or of rapidly decaying and dying on the same old feet. It can only accomplish the first by taking a firm grip on about fifty thousand important, influential gentlemanly persons and telling them firmly to shut up and do nothing if they don't want to be put to doing some most unpleasant work' (246).

Waugh had made gentle fun of Priestley as early as *Black Mischief*, and continued the campaign with glancing references in *Put Out More Flags*, *Scott-King's Modern Europe*, and various light journalistic pieces (EAR 352, 358). After dining with him in 1943, Waugh confided to his diary: 'J. B. Priestley, pathetically vain'; 'He sees himself as a man of great responsibility as the epitome of the Common Man' (D 537). The depth of their mutual dislike would explode into print only in 1957, when Priestley attacked the writer of *Gilbert Pinfold* for attempting, although really 'an author', to set up as a 'Catholic landed gentleman' – thereby, in Priestley's mind, 'going over to the enemy'. Waugh replied:

> There was, indeed, a *trahison des clercs* some twenty years back which has left the literary world much discredited. It was then that the astute foresaw the social revolution and knew who would emerge top dog. They went to great lengths to suck up to the lower classes, or, as they called it, to 'identify themselves with the workers'. Few excelled Mr Priestley in his zeal for social justice. It is instructive to reread his powerful novel *Blackout in Gretley*, which was written at a very dark time in the war when national unity was of vital importance. Its simple theme is that the English upper classes were in conspiracy to keep the workers in subjection even at the cost of national defeat.
>
> (EAR 528–9)

There follows a hilarious – and quite accurate – summary of the novel's plot, ending with quotation of Priestley on 'gentlemanly persons'.

Waugh's response to the ideology of the 'people's war' included an increasingly strident cult of the 'gentleman' (England's 'sole, unique, historic creation': (EAR 313)) and sour portrayals of the 'common man' and those he called with deliberately provocative condescension 'the labourers'. In 1942 he objected to a book on *British Dramatists* by Graham Greene: 'Mr. Greene subscribes to the popular belief in "the People". An American statesman has announced that this is "the century of the common man", and it is not to be wondered at that during the last ten years English writers have sought conspicuously to flatter the rising, and revile the falling, powers in the land, for they are by tradition a sycophantic race' (EAR 272).

Waugh was far from alone in deriding the idea of a 'century of the common man', the phrase popularized by Henry Wallace, Roosevelt's socialist vice-president and a professed admirer of Stalin. In February 1942, Henry Luce had argued in 'The American Century' – probably the most widely read essay ever published in *Life* – that a just and free post war settlement would not emerge from a 'people's war' ideology, but only by abandoning New Deal welfarism; he singled out Wallace among those who mistakenly hoped for prosperity through planning. Wallace responded in May with a speech on 'The Price of Free World Victory':

> Some have spoken of the 'American Century'. I say that the century on which we are entering – the century which will come out of this war – can and must be the century of the common man.... The march of freedom of the past one hundred and fifty years has been a long-drawn out people's revolution.... If we really believe that we are fighting for a people's peace, all the rest becomes easy.
>
> (Wallace 371–4)

The speech was later incorporated into Wallace's book *The Century of the Common Man* (1942), and soon provoked responses such as Max Beerbohm's, in his Rede Lecture on Lytton Strachey (1943):

> I doubt whether in the equalitarian era for which we are heading – the era in which we shall have built Jerusalem on England's smooth and asphalt land – the art of literature, which throve so finely and so continuously from Elizabethan to paulo-post-Victorian days, will have a wonderful renascence. We are told on high authority, from both sides of the Atlantic, that the present century is to be the Century of the Common Man. We are all of us to go down on our knees and clasp our hands and raise our eyes and worship the Common Man. I am not a learned theologian, but I think I am right in saying that this religion has at least the hall-mark of novelty – has never before been propagated, even in the East, from which so many religions have sprung.
>
> ('Strachey', 211–12)

What is crucial to realize in Waugh's use of the phrase, however, is his insistence that 'The Common Man does not exist. He is an abstraction invented by bores for bores' (EAR 302) – a theoretical counter created by a particular social and political agenda. The Hooper of *Brideshead* is a recognizable character. But he is more importantly a deliberately provocative composite symbol of the class whose supposed interests Waugh thought had come to dominate British wartime policy, a portent (as in the war trilogy Trimmer is a 'proletarian portent': US 240) of what socialism really means. Just as in the 1930s, in the face of socialist realism, Waugh protested by cultivating stylistic elaboration, in the 1940s and 1950s he created Hooper and Trimmer to insult not a lower class but his own: to provoke those who, championing 'the common man', had succeeded in bending national policy to their cause. It is not real-life Hoopers or Trimmers but socialism of the sort found in *Blackout in Gretley* that Waugh has in his eye when making the despicable (and upper-class) Ian Kilbannock tell Guy Crouchback: 'This is a People's War and the People won't have poetry and they won't have flowers. Flowers stink. The upper classes are on the secret list. We want heroes of the People, to or for the People, by, with, and from the People' (OG 130).

The depth of Waugh's alienation from the new England emerging from the war – and sympathy for the plight of such as Ambrose Silk – may be measured by a his 1943 review of Robert Graves and Alan Hodge's *The Reader Over Your Shoulder*:

> Artists of all kinds – but writers more than others – face a problem which cannot long be left unresolved. Society is changing in a way which makes it increasingly difficult for them to live at their ease. A few potential artists will doubtless be found to submit to the new restraints and, as state functionaries, busy themselves in public relations offices and Ministries of Rest and Culture, popularizing the ideas of tomorrow and the undertakings which, in peace, will replace the Giant Salvage Drives of today. For the more vigorous, however, the choice lies in the two extremes of anarchic bohemianism and ascetic seclusion. Each provides a refuge

from the state. The Bohemians will have a valuable function in teasing, it may be hoped to madness, the new bourgeoisie, but I believe it will be left to the ascetics to produce the works of art in which, if at all, English culture will survive.

(EAR 276)

(The 'salvage drive' to which Waugh refers was an effort to convert ornamental iron-work into war materiel, sometimes by confiscation; it had already elicited a letter from Waugh to *The Times* the previous March defending preservation of 'Victorian monstrosities' both for their artistic value and as 'symbols of independence and privacy', relics of a 'free and fecund' England that had 'rated liberty above equality': EAR 268.) To those like Herbert Read, whose *To Hell with Culture* (1941) sought to prosper the people's war by arguing that artists should embrace the emerging proletarian state, Waugh restated arguments seldom enunciated so clearly since the days of Pope and Congreve:

> Language must be preserved as a vehicle for accurate and graceful expression, and it is in danger of death from the decay of a stratified society. Aristocracy saved the artist in many ways. By its patronage it offered him rewards more coveted than the mere cash value of its purchases; in its security it invited him to share its own personal freedom of thought and movement; it provided the leisured reader whom alone it is worth addressing; it curbed the vanity of the publicist and drew a sharp line between fame and notoriety; by its caprices it encouraged experiment; its scepticism exposed the humbug. These and countless other benefits are now forgotten or denied. Its particular service to literature was that it maintained the delicate and unstable balance between the spoken and the written word.
>
> (EAR 276)

In the face of an increasingly intrusive egalitarian state, Waugh reasserted more forcefully than ever his Church's view of the merits, indeed the moral necessity, of social inequality. Against Graham Greene's acceptance of 'the new, complicated, and stark crazy theory that only the poor are real and important and that the only live art is the art of the People', he adduced 'the old, simple belief of Christianity that differences of wealth and learning cannot affect the reality and ultimate importance of the individual' (EAR 273). When in 1944 Harold Laski, Chairman of the Labour Party Executive, published a book arguing that Marxism was the logical historical successor to Christianity (and Russian Communism to Christian Rome), Waugh sent *The Tablet* one of his most effective reviews, 'Marxism, The Opiate of the People', ridiculing among much else Laski's assertion that '*The* problem that Christianity sought to solve' was not the fate of the soul but that of 'reconcil[ing] the existence of poverty [with] a state power which safeguarded the riches of the wealthy' (EAR 279). Later the same year, with arguments like Laski's in mind, he returned to the argument in *Brideshead*, giving Lady Marchmain the notorious speech on riches that leads Charles Ryder to cite the prooftext of the camel and the needle's eye. Waugh slyly managed to make Lady Marchmain's remarks both as provocative as possible to sensibilities such as Laski's and absolutely orthodox theologically:

'When I was a girl we were comparatively poor, but still much richer than most of the world, and when I married I became very rich. It used to worry me, and I thought it wrong to have so many beautiful things when others had nothing. Now I realize that it is possible for the rich to sin by coveting the privileges of the poor. The poor have always been the favourites of God and His saints, but I believe that it is one of the special achievements of Grace to sanctify the whole of life, riches included. Wealth in pagan Rome was necessarily something cruel; it's not any more'.[39]

V

Between the autumn of 1941, when he wrote *Put Out More Flags*, and the first six months of 1944, when *Brideshead Revisited* was completed, Waugh's failure to find a place in combat left him free to reestablish his literary life and friendships. When in London, he went daily to Heywood Hill's bookshop in Curzon Street, to gossip with Nancy Mitford, who worked there as a cerk, and other with old friends for whom it was a meeting-place: John Betjeman, Peter Quennell, Raymond Mortimer and the Sitwells.

He also visited the offices of *Horizon* and dined frequently with its editor, Cyril Connolly, with whom he had maintained a deep but uneasy friendship since 1928. Despite Connolly's agnosticism and Left politics, he and Waugh were united in literary and social tastes, love of food, wine and cigars; in their wit, and a common propensity to laziness and black boredom; and in a shared interest in architecture, antiques and the diversities of sexual desire. Waugh thought Connolly 'the most typical man of my generation' (HRC I15) and acknowledged their likeness in *Unconditional Surrender* by making a single character, Ludovic, the author of books clearly based on works each had written. They read each other's work with care and often echoed one another. When Waugh wrote in January 1945, 'The motto of privilege: Liberty. Leisure. Privacy' (D 608) – first formulation of his famous triad 'Liberty, Diversity and Privacy' – he was in fact echoing Connolly's *Horizon* editorial from the previous month: 'The State now sits by the bedside of literature like a policeman watching for a would-be suicide to recover consciousness, who will do anything for the patient except allow him the leisure, privacy and freedom from which art is produced'.[40]

In 1944 Connolly published (under the name 'Palinurus') a slender volume of *pensées* called *The Unquiet Grave* in which, in language learnt partly from Waugh, he began the long process of recanting socialism, especially as it is inimical to the artist: 'I live in an age when on all sides I am told...that the social and cooperative activity is the one way through which life can be developed. Am I an exception, a herd-outcast?...State Socialism in politics always goes with social realism in the arts, and eventually the position is reached that whatever the common man does not understand is treason' (27, 57). Waugh read the book that December, writing 'Well said, Palinurus' in the margin beside such comments as 'Literature is still best carried out through the individual unit' and 'fulfillment through participation in the communal life of an organized group...is tyranny'. But Connolly never adopted Waugh's religious faith: other passages arguing 'there can be no going back to Christianity' drew biting marginalia and the summary condemnation: 'There can be no genuine self-knowledge without some knowledge of God. But Cyril's elaborate "self-dismantling" is not the fruit of knowledge' (HRC I17).

Just as Guy Crouchback finds in the idle period after his first military engagement that 'without deliberation, he had begun to dissociate himself from the army in matters of real concern' (OG 161), matters of faith, never far from Waugh's mind, returned to the centre of his consciousness in the years between *Put Out More Flags* and his next novel. They also entered his public writing with a new explicitness, in the reviews of Greene and Laski, and in an amusing correspondence on education (a pressing topic for Catholics in the wake of R. A. Butler's proposed Education Bill) in the letters column of the *New Statesman*. In September 1943 the so-called Henshaw Report, a study commissioned in Bradford, purported to find that a greater proportion of children from Catholic than from Council schools became delinquents. Waugh's old bugbear Marie Stopes promptly wrote a letter to the *New Statesman* rehearsing the Henshaw data as proof that under any revised plan for education, Catholic schools should receive no public monies.[41] Fortified by months of debate on Butler's Bill in such journals as the *Tablet*, Waugh replied, questioning Stopes's statistics and commenting that her letter recalled the 'days of Titus Oates and Lord George Gordon': 'The truth, I think, is [that there] are still plenty of people about for whom the word "Catholic" acts as a drug stupefying all mental processes, and as long as these people are about we shall take good care to preserve our children from being taught either arithmetic or morals by them'. Stopes replied in turn, joined by another correspondent signing himself 'Medical Psychologist', whereupon Waugh put an end to the fracas:

'Medical Psychologist' chides me with not having 'taken the trouble to inquire' into his statistics. I plead, unashamedly, guilty for I was not brought up to regard the evasion of the police as the prime aim of education, nor has my subsequent observation of the world given me any reason to think that either the wickedest men or even the worst citizens are to be found in prison. The real enemies of society are sitting snug behind typewriters and microphones, pursuing their work of destruction amid popular applause....

No doubt by bringing my children up Catholics I am putting them in appreciable danger of imprisonment, but they must not reproach me with it. They belong to a Church whose most illustrious figures in any age and country have suffered the extremities of the law. Moreover, sir, a perusal of your own pages gives me the impression that, if things go as you wish, by the time they are hardened in crime, gaols will have grown so congenial and the rest of the country so heavy with restraints, that they will have the laugh on their innocent old father whom a Protestant education keeps on the right side of the law.[42]

In 1943 Waugh also renewed friendships with Gwen and Olivia Greene, who had been instrumental in his conversion a decade before, and with Hubert Duggan, dying at thirty-nine of tuberculosis. To Olivia, now hopelessly alcoholic, overweight and obsessed by a strange personal cult combining Catholicism and Communism, he offered guidance and consolation in a long and sad correspondence. Duggan had been raised a Catholic but allowed his faith to lapse; dying 'in blackest melancholy and haunted by delusions', he feared for his soul but hesitated to return to the Church. 'It seems in Hubert's mind that it would be a betrayal of Phyllis [de Janzé, his recently dead mistress] to profess repentance of his life with her' (D 552); 'Supernatural aid needed' (L 171).

The events of that October affected Waugh profoundly. Duggan's sister Marcella vehemently opposed his seeing a priest; his mother Lady Curzon was undecided. Waugh acted:

> I went to see Father Dempsey who is the Catholic chaplain for West London District, to consult him about Hubert.... He gave me a medal. 'Just hide it somewhere in the room. I have known most wonderful cases of Grace brought about in just that way'. When I got to Chapel Street Lady Curzon told me that it was not expected Hubert would live through the day. As Dempsey had gone out I went to Farm Street and brought back [its rector] Father Devas. Marcella did not want him to come in. She and Ellen were sitting by him supporting him in a chair saying, 'You are getting well. You have nothing on your conscience'. I brought Father Devas in and he gave Hubert absolution. Hubert said, 'thank you father', which was taken as his assent.
>
> ...late afternoon...Numerous doctors – one particularly unattractive one from Canada – Marcella more than ever hostile. Father Devas very quiet and simple and humble, trying to make sense of all the confusion, knowing just what he wanted – to anoint Hubert – and patiently explaining, 'Look all I shall do is just to put oil on his forehead and say a prayer. Look the oil is in this little box. It is nothing to be frightened of'. And so by knowing what he wanted and sticking to that, when I was all for arguing it out from first principles, he got what he wanted and Hubert crossed himself and later called me up and said, 'When I became a Catholic it was not from fear', so he knows what happened and accepted it. So we spent the day watching for a spark of gratitude for the love of God and saw the spark.
>
> (D 552–3)

Less than two weeks later Waugh began writing *Brideshead*, which re-enacts a nearly identical scene at Lord Marchmain's deathbed.[43]

It was just before Duggan's death, after nights of sitting up late 'talking about religion and socialism', that Waugh complained, 'I want to get back to work again', saying that he had experiences enough 'laid in the cellar, some still ripening, most ready for drinking' (D 547–8). But before work could begin, a transfer came through to a Special Air Services battalion for which he had volunteered, still hoping for combat, and in December 1943 he and Christopher Sykes moved to a 'secret villa' for a course in parachute training.

Jumping from a plane brought the forty-year-old Waugh a special joy:

> Parachuting is without exception the most exhilarating thing I have ever done. All the tedium of the last months has been worthwhile for the few seconds of first leaving the aeroplane. I felt absolutely no reluctance to jump.
>
> (L 174)

The first [jump] was the keenest pleasure I remember. The aeroplane was noisy, dark, dirty, crowded; the harness and parachute irksome. From this one stepped into perfect silence and solitude and apparent immobility in bright sunshine above the treetops.

(D 556)

So haunting did Waugh find these moments of escape from drab reality that he lovingly recalled them years later in Gilbert Pinfold's memory of a 'moment of liberation' when he was 'high on the back-stairs of mysticism' (GP 165–6), then again in *Unconditional Surrender*.

Guy jumped.... He experienced rapture, something as near as his earthbound soul could reach to a foretaste of paradise, *locum refrigerii, lucis et pacis*. The aeroplane seemed as far distant as will, at the moment of death, the spinning earth. As though he had cast the constraining bonds of flesh and muscle and nerve, he found himself floating free; the harness that had so irked him in the narrow, dusky, resounding carriage now almost imperceptibly supported him. He was a free spirit in an element as fresh as on the day of its creation.[44]

'Those who are conscious of another world, the world of the spirit', wrote Palinurus, 'acquire an outlook which distorts the values of ordinary life; they are consumed by the weed of non-attachment' (*Grave* 32). Something of that detachment underlies those many moments (also recreated in his fiction) when, looking in a mirror, Waugh saw not so much himself as 'the uncongenial fellow traveller who would accompany him through life' (MA 153). It underlies as well Waugh's physical courage, already visible in his travels of the thirties and so evident during the war as to be 'virtually a death wish' (Beevor, *Crete*, 221). He could, with complete honesty, congratulate a friend on turning fifty: 'It is a great thing to be old and I am sorry you are not older. Still you have definitely passed the watershed and that is everything' (L 249). The 'wish to die', Guy Crouch-back is told in the confessional, may be 'a quite good disposition', so long as it stems not from despair but a proper perspective on the relation of this world to the next. Nearly all the heroes of Waugh's early novels, from Paul Pennyfeather to Tony Last and William Boot, had sought some refuge *from* the alternatively drab and chaotic world outside; only with *Brideshead* and subsequent novels does it become clear what world 'all of us exiles' can properly withdraw *into*.

Injuring his leg on his second parachute jump, Waugh spent three weeks recovering, then applied in January 1944 for leave from the military to write his novel, provisionally titled *The Household of the Faith*. Carefully observing the protocols he had once disastrously ignored, Waugh applied in triplicate to his commander, the Secretary of State for War, and Brendan Bracken, citing among other reasons for such a remarkable request:

2. I have no longer the physical agility necessary for an operational officer in the kind of operations for which I have trained....
6. This novel will have no direct dealing with the war and it is not pretended that it will have any immediate propaganda value. On the other hand it is hoped that it

may cause innocent amusement and relaxation to a number of readers and it is understood that entertainment is now regarded as a legitimate contribution to the war effort.

7. It is a peculiarity of the literary profession that, once an idea becomes fully formed in the author's mind, it cannot be left unexploited without deterioration.

(D 557)

Permission granted, Waugh left for Chagford feeling 'full of literary power' (D 558) and looking forward to five uninterrupted months of writing.

'Military frivolities' soon intruded. In February came orders to report as aide-de-camp to a General Thomas, an assignment Waugh soon freed himself of by getting drunk in mess, spilling wine in Thomas's lap, and on being reprimanded replying, 'I could not change the habits of a lifetime for a whim of his' (D 559). ('It is extraordinary how much wine there is in a glass & how far it spreads if it is thrown with gusto' (L 181).) In March, 'like a rabbit from a hat', came a similar assignment; in April he was called back to duty for nearly a month, having by then come in the book 'to a suitable halting stage' – the division between 'Et in Arcadia Ego' and the events of ten years later in 'A Twitch Upon the Thread' – and so feeling that 'a week or two away from it may do no harm'. He was able to return to Chagford only in early May, when he 'painfully picked up the threads of a very difficult chapter of love-making on a liner' (D 559, 561, 564).

On D-Day, as others began to hope the war was in its final phase, Waugh crafted the climax of Ryder's memories:

> This morning at breakfast the waiter told me the Second Front had opened. I sat down early to work and wrote a fine passage of Lord Marchmain's death agonies. Carolyn [Cobb] came to tell me the popular front was open. I sent for the priest to give Lord Marchmain the last sacraments. I worked through till 4 o'clock and finished the last chapter – the last dialogue poor – took it to the post, walked home by the upper road. There only remains now the epilogue which is easy meat.
>
> (D 567–8)

The whole was finished on 8 June and the last batch of manuscript dispatched to his typist (with directions to change the names 'Charles Fenwick' to 'Charles Ryder' and 'Bridget' – taken from his sister-in-law Bridget Herbert Grant – to 'Cordelia'), leaving Waugh time to check quotations in the London Library and visit Pixton before returning to duty. He arranged for a private edition of fifty copies to be printed as Christmas presents for friends; the trade edition would have to await the new year.

VI

'Half an hour's scramble on the beach near Dakar; an ignominious rout in Crete. That had been his war' (US 217). So Guy Crouchback reflects in 1944 before taking up his final military posting in Yugoslavia. Substitute Bardia for Dakar, and Waugh that summer might have said the same. At the end of June, done with *Brideshead*, he returned to an army that seemed to have nothing for him to do. Rescue came, unexpectedly, from Randolph Churchill. 'He asked me to go with him to Croatia in the belief that I should be able to heal the Great Schism between the Catholic and Orthodox churches – something with which he has just become acquainted and finds a hindrance to his war policy. I accepted eagerly but, until yesterday, thought it unlikely to come off. I have had so many setbacks in the last three years' (D 568–9).

In 1944 Yugoslavia was only two decades old, a patchwork of mutually hostile Serbs, Croats and Slovenes (along with Italians, Hungarians and Bulgarians) – Catholic Orthodox, and Muslim – cobbled together at Versailles in 1919 of provinces from the Austro-Hungarian and Ottoman empires, as well as various quasi-independent states, all placed under a Serbian king. The confection never worked. In 1934 terrorists assassinated King Alexander and the monarchy moved into exile in London. In March 1941 Germany, planning its invasion of the Soviet Union, secured an alliance with what was left of the Yugoslav government; various resistance groups sprang up, spurring Winston Churchill's famous comment, 'Yugoslavia has found its soul'.[45] Germany and Italy thereupon invaded, setting up a series of puppet governments, including an Italian protectorate in Croatia (German after Italy's capitulation in 1943). By this time the main resistance group appeared to be the Serbian Chetniks led by Draža Mihajlović, loyal to the exiled King Peter; Britain supported Mihajlović. But after Germany began its attack on Russia, another resistance group emerged, one that claimed more genuinely national ambitions than the Chetniks: the Partisans, led by Josip Broz (Tito), a senior Comintern agent and Secretary-General of the then still small Yugoslav Communist Party.

To the West Tito himself was a shadowy figure until 1943, when William Deakin and Fitzroy Maclean parachuted into his headquarters, bringing back enthusiastic reports of Partisan zeal that, along with similar reports from the newly formed Special Operations Executive (Yugoslavia), led Churchill to switch support from Mihajlović to Tito. Maclean accordingly became head of a military mission (Macmis) to Tito, enlisting the Prime Minister's son Randolph as a demonstration of Britain's support. Privately, Deakin, Maclean and Winston Churchill came to understand that the Partisans, already embroiled in fighting other native groups as well as the Germans, had their own agenda: to divert German war efforts from the Russian front, meanwhile erecting a Communist Yugoslavia. But to solidify popular support for their new allies, Tito was throughout the war portrayed to the British public as a heroic nationalist freedom-fighter, one who meant when the conflict with Germany was over to sponsor religious toleration and free elections. This was the picture of Tito that Randolph Churchill himself accepted.[46]

Waugh went to Yugoslavia with some knowledge of the situation. In June 1943 he had noted 'a report in the *New Statesman* of an interview with returned Serbian guerrillas – anti-Mihailovic propaganda' (D 539). Catholic publications, fearful for co-religionists at the hands of Partisans seeking 'to use the period of German occupation as an opportunity to organize armed forces which, while ostensibly collected against the invader, would also be used against their own countrymen', gave Yugoslav affairs far more coverage than did the secular press, which treated the Balkans as a minor theatre in the war. From late 1943 onward, the *Month* and *Tablet* both argued that Tito's Partisans were at least equally devoted to bringing about a postwar Communist settlement as to aiding in the defeat of Germany.[47] Even as Waugh left for his new posting, news was leaking out of a Foreign Office report (received through the British delegation to the Vatican) of wholesale executions by Partisans in Slovenia of thousands of non-Communist natives. While Maclean continued to claim in his official reports that Tito practised religious toleration, twenty-seven Slovenian priests were murdered and seventy churches desecrated. 'When the truth [about Partisan activities] is published in detail', declared the *Tablet*, 'honest men in the world will be aghast' (15 July 1944, 29). With such reports in mind, Waugh understood his own purpose in Yugoslavia to be that of witness: to collect facts and, if necessary, make inconvenient truths known.

In July 1944 he proceeded with Randolph first to Bari, the Italian port where Macmis had its rear headquarters, then to Vis, an island off the Dalmatian coast where Maclean was briefing Tito before taking him to meet Winston Churchill. Here, taking advantage of the fact that the Partisan leader was so little known outside Yugoslavia that some even doubted his existence, Waugh initiated his longstanding joke of claiming that Tito was a woman, indeed a lesbian, referring to him as 'she' or 'Auntie'. (Weeks later he was still telling any who protested otherwise, 'Her face is pretty, but her legs are *very* thick' (HW 151).) But amidst 'Hammers, sickles and Communist slogans everywhere', he also noted: 'Too early to give any opinions but I have as yet seen nothing that justifies Randolph's assertion to the Pope that "the whole trend" was against Communism' (D 571–2).

Randolph's posting was to the Partisans' mainland headquarters deep in the Carpathian mountains at the old spa town of Topusko (the 'Begoy' of *Unconditional Surrender*), where he was to oversee Allied air-drops of supplies. He and Waugh flew in on 16 July; just before reaching the town their plane crashed, killing ten of the nineteen on board and leaving both badly burned. They were taken back to Italy to recuperate and returned to Topusko in September, whereupon Waugh set immediately to work, keeping an unusually full diary of his findings. On his first Sunday:

> Mass at 9 at Topusko church; half a dozen bourgeois, including two politicians of the Croat peasant party and a Dr Snoj of the Slovenian clerical party, and two soldiers. The remainder forty or so old devout peasant women. Randolph then drove me to investigate religious practices elsewhere – Glina . . . Four priests within six miles; no hindrance to worship except rival state organizations for youth and the military.
>
> (D 580)

Entries for succeeding weeks reveal grudging respect for the Partisans' devotion to duty and an effort not to overstate the evidence of religious persecution.

> Jews . . . said that a Jew had been killed by the bombing and his body robbed and stripped at once by the Partisans. This does not accord with what we know of them.
>
> (D 586)

[A Dominican prior] gave me heady white wine and told me that a letter had been sent to GSH recommending the execution of all connected with St. Blaise fête on grounds that it was religious. He also attempted to lie about priests being called up in Split. I caught him up and he had the grace to be confused.

(D 614)

Nonetheless, by December he had enough evidence to contact Maclean, seeking authority to make an official 'report on the religious situation' (D 596); 'an encouraging demand from Foreign Office for report on Church affairs' came through in January (D 612).

He also helped arrange the evacuation of Jewish refugees. But official duties were light, leaving plenty of time for boredom and for Waugh and Churchill to get on each other's nerves. The two men lived in close quarters; Churchill was often drunk while Waugh, who disliked the local liquor, remained unusually sober. 'Hour after hour Randolph trampled and trumpeted, talking, shouting, scratching, farting, belching and yawning; he tapped incompetently on the typewriter, bellowed into the telephone, and sat "clucking over the signals like an old hen"' (Hastings 469). Waugh was often rude, Randolph sometimes tearfully contrite. The arrival in October of their mutual friend Freddy Birkenhead brought temporary relief, though soon Birkenhead too lost patience.

Thinking the money well spent if it would keep Randolph quiet, Freddy and I have bet him £10 each that he will not read the Bible right through in a fortnight. He has set to work but not as quietly as we hoped. He sits bouncing about on his chair, chortling and saying, 'I say, did you know this came in the Bible "bring down my grey hairs with sorrow to the grave"?' Or simply. 'God, isn't God a shit'.

(D 591)

A German air-raid strained relations further. Despite angry shouts from Churchill to take cover, Waugh sauntered slowly along in plain view wearing the fine target of a white duffle-coat. On finally joining the rest of the mission in their trench, he protested Churchill's 'repulsive manners'. Churchill apologized, winning only the response: 'It wasn't your manners I was complaining of, it was your cowardice'.[48] Waugh soon requested yet another transfer.

In these extraordinary circumstances there arrived in November page proofs for the trade edition of *Brideshead*. As Waugh himself later recounted in inscribing them as a gift to Loyola College, a Jesuit institution in Baltimore which in 1948 awarded him an honorary doctorate: 'This set of pages proofs was sent in October 1944 from Henrietta Street to 10 Downing Street; from there it travelled to Italy in the Prime Minister's post bag, was flown from Brindisi & dropped by parachute on Gajen in Croatia, then an isolated area of "resistance"; was corrected at Topusko & taken by jeep, when the road was temporarily cleared of enemy, to Split; there by ship to Italy and so home, via Downing Street'.

The corrections Waugh made in Yugoslavia from 20 to 26 November, he wrote to Peters, were 'extensive & very important' (HRC E433): large excisions and deletions, and careful reworking of passages such as Anthony Blanche's dinner conversation with Charles Ryder. Among the passages wholly added at this stage were Charles's reflections on being given with Sebastian 'what I had never known, a happy childhood'; the letter from Sebastian ending 'Love or What you Will'; and long sections explaining the history of Brideshead Castle and Ryder's 'conversion to the baroque'.

Waugh's transfer came through at the end of November, a posting at Ragusa (Dubrovnik), which he reached in time for Christmas. His new role was as intermediary between the Partisans and British forces attempting to help speed what was now the German retreat. Tito had by this time openly allied himself with the Soviet Union, and the Partisans, increasingly confident of success, had grown openly hostile to the Allies. Waugh spent his days collecting further material on religious conditions, sorting through the requests of townspeople terrified of the coming regime and so seeking to emigrate, and distributing what food he could to the distressed, especially Catholics – activities that, to his pleasure, only fuelled Partisan dislike for the British in general and himself in particular. 'Looking back on the last two days I find that everything I have done, which is not much, has been benevolent – giving jobs to the needy, food to the hungry, arranging to get a Canadian moved towards Canada, helping a Dominican priest swap wine for flour. There are few in the Army can say this' (D 609–10).

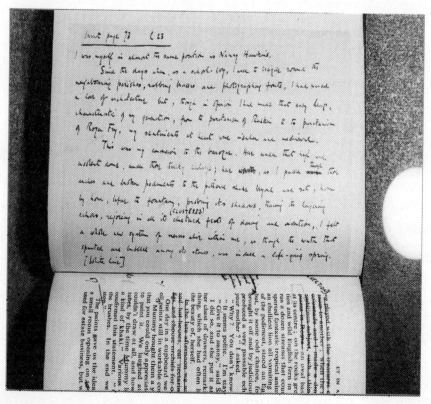

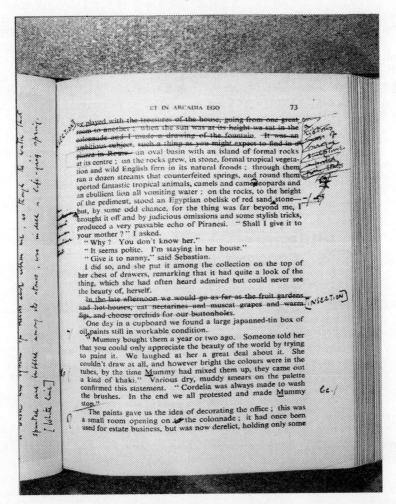

15–16 Page proofs of *Brideshead Revisited*, dropped by parachute to Waugh in Yugoslavia in 1944 and returned by diplomatic pouch via 10 Downing Street, later bound as a gift to Loyola College (Baltimore) in thanks for an honorary doctorate (Loyola College, Baltimore, Maryland).

Meanwhile he supported a local artist by sitting for a portrait bust – 'it will be the next best thing to having myself stuffed' – and enjoyed 'an authentic breath of Bloomsbury air', reading and annotating the copy of Connolly's *Unquiet Grave* sent by Nancy Mitford (D 608). Homesick and keen for responses to the private edition of *Brideshead*, he chided Laura for her too-brief comments on 'this book which I regard as my first important one' (L 195). As usual Nancy Mitford was his best source of gossip, though even she needed prodding: 'Do please keep your ear to the ground & report what they say. For the first time since 1928, I am eager about a book' (L 196).

By mid-February 1945 the Partisans had lost patience with what they called Waugh's politically 'incorrect' behaviour, contacted Bari, and secured his recall, effectively expelling him from Yugoslavia. Out of a job, Waugh sought and received official permission to travel to Rome to explain Croatian affairs to Vatican officials (including a brief audience with Pius XII himself). He returned to England in March, his first task completion of his report 'Church and State in Liberated Croatia' for Maclean and the Foreign Office.

Waugh had never pretended to a complete understanding of Yugoslav politics, but he had in a short time deduced much that subsequent history has tragically borne out. Assisted by his experience in Abyssinia, he soon realized that Jugoslavia was no unified 'nation' but a collection of factions often as murderous towards one other as to the Germans or Allies. Tito could not claim a national following; talk of the Partisan movement's 'inclusive, national character' was fraudulent. 'They want the Germans out so that they can settle down to civil war'.[49] In December 1944, noting the irony of Britain's simultaneous support for Tito's Partisans and opposition to a parallel movement in Greece, Waugh reflected sadly:

> Everyone here is worried about Greece.... The fault has come through the papers and politicians in England refusing to recognize that the Partisans everywhere are a homogeneous revolutionary army – instead we have called them 'patriots' and 'resistance groups' or 'armies of liberation' and put the word Communist, when used at all, in inverted commas as a German propaganda lie. In England apparently the thing is seen as an attempt by us to force an unwelcome royalist government on a democratic nation.
>
> (D 597)

Nor was he blind to the vices of Mihajlović and the Chetniks.[50] But he could not avoid the conclusion that in supporting Tito – and bringing over America to the same position – Britain was once again complicitous in abetting a greater evil. Wisely, Waugh did not in his official report make these arguments so directly as did publications such as *The Tablet*. Rather, he began by arguing that because the 'help given to the National Liberation movement by Great Britain has been extensive and, in the opinion of many observers, decisive', 'Some responsibility therefore rests with Great Britain for the consequence of its success'. Proceeding through a summary of evidence of religious persecution, he concluded simply:

> Great Britain has given great assistance to the establishment of a régime which threatens to destroy the Catholic Faith in a region where there are now some 5,000,000 Catholics. There is no hope for them from inside their country. Marshal Tito has paid lip-service to many liberal principles including that of freedom of worship. He may still be amenable to advice from his powerful Allies. If he were informed that the position of the Church under his rule is causing alarm, that it is not the policy of the Allies to destroy one illiberal régime to substitute another, that a Government which violates one of the principles of the Atlantic Charter cannot

be regarded as acceptable, he might be induced to modify his policy far enough to give the Church a chance of life.

(Sykes 370–2)

Even the committed Tito-supporter Maclean went on record that 'the report gives a reasonably fair picture' of Croat religious affairs, a view also borne out in a succession of postwar studies of the period.[51]

But there was of course by this time little Britain could do in Yugoslavia; Winston Churchill's efforts in the same direction had already failed. (In December 1945 Churchill confessed, 'I thought I could trust Tito...but now I am well aware that I committed one of the biggest mistakes in the war'.)[52] It is a measure of Waugh's seriousness in trying to do what little he could that within days of leaving Dubrovnik he had initiated efforts to return. 'A proposition has been made that mission officers may become consuls. It would be highly gratifying to return to the place I was expelled from, with great authority. It will give me the chance to help some of the unhappily stranded people of the place. So I have put in for this' (D 616). Back in England he followed up the request in person. Throughout March and April he was still 'very hopeful' of the appointment; as the time of waiting continued he also put in for a posting to the embassy in Athens, presumably for similar reasons. Only in May did he give up: 'I have the news that my application to go back to Jugoslavia has been refused and I am well content. Honour is satisfied. I am glad to have done all I could to go back and glad not to be going' (D 623, 627).

Waugh deplored not merely his government's policy in the Balkans but also its refusal to acknowledge the consequences of its acts. He wanted to circulate his report as widely as possible; Maclean and the Foreign Office wanted the opposite. After some inconclusive discussion as to whether it was covered by the Official Secrets Act, Waugh was told that he could discuss the report's contents but not publish it. He succeeded in persuading one MP to ask in the House what government meant to do to protect Croatian Catholics under the new regime. In a craven refusal to face facts, Foreign Secretary Anthony Eden replied: 'I cannot accept the implication that the assistance rendered by us to the National Liberation Movement of Yugoslavia in the struggle against Germany makes His Majesty's Government responsible for the internal administration of the Yugoslav state. This must remain the responsibility of the Yugoslav Government' (Hastings 480). Waugh wrote two letters to *The Times*, reviewed several books on the Balkans, and spoke to Catholic groups at Oxford, Cambridge and London University, attacking Britain's betrayal of Mihajlović.[53] There the matter rested until Eden invited Tito to visit England in 1952 – the same year Britain returned Mihajlović to Belgrade for 'trial' and execution – when, in a final effort to make the truth about Yugoslavia known, Waugh launched a campaign against 'Our Guest of Dishonour'.

As the war ended, tens of thousands of non-Communist Yugoslavs – including Mihajlović supporters forcibly 'repatriated' by the Allies – found their way into mass graves. Thus in the Balkans as in Poland, his own nation participated in what Guy Crouchback calls 'the dismemberment of Christendom' (US 180), accomplishing Germany's defeat at the cost of immense new human suffering, 'chaos and tyranny and famine and sheer wickedness throughout two-thirds of Europe'.

Like most Britons, Waugh knew little during the war of Churchill's private attitudes to these events. He knew Churchill's attitudes to the Soviet Union only through public speeches such as that delivered to the Commons after Yalta, just weeks before it became clear that Stalin would break all his promises about Poland: 'Marshal Stalin and the Soviet leaders wish to live in honourable friendship and equality with the Western democracies. I feel also that their word is their bond. I know of no government which stands to its obligations, even in its own despite, more solidly than the Russian Soviet Government' (Gilbert 827). He could know nothing of Churchill's complaint to Harold Macmillan at the Teheran Conference in 1943, 'The real problem now is Russia. I can't get the Americans to see it'; nothing about Churchill's intense, failed efforts late in the war to persuade America to contain what he called Russian imperial expansion; nothing about Churchill's advocacy in the months after Hiroshima that to end such expansion, the Soviet Union be threatened with nuclear attack.[54]

When peace came Churchill argued publicly the need, as he put it in the election campaign of 1945, to ensure 'that the simple and honourable purposes for which we entered the war are not brushed aside or overlooked in the months following our success, and that the words "freedom", "democracy" and "liberation" are not distorted from their true meaning' (Gilbert 844). But by then the damage was done. Many Christians shared Pius XII's view of the outcome of the war in Eastern Europe as the worst disaster for their faith since the Wars of Religion. Waugh's disappointment in British policy hardened during Churchill's later peacetime premiership into contempt for the man himself, so that he could write on Churchill's death in January 1965:

> He is not a man for whom I ever had esteem. Always in the wrong, always surrounded by crooks, a most unsuccessful father – simply a 'Radio Personality' who outlived his prime. 'Rallied the nation' indeed! I was a serving soldier in 1940. How we despised his orations.
>
> (L 630)

In *Men at Arms* it is 'On the day that Mr. Churchill became Prime Minister' that the ridiculous 'Apthorpe was promoted captain'.[55]

The fate of Poland and the Balkans haunts Waugh's succeeding work. In 1946, the preface to a new edition of *Campion* refers to 'saints in the prison camps of Eastern and South Eastern Europe' ('The hunted, trapped, murdered priest is amongst us again'); the heroine of 'Tactical Exercise' (1947) has a top-secret job 'concerned with setting up hostile and oppressive governments in Eastern Europe'; the story 'Compassion' (1949, later altered to form part of *Unconditional Surrender*) tells of religious persecution under the Partisans of Yugoslavia. In *Scott-King's Modern Europe* (1947), the hapless Dr Antonic explains the difference between the old Europe and the new:

'I am a Croat, born under the Habsburg Empire. That was a true League of Nations. As a young man I studied in Zagreb, Budapest, Prague, Vienna – one was free, one moved where one would; one was a citizen of Europe. Then we were liberated and put under the Serbs. Now we are liberated again and put under the Russians. And always more police, more prisons, more hanging'.

(SK39)

Meanwhile, on 28 May 1945, *Brideshead Revisited* was published.

6

Brideshead Revisited

The atmosphere of orthodoxy is always damaging to prose; and above all it is completely ruinous to the novel, the most anarchical of all forms of literature. How many Roman Catholics have been good novelists? Even the handful one could name have usually been bad Catholics. The novel is practically a Protestant form of art; it is a product of the free mind, of the autonomous individual.

George Orwell, 'Inside the Whale' (1940)

Clergy and religious denominations had always been a prominent feature of his books. There was reason behind the decision. His interest in people is not merely in their income groups, age-groups, their economic status. Had it been, he would, like Roger Simmons in *Work Suspended* have 'married an heiress, joined the Communist Party and become generally respectable'. He is interested in why they were born and where they are going after death.... Never a lover of his age he is now chiefly interested in how people prepare for the next. His last novel, *Brideshead Revisited* (1945) is an astonishing achievement. For here all the skill of the novelist has gone to elaborating the theme.

John Betjeman, 'Evelyn Waugh' (1947)

While writing *Brideshead*, the most densely complex and self-revealing of his works, Waugh grew convinced that it was not merely his best novel to date but a major work of art, a 'magnum opus'. 'I think perhaps it is the first of my novels rather than the last' (D 566); 'I believe it will go on being read for many years' (L 200). In Dubrovnik on 6 January 1945 – in a formulation later repeated in *Helena* – he was moved to interpret the signal achievement of this, his eighth novel and fifteenth published book, as proof that he had, though late, found his vocation:

I had never before realized how specially Epiphany is the feast of artists – twelve days late, after St Joseph and the angels and the shepherds and even the ox and the ass, the exotic caravan arrives with its black pages and ostrich plumes, brought there by book learning and speculation; they have had a long journey across the desert, the splendid gifts are travel-worn and not nearly as splendid as they looked when they were being packed up at Babylon; they have made the most disastrous mistakes – they even asked the way of Herod and provoked the Massacre of the innocents – but they get to Bethlehem in the end and their gifts are accepted, prophetic gifts that find a way into the language of the Church in a number of places. It is a very complete allegory.

(D 606)

He does not explain the allegory; do the 'black pages' pun on the pages of his book, the 'ostrich plumes' on what he knew was its luxuriant style?

'The whole thing', he wrote Peters, 'is steeped in theology' (L 185). For his first explicitly Catholic novel, Waugh had solicited expert help (for instance, from Ronald Knox on the deconsecration of a church). The first edition appeared with a 'Warning' on its dust-jacket (omitted in America):

> When I wrote my first novel, sixteen years ago, my publishers advised me, and I readily agreed, to prefix the warning that it was 'meant to be funny'.... Now, in a more sombre decade, I must provide them with another text, and, in honesty to the patrons who have supported me hitherto, state that *Brideshead Revisited* is not meant to be funny. There are passages of buffoonery, but the general theme is at once romantic and eschatological.
>
> It is ambitious, perhaps intolerably presumptuous; nothing less than an attempt to trace the workings of the divine purpose in a pagan world, in the lives of an English Catholic family, half-paganised themselves, in the world of 1923–39. The story will be uncongenial alike to those who look back on that pagan world with unalloyed affection, and to those who see it as transitory, insignificant and, already, hopefully passed. Whom then can I hope to please? Perhaps those who have the leisure to read a book word by word for the interest of the writer's use of language, perhaps those who look to the future with black forebodings and need more solid comfort than rosy memories. For the latter I have given my hero, and them, if they will allow me, a hope, not indeed, that anything but disaster lies ahead, but that the human spirit, redeemed, can survive all disasters.

The hero who offers limited hope in the face of inevitable disaster is its narrator Captain Charles Ryder, born like Waugh in October, 1903, whose memories, 'the memorials and pledges of the vital hours of a lifetime', comprise the story. A lonely young man 'in search of love' – and an artist in pursuit of beauty – Ryder follows a path that leads from lesser loves to greater, from human loves to God, though only when all is over does the act of retrospection itself enable him to understand the design of his life.

Time present, the setting of Prologue and Epilogue, is 1942: wartime, when the 'homeless, childless, middle-aged' Ryder finds that his love of the army has died. Book One, 'Et in Arcadia Ego', recalls the years 1923–6, the agnostic Charles's years at Oxford, his friendship with Sebastian Flyte, and the beginnings of his career as a painter. Book Two, 'A Twitch Upon the Thread', leaps ahead ten years – past ten 'dead years' that have included his marriage to Celia, shallow sister of his oafish Oxford friend 'Boy' Mulcaster – to 1936–9, to Ryder's love for Sebastian's sister Julia and, as war approaches, Lord Marchmain's return home to die.[1] All these memories culminate in the scene of Lord Marchmain's death, the moment to which, through the operations of an ironic providence as yet unrecognized by him, Ryder's whole life has been tending and which precipitates his conversion to Catholicism. 'I am delighted that you have become reconciled to *B.R.* in the end', Waugh wrote Knox, who like Laura and many Catholic friends was at first scandalized by the novel's loving recreations of Charles's earlier worldlinesses; 'It was, of course, all about the death bed. I was present at almost exactly that scene' (L 206).

Like many Catholic novels written for largely non-Catholic audiences, *Brideshead* is narrated for most of its length by a familiar modern type of unbeliever, one for whom others' faith is an 'enigma', 'but not one which I felt particularly concerned to solve'.

> I had no religion.... The view implicit in my education was that the basic narrative of Christianity had long been exposed as a myth, and that opinion was now divided as to whether its ethical teaching was of present value, a division in which the main weight went against it; religion was a hobby which some people professed and others did not; at the best it was slightly ornamental, at the worst it was the province of 'complexes' and 'inhibitions' – catchwords of the decade – and of the intolerance, hypocrisy, and sheer stupidity attributed to it for centuries. No one had ever suggested to me that these quaint observances expressed a coherent philosophic system and intransigeant historical claims; nor, had they done, would I have been much interested.
>
> (BR 76–7)

Ryder is thus a figure with whom unbelieving readers can identify – and, if the novel works, continue identifying as he is brought to faith. In this respect, quite aside from the novel's potent evocations of its characters' sufferings for their faith, Waugh's reviewers were right who found it a work of apologetic, even a 'Catholic tract'.

From the start, however, Waugh lards the story with hints that the narrator of 1942 has converted. In the Prologue Hooper tells Ryder of a service going on in Brideshead's 'R.C. church': 'More in your line than mine'.[2] At intervals we hear the voice of the older Ryder wryly commenting on the pretensions and errors of his younger self. When Charles leaves Brideshead after falling out with Lady March-main, he consoles himself with a display of adolescent sententiousness: 'I felt that I was leaving part of myself behind, and that wherever I went afterwards I should feel the lack of it, and search for it hopelessly, as ghosts are said to do'; 'I shall never go back'; 'I have left behind illusion. Henceforth I live in a world of three dimensions – with the aid of my five senses'. Amidst all this posturing the older Ryder cuts in: 'I have since learned that there is no such world' (149–50). Later, when Charles comments of a kindly monk at Fez, 'Poor simple monk, I thought, poor booby', the older Ryder interposes: 'God forgive me!' (189). Throughout *Brideshead*, readers must discriminate from what point of view emerge the judgments of a narrator who realizes that 'again and again' in life, 'a new truth is revealed ... in whose light all our previous knowledge must be rearranged' (71).

I The conversion of Charles Ryder

From the time of *Decline and Fall* and *Vile Bodies*, Waugh had drawn protagonists in a frustrated search for love. With *Brideshead* this search emerges as the central fact of human nature and for the first time finds its proper object. As the mature Ryder recognizes, 'to know and love one other human being is the root of all wisdom' (41): man is a being motivated by an inbuilt hunger for an adequate object of love, and our very sexuality may initiate a search that moves from the partial and transient to the permanent and complete. Just as Charles's painting progresses from landscape to human constructions (architecture) to the human figure (drawings of Julia), his loves form a series of steps like those on a Neoplatonic ladder, from Sebastian through Julia to God. Each lesser love is real and valuable, but at the same time inadequate: each is a means pointing beyond itself to a more satisfactory end. And because the progression embodies a providential design, each is a seeming detour or retrogression that in fact constitutes an advance.

'So through a world of piety I made my way to Sebastian' says Charles one Sunday in Oxford, not realizing that Sebastian will help lead him to that very piety. Raised by a distant father in a household without women, then sent to the adolescent 'bachelordom' of a boys' school, Charles's first love is a homosexual attachment to 'the most conspicuous man of his year by reason of his beauty' (26). In this first seeming detour and retrogression, Charles enjoys with Sebastian 'a brief spell of what I had never known, a happy childhood'. 'Alone together' at Oxford and Brideshead, free as yet of adult responsibilities, Charles and Sebastian enjoy an interlude of 'pastoral gaiety', a season in Arcadia. 'If only it could be like this always', says Sebastian, 'always summer, always alone, the fruit always ripe'. At first only the skull bearing 'the motto *Et in Arcadia ego* inscribed on its forehead' with which Charles decorates his room hints that the soul is never alone, that youth is called upon to mature, to die into adult responsibility.[3]

Critics have debated whether what Cara calls Charles and Sebastian's 'romantic friendship' is really homosexual. But Waugh is clear on the point (far more so than Alec had been in hinting such matters in *The Loom of Youth*). Looking back, Ryder admits that the relationship entailed a 'naughtiness … high in the catalogue of grave sins' – which could of course not be said of mere friendship. Lest we miss the point, Sebastian uses the same word shortly afterward in an off-hand reference to a newspaper report of 'Another naughty scout master'.[4] Suggesting a psychiatrist to treat Sebastian's drunkenness, Rex crudely adds, 'He takes sex cases, too' (146); and in one of the novel's many parallels between Books One and Two, Bridey tries to prevent Cordelia's dining with Sebastian and Charles, just as later he says his fiancée Beryl would not wish to visit Julia and Charles 'living in sin' (81, 250). Sebastian's Augustinian prayer, 'Oh God, make me good, but not yet', measures a pained awareness of what he must renounce, a pain as deep as Julia's in her decision to give up Charles rather than 'set up a rival good to God's' (77, 298). But just as Charles's drinking for pleasure differs from Sebastian's drinking to escape the claims of his conscience, Charles's homosexuality differs from Sebastian's. Charles's youthful homosexuality is merely a stage in a process of maturation, a process analogous to that whereby wine in fermenting first becomes quite 'undrinkable' so that later it may be all the more 'fit for the table' (41). Sebastian has no wish to grow up.

In Book Two it turns out that the 'magically beautiful' Sebastian was the 'forerunner' for Charles's more mature love for Julia, the sister who so much resembles him and who is now at the 'zenith' of the 'haunting, magical sadness' which is her beauty. 'I had not forgotten Sebastian. He was with me daily in Julia; or rather it was Julia I had known in him' (210, 265–6).

Such resemblance of brother and sister was in fact common in a class of tales about young men coming to maturity which, Paul Puccio has shown, provided an important source for *Brideshead*: the school novel, as practised from Thomas Hughes's *Tom Brown's Schooldays* (1857) and *Tom Brown at Oxford* (1861) to Waugh's own youthful favourite, Compton Mackenzie's *Sinister Street* (1913). These stories were often designed as if to teach Thomas Arnold's doctrine that the 'friendships' formed among boys in youth 'may be part of the business of eternity'; *Tom Brown's Schooldays* takes as one of its epigraphs the lines from Tennyson's *In Memoriam*: 'men may rise on stepping-stones / Of their dead selves to higher things'.[5] Along the way occur frequent speeches of advice from older students to younger (a kind of scene Waugh parodies in Charles's meetings with his cousin Jasper); sometimes boys bring one another to conversion. Often the schoolboy hero visits the sickroom of his closest friend, and eventually meets his family, his mother and especially his sister, whose physical resemblance to an already admired brother helps draw the hero from friendship to mature love and marriage. The title character of J. E. C. Welldon's *Gerald Eversley's Friendship* (1895) reflects of Ethel Venniker, sister of his school chum Harry:

> there was ... a presentiment of love in Gerald Eversley's relation to Miss Venni-ker. It lay in his old affection for her brother.... Miss Venniker was endowed in Gerald Eversley's view not only with her own charm, rare as it was, but with her brother's too. To be linked to her was to be linked to him, to him perpetually. The old schoolboy friendship would be consolidated, nay it would be sanctified by a deeper and holier sympathy.... Have I not known elsewhere instances of men who have loved the brother first, and then – with a still stronger love – his sister? ... blending ... the old love and the new?

In his months 'alone together' with Julia at Brideshead – the phrase, initially used of Charles and Sebastian, is repeated – Ryder hopes to inherit the house and go on living in that 'world of its own of peace and love and beauty' as in a new Arcadia.[6] Not yet converted, he does not recognize the source of Julia's sadness; he senses a progression in his development, but not yet that the progression has any end, musing to her that

> perhaps all our loves are merely hints and symbols; a hill of many invisible crests; doors that open as in a dream to reveal only a further stretch of carpet and another door; perhaps you and I are types and this sadness which sometimes falls between us springs from disappointment in our search, each straining through and beyond

the other, snatching a glimpse now and then of the shadow which turns the corner always a pace or two ahead of us.

(BR 265)

Knowledge of the end begins to come only at Lord Marchmain's death, after which – having so often told various Flytes that he doesn't and can't 'understand' them – Charles tells Julia 'but I do understand' why she must give him up (298).

The deathbed scene is elaborately prepared for. Spurred by Bridey's bland remark about 'living in sin', Julia, who like Sebastian has rebelled against but never lost her faith, gives way to increasingly frequent outbursts of 'anger' and even 'hate' – outbursts seemingly directed at Charles, actually at herself. Meanwhile Charles only 'dimly surmis[es]' the origins of these 'fierce moods' and the 'threat' to their life together that her faith represents. Thus without understanding his own motives he grows increasingly hostile to that faith, engaging in gleefully sophomoric antireligious arguments and seeking to prevent Lord Marchmain from seeing a priest.

When over Easter the priest is finally brought, there follows that most difficult of events to realize in fiction, a miracle. Out of love for his mistress Julia, Charles kneels to say an unbeliever's prayer, the old Stoic prayer 'Oh God, if there is a God'. 'I suddenly felt the longing for a sign, if only of courtesy, if only for the sake of the woman I loved'. Another, less detached prayer spontaneously follows. When Lord Marchmain then makes the sign of the cross, 'Ryder knows very well that his prayer has been answered, disastrously for his secular dreams of Julia and Brideshead Castle': in a penultimate turn of ironic providence, his very 'love for Julia has led him to lose her'.[7] Not merely the spectacle of the proud Marchmain humbling himself before God but the knowledge that he has witnessed God's action in the human realm shocks Ryder into belief. A 'phrase came back to me from my childhood' – in fact from the Easter service, that memorial to the bursting of the divine into history – 'of the veil of the temple being rent from top to bottom'.[8]

We are to understand that between 1939 and 1942 – between the final events of Book Two and the Epilogue, when he enters the chapel at Brideshead to utter 'a prayer, an ancient, newly learned form of words' (304) – Ryder has formally converted. Now, in the bleakness of wartime, he sees the army's cavalier destruction of house, grounds and fountain; only the hideous *art nouveau* chapel (whose carved oak looks as if 'moulded in plasticine', its metal-work like 'pock-marked skin') (36) survives intact. Surveying the destruction of beauties centuries in the making, Ryder recalls a phrase from the Lamentations of Jeremiah and momentarily despairs:

> The builders did not know the uses to which their work would descend; they made a new house with the stones of the old castle; year by year, generation after generation, they enriched and extended it; year by year the great harvest of timber in the park grew to ripeness; until, in the sudden frost, came the age of Hooper; the place was desolate and the work all brought to nothing; *Quomodo sedet sola civitas.* Vanity of vanities, all is vanity.

(BR 304)

Then Ryder passes beyond such despair, realizing that such Old Testament sentiments constitute 'a dead word from ten years back', a response by the old rather than the new man. ('How the city sits empty, that once was full of people', Jeremiah's lament for the destruction of the Temple, was also sung at matins on Maundy Thursday, at the beginning of the liturgy that concludes by celebrating the conversion of death into life at Easter.)[9] In what is the final fruit of his long process of retrospection, Ryder recognizes in both the war and his own life hints of a providential plan: a design by which, in the usual manner of providence, good is educed from ill, meaning from the seeming chaos of events. Just as the faith to which he has come is (literally) infinitely more important than whatever might have been the splendours of life at Brideshead with Julia, so the reopening of the ugliest part of the estate, the reconsecrated chapel, with its offer of grace to the 'surprising lot' of troops who use it, outweighs the destruction of its merely secular beauties.

> Something quite remote from anything the builders intended had come out of their work, and out of the fierce little human tragedy in which I played; something none of us thought about at the time: a small red flame – a beaten-copper lamp of deplorable design relit before the beaten-copper doors of a tabernacle.... It could not have been lit but for the builders and the tragedians, and there I found it this morning, burning anew among the old stones.
>
> (BR 304)

'The real meaning of history' turns out, in Christopher Dawson's words, 'something entirely different from that which the human actors in the historical drama themselves believe or intend'; Waugh himself explained his ending: 'the physical dissolution of the house of Brideshead has in fact been a spiritual regeneration'.[10] A brief final paragraph reveals the previously despondent Ryder now 'unusually cheerful', balancing and completing the Prologue's reference to the way browned-off soldiers 'got more cheerful' when 'they found themselves doing something with an apparent purpose in it'.[11] This sense of meaning in tragedy (not 'rosy memories' of pre-war life) is the 'hope' Waugh spoke of on the novel's dust-jacket.

II The Tragedians

To a protest from Nancy Mitford that Charles Ryder 'might have had a little more glamour', Waugh replied defensively, 'he is dim, but then he is telling the story and it is not his story. It is all right for Benvenuto Cellini to be undim but he is telling his own story and nobody else[']s' (L 196). *Brideshead*'s 'fierce human tragedy' belongs to all its players, to the Flytes as much as Ryder (who even before his conversion has 'the cloudy sense that the fate of more souls than one was at issue') (285). Its chief agent, as Waugh said, is providence, a divine will which overbears the rebellious wills of those in flight (the significance of the family name 'Flyte') from the demands of their faith – Sebastian, Julia and their father.

It is important to recognize that the Flytes are not an old Catholic family, just as Brideshead Castle is not, as its name might suggest, a medieval foundation.

The family turned Protestant with the Reformation. The marquisate came later yet, during the 'fat days' of 'the Georges', 'the days of growth and building' (291). The 'new house', built of stones from an older castle, was begun 'in Inigo Jones's time' (the seventeenth century, seed-time of such baroque masterpieces as Hawksmoor and Vanbrugh's Castle Howard) and continued over generations. The park is late eighteenth century, era of Capability Brown and Humphry Repton; the baroque fountain was brought from Naples in the early nineteenth. House and family thus recapitulate the history of English art and apostasy. Only on the brink of the twentieth century, through Lord Marchmain's 'recent and half-hearted' conversion at the time of his marriage (MGM 227), has the family returned to Catholicism. The chapel, the most recent addition to the estate, was a wedding-present to Lady Marchmain. All this – the estate he loves, the patrimony from which he derives his identity – Marchmain has abandoned, remaining in Italy after World War I, leaving behind his wife and family for an Italian mistress, excommunication, and self-imposed exile.

Initially the Flytes are as much an enigma to the reader as to Charles. To complicate our judgment Waugh metes out worldly graces to the disadvantage of the faithful, joining, in von Hügel's words, 'an apparent minimum of earthly gifts and a maximum of heavenly light' (*Letters* 159). Bridey and Cordelia, though opposite in personality – he coldly logical, she (as her name suggests) warm-hearted – are clumsy and physically plain, having inherited the hard features of their mother's family. Both share Lady Marchmain's piety, mixing talk of religion into daily affairs with the eagerness of Waugh's convert in-laws at Pixton, and her charities. Both are frustrated in their hope of a religious vocation (he as priest, she as nun); neither seems to share the brilliant possibilities open to Julia and Sebastian.

Only Sebastian and Julia have inherited their father's looks – and his fine taste. Bridey finds the beautiful Marchmain House 'rather ugly'; Cordelia finds the chapel – the only ugly room at Brideshead aside from Lady Marchmain's drop-ceilinged sitting-room – 'beautiful' (192, 82). Both Sebastian and Julia, while retaining the Catholicism in which they have been raised, have also inherited their father's rebelliousness, the strain of self-centred willfulness that leads him to choose exile and, in his final struggle against duty, to revise his will to disinherit his eldest son. (From youth Julia is distinguished from her con-temporaries by 'waywardness and wilfulness, a less disciplined habit'; Sebastian's life, Charles finds, is 'governed by a code of such imperatives' as 'I *must* have pillar-box red pyjamas', 'I *have* to stay in bed until the sun works round to the windows', 'I've absolutely *got* to drink champagne tonight': 160, 36.)

To those outside the faith Bridey seems especially obtuse – as Anthony Blanche says, 'a learned bigot, a ceremonious barbarian'. With his ridiculous matchboxes and ridiculous wife Beryl Muspratt, Bridey is by every worldly measure a fool. Charles finds him 'a mystery; a creature from underground' or from 'a moon-scape of barren lava'; 'neither had any understanding of the other, nor ever could'.[12] But Bridey is a fool sent to shame the wise. His 'mad certainties' and exquisitely inopportune 'bombshells', though they demonstrate in their complacency the same breath-taking lack of human sympathy that unfits him for the priesthood, are invariably correct: they are judgments *sub specie aeternitatis* jarringly intruded into a secular context. Bridey shocks Charles with his hope that Sebastian is alcoholic, but in fact has his brother's interests at heart: 'I hope it is dipsomania. That is simply a great misfortune that we must all help him bear. What I used to fear was that he just got drunk deliberately when he liked and because he liked'. Better physical illness than risk of hell; 'There's nothing *wrong* in being a physical wreck', 'no moral obligation to be Postmaster-General' (144–5). Bridey is equally right that 'It is a matter of indifference whether [Julia] choose to live in sin with Rex or Charles or both' (since in the eyes of God neither is her husband), and that this 'simple fact' is 'well known to her'.[13]

It is the demands of a faith he has never really lost that Sebastian seeks in Book One to escape.[14] 'Is it nonsense?' Sebastian asks Charles, 'I wish it were' (echoed later by Julia: 'How I wish it was [all bosh]!') (77, 255). Weak, homo-sexual and alcoholic, Sebastian knows he has much to renounce and atone. Thus his self-hatred ('I'm ashamed of myself'; 'I wouldn't love anyone with a character like mine'; 'I absolutely detest myself'); thus his 'deep, interior need' to 'escape from reality', to 'feel free', to 'go on running away, as far and as fast as I can'; thus, as the trustworthy Cara says, his remaining 'in love with his own childhood', symbolized by his teddy-bear. Sebastian's 'despairing prayer' is 'to be let alone', to be allowed to remain 'happy and harmless as a Polynesian', but since 'conscience and all claims of human affection' inevitably intrude with their demands that the soul grow up, 'his days in Arcadia were numbered'.[15]

Charles quickly learns that Sebastian is most unhappy (and most often drunk) at home and when reminded of his family. Their first visit to Brideshead elicits from Sebastian a waspishness to be seen again in Julia and Lord Marchmain at the end of the novel, for which he apologizes: 'Brideshead often has that effect on me'. 'The further we drove from Brideshead the more he seemed to cast off his uneasiness' (36, 37). But Charles mistakes the cause, supposing only that Sebastian hates his pious and meddlesome mother, whose clumsy (if well-intentioned) interference consistently exacerbates his drinking and unhappiness.

When Nancy Mitford asked, 'Are you or are you not on Lady Marchmain's side? I couldn't make out', Waugh replied: 'no I am not on her side; but God is, who suffers fools gladly'. 'Yes, Lady Marchmain is an enigma', he wrote Peters; 'I hoped the last conversation with Cordelia gave the theological clue'.[16] The reference is to Cordelia's explanation at the end of Book One – after Lady Marchmain has died, thinking herself a failure with her husband, Sebastian, and Julia – that 'when people wanted to hate God they hated Mummy', whose long-suffering piety constantly reminded them of their responsibilities to God (195). Like Bridey, Lady Marchmain is inept in a worldly way, even to the point of being taken in by the odious Samgrass, but right about eternals. Looking back, Ryder con-cludes of her: 'She accepted me as Sebastian's friend and sought to make me hers also, and in doing so, unwittingly struck at the roots of our friendship. That is the single reproach I have to set against her abundant kindness to me' (97).

Saintly but not a saint is Cordelia's trustworthy conclusion about her mother, and it is part of Waugh's genius in portraying Lady Marchmain to capture the

very human resentment that being loved and forgiven can cause. Given the
choice, who would elect even a near-saint for a parent? Descriptions of Lady
Marchmain as 'impatient of any relationship' short of 'intimacy' (98), as a
mother who feels 'Any failure in my children is my failure' and who 'likes
everything to be a present' (149, 56), suggest both a parent any child might
find suffocating and a woman who partakes of the divine. Thus Sebastian, Julia,
and, looking back, Ryder liken Lady Marchmain's sorrows to those of the Virgin
('her heart ... transfixed with the swords of her dolours, a living heart to match
the plaster and paint') and of Christ ('Mummy dying with my sin eating at her
... Mummy dying with it; Christ dying with it') (167, 252).

Once clear on Sebastian's relation to his mother, readers can unriddle Lord
Marchmain, whose drinking and self-imposed exile Cara, Bridey, Lady Marchmain, Cordelia and Ryder himself all parallel with Sebastian's. He too has failed
to grow up; he too – though from a different form of pride – has conflated the
religious demands he hates with the person of Lady Marchmain. Waugh himself
explained:

> The reason [for their separation] is never specified, but it is implied that it derives
> from two sources. First, a personal incompatibility which in turn causes the internal
> conflict in the characters of the two children, Julia and Sebastian.... Secondly,
> from Lord Marchmain's revulsion and flight from his religion, which he identifies
> with his wife and home – a revulsion which is overcome only on his deathbed.
>
> (MGM 227)

Nothing could be further from the truth than Lord Marchmain's claim never
to have been 'much moved by family piety' (280). Heir to a splendid history of
wealth, accomplishment, and responsibility, he told his wife on their marriage:
'You have brought back my family to the faith of their ancestors' (194). The
pompous phrasing (noted as such by Cordelia) discloses a fierce pride that
cannot bear playing second fiddle, cannot bear and so flees from the humiliating
acknowledgment that what has been freely given him by his wife and her faith
outweighs in ultimate importance all that he has brought to the marriage.
Unwilling to acknowledge that dependence, he 'commits a crime in the name
of freedom' (292), only to discover (like Sebastian) that there is no such freedom
from the demands on his soul.

In Venice Marchmain confesses that 'it is a disgraceful thing to inherit great
responsibilities' only to abandon them (88). Having abandoned his proper character, he creates for himself what even the young Charles recognizes as an
artificial personality: 'I was first struck by his normality, which, as I saw more
of him, I found to be studied' (87). The pose includes feigning 'entire indifference
to' his inheritance, but it fits uneasily, feeding what Cara calls the 'volcano of
hate' beneath. When he returns home to die, this hate, born of frustrated pride
and contained only with difficulty, flares out in cruelly 'waspish' jokes about those
around him that reveal 'a frame of malevolence under his urbanity' (278).

Still rebelling against all that his wife has stood for, Marchmain arranges to
die amidst the most splendid proofs of his worldly inheritance, the 'gilt mirrors

and lacquer' of the Chinese drawing-room and the Queen's Bed; he orders from storage 'the gold plate, which I had not before seen in use' (279). But it is not just such material appurtenances for which he has so long rebelled. His last long speech, so grievously misread by Edmund Wilson as Waugh's own celebration of aristocratic grandeur, serves to demonstrate how deeply Marchmain must humble himself in finally making the sign of the cross. His mind wandering, terrified of dying, the marquess vainly clings to life by rehearsing his family's noble history and his own place in it. He comes to the chapel: 'I gave it to her ... I built it for her', as if it and all it stands for were simply reflections of his own power and authority. Symbol of all he has tried to reject, the grace he has tried to refuse, he predicts that the chapel, since it was 'the last of the new house to come', will be 'the first to go' (293). Waugh has included the speech to make clear that Marchmain's final gesture of reconciliation is no 'small thing', no 'bare acknowledgment of a present' (the gift of God's grace freely given) (293), but a humiliating acknowledgment of dependence, and so of a lifetime's proudly mistaken priorities.

Sebastian's earlier, equally dramatic turn 'back to the Church' does not have the same effect on others, as yet unready to understand it. Sebastian's final, Christlike renunciation and self-abasement, his giving up of all the earthly things he loves – the substance of his holiness – was in fact present, unseen, in his earlier drunken misery. In taking up with the syphilitic, hopelessly unprepossessing Kurt (whose 'wound that wouldn't heal' suggests original sin), Sebastian begins a career of corporal works of mercy such as Cordelia and later Julia engage in. 'It's funny', he tells an uncomprehending Charles, 'I couldn't get on without him' – meaning, in a favourite phrase of von Hügel's, 'get on' to heaven.[17] Later Cordelia stresses that despite – indeed, because of – his 'suffering', Sebastian is at last 'happy' with Kurt, and 'quite happy' in his even more reduced state, pottering about 'a monastery near Carthage' (in the land of St Augustine), waiting to die. 'No one is ever holy without suffering', she explains, unknowingly forecasting what will happen to Charles himself; 'I've seen so much suffering in the last few years; there's so much coming for everybody soon'. Like the crucifixion itself, 'It's the spring of love' (266–71).

III Künstlerroman

'It's almost impossible', wrote Flannery O'Connor, 'to write about supernatural Grace in fiction' (*Works* 988). Novels commonly trade in psychological explanations of events, but no conversion, Waugh believed, is explicable merely psychologically; each comes through 'the unmerited and unilateral act of love by which God continually calls souls to Himself' (MGM 226.) The novelist who wishes to trace the operation of grace must thus construct a world in which two different orders of causation, the efficient and the final, operate simultaneously; psychology and teleology (whether characters know it or not) must cooperate.

In the order of final causes, Waugh recurrently likens Ryder's turn to faith to an avalanche on an arctic mountainside: a sudden, overpowering intrusion from without.[18] But since each human soul already contains a purpose within itself, an end it seeks to realize, the novel also traces in the order of efficient causation – of ordinary psychology – the process by which Ryder is prepared to receive grace. This Waugh accomplishes by casting the story not simply as a tale of conversion, but the conversion of a man whose vocation is to be an artist. (As he explained in 1946, one purpose of the novel is to suggest that 'God has a separate plan for each individual by which he or she may find salvation' (MGM 227).) In the Epilogue's final turn, Ryder recognizes in the story of his life a meaningful shape, a shape like that of a successful work of art. That he can understand his life this way is the fruit of his career as an artist.

With his conté crayons and expensive 'Whatman H. P'. drawing paper, Charles is headed for this career from the start, even before Anthony Blanche announces to him that he is 'that very rare thing, An Artist' (28, 49). From the outset, too, he possesses not only an intense sensitivity to beauty – to the beauty of fields and flowers, most often described as drenched in scent and rich in the colours white and gold, green and blue – but also an inchoate sense of natural beauty as a kind of gift or bounty. The novel hints as much with its many echoes of romantic poetry, Keats and Wordsworth and Browning, material Waugh had not often called on before. It may be the converted Ryder who calls on the language of Gerard Hopkins to evoke his first visit to Brideshead on a June day 'when leaf and flower and bird and sun-lit stone and shadow seem[ed] all to proclaim the glory of God', and who describes Julia in youth:

> through those halcyon weeks Julia darted and shone, part of the sunshine between the trees, part of the candlelight in the mirror's spectrum, so that elderly men and women, sitting aside with their memories, saw her as herself the blue-bird.... she brought to all whose eyes were open to it a moment of joy, such as strikes deep to the heart on the river's bank when the kingfisher suddenly flames across dappled water.[19]

But the older speaker is drawing out notions already present, if unformed, in his earlier responses. Just as the younger Charles 'believed [him]self very near heaven, during those languid days at Brideshead', the older self develops such feelings into the suggestion that 'perhaps the Beatific Vision itself has some remote kinship with this lowly experience' (71).

In *Brideshead* even eating – in the earlier novels a shorthand indication of wayward appetite[20] – can be redeemed; even the beauty of wine and fine cooking point to something higher. Dining in Paris with Rex Mottram, it is the older Ryder who intrudes the pun, last used in *Decline and Fall*, between souls and soles:

> 'Ma Marchmain won't do anything about [her health]. I suppose it's something to do with her crack-brain religion, not to take care of the body'.
> The sole was so simple and unobtrusive that Rex failed to notice it.
>
> (BR 154)

But even at the time, Charles hears a message in the 'beauty' of the wine they drink (though one still framed in the pretentious language of his adolescence): 'This Burgundy seemed to me, then, serene and triumphant, a reminder that the world was an older and better place than Rex knew, that mankind in its long passion had learned another wisdom than his'; it 'whispered faintly ... words of hope' (155). Later, after a day of inspired painting at Marchmain House, he feels himself a man 'of Browning's Renaissance': 'I had my finger in the great, succulent pie of creation' (196).

Such moments develop what was already implicit in Charles's idyll with Sebastian, a kind of secular communion: 'under a clump of elms we ate the strawberries and drank the wine', 'the sweet, golden wine' seeming, in one of Waugh's favourite expressions, 'to lift us a finger's breadth' above reality.[21] The beauty to which Charles responds even in food is invested from the start with implicit eschatological significance, as a sign of (and call to) what in the sonnet 'To what serves Mortal Beauty?' Hopkins calls 'God's better beauty, grace'. (In 1945 Waugh wrote to a friend, explaining his dislike of Picasso: 'There is an Easter sense in which all things are made new in the risen Christ. A tiny gleam of this is reflected in all true art' (L 215).) As the story of an artist drawn by beauty to grace, *Brideshead* in effect turns on its head James Joyce's tale of secularization in *A Portrait of the Artist as a Young Man* (1916).

As he matures Charles ascends through a hierarchy of kinds of beauty and art as through a hierarchy of loves. In art as in love, he must retrogress to a kind of childhood before he can progress. Before succeeding as a painter he learns (like a romantic poet) to see nature innocently, rather than through the modernist aesthetic theories he has imbibed. And once again the Flytes serve as catalysts, first of all Sebastian, whose gift at Oxford of 'golden daffodils' makes everything else in Charles's rooms – including especially a screen from Roger Fry's Omega Studios – seem unreal (31).

Charles enters Oxford a devotee of modernism, of 'the puritanism of Roger Fry' (73) and Clive Bell. Soon after, his bookish friend Collins, later to become an authority on Byzantine art, explains in theoretical terms 'the fallacy of modern art': the contradictoriness of the doctrine of 'Significant Form', which outlawed representations designed to point to deeper meanings, beyond the visual surface of the canvas. 'The whole argument from Significant Form stands or falls by *volume*. If you allow Cézanne to represent a third dimension on his two-dimensional canvas, then you must allow Landseer his gleam of loyalty in the spaniel's eye'. But it takes Sebastian to drive home in a practical way the fallacy of a theory of 'aesthetic emotion' that sunders beauty from living nature (and therefore also from nature's God):

> it was not until Sebastian, idly turning the pages of Clive Bell's *Art*, read: ' "Does anyone feel the same kind of emotion for a butterfly or a flower that he feels for a cathedral or a picture?" Yes, *I* do', that my eyes were opened.[22]

Soon after, Sebastian begins Charles's aesthetic education afresh, insisting they visit the Botanical Gardens 'to see the ivy', 'more different kinds of ivy than I knew existed' (31). Having recovered a direct apprehension of natural beauty, Charles begins through a series of steps to realize his artistic vocation. By inviting him to stay at Brideshead, Sebastian again serves as guide: 'It was an aesthetic education to live within those walls' (72). It is the complex beauty of Brideshead, not simply the Flytes' wealth, that immediately attaches Charles. Since schooldays he had 'nursed a love of architecture', bicycling to local churches to rub brasses and photograph fonts, but his tastes had remained 'insular and medieval'. Amidst Brideshead's 'clustered feats of daring and invention', he undergoes a 'conversion to the baroque' (73), the manner of the Catholic Counter-Reformation. His openness to the baroque signals an openness to the values that inform it, his artistic 'conversion' prefiguring his later religious conversion.[23]

Here Sebastian sets Charles to draw the fountain, with its panoply of represented plant and animal life (represented natural beauty), resulting in the first in a sequence of signal moments of artistic inspiration. 'I see [the fountain] as a combination of three famous works of Bernini', the Counter-Reformation master, Waugh wrote in 1946: the Trevi, the central fountain of the Piazza Navona, and the elephant surmounted by an obelisk which stands nearby, before the church of Santa Maria sopra Minerva (MGM 227). The novel conjures up just such a monument of lavishly varied yet unified elements, reflecting the bounteous plenitude of creation:

> It was an ambitious subject for an amateur – an oval basin with an island of formal rocks at its centre; on the rocks grew, in stone, formal tropical vegetation and wild English fern in its natural fronds; through them ran a dozen streams that counterfeited springs, and round them sported fantastic tropical animals, camels and camelopards and an ebullient lion all vomiting water; on the rocks, to the height of the pediment, stood an Egyptian obelisk of red sandstone – but, by some odd chance, for the thing was beyond me, I brought it off and by judicious omissions and some stylish tricks, produced a very passable echo of Piranesi.
>
> (BR 72–3)

Charles's 'stylish tricks', like the castle's 'tricky ceilings' (73), echo the 'devious ways' by which, he later comes to realize, providence works its surprising effects: moments of artistic inspiration point to and prepare for a higher inspiration (162). 'I felt a whole new system of nerves alive within me, as though the water that spurted and bubbled among [the fountain's] stones was indeed a life-giving spring' (73).

From this point onward Charles's moments of artistic success closely track his spiritual development: like Beseleel's, his craftsmanship turns out a gift of the spirit.[24] Alone with Sebastian in the Arcadia of Brideshead, he next attempts 'a romantic landscape': 'The brush seemed somehow to do what was wanted of it' (74). But this is 'a landscape without figures'; Charles recognizes that he is not yet adept enough to attempt the human form. Two years later, after studying in Paris, he receives from Bridey his first commission, the work that turns him toward a career in architectural painting: memorializing Marchmain House before it is torn down to make way for a block of flats. As he paints, afternoon light 'fresh green from the young trees outside' streams in through the windows: still nourished by the beauty of creation which it is art's duty to imitate, he is given a third moment when 'I could do nothing wrong.... There were no difficulties; the intricate multiplicity of light and colour became a whole; ... each brush stroke, as soon as it was complete, seemed to have been there always' (192–3). Once again he is 'buoyed and exhilarated', deeply 'alive', gripped by an 'intensity and singleness and the belief that it was not all done by hand' which he identifies as 'inspiration' (199). As the painting reaches 'completeness', so Charles himself moves toward teleological fulfillment, a realization of his artistic vocation.

Charles's choice of professional subject-matter – buildings, whose completion over time, like that of inspired paintings, seems 'not all done by hand' – stems once again from an attitude analogous to, and so a preparation for, belief in providence. He explains his choice in a passage that looks forward to the Epilogue's final recognition that 'Something quite remote from anything the builders [of Brideshead] intended has come out of their work'.

> I became an architectural painter. I have always loved building, holding it to be not only the highest achievement of man but one in which, at the moment of consummation, things were most clearly taken out of his hands and perfected, without his intention, by other means.
>
> (BR 198)

But the analogy remains flawed and incomplete, as the remainder of the sentence, shifting to past tense, suggests:

> and I regarded men as something much less than the buildings they made and inhabited, as mere lodgers and short term sub-lessees of small importance in the long fruitful lives of their homes.
>
> (BR 198)

Charles's preference at this stage for buildings over people bespeaks a confusion of ends and means – a confusion whose fruit is a sharp detour from self-realization: his trip to paint the deserted ruins of Mexico. Though reviewers claim to find 'a new and richer note' in his Mexican paintings, Anthony Blanche rightly dismisses them as 't-t-terrible t-t-tripe'; though reviewers find that in them 'Mr. Ryder has at last found himself', even Celia knows that they are not 'quite *you*' (201, 236).

The crucial distinction between ends and means has been introduced long before by Bridey – appropriately, in a conversation about architecture and wine. Bridey asks Charles whether he thinks the chapel 'Good Art':

> 'Well, I don't quite know what you mean', I said warily. 'I think it's a remarkable example of its period. Probably in eighty years it will be greatly admired'.
> 'But surely it can't be good twenty years ago and good in eighty years, and not good now?'
> 'Well, it may be good now. All I mean is that I don't happen to like it much'.
> 'But is there a difference between liking a thing and thinking it good?'
> 'Isn't that just the distinction you made about wine?'
> 'No. I like and think good the end to which wine is sometimes the means – the promotion of sympathy between man and man. But in my own case it does not achieve that end, so I neither like it nor think it good for me'.
>
> (BR 82–3)

The difference between 'liking a thing' and 'thinking it good' which seems opaque to Bridey, so little has it troubled him, has of course been the source of Sebastian's torment, of the war within him between the orders of nature and grace. More specifically, Bridey distinguishes liking a thing as a means and thinking it good as an end in itself. In the largest perspective, since the end of each soul is salvation, all natural activities, even art, constitute not ultimate goods but lesser means: even art, to be 'good', must be good *for* something. In acknowledging that the chapel may be artistically 'good' but that he doesn't like it, Charles registers a preliminary awareness of the hierarchic relation of ends and means, leading Bridey to conclude the discussion: 'Of course, you are right really. You take art as a means and not as an end. That is strict theology, but it's unusual to find an agnostic believing it' (84).

Nothing in the realm of nature is an end in itself: so Waugh argues in the first of his novels devoted explicitly to his religious faith, casting Ryder's story as a progression through a series of stages or stepping-stones – 'forerunners' – each of which has its ultimate meaning not in itself but in that to which it leads. To mistake a means for an end – as Anthony Blanche (like Ambrose Silk) takes art as an end in itself – is to remain frozen in a lower stage of development, not to realize one's full humanity. Blanche, 'ageless as a lizard, foreign as a Martian' (30), retains both the homosexuality and view of art Charles outgrows. (In 1936 Charles finds that 'Blanche had not changed from when I last saw him; not, indeed, from when I first saw him' (236).) During his apprentice years 'under the spell of Sebastian', even while he didn't 'particularly like' Blanche, Charles found himself 'enjoying him voraciously, like the fine piece of cookery he was': the aesthete did 'more than entertain'; he 'transfigur[ed] the party, shedding a vivid, false light of eccentricity' so that even prosaic students 'seemed suddenly to become creatures of his fantasy' (38, 30). But just as means differ from ends, what is appropriate to youth may be inappropriate in, and so may damage, maturity. Charles last sees Blanche in the aesthetically deplorable surroundings of a gay bar: 'The place was painted cobalt; there was cobalt linoleum on the floor. Fishes of silver and gold paper had been pasted haphazard on ceiling and walls' (237). With its smells of cats, gin and cigarette-ends, the Blue Grotto Club is a grotesque parody of the scents and colours Charles has enjoyed, especially of the beauty of Brideshead – and of Lady Marchmain's sitting-room there, its walls 'stripped and washed blue' (112), Mary's colour.

Each soul, the mature Ryder recognizes, fully realizes its own individuality only through realizing its God-given purpose. The 'hours of afflatus in the human spirit' which are 'the springs of art' are also 'in their mystery, akin to the epochs of history': 'rare, classic periods' apart from which 'the human soul' is 'seldom single or unique' (197). Failure to progress toward this end is to remain not 'a complete human being at all', but only 'a small part' of one, 'pretending to be whole', as Julia says of Rex and Ryder of himself in his dead years (177, 200). In its appropriate time and place Blanche's art helped those around him to begin the process of realizing themselves as individuals: after he left Oxford, his friends 'lumbered back into the herd from when they had been so capriciously chosen and grew less and less individually recognizable' (96). But because he does not grow beyond taking art as an end, Blanche, though he may be a fine judge of Charles's Mexican paintings, reduces himself (again like Ambrose Silk) to a mere 'type'.[25]

Charles makes a version of Blanche's mistake of confusing the ends of art with those of life – and a more sophisticated version of his own earlier mistake of reading natural beauty through the lenses of the theory of Significant Form – when he treats Julia's outburst by the fountain as merely typical, merely a scene from a play or a restaging of Holman Hunt's painting *The Awakening Conscience*. Julia rightly responds to this denial of their individuality and purpose:

> 'Oh, don't talk in that damned bounderish way. Why must you see everything secondhand? Why must this be a play? Why must my conscience be a Pre-Raphaelite picture?'
>
> (BR 255)

(Later Lord Marchmain, still rebelling against his individual vocation, makes the same mistake, telling Charles of the stage-set he has carefully assembled to showcase his coming death: 'You might paint it, eh – and call it "The Death Bed"?' (279).)

After painting Marchmain House (in the interval between Books One and Two of the novel), Charles enters his dead years: 'For nearly ten years I was thus borne along a road outwardly full of change and incident, but never during that time, except sometimes in my painting – and that at longer and longer intervals – did I come alive as I had been during the time of my friendship with Sebastian' (198). At his nadir, his love for Celia like his artistic inspiration dead, he retrogresses on his trip to Mexico from civilization to barbarism, from painting buildings 'in the last decade of their grandeur' to empty ruins. Frozen in his progress, Charles is not changed at all by his adventure, as he confesses to Celia (in an echo of Cardinal Newman):

> 'I don't believe you've changed at all, Charles'.
> 'No, I'm afraid not'.
> 'D'you want to change?'
> 'It's the only evidence of life'.[26]

Just as 'It needed [Blanche's] voice from the past to recall' Charles to a recognition of what is wrong with his Mexican paintings (237), it takes the return of Sebastian's beauty in Julia to draw him on to the next, higher phase of art: painting the human form. 'I never tired of painting her, forever finding in her new wealth and delicacy' (242).

At this point what we see of Ryder's development in painting stops; his conversion and the coming war bring his second idyll in Arcadia – and the beauty of the house itself – to an end. The last of Ryder's works of art to which we are introduced is not a painting, not a work of visual art at all. Rather it is the series of memories which finally, in the Epilogue, are revealed in full meaningful shape to constitute the realization of a vocation: the 'memorials and pledges of the vital hours of a lifetime' that comprise *Brideshead Revisited*. *Brideshead* thus points forward to *The Loved One* and *Gilbert Pinfold*, both of which end with the protagonist sitting down to write the novel we have just read.

Perhaps Waugh meant in this way to emphasize that, like the 'charm' the novel mentions so much, neither earthly beauty nor its imitation in art, though each may be valuable as a means, constitutes an ultimate good. In the years after *Brideshead* he often returned to the argument first raised in *A Handful of Dust*, his complaint against what he called the 'mysticism of Art': the mistake of 'those who, lacking other objects of reverence, now attribute a priest's, even a martyr's, sanctity to the artist' (EAR 348), and who suppose that imaginative experience can somehow substitute for revealed religion. In a correspondence in 1949 with David Cecil, whom he thought guilty of such mysticism, Waugh wrote that each soul 'is born with a longing for God and Beauty', but 'I can't think of a single Saint who attached much importance to Art'. Art is 'humanism' and therefore 'recreation', 'a harmless way for ... men to occupy their leisure and earn their living'; it cannot 'reconcile man with his unhappy predicament on earth'. 'Perhaps in the Providence of God the unqualified hideosity of Modern Art has been sent us to scourge us for just this aberration' of confusing art with religion (L 303, 305).

IV Captain Ryder and Captain Waugh

Brideshead appeared in May 1945 with a dedication to Laura and the Author's Note: 'I am not I; thou are not he or she; they are not they'. Waugh had already told Dorothy Lygon, 'It's all about a family whose father lives abroad, as it might be Boom [Lord Beauchamp] – but it's not Boom – and a younger son: people will say he's like Hughie, but you'll see he's not really Hughie – and there's a house as it might be Mad [Madresfield], but it isn't really Mad' (HW 53). Thus invited, Waugh's friends immediately began identifying the novel's characters and settings. Maurice Bowra recognized himself in Mr Samgrass; Sebastian's teddy-bear Aloysius recalled John Betjeman's Archie. Alec Waugh heard Evelyn Gardner's voice in Celia Ryder's; Dorothy Lygon wrote, 'Sebastian gives me many pangs' for his resemblance to the dead Hugh, with whom Waugh had planned to share rooms during his final term at Oxford.[27] No response survives from Brian Howard, source of Blanche's stammer and depravity; Harold Acton generously found Waugh's chapters on Oxford in the twenties 'the only successful evocation of the period that I know'.[28]

It was easy for friends to identify Ryder with the Waugh who had stayed in their country houses, especially in the years after his first marriage when, like Ryder, he escaped to the tropics, collecting material for novels that (like Ryder's Mexican pictures) focused 'the frankly traditional battery of his elegance and erudition on the maelstrom of barbarism' (BR 201). Though Brideshead Castle is patterned mainly after Castle Howard – also damaged in wartime, not by soldiers but a fire started by an evacuee schoolgirl that in 1940 destroyed the dome and most of the rooms on the south front – its chapel is based on the chapel built at Madresfield by P. C. Harwick in 1867, 'the most complete realisation of Arts and Crafts theory in Britain'.[29] More even than Beauchamp's son Hugh, Sebastian recalls Alastair Graham, also a drunkard, and the child of a strong-willed mother. Graham had in fact once written to Waugh, in a letter signed 'With love from Alastair, and his poor dead heart' (and which enclosed a nude photograph of himself):

> I have found the ideal way to drink Burgundy. You must take a peach and peel it, and put it in a finger bowl, and pour the Burgundy over it. The flavour is exquisite.... will you come and drink with me somewhere on Saturday? If it is a nice day we might carry some bottles into a wood or some bucolic place, and drink like Horace.
>
> (Hastings 108)

Even readers who did not know Waugh personally identified author and narrator; many supposed Waugh, like Ryder, a recent convert.

Specific parallels with Waugh's own life are thickest in Book One, which readers have generally found more evocative than the later chapters about Julia. In Book Two the painter of *Ryder's Country Seats* and *Ryder's English Homes* resembles less the Waugh who had turned from drawing to writing than John Piper – and even more, as Caroline Dakers suggests, Captain Dick Wyndham. Wyndham, a wealthy amateur painter who in the 1930s mounted two private showings in London of his 'Paintings of Country Seats and Manor Houses', was an acquaintance of Waugh and close friend of Cyril Connolly and Peter Quennell (and already the original for Richard Whittingdon in Wyndham Lewis's *Apes of God*). In 1935, at the same time as Ryder, he travelled to Africa to escape an unhappy marriage and rejuvenate his art. (In *Brideshead*, a careless reporter writes, after viewing his Mexican paintings, of 'socialite artist Ryder, who has abandoned the houses of the great for the ruins of equatorial Africa' (233).) Wyndham's trip issued in an illustrated book (1936) and an exhibition of African paintings (1937), both titled *The Gentle Savage* (and both of notably poor quality).[30]

Brideshead most reveals its author not in parallels with specific persons or events but in the ways Waugh explores his own spiritual passages – for instance, his own early homosexuality. The subject had arisen in nearly all his previous novels; *Brideshead* seems to lay a ghost. Since Oxford and Alastair, Waugh had associated homosexuality with art and escape from convention, freedom and indulgence of pleasure. Throughout his life he maintained affectionate friendships with various 'buggers', and in 1949 complained to Nancy Mitford of the treatment of homosexuals on the New York stage: 'they all commit suicide. The idea of a happy pansy is incomprehensible to them' (L 306). With a breadth of tolerance for human nature then rare among Catholic moralists, Waugh called publicly for 'compassion' toward the diversities of human desire:

> 'Normality' is certainly an almost meaningless expression. The absolute norm is an abstraction from which all men vary in greater or less degree. Moral theologians postulate a Natural Law and from it deduce a code of the licit and illicit that corresponds very slightly with the common observation of human behaviour. Much that seems 'normal' is forbidden, much that seems repugnant or absurd is

allowed. The vagaries of human lust are fully catalogued. They have been publicized and we have become less xenophobic in condemning eccentricity.[31]

But he also believed that in their 'lawlessness' there is 'a radical difference
between heterosexual and homosexual relationships' (EAR 511). From the
charming Captain Grimes to the thoughtful and gifted Ambrose Silk, from the
merely wayward Miles Malpractice to the more obviously vicious Anthony
Blanche and Mr Samgrass, Waugh's homosexual characters are also prey in
varying degrees to rootlessness and self-centredness; their lives are fascinating,
but insecure and finally unsatisfying.

'There's a home and family waiting for every one of us', lamented Grimes in
1928: 'We can't escape' the 'impulse of family life', 'try how we may'; 'if by
chance we have escaped the itch ourselves, Nature forces it upon us another
way' (DF 131–2). In the 1930s, homosexuality was a part of himself that, 'in the
atrophy endemic to all fruitful marriages' – as *Put Out More Flags* strikingly
describes Barbara Sothill's turn from adolescence to mature life with a husband
and a home of her own – Waugh was content to 'let waste and die' (POMF 14).
But those early experiences remained important to him, and Waugh was a man
consumed with a need to find meaning in the pattern of his life. In the forties,
beginning with *Put Out More Flags*, he began from the security of marriage to
work out in his fiction a way to redeem that pattern. Ambrose Silk brought to
life with ambivalent sympathy a man he deeply understood. With *Brideshead*
youthful homosexuality comes into focus as a kind of fortunate fall – fortunate so
long as it is eventually put away with other childish things, and once safely put
away available like other youthful pleasures for nostalgic reminiscence. In the
years after *Brideshead* Waugh grew increasingly willing to discuss that side of his
life he had once sought to obliterate by burning his Oxford diaries.[32]

Brideshead also lingers over lost pleasures in its highly elaborated style, what Rose
Macaulay called its 'orchidaceous luxury of bloom'. '[Y]ou may have overdone the
semi colons a bit', wrote Henry Yorke, 'yet even then the regret with which the
whole book is saturated is beautifully carried out in the long structure of your
sentences'.[33] Like many in the grey days of rationing, queues and restricted travel,
when oranges, bananas and even (after the Germans occupied Brittany) onions
became prized rarities, and when new clothes and furniture were available only in
a few government-approved 'utility' designs, Waugh indulged compensating
memories of a golden past. As Cyril Connolly had foretold as early as 1939, the
war years saw an outpouring of autobiographies and memoirs of childhood. The
wartime deprivations that led to *Brideshead*'s evocation of languid summer afternoons, plover's eggs and lobster, 'melon and prosciutto on the balcony' in Venice,
and the splendours of Brideshead (which calls forth 'ample civilized allusion, to
Quattrocento portraiture, Lear on the heath, the Duchess of Malfi, Ruskin and
Pre-Raphaelitism') also produced the hungry luxuriousness of *The Unquiet Grave*
(with its memories of truffles, brioches and roast coffee in the south of France) and
the jewelled prose of Osbert Sitwell's otherwise unaccountably popular autobiography *Left Hand, Right Hand!* (1941–9), whose 'verbal plethora' is a rebellion
against wartime scarcity and utilitarianism.[34]

For Waugh, stylistic elaboration was the token of another way in which he was coming in the mid-1940s to find meaning in the pattern of his life: an emerging sense that he was not merely a man who happened to make a living from books but an author by vocation. While writing *Brideshead* he had reflected that 'English writers, at forty, either set out prophesying or acquiring a style. Thank God I think I am beginning to acquire a style' (D 560). Letters to friends start to be filled with lectures on fine points of etymology and usage.[35] In 1946 he announced that henceforward his novels would be characterized by 'two things to make them unpopular: a preoccupation with style and the attempt to represent man more fully, which to me, means only one thing, man in his relation to God'. In the face of a 'disintegrated society', the 'dark age opening' wherein 'scribes may play the part of monks after the first barbarian victories', his special call to service was to be a Catholic artist 'creat[ing] little independent systems of order of his own' (EAR 302, 304). Having found his own vocation, he increasingly took vocation as his theme: *The Loved One*, *Helena* and *Sword of Honour* are all in different ways studies of vocation, of the unique tasks God has chosen for each's hero to accomplish.

Like Connolly, Waugh later grew embarrassed at his luxuriant wartime prose. In 1950 he wrote to Graham Greene that he had 'reread *Brideshead* and was appalled': 'it won't do for peace-time' (L 322). He began a revision, introduced when it was finally published in 1960 by the apology: 'It was a bleak period of present deprivation and threatening disaster – the period of soya beans and Basic English – and in consequence the book is infused with a kind of gluttony, for food and wine, for the splendours of the recent past, and for rhetorical and ornamental language, which now with a full stomach I find distasteful'.[36] In *Unconditional Surrender*, Corporal Ludovic produces a best-selling novel which is transparently a pastiche of *Brideshead*: a 'very gaudy, almost gorgeous tale of romance and high drama' set among the Marmaduke family, 'whose heroine was the author' and that 'for all its glitter' was 'not a cheerful book': 'Melancholy suffused all its pages and deepened towards the close'. At the same time Ludovic wrote, Waugh confesses, 'other English writers, averting themselves sickly from privations of war and apprehensions of the social consequence of the peace', were also turning from their 'drab alleys ... into the odorous gardens of a recent past transformed and illuminated by disordered memory and imagination' (US 242–3).

The preface to the revised *Brideshead* also apologises for such 'grosser passages' as 'Julia's outburst about mortal sin'. But these passages – 'never, of course, intended to report words actually spoken' ('They belong to a different order of writing') – cannot, Waugh argues, wholly be excised; they remain essential to the book.[37] In fact they capture what in 'Fan-Fare' he had identified as the two sides of his vocation, attention to style and to man's relation to God. Transitions within a novel to 'different orders of writing' – exercises in generic mixture, like that which ended *A Handful of Dust* – had always been one of his favoured devices for shedding a new, higher, usually unfavourable light on events. In Julia's speech the displacement of realism signals the divine order supervening on the human.

Brideshead's Epilogue details the destruction of nearly everything the novel's luxuriant style has evoked, in a conclusion whose bleakness reflects not only Waugh's sense that the war had ended a world, but also a pessimism at the heart of his faith and his very sense of life. Like many believers, Waugh habitually connected growth in faith with psychological maturity.[38] But for him as for Ryder and Barbara Sothill, maturity brought atrophy and loss. He always found it easier to evoke the pleasures to which the soul must die in growing up than any compensating satisfactions; already in 1928, the Oxford life to which Paul Pennyfeather returns in order to prepare for the priesthood is humdrum compared to the worlds he leaves behind. Waugh had himself as much as Ronald Knox in mind when he described his friend's youth:

> Ronald had no desire to grow up. Adolescence, for him, was not a process of liberation or adventure. Manhood threatened him with tedious duties and grave decisions.... He grew up slowly. Each stage of his growth imposed a burden; each enlargement of spirit, the loss of something fond.
>
> (K 79)

> Ronald had a hard road ahead and he was taking it easy, preferring to loiter among friends and sentimental memories, which offered mere reflections of the light that was his true goal. But these distractions came from God, and he was content to remain by the wayside....
>
> (K 71)

'All my life they've been taking things away from me' Sebastian tells Charles of his family. 'All the agonies and annoyances of growing up, which may last a lifetime', Waugh wrote in 1952, 'spring from the slow, necessary realization of the truth of the fall of Adam, and of the exiled condition of his progeny' (EAR 430).

The Flytes consistently tell Ryder of their faith that, as Sebastian says, 'happiness doesn't seem to have much to do with it' (80). When Charles, near tears, explodes to Bridey, 'It seems to me that without your religion Sebastian would have the chance to be a happy and healthy man', Bridey replies evenly: 'Its arguable. Do you think he will need this elephant's foot [waste-basket] again?' (129). Charles may be right, Bridey concedes; but if Catholicism is true, the point is trivial. *Brideshead*'s final, understated invocation of hope is locally effective, but an overpowering bleakness remains, a sense of loss like that Cordelia feels when the Brideshead chapel is closed, 'as though from now on it was always going to be Good Friday'. One American reader wrote to Waugh expressing a not uncommon reaction to the novel: 'Your *Brideshead Revisited* is a strange way to show that Catholicism is an answer to anything. Seems more like the kiss of Death' (EAR 304).

Waugh was of course on firm theological ground in suggesting that grace does not compensate for nature in nature's own terms. In manuscript he had given the novel an epigraph from Hebrews: 'Non enim habemus hic manentem civitatem'.[39] But *Brideshead*'s ending remains disturbing in a story that began by casting its hero's progress as an ascent through kinds of beauty and love.

Its final scenes of destruction and renunciation suggest less a transition to 'God's better beauty' than a stark conviction of the *truth* of faith – a conviction that, as a character in Muriel Spark's *The Comforters* says, 'the True Church was awful, though unfortunately, one couldn't deny, true' (89–90). The beautiful fountain gives way utterly to the aesthetically deplorable chapel; Cordelia explains that suffering is 'the spring of love', but it is suffering as loss, not love, that suffuses the novel's final pages. In all this *Brideshead* once again captures Waugh's sense of the shape of his own experience from the twenties through to the war.

But it was not a self-understanding with which he could remain satisfied. Waugh came to recognize that it had been the glamour of suffering like that of Charles, Julia and especially Sebastian – whose last days as described by Cordelia have the flavour of a medieval saint's life – which shored up *Brideshead* 's ending, by substituting for loves and beauties lost. And if Charles finally finds a family not among the Flytes but in the household of the faith, that faith is itself sometimes glamourized. Catholics are not 'like other people', Sebastian tells Charles. True, Catholics sent their children to separate schools, and until 1897 were prohibited by the hierarchy from attending Oxford or Cambridge; but Sebastian continues: 'they're a clique – as a matter of fact, they're at least four cliques all blackguarding each other half the time'; 'they've got an entirely different outlook on life; everything they think important is different from other people' (80).

'Smugness', wrote Flannery O'Connor, 'is the great Catholic sin' (*Works* 983). That Waugh came to recognize *Brideshead* 's exclusivism and glamourization of suffering as faults is attested by his subsequent attempts to correct them, most obviously in the war trilogy but already in essays such as 'Come Inside' (1949) and the novel he began next after *Brideshead*, *Helena* – another tale of a convert's vocation, but one that ends not in heroic renunciation but modestly satisfying fulfillment. Like all Waugh's characters who undergo development, Helena finds growing up a continued process of loss – 'All her life Helena's sleep had been full of dreams and always, daily ... she opened her eyes on a scene of loss' – but one expression of her sanctity is her willing acceptance of the process wherein 'by imperceptible stages and without regret [she] lost her youth' (H 147, 67). Most strikingly, *Helena* radically transforms what in Waugh's earlier fiction had been the persistent theme of the need to man the barricades, to maintain the wall between barbarism and Christian civilization.

In a much-quoted speech the young Helena's husband Constantius explains of the Roman wall in Swabia:

'I'm not a sentimental man ... but I love the wall. Think of it, mile upon mile, from snow to desert, a great girdle round the civilized world; inside, peace, decency, the law, the altars of the Gods, industry, the arts, order; outside, wild beasts and savages, forest and swamp, bloody mumbo-jumbo, men like wolf-packs; and along the wall the armed might of the Empire, sleepless, holding the line. Doesn't it make you see what The City means?'

(H 47)

The image recalls what Wilfrid Ward called the 'fortress' or 'siege mentality' personified by Pius IX and typical of the Roman Church until well after World War II. Waugh had often likened his religion to such a wall: 'Quite right to suppress them' concludes *Decline and Fall*, as Paul Pennyfeather surveys deviations from orthodoxy. But in the years after *Brideshead* his thinking changed. He continued to treat civility in these terms – 'My generation has not set a good example of defence', argues a 1962 review of some books on etiquette; 'Let the young man the walls' (EAR 592) – but not religion. At a pivotal moment in *Sword of Honour*, Guy Crouchback will be rebuked by his father for thinking of his church as such a barrier, and in *Helena* itself, the description of the Roman wall as a 'great girdle round the civilized world' comes not from Waugh's heroine but the small-minded Constantius, to whom Helena replies: 'Must there always be a wall? ... Instead of the barbarian breaking in, might The City one day break out? ... couldn't the wall be at the limits of the world and all men, civilized and barbarian, have a share in The City?' (H 48–9). Later in the novel she learns the meaning of this youthful insight when Pope Sylvester defines the Church as 'the whole of fallen man redeemed'.

Waugh was constitutionally incapable, of course, of pursuing such sentiments to the point of adopting the Abbé Huvelin's famous advice: 'Connaître son temps avec amour'.[40] In the spring of 1945, while most Britons eagerly looked forward to the war's conclusion, he wrote in his diary: 'No exhilaration anywhere at the end of the war'; 'The war news continual successes in the destruction of central Europe'; 'Gloomy apprehension of V Day. I hope to escape it'; 'Conversation mostly despondent at the collapse of Europe, the advance of Russia, heathenism'; 'Recommended catacombs' (D 624–5). In May, as VE day was announced, he mused how the war had taught him he was not a 'man of action' but an artist. On learning that he was not to return to Yugoslavia, he turned his attention to his long-deferred novel about St Helena, remarking (in language once again borrowed from Cyril Connolly): 'I thank God to find myself still a writer and at work on something as "uncontemporary" as I am'.[41] By September he was free of the army and, the nuns having left, back with Laura at Piers Court.

7

A People's Peace (1945–1950)

[Mrs. Belton] was only behaving like most other people who had taken six years of war with uncomplaining courage and were now being starved, regimented, and generally ground down by their present rulers.... the endless struggle to get food and clothes, and the nastiness of the food and the clothes when you got them... the endless waits at the Food Office and the Fuel Office... the increasing inquisitioned prying of officials into private affairs, were all bringing people into a state of dull resentful apathy with no hope of relief.

'Lots of people say they are going to emigrate', said Mrs. Belton... 'I wonder if we could go into the village alms-houses when we are a little older. My husband's great-grandfather built them, so it would be quite reasonable'.

'I'm quite sure you couldn't', said Mrs. Carton. 'Homes for the aged middle class won't come in our time, and by the time they do come there probably won't be any middle classes. And when They have exterminated the middle classes, England won't be any better'.

Angela Thirkell, *Love Among the Ruins* (1948)

A few years earlier the British had emerged with the status of heroes from a long and bitter war in which, but for their stubbornness and daring, the greater part of mankind would have lost their liberties.... Of this interlude of greatness, all outward and some inward traces had been expunged with remarkable celerity. By processes which nobody really understood, the heroes, unarming, had converted themselves into mice – mild, well-regulated, apprehensive little creatures who scurried about their bureaucratic cage which other and more knowing mice had built for them. As mice go, they were remarkably well off; and many of them accepted mousehood gladly enough, for it involved no risks of any kind, and although enterprise was frustrated and indeed penalised, the lack of it was perfectly *comme il faut*. Yet even in these, and still more in the others who clung to an old-fashioned view of the relations between the individual and the State, the memory of the days when they had been something more than mice was still alive and strong.

Peter Fleming, *The Sixth Column* (1951)

The public persona of Waugh so dear to journalists and cartoonists – the crusty conservative who would not vote because he did not 'aspire to advise my sovereign in her choice of servants' (EAR 537), the reactionary die-hard so at odds with modern life as to abjure even such conveniences as the telephone – was incubated by the war and fully fledged by the elections of July 1945. With its ringing manifesto, 'The Labour Party is a Socialist Party, and proud of it. Its ultimate aim is the establishment of the Socialist Commonwealth of Great Britain', Labour won a clear majority; jubilant Labour MPs sang 'The Red Flag' in the Commons chamber. 'The significance of the election', declared the new Minister of Health Aneurin Bevan, 'is that the British people have voted deliberately and consciously for a new world' (Foot 2: 18). Like most of his friends, Waugh found Labour's victory a 'prodigious surprise' and an 'overwhelming defeat' (D 629).

The new government immediately set about to scale the 'commanding heights' (in Bevan's phrase, borrowed from Lenin) – instituting policies of nationalization, public welfare and income redistribution aimed at the ideal of a 'classless society'. To finance its policies (and because of immense debts left by the war), government maintained and even deepened the austerity of rationing and high taxes. 'We are at peace – in theory, anyhow', complained the Labourite journalist J. L. Hodson; 'Or is it that one war is over and we're now in the middle of another one? A civil war?' (Hennessy 115, 283). Waugh dubbed the new regime the 'Attlee terror'. 'The French called the occupying German army "the grey lice". That is precisely how I regard the occupying army of the socialist government' (D 663). For two years he considered emigration.

It is easy to forget how many writers – not only famous exponents of England's postwar decline like T. S. Eliot, but popular writers such as Elizabeth Bowen, Peter Fleming, Angela Thirkell and T. H. White – shared this disgust of the new policies of regulation and social levelling. In *Peace Breaks Out* (1946), Angela Thirkell's Mrs Moreland announces the arrival of a 'Brave and Revolting New World': 'It is really good-bye to everything nice forever' (153, 273). In 1950, after five years of Labour rule, White began a book on eighteenth-century social life with the remark, 'Well, we have lived to see the end of civilization'. He reviewed the new ministers' most notorious public statements about private wealth: Margaret Bondfield's boast on having forced the Duke of Norfolk from his house, 'We had our revolution during the war. We did not cut off their heads, we only cut off their incomes'; the comment of Emmanuel Shinwell, Minister of Fuel and Power, on the basis of Labour support: 'We know that the organised workers of the country are our friends. As for the rest, they don't matter a tinker's cuss'; and Bevan's unforgettable characterization in 1948 of Tories as 'lower than vermin'. 'It is useless to whine', White reflected; 'It has happened. It is the logical result of our half-baked Victorian humanitarianism...now we are done for'. Since 'it is no longer possible to be a gentleman', White resolved to console his 'old age by running away', recreating in his imagination 'the grand old days' of a 'civilization which we shall never see again' (*Scandal* 15–17). He was only forty-three when these words were published, three years younger than Waugh; but home seemed a foreign country, and he felt old.

Waugh too felt himself an aged exile in the postwar world. 'I strain forward to senility', he told Nancy Mitford in 1946, on his forty-third birthday (L 238); he told Alec that 'since 1945' he had 'felt fifty years old' (HRC E1371). Waugh's malaise ran deeper than White's nostalgia for the lost splendors of Knole and Stowe. 'Why am I not at ease?' he mused in 1946; 'Why is it I smell all the time wherever I turn the reek of the Displaced Persons' Camp?' (D 662). With Scott-King's 'peculiar relish in contemplating the victories of barbarism' (SK 2), he followed the newspapers' daily reports of the continuing suffering of millions in Eastern Europe: 'News of the world still horrible' (D 662); 'Thousands have died and are dying today in torture for the Faith' (L 381). The news reports were brought home sharply by real displaced persons claiming his charity. Between 1946 and 1950, he corresponded with Hilde Bertram, a Catholic refugee he had tried to help in Yugoslavia; since then she had been moved from prison to prison, lost her husband, and finally been sent, desperately poor and with a young daughter to support, to a refugee camp in Austria. Waugh sent food parcels and offered her a job in his own house. At the same time he worked to help his distant relative Zarita Mattay, trapped in transit camps abroad, to emigrate with her family to Australia, and paid for her mother to enter an English nursing home before joining them. Mattay wrote to him in 1948 from one refugee camp: 'I do not think I shall ever be able to express to you in words what I feel about your attitude to us & our problems' (ST2 222).

Haunted by what seemed the war's disastrous results both abroad and at home – enormous suffering and religious persecution in the 'liberated' nations; 'the planners' reshaping England on principles akin to those of the engineers of that suffering – Waugh despaired not only of England but the 'Modern World'. The phrase was now often on his pen, suggesting 'a barbarism and evil so complete as to be past human help' (Gallagher, EAR 292).

> In the natural order the modern world is rapidly being made uninhabitable by the scientists and politicians. We are back in the age of Gregory, Augustine and Boniface, and in compensation the Devil is being disarmed of many of his former enchantments. Power is all he can offer now; the temptations of wealth and elegance no longer assail us. As in the Dark Ages the cloister offers the sanest and most civilized way of life.
>
> And in the supernatural order the times require more than a tepid and dutiful piety. Prayer must become heroic.
>
> (EAR 369)

From the 'catacombs' one might survey the 'rapid decay' of 'Western culture' and pray for aversion of the 'disaster ahead' (L 215, 241).

'I am anxious to emigrate, Laura to remain & face the century of the common man', Waugh wrote to Nancy Mitford (who, though she claimed to be a socialist, had already moved to Paris). 'She is younger, braver, & less imaginative than I. If only they would start blowing up the place with their atoms' (L 236). When new government building projects threatened even the village of Stinchcombe, he put Piers Court on the market and sought to move, if not like his friends John and Daphne Acton to Africa, at least to a castle in Ireland in which 'to immure myself and family' (L 251).

> Throughout the day constantly recurring thoughts of Ireland. Not so much of what I should find there as what I should shake off here.... The certainty that England as a great power is done for, that the loss of possessions, the claim of the English proletariat to be a privileged race, sloth and envy, must produce increasing poverty; that this time the cutting down will start at the top until only a proletariate and a bureaucracy survive. As a bachelor I could contemplate all this in a detached manner, but it is no country in which to bring up children. But how long will Liberty, Diversity, Privacy survive anywhere?
>
> (D 661–2)

A series of house-hunting trips to Ireland turned up two appealing properties. An offer for one was hastily withdrawn when the next day's newspaper announced a Butlin's Holiday Camp scheduled for construction nearby; the other proved too expensive so long as Piers Court remained unsold.

Personal discomfort of course fuelled Waugh's wish to escape. At just the moment when he had achieved international success, politicians seemed to thwart any enjoyment of its fruit. The new government foresaw continuing wartime rationing for five more years, with all the apparatus of identity cards, coupons, 'points' and 'personal points', and different tickets for milk, food, clothing, coal and petrol. The basic weekly ration for adults when Clement Attlee became Prime Minister – 1s 6d of meat, 2.5 pints of milk, one egg – was soon cut back; bread, never rationed in wartime, was added to the list in 1946 by Minister of Food John Strachey; in 1948, petrol for individuals was limited to ninety miles' worth per month. Paper rations diminished each year from 1946 to 1949, leading to comments such as V. S. Pritchett's that British authors were 'annulled in effect by the inflation and the shortage of paper'.[1] Waugh complained of 'Balkan austerity'. 'We have practically no meat – two meals a week – and live on eggs and macaroni, cheese (made by Laura), bread and wine; very occasionally we get a rather nasty fish' (D 637). He acknowledged a gift of food from Randolph Churchill, then working in America: 'It was a sublimely meritorious act to send me a cheese' (RC 4–5).

Meanwhile wartime levels of taxation remained in effect: a basic rate on income of nearly fifty per cent, which with the addition of supertax meant a top marginal rate that between 1941 and 1953 never fell below 97.5 per cent.[2] All Waugh's writing in the years following the Labour victory brings to life what 'Tactical Exercise', published in 1947 – Labour's most difficult year, when a record cold winter resulted in coal strikes, fuel shortages and unemployment of two million – calls 'the vast net of governmental control' woven by 'the new, alien, occupying power'. This tale, which Cyril Connolly thought 'subtle & perfect', is memorable less for its slender plot – a husband and wife each determined to murder the other – than its description of the reduced circumstances in which two members of 'what's left of the middle class' live.[3] 'Furniture was unprocurable, furnished flats commanded a price beyond their income, which was now taxed to a bare wage', so the couple move into her parents' house in Hampstead, a once 'substantial Georgian villa' now cold for lack of coal and in hopeless disrepair. (In January 1947 the Ministry of Works ruled that no more than £10 could be spent on private repairs without permission from local authority.) Elizabeth Verney has a job in the bureaucracy but her husband John, a wounded veteran just discharged, cannot find work and so spends his day 'in the queues', doing the shopping. 'There had been less to annoy him before the war'.

One escape from 'Welfaria' was writing, especially about vanished times and places. Just as the war itself had fostered a flood of memoirs and autobiographies, postwar writing too tends to be retrospective, to linger in a spacious world of vanished comforts and country houses.[4] As hostilities ended Waugh turned first to *Helena*, whose opening sections appeared in the Christmas issue of *The Tablet* in 1945; by January 1946 he completed what would become the first three chapters. But progress soon slowed, partly because of the historical research the novel required, partly because, in the wake of *Brideshead*, he was under no financial pressure to write. Meanwhile, in October 1945, he reread his Lancing diaries and began 'a novel of school life in 1919 – as untopical a theme as could be found' (D636). *Charles Ryder's Schooldays* was to be a prequel to *Brideshead*; wisely abandoned after a few pages, the fragment was first published only in 1982.[5]

Another escape, though limited by currency restrictions, was travel. Excerpting passages from his first four travel books for publication in *When the Going Was Good* (1946), Waugh seemed to say farewell to this prewar pleasure: 'There is no room for tourists in a world of displaced persons', of refugees and barbed wire (WGG 9). (As Peter Fleming noted, Waugh arranged his excerpts to begin in a bar and end on a battlefield (CH 290).) A year later his protagonist Scott-King, hoping for 'hot oil and garlic and spilled wine', is lured abroad from an England still eating dried eggs – that wartime 'triumph of modern science' – only to enter a new world of 'embarkation papers, medical cards, customs clearance slips, currency control vouchers, passports, tickets, identity dockets, travel orders, emigration certifications, baggage checks and security checks'. 'This was not how he used to travel'.[6] But despite such difficulties, Waugh managed in the postwar years to travel nearly as often as in the thirties, though now (because of currency restrictions) necessarily more briefly. Such restrictions kept him at home only once, preventing a trip to America to collect an honorary degree – cause for an angry letter to *The Times*.[7]

In April 1946 he observed the trials in Nuremburg as a guest of the British delegation – he probably hoped to write about them as Rebecca West was doing for the *Daily Telegraph* and *New Yorker* – and stopped afterward to renew contact with the Coopers, now established in the British Embassy in Paris. He collected too little material for an essay about the trials, but a trip to Spain two months later inspired *Scott-King's Modern Europe*. In August 1947 he visited Stockholm, Oslo and Copenhagen as a reporter for the *Daily Telegraph*. A trip earlier the same year to negotiate the filming of *Brideshead* resulted in *The Loved One* (1948) and became the first of four happy visits to the United States. He returned in 1948 to begin researching an article for *Life* on the Catholic Church in America, and in 1949 and 1950 to lecture and enjoy his fame in the country he described to Nancy Mitford, deliberately tweaking the anti-Americanism of the creator of Hector Dexter, as 'the most wonderful health resort in the world' (L 336). In

January and February 1951 he travelled to Israel and Turkey with Christopher
Sykes, again at *Life*'s expense; in 1952 he went on his own to join the celebration
in Goa of the four hundredth anniversary of the death of St Francis Xavier, start
of a lifelong fascination with India.[8] Meanwhile, through careful shepherding of
foreign earnings as 'nest eggs' to circumvent the currency restrictions, he
managed to 'escape regularly' (TA 12) for holidays in Paris and Monte Carlo,
Rome, Florence and Sicily, visiting old friends like Harold Acton and bringing
back luxury goods then still hard to find in England outside the black market –
cheese, wine, perfume, toys for the children. It galled him to watch other nations
recover from the war more quickly than England.

Only in 1947 ('this third year of the Occupation'), while visiting Scandinavia,
did Waugh finally decide not to emigrate. He thought he saw in Sweden 'some
such state as ... the English voter dimly aspired to create at the general election'
of 1945:

> They are secularized from infancy by the omnicompetent state and as a result are
> unique in history in having no religion at all....
>   The state is supreme, but humane; hereditary class distinctions barely exist, and
> taxation has brought the level of diminishing returns so low that the only serious
> labour problem is middle-class absenteeism. Domestic service has been abolished,
> and with it the private house. Almost everyone in Stockholm inhabits a tiny
> flat....Nothing except the changing of the royal guard is at all disorderly. At the
> universities technology is dominant; there are no debating societies.
>
>   (EAR 339–43)

Something like a missionary purpose of standing against England's travelling
down the same road was part of what persuaded him to stay.

> During my tour I decided to abandon the idea of settling in Ireland. Reasons (1)
> Noble. The Church in England needs me. (2) Ignoble. It would be bad for my
> reputation as a writer. (3) Indifferent. There is no reason to suppose life in Ireland
> will be more tolerable than here....The Socialists are piling up repressive meas-
> ures now. It would seem I was flying from them. If I am to be a national figure I
> must stay at home.
>
>   (D 689)

Waugh understood that he could only 'make-believe to be detached from the
world' (D 640); even while considering emigration, he set out to be a 'national
figure' by taking up rebellious arms against the new England.

I

His first salvo against the Welfare State was 'What to do with the Upper Classes:
A Modest Proposal', written to annoy readers of the *New Statesman* (and so
successfully annoying that no British magazine would accept it).[9] The essay is
the satiric equivalent of Churchill's notorious 'Gestapo' speech of the 1945
election campaign, which had warned voters that socialism was 'inseparably
interwoven with Totalitarianism' and that to achieve its goals, Labour would

have to bring in 'some kind of Gestapo' (Gilbert 846). Waugh similarly predicts that the 'classless society, if and when it comes, will not be the fruit of purely English methods' but of '"social engineering" of the sort that is prevalent in half of what was once Europe' (EAR 313).

Moreover, Waugh argues, the effort to 'exterminate' Britain's 'gentlemen' will impoverish, not enrich, 'the workers'. 'By common agreement we are in need of exports' (Labour's effort to right Britain's balance of trade, summarized in the slogan 'Export or Die', had produced many absurd restrictions, such as that permitting only plain white china for sale at home, reserving all patterned products for export). But British trade and tourism depend, Waugh asserts, on the prestige-value of its goods and services, prestige associated with its class structure. His Swiftian solution: apartheid, 'a system of "native reservations" of the kind established in Africa and the USA', but for the upper classes. The products and appeal to tourists of these internment camps would attract the dollars necessary for British workers to have 'the exotic luxuries they had learned to enjoy'. Such enclaves would not only provide a useful function for parasitic peers; 'unprogressive people of the middle class' – including, by implication, Waugh himself – 'should be encouraged to make their modest homes there' as well.

Underpinning this prophecy of what we now call the 'heritage industry' are two of Waugh's constant themes: the freedom and rich variety fostered by England's 'elaborate and flexible class structure'; and the incompatibility of equality, especially forced equality, with liberty.

Similar provocations followed, including a detailed attack on the socialist future envisioned by Cyril Connolly in *Horizon*.[10] At a time when 'class difference' suggested to common opinion an injustice to be overcome, Waugh flaunted his belief in the advantages of what T. S. Eliot called 'a healthily *stratified* society'. He praised a new novel by Antonia White: 'As every truthful account of the English must be, this story is vividly class-conscious'; a review otherwise celebrating the young Angus Wilson's *Hemlock and After* (1952) explains that it is the Left, not Waugh, that is unhealthily preoccupied by social distinction:

> There seem two prepossessions of Mr Wilson's which greatly detract from his power as an artist. Perhaps they are Marxist in origin. One is his hypersensitivity to class. Nowhere except perhaps in parts of Asia, is the class structure as subtle and elaborate as in England.... Many writers have found a rich source in this national idiosyncrasy. Few writers have a sharper nose for class than Mr Wilson. But when he defines he seems to condemn. It is as though he found something obscene in the mere fact of class membership. Can he be troubled by remote dreams of The Classless Society?[11]

'Stable and fruitful societies have always been elaborately graded', he wrote in 1960. 'The ideal of a classless society is so unnatural to man that his reason, in practice, cannot bear the strain' (TA 165).

Essays like 'What to Do' were designed as provocations, but, as is usual in satire, their implied positive values were thoroughly commonplace. John Verney's feeling in 'Tactical Exercise' that 'there had been less to annoy him before the war' echoes through hundreds of contemporary news stories and unhappy

letters to editors, complaints sent by such familiar types as the 'middle-aged
school master now much reduced' (Hopkins 154–5) – a figure Waugh brings to
life in Scott-King. Waugh's polemics amplify the anti-socialism of an increasingly
self- conscious (and increasingly discussed) 'middle class' – 'the rest', as opposed
to the organized manual workers whose interests Labour was thought to represent – who considered themselves the losers after 1945 and were quick to accuse
Labour of waging 'class warfare'. Little in Waugh's postwar political writings
cannot also be found in Roy Lewis and Angus Maude's historical survey of the
endangered *English Middle Classes* (1949) or John Bonham's famous sociological
analysis, *The Middle Class Vote* (1954). Like John Verney, members of what Orwell
called 'the sinking middle class' complained of paying high taxes to finance new
housing for workers while they themselves could not afford to move, and more
generally of government policies designed to ensure that while workers' incomes
rose markedly, their own fell. 'My class is on the up and yours is on the down',
Aneurin Bevan told R. A. Butler; in 1948 the *Economist* reported that while real
net wages had risen between ten and thirty five per cent over the previous
decade, salaries had fallen between twenty and thiry per cent.[12] Lewis and
Maude presented 'the progressive impoverishment of the middle classes' under
Labour as a truth universally acknowledged, nearly as universally as that 'the
survival of England, and the success of England's message to the world, depends
upon the best of middle-class social attitudes becoming widespread throughout
society' (337, 345). They mourned the extinction of a middle class whose 'freedom and independence, based upon a secured income and a high standard of
living', had in the past fostered a 'creative' and 'critical spirit' which had served
as society's bulwark against 'the abuse of power' and 'given freedom to experiment in art, in science, and in politics' (ch. 6).

Waugh joined many writers whose watchwords during the Labour years were
'privacy', 'diversity' (or 'variety'), 'freedom' and 'individuality', who criticized
'bureaucracy' and thought themselves 'a beleaguered group, battling against
insurmountable odds'.[13] As *The Loved One* and *Love Among the Ruins* would argue
most forcefully, individual 'personality' itself seemed threatened by the new
order. Ronald Knox suggested in 1945:

> Mankind has abdicated, within a life-time, all those rights which we used to include
> under the notion of political liberty. To be free, in these days, means at best to be
> bullied by your own fellow countrymen rather than by foreigners. . . . Your property
> is yours only on sufferance; you must hand on no traditions to your children except
> what the State approves. Even where we still hold out against ochlocracy, and
> enjoy democratic institutions, the shackles of State control tighten round us daily;
> inspected here, directed there, we find the area of individual choice continually
> shrinking, our daily lives increasingly conditioned from above. . . . we are not the
> *men* we were; in all those daily contacts which make citizens of us, our personalities
> are being ruthlessly abridged.
>
> (*Atom* 145)

On the eve of the 1951 elections Peter Fleming entered a plea for 'someone with
a personality, someone who's a bit of a hero' (*Sixth Column* 46).

Nor were such fears voiced only by Conservatives. Even from the Left the late forties heard repeated warnings such as John Lehmann's about the newly urgent need 'to assert the rights and dignities of the individual human being against the pretensions of the state'. 'There must be constant endeavour to resist encroachments by the State which endanger human personality' warned the Lambeth Conference in 1948; in 1949, the political scientist Donald MacRae, celebrating Labour's accomplishments, nonetheless diagnosed 'a massive indifference to the true content of life, the creation of personality'.[14] Connolly and Waugh's fears that the arts might not survive social levelling were also variations on a commonplace. In *The God that Failed* (1949), Stephen Spender defended his rejection of Communism (though not socialism) on the ground that the 'the artist is an individualist' and that his 'creative spirit', like the 'passion for individual freedom' itself, is ineluctably 'bourgeois'. In his essay, *The Arts Under Socialism* (1947), even J. B. Priestley confessed that 'The artist wonders rather dubiously about the Socialist atmosphere of cooperation, committees, and common sense'; 'he is doubtful about a society' that inhabits only 'nice bungalows and tidy communal flats', and 'is ready, secretly perhaps, to regret' the abolishing of 'social inequalities'. In Malcolm Muggeridge's simpler formulation, 'Leftism has arrived and is installed in Westminster'; 'They are bores'.[15]

It is significant that in 'Tactical Exercise' Waugh makes John Verney not a Tory but a Liberal. A Conservative almost by birth, Waugh grew increasingly aware how little different were his own party's policies from Labour's, and so was sympathetic to that strain of Liberalism (typified for instance by Friedrich Hayek's 1944 best-seller, *The Road to Serfdom*) which preached individual enterprise and predicted from socialist pursuit of a classless society not equality but the emergence of a two-class state.[16] When Elizabeth Verney defends the need for austerity, saying 'I know it's maddening, John, but you realize it's the same for everyone', her husband explodes: 'That's what all you bureaucrats want. Equality through slavery. The two-class state – proletarians and officials'. Attacking Connolly, Waugh wrote (in a deliberately archaic vocabulary): 'We live under a regime which not only discriminates against, but makes it an avowed purpose to exterminate, the nobility, gentry, yeomanry, burgesses and vagabonds, and to produce the modern two-class State of officials and proletariat'. Auberon Waugh later said that his father's politics 'were far closer to the Manchester School' than 'to the Conservative right wing'.[17] He of course remained a (non-voting) Conservative in part because he recognized that unlike the Liberals, who were nearly wiped out in the election of 1945 (they retained only twelve seats), Conservatives might still win workable majorities. 'I hope to see the Conservative Party return with a substantial majority', he wrote during the campaign of 1959; 'I recognize that individually some of the Liberal candidates are more worthy than many of the Conservatives, but any advantage to them can only produce deplorable instability' (EAR 537).

Waugh remained a Tory also because of his vision of what constituted a just and free society, an ideal perhaps best summarized in a preface he wrote in 1962 for the American publicist Timothy McInerny's political manifesto, *The Private*

Man. After the opening and closing statements of *Robbery Under Law*, the preface is Waugh's best formulation of his own political philosophy:

> Civilization is, under God, the free association of free men. Man is born in a family and by nature should be fed and taught in a family until he is of an age to take on the responsibilities of parenthood. A man's true freedom is in direct proportion to his power to control the production of the necessaries of family life.... The majority, the public man, the common man, the State, the spirit of the age – the many headed, many named monster knows that the strongest force opposed to him is property....
>
> It has often been pointed out that Liberty and Equality are irreconcilable.... Men are not naturally equal and can only seem so when enslaved.... Men are distinguished by the variety and degree of their natural faculties. Therefore the proper structure of a healthy State is pyramidical. The organic life of society should be a continuous process of evolving an aristocracy. In a healthy society there should be no impassable barriers of hereditary caste keeping down the individual; recruitment into the aristocracy should be fostered; nor should there be rigid privilege which preserves in authority men who prove themselves unfit for it; but, by and large, the most valuable possession of any nation is an accepted system of classes, each of which has its proper function and dignity. At the head – I am not sure that McInerny would agree with me in this particular – is the fount of honour and justice; below that men and women who hold office from above and are the custodians of tradition, morality and grace; when occasion arises ready for sacrifice but protected from the infection of corruption and ambition by hereditary possession; the nourishers of the arts, the censors of manners. Below that the classes of industry and scholarship, trained from the nursery in habits of probity. Below that manual labourers proud of their skills and bound to those above them by common allegiance to the monarch. In general a man is best fitted for the tasks he has seen his father perform.
>
> Neither Mr McInerny nor I can hope to see such a State in its completeness – it has never existed in history nor ever will; but both our nations are yearly drifting further from this ideal. It is not enough to say: 'this is the spirit of the age' and to deplore it, for the spirit of the age is the spirits of those who compose it and the stronger the expressions of dissent from prevailing fashion, the higher the possibility of diverting it from its ruinous course.

(EAR 580–3)

Though in *Pinfold* Waugh labels his own views 'idiosyncratic Toryism', it is hard to imagine a more conventionally conservative statement; what made such views seem idiosyncratic was the drift into Welfarism of the postwar Tory party itself.[18]

Among his polemical 'expressions of dissent from prevailing fashion', Waugh cultivated his role as national figure through an ever more visible public persona of flamboyant anachronism: a man who in spite of the war's seeming to have ended the custom dressed for dinner even at home, and who flaunted such badges of inequality as his membership in that 'refuge from the hounds of modernity', White's Club (L 289). There now emerges Waugh the 'supersnob', as Arnold Lunn named the pose, recalling Waugh's pleasure in 'poking fun at devout egalitarians':

Once, when we crossed the Atlantic together, Waugh, who was of course traveling first class, accepted an invitation to dine with me. I was traveling second class and, as he entered the dining room, he sniffed and said, 'Curious how one can smell the poor'. This amused me but some of those to whom I have told this story were not amused. And it was that kind of person whom Waugh delighted to shock by particularly outrageous performances in his favorite comic role, the supersnob.

(Lunn 189–90)

The story was often retold in distorted versions, for instance by Kingsley Amis, who in 1975 had Waugh shout the words for all the second-class diners to hear. This public pose reinforced the provocations of Waugh's fiction, such as the reference in *Men at Arms* to Guy's 'little household, twenty strong' (disbanded at a time when servants were 'everywhere' being dismissed) that Amis recognized as 'almost certainly put in specially to annoy the Labour Party'.[19]

And in a kind of living protest, Waugh continued his fight against the century of the common man by recreating at Piers Court an earlier, more spacious manner of life – and making sure the rest of the world knew about it. Inclination and ideology converged in his increasingly lavish decoration of house and garden, creating a well-advertised bastion from behind whose gates (embellished with the famous plaque 'No Admittance on Business') he gave gnomic interviews and lobbed grenades in the form of exquisitely worded letters to editors of magazines and newspapers – more than 100 of them before his death – on topics from modern art and taxes to Catholic ritual and the death penalty. As he gaily confessed of himself in *Gilbert Pinfold*, 'by the narrow standards of his age his habits of life were self-indulgent and his utterances lacked prudence' (GP 6).

II

What brought such national prominence and underwrote its expense was the success of *Brideshead*. *Brideshead*'s most important immediate effect was to make Waugh richer than he had ever been before; its most lasting effect, as he said in 1960, to lose 'me such esteem as I once enjoyed among my contemporaries' (BR 29).

Even before publication he wrote to Laura from Yugoslavia: 'We are stinking rich. Do get magnificent furs if it is not a foolish time' (L 197). Successful in England, in America the novel became a Book-of-the-Month Club selection; sales neared a million copies. In March 1945, Waugh's account with Little, Brown stood at $219.45; a year later it contained $97,670.98 – more than the sum of all his previous earnings (McNamara 235). In July 1945, in the first flush of *Brideshead*'s success, he wrote in his diary: 'The Americans have made it their Book of the Month, which is worth £10,000 down and a probably further £10,000 from cinema rights. In order to avoid paying four-fifths of this to the State I am arranging, if possible, to fix my gross income for the next five years at £5,000 a year' (D 628). He was now in a position to accept only what journalistic assignments he chose, and for these to command the very highest fees – from *Life*, a dollar a word.

Nothing could have been more dangerous for a man who had never saved, refused to keep records (a trait Laura shared), and indeed often went astray in simple arithmetic. ('I shall think of you for about 17 hours in the 24 and dream of you for the other five', he to wrote Laura during their courtship (L 107).) Before marriage, on the very day he received the Hawthornden Prize, only the efforts of Peters in a local police court had kept him from imprisonment for debt; even after taking on the responsibilities of a family, he could discover £2000 more than he expected at his bank, or, as he told Nancy Mitford in January 1950, a huge overdraft:

> Well last week I said to Laura 'are you sure you arent over-drawn at the bank?' 'No, I don't think so. I'm sure they'd tell me, if I were'. 'Well do ask'. So she did and, my dear, she had an overdraft of £6,420 which had been quietly mounting up for years. There is no possible way to pay it off, as her capital is in trust and for me to earn that much more, I should have to earn about 150,000....I shall have to go to prison but that is hell nowadays with wireless & lectures & psychiatry. Oh for the Marshalsea.
>
> (L 318)

Waugh chose to limit his annual income to £5000 because with surtax, as he advised Graham Greene when *The Heart of the Matter* proved successful, 'it is simply not worth while earning more than a gross £5000 a year nowadays'. At that income, marginal tax rates ('the rate of diminishing returns') rose to seventy-five per cent, discouraging further earning.[20] Thus from 1945 until the early fifties – as long as the *Brideshead* money held out – Waugh published little fiction, and that uncharacteristically short. 'Further effort', as Gilbert Pinfold explains, 'could only bring him sharply diminishing rewards' (GP 17). 'It is impossible now to be rich but it is possible to be idle' (L 278); 'Success has brought idleness as its dead fruit' (D 698). *Helena* (1950) and *Men at Arms* (1952), both long in planning, appeared only when new earning became necessary.

High tax rates also stimulated Waugh's charity: from 1948 onward, he donated the proceeds from translations to Catholic charities in the countries concerned; proceeds from *Scott-King's Modern Europe* and reissues of *Vile Bodies* went to the Jesuits; more writing than ever went for free to *The Tablet* and *The Month*. 'I can't afford to earn like this', he wrote to Peters in 1949; 'This is getting desperate. We must get rid of the whole cinema rights of *Scoop* to the Jesuits if the deal goes through' (HRC E638).

Meanwhile, amidst widespread complaints of a nation forced to become more or less criminal to survive, Waugh like many Britons became adept in tax-avoidance.[21] Wherever possible he took payment in kind – a Ford station-wagon from *Good Housekeeping*, delivered through Ireland and later sold for £700 cash; a case of 'Champagne, the shortest road out of Welfaria' (L 315) per thousand words of *Wine in Peace and War* (1947), a charming pamphlet written for the wine merchants Saccone and Speed, employers of Mary Lygon's husband Prince Vsevolode.[22] Proceeds from the sale of review books were free of tax, as were judgments in libel suits – a motive for attending carefully to press cuttings that would later pay handsomely. Most of all, the Revenue needed never know of expenses paid by others for his business travel (or so Peters and Waugh thought), leading to frequent reminders to those who paid his way to America: 'luxury not lionization is the thing'; 'I don't want to take a penny out of America but I want to travel and live there in fat style'.[23] For 'The American Epoch in the Catholic Church' (1949), *Life* paid $1000 as fee, $4000 in expenses. (Eventually Waugh paid back taxes on such income.)

That Waugh profited from *Brideshead* at all was chiefly due to the financial acumen of A. D. Peters. In 1944–5, unhappy with the chapters on Julia, Waugh suggested drawing out the novel to two or three volumes; Peters persuaded him that novels in more than one volume did not sell. Peters persuaded Chapman & Hall to risk enough rationed paper for a trade edition in May 1945 of 10,000 copies (for which Waugh received an advance of £1113), introduced Waugh to taking payment for writing in the form of 'expenses', and oversaw his foreign 'nest eggs'. Most important, it was Peters who devised a way to forestall the inevitable result had Waugh simply, as he wished, transferred *Brideshead*'s American profits to England. ('Your Government and ours between them [would] get nearly all the money', Peters wrote to Alfred MacIntyre at Little, Brown.)[24] He arranged for Little, Brown to retain Waugh's earnings on account, paying them out in twice-yearly sums of $5000. This system permitted Waugh to avoid the full burden of supertax and to profit from the weak pound against the strong dollar, stretching his income from *Brideshead* into the 1950s.[25]

Peters's wisdom is clearest in his grasp of the American literary market and early understanding that overseas financial arrangements were fast becoming more important to his authors than British. (As Waugh told Nancy Mitford in 1949, 'it looks as though soon one American reader will be worth ten Europeans' (L 307).) In 1945, despite Waugh's impatience, Peters insisted that American publication of *Brideshead* be deferred until the following January. He knew that the Book of the Month Club was considering the novel; by January the Club would have made its choice, which if favourable would result in a first printing by Little, Brown of 300,000 copies rather than 10,000. In January, too, the United States after long discussion was to reverse its policy of taxing American earnings by foreign authors.

Peters understood the economics of paperback publishing better than his client, who never fully grasped that the small return per copy from mass-market paperbacks might dwarf the profits of hardback sales.[26] In 1953 Peters negotiated the sale of Waugh's American paperback rights to Gulf and Western for $45,000. And Peters knew that however much his authors earned from the sales of books, there was potentially even more profit in subsidiary rights such as film options, and that once again the highest offers came from America. In 1955 he orchestrated the negotiations with American print-publishers and film studios by which in four weeks – before a single review appeared – *Island in the Sun* earned Alec Waugh $250,000. Though only one of Waugh's novels (*The Loved One*) was filmed in his lifetime, Peters ensured that his client received a fairly regular income from the sale of options.[27] Nowhere was Peters shrewder than in his handling of the film rights for *Brideshead*. In 1945, Metro-Goldwyn-Mayer had an old contract with Waugh, soon to run out, whereby it could buy the option on any new novel for $20,000. Peters carefully delayed entering negotiations over film rights for Waugh's new best-seller until the contract had expired, with the result that when the studio sought *Brideshead* it had to offer $140,000. (Had the deal gone through, we might not possess *Sword of Honour.*)

In only one instance did Peters's financial planning serve Waugh ill. In December 1949, while negotiating what promised to be a highly profitable deal with Penguin, he wrote to his suspicious client:

> Penguins would not hurt your ordinary sales and might increase the demand for your future books. [They] want to put out ten... novels in 1951.... As there is a lot of money involved, I suggest that you assign these cheap rights to a Trust for the benefit of one or more of your children. You save tax, ensure their future to some extent, and can also draw on the income for the Trust for their education and maintenance if the Deed is skilfully drawn up.
>
> (8 Dec. 1949, HRCT)

Peters estimated that Waugh could thereby save £700 in taxes annually. Waugh soon saw the wisdom of an arrangement that friends such as Ann Rothermere and Rebecca West were also adopting, and in August 1950 Peters's solicitor W. A. Evill drew up a deed of trust naming Peters and Evill as trustees and the Waugh children as beneficiaries. Into the trust went a £1000 advance from Penguin and all Waugh's unassigned copyrights (in effect, all revenue from his previous works); he and Laura were to live on the earnings from future publications. With the trustees' permission, Waugh in turn could draw on the trust for such expenses as the children's school fees, indeed for anything that could be termed an 'investment'. 'By all means install a new fireplace', Peters wrote as trustee that December; 'It is essential to keep the children warm'.[28] With funds from what he called his 'Save the Children Fund' Waugh was soon buying paintings, furniture, silver and rare books; in the sixties, when money was short, he began to sell his own manuscripts to the trust.

The Save the Children Fund thus helped underwrite Waugh's life at Piers Court while serving as the vehicle for the only kind of investment he knew well how to make: a shrewd collector, he acquired objects whose value over subsequent decades vastly increased. Where Evill and Peters went wrong was in supposing that funds taken from such a trust were free of tax. Already in 1951 the Inland Revenue began inquiring into the trust, and hostile newspapers began speculating about its value.[29] Years of worrisome correspondence between Peters and the authorities followed, and for the rest of his life, as his income seemed steadily to decline, Waugh was haunted by the idea that at any moment he might become bankrupt, reducing Laura and the children to poverty.

III

The effects of *Brideshead* on Waugh's reputation occurred in two phases. When the trade edition of the novel first appeared in 1945 reviews were mainly laudatory. *The Tablet* called it 'a great apologetic work in the larger and more humane sense'; the *Spectator* found it Waugh's 'most ambitious novel and his best' and praised its *lack* of Catholic 'exclusiveness'. In the *Sunday Times* Desmond MacCarthy too found it Waugh's best novel and warned that 'unintelligent and timid Catholics' might be offended.[30] Among the dissenters only Waugh's old foe the *New Statesman* clearly signalled what was to come, resurrecting the complaint first made years before by Ernest Oldmeadow: Henry Reed found *Brideshead* a 'gaudy novelette' of 'overpowering snobbishness', a work whose epigraph should have been 'How beautiful they are, the lordly ones' (CH 239–40). Waugh noted in his diary a week later: 'Most of the reviews have been laudatory except where they were embittered by class resentment' (D 628).

In December 1945, primed by Waugh, Randolph Churchill wrote to introduce members of the Book of the Month Club to *Brideshead*'s author:

> The character and writings of Evelyn Waugh have combined to make him one of the most controversial figures in England today. Even his severest critics admit him to be one of the three or four finest living writers of English prose; yet his recent writings have provoked an astonishing exhibition of irritation and even anger in leading intellectual circles in London.... [The] intellectuals of Bloomsbury suffer from [a] form of intellectual snobbism – proletarian snobbism.[31]

This titillating sales-pitch was not wholly true when Churchill wrote it. But it does capture Waugh's sense of himself as embattled, and it presages the tone of his attacks on the new socialist regime in the course of the coming year. By the end of 1946 Waugh had helped bring such irritation and anger into being.

He was now the much talked-about best-selling author, recipient of fan mail (especially from Americans) to which he delighted in crafting wittily dismissive replies. 'An offensive letter from a female American Catholic. I returned it to her husband with the note: "I shall be grateful if you will use whatever disciplinary means are customary in your country to restrain your wife from writing impertinent letters to men she does not know"' (D 643). In 1946, while Waugh's new fame lent added visibility to his attacks on the Left, there began to appear long essays reviewing his career, summarizing his political and social views and showing how these affected his most recent novel. All were by writers publicly and profoundly antipathetic to his politics, and all condemned *Brideshead* in terms that set the tone of highbrow response to the novel for the next twenty-five years, opening the way for such later summary judgments as 'It's bad taste to like *Brideshead*' (Howarth 77) and Brigid Brophy's famous remark in the *New Statesman*, 'In literary calendars 1945 is marked as the year Waugh ended' (CH 161).

The critical backlash began in earnest in January 1946, when the *New Yorker* carried a review by America's most influential highbrow critic, Edmund Wilson. Famously anti-Catholic and anti-conservative – in 1936 he had declared that 'you feel in the Soviet Union that you are at the moral top of the world where the light never really goes out' (*Travels* 321) – Wilson could hardly be expected to praise *Brideshead*; he was especially stung by seeing his own lavish praise of *Decline and Fall, Vile Bodies, A Handful of Dust Scoop* and *Put Out More Flags* splashed on Little, Brown's dust-jacket. Waugh had also recently insulted Wilson. During a supper party at Cyril Connolly's in 1945, despite warnings to avoid the topic, Waugh had questioned Wilson about his British publisher's fears that *Memoirs of Hecate County* might be subject to the laws against pornography. After a hilarious series of innocent-seeming probings, Waugh concluded: 'Mr Wilson, in cases like yours I always advise publication in Cairo' (Sykes 385). The next day he 'chucked [an] appointment to show London' to this 'insignificant Yank' (D 625).

In his masterful hatchet-job for the *New Yorker*, Wilson professed to find *Brideshead* a 'bitter blow'. The fine writer of 'comic' novels 'no longer knows his way' when he tries to enter the 'normal world'; the result is 'mere romantic fantasy' and writing riddled by cliché. Admitting himself 'unsympathetic by conviction' to Waugh's religion, Wilson argued that 'what has caused Mr. Waugh's hero to plump on his knees is not, perhaps, the sign of the cross but the prestige, in the person of Lord Marchmain, of one of the oldest families in England':

> For Waugh's snobbery, hitherto held in check by his satirical point of view, has here emerged shameless and rampant. His admiration for the qualities of the older British families, as contrasted with modern upstarts, had its value in his earlier novels, where the standards of morals and taste are kept in the background and merely implied. But here the upstarts are rather crudely overdone and the aristocrats become terribly trashy, and his cult of the high nobility is allowed to become so rapturous and solemn that it finally gives the impression of being the only real religion in the book.
>
> (CH 246)

In a concluding sneer Wilson predicted that *Brideshead* 'will prove to be the most successful, the only extremely successful, book that Evelyn Waugh has written, and that it will soon be up in the best seller list some where between *The Black Rose* and *The Manatee*'.

'I seem to be in the way of a good deal of critical attention', Waugh wrote that December; 'This morning *Horizon* arrived with a long article by Rose Macaulay advising me to return to my kennel and not venture into the world of living human beings' (D 667). Macaulay examined such previously little-noticed books as *Waugh in Abyssinia* ('a fascist tract') to argue that there were two Waughs: a fine writer of 'totally amoral' farces which in their extravagance had nothing to do with 'real life', and a writer of politically partisan non-fiction in which 'strangely fierce intolerances and phobias' conspired to corrupt both his judgment and his style. *Brideshead*, whose 'snobbery' she traces to 'adolescent surrender to glamour', is a sad instance of the intrusion of the second kind into the first. 'His genius and his reputation seem to stand at the crossroads; his admirers can only hope that he will take the right turning' (Macaulay 376). With Wilson and Macaulay thus begins a new generation of misguided distinctions between Waugh's 'earlier' and 'later' fiction (pre- and post-*Brideshead*); a chorus of postwar critics once again advises a return to his supposed 'early manner' – to the funny novelistic practice they had in fact rarely understood.

In the same month Macaulay's essay appeared, the political and religious progressive Conor Cruise O'Brien published another long retrospective review,

'The Pieties of Evelyn Waugh', in the Catholic *Bell*. Unlike Macaulay, O'Brien claimed to have found Waugh's earlier novels all too meaningful – from the start 'Waugh's political outlook is the expression of his social prejudices'; with *Brideshead* his 'almost mystical veneration for the upper classes' becomes a 'private religion, on which he has superimposed Catholicism'. According to O'Brien, Waugh damns the likes of Hooper simply because his lower-class soul 'is nothing to compare with the genuine old landed article'; O'Brien clinches his case by citing Lady Marchmain's speech on riches, which shows that 'In Mr. Waugh's theology, the love of money is not only not the root of all evil, it is a preliminary form of the love of God' (CH 255–63).

'I was pleased with *Brideshead Revisited*', Waugh wrote to John Betjeman in 1948, 'which everyone tells me was a great disgrace' (L 270). Wilson and O'Brien of course misread the novel, not only in small ways – Wilson claimed that before his conversion Ryder 'stoutly defended his Protestantism', O'Brien that at the end Ryder leaves the chapel 'empty of worshippers' – but also programmatically. *Brideshead* never 'damns' Hooper – it never judges Hooper in religious terms at all; and it is precisely the spectacle of Lord Marchmain *renouncing* pride of pedigree that marks his own atonement and leads to Ryder's conversion. Much more accurate than Wilson or O'Brien's would be a description of *Brideshead* as a story of how Catholicism infects and finally destroys a noble old Protestant family. The novel had not confused social and religious values, but it did provide an opening for such criticism by concerning itself with both.[32] Wilson and O'Brien's reviews were soon reprinted in collections, to be read and echoed by hostile critics for years to come.

Waugh seldom replied to hostile criticism of his writing, but he did quarrel with attacks on his character. 'I dont much mind the papers saying I am beastly, which is true, or that I write badly, which isn't. What enrages me is wrong facts' (L 336). Like Oldmeadow a decade earlier, Wilson and O'Brien had impugned his faith. He replied to Wilson in 'Fan-Fare' (1946), an essay for *Life* which originated when Waugh refused an earlier proposal for a picture-story about the people on whom his characters were based. Framed as a response to his many American correspondents, the essay presents Waugh's own account of his development and new sense of vocation. He rebuts 'the charge of using clichés' ('I think to be oversensitive about clichés is like being oversensitive about table manners') and 'the charge of snobbery' ('Class-consciousness, particularly in England, has been so much inflamed nowadays that to mention a nobleman is like mentioning a prostitute sixty years ago'). Wilson appears by name only when the topic is religion:

> I have already shaken off one of the American critics, Mr Edmund Wilson, who once professed a generous interest in me. He was outraged (quite legitimately by his standards) at finding God introduced into my story. I believe that you can only leave God out by making your characters pure abstractions. Countless admirable writers, perhaps some of the best in the world, succeed in this.... They try to represent the whole human mind and soul and yet omit its determining character – that of being God's creature with a defined purpose.[33]

To O'Brien's more direct imputations of bad faith, Waugh replied in a letter to the *Bell* that at the time of his conversion to Catholicism, 'My friends were fashionable agnostics and the Faith I then accepted had none of the extraneous glamour which your reviewer imputes to it'; he asked of his portrayals of the millionaire Rex Mottram and Lady Celia Ryder, 'Why did my reverence for money and rank not sanctify these two?' (CH 270–1). He would continue to answer direct attacks on his faith, for instance in 1960 when Frank Kermode suggested once again that in Waugh's 'Papist history and theology', religion is 'inseparable from class': 'Your reviewer's theme has long been tedious to me, but as it impugns my good faith as a Catholic.'[34] Such reiterated explanation had by then become tiresome; when one interviewer raised the old chestnut once again, Waugh's reply was simply: 'Nonsense' (Ryan 42).

From *Brideshead* onward, starting with *When the Going Was Good* and *Scott-King's Modern Europe*, reviewers would ground their remarks in generalizations about Waugh's now well known 'views'. As Malcolm Bradbury argued in 1964, after *Brideshead* Waugh's critical reputation 'diminished, and largely for this simple reason': his 'distrust of total democracy' and 'snobbery' (CH 456). Had *Waugh in Abyssinia* and *Robbery Under Law* been more widely read, or his prewar novels better understood, the trouble might have begun earlier; after *Brideshead* and during the Labour years, it was inevitable. Gilbert Pinfold's claim in 1957 to regard 'his books as objects which he had made, things quite external to himself to be used and judged by others' (GP 2) was a useful pose for a writer by then long used to reviews which ritually praised his prose style before turning to the real work of damning his politics. Waugh had of course brought such criticism upon himself, by his newly explicit advocacy – and by championing a point of view so at odds with the fashions of his time. If after the war he embraced writing as a vocation (and came to regret not receiving a knighthood), he must also have known that his very outspokenness unfitted him for public employments and honours.

Attacks on Waugh's 'snobbery' (and in the fifties on his setting up as a 'country squire') were of course mainly a way of attacking his politics. And by making not just his books but his life an advertisement for his views, Waugh made it inevitable that reviewers would use his books as pretexts for discussions of their author. 'All the reviews of *Scott-King*, instead of being about the book, have been about me saying that I am ill-tempered and self-infatuated', he complained in 1947: 'It hurts'.[35] The writer of 'expressions of dissent' designed to divert Britain 'from its ruinous course' had to walk a fine line: personal publicity both amplified his message and boosted sales; but if the publicity became too hostile, sales would suffer and the messenger cease to be taken seriously.

It would be foolhardy to attempt wholly to exculpate Waugh of the charge of snobbery, or at least rudeness (especially when drunk). There are too many stories like the one Mary Lygon told of his response over her dinner-table to some tedious praise of *Brideshead*: 'I thought it was a good book but if a common boring American woman like you says it's good, it must be very bad' (WM 27). But it is noteworthy how many of the famous stories, like Amis's version of

Waugh's joke to Arnold Lunn, turn out not to be true. Critic after critic has retailed the tale (first put into circulation by A. P. Herbert in an after-dinner speech in 1952) of Pius XI rebuking Waugh during an audience: 'But Mr. Waugh, you must remember that I am a Catholic too'. Who was present to hear such a remark? If the story has any basis at all – it was also told of Clare Luce – it must first have been told by Waugh as a joke against himself. By 1952 he could complain with justice to Diana Cooper, 'as all epigrams get attributed to Ronnie Knox, all rudeness gets attributed to me. Beasts come to me and say: "I heard something amusing you said the other day" and then recount an act of hideous boorishness without the shadow of reality'. 'Fact is', Nancy Mitford told him, 'the public looks upon you as the Rev. Brontë and is fearfully disappointed if you don't rush at journalists with a poker'.[36]

But the crucial point is the deliberateness and rationale of Waugh's offensive gestures, designed to be what only very few recognized at the time: a form of 'corrective snobbery'.[37] As Auberon Waugh has said, his father nurtured his 'romantic attachment to the aristocratic ideal' especially 'when he discovered how much it annoyed people' ('A Death' 562). Friends like Nancy Mitford celebrated 'the real bonhomie behind that mask of iron' (NM 250); Ann Fleming recognized a deliberate pose:

> Some may have been permitted to telephone Evelyn, to me it was forbidden, though I once broke the rule. Some hours after he left our house in Kent for a hotel nearby, a telegram arrived for him; it seemed to me urgent. . . . I telephoned and was crushed. 'Your manservant should have delivered it', he said reproachfully and rang off. He knew perfectly well that I had no manservant, though these obsolete and useful persons were part of his act.
>
> (HW 239)

To advertise his opposition to a socialist regime of 'politicians buying votes with my money' (L 365), Waugh wrote, spoke and lived in a way that inevitably brought charges of snobbery; so accused, he inflamed critics further by playing up to the role, as when asked by an interviewer in 1962 why his novels had given no 'sympathetic or even full-scale portrait of a working-class character':

> I don't know them, and I'm not interested in them. No writer before the middle of the nineteenth century wrote about the working classes other than as grotesques or as pastoral decorations. Then when they were given the vote certain writers started to suck up to them.
>
> (Jebb 114)

The result of this dangerous game was that while Waugh's novels continued to sell and often to be celebrated, there began in the late forties to emerge a kind of rage among more liberal critics, rage that would explode in the decade to follow.

IV

Despite tepid reviews, *Scott-King's Modern Europe*, a 'long short story about my trip to Spain', sold over 14,000 copies when it was published in December 1947 (1949 in America). Douglas Woodruff, editor of *The Tablet*, had invited Waugh to join in attending a celebration of the fourth centenary of Francisco de Vittoria, theorist of international law and greatest of a great line of Renaissance philosophers at the University of Salamanca. It was Waugh's first experience of the international academic conference circuit, which he came to despise; *Scott-King* scoops many later satires on the same subject such as Arthur Koestler's *The Call Girls* (1965), whose title refers not to prostitutes but academic symposiasts. Except that when the festivities were over Waugh and Woodruff were left to arrange their own transport home, the trip bore no relation to Scott-King's disastrous and disillusioning exposure to a 'Modern Europe' of tyranny, displaced persons and illegal refugees. Nonetheless, the obscure, aging classics master Scott-King, who feels himself an exile in postwar Britain ('he was a Mediterranean man') and whose 'precise and slightly nasal lamentations of modern decadence were widely imitated', is clearly a version of Waugh himself – the first fictional presentation of the new persona Waugh had unveiled in 'Fan-Fare'.

In 1946, amidst Labour's campaign to redirect education into technical and scientific fields – what Waugh liked to dismiss as 'stinks' – Scott-King watches 'his classical colleagues fall away', 'replaced by physicists and economists from the provincial universities'.[38] In these bleak circumstances he is invited to Neutralia, a tiny Mediterranean nation so named because like Franco's Spain it 'kept out of the second World War'. The historical events that have given birth to this 'typical modern state' comprise a catalogue reminiscent of Jonathan Swift:

> Let us eschew detail and observe that for three hundred years [Neutralia] has suffered every conceivable ill the body politic is heir to. Dynastic wars, foreign invasion, disputed successions, revolting colonies, endemic syphilis, impoverished soil, masonic intrigues, revolutions, restorations, cabals, juntas, pronunciamentos, liberations, constitutions, *coups d'état*, dictatorships, assassinations, agrarian reforms, popular elections, foreign intervention, repudiation of loans, inflations of currency, trades unions, massacres, arson, atheism, secret societies.... Out of it emerged the present republic of Neutralia, a typical modern state, governed by a single party, acclaiming a dominant Marshal, supporting a vast ill-paid bureaucracy whose work is tempered and humanised by corruption.[39]

Again like Spain, Neutralia attempts to regain its standing in the international community through cultural congresses such as a celebration of the tercentenary of its best-known son (and Scott-King's special subject), the obscure neo-Latin poet Bellorius, author of a forgotten poem about an island utopia.

It soon becomes clear that Scott-King's invitation has been made under false pretences. The ceremonies turn out to be a 'plot' to trick the conferees into laying wreaths not to Bellorius, but at a monument to the Marshal; when photographs of the event appear in European newspapers, Scott-King and his colleagues are branded 'Reactionaries' and 'Fascists'. A Swiss and a Chinese delegate thereupon leave the group, only to be murdered by 'partisans' in the hills; two South American students attached to the conference are imprisoned. Scott-King alone remains to participate in the unveiling of Bellorius's statue, offering 'from the heart' a speech in Latin:

He said that a torn and embittered world was that day united in dedicating itself to the majestic concept of Bellorius, in rebuilding itself first in Neutralia, then among all the yearning peoples of the West, on the foundations Bellorius had so securely laid. He said that they were lighting a candle that day which by the Grace of God should never be put out.

(SK 66)

The words echo Hugh Latimer's to Nicholas Ridley when the two were burnt at the stake by Queen Mary in 1555 for their Protestantism.[40] Both men were to Waugh traitors to the truth; the allusion signals the illusoriness of hopes of progress by political means. Scott-King himself is soon shaken from such illusions by the ordeal of escaping from Neutralia via an underground, run in covert cooperation with the state, devoted to smuggling uncredentialled persons abroad and making dissidents 'disappear'. 'Welcome to Modern Europe' says one of its leaders, a woman with 'the face of a *tricoteuse* of the Terror'.

In a parody of the final chapter of Jane Austen's *Mansfield Park* ('Let other pens dwell on guilt and misery'), Waugh declines at the end of this 'light tale' about a 'summer holiday' to speak 'of those depths of the human spirit, the agony and despair' of Scott-King's perilous escape: a voyage that lands him not home but stark naked in 'No. 64 Jewish Illicit Immigrants' Camp, Palestine' (83, 85–6). Cured of illusion, Scott-King returns to England and a headmaster who tries to persuade him to give up classics for 'economic history'.

> 'Parents are not interested in producing the "complete man" any more. They want to qualify their boys for jobs in the modern world. You can hardly blame them, can you?'
> 'Oh yes', said Scott-King. 'I can and do'....
> 'But you know, there may be something of a crisis ahead'.
> 'Yes, headmaster'.
> 'Then what do you intend to do?'
> 'If you approve, headmaster, I will stay as I am here as long as any boy wants to read the classics. I think it would be very wicked indeed to do anything to fit a boy for the modern world'.
> 'It's a very short-sighted view, Scott-King'.
> 'There, headmaster, with all respect, I differ from you profoundly. I think it is the most long-sighted view it is possible to take'.
>
> (87–8)

The most penetrating review of *Scott-King* came from George Orwell, who recognized how the novel played on widespread fears in the late forties that another European war was already brewing:

> Nowadays, it is implied, only the middle-aged have scruples or ideals; the young are born hard-boiled.... The modern world, we are meant to infer, is so unmistakably crazy, so certain to smash itself to pieces in the near future, that to attempt to understand it or come to terms with it is simply a purposeless self-corruption. In the chaos that is shortly coming, a few moral principles that one can cling to, and perhaps even a few half- remembered odes of Horace or choruses from Euripides, will be more useful than what is now called 'enlightenment'.
>
> (CH 294–6)

Orwell criticized Waugh's giving Neutralia characteristics of both Fascist and Communist dictatorships, but the equivalence of totalitarianisms, Left and Right, is precisely Waugh's point. Waugh had differed from Catholic conservatives over Spain in the thirties; a decade later he is still critical of Franco's regime, so much so that Woodruff, as a prominent Catholic layman, refused *Scott-King*'s dedication. Waugh thereupon dedicated the story instead to Woodruff's wife Mia, 'coniugis prudentioris audaci coniugi' – 'To the lion wife of a churchmouse husband', as he wrote in her copy (HW 126).

Other reviewers thought Neutralia some Soviet satellite, or, because ruled by a 'Marshal', Yugoslavia. (One working title for the story had been *Ten Days that Shook Scott-King*, after the Soviet hireling John Reed's popular hymn to the Bolshevik Revolution, *Ten Days that Shook the World* (1919).) There are touches as well of Fascist Italy ('syndico-radicals'), socialist Mexico (a 'General Cardenas'), and most topically Greece, where even as Waugh wrote, Communist guerrillas were attempting to topple the British-supported government. Waugh's chief target in *Scott-King* was Franco's Spain, but he meant the satire to be generally applicable. In a Cold War mood he wrote to Peters that if the story were filmed, 'Neutralia should cease to be Spain & become a Soviet satellite, thus giving topical patriotic point' (L 264).

Scott-King is a minor work, full of easy jabs at England under Labour – 'Here things are very expensive', says one Neutralian, 'but there is plenty for all who pay, so our people do not strike but work hard to become rich. It is better so, no?' (22) – and full as well of material recycled from earlier novels, especially *Scoop*. In 1949 Waugh told an interviewer, 'If I'd rewritten it now I should get into it more of the real horror, less of the fascination of travel'.[41] But at the same time, Scott-King himself is the first of a new kind of Waugh hero, not merely 'dim' but also 'blasé', a simple man who comes to full understanding of the ills of 'modern Europe' and elects limited rebellion from the safety of an honourable retreat. He is also, uniquely among Waugh's heroes, repeatedly identified as an 'intellectual' (9, 47, 48, 72). That Waugh should have used such a term of a hero – and a character clearly modelled on himself – once again reflects his response to the growing criticism of *Brideshead*.

Edmund Wilson's most wounding remark about *Brideshead* was perhaps his sneering prophecy of its popularity, which Waugh would recall fifteen years later in *Unconditional Surrender*:

> 'Ludovic's *Death Wish* has *got* something, you know'.
> 'Something very bad'.
> 'Oh yes, bad; egregiously bad. I shouldn't be surprised to see it a great success'.
> (US 262)

(Ludovic's novel sells a million copies in America despite being 'tosh' (US 310).) For years Waugh's pose had been that of anti-intellectual and amateur, a believer like Dr Johnson that all publicity is good publicity. Now, just as he became sure of his vocation, not only were reviewers united in focusing first on his politics, secondarily on his artistry; they could dismiss him as just the sort of popular writer whose work would be selected by the Book of the Month Club. *Time* magazine noted wryly in 1948: '*Brideshead* was the first of Waugh's novels to become a U. S. best-seller. His fans had reluctantly winked at the fact that he is a conservative and a Roman Catholic convert. But popular? No literary cult can tolerate popularity in its prey. The boys were preparing to dump Evelyn' (CH 301).

It was *Brideshead*'s success that led to Waugh's promise in 'Fan-Fare' that his future novels would be 'unpopular', and, for a few years at least, to his indulgence toward the 'intellectual'. In the same year *Scott-King* appeared he told readers of the *Daily Telegraph* that 'intellectuals' 'throughout the West are now turning to formal Christianity' (EAR 343). Meanwhile he offered his next novel for free to Cyril Connolly, in Waugh's view the 'leader of the English intellectuals' (EAR 312), for publication in *Horizon* – a magazine whose readership differed as much as possible from Book-of-the-Month subscribers. He hoped (in language once again borrowed from Connolly) that such publication would help in 're-establishing my popularity in highbrow circles'.[42] The effort succeeded: partly because of its veneer of fashionable anti-Americanism, *The Loved One* was the first (and only) of Waugh's novels to be noticed by F. R. Leavis's *Scrutiny*. But of course Waugh's irenic mood did not last. He had already told Diana Cooper in 1946 that '*Brideshead* is having a disquieting success among the Yanks so I am writing a novel about the Empress Helena which will put the kybosh on that' (DC 82–3). In 1948, again looking ahead to *Helena*, he wrote to Nancy Mitford: '*Loved One* is being well received in intellectual circles. They think my heart is in the right place after all. I'll show them' (L 273).

V

At the end of January 1947, while Britain suffered its worst winter in a century, Waugh left to negotiate the film rights to *Brideshead* and enjoy with Laura the first of his postwar American holidays. At every stage of the trip MGM provided luxury as well as lionization. After a happy week in New York at the Waldorf during which Laura spent $2000 on new clothes – Waugh was delighted to find her outspending his own efforts to shake off British austerity – they proceeded cross-country on the *Twentieth Century* ('the pride of the US railways – rightly'; 'The dinner absolutely excellent' (D 672)) and arrived in Beverly Hills in early February, where, he reported to Peters, the social life was 'not as generally described', but 'gay & refined' (L 247). There were old friends on hand, Iris Tree and Randolph Churchill; Waugh made a pilgrimage to the Disney studios, whose cartoons he had long admired, and met favourite stars such as Merle Oberon, Anna May Wong and Charlie Chaplin. He attended a private screening of Chaplin's new film *Monsieur Verdoux*, which when it opened later that year in Britain he acclaimed (despite Chaplin's 'socialism and pacifism') as a work of 'genius' (EAR 337). In such easy circumstances (and to keep the 'yanks' off balance) Waugh's playfulness came to the fore. At a party arranged for him at Louis Mayer's palatial house, he stopped conversation by declaring with 'cherubic innocence': 'How wise you Americans are to eschew all ostentation and lead such simple, wholesome lives! This really is delightful. Who'd even want to live in the main house when he could have this charming gatehouse instead!' (ST2 188).

MGM had offered $140,000 for *Brideshead* (less four weeks' expenses, set in Hollywood style at $2000 a week). It was the 'only one chance in his life', Peters recalled, 'of making a really big killing' (WM 29). Despite the sometimes blasé tone of his references to the negotiations, Waugh very much wanted the money. *Brideshead*'s sales were already waning, and he was increasingly unsure how long he would be able to maintain what *The Loved One* calls 'maximum earning capacity'. But he also insisted on 'full Molotov veto rights' over any treatment of his best book to date.

Predictably, given the novel's publicity – its American dust-jacket advertised 'an extraordinary love story' set among 'the rich, the beautiful, and the damned Marchmains' – it soon became clear that MGM viewed '*Brideshead* purely as a love story. None of them see the theological implication' (D 673). Waugh wrote a five-page memorandum outlining his understanding of the novel and suggesting various changes to help turn it into a successful film (such as down-playing Ryder to focus wholly on the Marchmains). But the writers 'lost heart as soon as I explained . . . what *Brideshead* was about' (D 675).

Waugh had arrived in Hollywood at the worst possible time. In 1946, the Hays-Johnston Office and the Hollywood Production Code, both strongly supported by the Catholic League of Decency, were at the height of their power and authority. The Hays Office was already enmeshed in public battles with Howard Hughes over Jane Russell's exposure in *The Outlaw* and with David O. Selznick over *Duel in the Sun*; soon the chief censor Joseph Breen would find Darryl Zanuck's *Gentleman's Agreement* objectionable because its divorcée heroine lent a 'flavor of acceptance and even tacit justification of divorce', a topic suitable for treatment on film only 'when it was obtained against the wishes, and generally over the objections, of the sympathetic lead' (Leff 143–4). On the very day Waugh presented his memorandum, Monsignor Fulton Sheen, Rabbi Sidney Goldstein, and the Rev. Harry Emerson Fosdick launched a nationally publicized campaign against the sexual mores purveyed not only on film but through the lives of Hollywood stars themselves.

In line with the Production Code's requirement that homosexuality 'not even be hinted at in motion pictures', Waugh was quite willing to write Anthony Blanche out of any film version of *Brideshead*. But this left Charles and Julia's adulteries – a subject, according to the Code, that 'must not be explicitly treated, or justified, or presented attractively' – and their divorces. He insisted that the story required explicitness about both:

> there must be an impediment to the marriage of Julia and Charles. Otherwise, since Julia's marriage to Rex has never been ecclesiastically valid, there is no reason why she should not marry Charles and provide a banal Hollywood ending. I regard it as essential that, after having led a life of sin, Julia should not be immediately rewarded with conventional happiness. She has a great debt to pay and we are left with her paying it.
>
> (MGM 229)

It was this demand that killed the project. Waugh's producer Leon Gordon, worried by what he called the novel's 'many obstacles from a censorable angle', laid the whole question before Joseph Breen in a letter asking whether 'they can be ultimately surmounted or if the cuts necessarily go so deep as to destroy the story'. (For good measure, Gordon included with his query a sheaf of the novel's worst reviews, including O'Brien's from the *Bell*.) Breen replied unequivocally on 13 March: 'this story, in its present form, is unacceptable'.[43] On 15 March Waugh cabled Peters, 'Censor forbids film of *Brideshead*' (EAR 530). He and Laura left Hollywood in March 'as we had come, in effortless luxury' (D 675).

It is a measure of Waugh's angry disappointment that on reaching New York he offered *Life* an interview attacking Hollywood censorship. *Life* refused, but back in London the *Daily Telegraph* offered £100 each for up to three articles on his trip. The result was 'Why Hollywood is a Term of Disparagement' and 'What Hollywood Touches it Banalizes'.[44] The essays present a long and varied bill of complaint: the film industry's myriad unions ensure that every film must bear the expense of 'redundant labour'; so unable are screenwriters 'to follow a plain story' (even when that story has been a 'Book of the Month') that one wonders why studios 'trouble to purchase rights'. But it is Hollywood's commitment to 'the great fallacy of the Century of the Common Man' – that 'a thing can have no value for anyone which is not valued by all' – which, by leading both to 'gross quantitative standards' and censorship so sweeping that all incisiveness is lost, has done most to prevent the cinema from growing into the major art form it might have become. Like Ruth Inglis in *Freedom of the Movies* (published later the same year), Waugh pleads for a system of supervision that would permit films which appeal to adults as well as children:

> In fact, no one really knows what will corrupt anyone else.... But when all this is said it remains broadly true that some films may be harmless to adults and harmful to children. This, with all the essential finer distinctions, the Americans ignore, and the function of the Hays Office is to enforce a code which forbids the production of any film which can be harmful to anyone, or offend any racial or religious susceptibility. No such code is feasible in a heterogeneous society.
>
> (EAR 330)

In what can only be a reference to *Brideshead*, he supplies an instance of the 'vagaries of the Hays Office':

> A script was recently condemned as likely to undermine the conception of Christian marriage. The story was of an unhappy married man and woman who wished to divorce their respective partners and remarry one another. They institute proceedings, but in the end refrain from remarriage precisely because they come to realize that this would not constitute Christian marriage. At the same time the excellent film *The Best Years of Our Lives* was being acclaimed as the embodiment of healthy American domesticity. That story depends for its happy end on the hero being deserted by his Bohemian wife and thus being free to marry the banker's innocent daughter. This was passed because it was never specifically stated that a divorce would have to intervene.[45]

Thus neutered, films create a false vision of an American Eden, perpetuating 'a conception of innocence which has little relation to life' – the theme also of his next novel.

VI

Friends suggested that while in Los Angeles Waugh visit both a pets' cemetery and the extraordinary 300-acre funeral park, Forest Lawn. He soon reported to Peters the discovery of 'a deep mine of literary gold' (D 675).

> I am entirely obsessed by Forest Lawns & plan a long short story about it. I go there two or three times a week, am on easy terms with the chief embalmer & next week am to lunch with Dr HUBERT EATON himself ['The Builder', model for *The Loved One*'s Dr Kenworthy, 'The Dreamer']. It is an entirely unique place – the *only* thing in California that is not a copy of something else.... I have seen dozens of loved ones [Eaton's euphemism for corpses] half painted before the bereaved family saw them.
>
> (L 247)

He brought home copies of the official *Art Guide of Forest Lawn* and Ray Slocum's *Embalming Techniques* (1937), both of which contributed specific details to *The Loved One*. From Slocum Waugh learnt of trimming cards to shape a corpse's lips, of special compounds to close recalcitrantly 'firmed' eyes, and massages to undo the marks left on a body by strangulation. The story told by one of Whispering Glades's saleswomen of a couple killed in a car crash, leaving two daughters 'comfortless' because their parents had failed to make 'before need arrangements' for burial, comes directly from the *Art Guide*, as does her advice to avoid 'morbid reflexions' by facing death squarely – exactly what, in Waugh's view, the Hollywood cemetery failed to do.[46]

In April 1947 he wrote an 'essay for *Life* about death' (D675), a picture-story about Forest Lawn entitled 'Death in Hollywood'.[47] *The Loved One: An Anglo-American Tragedy* went through numerous drafts between May and September; it first appeared in *Horizon*, occupying the entire February 1948 issue. With its opening flattery of *Horizon*'s readers (presumably able, unlike the subscriber in the story, to understand its avant-garde contents), 9500 copies sold out immediately. 'I wish it were 19,000' wrote Connolly, but the tale's very unavailability helped guarantee hardback sales later in the year.[48]

Hardback publication was delayed by publishers' requests for changes and fears of libel. For Little, Brown, Waugh excised passages such as Mr Joyboy's comment: 'The skull drained very nicely. Practically no massage was needed. I removed the tongue and filled the mouth with cotton wool to support the cheeks which showed a tendency to sag'. To quell fears of a libel action from Dr Eaton, Waugh added a prefatory disclaimer and persuaded a titled friend, Baron Stanley, 'to add a codicil to his will stating that on his death he wished his body to be transported to Los Angeles for burial in Forest Lawn, as he understood that this cemetery bore some resemblance to the beautiful one so movingly described by his friend Mr Evelyn Waugh' (Sykes 419). (The potentially expensive codicil was removed when the danger had passed.) The hardbound edition finally appeared, illustrated by Stuart Boyle and dedicated to Nancy Mitford, in July in America and October in Britain – the only occasion on which one of Waugh's novels made its first hardcover appearance in the United States. Once again circumstances boosted sales: news of enthusiastic American responses, including a six-column review in *Time*, reached England weeks before copies were available.

Even before visiting California Waugh had proposed to his agents a tale embodying what would be *The Loved One*'s major theme: 'The moral, which needs emphasis more in this century than in any of which we have record, is that a complete life can only be lived when the fact of Death is kept steadily in mind' – that 'life is not a freehold but a precarious tenancy recoverable by the landlord' (HRC E523). 'Death in Hollywood' details how Forest Lawn evades death's meaning and importance:

> Dr. Eaton has set up his credo at the entrance. 'I believe in a happy Eternal Life', he says. 'I believe those of us left behind should be glad in the certain belief that those gone before have entered into that happier Life'...Dr. Eaton is the first man to offer eternal salvation at an inclusive charge as part of his undertaking service....
>
> We are very far here from the traditional conception of an adult soul naked at the judgment seat and a body turning to corruption. There is usually a marble skeleton lurking somewhere among the marble draperies and quartered escutcheons of the tombs of the high Renaissance; often you find, gruesomely portrayed, the corpse half decayed with marble worms writhing in the marble adipocere. These macabre achievements were done with a simple moral purpose – to remind a highly civilized people that beauty was skin deep and pomp was mortal. In those realistic times hell waited for the wicked and a long purgation for all but the saints, but heaven, if at last attained, was a place of perfect knowledge. In Forest Lawn, as the builder claims, these old values are reversed. The body does not decay; it lives on, more chic in death than ever before, in indestructible Class A steel-and-concrete shelf; the soul goes straight from the Slumber Room to Paradise, where it enjoys an endless infancy....
>
> (EAR 335–7)

In the same way Whispering Glades eschews all 'conventional and depressing' memorials such as 'wreaths or crosses'; its embalmers turn death's 'grim line of endurance' into 'Radiant Childhood smiles'. Its consoling promise is that upon (suitably expensive) burial, all loved ones embark 'on the greatest success story of all time', 'the success that waits for all of us whatever the disappointments of our earthly lives'. 'Pass the buck', its saleswomen tell customers with unwitting irony, 'Whispering Glades can take it'.[49]

As an antidote to euphemism and the evasion of mortality, *The Loved One* evokes death's unblinkable facts in a series of calculated assaults on readers' sensibilities. The process begins with some prophetic remarks delivered by veteran Hollywood script-writer Sir Francis Hinsley to Waugh's hero Dennis Barlow, a war poet who on failing to find regular film work has taken a job at the Happier Hunting Ground.

'Did you see the photograph some time ago in one of the magazines of a dog's head severed from its body, which the Russians are keeping alive for some obscene Muscovite purpose by pumping blood into it from a bottle? It dribbles at the tongue when it smells a cat. That's what all of us are, you know, out here. The studios keep us going with a pump. We are still just capable of a few crude reactions – nothing more. If we ever got disconnected from our bottle, we should simply crumble'.

(LO 10)

When Megalopolitan Studios (MGM) disconnects the pump – when it fires him – sloth turns to despair and Hinsley hangs himself, leaving Dennis to arrange his funeral at Whispering Glades. There a 'mortuary hostess' provokes a second disturbing image as she asks whether Dennis's 'Loved One' was 'Caucasian' (like Forest Lawn, Whispering Glades excludes Negroes and Chinese):

'Well, let me assure you Sir Francis was quite white'.
As he said this there came vividly into Dennis's mind that image which lurked there, seldom out of sight for long; the sack or body suspended and the face above it with eyes red and horribly starting from their sockets, the cheeks mottled in indigo like the marbled end-papers of a ledger and the tongue swollen and protruding like an end of black sausage.

(LO 38)

(The corpse's vivid colours hint that race matters nothing in death.) But these hideous images pale beside the sight of Sir Francis's corpse 'transfigured' by embalmer and cosmetician:

the face which inclined its blind eyes towards him – the face was entirely horrible; as ageless as a tortoise and as inhuman; a painted and smirking obscene travesty by comparison with which the devil-mask Dennis had found in the noose was a festive adornment, a thing an uncle might don at a Christmas party.

(LO 65)

Meaninglessness, Waugh suggests, is more terrifying than the fearful, but at least humanly comprehensible, prospect of the Four Last Things.

The novel finds such meaninglessness everywhere in American life. The same point emerges through a series of references to savourless foods: to American 'nutburgers' ('It is not so much their nastiness as their total absence of taste that shocks one'), and especially that new hybrid so recurrently mentioned as to become a symbol, Kaiser's Stoneless Peaches.

A peach without a stone. That was the metaphor of Frank Hinsley. Dennis had once tried to eat one of Mr. Kaiser's much-advertised products and had discovered a ball of damp, sweet cotton-wool. Poor Frank Hinsley, it was very like him.

(LO 73–4)

Just as Whispering Glades replaces real bees (which sting) with mechanically reproduced buzzing, Americans have bred fruit without the hard seed at its core, without the hard seed of new life that gives the fruit its taste – just as death, judgment and the afterlife alone give meaning to earthly life. Evade this hard doctrine, deny the meaning of death, and a culture becomes empty and tasteless, because spiritually dead.

Waugh wrote to Peters that he feared *The Loved One* might come 'rather poorly after an article in *Life* ['Fan-Fare'] in which I declared that I would only write religious books in future' (HRC E523). But the novel in fact suggests a Catholic alternative in the same way his earliest fiction had, by negation. 'Deprived of the sacraments, imaginative minds invent all kinds of fetishes for themselves'; in southern California, 'countless preposterous cults' seek to sugar over the facts of death (EAR 377, 335). The novel brims with references to non-Christian cultures and creeds, some glancingly alluded to (the 'Hindu Love Song', 'Egypt of the Pharaohs', the 'Guru Brahmin', the 'Grand Sanhedrin'), others, like the newly fashionable French existentialism, lingered over to be the more thoroughly exploded: 'Sir Ambrose . . . lived existentially. He thought of himself as he was at that moment, brooded fondly on each several excellence and rejoiced' (7). Aimée Thanatogenos takes her Christian name from Aimée Semple Macpherson, in whose Four Square Gospel her father lost his money (whereupon her mother 'took to New Thought and wouldn't have it that there was such a thing as death'); predictably, she now has no religion ('because I was progressive at College') except to think herself 'ethical'. At his lowest point – when he is most at risk of thralldom to the dead world around him – Dennis plans to quit the Happier Hunting Ground (where he buries such animals as 'a non-sectarian chimpanzee') and take up the more remunerative career of 'non-sectarian clergyman'. Punctuating all these references to other creeds is another sequence of hints intended to call to mind the true faith the others deny, references to 'atonement' and 'martyrdom' that culminate in the address of the Heinkels, who have just lost their pet Sealyham: '207 Via Dolorosa, Bel Air'.

Developing themes first launched in *Vile Bodies* and 'Excursion in Reality', Waugh everywhere stresses that in parallel with Whispering Glades, the other great false church of southern California is the film industry. To each worker at the studios is 'given a span of life between the signature of the contract and its expiration; beyond that lay the vast unknowable'; 'Liturgy in Hollywood is the concern of the Stage rather than of the Clergy'.[50] Having worked in both, Dennis inchoately recognises the connexion of studio and cemetery, one falsifying life, the other death:

> When as a newcomer to the Megalopolitan Studios he first toured the lots, it had taxed his imagination to realize that those solid-seeming streets and squares of every period and climate were in fact plaster façades whose backs revealed the structure of bill-boardings. Here the illusion was quite otherwise. Only with an effort could Dennis believe that the building before him was three-dimensional and permanent; but here, as everywhere at Whispering Glades, failing credulity was fortified by the painted word.
>
> (LO 33–4)

(The passage seems to have supplied Tom Wolfe with the title of his satiric history of modernist aesthetics, *The Painted Word* (1975).)

One casualty of the novel's spiritually dead world is individuality, which, Waugh always believed, demands cultural rootedness; it cannot exist apart from participation in an informing and enlivening tradition – national, cultural and finally religious. Without such roots, there cannot thrive any real personality, only the uniformity Dennis finds throughout America, in its food, speech, education, dress and especially its women. Whispering Glades promises not merely happiness but 'individuality' in death: 'Normal disposal is by inhumement, entombment, inurnment or immurement, but many people just lately prefer insarcophagusment. That is *very* individual' (36). This speech comes, ironically, from one of 'that new race of exquisite, amiable, efficient young ladies whom [Dennis] had met everywhere in the United States' (35). And as Whispering Glades falsifies individuality in death, Megalo (which keeps on staff a 'Director of Personality') 'creates' personality in life. Francis Hinsley vies with another studio-god (also a suicide) for the honour of having brought the star Juanita del Pablo 'into existence':

> Poor Leo bought her for her eyes. She was called Baby Aaronson then – splendid eyes and a fine head of black hair. So Leo made her Spanish. He had most of her nose cut off and sent her to Mexico for six weeks to learn Flamenco singing. Then he handed her over to me. *I* named her. *I* made her an anti-Fascist refugee. *I* said she hated men because of her treatment by Franco's Moors. That was a new angle then.
> (LO 5)[51]

Her 'personality' remade in Hollywood once already, there is no reason Baby/Juanita cannot (like King's Thursday in *Decline and Fall*) be remade over and over again; as Aimée points out, 'Once you start changing a name, you see, there's no reason ever to stop' (77). Soon, under pressure from the Catholic League of Decency to make 'healthy films', the studio pulls out her teeth and bleaches her hair in order to transform her from Spanish refugee into 'Irish colleen'. (In 1952 Waugh reflected to Nancy Mitford of his earlier desire to move to Ireland: 'once one pulls up roots & lives abroad there is no particular reason for living anywhere. Why not Jamaica? Why not Sicily? Why not California?' (L 373).)

Can love exist in a void?' Waugh asked audiences during his American tour in 1949 (Lecture 301). The dangers posed by modernity to individuality, art and love had occupied Waugh since the beginning of his career, and became explicit in *Brideshead*. In the years that followed, he made his way with difficulty through Fr D'Arcy's 'very important' philosophical treatise *The Mind and Heart of Love* (DC 88), and announced his continuing interest in the titles of *The Loved One* and *Love Among the Ruins*.[52]

The latter, begun in 1949 but not published until 1953, recapitulates in starker form most of *The Loved One*'s aims and techniques. Both begin with a disorienting opening scene: in *The Loved One* what seems a jungle reveals itself as Los Angeles; in *Love Among the Ruins*, an elegant country house turns out a prison. In both, identity is undermined by what the forties called 'materialism', the fifties 'mass culture' – attitudes that deny the meaning of human life and death. (In the socialist future of *Love Among the Ruins*, it is not film studios but 'the State' that has 'made' Waugh's hero Miles Plastic; 'Be careful', a bureaucrat tells him, 'that's your Certificate of Human Personality you've dropped – a *vital* document': LAR 5, 14.) In both, the hero is a man spiritually stunted but, unlike those around him, not wholly dead – one who manifests a small spiritual spark, partly through his appreciation of art, partly by falling in love. In both, it is a woman uniquely different from those around her who immediately attaches the hero: a woman like himself, a fellow exile, in fact an artist, though of a wholly decadent kind.

Aimée Thanatogenos ('the loved one born of death') instantly attracts Dennis Barlow because as 'sole Eve in a bustling hygienic Eden, this girl was a decadent'; amidst the uniformity of American womanhood, she seems 'unique'. '[B]rain and body were scarcely distinguishable from the standard product, but the spirit...' (45, 117). 'Eve' suggests a soul, capable of temptation and fall, unlike the novel's other characters (none, in Graham Greene's phrase, 'men enough to be damned'); Dennis first gets to know her in a garden.[53] Possessed of at least the vestigial remains of 'spirit', Aimée in turn is drawn to Dennis because he is a poet. She proudly views her job composing corpses into sources of 'consolation' as a form of 'art'; like the waifs of *Vile Bodies*, she hungers for permanence, if only of an aesthetic kind. 'Do you think anything can be a great art which is so impermanent?' she asks; 'I've seen painting [on a corpse] not ten years old that's completely lost tonality' (76). Though decadent, it is Aimée's mysticism of art that provides the hint of spiritual possibility in her which attracts Dennis, scion 'of an earlier civilization with sharper needs' – and that makes possible the 'Anglo-American Tragedy' of the novel's subtitle, her suicide, which Waugh casts as a grotesquely debased Greek tragedy:

> An umbilical cord of cafés and fruit shops, of ancestral shady businesses (fencing and pimping) united Aimée, all unconscious, to the high places of her race. As she grew up [in America] the only language she knew expressed fewer and fewer of her ripening needs... [but] Attic voices prompted Aimée to a higher destiny; voices which far away and in another age had sung of...Alcestis and proud Antigone.
>
> (LO 117, 130)

Neither Aimée nor Dennis is a character for whom the novel elicits much sympathy. Aimée's broken heart, Waugh writes blandly, is merely 'a small inexpensive item of local manufacture'; Dennis is a mediocre poet, a plagiarist, a blackmailer, 'a liar and a cheat' (118) – like Adam Fenwick-Symes and Basil Seal, a cad. 'There is an ineradicable caddishness about all my heroes – Dennis too, I'm afraid', Waugh wrote to Connolly, who had complained of his 'heart-lessness' (HRC E62). Reviewers also complained of *The Loved One*'s 'cruelty', but Waugh's point is that a dead world fosters nothing better than spiritual cripples.

In portraying Dennis as 'a young man of sensibility rather than sentiment' (31) Waugh also signalled his intention to avoid the charges of sentimentality levelled against *Brideshead*. In the course of composition he came to understand *The Loved One* not only as a meditation on love in a spiritually dead world, but also a tale of artistic vocation; he went back over his manuscript to insert the numerous passages in which Dennis's 'Muse' speaks to him of his unique task, of that 'something in Whispering Glades that was necessary to him, that only he could find' (69).

> the Muse nagged him.... There was a very long, complicated and important message she was trying to convey to him. It was about Whispering Glades, but it was not except quite indirectly, about Aimée. Sooner or later the Muse would have to be placated.
>
> (LO 90)

Aimée's death frees Dennis from Hollywood, allowing him to return to England; more importantly it frees him as a writer.

> On this last evening in Los Angeles Dennis knew he was a favourite of Fortune. Others, better men than he, had foundered here and perished. The strand was littered with their bones. He was leaving it not only unravished but enriched. He was adding his bit to the wreckage; something that had long irked him, his young heart, and was carrying back instead the artist's load, a great, shapeless chunk of experience; bearing it home to his ancient and comfortless shore; to work on it hard and long, for God knew how long. For that moment of vision a lifetime is sometimes too short.
>
> (LO 143–4)

Dennis's 'artist's load' echoes an earlier 'load', the dead Sealyham that early in the novel he carried out from 207 Via Dolorosa. We are to understand that he returns to England to write something very like *The Loved One* – perhaps, in 'God knew how long', to become a Christian artist like Evelyn Waugh.

VII

In 1946 Waugh began reading Henry James (D 663). One fruit of this new source of pleasure is Dennis Barlow's recognition that in his relations with Aimée he has 'become the protagonist in a Jamesian problem', a confrontation between 'American innocence and European experience' (LO 105). Remarkably, Waugh often insisted that this strand of *The Loved One* was the central one: he told Peters that the story 'should not be read as a satire on morticians but a study of the Anglo-American cultural impasse with the mortuary as a jolly setting', and Cyril Connolly that its main theme was 'the Anglo-American impasse' (HRC E555, L265). There had been many tales about Americans abroad; *The Loved One* is among the first of a literary kind that was to grow increasingly popular after the war: stories of Englishmen (in Malcolm Bradbury's title of 1965) *Stepping Westward* to America.

Nervous that *The Loved One* might alienate American customers, Waugh had toyed with the idea of publishing only in Britain. (Peters, who disliked the tale, advised publishing nowhere.) But Waugh knew that dismissive comments about America – of which the novel's most extreme instance is Ambrose Abercrombie's remark, 'Wonderful country, splendid lot of people, but no one who was really fond of dogs would bring one here' (137) – were a sure way to recapture highbrow approval in both countries. Then as now, American intellectuals were quite used to, even eager for, satires on American uniformity and materialism (and on Hollywood). In both America and England, *The Loved One* enjoyed more widespread critical understanding than had any other of his novels.

The Loved One's concern with Anglo-American relations also reflects their uneasy state in the late forties. The topic was everywhere as Britain found itself, no longer a great power, increasingly dependent on its American allies – a 'very ignoble thing', Ernest Bevin said in 1947, even while working to further that alliance through such means as NATO (Porter 272). The heyday of the New Deal past, Americans were suspicious of the Britain's new socialist government; Britons were inevitably both grateful and resentful as America, which seemed not to acknowledge the depth of England's wartime sacrifices, offered loans but (before Marshall aid) only on the harshest terms. Britons could not but be fearfully curious about the nation which seemed so successfully to be exporting not only its produce but its 'way of life'. Analyses such as *The American People: A Study in National Character* (1948), a work of cultural anthropology by Geoffrey Gorer (a British student of Margaret Mead), became English best-sellers. 'A generation ago', Waugh wrote in a 1949 essay that cites Gorer, developments in America 'caused mild amusement as the eccentricities of a likeable but remote people. Today they are studied as portents of the development of the whole world' (EAR 380).

Efforts to understand America were in part efforts to understand the road Britain itself was travelling, attacks on America a way to register discontent with such changes. The TLS made clear (in the only review to notice its concern with science, the engine of American mass culture) that *The Loved One* directed its satire not only at the United States but Europe as well:

> In this age of materialism, dominated by the principles of Marx, Freud or Henry Ford, dissident writers have taken refuge either in a well-bred irony derived from James or more recently in religion. The growing strength of the new school of Roman Catholic writers, of whom Mr Evelyn Waugh must be claimed as one, suggests that the humanism of Mr Forster and his followers has proved an inadequate weapon against the attacks of the Philistines, armed as they now are with both philosophy and science. The time has come again for the transcendental answer.... Mr. Waugh has gone to the country where man has achieved his greatest material triumphs in order to expose the hollowness of the pretensions of modern civilization as a whole.
>
> (CH 304, 306)

If the America of *The Loved One* is spiritually dead, Britain, as Dennis says, is 'dying' (121); the parallel between *The Loved One* and the 'near future' imagined in *Love Among the Ruins* suggests a belief that socialist Britain would soon overtake America in many of the same directions of change. Long before *The Loved One*'s attack on the uniform mediocrity of American products and people, Waugh complained (like Angela Lyne) of a decline of skilled craftsmanship in England brought on by the war and accelerated afterward; *Love Among the Ruins* imagines a near future in which nothing is well made and nothing works.

Waugh's anti-Americanism had always been in part a fashionable pose, and though he was capable of such grand gestures as smashing a hotel window to protest American air-conditioning, repeated visits changed his attitudes to the United States. In 1949 he criticized V. S. Pritchett for indulging 'the prevalent distaste for Americans', adding that 'It is interesting to observe the stages by which in recent years the mild derision of an ancient civilisation for the *parvenu* has been transformed into the rancour of the under-dog snarling at its bene-factor'. He told an interviewer in New York who recalled George Orwell's claim that if he 'had been rude to America in *The Loved One*', *Scott-King* was 'equally rude to Europe': 'Not equally. People said I was harsh toward America. Not at all. I was harsher toward Europe. I've more despair for Europe than for America. There's much more wrong *there* than here'.[54] Such comments were not mere efforts to please American customers. 'New York was delightful', he wrote Diana Cooper; 'I have come round to your love of it' (DC110). Waugh's views changed especially during his second and third American trips, spent gathering information for one of his most ambitious essays, 'The American Epoch in the Catholic Church'. With Randolph Churchill's help, Waugh per-suaded the ardent convert Clare Booth Luce of *Life* to pay $5000 for an essay intended, like many other recent pieces by Catholic visitors to America, to inform 'European Catholics about the character of their future leaders'.[55]

On these visits Waugh lectured to and interviewed Catholics in New York, Boston, Baltimore, Chicago, St Louis and New Orleans; he got as far west as Milwaukee and north to Canada. He made new friends (such as Anne Free-mantle, with whom he corresponded for years after and who in 1960 wrote a memoir of their contacts), and met others with whom he had previously corre-sponded.[56] He was especially eager to meet Dorothy Day, a founder of the Catholic Worker Movement, and to observe her work feeding New York's poor. (Long afterward, Day recalled meeting the author she had admired, who for all his differing politics promptly made over some of his American royalties to support her organization.)[57] He twice visited Thomas Merton, a Trappist at the monastery of Our Lady of Gethsemani in Kentucky, whose popular auto-biography *The Seven-Story Mountain* he had read when it appeared in America in 1948 and found 'immensely moving' evidence that 'American monasticism may help save the world' (L 283). Tom Burns asked Waugh to edit the book for English publication, a massive task (including cutting about a fifth of Merton's windy text) that he completed, brilliantly, in a week, producing *Elected Silence* (1949). An engaging correspondence ensued in which Waugh offered a grateful Merton literary advice – 'you tend to be diffuse.... It is pattern-bombing instead of precision bombing. You scatter a lot of missiles all round the target instead of concentrating on a single direct hit' – and a copy of Fowler's *English Usage*; despite their manifold political differences, Merton in turn joined the ranks of Waugh's spiritual advisers.[58]

Given its broad scope, 'The American Epoch', though only 6000 words long, took a year to research and three months to write; the result was an immense success when it appeared in *Life* in September 1949 and eight weeks later in *The Month*. Amidst anecdotes of American idiosyncrasies (such as a 'plastic crucifix which, I was assured, had the advantage that you could "throw it on the ground and stamp on it"'), Waugh managed a shrewd survey: of the 'stupendous feat' whereby 'without help from the State – indeed in direct competition with it – the poor of the nation have covered their land with [Catholic] schools, colleges and universities'; of the role of the Irish in the American church ('The problem with the Irish is to guard them from the huge presumption of treating the Universal Church as a friendly association of their own'); and of the special challenge to religious consciences and institutions posed by American secularism ('the neutral, secular State can only function justly by keeping itself within strict limits. It is not for a foreigner to predict how long the government of the United States will resist the prevalent temptation to encroachment. He merely notes admiringly and gratefully that hitherto the temptations have been largely resisted').[59]

Waugh had asked to meet not only 'prominent preachers' but also ordinary believers, especially 'negroes & Mexicans' (L 283), whose 'heroic fidelity' he celebrated: 'honour must never be neglected to those thousands of coloured Catholics who so accurately traced their Master's road amid insult and injury'. A moving passage, soon to be echoed in *Helena*, describes Ash Wednesday in New Orleans:

> The Roosevelt Hotel overflowing with crapulous tourists planning their return journeys. How many of them knew anything about Lent? But across the way the Jesuit Church was teeming with life all day long; a continuous, dense crowd of all colours and conditions moving up to the altar rails and returning with their foreheads signed with ash. And the old grim message was being repeated over each penitent: 'Dust thou art and unto dust shalt thou return'. One grows parched for that straight style of speech in the desert of modern euphemisms, where the halt and lame are dubbed 'handicapped'; the hungry, 'under-privileged'; the mad, 'emotionally disturbed'. Here it was, plainly stated, quietly accepted, and all that day, all over the light-hearted city, one encountered the little black smudge on the forehead which sealed us members of a great brotherhood.
>
> (EAR 382)

Beyond American Catholicism, Waugh comes close to celebrating 'Americanism' itself:

> Unhappily 'Americanism' has come to mean for most of the world what a few, very vociferous, far from typical, Americans wish to make it. The peoples of other continents look to America half in hope and half in alarm.... There is a purely American 'way of life' led by every good American Christian that is point-for-point opposed to the publicized and largely fictitious 'way of life' dreaded in Europe and Asia. And that, by the Grace of God, is the 'way of life' that will prevail.
>
> (EAR 387–8)

The passage is remarkable, coming only fifty years after the series of repudiations by Leo XIII, a figure Waugh deeply admired, of democracy, liberty of conscience and separation of church and State that culminated in Leo's wholesale condemnation of theological 'Americanism' in the letter *Testem benevolentiae* (1899).[60]

Waugh's new attitude rested as much on political as religious grounds. 'The U.S.A'., in the words of the publicity flier for his 1949 visit – the year NATO formed – 'is assuming leadership of the "West"' (ST2 235). Whereas in 'Compassion' (1949) it is British officialdom that rescues the Jews of Begoy, in *Unconditional Surrender* (1961) their liberators become 'a private charitable organization in America' (UC 302). From Yugoslavia and Greece to Vietnam, Waugh supported America in the Cold War, even its decision in 1956 not to assist Anthony Eden (whom Waugh called simply 'Jerk') in Suez (L 477–8). 'Don't want to be published at all by communist countries', he told Peters in 1949; 'They might use *Loved One* as anti-American propaganda' (L 295). These Cold-War commitments hover in the background even of *Helena*, published in the midst of the Korean conflict. 'There's the split between East and West, which is almost topical', he told Harvey Breit (1957, 148–9). The strife of Helena's time seemed to parallel world affairs in 1950:

> Poetry was dead and prose dying. Architecture had lapsed into the horny hands of engineers....An enormous bureaucracy was virtually sovereign, controlling taxation on the sources of wealth, for the pleasure of city mobs and for the defence of frontiers more and more dangerously pressed by barbarians from the East. The civilized world was obliged to find a new capital.
>
> (EAR 408)

In 1958 Waugh condemned the Museum of Modern Art's famous travelling show *The Family of Man*, a tendentious collection of photographs of vulgar American comfort set beside portrayals of poverty elsewhere, as 'flagrant anti-American propaganda' (L 504). As the new culture of the 1960s swept Britain, he argued that 'Americans are immensely the superiors of the English' in matters of etiquette (EAR 591); he refused an offer from *Esquire* for an article on the 'crudeness' of American writers on the ground that they were far more 'literate' than their young English counterparts (HRC E1299). Once a symbol of sterile uniformity, America became for Waugh the bastion of his cherished 'individuality' and 'diversity'. 'It is delightful to be reminded that "our cousins across the Atlantic"', he wrote in an enthusiastic review of Leo Rosten's stories, 'are, very few of them, Colonial Dames and Daughters of the Revolution', but instead comprise mainly 'Kaplans and Mitnicks, Tarnovas, Plonskys, Matsonkases and Rodriguezes. It makes that enigmatic people very much more loveable'.[61]

8

The Post of Honour is a Private Station
(1948–53)

'You don't understand modern politics, mamma. There are no private lives nowadays.... When the historians come to write of me, they will say that if I wish to
live, I must determine to rule.'

'Oh *history*. I've read quite a lot sitting alone here year by year. Keep out of
history, Constantine. Stay and see what I have done, the clearing and draining and
planting. That is something better than history.'

Helena (1950)

I have never gone into public life. Most of the ills we suffer are caused by people
going into public life.... I have raised a family and paid such taxes as I find
unavoidable. I have learned and practised a very difficult trade with some fair
success.

Campaign speech, Edinburgh University (1951)

By 1948 Waugh had re-established a social life nearly as active as that he
enjoyed when first bursting on the literary scene in 1928–30. A stream of old
and new friends visited Piers Court, whose decoration proved a continuing
source of pleasure; the London social season revived, and with it his extended,
boozy stays in the Hyde Park Hotel. His family grew – James was born in June
1946, Michael Septimus in July 1950 – as did his correspondence, charities and
efforts at proselytization.

'To live in the past is very expensive' says a character in Orwell's *Coming Up for
Air*, 'you can't do it on less than two thousand a year' (19). 'I go out shopping after
luncheon a bit tight & buy such peculiar things', Waugh wrote to Nancy Mitford
from London: 'a 1/2 ton marble 2nd Empire Clock' and for 200 guineas 'a solid
silver 1830 candelabrum as tall as myself'.[1] When in early 1948 John Betjeman
found some 'very dark 1860 Gothic' wallpaper too funereal for his taste, Waugh

17 Piers Court: family group in the Greek folly (Private Collection).

18 Piers Court: the 'Edifice' that Waugh hoped to decorate with human skulls (Hulton Getty).

quickly bought it for use in a guest room (whose woodwork he painted a sharply contrasting pink). 'Please come & stay when the room is finished. It will be a nightmare' (L 267). He shopped for narrative paintings of his favourite period – 'I really only like pre-Great-Exhibition post-Waterloo art' (L 270) – and acquired Karl Swoboda's *The Connoisseurs* and Robert Musgrave Joy's pair, *The Pleasures of Travel, 1751* and *1851.* (Joy's first painting depicts a stage-coach robbery, the second the comforts of Victorian railway travel; Waugh commissioned Robert Eurich to produce a companion piece, *The Pleasures of Travel 1951*, showing in gruesome detail the passengers in an aeroplane about to crash.) Soon he could boast a collection including works by Joy, Swoboda, Rossetti, George Smith, Holman Hunt, Arthur Hughes, Augustus Egg, John Atkinson, Rebecca Solomon,

19–20 Robert Musgrove Joy, *The Pleasures of Travel 1751* and *1851* (Private Collection).

21 Richard Eurich, *The Pleasures of Travel 1951*, commissioned by Waugh in 1952. From beneath the clergyman's newspaper slides a copy of the new Penguin edition of *Decline and Fall* (Private Collection).

22 The dining room at Piers Court (*Country Life*).

Richard Cooper, Van Vitallius and Zurbarán. In 1949, he turned his attention to the gardens, hiring a firm to have his grounds 'made much uglier at terrible expense' (L 300). There sprang up serpentine walks, a fernery and two follies: a ruined Greek temple, its Ionic columns artfully disposed in various states of decay and a grotto (known in the family as 'The Edifice'). To embellish the last he advertised in the *Tablet, Country Life* and *The Times* for human skulls – but was unable, he told interviewers, to acquire the skull of the editor of the *New Statesman* (Allsop). He equally regretted bidding too low at a local house-sale for 'twelve eight foot Caesars in marble bustos' (DC 125).

Into this world were invited a stream of visitors: the Hollises, Woodruffs, Cyril Connolly, Graham Greene and Catherine Walston, Patrick Kinross, Maurice Bowra, Ronald Knox and Camilla and Christopher Sykes. In 1946, the Waughs met their neighbours Frances and Jack Donaldson, who though socialists became lifelong friends and frequent guests. Years later, in an effort to rebut hostile obituaries, Lady Frances would publish *Portrait of a Country Neighbour* (1968), a thoughtful profile of Waugh the father and friend, full of stories such as Waugh's suggestion to his daughter Teresa during a sight-seeing tour that included the tomb of Henry VIII, 'Yes, you may spit on that'. The children were taught to chant when passing local houses: blessings on those in parental favour ('God bless Colonel Brown. They shall prosper that love him. Peace be within his walls and prosperity within his palaces'), maledictions on reprobates such as the owner of a local condom factory (Donaldson 46, 41). When old enough to dine downstairs, the children were encouraged to tease guests and entertain the table with prepared speeches (always beginning, by family tradition, with the formula, 'Unaccustomed as I am to public speaking …'). Indulgent but demanding, Waugh adopted what he called the role of 'Victorian paterfamilias', happiest when the children returned to the nursery or, later, to their boarding schools. But he was also unusually able to enter into their games and happy to take on the task ceded by Laura of corresponding when they were away, crafting playful letters any child might delight in receiving.

In 1948, Fr D'Arcy introduced Philip Caraman, SJ, the new editor chosen to revitalize *The Month*. Waugh immediately offered, for free, the unpublished 'Compassion' (meanwhile telling the BBC it couldn't afford to commission a story from him). Caraman became a frequent visitor to Piers Court, sometimes saying Mass there for the family. That year, too, Waugh got to know Pamela Berry and Laura's distant cousin Ann Charteris, Lady Rothermere (later Ann Fleming), famous as a hostess who might on one evening insist that her guests speak only Latin, on another that they stand atop her dining table and sing. Both women joined Nancy Mitford and Diana Cooper in the ranks of Waugh's well-placed gossipy correspondents. He revived his old friendship with Daphne Vivian, now Marchioness of Bath, visiting often at Longleat (where he also saw Olivia Greene, impoverished and partly mad, living with her mother in an outbuilding on the estate).

The most unexpected friendship of these years was with George Orwell, a relation of mutual admiration that grew into friendship during the last year of Orwell's life. Despite political differences, their opinions converged on matters from what Orwell called the 'emotional shallowness' of the Left ('They take their cookery from Paris and their opinions from Moscow') to the betrayal of Mihajlović in Yugoslavia; even before the war, Catholics scented in Orwell a potential ally in the crusade against Communism.[2] They discussed each other's work with manifest pleasure and respect.[3] Orwell sent Waugh copies of both *Animal Farm* and *1984*; surviving letters between them indicate a larger correspondence perhaps now lost. ('I think your metaphysics are wrong', Waugh wrote on receiving *1984*. 'You deny the soul's existence....The Brotherhood which can confound the Party is one of love'.) They first met when Connolly arranged a visit to Orwell (then reading through Waugh's works for a 5000-word article for *Partisan Review*) in hospital; Waugh reported that he thought Orwell – probably because of his physical suffering – 'very near to God'.[4]

Waugh's often extraordinary generosity extended especially to fellow-Catholics and fellow-writers: Moray McLaren and Alfred Duggan owed their careers and, both thought, their lives to him. McLaren gratefully recounted Waugh's spiritual and financial intervention during the period of his despair after the war, including a letter that read simply, 'You must be very hard up; I am not. Here is a cheque. Cash it and forget about it' (WM 27–8); Waugh guided the impoverished Duggan into the new career of historical novelist, puffed his works in the *Spectator* (18 Nov. 1955, 667–8) and raised money for his widow. In the same spirit, he continued to hound non-Catholic friends to consider conversion, efforts that bore fruit in 1947, when he stood godfather to Elizabeth Pakenham and in 1948, when a long theological correspondence with John Betjeman unexpectedly precipitated the conversion of his wife Penelope.[5] Catholic friends who strayed – especially Clarissa Churchill, Winston's niece, who in 1952 married the divorced Anthony Eden outside the Church – found themselves recipients of anguished remonstrances (L 378–82).

I

Waugh's life of St Helena, mother of Constantine and 'inventor' (i.e., discoverer) of the True Cross, was at last finished in March 1950 and published that October. Fifteen years had passed since the visit to Palestine which had suggested the idea for such a 'semi-historic, semi-poetic fiction' (HP 2), five since he began writing: the longest he ever worked on a novel. The short book chronicles sixty years, from Helena's pagan youth to her pious old age. For the details of life in the fourth century Waugh had read widely and consulted authorities both Jewish and Christian; John Betjeman supplied information about Anglican churches dedicated to Helena, his wife Penelope (to whom the novel is dedicated) details about girls' sexual pleasure in horseback riding.

Waugh thought the result a 'MASTERPIECE' (L 312). Its dust-jacket proclaimed, 'Technically this is the most ambitious work of a writer who is devoted to the niceties of his trade'; he told Sykes 'It's far the best book I have ever written or ever will write' and repeated the assertion for years after, telling a series of baffled interviewers that of all his novels *Helena* was the 'best written', on 'the most interesting theme'. According to Harriet Waugh, *Helena* was 'the only one of his books that he ever cared to read aloud to the whole family'.[6]

Reviewers, Aubrey Menen noted, 'disagreed violently' about the book; none of Waugh's novels so clearly demonstrated what W. G. Allen called the 'handicap' of having 'two quite different reading publics'. The Catholic press shared Waugh's judgment: both Menen and Fr D'Arcy hailed a 'masterpiece', 'a model for a new sort of novel' in an otherwise uncreative period.[7] But except for John Mortimer's guarded praise in the *Sunday Times* ('Admit, while you are reading this book, his point of view and you may conclude, as I do, that it is his finest achievement'), notices in what Waugh called the 'rationalist press' ranged from tepid to vitriolic. Philip Toynbee wondered why Waugh had troubled to write such a trifling '*opera bouffe*' at all, since had he lived in Rome he would have embraced not the Christianity of the slaves but the paganism of the emperors; Henry Reed complained that 'Every eighteen months or so, right in the centre of our ravaged literary scene, Mr. Waugh is plumped down before us, a halo on his head, a scowl on his face; and up goes a hierophantic chorus'.[8] 'Most of the reviews I have seen have been peculiarly offensive', Waugh wrote to Graham Greene. Christopher Sykes believed that the 'indifferent reception given to what Evelyn believed to be by far his best book was the greatest disappointment of his whole literary life'.[9]

Undeterred, Waugh pressed Sykes to arrange a radio dramatization of the novel for the BBC Third Programme, aired in December 1951. Flora Robson read the role of Helena, John Gielgud Constantine. The evening before, Waugh himself offered an introductory commentary: 'The book was not as popular as I had hoped. Several frankly inquired why I had written it. This evening I will try to give my reasons' (ST2 300). Under the title 'St. Helena Empress', his remarks appeared the following January in the *Month* and again as the first half of *The Holy Places*. They eventually inspired Frederick Stopp, a Germanist at Cambridge, to write 'Grace in Reins', a long retrospective review for the *Month* containing the most thoughtful explication any of Waugh's fiction had yet received. Delighted, Waugh wrote to its author; 'Freddie' and Elizabeth Stopp soon visited Piers Court and became family friends. With Waugh's help Stopp eventually produced *Evelyn Waugh: Portrait of an Artist* (1958).

Stopp compared the fulfillment of Helena's quest with Ryder's turn to faith in *Brideshead*:

> Helena's discovery of the True Cross is the avalanche which has been impending all her life. But the special interest of this book is that, by choosing as the central character one about whose life almost nothing else is known but this one supreme, final and yet constitutive act, the author has a clear field in which to build up the total rounded picture of a life and a social and historical setting whose every line of development converges on to that point. Legendary in its beginning and its end, historical in its middle course, the book is a striking representation in artistic form of that living and inherited historicity which is known as the tradition of the Church.
>
> ('Grace in Reins' 76)

Both novels explore the interpenetration of the natural and supernatural, nature and grace, in the lives of characters whose natural instincts lead them to embrace and fulfill divine purpose. Just as he had stressed the teleological patterning of *Brideshead* by having Ryder say not 'I saw Sebastian in Julia' but 'it was Julia I had known in him', Waugh told his BBC audience that Helena 'might claim, like that other, less prudent queen' (Mary Stuart), 'In my end is my beginning' (EAR 408). (Lest we miss the point, Helena is associated at the end of the novel with the island of 'Telos' H 261.) Waugh's artistry consists once again in creating a character whose habits of mind comprise a preparation for and lead by a series of waystations or forerunners to, the unique, unrepeatable act that completes her life and seals her sainthood.

We first see Helena in the schoolroom. Following what Gibbon called the 'recent' legend 'invented in the darkness of the monasteries' of Helena's British origin (Gibbon 1: 403), Waugh makes her the daughter of King Coel, the merry old soul of rhyme. (In the first of the novel's many buried jokes, an old soldier grumbles that Coel – whose orchestra contains 'three strings' – 'lacks Gravity'.) Princess Helena is a practical, common-sensical girl always asking questions, questions that seem childlike to the worldly folk around her: where are the actual ruins of Troy, ancestral home of the exiled Britons? what do the Mithraists believe and on what evidence? How can we know? Her myriad questions suggest an inbuilt yearning for 'something to be sought which she had not yet found' (H 124), for an ideal of whose nature she is as yet unaware. Impatient of fable, she asks always for hard facts. To the purveyors of poetry and mystery she responds, 'Why will no one ever talk plain sense to me? ... All I want is the simple truth' (60), or with a blunt 'Rot' or 'Bosh'; at a highfalutin' lecture on Gnosticism she breaks into giggles. She at last finds her hard facts in the solid baulks of wood on which a historical, not mythical, god died and in this act of discovery 'come[s] to the end of all her questions' (241).

The novel's other characters serve to contrast with Helena's inspired simplicity. Her questing spirit draws her to her husband Constantius, a practical man and constant questioner much like herself. But as she travels from her home to his, increasing her sense of exile, Contantius turns out a lesser man than Helena thought: a 'small, cold soul' whose inquiries aim only at power. 'His need was simple; not today, not tomorrow, but soon, ... Constantius wanted the World' (24). (In one of the novel's many puns, Helena learns of her husband, 'The Divine Aurelian thinks the world of him'; by contrast, once she has found the Cross, Helena 'tells' and 'gives to' the world.) Constantius' 'world' is a much more limited affair than Helena's: he values the Roman Wall for keeping the 'incurable barbarians' out; she asks, not yet fully understanding her own meaning, whether Rome might 'one day break out' and 'all men, civilized and barbarian, have a share in The City' (48). Constantius rises through treachery, murder and magic, in the process destroying Helena's illusions about the grandeur of the earthly Rome she once wished so much to visit. Embodying the 'Power without Grace' she later diagnoses in their son, Constantius is soon murdered.[10]

Midway through the story, in a chapter titled 'The Post of Honour is a Private Station', Helena – middle-aged, divorced and disillusioned, still pagan, her husband dead and son taken from her – thinks her life over. She has moved to Dalmatia, on the Yugoslav coast Waugh knew well, and wishes only to cultivate her estate, advising Constantine on one of his rare visits: 'Keep out of history' (112). But providence has other plans and makes use of the most unlikely instrument: politics. Her life in danger, Helena is hurried off to Trèves; here she meets Lactantius, a Christian who at last gives simple, factual answers to her questions:

> 'Tell me, Lactantius, this god of yours. If I asked you when and where he could be seen, what would you say?'
> 'I should say that as a man he died two hundred and seventy-eight years ago in the town now called Aelia Capitolina in Palestine'.
> 'Well, that's a straight answer anyway. How do you know?'
> 'We have the accounts written by witnesses. Besides that there is the living memory of the Church....'
> 'Well, that's all most interesting'.
>
> (130–1)

Meanwhile Constantine, now emperor, has officially recognized Christianity. In what Waugh (echoing Newman's 1852 sermon on the restoration of the Catholic hierarchy in England) calls a miraculous 'Second Spring', the City at last 'breaks out' as the young Helena had hoped: 'from every altar a great wind of prayer gathered and mounted, lifted the whole squat smoky dome of the Ancient World, swept it off and up like the thatch of a stable, and threw open the calm and brilliant prospect of measureless space'. Among so many others, Helena too converts:

> None knows when or where. No record was made.... Privately and humbly, like thousands of others, she stepped down into the font and emerged a new woman.... She was one seed in a vast germination.... The strong, questing will had found its object; the exile her home.
>
> (140)

'I think from the non-Catholic reader's point of view it's a pity you don't tell about the conversion', wrote Nancy Mitford (NM 205). Waugh pushed Helena's conversion so far offstage not merely because we have no record of the event but to avoid a scene like Marchmain's deathbed, for which *Brideshead* had been so criticized. He also needed to avoid giving the story a premature completion. At this point the woman who began, like Tony Last, in search of a City, has given up on mythic Troy and learnt the corruption of Rome; she has found her true citizenship not in these earthly cities but the Household of the Faith. But her vocation, the end signalled by her beginning, is to be completed only in Jerusalem. (Waugh's working title for the novel was *The Three Quests of the Dowager Empress*.)

In chapter 1 the young Helena's tutor reads to her of her namesake Helen of Troy, who gave up everything for love. In a Homeric passage probably 'the interpolation of a later hand' (in fact Waugh's own), Venus approaches Helen, saying 'Come, Paris is waiting on his carved bed, radiant'. 'Laughter-loving

Venus set a chair for her by the bed' (14). Only in the novel's final chapter, in Palestine, seated on an ivory chair while servants dig, does the aged Helena, guided not by pagan Venus but the spirit of Christian love, find her lover's 'bed' in the carved wood of the Cross. The same sense of love transfigured and consummated is suggested through the novel's frequent references to Helena's horsemanship. In chapter 1, while falling in love with Constantius, she had imagined herself a horse being ridden – a 'symbol of erotic struggle and surrender, of the integration of two natures and two wills in intimate fusion' (Stopp, 'Grace', 83). At the end, having found the Cross, she is the horse once again, now in the service of a divine huntsman: 'Hounds are checked, hunting wild. A Horn calls clear through the covert. Helena casts them back on the scent' (H 265).

To his BBC audience Waugh explained this 'scent', i.e., the importance of Helena's discovery:

> she was not merely adding one more stupendous trophy to the hoard of relics.... She was asserting in sensational form a dogma that was in danger of neglect.... In the academies of the eastern and south-eastern Mediterranean sharp, sly minds were everywhere looking for phrases and analogies to reconcile the new, blunt creed for which men had died, with the ancient speculations which had beguiled their minds and spiced their logic... The situation of the Church was more perilous, though few saw it, than in the days of persecution.
>
> (EAR 409–10)

Gnostic mysticisms were fashionable among intellectuals; theological parties like the Arians debated fine points. The trend is typified by Constantine's silly, vicious wife Fausta, 'an epitome of the high politics of the age', who complains of the Council of Nicaea's refusal to agree with Arius on a point so fine that even Waugh's proofreaders couldn't keep it straight:

> 'You see none of the Western bishops have got a new idea in their heads.... they don't realize they've got to move with the times... "That's the faith we've been taught," they said. "But it doesn't make *sense*," said Arius. "A son *must* be younger than his father." "It's a mystery," said the orthodox, perfectly satisfied, as if that explained everything... . I mean, we must have Progress. Homoiousion is definitely dated. *Everyone* who really counts is for Homoousion – or is it the other way round.... Theology's terribly exciting but a little muddling. Sometimes I almost feel nostalgic for the old [Mithraic] taurobolium, don't you?'
>
> (150–2)[11]

Even Constantine – in his mixture of vanity and despair one of Waugh's finest tragicomic creations – is crazed with symbols and speculation. Just as Fausta (in blasphemously Marian language) thinks herself chosen 'alone among women' as God's 'especial favourite and consort', Constantine speculates that God will 'dispense with all that degrading business of getting ill and dying and decaying' by assuming him directly into heaven. (Assumption into heaven was a lively theological issue when Waugh wrote *Helena*.)[12] 'Everything about the new religion was capable of interpretation, could be refined and diminished; everything except the unreasonable assertion that God became man and died on the Cross; not a myth or an allegory', but 'a matter of plain historical fact' (EAR 410), of which the planks of wood discovered by Helena serve as timeless reminder. 'I bet He's [God's] just waiting for one of us to go and find it', she tells Pope Sylvester, amidst a discussion of Christianity's many new converts, some of whom 'don't seem to believe anything at all', while others make of their religion 'a game of words'; 'Just at this moment when everyone is forgetting it and chattering about the hypostatic union, there's a solid chunk of wood waiting for them to have their silly heads knocked against' (H 209). In finding the Cross, Waugh wrote to Betjeman, Helena 'snubbed Aldous Huxley with his perennial fog' – Huxley's comparative-anthropological argument in *The Perennial Philosophy* (1945) that all religions are variants of a few basic myths – 'by going straight to the essential physical historical fact of the redemption' (L 340).

Helena's contempt for theological speculation is a far cry from Waugh's youthful celebration of 'the science of simplification' in *Remote People*. Though Waugh never stopped arguing that philosophic argument and historical evidences could serve as a foundation for faith – 'I can never understand why everyone is not a Catholic' he told Nancy Mitford in 1949 (L 307) – the supernaturalism of *Helena*, with its stress on the cult of relics (hardly a popular stand in 1950) and on the 'unreasonableness' of Christianity, captures the development in his faith over the years since his conversion. As Helena tells Lactantius, 'It all seems to make sense up to a point and again beyond that point. And yet one can't pass the point' (88). ('Don't follow emotions follow reason', Waugh counselled John Betjeman, immediately adding, 'The final step must be a step in the dark'(L 244–5).) Helena's offstage conversion begins in argument but is completed only by grace, just as in Palestine she finds the Cross not by natural means but only with the help of a God-sent vision of the Wandering Jew.[13] For all the novel's emphasis on historical 'fact', Waugh was quite willing to admit the possibility that Helena's cross might not have been genuine, telling BBC listeners, 'Even so her enterprise was something life-bringing' (EAR 409).

Even sympathetic reviewers were unnerved by the presence in a novel of such evidently pious intent of so many jokes, especially what Waugh called its 'willful, obvious anachronisms', 'introduced as a literary device'.[14] Helena speaks the slang of modern London; the novel's soldiers (and soldiers' wives) recall their counterparts in World War II; in a fine scene, Constantine dresses down a sculptor who is the ancient equivalent of Roger Fry, a 'modern artist' who has nothing but bemused contempt for 'representational work'.[15] Constantine's reflection that historians will say that to live, he had to rule, anticipates by fourteen hundred years Gibbon's remark, 'The throne was the object of his desires; and had he been less actuated by ambition, it was his only means of safety. He was ... sufficiently apprised that, if he wished to live, he must determine to reign'.[16] Explaining his utopian dream of leaving 'imperfect' Rome for a shining new capital in the East, Constantine tells Helena 'I've got the site, very central; it will make a sublime port' (204, punning on the traditional name of the Topkapi Gate, the 'Sublime Porte'). When he off-handedly makes his famous Donation ('Take the place. It's all yours. I am leaving and I shan't come back') a nearby cleric muses, 'But I rather wish we had it in writing all the same' – to which another replies: 'We will, monsignore. We will' (203, 205). On the basis of such passages, the *Christian Science Monitor* concluded that the novel could be read as anti-Christian satire (21 Oct. 1950, 10).

But, as in many more recent historical novels (such as Peter Ackroyd's *Hawksmoor* and John Crowley's *Ægypt*), Waugh's deliberate use of anachronism serves both to point up parallels between past and present and to suggest a perspective from which time itself, as he wrote elsewhere, 'is a human conception & limitation' (L 246). Nowhere is this more clear than in one of Waugh's most daring exercises in generic mixture, comparable to the Brazilian sequence in *A Handful of Dust*: the novel's description of the false witch hired by Fausta to persuade Constantine to murder her in-laws. '[S]uddenly seized by a demon and possessed', the young girl steps 'off the causeway of time' to sing a genuine prophecy. In the tempo of a 'jazz disc', her song begins 'Zivio! Viva! Arriba! Heil!' and in a versified mélange of totalitarian slogans and West-Indian Negro slang foretells the fate of all Power without Grace: 'The world was his baby, but baby got sore'.[17]

Other readers were less concerned to unravel the carefully patterned meaning of Helena's quest than to find evidence of the author's famous snobbery and right-wing politics. According to John Raymond in the *New Statesman*, the author of *Helena* 'took time off from savaging the lesser breeds' to tell the story of one of his favourite character-types, 'the clear-eyed, clean-limbed, daughter of Diana, with a niche in Debrett' who like all his converts 'gets to Heaven the back way, by having the right kind of Nanny'. Waugh let the insult pass, but when Fr Gerard Meath suggested in *The Tablet* that his heroine becomes a saint through 'her aristocratic inheritance' rather than 'the power of the Holy Spirit', he both replied in angry letters and threatened a libel suit.[18]

He had of course deliberately chosen an aristocrat saint. In the spirit of Lady Marchmain's speech on riches he told John Betjeman: 'I liked Helena's sanctity because it is in contrast to all that moderns think of as sanctity. She wasn't thrown to the lions, she wasn't a contemplative, she wasn't poor & hungry, she didn't look like an El Greco. She just discovered what it was God had chosen for her to do and did it' (L 339–40). Though no martyr, Helena does conform to conventional notions of sanctity; critics like Raymond, eager to find evidence of class bias, ignored her humility, which deepens as her rank rises. The young princess loses her pride of family when she leaves Britain; while her husband and son take control of the Roman world, she goes 'privately and humbly' to baptism; as Empress Dowager she chooses 'a single small room among the nuns of Mount Zion where she did her own housework and took her turn waiting at table' (H 140, 227). This side of Helena's character, too, is implicit in her beginning. Her youthful pleasure in consorting with grooms and sailors prefigures what she later experiences when attending a crowded Roman mass: the kind of brotherhood Waugh himself had felt in Mexico and New Orleans and would again in Goa.

A few years earlier Helena would have shrunk from them, would have had a posse of guards whacking and barging to clear a little cloister for her to move and breathe in. 'Odi profanum volgus et arceo'. That was an echo from the old empty world.... The barrow-man grilling his garlic sausages in the gutter, the fuller behind his reeking public pots, the lawyer or the lawyer's clerk, might each and all be one with the Empress Dowager in the Mystical Body.... There was no mob, only a vast multitude of souls.

(H 145–6)

'Others a few years back had done their duty gloriously in the arena. Hers was a humbler task, merely to gather wood. That was the particular, humble purpose for which she had been created' (259–60).

'Evelyn thought *Helena* his most perfect novel', wrote Martin D'Arcy, 'because his own personal thesis was best put forth in it: that God put man on this earth to do a special task'. There was of course nothing unusual in the idea of vocation itself; generations of Catholics (and Protestants) had embraced notions of vocation both general (that common to all Christians) and particular (one's own calling).[19] Waugh's 'personal thesis' was of vocation as a call to a 'single, peculiar act of service', some unique act 'which only we can do and for which we were each created' (EAR 409–10). The idea had been implicit in *The Loved One*; it is first clearly stated in his 1946 attack on Connolly, which refers to 'a particular task for each individual soul, which the individual is free to accept or decline at will and whose ultimate destiny is determined by his response to God's vocation' (EAR 310).

Waugh was fascinated especially by the idea of a heroism in humble tasks, services which though small can give some meaning to a life, some role in the divine plan. Sebastian Flyte cares for the egregious German deserter Kurt; Guy Crouchback succumbs in wartime to a series of false notions of heroic purpose before recognizing and embracing that 'small service which only he could perform, for which he had been created. Even he must have his function in the divine plan. He did not expect a heroic destiny' (US 81). Waugh too developed his idiosyncratic notion of vocation during the war years, when he had so often found himself frustrated and bored, unable to serve – when, as he complained in his diary, his life seemed meaningless and empty, 'without any task' (531). At a low point in 1943, he could write '[I] don't want to influence opinions or events'; 'I don't want to be of service to anyone or anything' (D 548). The cure for Guy's 'emptiness' and 'apathy' is service to Virginia's child and the Jews of Begoy; the thawing of Waugh's own wartime 'ice age' (DC 85) came through his invigorating, signal service at Hubert Duggan's deathbed, followed by the exhilarating months of writing his first explicitly Catholic novel, *Brideshead* – the book that seemed to confirm his new sense of his writerly vocation – and his work in Yugoslavia. Small services, but real and uniquely his own.

The author of *Helena* projects himself into the figure of the Christian convert Lactantius, 'the greatest living prose stylist' of Constantine's silver age, a man who 'delighted in writing, the joinery and embellishment of his sentences, in the consciousness of high rare virtue when every word had been used in its purest and most precise sense, in the kitten games of syntax and rhetoric' (119–20). Lactantius helps bring Helena to faith, just as Waugh had helped Penelope Betjeman – of whose personality, he freely acknowledged, Helena was 'primarily a portrait'.[20]

Elsewhere Waugh was at pains to undermine the 'mysticism of art', stressing how small a service the writer offers: 'The Church and the world need monks and nuns more than they need writers. These merely decorate. The Church can get along very well without them' (EAR 387). But *Helena* allows Lactantius – using another anachronistic pun – to defend his literary vocation as a calling less than that of the martyrs but nonetheless considerable.

> 'It needs a special quality to be a martyr – just as it needs a special quality to be a writer. Mine is the humbler rôle, but one must not think it quite valueless.... You see it is equally possible to give the right form to the wrong thing and the wrong form to the right thing. Suppose that in years to come, when the Church's troubles seem to be over, there should come an apostate of my own trade, a false historian, with the mind of Cicero or Tacitus and the soul of an animal' and he nodded towards the gibbon who fretted his golden chain and chattered for fruit. 'A man like that might ... be refuted again and again but what he wrote would remain in people's minds when the refutations were forgotten. That is what style does – it has the Egyptian secret of the embalmers. It is not to be despised'.
>
> (122)

At the end of the novel Helena's bones are deposited in the church of Ara Coeli, on whose steps 'Edward Gibbon later sat and premeditated his history' (in manuscript, 'his great work of slander') (264). Waugh included not only Lactantius but himself among those for whom Helena prays at Epiphany, in a passage that was a revision of Waugh's own Epiphany meditation made in Yugoslavia in 1945 – and that, Laura said later, Waugh thought one of the best passages he ever wrote (Phillips 95):

> 'Like me', she said to [the Magi], 'you were late in coming.... Yet you ... were not turned away. You too found room before the manger. Your gifts were not needed, but they were accepted and put carefully by, for they were brought with love. In that new order of charity that had just come to life, there was room for you, too...'.
>
> 'You are my especial patrons', said Helena, 'and patrons of all late-comers, of all who have a tedious journey to make to the truth, of all who are confused with knowledge and speculation, of all who through politeness make themselves partners in guilt, of all who stand in danger by reason of their talents'. ...
>
> 'For His sake who did not reject your curious gifts, pray always for all the learned, the oblique, the delicate. Let them not be quite forgotten at the Throne of God when the simple come into their kingdom'.
>
> (H 239–40; cf. above, 223–4)

II

Waugh's 'personal thesis' of special, individual purpose was a source of comfort to a man prone all his life to black melancholy, to a depressive sense of life's featureless emptiness. Since youth he suffered bouts of boredom like those recorded in the three 'Nightmares' of *Remote People* and explored in *Vile Bodies* and *A Handful of Dust*. He always cherished the individual and peculiar as against the mere 'type'; during his attacks of boredom all such distinctions seemed flattened out. His religious faith did not alleviate his melancholy, but only changed its direction.

It is not that Waugh was harrowed by religious doubts, though he doubtless suffered his share of these.[21] Rather it was the firmness of his belief in the unimportance of this life compared with the next which fed his depression, threatening always to convert his responses to the world, either of love or hate, to boredom. 'The Christian writer knows that five minutes after his death it will not matter to him in the least whether his books are a success or not', he told the Newman Society in 1956 (from which it followed, as he told American audiences, that 'artistic integrity is really pride').[22] 'Displeasure takes the shape of boredom with me nowadays', he noted in 1955 (D 737). The same sense of emptiness afflicts all Waugh's subsequent heroes:

> The tiny kindling of charity which came to [Gilbert Pinfold] through his religion sufficed only to temper his disgust and change it to boredom.... At intervals during the day and night he would look at his watch and learn always with disappointment how little of his life was past, how much there still was ahead of him. He wished no one ill, but he looked at the world *sub specie aeternitatis* and found it as flat as a map.
>
> (GP 7–8)

> Depressive doubts ... are common to a certain kind of artist ... but there were also in Ronald [Knox] the seeds of a weakness that was not a matter of mood; not the product of indigestion or influenza or the chill winds of March. The vision of himself *sub specie aeternitatis* threatened and but for his reserves of spiritual strength might have overwhelmed him, with the sense of futility in all his occupations.
>
> (K 247–8)

> As for Guy, he had recognized from the first a certain remote kinship with this most dissimilar man [Ivor Claire], a common aloofness, differently manifested – a common melancholy sense of humour; each in his own way saw life *sub specie aeternitatis*.....
>
> (OG 110)

In this state – 'sadness in the face of spiritual good', as he would define it in a late essay on the sin of 'Sloth' – one loses not belief itself, but its animating energy. 'Love of his fellow men also dies in him'; he is 'Eaten by apathy, self-pity and the sense of futility' (EAR 573–4). The essay supplies a fine analysis of Guy Crouchback, who also 'had no wish to persuade or convince or to share his opinions with anyone' (MA 10). Waugh wrote of himself in 1947:

> my prayers tepid....I have no human contacts here....Mystics spend half their lives in doubt and despondency, half in exultation. How can one claim that one

half is valid evidence and not the other? But to aim at anything less than sanctity is not to aim at all. Oh for persecution!

(D 676)

His letters and diaries from the late forties onward contain numerous prayers for 'charity' and self-lacerating analyses of his lack of it.

Yesterday Laura announced to me that a stone vase had fallen from a pillar on the head of one of my workmen. 'Oh dear is it badly broken?' 'It's bleeding profusely'. 'No no I mean the vase'. This came out quite instinctively. How to reconcile this indifference to human beings with the obligation of Charity. That is my problem. But I am sure that Dickensian geniality is as far from Charity as my indifference.

(DC 88)

Such passages are less atonements for his famous rudeness than efforts made while despondent to kindle some feeling for the life around him, some interest in a world that seemed often to have gone blank. 'Church again', Waugh noted in his diary in January 1954; 'My prayer is now only, "Here I am again. Show me what to do; help me to do it"' (D 722). Soon Guy Crouchback will also pray:

'I don't ask anything from you'; that was the deadly core of Guy's apathy.... That emptiness had been with him for years now, even in his days of enthusiasm and activity.... Enthusiasm and activity were not enough. God required more than that. He commanded all men to *ask*.

In the recesses of Guy's conscience there lay the belief that somewhere, somehow, something would be required of him; that he must be attentive to the summons when it came.... 'Show me what to do and help me to do it', he prayed.

(US 80–1)

The story of a life joyously fulfilled through service, *Helena* is Waugh's only straightforwardly hopeful (indeed cheerful) book. The heroine's emotions spill over even into its descriptions of springtime scenery, the most lavish natural descriptions to be found anywhere in Waugh's fiction. But it is notable that Helena completes her vocation only at the end of a long life, after which she 'sail[s] away, out of authentic history'. Waugh was never able to give satisfying imaginative form to an ordinary, active life of faith, to the life that comes after vocation is recognized. Edmund Campion had the luxury of being martyred young; what awaits Charles Ryder and Guy Crouchback after regeneration is only dimly gestured toward and seems mainly a time of waiting. So Waugh's own life often seemed to him after the war, the process of his maturing – of loss – over:

Yes, I am serenely happy, swathing myself in layers of middle age; the crisis over, the doctor's bag packed, I placidly doing cross-word puzzles at the bedside of the patient for whom all hope has finally been abandoned. After ten years fretfulness I am quite reconciled to the decline of the West.... I am very grown up. All growing pains over. Only prostate ahead.

(DC 82, 84)

III

'Something must be done to protect the holy places, something, also, to accommodate visitors' muses the bishop of Aelia Capitolina toward the end of *Helena* (221). So Pius XII also argued in an increasingly urgent series of encyclicals beginning at the time of Israel's independence in May 1948.[23] The end of the British Mandate brought to Palestine not peace but new fighting between Jews and dispossessed Arabs; the United Nations, which stepped in next, was even less able to resolve conflict than had been the British. Jerusalem was divided, its shrines crumbling. Israel claimed sovereignty over the entire city; Pius called on the faithful to support the United Nations's efforts to enforce its declarations of Jerusalem's international status. *Helena* contained Waugh's first response to that call. He answered it more fully in 1951 with an essay on 'The Defence of the Holy Places'.

The problem of Jerusalem had already surfaced obliquely in *The Loved One*, whose uncharacteristically harsh references to Jews reflect Anglo-American tension over Palestine even before the end of the Mandate.[24] In 1950, Waugh proposed an article on the shrines to *Life*, which readily offered $5000 and engaged Christopher Sykes to produce a parallel article on Turkey. Sykes cheerfully planned the trip while Waugh wrote him notes in their old manner: 'I know what it is you want to stay where you can have women in your rooms you filthy beast well you wont not with me see we are going somewhere respectable with no goings on except a game of cards with a crook or maybe a bit of buggery but no filthiness with women while I am around please make up your mind to that' (L 344). It was the last occasion on which Waugh and his future biographer were in regular contact. The two set out in January 1951, stopping first in Rome, where Waugh tried unsuccessfully to persuade Vatican officials to permit the consecration of a private chapel at Piers Court; for a leisurely month they visited Damascus and Beirut, Tel Aviv and Jerusalem and finally Ankara. By summer Waugh had finished what he thought an especially fine essay, which to his irritation *Life* held back for its Christmas issue. To ensure wide circulation, he arranged for 'The Defence' to appear in 1952 in *The Month* and again as half an elegant limited-edition volume on *The Holy Places*, published by the Queen Anne Press (where Ian Fleming was editor) and dedicated to Frank and Elizabeth Pakenham.

Having closely followed England's struggles under the Mandate, Waugh opposed Zionism. His position was confirmed in 1947, when it became clear that Palestinian Jews were being supported against Britain by Soviet arms funnelled through Czechoslovakia.[25] He thus arrived in Jerusalem in 1951 sympathizing with Palestinian Arabs 'stampeded' from their homes and now living 'in destitution' 'in the wastes of Jordan' (EAR 412). But he quickly came to detest both sides, as he wrote in early February to Laura from the Jordanian zone of the city:

Both Jerusalems are full of huge cars flying UNO flags while both countries starve. Here there are half a million absolutely destitute & hopeless Arab refugees from Israel. Israel, starving & houseless, is importing 25,000 Jews a month from

Mesopotamia, Abyssinia, the Yemen, everywhere. Neither side has any housing & both carefully demolish whole villages where enemies have lived. All are stark mad & beastly & devoid of truth.

(L 345)

In such circumstances, he rightly saw, United Nations efforts were doomed. His essay for *Life* began:

> On one side a people possessed by implacable resentment, on the other by limitless ambition; between them a haphazard frontier determined by the accidents of battle and still, in spite of the truce, the scene of recurrent acts of atrocity and revenge; on that line and cut through by it, the most sacred city in the world.... On 11 December 1948, the General Assembly of the United Nations proclaimed Jerusalem unique and granted it international status.... Now by a double act of aggression as flagrant as the invasion of South Korea, the city has become a battleground temporarily divided between two irreconcilable enemies. One voice only is heard reproaching the nations with their betrayal – the Pope's; but ... [t]he great opportunity has been lost.

(EAR 410–1)

Waugh therefore used the essay mainly to plead for the shrines, especially the 'supreme treasury': the Church of the Holy Sepulchre (where he and Sykes had been profoundly moved by an all-night vigil), now 'visibly falling to pieces'. Under the intricate arrangements of the 'Status Quo', various faiths – Latins, Greeks, Abyssinians, Armenians – all had rights in the dilapidated church; none was able to undertake its reconstruction. Some suggested the structure be levelled to make way for separate churches for each. At the end of his essay, in a passage described by one reviewer as 'profound to the point of inspiration',[26] Waugh condemned this plan as false to the nature of the Christian community, full of faults and fiercely divided, but still essentially one:

> One has been in the core of one's religion. It is all there, with all its human faults and its superhuman triumphs and one fully realizes, perhaps for the first time, that Christianity did not strike its first root at Rome or Canterbury or Geneva or Maynooth, but here in the Levant where everything is inextricably mixed and nothing is assimilated..... Our Lord was born into a fiercely divided civilization and so it has remained. But our hope must always be for unity and as long as the Church of the Sepulchre remains a single building, however subdivided, it forms a memorial to that essential hope.

(EAR 420)

At the end of February 1951 Waugh returned to a nation preparing for the Festival of Britain, whose 'monstrous constructions', the modernistic Dome of Discovery and Skylon, Guy Crouchback watches rise on the south bank of the Thames at the end of *Unconditional Surrender*. Many were suspicious of the project, at least before its gates opened in May: the *Daily Express* debated the propriety of spending ten million pounds on a 'socialist extravagance' at a time of war and economic hardship; Sir Thomas Beecham called it 'a monumental piece of imbecility and iniquity'. Noël Coward sang in 'Don't Make Fun of the Fair':

> Take a nip from your brandy flask,
> Scream and caper and shout,
> Don't give anyone time to ask
> What the Hell it's about.

(Frayn 322)

Waugh's contributions to the 'Festival spirit' included a sour letter to *The Times* (24 May, 5), veiled satire in an unmarketable story called 'A Pilgrim's Progress' (later to become *Love Among the Ruins*) and a BBC broadcast making fun of the National Book League's exhibition at the fair of the 'hundred best books' by contemporary authors. He castigated the atheism and socialism of the League's judges and – a view he would raise often in coming years – the general poverty of current writing. 'There are no towering geniuses whom they have ignored'; 'We happen now to have struck a bad patch' (EAR 400).

In October, for a lark, Waugh agreed to stand for election as Rector of Edinburgh University. His qualifications, he asserted in his sole campaign speech, were merely 'negative': 'I have never gone into public life' (EAR 406). He seems to have taken less interest in the other elections of that month, wherein after six years of Labour rule the Conservatives, under the slogan 'Set the People Free' (from the socialism that had 'stopped, stifled, even strangled' Britain's economic recovery from the war), were returned with a narrow majority and Winston Churchill once again became Prime Minister. Angela Thirkell celebrated the Conservative victory by naming her novel for 1951 *Many Happy Returns*; many of Waugh's friends were passionately involved in the campaign. Peter Fleming's *The Sixth Column*, published in the summer of 1951, was an elaborate propaganda effort to persuade voters to reject a regime of 'more restrictions on enterprise, more temptations to the enterprising to become dishonest in order to get round the restrictions, more bogus equality, more and more security until it's illegal as well as unnecessary to take a risk'.[27]

Withdrawing from public causes, Waugh ignored both the campaign and its result. After the 1945 elections he had spoken of living to 'see the Restoration' (L 263), but by 1951 he recognized that a change of government would bring no real change in policy. For all his campaign talk about the need to 'roll back' socialism, Churchill himself argued in his first major speech after reassuming power that what the nation needed was 'several years of quiet steady administration, if only to allow socialist legislation to reach its full fruition' (Porter 280–1). To congratulations on the election results, Waugh replied fiercely, 'The Conservative Party have never put the clock back a single second' (Donaldson 15); he predicted to Nancy Mitford, 'Now that there is a tiny Conservative Majority, the persecution of the rich by the politicians will be greatly intensified so that they can display class impartiality' (L 358). That the Conservative government largely continued Labour policies soon became a commonplace. Just as journalists coined the word 'Butskellism' (conflating outgoing Labour

Chancellor Hugh Gaitskell and his Tory Successor R. A. Butler), *Love Among the Ruins* imagines a Welfare Britain of the near future ruled by a Tory-Labour Coalition.

IV

In 1951 Waugh's mind was not on elections but the novel which for years he had planned as the culmination of his career. He had long hinted that the events of the Second World War merited 'a place in literature' and had not yet received 'the epic treatment they deserve' (EAR 320, 321). The public learned of his plan only in 1949, when an assistant editor of the *New York Times Book Review* got the scoop that he intended 'a novel or two novels about the war', 'a study of the idea of chivalry' (Breit 1956, 45). Friends knew earlier. 'I have two shots in my locker left', he told Nancy Mitford in 1946, 'My war novel and my autobiography. I suppose they will see me out' (L 238). In the spring of 1951 he reread his wartime diaries; in June, on a visit to Chantilly to be near Diana Cooper, he began 'scribbling away hard at my maximum opus', provisionally titled *Honour*. 'I think it is frightfully funny. A bad sign' (L 356).

That summer Anthony Powell published *A Question of Upbringing*, the first novel in his sequence *A Dance to the Music of Time*; soon Waugh was also reading Ford Madox Ford's '*very* good' novels of World War I (DC 127), *The Good Soldier* (1915) and the tetralogy *Parade's End* (1924–8), both of which suggested ideas for *Sword of Honour*. Waugh, too, planned a series of 'four or five' novels, as he told Clarissa Churchill, 'which won't show any shape until the end' (L 363–4). Treating the same period as *Put Out More Flags* (from 1939 through the Phoney War to Dunkirk), *Men at Arms* appeared in September 1952 with the notice that it was the start of a trilogy. It was to be 'the first comic turn of a long music-hall show', he told Ann Fleming, 'put on to keep the audience quiet as they are taking their seats. If I ever finish writing and if anyone ever reads, the succession of volumes that I plan to follow it, it will make some sense' (L 379–80).

A review of J. F. Powers's *Prince of Darkness* written early in 1949 (at about the same time he began 'Compassion') had as much as announced what would be the trilogy's central theme:

> 'Prince of Darkness' is a magnificent study of sloth – a sin which has not attracted much attention of late and which, perhaps, is the besetting sin of the age. Catholic novelists have dealt at length with lust, blasphemy, cruelty and greed – these provide obvious dramatic possibilities. We have been inclined to wink at sloth; even, in a world of go-getters, almost to praise it. An imaginative writer has advantages over the preacher and Mr. Powers exposes this almost forgotten, widely practised, capital sin, in a way which brought an alarming whiff of brimstone to the nostrils of at least one reader.
>
> (EAR 374)

Waugh's later essay on 'Sloth' (written in 1962 for a *Sunday Times* series on the seven deadly sins) defines the sin itself:

> What then is this Sloth which can merit the extremity of divine punishment?

St. Thomas's answer is both comforting and surprising: *tristitia de bono spirituali*, a sadness in the face of spiritual good. Man is made for joy in the love of God, a love which he expresses in service. If he deliberately turns away from that joy, he is denying the purpose of his existence. The malice of Sloth lies not merely in the neglect of duty (though that can be a symptom of it) but in the refusal of joy. It is allied to despair.

(EAR 573)

Men at Arms introduces Guy Crouchback as a man who even before the outbreak of war feels as had Waugh when he wrote in 1943 of 'dissociating myself very largely with the rest of the world'. 'Destitute, possessed of nothing but a few dry grains of faith', Guy has 'no wish to persuade or convince or to share his opinions with anyone'; we hear from the start of his 'old despair' and at the end of his 'increasing sloth' (MA 32, 11, 296).

Into that wasteland where his soul languished [Guy] need not, could not enter. He had no words to describe it . . . . There was nothing to describe, merely a void . . . . It was as though . . . he had suffered a tiny stroke of paralysis.

(MA 7)

'Even in his religion he felt no brotherhood'. Like Waugh, he sometimes 'wished that he lived in penal times'; in the manner of R. H. Benson's *Lord of the World*, 'Sometimes he imagined himself serving the last mass for the last Pope in a catacomb at the end of the world'.[28] Joining a crusade against 'the Modern Age in arms' seems to offer an opportunity for service, for commitment to a cause larger than himself.

Reviews confirmed Waugh's fears that *Men at Arms* alone might not give an adequate sense of the trilogy's direction. He introduced Guy on the dust-jacket as 'a romantic, spiritually crippled and socially isolated, numbed and desiccated by previous misfortune' who enlists because he 'sees in war the hope of personal revitalization'. But the pattern of disillusion and regenerative suffering that over the trilogy brings Guy from isolation to charity and an active faith is barely visible from *Men at Arms* alone, which ends with Guy still mired in romantic illusions of soldiering. It would be two years before Stopp, in 'The Circle and the Tangent', an essay written with Waugh's help, offered the first sustained critical exploration of the novel's main concerns.

The war would revitalize Guy, Waugh told his biographer, but only ironically, by bringing him to the 'realization that no good comes from public causes; only private causes of the soul' (Stopp, *Portrait*, 46). ('*Men at Arms* was a kind of uncelebration. Guy has old-fashioned ideas of honour and illusions of chivalry; we see these being used up and destroyed by his encounters with the realities of army life' (Jebb 112).) Meanwhile the long lapse of time before further volumes appeared – three years for *Officers and Gentlemen*, six more for *Unconditional Surrender* – meant that few readers approached subsequent volumes with a clear sense of what had come before. Consensus that the trilogy (in Cyril Connolly's phrase) constitutes 'the finest novel to come out of the war' (CH 430) would emerge only after Waugh's death.

Nor does *Men at Arms* suggest the brilliance of the volumes to follow. Despite his confidence while starting to write, Waugh soon developed 'a sad suspicion that it is very dull' (DC 118): that his jokes 'about WCs' went on too long and that the whole was 'slogging' and 'inelegant' (L 366, 363). In February 1952 he told Graham Greene: 'I finished that book I was writing. *Not* good. Of course all writers write some bad books but it seems a pity at this particular time' (when, the *Brideshead* money exhausted, he wanted another best-seller). 'It has some excellent farce, but only for a few pages. The rest very dull. Well, the war was like that' (L 370). Most of all he worried that his story was 'all falling to bits' – that its main theme was getting lost in a thicket of minor characters and situations (L 365). The last point was quickly made in a shrewd review by Connolly, still smarting from a presentation copy inscribed 'To Cyril, who kept the home fires burning'. (He had served during the War as a fire-watcher.) Dull 'beer' rather than Waugh's usual 'champagne', Connolly declared (CH 337), a judgment with which Waugh agreed: 'You ... have clearly defined all that I dislike in the book. "Beery" is exactly right' (L 383). His consolation was 'that there is simply no competition these days', when 'in any branch of literature from detective stories to theology, we are reading precisely the same writers as we were reading eighteen years ago' (EAR 421). 'My unhappy novel is having the reception it deserves – large sales and sharp criticism' (DC 143). No other part of the trilogy was so much trimmed in the one-volume *Sword of Honour* of 1965.

In writing *Men at Arms* Waugh did not yet know exactly how the sequence would work itself out. One plan was to follow up with a second volume on Dunkirk. He advertised for and questioned men who had been present there, but the effort was 'useless'; 'I should have realized that one cannot live other people's experiences'.[29] A general outline of the whole was nonetheless clear in his mind from the first. The story 'changed a lot in the writing', he said in 1962, but 'both the sword in the Italian church' (the sword of the failed crusader Roger of Waybroke, to whom Guy dedicates himself at the start of *Men at Arms*) and the sword of Stalingrad (symbol in *Unconditional Surrender* of the war's failure as holy public crusade) were 'there from the beginning' (Jebb 113). From the start Waugh planned Guy's crusade, like Sir Roger's, as a failure, but a fortunate failure that would breed private spiritual regeneration. In January 1954, even before completion of *Officers and Gentlemen*, he specifically excluded 'Compassion' from republication in *Tactical Exercise* (a collection of stories for the American market) on the ground that it would 'form part of Vol III' (HRC E846-7).

Further evidence of Waugh's sense of the trilogy's larger design comes in a letter of September 1952, replying to Connolly's review: 'all the subsidiary characters, like "Trimmer" & "Chatty Corner" & "de Souza" will each have a book to himself. Anyway the theme will see me out – that is the humanizing of Guy' (L 383). *Men at Arms* carefully establishes the characters of Trimmer ('marked for ignominy', 'he was the only member of the batch whom Guy definitely disliked'), cowardly and opportunistic Ian Kilbannock and the 'cynical' de Souza, all important in later volumes (MA 48-9). The letter to Connolly also makes clear Waugh's plan to conduct the whole by detailing Guy's interaction with a series of characters who mirror parts of himself: who embody his various illusions, dangerous tendencies, and saving possibilities. In *Men at Arms* Guy is made to resemble three other characters: his older brother Ivo, his father and his fellow-officer Apthorpe.

'The character of the Crouchback family', Waugh told the journalist W. J. Igoe, is one 'of withdrawal from the world, at its lowest in mad Ivo, at its highest in the father' (and, presumably, in Guy's nephew Tony's later decision to become a monk) (L 571). Between these alternative versions of the family trait lies Guy's reclusiveness and failure of sympathy for others – his spiritual sloth. For eight empty years since his wife Virginia deserted him, from 1931 to 1939, Guy has lived alone in Italy, 'deprived of the loyalties which should have sustained him', celibate in a villa which to the rest of the family has been 'a place of joy and love' (MA 4–5). His Italian neighbours do not find him 'simpatico'; even his plantings fail to grow. In this spiritual void he is haunted by the memory of his brother Ivo, who in 1931 went mad through an 'excess of melancholy', barricaded himself alone in a room and starved himself to death. 'Guy and Ivo were remarkably alike'; 'Ivo's death sometimes seemed to Guy a horrible caricature of his own life' (17, 12). Ivo's despair and suicide point an extreme example of where Guy's own sloth might lead if not converted through faith to better uses.

That conversion comes in later volumes as Guy learns to emulate another character he already resembles physically: his saintly old father, a man of 'tolerance and humility' (MA 34) and unfailing piety. 'Despite the forty years that divided them there was a marked likeness between Mr. Crouchback and Guy' – except for the old man's 'expression of steadfast benevolence', which in Guy is 'quite lacking' (33). Waugh explained in his jacket copy: 'The abiding values which co-existed with and survived all the political clap-trap' of the war years 'are personified in the hero's father'. Old Mr Crouchback's function in the trilogy, he told Stopp, was 'to keep audible a steady undertone of the decencies and true purpose of life behind the chaos of events and fantastic characters. Also to show him as a typical victim (parallel to the trainloads going to concentration camps) in the war against the Modern Age' (*Portrait* 168).

But the character Guy most resembles in *Men at Arms* is his 'doppel-gänger' (128) Apthorpe, who gives his name to the novel's three sections: 'Apthorpe Gloriosus', 'Apthorpe Furibundus' and 'Apthorpe Immolatus' (the triumph, lunacy and slaying of Apthorpe). He is Guy's equal in age (thirty-six in 1939, the same age as Waugh) and joins the Halberdiers on the same day; both are called 'Uncle' by younger officers; lamed by similar knee injuries, the two become 'like a pair of twins' (116). With his collection of arcane field gear and odd bits of military knowledge (reminiscent of Alastair Trumpington's fascination with swords and Sam Browne belts in *Put Out More Flags*), Apthorpe embodies the most immature side of Guy's self-understanding and search for fellowship in the army.

Like boys at play, Apthorpe and Guy vie with their Brigadier, the fantastic Ritchie-Hook, for control of Apthorpe's 'thunder-box' (antiquated military slang for an antique field latrine), a possession that suggests the outdatedness of the military ideals of all three, indeed their reversion to a kind of infantile stage. For Guy the games of the thunder-box, 'those mad March days and nights of hide-and-seek', supply happy 'childlike memories' (193); Apthorpe, tucked up in a 'high collapsible bed', resembles 'a great baby in a bassinette' (204). At his most Apthorpean, Guy temporarily adopts moustache and monocle, making himself look, he thinks, 'every inch a junker'. (The 'rolled gold' of the monocle and its 'false leather purse' parallel the 'faery gold' of Apthorpe himself (129, 131).) But as the war grows serious – as the Phoney War gives way to Dunkirk – Apthorpe's fantasies look more and more like dangerous lunacy; he is eventually revealed as a fraud and killed (accidentally) by Guy, his death signalling the end of an illusion and an important stage in Guy's maturation.

In all this *Men at Arms* recapitulates the movement of Book I of *Brideshead*. Like Charles Ryder with Sebastian, Guy experiences with the Halberdiers 'something he had missed in boyhood, a happy adolescence' (MA 50). The novel as a whole is structured as a series of regressions which enable later progress. On enlisting Guy comes boyishly to 'love the whole Corps deeply and tenderly' (58) and thereby to suppose that a 'ghost had been laid ... which had followed him for eight years'; 'that airy spirit could never again block him, he thought' (102). At this early point in his development Guy confuses lesser goods with greater, the army with that true fellowship that can come only through renewed religious faith (and that alone will eventually lay his 'ghost').

> In youth he had been taught to make a nightly examination of conscience and an act of contrition. Since he joined the army this pious exercise had become confused with the lessons of the day. He had failed dismally in the detail of the pilearms.... There was much to repent and repair.
>
> (MA 63)

Only in *Officers and Gentlemen* will Guy begin 'to dissociate himself from the army in matters of real concern' (OG 161) – to distinguish means and ends, soldiering from the demands of the spirit.

The Halberdier barracks to which he is sent after first joining the army, Guy realizes in hindsight, was the site of 'his honeymoon, the full consummation of his love' for the Corps (MA 91). From its camaraderie and comforts he is next moved for training to the dismal Kut-al-Imara House, Southsand, a disused school. Here during a chilly Lenten season Guy finds 'the Preparatory School way of life completely recreated', first experiences military inefficiency and suffers momentary doubts.[30] But on Ash Wednesday the stern but playful form-master Ritchie-Hook reappears armed with collapsible spoons and dribble glasses and preaching the military art of 'biffing' and booby-traps. Ritchie-Hook takes over training himself, leading Guy in another regression to succumb again to 'the old, potent spell' of the military. So powerful is this 'big magic' that he tries while on leave (ironically, on St Valentine's Day) to seduce his ex-wife Virginia. (Two volumes later, when Virginia asks what led to the attempt, Guy answers accurately, 'That wasn't love'; 'Believe it or not, it was the Halberdiers': US 186.) The result is a finely realized scene, strategically placed at the centre of the novel, of Guy's humiliating rejection. But as in *Brideshead*, lesser goods lead to greater and providence makes use of the unlikely instruments to educe good from ill. A fortuitous series of drunken phone calls from Apthorpe derails the seduction that, if successful, would have delayed Guy's spiritual progress.[31]

In a third regression, Guy returns after his humiliation by Virginia to Southsand, which now seems 'a place of solace'. 'Hotel and Yacht Club would shelter him, he thought.... Mist from the sea and the melting snow would hide him. The spell of Apthorpe would bind him and gently bear him away to the far gardens of fantasy' (166). There follows the sequence of the thunder-box, then, after further disappointments, the raid on Dakar – the 'Operation Truslove' Guy has fondly imagined in terms of 'gloriously over-Technicoloured' movies (always in Waugh a sign of illusion) and his boyhood reading.[32] For his courageous participation in the raid Guy earns only a black mark with the Corps; in a final scene, his kindness in bringing the customary bottle of whisky to Apthorpe in hospital results in Apthorpe's death and a yet deeper black mark.

Though Apthorpe's death marks the end of Guy's most youthful illusions of military comradeship and heroism, *Men at Arms* leaves its hero still far from spiritual maturity. He has learned to say 'Here's how' while drinking with fellow-soldiers, but a final scene with a Goan steward, a Catholic towards whom Guy's 'heart suddenly open[s]' (277) but with whom he can establish no human contact, makes clear how far he has still to travel on the road to charity as he 'crouches back' to a living faith like his father's. Even the adulterous, ironically named Virginia, a descendant of Brenda Last, seems by comparison not a callous betrayer but generous, warm-hearted, sympathetic – all that Guy is not.

Reviewers were frankly confused. The novel's dedication 'To Christopher Sykes, Companion in Arms' suggested lightly veiled autobiography, a work to be read as John St John read both *Put Out More Flags* and *Men at Arms*: as gentle, even loving satire on army life. It was equally possible to find the novel a celebration of military heroism (the first instalment of a story in which the brotherhood of army life *succeeds* in revitalizing Guy); or a parable of the need to replace secular values with higher ones; or simply a celebration of the 'unequalled dottiness of the English'.[33] Even the *Tablet*'s friendly reviewer argued obtusely that 'Guy's slightly self-conscious Catholicism is a distraction from the main theme of the novel' (13 Sept. 1952, 211).

'On the whole *Men at Arms* is good-tempered Waugh', wrote John Raymond in the *New Statesman*, 'and therefore Waugh at his second best'. Raymond noted as well the presence of Waugh's 'newer and more irritating mannerisms': 'Why ... must his characters be forever splashing each other with holy water?' (CH 339). Critics further to the Left were more forthright: 'too elementary for adult belief' (Edwin Muir); 'an orgy of adolescent sentiment' – 'Let God look after the well-being of the Anglo-Catholic aristocracy and let Evelyn Waugh, to the delight of his readers, return to their follies' (Joseph Frank). Delmore Schwartz revelled in contempt:

Waugh appears to be saying to the reader: I see the stupidity, foolishness and triviality of human beings just as much as you do, but I draw a different conclusion:

human beings are ridiculous without religious belief and they are just as ridiculous when they are possessed by religious belief, but at least when they are truly religious, they have a touching, pathetic, bewildered quality which makes possible a little compassion amid one's overwhelming contempt. If this is all that Catholicism means to Waugh, then any old religion and any old myth would serve as well and as vainly; and since it is all the meaning it has in his recent novels, no great fantasy is required to read them as the fiction of an *agent provocateur* in the pay of a society for the propagation of atheism ..... [T]he daring and the gaiety of the books which made Waugh justly famous, have been succeeded by what can only be described as a bored titter.[34]

As the first volume of what was clearly intended as a major work, *Men at Arms* seemed to demonstrate that the old Waugh was gone forever, that the master had lost or abandoned his satiric gift. The novel won the James Tait Black prize ('£185 free of tax – I have to earn about £800 to get that'), but in the main, Waugh noted of his reviews, 'I am coupled always (greatly to my honour) with Hemingway as a "beat up old bastard"' (DC 160, 143).

V

The chief villain in *Scott-King* and *Helena* was 'politics'; *Men at Arms* began a long fictional demonstration that 'no good comes from public causes'. Soon Waugh would celebrate Gilbert Pinfold's catacomb mentality, his policy of 'burrow[ing] ever deeper into the rock' (GP 6). The early fifties saw Waugh's last efforts at direct intervention into public political affairs: what he liked to call his 'Tito Tease', and, after two years of revisions, publication of *Love Among the Ruins* (1953).

In September 1952, Foreign Secretary Anthony Eden met in Yugoslavia with Tito, then enjoying enthusiastic Western support (including generous financial and military aid) for his break with Stalin. Later that autumn, Churchill and Eden invited Tito to make a state visit to England. Appalled, Waugh wrote to Peters: 'Would any popular paper print an article from me abusing Eden for inviting Tito here? If they would, the price would not be important provided I could be as truthful as I liked in the words I liked' (HRC E770). 'Our Guest of Dishonour', run on the front page of the *Sunday Express* on 30 November, succeeded beyond his hopes in sparking national, even international debate.

After a summary of the Yugoslav situation as he had known it in 1944 (Tito 'was busy then, as now, in the work for which he has a peculiar aptitude – hoodwinking the British') and brief reference to the postwar bloodshed whereby Tito solidified his regime, Waugh rises to magisterial contempt:

Do [politicians] really suppose that Tito, who has betrayed in turn emperor, king, friends and finally his one consistent loyalty to Stalin, will prove a trustworthy friend to *them*? ... there is a loyal multitude of Her Majesty's subjects who recognize in him one of the six or seven most deadly and most powerful enemies of all they hold holy. Tito is seeking to exterminate Christianity in Yugoslavia. ... Our leaders are properly cautious of offending religious and racial minorities. Mr Eden would not invite the country to feast and flatter a notorious Jew-baiter. Only when Christianity is at stake do our leaders show bland indifference.[35]

23 Anthony Low cartoon provoked by Waugh's 'Tito Tease' of 1952–3. Evelyn Waugh and Graham Greene appear in the lower left (*Manchester Guardian*/Bodleian Library, Oxford).

In the context of official refusal to admit wartime mistakes and Cold War enthusiasm for any chink in the Soviet armour, Waugh's was a heroic statement. Government spokesmen defended Eden; the Left defended Tito. Waugh followed up with interviews, a half-dozen letters to editors and a public lecture at Glasgow organized by the Catholic Truth Society to 'over 3000 people [who] paid cinema prices to proclaim their disapproval' of Tito's visit (DC 161). Waugh found himself for the first time the subject of political cartoons; even the foreign press took notice. In America, *Time* praised his efforts and observed that he was soon joined by Archbishop Cambell of Glasgow, who called Tito a 'modern Nero', and Bishop Heenan of Leeds, who threatened that Tito would receive 'a warm reception in this country'; even softspoken Cardinal Griffin allowed himself to be quoted: 'To say that we find it difficult to understand why this invitation was extended is an understatement'.[36] Soon Waugh received letters of support from 'Christians of all denominations all over the country'.[37] Graham Greene weighed in on his side, as did some hard-line Stalinists such as James Klugmann, who used the occasion to continue the attack on the Marshall's deviationism which he had begun in *From Trotsky to Tito* (1951).

Tito's visit – his first trip outside Yugoslavia since 1948 – went forward without incident and amidst great public acclaim. Lord Fisher, Archbishop of Canterbury, was 'photographed beaming benevolently at a man who, in an overwhelmingly

Christian country, had just abolished the Christmas holiday' (Beloff 151). Waugh had once again served as witness, awakening some consciences and embarrassing some in the government; it was a superb farewell performance. In 1954 the *Express* group offered him 100 guineas for a leader attacking Nehru's visit to London, in 1956 for another on a proposed visit by Khrushchev. Waugh refused both offers, commenting on the second occasion that the visits of Tito and Khrushchev were not parallel. In the case of Tito, 'an imposture was being attempted on the British public by representing Tito as a gallant ally when in fact he had been a treacherous enemy and as a liberal statesman when he was in fact a doctrinaire Marxist persecuting the Church in a way of which the general public were kept ignorant'. Khrushchev by contrast was a professed foe: there is 'nothing unchivalrous about eating with open enemies'.[38]

In May 1953, while the nation celebrated the coronation of Elizabeth II, Waugh pointedly stayed at home, declining an offer of £250 to report the event.[39] He was disgusted by popular talk of a 'new Elizabethan age': 'rebunking', said the author of *Campion*. He had finished *Love Among the Ruins* (begun as *A Pilgrim's Progress*) the previous winter, but mischievously delayed publication until the day before the coronation; he had his own copy bound in sheets of coronation stamps. Subtitled *A Romance of the Near Future*, the novel joined many other nervous diagnoses – Henry Green's *Concluding* (1948), Aldous Huxley's *Ape and Essence* (1949), Orwell's *Nineteen Eighty-Four* (1949), Koestler's *Age of Longing* (1951) and Fleming's *Sixth Column* (1951) – of how the war and its aftermath were changing Britain and Europe.

   Product of three years' intermittent but painstaking work, *Love Among the Ruins*, though slender, is like *Helena* among Waugh's most highly finished, densely allusive novels. It was also his first to suffer near-total critical failure. Various versions were rejected by the *Atlantic, Colliers, Cosmopolitan, Esquire, Flair, Harper's, Ladies' Home Journal, Life*, the *New Yorker*, the *Saturday Evening Post* and the *Sunday Times*; alone of his finished novels it was never published separately in America, appearing only in the anthology *Tactical Exercise* (1954).

   The tale opens at Mountjoy Castle on a 'rich, old-fashioned Tennysonian night': 'In the basin the folded lilies left a brooding sweetness over the water. No gold fin winked in the porphyry font and any peacock which seemed to be milkily drooping in the moon-shadows was indeed a ghost, for the whole flock had been found mysteriously and rudely slaughtered a day or two ago'. Waugh echoes the most famous portion of Tennyson's *The Princess*:

   Now sleeps the crimson petal, now the white;
   Nor waves the cypress in the palace walk;
   Nor winks the gold fin in the porphyry font....
   Now droops the milkwhite peacock like a ghost....
   Now folds the lily all her sweetness up....

Succeeding passages self-consciously recall Shakespeare, Emerson, Tacitus and – aptly for a story about a world like that of *The Loved One*, sterile, loveless and

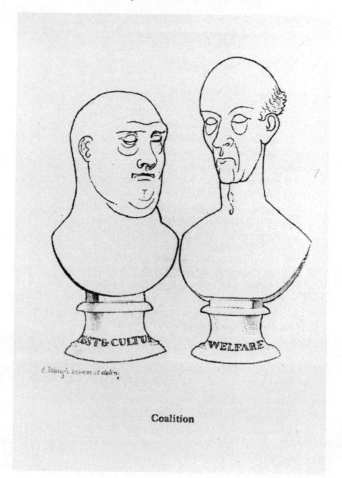

Coalition

24 Waugh's drawing for *Love Among the Ruins* (1953) of the plain-spoken Minister of Rest and Culture and the stiffly formal Minister of Welfare.

dead – Seneca on suicide.[40] The novel's opening descriptions of the weather – despite the best efforts of the 'State Meteorological Institute', 'The weather varied from day to day and from county to county as it had done of old, most anomalously' – draw on R. H. Benson's *Lord of the World*, as do its descriptions of state-sponsored euthanasia.[41] As Sykes noted, Waugh's socialist 'near future', in which even the family is bureaucratized – and orphans are a specially privileged class – pays homage as well to Max Beerbohm's parody of H. G. Wells in *A Christmas Garland* (1912), whose hero hopes for a 'Provisional Government of Female Foundlings', a brave new world of 'progress' wherein classical education is eradicated, the calendar decimalized and secularized and at age ninety all

25 Chancellor of the Exchequer Sir Stafford Cripps and Foreign Secretary Ernest Bevin (during wartime, Minister of Labour) (1949) (Times Newspapers Ltd).

citizens voluntarily enter a 'Municipal Lethal Chamber'.[42] Finally there are Waugh's illustrations, collages created with scissors and paste from engravings after Canova. Nearly all are ironic transformations of their originals. Waugh's frontispiece illustrates his hero and heroine Miles and Clara as Canova's Cupid and Psyche, but in a world that frustrates love, Cupid/Miles has lost his wings; a later illustration of the hospital where at Christmas-time Clara has an abortion borrows from Canova's '*Annunciation*'.[43] One illustration is entirely Waugh's own: his portrait of the Ministers of 'Welfare' and (in language reminiscent of Soviet bureaucracy) 'Rest and Culture', who look (and sound) suspiciously like Sir Stafford Cripps and Ernest Bevin.

The novel's density of literary, historical and religious allusion ironically counterpoints its evocation of a culture in decay because it has wilfully broken with all sustaining traditions. In 1948 Waugh mourned the passing of a shared culture that once provided a 'common ground' of communication for 'men of opposed views to discuss their differences intelligibly', but which modern education had eroded; he voiced concern over the loss of such 'cultural literacy' increasingly as he grew older.[44] His very title recalls both Angela Thirkell's 1948 novel of postwar austerity and Robert Browning's verse tale of a shepherd who surveys the ruins of a once-powerful city, come to grief because it did not value love. 'Love is best', Browning concludes; Waugh's civilization of the future, through its failure to preserve traditions of value, robs its citizens of the capacity for love.

Like that other 'new-born monster to whose birth ageless and forgotten cultures had been in travail' (the new King's Thursday of *Decline and Fall*), Miles Plastic, 'typical of a thousand others', embodies the culmination of history:

> The State had made him.
> No clean-living, God-fearing, Victorian gentleman, he; no complete man of the renaissance; no gentil knight nor dutiful pagan nor, even, noble savage. All that succession of past worthies had gone its way, content to play a prelude to Miles. He was the Modern Man.
>
> (LAR 5)

The 'Bevan–Eden Coalition' has ushered in the omnicompetent two-class state of workers and civil servants, a world wherein breakfast consists of 'State sausages' fried in 'State grease', and clothing (recalling the 'utility' fashions of wartime) is restricted to a uniform 'drab serge'. Psychology has replaced religion – 'on the first Friday of every month' children are 'psycho-analysed'.[45] Christian festivals linger only in folklore, like the 'obscure folk play' about 'maternity services before the days of Welfare' performed on 'Santa Claus Day'. Just as Britain's post-war governments launched the construction of massive New Towns, the landscape of *Love Among the Ruins* is covered with 'satellite cities', each centred on a glass-and-concrete 'Dome of Security' (a swipe at the Festival of Britain's Dome of Discovery, its modernist style suggestive also of civic architecture in what the Minister of Welfare calls 'our Great Neighbour to the East'). This new Britain is the culmination of twenty years of Leftist dreams:

> The Director [of the Euthanasia Centre] was an elderly man called Dr Beamish, a man whose character had been formed in the nervous '30s, now much embittered, like many of his contemporaries, by the fulfilment of his early hopes. He had signed manifestos in his hot youth, had raised his fist in Barcelona and had painted abstractedly for *Horizon*; he had stood beside Spender at great concourses of Youth and written 'publicity' for the last Viceroy. Now his reward had come to him.[46]

In such a spiritually dead world, 'personality' is merely a certificate and 'love' (now replaced by mandatory 'sex education') a word 'seldom used except by politicians and by them only in moments of pure fatuity' (29). In compensation the State offers its 'welfare-weary citizens' free euthanasia – a lively topic in the early fifties[47] – though as money grows short it considers charging for the service (as in 1949 Labour imposed charges in the Health Service).

Love Among the Ruins opens with Miles Plastic serving a prison sentence for arson. A long history of penal legislation and reform drew Waugh back to the themes he had raised through Sir Wilfred Lucas-Dockery a quarter-century before.[48] Because in the new penology of Welfare 'there are no criminals', 'only the victims of inadequate social services' – 'it was a first principle of the New Law that no man could be held responsible for the consequences of his own acts' – convicts are sentenced not to hard labour but to the pre-Welfare luxury of

Mountjoy ('Malfrey' in manuscript, the Sothill's house from *Put Out More Flags*), where as restitution for earlier deprivation they undergo a rehabilitative regimen of classical music and 'remedial repose' (8, 10). Suddenly declared cured, Miles is torn from these splendours so that he may take his first step as a civil servant on the 'non-competitive ladder'.

Like Dennis Barlow in *The Loved One*, the spiritually starved and maimed Miles falls immediately in love with a woman all unlike her surroundings: Clara is beautiful, cherishes in the paintings she has inherited from her mother a few fragments of the better world before Welfare, and oddest of all, wishes to continue living. With her unwilling arrival at the Euthanasia Centre, 'hope appeared'. She is also an artist: 'it's just because I could dance that I *know* life is worth living. That's what Art means to me'.[49] But like Aimée Thanatogenos's, Clara's is a decadent aestheticism. Because 'you can never dance really well again after you've had a baby', she has tried to have herself sterilized through a surgical procedure Waugh calls – after the Communist Jack Klugmann – 'Klugmann's Operation'.[50] The failed operation's only effect is her golden beard – like the operation that caused it, a distortion of human nature, but another difference from other women that attracts Miles. When she becomes pregnant by him, Clara chooses art over life, modernity over love and human nature. In the central scene of the novel, she aborts their child and through a second surgical procedure disposes of her beard by having the skin of her face replaced with plastic. The result is an unsettling image reminiscent of *The Loved One*: 'something quite inhuman, a tight, slippery mask, salmon pink' that 'takes grease-paint perfectly'.[51]

It is the third time Miles has been betrayed by love and beauty – seduced into hoping that life might have something to offer beyond Welfare, then brought up short. On growing up he was thrust by the bureaucracy into a job washing dishes at an Air Force training facility; after prison, into emptying waste-baskets at the Euthanasia Centre. But 'he had known better than this. He had known the tranquil melancholy of the gardens at Mountjoy. He had known the ecstasy when', in his first act of arson, 'the Air Force Training School had whirled to the stars in a typhoon of flame' (21). Now, betrayed by Clara, his child killed, Miles reacts in the only way his stunted nature knows: by destroying his betrayer, the source of hope that has caused him only pain. He sets fire to Mountjoy.

> The scorched-earth policy had succeeded. He had made a desert in his imagination which he might call peace. Once before he had burned his childhood. Now his brief adult life lay in ashes; the enchantments that surrounded Clara were one with the splendours of Mountjoy; her great golden beard, one with the tongues of flame that had leaped and expired among the stars.... He ate his sausage with keen appetite and went to work.
>
> (LAR 43)

Beauty destroyed, Miles seems wholly 'cured' of his brief excursion into humanity and hope. 'The conditioned personality recognized its proper pre-ordained environment'; 'The Modern Man was home'. But in a final sequence, his small, starved spark of humanity reasserts itself. He has been recruited by the bureaucracy to marry a hideous Miss Flower and tour the country lecturing on model prisons:

> In perfect peace of heart Miles followed Miss Flower to the Registrar's office.
>   Then the mood veered.
>   Miles felt ill at ease during the ceremony and fidgeted with something small and hard which he found in his pocket. It proved to be his cigarette-lighter, a most uncertain apparatus. He pressed the catch and instantly, surprisingly there burst out a tiny flame – gemlike, hymeneal, auspicious.
>
>   (LAR 51)

The lighter's 'uncertainty' frames the 'anomalous' weather with which the novel began. In neither case can the State bring nature wholly to heel. Human nature – love – will out, though in the world of Welfare its only outlet be an 'ecstasy' of destruction.

9

Retrospective: Shaping a Life
(1953–1966)

Some kind reviews of *Love Among the Ruins*. Most positively abusive. . . . Everyone on the watch for declining powers.

Diary, 5 June 1953

There is no unanimity as to the exact moment of my decline; some put it eight, some twenty-five years ago, some this month.

'Mr. Waugh Replies' (1953)

Very soon, perhaps the next time I write a book, I shall be humiliated by the lack of interest shown and shall look back on these as years of plenty.

Diary, 25 June 1955

It is the season when American tourists persecute me. They have fallen in numbers with my fall from fame.

Waugh to Ann Fleming, 2 Sept. 1959

This novel . . . lost me such esteem as I once enjoyed among my contemporaries.

Preface to *Brideshead Revisited* (1960)

This book found favour with the critics who date my decline from it.

Preface to *A Handful of Dust* (1964)

Even though he still writes, [Waugh] offers mainly a period interest. He is essentially a pre-war novelist, and the post-war interest in him is a kind of hangover, a nostalgic reaction, socially, but not critically, interesting.

Graham Martin, *Penguin Guide to English Literature* (1961)

'My life ceased with the war', Waugh told Nancy Mitford in 1954. 'When I have squeezed the last thousand words out of that period I shall have to cast back to my still unravished boyhood' (L 432). Family responsibilities, the years of austerity, and simply growing up conspired to end the life of adventure that had nourished his earlier fiction. There would come again in the events that led to *Gilbert Pinfold* (1957) what Waugh had found at Forest Lawn, the uncovenanted blessing of experience suitable for novelization; he would also write two more major works of non-fiction, *Ronald Knox* (1959) and *A Tourist in Africa* (1960). But Waugh knew the war novel – product of fifteen years of thought, from 1945 to 1961 – would be his *maximum* as well as *magnum opus*. He called it 'Operation Lifetime' (DC 141); in 1958, after finishing *Knox*, he wrote to his agents that he had 'only a year or two ahead' of 'original work'. 'Soon I shall have to jump at every chance of writing the history of insurance companies or prefaces to school text-books'; 'while I have any vestige of imagination left, I must write novels' (L 507).

Waugh was only fifty-four when he made this (correct) assessment that he had but a few years of novel-writing left. He already thought himself 'an elderly writer' (L 536), the representative of a passing generation; and he had long predicted that he would not live much past sixty.[1] In the 1950s such predictions were fortified by growing physical ills: arthritis, rheumatism, sciatica, rotting teeth, deafness, and the cumulative effect of three decades of heavy drinking and drugs to combat 'insomnia, the occupational disease of writers' (K 238). It took half a week to recover from trips to London, binges that ended, he complained, in sending flowers to hostesses in apology for drunken behaviour whose details he couldn't recall.

Waugh's writing now becomes self-consciously the work of an old man, full of references to the different world of his youth, 'years and years ago' (EAR 508). It was a role he had long planned for and determined, so far as possible, to enjoy. He always nurtured a strong sense of the duties and foibles appropriate to each of life's stages. His first essays on youth, with their strident claims that 'Elderly people should not make themselves ridiculous by pretending to belong to the younger generation', argued that it was not the task of the old to 'keep up' or 'stay young', but precisely to do the duty of the old; a 1962 essay on etiquette argued that 'In normal civilizations it is the old who are the custodians of the tribal customs. It is their duty to transmit them. The young can enjoy flouting them until they themselves age'.[2] The principle extended from social to literary behaviour. The 'Brain-Wain-Amis' school of novelists, he told an interviewer in 1960, 'have never had the faults of youth, which should be pretentiousness, affectation, over-embellishment, the use of recondite words, all being fined down by discipline and developing taste to good prose'.[3] For himself, age meant the creation in *Knox*, *Unconditional Surrender* and *A Little Learning* of the finely chiseled prose, simple yet lapidary, whose 'carefully outmoded elegance', as Anthony Burgess said, 'evokes an England of firmer tastes and more powerful convictions', fixing 'the writer at an immovable frontier, administering the laws of a dead empire' (CH 471).

Even debility provided opportunity to embellish his persona. 'I am quite deaf now', he wrote in 1953 on losing the hearing in one ear; 'Such a comfort' (L

396). Arthur Waugh had used an ear-trumpet; in *Brideshead*, Sebastian writes to Charles: 'There are too many people here, but one, praise heaven! has an ear-trumpet, and that keeps me in good humour' (BR 40). Eager to acquire such an object himself, Waugh advertised in *The Times* and in 1956 selected a blackened tin Edwardian model, seventeen inches long when extended. 'My ear trumpets are a great convenience and a great success socially' (DC 234). He made sure photographers captured this symbol of the impasse between himself and the modern world, and at a luncheon marking *Pinfold*'s publication snubbed Malcolm Muggeridge by pointedly lowering the contraption when Muggeridge began a speech, raising it when he ended.

The public persona Waugh had laboured to create was now well established in the national mind. Much of his work depends on readers' recognizing it – most of all *Gilbert Pinfold*, but also lesser works such as *Tourist in Africa*, which reflects of a group of nuns who 'did not seem notably joyous': 'But who am I, of all people, to complain about that?' (TA 30). Magazines and newspapers ran a steady stream of 'profiles' and reviews; the briefest of meetings with him spawned articles; there was copy in his agreeing to give an interview, his children's travel plans, even his favourite parlour games.[4] Publicity was good for business, and to the end of his life Waugh presented a formidable front to the world. But in the early 1950s there lurked behind that front a growing depression, rooted in ill health, declining finances and fears – exacerbated by increasingly hostile reviews – that, as *Pinfold* puts it, he might be 'written out'.

'My poverty is very irksome', he wrote to Nancy Mitford; 'It is often in my mind' (L 354). In 1950 David O. Selznick's idea for a film of *Brideshead* from a screenplay by Graham Greene seemed to promise rescue, but the plan collapsed. There had been Laura's £6400 overdraft; the Inland Revenue began inquiries into his past earnings, and in 1951 demanded six years' unpaid supertax on film contracts and 'expenses'. Such setbacks spelt retrenchment. His account with Little, Brown stood at over $50,000 (subject to tax upon disbursement), but he was haunted by fears of soon being unable to support his family. The heyday of Piers Court was over.

Peters visited Stinchcombe in January 1952 to offer counsel, writing soon after: 'if you can maintain a spending figure of £4000 a year, as I am sure you can, the reduction of your standard of living need not be quite so drastic as you think. You should be able to keep a reasonable staff to run the house and still come out square. The hardest thing of all is to pay back income tax out of current earnings. That is practically impossible' (ST2 302). Waugh complained half jokingly to Nancy Mitford:

So I have been doing sums for weeks & find I am hopelessly ruined (financially *not* morally). So I have come to a Great Decision to Change my Life entirely. I am sacking all the servants (five does seem a lot to look after Laura & me in a house the size of a boot) and becoming Bohemian. I shall never wear a clean collar again or subscribe to Royal Lifeboat Fund and I shall steal peoples books & sell them & cadge drinks in the Savage Club by pretending to know you. It is no good trying to live decently in modern England. I make £10,000 a year, which used to be thought quite a lot. I live like a mouse in shabby-genteel circumstances, I keep no women or horses or yachts, yet I am bankrupt, simply by the politicians buying votes with my money.

(L 365)

He reduced his staff to two dailies; to make money quickly he accepted work on a screenplay from Carol Reed, had his library valued for sale to the trust, and inquired whether the Queen Anne Press might print a collection of his journalism under the title *Offensive Matter.*

To his description of *Men at Arms* as a 'bad book', Graham Greene had responded loyally: 'You're completely crazy when you think it is not up to the mark – I think it may well be the beginning of your best book' (ST2 308). But in two years the novel sold only 19,000 copies – a fiftieth of the sale of *Brideshead*. Then came *Love Among the Ruins*, which for all its thinness took three years to complete, earned practically nothing, and despite respectful expressions of disappointment from friends such as Cyril Connolly (and positive enthusiasm from the TLS) unleashed a new flood of hostile criticism. 'I have been much upset by violent & inaccurate abuse in the Beaverbrook press', he wrote to Christopher Sykes in June 1953 (L 404), and in the same month uncharacteristically answered his attackers in an article for the *Spectator* entitled 'Mr. Waugh Replies'.

'Reviewers can greatly encourage or cruelly wound a young writer, perhaps also a very old one, fearful of failing powers'. Claiming an exception for himself (as 'middle-aged'), 'Mr. Waugh Replies' proceeds with remarkable objectivity to 'examine the work of the modern reviewer in the single light of my own latest book which has been pretty generally condemned'. Its chief exhibits are Nancy Spain's comment in the *Daily Express* that on reading *Love Among the Ruins* she 'yawned and yawned and yawned'; Milton Shulman's prediction in the *Sunday Express* that in future only snobs would enjoy his books (this, Waugh notes, although *Love Among the Ruins* is his only novel 'in which there appears no member of the upper class, either as buffoon or heroine'); and most personally offensive of all, George Malcolm Thompson's review in the *Evening Standard*, which assembled the remarkable bill of complaint: Waugh dislikes oysters; is 'sensitive about his short stature'; resembles 'an indignant White Leghorn'; is a 'prig'; advocates slavery. His peasant ancestors left the Church of Scotland because the Scots stopped burning witches. Thompson came to the novel itself only in his final sentences: 'Some of the illustrations to *Love Among the Ruins* are by the author. They are not very good either'. Waugh scented conspiracy: 'This unanimity of the Beaverbrook press is striking. All abuse, not so much my little book, as me, in terms which, used of a coal-miner, would precipitate a general strike'.[5]

Such notices could not but erode confidence, though once again Waugh took comfort in knowing that even his lesser works stood out at a time when, as Stephen Spender said in 1953, 'the novel seems to have halted'. 'The great thing is that there is simply no competition these days', he reflected often while awaiting reviews of *Men at Arms*.[6] His generous tributes to younger writers such as Angus Wilson, Muriel Spark and V. S. Naipaul stressed the rarity of their talent. 'Our whole literary world is sinking into black disaster', he told the

Newman Society in 1956; 'I am sure that those who live for the next thirty years will see the art of literature dying'.[7]

Among those new works he did *not* praise were such products of 'the Movement' and the 'Angry Young Men' as John Wain's *Hurry on Down* (1953), Kingsley Amis's *Lucky Jim* (1954), and John Braine's *Room at the Top* (1957). Beginning in 1955, Waugh became well known for attacks on what he called the 'Amis-Wain-Braine' school, 'the modern Teddy-boy school of novelist & critic', and 'l'École de Butler' ('the primal men and women of the classless society' who swelled the universities thanks to the Butler Education Act).[8] Waugh's sneers were neither the first nor the most violent insults traded between established senior authors and an equally hostile younger generation who celebrated the 'provincial' above the 'metropolitan', attacked the 'country-house school' in fiction, and called for novelists to come to terms with the new reality of the Welfare State. Already in 1953 Spender cited a literary 'rebellion of the Lower Middle Brows' – 'class-conscious young people' led by an 'inferiority complex' to oppose all things 'stylish' or 'classy', 'concerned not with inventing values of life, but with communicating information about their working-class origins, or the Red Brick University' (where as teachers they 'equate literature with sanitary engineering').[9] In a retrospective review of *Lucky Jim* for the Christmas 1955 issue of the *Sunday Times*, Somerset Maugham famously proclaimed:

> *Lucky Jim* is a remarkable novel. It has been greatly praised and widely read, but I have not noticed that any of the reviewers have remarked on its ominous significance. I am told that today rather more than sixty per cent of the men who go to the universities go on a government grant. They are the white- collar proletariat. They do not go to the university to acquire culture, but to get a job, and when they have got one, scamp it. They have no manners and are woefully unable to deal with any social predicament. Their idea of a celebration is to go to a public house and drink six beers. They are mean, malicious, and envious. They will write anonymous letters to harass a fellow undergraduate and listen in to a telephone conversation that is no business of theirs. Charity, kindness, generosity are qualities which they hold in contempt. They are scum.
>
> (Morgan 87–8)

While Amis mocked the 'nostalgia for style nowadays among people of oldster age-group or literary training' (and declared 'Style, a personal style, a distinguished style' mere 'idiosyncratic noise'), Waugh wrote 'Literary Style in England and America' (1955), renewing his campaign for 'elegance' and 'individuality' in a survey of modern writers that pointedly omits all reference to the Movement.[10] Though he had often complained of it before, the last item in *Pinfold*'s much-quoted catalogue of dislikes – 'plastics, Picasso, sunbathing and jazz' (GP 7) – was probably aimed in 1957 at the well-advertised musical tastes of Amis and Larkin. It seems equally likely that, just as Waugh's term 'Teddy-boy' suggests mannerless adolescent machismo, his new openness in the 1950s about his past homosexuality and continuing appreciation for male beauty was partly a response to the Movement's well-known tendency to gay-bashing, another way in which younger writers distinguished themselves from the older literary establishment.[11]

Waugh's sneers diminish at the end of the decade, when even newspaper critics turned against the Movement they had earlier helped to create. In 1958 he wrote to an American friend who had praised *Lucky Jim*: 'I don't think much of Mr. Amis but he has admirers as discerning as Anthony Powell so there must be something in him'.[12] But younger writers' fascinated hostility to Waugh did not soon abate, in part because so many found their claims to novelty undercut by an older writer who anticipated by a generation their own rejection of literary modernism and 'Bloomsbury', of the obscurities of James Joyce and the Virginia Woolf novel of sensibility. (Many reviewers noted similarities between *Lucky Jim* and *Decline and Fall*; soon Amis's novels were greeted as 'fish-and-chips Waugh'.)[13] When in 1957 Amis announced a new 'golden age of satire', of fiction that blends 'the violent and the absurd, the grotesque and the romantic, the farcical and the horrific within a single novel', he laboured unconvincingly to distinguish this 'new' mode from what had long been Waugh's practice. Over the next two decades, in a stream of hostile essays and reviews, Amis would evince a fascination 'so intense that he devotes more pages to [Waugh] than to any other writer'.[14]

As younger writers took over the review pages of the once-dependable *Spectator* and *Observer*, treatment of Waugh in the press hardened. The opponent of modern liberalism was now portrayed as a monster of bigotry whose writing lacked all contemporary relevance. *Officers and Gentlemen* would be greeted as 'the quintessence of silliness', 'crazed by snobbery and nostalgia' ('Waugh has bitten off considerably more than his little teeth can chew'). The TLS used *Gilbert Pinfold* to launch an attack on its author as a 'lightweight', a 'freak talent' who never had 'much to say'.[15] Others simply pretended to ignore him:

> As for Mr. Waugh, his principal work in recent years has been the trilogy *Men at Arms*, which I gave up reading about half-way, feeling hooperish and as if eavesdropping. There is no reason why Mr. Waugh should not talk, in print, to himself and a few friends, but it would be pointless for a critic to comment on the monologue.
>
> (O'Brien, *Maria Cross*, vii)

As Donat Gallagher notes, 'The *Observer* critic who wrote, "Like most reviewers, I am of a conventionally liberal turn of mind; and the problem with which Mr. Waugh confronts us, is how to do him justice in spite of his views", was smug but almost uniquely self-aware. Despite his stated concern for justice, however, ... this same critic went on to describe *Unconditional Surrender* as "misanthropic", "lunatic McCarthyism", "painfully gushing and vulgar", "fantastically confused in values" and "appealing in the same way as the *Queen* magazine", without once recognizing the existence of, let alone confronting, the novel's themes or the historical viewpoint on which it is based'.[16]

I

On finishing *Men at Arms* Waugh turned down offers for other work (including a life of the recently canonized Thomas More) to continue 'toiling away at the war saga' (HRC E743), and in March 1953, on finishing *Love Among the Ruins*, settled down to work on volume two, provisionally titled *Happy Warriors*. 'Mr. Waugh Replies' appeared in July; that August, he agreed to record an unscripted radio interview for the BBC's series *Personal Call* (to be aired only in the Far East). For years Waugh had avoided such public performances, usually by demanding excessive fees. 'In order to earn a living (ha ha) it is unavoidable that one expose oneself to ridicule & obloquy now & then', he told John Betjeman in 1946, 'but the BBC pay so little & expect so much time & trouble that it is not worth while' (L 230). The next year he instructed Peters: 'Price for television £50 in a false beard. With the natural face £250' (L 253). Broadcast media did not permit the kind of carefully controlled self-presentation he achieved in print. But at a time of poor sales he needed publicity.

In August 1953 the BBC's Stephen Black (renamed Angel in *Pinfold*) arrived with a truckload of sound equipment at Piers Court; the whole family watched as their famous father answered questions about his early life and social attitudes. (Auberon, thirteen, observed that Black 'did not seem to like my Father very much'.)[17] Hoping to penetrate Waugh's celebrated privacy further, the BBC requested another interview, now for the domestic series *Frankly Speaking*. After haggling for an unusually high fee (forty guineas plus £8 expenses) Waugh went up to London in September, to be grilled by a panel of three (Black, Jack Davies and Charles Wilmot). Thinking his initial performance too unguarded – 'Politics & sociology are not really my subjects', he told his BBC contact (ST2 336) – Waugh asked to record the interview again. A composite version of the two recordings was aired on 16 November.

'My broadcast was pretty dull', he told Nancy Mitford in a judgment to be repeated in *Pinfold*; 'They tried to make a fool of me & I don't believe they entirely succeeded'.[18] The interview bears out both halves of Waugh's impression. None of his books is so much as mentioned by name: the interviewers were not interested in Waugh the writer, only the famous curmudgeon. Waugh parried insults (and invitations to insult others) in the face of questions such as 'Have you ever really wanted to obliterate anybody, to kill somebody for example?'; 'What sort of faces do you dislike?'; 'Do you still, at your present age, ever do anything with your hands at all?'[19]

> **BBC**: Do you, generally speaking, like the human race? Do you like crowds, for example, or do you fly from them?
> **Waugh**: Loathe crowds. Liking the human race is the prerogative of God, not of a human being, because a human being can't know the human race.
> **BBC**: Do you find it easy to get on with the man in the street?
> **Waugh**: I never met such a person.
> **BBC**: Do you like people generally when you meet them in trains or buses, or on a ship? . . .
> **Waugh**: I clearly can't make myself understood! There is no such thing as a man of the street. There is no ordinary run of mankind. There are only individuals who are totally different. And whether a man is naked and black and stands on one foot in the Sudan, or is clothed in some kind of costume in the baths of England, they are still individuals and entirely different characters.

Determined to elicit outrageousness, his interviewers turned to capital punishment:

BBC: You are in favour of capital punishment?
Waugh: For an enormous number of instances.
BBC: And you yourself would be prepared to carry it out?
Waugh: Do you mean actually doing the hangman's work?
BBC: Yes.
Waugh: I should think it very odd to choose a novelist for such a task.
BBC: Supposing they [were] prepared to train you for the job. Would you take it on?
Waugh: Well, certainly.
BBC: You would?
Waugh: Certainly!
BBC: Would you enjoy such a job, Mr. Waugh?
Waugh: Not in the least.

When Waugh confessed pleasure in religious spectacles, his interviewers made their contempt clear:

BBC: You're enjoying a spectacle, apart from the festival itself, of crowds. And yet crowds you don't like.
Waugh: Well, I shouldn't really wish to be mixed up in a crowd of people slashing themselves with daggers and going into ecstatic frenzies, you know. I'd sooner be in an upper window looking down on them.
BBC: You like, in fact, generally speaking, to be in an upper window looking down.

The *Spectator*'s 'Notebook' column commented the next week: 'I never heard an interview conducted in public on such ill-natured terms' (20 Nov. 1953, 557).

By this time 25,000 'excellent' words of *Happy Warriors* were done, but the novel stalled. Autumn and winter were particularly cold; Waugh suffered mind-numbing rheumatic pain; his insomnia grew acute. From various doctors he had accumulated prescriptions for sleeping drugs, including bromide and chloral (ingredients, when mixed with alcohol, of the famous 'Mickey Finn'). The drugs were meant to be diluted in water, but Waugh splashed them together, careless of dosage, in crème de menthe – and as a pain-killer during the day, in gin. He spent days sitting before the fire, bored, in pain, depressed. 'Intense cold. Sat like hibernating badger all day'; 'Clocks barely moving. Has half an hour past? no five minutes' (D 724, 722). 'I am stuck in my book from sheer boredom', he told Nancy Mitford; 'I know what to write but just cant make the effort to write it' (L 415). Unable to work, he allowed himself to be goaded by a gross insult from Hugh Trevor-Roper into an acrimonious controversy over Reformation history in the letters column of the *New Statesman*.[20]

Uncertain mental as well as physical health deepened Waugh's depression. In September he had told John Betjeman: 'My memory is not at all hazy, just sharp, detailed & dead wrong' (L 410). To cheer his old friend on his fiftieth birthday, Betjeman offered a present of the kind both men treasured: an elaborate Victorian washstand designed by William Burges, inset with panels painted by Sir Edward Poynton. Waugh inspected this prize in Lord Kinross's London house, but when it finally arrived at Piers Court was sure a piece was missing: an ornamental bronze spigot that he could recall in detail. Kinross recalled no such part; the movers knew of none; Betjeman, to whom at the end of December Waugh sent a drawing and the question 'Did I dream this or did it exist', could only reply, 'There was never a pipe'. 'I must see an alienist', Waugh mused in January; 'These delusions are becoming more frequent'.[21] Laura, equally worried, called in a doctor who recommended a complete change of scene. Waugh had not revealed the extent of his self-medication, but, mindful of Rossetti's example, knew that he 'had been accumulatively poisoning' himself (L 418) and resolved to give up soporifics. 'Oh I have been ill', he wrote to his daughter Margaret. 'First a cold & then agonising rheumatism. So I am jumping into the first available ship. She goes to Ceylon. I shant come back until I have finished my book, but I hope I shall do that on the voyage' (L 417).

The result was the journey later recast as *The Ordeal of Gilbert Pinfold*. Laura wanted to accompany her husband but was kept at home by a lawsuit over the farm. On 29 January, 1954, having packed only a few days' supply of sleeping drugs, Waugh boarded from Liverpool a ship bound for Rangoon. Four days out he wrote home:

> Pretty empty and the passengers pleasant. The chief trouble is the noise of my cabin. All the pipes and air shafts seem to run through them. To add to my balminess there are intermittent bits of 3rd Programme talks played in private cabin and two mentioned me very faintly and my p.m. took it for other passengers whispering about me. If a regular rural life out of doors doesn't work the trick I'll see an alienist. But I want to be back with you now.
>
> (L 418)

The trouble was worse than Laura knew. He had begun hallucinating voices, including that of Stephen Black; he seemed to know by telepathy that his cables home were being shown among the passengers, various of whom were in league against him; he was sure he overheard a murder. One fellow-passenger later reported seeing Waugh 'talking into the toast rack' and addressing electric lamps as if they were radio transmitters (Carpenter 434). On 8 February he to wrote Laura that he had disembarked in Egypt and planned to fly on to Colombo. 'I must have been more poisoned that I knew'; 'I found myself the victim of an experiment in telepathy which made me think I was really going crazy' (L 418). But the voices followed him to Ceylon: 'It is rather difficult to write to you because everything I say or think or read is read aloud by the group of psychologists whom I met in the ship. I hoped that they would lose this art after I went on shore but the artful creatures can communicate from many hundreds of miles away' (L 419).

Anxious at what was obviously a serious mental disorder, Laura consulted the Donaldsons. Frances Donaldson recalled in her *Portrait of a Country Neighbour* the events that followed. Jack generously agreed to fly out to Ceylon, but on 18

February before he could do so, Waugh himself announced that he was return-ing home. Laura went to the Hyde Park Hotel in London to meet a husband still hearing voices and now half-convinced that he was suffering demonic posses-sion. A phone call to the BBC convinced him that Stephen Black could not have been on board the ship to Egypt, but the voices continued. Laura called in Fr Caraman (*Pinfold*'s 'Fr Westmacott'), from whom he abruptly requested exorcism. Caraman in turn telephoned Eric Strauss, chief psychiatrist at St Bartholomew's Hospital, also a Roman Catholic (and Graham Greene's therapist), who came immediately to the hotel and after a few questions diagnosed Waugh's hallucina-tions as a simple case of bromide poisoning. Strauss prescribed rest and a new soporific, paraldehyde (which, despite its marked odour, Waugh would take for the rest of his life); the voices, already fading, soon disappeared entirely.[22]

Knowing how the tale of her husband's illness might be twisted by a hostile press, Laura had sworn the Donaldsons to secrecy. But Waugh – perhaps realizing complete secrecy was impossible – chose instead to advertise what had happened. 'I've been absolutely mad', he shouted to friends for all to hear; 'Clean off my onion!' (Hollis, *Oxford*, 82). A year later he would also have the idea of retelling the story in fictional form. Meanwhile, he returned in June to *Happy Warriors*, his quiet life interrupted only by occasional visitors – in the spring, Frederick Stopp, who had secured Waugh's cooperation 'to write my "life"' (D 722) – and in December by the death of his mother at eighty-four.

A draft of *Happy Warriors* – 'shorter than *Men At Arms*, but rather better', he told Peters (HRC E869) – was finished at the beginning of November 1954, just as his collection of stories *Tactical Exercise* appeared in America. From November to January Waugh revised his manuscript, then celebrated by spending two months in Jamaica, visiting the Brownlows and then moving on to the Flemings at Goldeneye, where Ian worked on *Moonraker*, latest of what Ann liked to call his 'horror comics' (LAF 153).

There was much to celebrate. After his depression and attack of 'Pinfoldism', Waugh had not been sure he would be able to finish the novel at all. On completing the draft in November he had sent Peters copy for its dust-jacket, announcing both a change of title and doubts of his ability ever to produce a third volume:

> *Officers and Gentlemen* completes *Men at Arms*. I thought at first that the story would run into three volumes. I find that two will do the trick. If I keep my faculties I hope to follow the fortunes of the characters through the whole of the war, but these two books constitute a whole.... *Men at Arms* began with its hero inspired by illusion. *Officers and Gentlemen* ends with his deflation.

The same month he wrote Nancy Mitford: *Officers and Gentlemen* 'is short & funny & completes the story I began in *Men at Arms* which threatened to drag out to the grave' (L 433).

But by the time the novel was published in June 1955, Waugh's confidence had returned. Soon he was outlining detailed plans for the trilogy's conclusion to Frederick Stopp and Maurice Bowra (L 444). 'Bad reviews of *O. and G.* in

England, good ones from New York', he noted in his diary that July; 'I am quite complacent about the book's quality. My only anxiety is about American sales. It would be very convenient to have another success there' (D 729).

To ensure such sales, Waugh agreed to a televised interview with Dave Garroway for NBC's *Today* show, to be recorded at Piers Court on 30 June and aired on the eve of *Officers and Gentlemen*'s American publication. He accepted $100 for what he expected would be only a few hours' work; the event proved another inquisition, but not one that haunted his imagination. Reinvigorated, Waugh was playful.

> The television people came at 10 and stayed until 6:30.... They filmed everything including the poultry. The impresario kept producing notes from his pocket: 'Mr. Waugh, it is said here that you are irascible and reactionary. Will you please say something offensive?' So I said: 'The man who has brought this apparatus to my house asks me to be offensive. I am sorry to disappoint him'. 'Oh, Mr. Waugh, please, that will never do. I have a reputation. You must alter that'. I said later, not into the machine: 'You expect rather a lot for $100'. 'Oh I don't think there is any question of payment'.
>
> (D 726–7)

No tapes of the interview survive; one quotation appeared in a profile of Waugh by Bernard Kalb:

> 'We have a proverb in my country...that a hen should not count her chickens before they are hatched. The cares of a large household make it desirable for me to continue at work for many years to come. I pray that I retain my faculties until my youngest child has completed his education. I have in mind at least one (probably more) study of the characters in these two books [*Men at Arms* and *Officers and Gentlemen*]. Perhaps a third volume may appear in 1957. Modern taxation makes haste unprofitable – I hope and believe to the benefit of literature'.
>
> (*Saturday Review*, 9 July 1955, 10)

II

The 'second stage of his pilgrimage, which had begun at the tomb of Sir Roger' (OG 17) takes Guy Crouchback through 1941 and 1942, from the aftermath of Dakar to the aftermath of Crete. *Men at Arms* ended with the unauthorized 'Operation Truslove' at Dakar, after which Guy's colonel told him, 'By all justice I ought now to be drafting a citation for your M.C. Instead of which we're in the hell of a fix' (MA 293). At the start of *Officers and Gentlemen*, Ritchie-Hook and his men are rescued from disgrace and inaction by a directive from Churchill himself; Guy moves from a dull desk-job in England with the middle-class Halberdiers to a temporary posting with the upper-class Commandos. The bulk of the novel – and some of Waugh's finest writing – traces Guy's training with the Commandos in Scotland and fighting with them in the shambles of Crete, his 'island of disillusion' (OG 241). Finally, through another intervention from above (by Mrs Stitch), Guy ends once more in England and 'the old ambiguous world': once more a Halberdier, inactive and – though his performance

on Crete was 'wholly creditable' (334) and should again have won him a medal –
in disgrace. Beneath a carefully fragmented plot (designed to convey the dis-
jointedness of wartime experience), the novel is tightly organized: a web of
parallel characters and situations, significant montages and historical allusions
establish Waugh's central theme that Guy has been wrong in identifying modern
warfare with a religious crusade, and most wrong in making the equation of the
novel's title.

As the story opens, 'an act of *pietas* was required of him, a spirit was to be
placated' (18): Guy must fulfill a promise to the dying Apthorpe to pass on
Apthorpe's enormous kit to his old friend Chatty Corner. In a regression that
enables progress, the act of laying Apthorpe's ghost takes Guy to the island of
Mugg in Scotland, described in a delightful pastiche of Dr Johnson on the
Hebrides:

> This Isle of Mugg has no fame in song or story. Perhaps because whenever they
> sought a rhyme for the place, they struck absurdity, it was neglected by those
> romantic early-Victorian English ladies who so prodigally enriched the balladry,
> folk-lore and costume of the Scottish Highlands.... It lies among other mono-
> syllabic protuberances. There is seldom clear weather in those waters, but on
> certain rare occasions Mugg has been descried from the island of Rum in the
> form of two cones. The crofters of Muck know it as a single misty lump on their
> horizon. It has never been seen from Egg.
>
> (OG 55)

Here Corner reveals the truth about Apthorpe, no real Africa hand but merely a
salesman for a coffee concern. In a 'holy moment' – 'Suddenly the wind
dropped' (71) – Corner signs for Apthorpe's gear and so frees Guy to proceed
in his military career. The whole sequence sets the events of the novel on a
quasi-mythic plane; there follow a series of allusions to figures of heroic legend,
Achilles, Hector, Hercules, Philoctetes, Jason, Miltiades, Circe and Cleopatra,
all painfully inappropriate to the context in which they occur: a story that traces
the rise of Trimmer and fall of Ivor Claire.

Trimmer, the 'proletarian portent', becomes a national hero through the
connivance of two self-seeking 'accomplices in fraud', General Whale and his
publicist Ian Kilbannock. As the war grows more serious, the Ministry of
Information 'want a hero of just Trimmer's specifications' – i.e., his 'sex appeal'
– 'to boost morale and Anglo-American friendship' (206). In turn, General
Whale, none of whose planned raids (raids potentially so bloody as to have
won him the nickname 'Brides-in-the-Bath') has yet been enacted, needs to
impress his superiors with a splashy success story so the Commandos won't be
disbanded and his own office shut down.[23] 'On Holy Saturday 1941' and into the
next morning, as 'all over the world' the *Exultet* is sung, Whale and Kilbannock
plan the bogus Operation Popgun (151, 154). 'That ought to do it', they say
cynically when Kilbannock finishes the equally fraudulent news release by which
Trimmer the deserter from the Argylls is reborn as 'the Demon Barber', hero of
the national press (199). For his part in the ruse, Trimmer receives the medal Guy

should have won at Dakar. But Popgun's success also guarantees the future of the Commandos, and so Guy's chance for battle on Crete.

Trimmer is a merely comic figure, without the stature of his literary ancestor Hooper; Waugh blames Trimmer's apotheosis squarely on the villains who have created him, especially Lord Kilbannock. Established in *Men at Arms* as a man who plans to use the war to make his career, Ian has already hoodwinked Guy into helping the cowardly martinet Beech become a member of Bellamy's; we last see him pimping for Trimmer, pressing Virginia to 'keep him in spirits' during the Demon Barber's lecture tour. The fabrication of a proletarian hero in Operation Popgun has in fact provided Ian an occasion to join political ideology with personal advancement: 'I've been pretty red ever since the Spanish war' he tells Guy, showing 'the democratic side of [his] character' (128). 'Flowers stink': the 'people's war' has no room for 'upper class' heroes, the 'Fine Flower of the Nation' (130).

Guy easily detects that Kilbannock is no gentleman; the fall of his friend Ivor Claire forces a more wrenching revision of perspective.

> Ivor Claire was another pair of boots entirely, salty, withdrawn, incorrigible. Guy remembered Claire as he first saw him in the Roman spring in the afternoon sunlight amid the embosoming cypresses of the Borghese Gardens, putting his horse faultlessly over the jumps, concentrated as a man in prayer. Ivor Claire, Guy thought, was the fine flower of them all. He was quintessential England, the man Hitler had not taken into account, Guy thought.
>
> (OG 146-7)

But Ivor only resembles 'a man in prayer'; though a decorated officer, he is neither hero nor even gentleman. He won his MC, we learn from Trimmer, 'At Dunkirk, for shooting three territorials who were trying to swamp his boat' in the evacuation (63–4). Guy has managed to ignore this and other signs of the Ivor who will desert on Crete: his cheating during a training exercise on Mugg; his confession to Guy at Cape Town that he 'longed for a torpedo' to hit their troopship, leaving 'myself, the sole survivor, floating gently away to some nearby island' (141). As he meditates desertion, Ivor seeks to excuse his cowardice through a politics like Ian's: 'when we are completely democratic, I expect it will be quite honourable for officers to leave their men behind' (295).

In hospital, shattered by his Cretan experience, Guy recalls (and nearly becomes) the despairing Ivo. 'His brother Ivo had been silent, too, Guy remembered' (304, a passage that frames his incipient despair at the start of the novel, when, unable to locate Chatty Corner, he imagined himself dwindling into 'a gentler version of poor mad Ivo': 47). But once again, as in the case of Trimmer and Operation Popgun, the issue is not one man's misdeeds but the participation of officialdom in them. Guy is shocked less by Ivor's desertion than the determination of Tommy Blackhouse and Julia Stitch to keep the affair quiet (she out of Forsterian loyalty to a friend, he because the trouble of a court-martial would violate his precept, 'never cause trouble except for positive preponderant advantage').

Guy lacked these simple rules of conduct. He had no old love for Ivor, no liking at all, for the man who had been his friend and proved to be an illusion. He had a sense, too, that all war consisted in causing trouble without much hope of advantage.[24]

Ironically it is Guy who reminds Julia Stitch of Ritchie-Hook's zeal in pursuing deserters, raising inter such fears for Ivo that she consigns him to a slow boat home and inexplicable, unearned disgrace. In a final interview, this tarnished goddess of modernity gives Guy a Judas-like 'fond kiss' before criminally disposing of a letter containing a dead soldier's identity disc (thinking it Guy's written evidence of Ivor's guilt).

The man who has saved Guy's life, shepherding him from Crete back to Egypt over countless days in an open boat, is a new character, added to the novel late in the process of composition: Claire's mysterious soldier-servant Corporal-Major Ludovic. A 'thoughtful corporal' who 'keeps a diary' (as Koestler famously described the type), Ludovic resembles Ian and Trimmer (in his gift of tongues), Ivor (who is quick to defend him), and, most ominously, Guy himself.[25] Like Guy (whom he understands uncannily well), Ludovic puzzles over moral-theological questions, and is drawn to suicide (OG 299–301); just before murdering Major Hound, Ludovic occasions an unholy moment that frames the 'holy moment' with which the novel began: 'Suddenly, for no human reason, a great colony of bats came to life in the fault of the cave, wheeled about, squeaking in the smoke of the fire, fluttered and blundered and then settled again, huddled head-down, invisible' (272). Waugh could have lavished such attention on this new character only because he foresaw something of Ludovic's role in the final volume of the trilogy. Ludovic's stamina waxes as Guy's strength wanes, a process reversed in *Unconditional Surrender*, where Ludovic emerges full-blown as Guy's antitype.

'War is a gentleman's occupation', Waugh had once claimed (van Zeller 285); Guy too (as Ludovic notices) has wanted 'to believe that the war is being fought by such people. But all gentlemen are now very old' (OG 248–9). *Officers and Gentlemen* regularly recurs to one such spiritual beacon: old Mr Crouchback re-enters the story in its opening pages and, in a telling montage, immediately after Operation Popgun. (Waugh removed a third appearance at the end of the novel, presumably because such a curtain-call would have been heavy-handed.) Like Arthur Waugh, old Mr Crouchback donates his services as a school-teacher while younger men fight. He remains a model of honourable simplicity, but the new ideology of the people's war has worn him down into a 'gentle, bewildered old man' (28). On being told that he cannot send food to his nephew in a concentration camp (but must instead 'share things equally'), he protests:

'After all, *any* present means that you want someone to have something someone else hasn't got. I mean even if it's only a cream-jug at a wedding. I shouldn't wonder if the Government didn't try and stop us praying for people next. . . . I'm not much of a dab at explaining things, but I *know* it's all *wrong*.'

(OG 28–9)

Waugh himself wrote to the *Spectator* in 1946, supporting Victor Gollancz's campaign against the government ban on food parcels for the defeated Germans:

> surely the prohibition lies at the heart of Socialism? Conscience has been nationalised. Private charity, like private thrift, has no place in the world Mr Gollancz has striven so conspicuously to create. The law which forbids selfishness, forbids with equal justice unselfishness. Our food is not our own property by right of purchase to dispose of as we think fit; it is a ration allowed us by the State in order, as has been made clear in the Parliamentary replies quoted in Mr Gollancz's recent pamphlet [a portfolio of photographs of starving German children entitled *Is It Nothing to You?*], to keep us strong to work for the State. In this, as in all matters, the State is the sole judge of what is best for us.
>
> There are many of us who deeply resent this principle, but it is hard to see what right Mr Gollancz has to complain. He has probably done more than any living man to secure its popular acceptance.
>
> (1 June 1946, quoted in Edwards 421)

III

On the occasion of *Officers and Gentlemen*'s appearance, Lord Beaverbrook's *Sunday Express* ran a profile of Waugh by Joseph Pitman, an article of a now an all-too-familiar sort. Citing Waugh's advance notice of the novel (about how Guy begins in illusion and ends in deflation), Pitman suggested that 'There are some who would like to apply the same process to Mr. Waugh himself'. 'Reared in Golders Green', the 'Boswell of our older aristocracy' is no member of the class he apes: Waugh 'paid for his own coat of arms' with 'his own hard cash', won 'from the common, book-buying millions'.[26] Alec wrote at once, volunteering to correct at least the mistake about the coat of arms. The profile seemed one more instance of the 'strange unanimity' of the Beaverbrook papers, perhaps guided by Beaverbrook himself. To the old accusations of snobbery, rudeness and insincere faith was now added another that would dog him for the rest of his life: that he had set up as a country 'squire' – a 'scribbling squire', in the words of another reporter, living a 'crested, cross-patch charade'.[27]

This new accusation dated from an occasion when not only readers of *Country Life* but the general public had a chance to observe Piers Court. On 14 August 1954, the Waughs held an open house for the benefit of their parish church. Waugh issued posters and magazine advertisements, and paid the Poor Clares to pray for good weather. (Five minutes before the fête began, rainy skies cleared.) Visitors from as far as London paid a shilling to tour his house and grounds. The event was later memorably described by Frances Donaldson and in a delightful (if partly fanciful) memoir by Edward Sheehan, a reporter for the *Boston Globe* visiting for the weekend whom Waugh dragooned into helping rearrange furniture and sell muffins. In the garden, the children sold tickets to a hut mysteriously marked 'Holy Fryer' (inside hung an old frying pan); indoors young Rose Donaldson served as guide, reciting a carefully memorized patter: 'Ladies & Gentlemen, this is Sir Max Beerbohm's famous caricature of Sir Ernest Cassel. Pray notice the gross Jewish features so strongly transmitted to Lady Mountbatten' (DC 197). William Douglas-Home having telephoned for permission to report the fête in the *Sunday Express*, Rose recited of two paintings by Rebecca Solomon, *The Industrious Student* and *The Idle Student*: 'This one is reading for honours – this one for pluck. The newspaper that can be seen in the pocket of the second one is a kind of rag, the equivalent of, one might say, today's *Sunday Express*' (Donaldson 49). Another American present, Joseph Crowley – from that day onward one of Waugh's friends, correspondents, and, in one remarkable instance, literary advisors – recalls the occasion as well, and supplies useful correctives to Sheehan and Donaldson's accounts.[28]

Waugh thoroughly enjoyed hosting so fantastic a party and showing off the fruit of years of serious thought given to decoration, but he soon paid a steep price. Douglas-Home published a snide account in the next day's *Sunday Express* under the title 'Waugh Locks Up Lambs as his "Public" Tours his Treasures'; in October, an anonymous profile in *Truth* spoke of the 'bogus squire' of Stinchcombe, a snobbish 'climber' who in his desire to be accepted as a 'member of the ruling class' was now opening his house (like some baronial mansion) 'to the paying public'.[29]

Waugh's sense of a Beaverbrook conspiracy grew stronger in June 1955, when Nancy Spain, now a familiar personality on television's *My Word* programme as well as book reviewer for the *Daily Express*, mounted a second attack on him. Hoping to add an essay on Waugh to her series *A Cool Look at the Loved Ones*, Spain telephoned at breakfast time on 21 June to ask whether she and a friend, Baron Noel-Buxton, might come to Piers Court for an interview. Laura refused, but at 7:45 that evening journalist and peer arrived nonetheless. Two days later Spain ran a column recalling their reception:

> I rang the bell. Mrs. Waugh, a beautiful woman in a twin set and slacks, came immediately, sighed deeply and leaned against the door jamb. I said who we were. She said she was afraid we could not stay, when I heard a voice calling: 'Who is it? ... Go away, go away! You read the notice, didn't you? No admittance on business!' Lord Noel-Buxton is rather a tall man. He stood his ground, blinking, looking down at Mr. Waugh, who is a rather short man. 'I'm not on business', was the answer. 'I'm a member of the House of Lords'.
> ('My Pilgrimage to See Mr. Waugh', *Daily Express*, 23 June 1955, 6)

For years to come, the scene of Spain and Noel-Buxton on the doorstep would be a favourite subject of Waugh family charades. At the time, Waugh converted his irritation into the hilarious public rebuke 'Awake My Soul! It is a Lord', originally written for *Punch*, then revised (when *Punch*'s editor Malcolm Muggeridge found the first version libellous) for the *Spectator*. 'I am sometimes accused of a partiality for lords', the article began, addressing at the outset what had been the main charge of the Beaverbrook press. A fine recital of events follows (including Waugh's going out to see whether, rebuffed at his front door, the intruders were 'slipping round to suck up to the cook'), then the summing-up:

> We have many sorts of lord in our country. ... In Lord Noel-Buxton we see the lord predatory. He appears to think that his barony gives him the right to a seat at the dinner-table of any private house in the kingdom.
> Fear of this lord is clearly the beginning of wisdom.
> (EAR 470)

To tweak Nancy Spain, Waugh also included a passage repeating in stronger terms the argument of 'Mr. Waugh Replies':

> The popular papers are fitfully aware, I believe, that there are spheres of English life in which they hold a negligible influence. The fifty or sixty thousand people in this country who alone support the Arts do not go to Lord Beaverbrook's critics for guidance. So it is that artists of all kinds form part of the battle-training for green reporters. 'Don't lounge about the office, lad', the editors say, 'sit up and insult an artist'.
>
> (EAR 468)

When the article appeared Waugh received 'a mountainous mail from people as different as Edith Sitwell and Violet Bonham Carter, telling me of sufferings at [Nancy Spain's] hand in the past'. From America P. G. Wodehouse wrote of his experience with a reporter who had 'prattled away all smiles', then produced 'a stinker about me for his beastly gutter rag': 'It just shows that the Waugh method is the only one for dealing with the *Express*. "Ptarmigan, throw this man out and see that he lands on something sharp."'[30] Correspondence also poured into the *Spectator* – mainly defences of the hapless baron, but also a letter of support from Nancy Mitford: 'it is no wonder if elderly writers become bad-tempered. Dogs which are constantly baited turn savage' (22 July 1955, 122). Noel-Buxton wrote to explain that Waugh was 'entitled to be angry with Miss Spain' but not with him, because he had never uttered the words she attributed to him about not being on business (15 July, 94). (The opportunity was too good to pass up; Waugh swooped: 'Finding he has made an ass of himself, [Noel-Buxton] turns on the lady whom he chose to escort, and publicly calls her a liar. Has Miss Spain no brother? Has the editor of the *Daily Express* no horse-whip?': 22 July, 121.) Spain in turn reasserted that the famous words *had* been uttered, provoking yet another letter from Noel-Buxton trying to reconstruct his remarks, with results funnier even than his supposed original statement: 'I said to Nancy Spain that one of the main things [about Waugh's rebuff] was the insult to herself as a woman. Secondly, it was, I felt, an insult to the House of Lords as an institution' (29 July, 166).

A decade later Waugh wrote to Nancy Mitford: 'When Lord Noel Buxton and your friend Miss Spain intruded in my house I put it on the market the next day because I felt it was polluted' (L 636). The remark is of course an instance of that favourite Waugh pastime, fantastic myth-making. His health restored and in fine fighting shape, Waugh was bored by his year's enforced rest and wished to flee an area rapidly losing its rural character to motorcycle trippers and the condom factory recently erected nearby. In July 1955 he wrote to his estate agents:

> You may remember that you came here about nine years ago when I had an idea of moving to Ireland.
>   Now I have an idea of moving anywhere. I am sick of the district. . . . I don't want the house advertised. But if you happen to meet a lunatic who wants to live in this ghastly area, please tell him.
>
> (L 443)

The garden fête had alerted him to the dangers of advertising; when advertising became necessary, the *Daily Mail* ran a picture-story about his 'search for a new Brideshead' under the headline 'THE WAUGHS MOVE ON: Ten-bedroom, 40-acre home is not big enough. IF YOU HAVE THREE SONS AND THREE DAUGHTERS, HOW BIG A HOUSE DO YOU NEED?' (2 May 1956, 3).

Meanwhile his war with the press continued. In March 1956, when John Wain panned P. G. Wodehouse's *French Leave* in the *Observer*, Waugh wrote a letter defending his aged 'Master'; Wain in turn replied that Waugh's remarks could carry little weight, since he was not a 'critic' (L 461). This strange mode of rebuttal spurred Waugh to an essay arguing that 'In a civilized society everyone is a critic'; 'Does [Wain] regard them as imposters because they have not taken classes in English literature?'[31] The essay began with a survey of the decline of British book-reviewing, including a swipe at Nancy Spain and her colleagues:

> An investigation has been made in the book-trade to determine which literary critics have most influence on sales. I remember the time when the *Evening Standard* was undisputed leader.... Things have changed. The Beaverbrook press is no longer listed as having any influence at all. The *Observer* heads the poll, with the *Sunday Times* as runner-up.
>
> (EAR 507)

Three weeks later Spain replied in the *Daily Express* under the title, 'Does a Good Word from Me Sell a Book?':

> There is a war between Evelyn Waugh and me. He said, some weeks ago, in a literary weekly, that the Express has no influence on the book trade. The Express, he complains, sold only 300 of *his* novels. He once had a book chosen by the Book Society, so that sold well. But the total first edition sales of all this other titles are dwarfed by brother Alec. **ISLAND IN THE SUN** (*Cassell, 16s.*), foretold by me as this year's runaway Best Seller, has now topped 60,000 copies as a direct result of my Daily Express notice. So the publisher told me yesterday.
>
> (17 March 1956, 6)

'I have waited a long time to catch the *Express* in libel', Waugh wrote to Peters with evident satisfaction; 'I think they have done it this time' (L 468). Peters agreed. Waugh had before him the example of Randolph Churchill, recently awarded £5000 when *The People* called him 'chief among' the 'paid hacks, paid to write biased accounts of the' General Election of 1955.[32] Hungry for victory against the corporation press he had so long despised, Waugh sued; Spain counter-sued (on the ground of his remark, 'The Beaverbrook press is no longer listed as having any influence at all'). A note from Ann Fleming confirmed that Beaverbrook himself was now personally involved in the attacks by his employees (LAF 179).

In the year it took for the cases to come to court, Waugh began work on *Pinfold*. That October he wrote in his diary: 'I have worked hard every day lately. Not today. Rebecca West has libelled me, according to the *Daily Express*' (D 770).

The paper had indeed libelled him again – and much more seriously – in a story by its literary editor Anthony Hern about a new edition of Rebecca West's *The Meaning of Treason*.

By 1956, revelations of collaboration and spying had inspired a stream of books: Alan Barth's *The Loyalty of Free Men* (1951), Cyril Connolly's *The Missing Diplomats* (1952), Alan Moorehead's *The Traitors* (1952) and C. P. Snow's *The New Men* (1954). But the first and best of these was West's *Meaning of Treason*. Its first edition (1947), mainly about William Joyce (Lord Haw-Haw), traced the roots of wartime treachery to the internationalism of the twenties and thirties, when, in the wake of World War I, 'nationalism' and even 'patriotism' seemed to advanced thinkers not virtues, but causes of conflict. In 1952, West updated her analysis to treat the new kinds of traitor represented by Klaus Fuchs, Alan Nunn May and the stylish Guy Burgess and Donald Maclean. For a third, paperback edition in 1956, following the scandal of Kim Philby (the 'Third Man'), West again broadened her discussion, adding a paragraph about literary figures who had, in her view, so far glamourized cosmopolitanism and 'style' as to create 'a climate in which the traitor flourishes'. She made the mistake of naming names, and under the screamer headline 'REBECCA WEST ATTACKS EVELYN WAUGH & GRAHAM GREENE', Anthony Hern made the mistake of quoting her 'breath-taking denunciation':

> they have created an intellectual climate in which there is a crackbrained confusion between the moral and the aesthetic.... People who practise the virtues are judged as if they had struck the sort of false attitude which betrays an incapacity for art, while the people who practise the vices are regarded as if they had shown the subtle rightness of gesture which is the sign of the born artist.... For many years... Waugh has been implying that the worthless and dissolute are more worthy than people who are in fact worthy and who keep sober.

'This is the most devastating exposure of the essence of treachery yet made', Hern concluded.[33]

All this is a perverse misreading of Waugh, whose views differed little from West's own. For years he too had protested confusion between the moral and the aesthetic; since *Labels* he had celebrated 'nationality' and 'patriotism'. West's accusations seem based on a careless reading of *Put Out More Flags* and *Brideshead*. She certainly had not paused over the case of Ivor Claire in *Officers and Gentlemen*, whose expert horsemanship might have reminded her of William Joyce's similar skill, and whose argument in favour of desertion – 'I was thinking about honour. It's a thing that changes, doesn't it?' (OG 295) – pointedly recalls Talleyrand's famous maxim: 'La trahison – c'est une question du temps'.[34]

All Waugh's libel suits were settled in his favour over the winter of 1956–7. Pan Books (a division of Macmillan) withdrew its edition of *The Meaning of Treason* from sale as soon as Waugh entered his suit, and on 13 December admitted in court that the book's treatment of him was 'indefensible and unfair'. 'The plaintiff for his part recognised that the sudden withdrawal of the book would have caused the defendants acute financial loss and did not press any claim for damages', settling only for costs.[35]

The cases against Beaverbrook's papers, reported daily in *The Times* and *Express*, were more elaborate and expensive affairs. Both sides retained some of the nation's most distinguished lawyers; had Waugh lost, his legal' fees would have been a crushing financial blow.[36] A week before trial, Beaverbrook offered to settle the case against Spain, but Waugh, having taken 'the precaution of telling the Dursley parish priest that he should have 10%' of any winnings to help repair his church's roof (L 486), persisted. On 19 February began a proceeding that included testimony by Laura (about Miss Spain's 'invasion' of Piers Court), Alec (who came from Tangier to discuss the brothers' relative sales), Peters and Waugh himself. The case was effectively decided when Spain admitted under cross-examination 'that she had not taken any steps before [her] article was published to ascertain whether it was true or not', but Waugh's lawyers did not succeed in proving the connivance of Beaverbrook himself.[37] After two hours' deliberation the jury decided in Waugh's favour, awarding him £2000 plus costs. 'Miss Spain behaved in a gentlemanly way & congratulated me and I sent her a bottle of pop'.[38]

The last case, against Hern and the *Daily Express*, was a simpler matter. Waugh had invited Graham Greene to join the suit, but Greene refused, preferring instead to mount his own campaign of ridicule against the paper.[39] The case was heard in late March. By then Waugh had finished *Pinfold*, including one passage that Peters, when he read it in manuscript, warned would be imprudent to print while the last libel suit was pending:

> [Pinfold] subscribed to a press-cutting agency excusing this weakness on the grounds that it might one day provide a tax-free increment in the form of damages for libel.... Once a month, on the average, he would receive one of these little biographies. He read them attentively, noted the inaccuracies, and held his fire. One day they would go too far and he would take them to court. Then he would add to his collection of Pre-Raphaelite paintings and restore his depleted cellars.

'In view of my forthcoming reappearance in the courts I have to be careful what I publish', Waugh agreed; on Peters's advice he deferred publication of the novel until after the trial, thereby also foregoing an offer of serialization from *Life*.[40]

On 4 April Beaverbrook Newspapers admitted in court 'that there was not a vestige of justification for [Hern's] cruel attack on the plaintiff' and agreed to print an apology. Waugh was awarded £3000 plus costs – bringing his total winnings to £5000, the same as Randolph Churchill's. He promptly ordered a carpet, a copy of a design displayed in 1851 at the Great Exhibition, with which to 'Victorianize' his new house.

IV

The previous June, even before finding a new property, Waugh sold Piers Court for £9500; in September he and Laura selected Combe Florey, near Taunton and only twenty miles from Pixton. The rambling sandstone structure, begun in 1675 and rebuilt under George II, was ready for occupancy by Christmas 1956.

26 At Combe Florey, Somerset. The 'Betjeman Bequest' (the washstand by William Burges mentioned in *The Ordeal of Gilbert Pinfold*) and above it, a Cistercian Monk by Zurbarán (Mark Gerson).

He made over its sixteenth-century gatehouse (after again failing to receive authorization for a private chapel) as living quarters for the older children Teresa and Bron; Laura took over farming its forty acres.

'Laura has moped a little at seeing [Piers Court] dismantled'; 'I am delighted, elated, exhilarated' (D 770, L 477). Combe Florey was both larger and £2000 cheaper than Piers Court. Waugh spent the difference on a flurry of decorating ('candelabra, carpets, fireplaces', a painting by Arthur Grimshaw – 'I have been buying objects like a drunken sailor'), and instructed his agents not to 'reveal my

27 Waugh's library at Combe Florey (Mark Gerson).

new address. Literary Garbo' (L 484, 492). Combe Florey 'will be a suitable place to end my days', he told Ann Fleming – 'there is a lunatic asylum bang next door which is valuable' (LAF 186). 'My only sorrow [is that before moving] I shant quite finish the barmy book, which is going to be quite long but I believe funny' (L 477). The 'barmy book' would be his last and subtlest reply to all those critics whose obloquies had risen to the point of libel.

In the novel, Gilbert Pinfold calls his brush with madness a 'hamper' of 'fresh, rich experience', and puts aside his work-in-progress to exploit such 'perishable goods' before memory fades (GP 184). Waugh himself did not consider writing about his trip to Ceylon until a year afterward, in January 1955; the book he put aside to write *Pinfold* was thus not *Officers and Gentlemen* but, as he told an American interviewer, the final volume of his trilogy.[41] Writing began in earnest that autumn; Waugh worked on the novel amidst his developing libel actions and completed it in January 1957, soon after the move to Combe Florey. *The Ordeal of Gilbert Pinfold: A Conversation Piece* appeared in July, dedicated to Daphne Fielding. To Waugh's disappointment, Chapman and Hall failed to secure a 'horror' by the painter Francis Bacon to embellish its dust-jacket (L 482).

Borrowing a phrase from James Joyce (and perhaps from Stopp's soon to be published *Evelyn Waugh: Portrait of an Artist*), *Pinfold* opens with a 'Portrait of the Artist in Middle Age', proceeds through a rendition of the hero's hallucinations on a trip to Ceylon, and ends with Pinfold sitting down to write the narrative we have just read. The ending was probably inspired by Muriel Spark's first novel, *The Comforters*. A fellow-convert, Spark had been received into the Church in 1954 by Fr Caraman; another mutual friend and fellow-Catholic, Gabriel Fielding, sent Waugh an advance copy of her novel in hopes of a quotable puff. To Spark's delight Waugh offered the phrase 'brilliantly original and fascinating' (L 477) and went on to praise the book in a talk to the PEN Club and in a generous review for the *Spectator*, where he announced, five months before *Pinfold*'s publication, 'It so happens that *The Comforters* came to me just as I had finished a story on a similar theme and I was struck by how much more ambitious was Miss Spark's essay and how much better she had accomplished it' (EAR 519). Spark's writer-heroine hears voices which seem to be writing the story of her life – the story we are reading – and in the end frees herself from them only by writing a novel of her own (about characters who feel themselves to be characters in a novel). Though he had already experimented with reflexive endings in *Brideshead* and *The Loved One*, Waugh added *Pinfold*'s ending only after reading Spark.

As he had made no secret of his madness in 1954, Waugh now advertised *Pinfold* as straightforward autobiography. He announced at a Foyles literary luncheon on the day of publication: 'Three years ago I had a quite new experience. I went off my head for about three weeks'.[42] The American edition declared in its preface: 'Mr. Waugh does not deny that "Mr. Pinfold" is largely based on himself'. Thus invited, reviewers were prompt to treat the book as a confession rather than a novel, and so to offer not literary criticism but psychological analysis of Pinfold/Waugh's case history. Most took the route of John Lehmann, who argued that Pinfold's sharply accusatory voices, expressive of repressed guilts and erotic fantasies, constituted 'the revenge of his nature' – the bubbling up of Pinfold/Waugh's troubled unconscious, long buried beneath what the novel itself admits is a carefully crafted public shell.[43]

Later critics, attending to Pinfold's frequent references to the 'bestial', his initial failure to pray or hear Mass, and the way his voices echo and are sparked by various literary works, have added further readings of the novel: as a parable of the barbarian within; of religious loss and regeneration; and of the fragile and dangerous processes of literary creation. All these readings seem misguided – and exactly the kind of speculation Waugh meant his odd book to evoke. Despite his protestations, the story is not straightforwardly autobiographical (both Sykes and Donaldson noted sharp differences between *Pinfold* and the account Waugh had cheerfully retailed in the days after his return from Ceylon); Waugh, who classed 'psychoanalysis' among those other diseases, 'socialism, modern painting, agnosticism', was not a man to bare his soul before the public without some carefully contrived purpose. Nor has any psychological reading of *Pinfold* yielded a novel of the thematic density and coherence characteristic of all his other works.[44]

Pinfold is not really a novel like Waugh's others at all, but a kind of mock-novel: a sly invitation to a game. Having long complained of a prying and hostile press, Waugh now offered his critics the materials with which to construct the most searching portrait of himself yet – and waited to see who would take the bait. In Alan Brien's colourful description, Waugh 'rounded on his pursuers, ... swallowed them, and regurgitated them, harmless and picturesque as fossils in marble, embalmed in an autobiographical novel' ('Permission', 462).

The materials are skilfully chosen. Mixing easily recognizable truths with equally obvious falsehoods, *Pinfold* paints a sadder, more genial Waugh than had his enemies, a man more deeply troubled than they had conceived, and one capable of harsh self-criticism. The first chapter is an exercise in selective self-revelation conducted mainly as a meditation on his public image; here and later Waugh takes every opportunity to remind readers of those recent occasions when his character had been most offensively maligned. 'He's quite capable of taking you to the courts', say the voices; the book even responds obliquely to the allegations of Rebecca West. Against accusations that he is a traitorous spy, Pinfold stresses that 'in an old-fashioned way he was patriotic' (GP 94, 109).

The voices make some charges obviously false of Waugh (that he is impotent, a Communist, an 'old queen', secretly a Jew), others that touch on his real concerns (he is 'written out', a 'typical alcoholic', deeply in debt, lies on his tax returns, wishes to die, yearns sexually for a young woman named Margaret).[45] Most of all, they echo accusations that had surfaced in scores of profiles and reviews. Pinfold's novels are morbidly sentimental and cloyingly religious; he is a 'fascist' (either by party affiliation, or simply because he speaks 'ill of democracy'); a 'snob'; an *arriviste* ashamed of his origins; 'il n'est pas de notre société'.[46] 'His religious profession was humbug, assumed in order to ingratiate himself with the aristocracy'; 'It goes with being Lord of the Manor' (79, 116).

The game worked: his enemies were suitably puzzled. From 'the recesses of Mr. Waugh's mind', wrote Philip Toynbee in the *Observer*, have come 'the self-revelations of a remarkably honest and brave man who has also allowed us to see that he is a likeable one'; 'Whatever will he do next?' (CH 386). His real opportunity came in August, when J. B. Priestley published a retrospective review in the *New Statesman*. Claiming that 'it is not Mr. Waugh but Gilbert Pinfold who is the subject of this essay', Priestley proceeded to the attack:

> if Pinfold imagines his troubles are over, he is a fool. ... they are right, these voices, when they tell him that he is a fake. ... He is an author pretending to be a Catholic landed gentleman. ... [pretending to] represent some obscure but arrogant landed family that never had an idea in its head. ... Pinfold must step out of his role as the Cotswold gentleman quietly regretting the Reform Bill of 1832. ... He must be at all times the man of ideas, the intellectual, the artist, even if he is asked to resign from Bellamy's club. ... If authors and artists in this country are not only officially regarded without favour but even singled out for unjust treatment – as I for one believe – then the Pinfolds are partly to blame.
>
> (CH 388–91)

Waugh responded in the his best manner with 'Anything Wrong with Priestley?'
'Unless I am misinformed, Mr. Priestley was at my age a landed proprietor on a scale by which my own modest holding is a peasant's patch'. (Priestley owned two country houses, one Georgian, the other a Victorian mansion with two

thousand acres on the Isle of Wight; for trips to London he kept a flat in the Albany.)

> Naturally I hunger for Mr. Priestley's good opinion and would like to keep my sanity for a few more years. I am an old dog to learn new tricks but I dare say I could be taught an accent at a school of elocution [a reference to the broad Yorkshire accent Priestley laboured to retain]. I should not find it beyond me to behave like a cad on occasions – there are several shining examples in the literary world. My hair grows strongly still; I could wear it long. I could hire a Teddyboy suit and lark about the dance halls with a bicycle chain. But would this satisfy Mr. Priestley? Would he not be quick to detect and denounce this new persona? 'There was Waugh', he would say, 'a man of humane education and accustomed to polite society. Tried to pass as Redbrick. No wonder he's in the padded cell'.
>
> (EAR 528)

Priestley had argued that the roles of 'artist' and 'gentleman' are 'incompatible' – that 'real' artists demonstrate 'distaste for the upper classes' and support for the 'Welfare State', and that Pinfold Waugh had therefore 'gone over to the enemy'. Waugh in turn responded, in reviewing Connolly's *Enemies of Promise*, by diagnosing in his opponent both inconsistent Leftism and an 'itch of persecution mania'. 'I say, Priestley, old man, are you feeling all right?'

V

Pinfold done, Waugh hoped in March 1957 to spend some of his libel proceeds on a holiday in Monte Carlo for Laura, who loved gambling. Instead they accompanied an ailing Ronald Knox, recently diagnosed with liver cancer, for a holiday in a seaside hotel at Torquay. Waugh had first heard Knox preach in 1924; they met during the Oldmeadow affair, when Knox was Catholic chaplain to Oxford undergraduates. In the years that followed, the two met rarely but had many friends in common. In 1937 Knox met and developed a deep attachment to Daphne Acton; the affection was mutual, and from 1938 he was private chaplain to the Actons at Aldenham, where he produced his translation of the Bible. After the war, when the Actons fled the Welfare State for Rhodesia, he accepted an invitation to live with Katherine Asquith at the Manor House at Mells.

Waugh came to know Knox well only during the War, after which the priest often visited Piers Court. Both men shared a love of verbal play and distaste for what Knox (who liked to say that the last really useful human invention was the toast-rack) called, simply, 'this revolting age' (K 272), especially the course steered by the postwar Labour government. In 1948 Waugh contributed a long essay on Knox to Cyril Connolly's *Horizon* series on *The Best and the Worst* in modern writers, and in 1949 edited a selection of his sermons; in 1950, Knox dedicated his most substantial work of scholarship to Waugh (a study of religious *Enthusiasm* in the seventeenth and eighteenth centuries that Waugh hailed as 'the greatest work of literary art of the century') and chose Waugh as his literary executor.[47]

Publishers had often approached Knox for an autobiography, a companion to the story of his conversion already told in his *Spiritual Aeneid* (1918). Seeing Knox often in his last months, Waugh offered in June 1957 to write the book his friend was unable to compass. Knox accepted, with the result that his death that August, as Waugh told Diana Cooper, 'transformed my life. Instead of sitting about bored and idle I am busy all day long, both writing his life and managing his affairs' (DC 244). A far more daunting task than *Campion*, the biography of Knox was to be Waugh's most ambitious work of non-fiction, requiring months of research into Knox's family, personal history and voluminous writings, and into intricate details of the Anglican and Catholic hierarchies. There were scores of friends and associates to interview (Waugh acknowledges eighty-seven in his preface), thousands of letters and documents to digest. In September 1957, refusing other work, he told Peters the book might take two years and would be 'a magnum opus'. It took eighteen months and, as Peters noted afterward, 'seems more important to him than anything else he has written'.[48]

One indispensable source was Lady Acton, happy to share her memories of Knox at Aldenham. In February 1958 Waugh flew to Rhodesia for a three-week stay with Daphne and Sir John, their ten children and three grandchildren, at their farm, M'bebi, outside Salisbury. 'Rhodesia is not an interesting country', he reported to Ann Fleming; but he was enchanted by the household at M'bebi:

> Children were everywhere, no semblance of a nursery or a nanny, the spectacle at meals gruesome, a party-line telephone ringing all day, dreadful food, an ever present tremendously boring ex-naval chaplain, broken aluminum cutlery, plastic crockery, ants in the beds, totally untrained black servants (all converted by Daphne to Christianity, taught to serve Mass but not to empty ash trays). In fact everything that normally makes Hell but Daphne's serene sanctity radiating super-natural peace. She is the most remarkable woman I know.
>
> (L 504–5)

In March Waugh received an invitation to Downing Street to discuss Harold Macmillan's memories of Knox, who had been his tutor in 1910 (during Knox's struggle to decide between Anglicanism and Rome) and a friend ever since.

In June came news that Bron, completing his National Service with the army on Cyprus, was critically injured: while inspecting a gun, he had emptied a round of machine-gun fire into his own chest. Laura flew out, stayed in Cyprus for a month, then accompanied Bron back to London to begin a year's further hospitalization. (During visits at this time, Auberon wrote later, 'I began to be quite fond of my father, never having liked him much in childhood or early youth' (*Will This Do* 112).) In November Olivia Greene died of breast cancer in Bath. But by Christmas 1958 a manuscript was finished; Waugh put it out to bid, and turned down offers from Burns & Oates and Longmans to accept an advance of £3000 from Chapman & Hall. Delayed by further research and a printers' strike, *The Life of the Right Reverend Ronald Knox, Fellow of Trinity College, Oxford, and Pronotary Apostolic to His Holiness Pope Pius XII* appeared in October 1959, dedicated to Knox's patrons and Waugh's friends Katherine Asquith and Daphne Acton.

The authorized biography of a world-famous humourist and Catholic apologist was widely and generously reviewed. The book reduces masses of information to order without sacrificing brevity or interest; it brilliantly evokes the period of Knox's conversion to Catholicism – what such a move meant socially, doctrinally and to Knox's devoutly Anglican family. But nearly all readers agreed that Waugh left the heart of the believer (and the spiritual distinction of the beloved pastor) largely unexamined; the book's celebrated discretion borders on impersonality. 'It is an extremely good biography: beautifully clear, ... never uncritical, never dull', said the TLS, but he asks us to take Knox's 'genius' and 'sanctity' 'largely on trust'. 'The central mysteries are still hidden', agreed Maurice Bowra (CH 396–7, 406).

Waugh himself recognized the problem, explaining in the preface that his 'primary purpose [was] to tell the story of [Knox's] exterior life, not to give a conspectus of his thought'. '[A] lot of people will say that I miss his essential point and of course they will be right', he told Daphne Action, reasoning that Knox's choice of biographer meant that he 'wanted to be treated as a man of letters rather than of prayer'. But Knox's literary accomplishment also gets surprisingly little critical attention, less than in the *Horizon* essay of 1948.[49] Waugh left ample room for further books such as Thomas Corbishley's *Ronald Knox the Priest* (1964), Robert Speaight's *Ronald Knox the Writer* (1965) and the family portrait of *The Knox Brothers* by Ronald's niece Penelope Fitzgerald (1977).

The sharpest criticisms of the biography came not in the secular press but from fellow Catholics. While asserting (rather than illustrating) Knox's spiritual attainments, Waugh had cast the biography as the tale of a richly talented and sensitive man who, after a brilliant career at Oxford and in the Anglican Church, languished unappreciated by a Catholic hierarchy that never gave him 'adequate official honours' and never 'fostered his genius' (K 176, 241). Condemned by Cardinal Bourne at the outset of his Catholic career to a decade of school-teaching at St Edmund's, Knox laboured for a year on a revised *Manual of Prayers* that the hierarchy first solicited then unceremoniously repudiated: 'It is an example of the official frustration of his talents' (292). His greatest disappointment arose over the translation of the Bible, on which he worked 'alone' and 'without encouragement', rewarded by Cardinal Griffin with a stipend of only £200 a year. Thus for 'a few hundred pounds the Bishops acquired a thriving property, which at the time of Ronald's death had yielded some £50,000'; 'no word of thanks was ever said to him for this substantial benefaction' (273).

Shortly before publication Mgr John Barton, senior censor, warned Waugh, 'It is, as you are no doubt aware, a sort of unwritten law that bishops are not criticized or discussed to their disadvantage in any public way'.[50] Catholic reviewers were quick to defend Cardinals Bourne and Griffin and to suggest that there was another side to the affair of the affair of the *Manual of Prayers*.[51] Douglas Woodruff pointed out in the *Tablet* that had Waugh read further in Knox's correspondence with Griffin, he would have learnt that in 1947 Knox himself refused further payment for the Bible translation. Waugh sent a letter of apology to the *Tablet* and corrected these and other mistakes in later editions.[52]

What led Waugh to paint so partial a portrait, thus compromising his major work of scholarship? He had of course many dissatisfactions with the hierarchy, and a personal grudge against Cardinal Bourne. But it was finally Knox's own frequently voiced sense of the downward trend of recent history, so congenial to Waugh, that led him to cast Knox less as valued priest than modernity's garlanded victim. Knox shared the political and social opinions Waugh scatters through the biography – of the 'sadder and duller generation' of writers educated after 1914; of 'the drab and sour period of victory' after 1945, a time of 'social revolution' when the Butler Education Act 'overcrowd[ed] the University'. The book often intrudes such sentiments without substantiating them from Knox's works or conversation, making it easy for readers to diagnose a case of 'Waugh projecting on [Knox] his own discontents'. The book's most penetrating psychological insights apply at least as well to Waugh himself as to Knox; as Angus Wilson noted, 'It is a portrait uncomfortably in tune with the mood of *Men at Arms* and *Officers and Gentlemen*'.[53]

It is thus no surprise that in its ostentatiously chaste, formal, old-fashioned prose, *Knox* points forward to *Unconditional Surrender* and to Waugh's own self-presentation in *A Little Learning*. With its elaborate title redolent of past centuries, Johnsonian sentences and laboured puns ('intractable clergymen' during the Oxford Movement), *Knox* establishes its subject as the representative of a classic tradition latterly in decline. Though we learn that in later editions of his works Knox added translations of Latin passages 'for the benefit of a generation educated differently from his own' (166), Waugh pointedly leaves most of his Latin untranslated. In writing *Knox* he was polishing the persona, 'hard, bright and antiquated as a cuirass' (GP 9), soon to be presented to the world in his autobiography.

VI

Knox 'is selling like warm cakes', Waugh told Daphne Acton soon after publication (L 529). Elsewhere he was more forthright: 'At this rate, I shall end my life writing a history of the cobbler industry' (Buckley 1376). Having spent so long on a book that earned little beyond its advance, Waugh needed both an infusion of cash and a holiday. Still hoping to revisit India for an essay about Indian Christianity on the model of 'The American Epoch in the Catholic Church', he asked Peters to find a magazine willing to subsidize winter travel.[54] Peters arranged instead a trip to Africa, to be paid for by the Union Castle shipping line: in return for publicity, Waugh would receive £500 plus £1500 in expenses. On January 28, 1959 – between finishing the manuscript of *Knox* and the arrival of proofs – Waugh left for a brief visit to Lady Diana in Genoa before shipping out for a two-month tour of Kenya, Zanzibar, Tanganyika, Southern Rhodesia (where he again stayed with the Actons) and South Africa.

The trip was uniformly happy, so enjoyable that Waugh reported becoming 'a very different creature – all melancholia gone'; for weeks after returning in April, he wrote gaily to friends of being 'rejuvenated by trundling round Africa', and in October told Ann Fleming that 'trying to write about my African jaunt...is hard going because I can only be funny when I am complaining about something and everyone was so decent to me'.[55] He passed the summer at Combe Florey, 'entirely delicious' that year, making small stabs at the travel book, beginning a revision of *Brideshead* requested by Chapman and Hall, and exchanging playful letters with friends. Auberon returned from a visit to Italy, fully recuperated, bearing tales of Harold Acton and the manuscript of a startlingly able first novel (*The Foxglove Saga*); with all the children present, Waugh invited Mark Gerson to come and photograph family, house and grounds. But for disappointments at the summer's beginning and end – in May the offer of a CBE rather than the knighthood he hoped for, in October Catholic reaction to *Knox* – Waugh would not enjoy a period of such unalloyed content for the rest of his life.

That autumn Peters announced that Waugh's American nest-egg (his account with Little, Brown) was not only exhausted but $10,000 overdrawn. Though eager to return to the war trilogy, Waugh proposed another biography, a life of Holman Hunt, but such a book would take too long before realizing profits. Journalism had always been his mainstay in such circumstances. But he now had trouble selling the serious pieces he most wanted to write; editors wanted 'vintage' Waugh, exercises in saleable curmudgeonliness such as a series on 'A Space Man's Report on Us' offered by the *Sunday Dispatch*. 'It's no good quarrelling with my bread and butter at my age', he told Peters; if editors want 'drivel', then he would 'learn to drivel'.[56]

That December the *Daily Mail* carried just such a 'challenging' essay, written for inclusion in a series of predictions about what the decade of the 1960s would bring: 'I See Nothing But Boredom... Everywhere.' At the height of the Campaign for Nuclear Disarmament's protests against American nuclear bases in Britain, Waugh began arrestingly:

> I am not the least nervous about the much-advertised threats of the nuclear scientists: first, because I can see nothing objectionable in the total destruction of the earth, provided it is done, as seems most likely, inadvertently. If it is done in malice someone will have behaved culpably. But every well- instructed child knows that the world is going to end one day.
>
> (EAR 538)

The rest of the essay rings changes on the (commonplace) theme that with the emergence of a 'classless society', 'we are fast losing all national character'. 'Now all those things that gave the salt to English life and were the raw material of our Arts are being dissolved' in 'drab uniformity'; soon 'all buildings will look the same, all shops sell the same produce, all people say the same things in the same voices'.[57]

The African travel book was finished in December 1959; in the new year, the *Mail* offered Waugh £2000 for four travel articles about European cities, financing winter trips with Laura to Rome, Monte Carlo and Venice, and with Meg to Athens. That spring Waugh earned $1000 by reading from his works for Verve Records – half an hour of dialogue from *Vile Bodies*, half an hour of delightfully rendered scenes from *Helena*. In June he wrote to Tom Driberg: 'I have let myself in for cross-examination on Television by a man named Major Freeman who I am told was a colleague of yours in the Working Class Movement' (John Freeman, once a Labour MP, later editor of the *New Statesman*); 'Do you know anything damaging about him that I can introduce into our conversation if he becomes insolent?' (L 544). To stimulate sales, Waugh had accepted an invitation to appear on the BBC's television series *Face to Face*, more than half hoping that his demand for the extraordinary fee of £250 would cause the deal to fall through. But 'The BBC have called my bluff' (HRC E1156). (The series had already included interviews with Nurbar Gulbenkian, Carl Jung, Martin Luther King, Bertrand Russell and Adlai Stevenson; a specialist in childhood memories and traumas, Freeman had managed during one broadcast to reduce his famous subject to tears.)

The interview was televised on 26 June 1960, and has ever since been cited as another instance of Waugh's famous hostility to invaders of his privacy. But anyone who watches the interview today will find that except for one coy reference by Waugh to how 'everyone thinks ill of the BBC', all the hostility was on Freeman's side. 'Are you a snob?' Freeman asked; is 'your life in the country' a 'charade'? Did Waugh brood over 'all the adverse criticism' of his work? 'Are you ever rude to . . . nuns and priests and people of your own faith – or is this something you reserve for outsiders?' 'Do you feel the need to belong to an organisation all the time?' Did the more odious accusations made by Pinfold's voices reflect what Waugh's neighbours were saying of him? 'What do you feel is your worst fault?' (answer: 'irritability'). Waugh parried the usual questions about himself as 'squire' by explaining that 'The country to me is a place where I can be silent'; asked why he had nonetheless agreed to be interviewed, he replied with perfect deadpan: 'Poverty. We've both been hired to talk in this deliriously happy way'. Freeman's fascination with childhood ensured that much of the interview was wasted, and amidst his rapid-fire questions Waugh often had to interrupt to answer fully. But throughout, Waugh remained wryly friendly, answering with striking honesty and sometimes even volunteering modestly embarrassing facts about himself. 'To my literary and aesthetic tastes, to the problems of construction and style, to the places where I had travelled and the people I had met, to my habits of work, to all in fact which constitutes the literary life, [Freeman] was indifferent', he commented later.[58]

In July the revised *Brideshead* appeared, followed in August by Auberon's *Foxglove Saga* – 'very funny, I thought' (L 541). *A Tourist in Africa* (excerpts from which also ran in the *Spectator*) had been ready in proof since May, but with his usual grasp of publicity Waugh asked that publication be delayed until the autumn so that each publication (and the BBC interview) might enjoy its own success and contribute to that of the next. His last travel book appeared in September 1960.

'I am not sending you or any of my honoured friends a copy of my African pot boiler because I despise it', he told Ann Fleming (L 549). Partly from laziness, the book was 'a stylistic experiment: a travel diary rather than a connected narrative, composed in short sentences (often fragments) designed to convey immediacy.

28*th December* 1958. On the third day after Christmas we commemorate the massacre of the Holy Innocents. Few candid fathers, I suppose, can regard that central figure of slate in Breughel's painting in Antwerp without being touched by sympathy. After the holly and sticky sweet-meats, cold steel....

Last year I went to Central Africa but saw nothing. I flew there and back and spent a month in purely English circumstances cross-examining authorities on the book I was writing. Africa again without preoccupations with eyes reopened to the exotic. That's the ticket.

(TA 11, 13)

There are fine set-pieces such as an encounter in Rhodesia with officious bureaucrats busily assembling meaningless statistics – 'Here, fully displayed, are the arts of modern government for which, it is popularly believed, the native races are not yet far enough advanced' (116) – interspersed with brief historical essays, mainly on past colonial follies, the fault of politicians both Right and Left. 'It is wrong to represent bureaucracy as an evil contrived only by socialists. It is one of the evidences of original sin' (14–15).

Since 1960 critics have generally agreed with Cyril Connolly's judgment that, on purely literary grounds, *A Tourist* was 'quite the thinnest piece of book-making which Mr. Waugh has undertaken' (CH 415), and it has been easy after making this judgment to dismiss the book's argument as well. Its claim to be the work not of a traveller but simply a tourist, one who eschews 'problems' and seeks 'only the diverting and the picturesque' (TA 163), has led readers to conclude that the complexity of African politics simply overwhelmed him – that 'as a serious political statement [*A Tourist*] is largely negligible' (CH 51). But Waugh's studied gestures of modesty more likely stemmed from his awareness of adding to what was already a flood of books on problems of such complexity as to resist all easy generalization. 'From Algeria to Cape Town the whole African continent is afflicted by political activities which it is fatuous to ignore and as fatuous to dub complacently an "awakening". Men who have given their lives to the continent can do no more to predict the future than can the superficial tourist' (TA 164).

Politically informed readers found enough substance in the book to differ violently over it. Reviewers on the Left were especially discomforted to find an attack on racialism conducted from a distinctly conservative point of view: the angry young Alan Sillitoe ridiculed Waugh's 'alien values' and the 'curious, falsely attractive sense of tolerance of a caste-bound mind'; Basil Davidson, a popular historian and travel-writer whose works included a Marxist study of *The African Awakening* (1955), called Waugh's political opinions 'often silly and nearly always out of touch with reality'. On the Right, Anthony Allott, a historian of African law at the University of London, found 'little, either of fact or interpretation, with which one can disagree'. Allott made clear what was at stake in all these responses: 'To say that this book shows a well-balanced and objective appreciation of some of the problems of East and Central Africa is perhaps merely to say that the reviewer shares the prejudices of Mr Waugh' (CH 418, 412–13).

For all its lightness of touch, *A Tourist* is arguably Waugh's wisest travel book, certainly his most accurately prophetic. Its theme had already been stated in 'I See Nothing But Boredom': 'The foundation of empires is often an occasion of woe; their dissolution, invariably; and I believe that the peoples of Asia and Africa who have lately enjoyed British rule are in for great distress'.[59] In retrospect we can now see 1959–60 as a watershed year when Britain and France greatly accelerated their rush to decolonialize, leaving behind a series of jerry-built 'constitutional' states that would one by one suffer military coups and single-party rule – seventy five such coups by 1970, in a sad and bloody litany that includes the names of Nkrumah, Kasavubu, Lumumba, Tsombe, Mobutu, Kenyatta, Kaunda, Youlou, Maga, Mba, Gadafi, Banda, Macias Nguema, Bokassa, Sékou Touré, Obote, Tombalbaye, Malloum, Kerekou, Bourguiba, Amin.

A Tourist seems in fact a self-conscious, valedictory rewriting of *Remote People*, to which it more than once refers. The pragmatism and pessimism of 1931 remain: 'Cruelty and injustices are endemic everywhere'; 'Tribal wars and slavery were endemic before [the white man] came; no doubt they will break out again when they leave' (TA 167, 151). But to such sentiments Waugh now adds a far more thoroughgoing refusal to celebrate European institutions. *Remote People* had found charm in settlers' efforts to establish 'Barsetshire on the equator'; *A Tourist* evinces no nostalgia for what he had once called 'the free and fecund Victorian age'. 'As for the nineteenth century, which is popularly supposed to have been so free...'; 'It is hard to realize now that at the time of the Diamond Jubilee many men of good will and intelligence thought the Pax Victoriana a reality' (TA 14, 151). The narrator's search for 'the exotic' is rewarded not by the Alice-in-Wonderland joys of 1931, but the very grim spectacle of a continent losing its distinctive character and being laid waste by politics (both processes symbolized by the hideous modernist buildings everywhere displacing native styles). Everywhere burgeons a new class of bureaucrats – in Tanganyika, 'the number of officials has doubled since 1945' – and with them 'the universal process of offices becoming larger and private houses smaller' (65, 46). Like *Remote People*, *A Tourist* climaxes with a vignette of the 'one valuable thing' the Europeans brought, here realized in Father Groeber's Serima Mission, where under the aegis of the universal Church, a distinctively African religious and artistic culture temporarily prospers. But in what is perhaps Waugh's most striking revision of his earlier book, where *Remote People* had been flippant on the issue, *A Tourist* ends with a discussion of racialism as simply 'insane'. In a brilliant phrase, Waugh describes the two-class state created by South African apartheid – yet one more instance of modern failure to understand that 'Stable and fruitful societies have always been elaborately graded' – as 'egalitarianism literally cracked' (165).

A Tourist bases its gloomy predictions partly on Waugh's familiar argument that in areas of tribal, racial and cultural diversity, claims to represent the 'nation' generally mask other, less creditable aims; partly on an analysis put into the mouth of a nameless priest in the mountains of Tanganyika:

Then the old priest who was guiding us, an Italian long habituated to Africa, spoke of African 'nationalism'. The mistake, he said, was to introduce 'Africanization' through politics instead of through service. None of the young men now filling the lower government offices should have been sent from England. Natives should have filled those places and an all-African administration should have been built up from the bottom. Instead we contemplated handing over the highest posts to men who had nothing except the ability to make themselves popular. Like everyone else I met he spoke well of Mr. Nyerere, but he doubted the ability of his party to govern.

It was not a new point of view, but the speaker gave it authority.

(TA 111)

As many have argued, Britain in its rush to decamp from Africa left behind not political institutions but simply politicians. (Nyerere's party indeed failed to govern; in 1964 Nyerere emerged as Tanzania's charismatic dictator, leader of what he called 'a democratic one-party state'.)

VII

'As soon as *Knox* is done', Waugh told Peters, 'I must start a novel – get it done while I have inventive strength left' (HRC E1063). After finishing *A Tourist* and his tour of Mediterranean cities, he turned down an offer of $5000 a year from the *National Review* for twice-monthly essays of 2000 words ('higher pay by far than we have ever given before') to begin his last novel (Buckley 1376). By August 1960, under the working titles *Chivalry* and *Conventional Weapons*, 30,000 words were done (taking the story to Mr Crouchback's funeral); *Unconditional Surrender* was completed in April 1961 and published that October, with a dedication 'To my daughter Margaret, Child of the Locust Years'. He renamed the book in response to a letter from Jocelyn Brooke (who had also chosen *Conventional Weapons* as title for a novel); because another *Unconditional Surrender* had appeared in America, Little, Brown insisted on yet a different title for the US edition. 'Which will help the poor reviewers to understand better? That's really all that matters', Waugh wrote, suggesting alternatives – *Peace without Honour, Honour Comes a Pilgrim Grey, The Sword, Quixote in Modern Dress, Uncle Tom's Cabin & the Seven Dwarfs* – from which his editors selected *The End of the Battle*.[60]

After a decade of setbacks and doubts, Waugh had produced what today many consider his finest achievement. That he could complete so complex a novel (both in itself and as the culmination of his trilogy) in only twelve months was the result of years of planning. At least since 1954 he had known that he would incorporate material from 'Compassion'; in 1955, he asked Ann Fleming for 'some particulars about abortion in wartime for my next volume' (D 736). By 1959 he had hired Joan Saunders of Writers and Speakers Research to provide information about air-raids, buzz-bombs and the object that had already given its name to the Prologue of *Men at Arms* and would later serve as title for the trilogy as a whole: the Sword of Stalingrad, officially known as the 'Sword of Honour', commissioned by George VI in February 1943, exhibited to large crowds in Westminster Abbey from 29 to 31 October, and presented by Churchill to Stalin at the Teheran Conference that November.[61]

After a 'Synopsis of Preceding Volumes' and a brief account of Guy's 'Locust Years' (his 'two blank years' after Crete failing to find his way back into battle), the story opens on Guy Crouchback's fortieth birthday in 1943. Crowds of

Londoners stand on line to view the sword, displayed like a cross 'upright between two candles, on a table counterfeiting an altar...hard by the shrine of Edward the Confessor and the sacring place of the kings of England', but Guy is 'not tempted to join them in their piety' (US 18–19). Waugh denies its official name to this debased modern analogue of the sword of Sir Roger on which Guy dedicated himself in *Men at Arms*. Instead, in tribute to the disillusioning corruptions of modern politics, he calls it only 'State Sword', and traces its inspiration to the bogus hero of Operation Popgun.

> 'By the way, do you realize it was Trimmer who gave the monarch the idea for this Sword of Stalingrad? [Baron Kilbannock tells his wife]. Indirectly, of course. In the big scene of Trimmer's landing I gave him a "commando dagger" to brandish. I don't suppose you've ever seen the things....A few hundred were issued. To my certain knowledge none was ever used in action....They were mostly given away to tarts....Well, you know how sharp the royal eye is for any detail of equipment. He was given a preview of the Trimmer film and spotted the dagger at once. Had one sent round...and the final result was that thing in the Abbey'.
>
> (US 48)

'First of the two bastards Trimmer fathers in the book', the sword symbolizes the Russian alliance, the cataclysm which convinces Guy that the war will be lost spiritually even as it is won militarily, and so that 'Personal honour alone remains'.[62]

The main story ends a year later with the 'unconditional surrender' not of the Fascist enemy but of Guy himself, to providence and a renewed religious faith. After a climactic confession of previous sins, Guy learns to embrace his calling: to a life not of public crusading for universal justice, but a humble pilgrimage of private charity and devotion. Like *Brideshead* – of which it is in many ways a revision – the trilogy's largest subjects are 'the operation of divine grace' and the 'limited hope' available in a world beset by disaster.

In 1939 Guy had thought 'there was a place for him' in a crusade against 'the Modern Age in arms' (MA 5); by 1943, he sees no place for himself in a war which 'it doesn't seem to matter now who wins' (US 8). But the subversion of Allied war aims that completes Guy's disillusion with soldiering – especially when, in Yugoslavia, he becomes himself an unwilling instrument in the subversion of a once-Christian nation – also begins his spiritual renewal. Guy makes his recovery by recognizing, and rejecting, a world now seen to be populated not by the wayward child-warriors of *Men at Arms* or the seemingly gallant heroes of *Officers and Gentlemen*, but very adult forms of corruption and betrayal. An object of 'veneration', the Stalingrad sword which organizes *Unconditional Surrender*'s first chapter symbolizes the new secular religion embraced by so many of the novel's characters: the Communism of De Souza, Gilpin, Joe Cattermole, Susie, the 'Loot' and Sir Ralph Brompton, whose 'special care' at this late stage of the war is 'Liberation'. 'Wherever those lower than the Cabinet and the Chiefs of Staff adumbrated the dismemberment of Christendom, there Sir Ralph might be found'; 'Tito's the friend, not Mihajlovic', he reminds his acolytes.[63] *Unconditional Surrender* dramatizes what since 1930 Waugh had thought the great battle of modern times, between (Catholic) Christianity and Communism, the only religions that could any longer command assent. His vision of an international Communist conspiracy predictably led reviewers like Philip Toynbee to accuse him of 'lunatic McCarthyism'.

Unconditional Surrender was of course a product of the Cold War, conceived in the wake of Burgess, Maclean and Philby; after Rebecca West's libel, Waugh was doubtless glad of an occasion to make his commitments unambiguously clear. He was no admirer of Senator McCarthy. But he did believe that a Communist conspiracy existed during and after the war, furthered by spies and by 'officials who were working for the local Communist Parties rather than for their own country'.[64] He had seen its workings first-hand in Yugoslavia. Recent studies of Communist infiltration into Britain's wartime mission there strikingly confirm the accuracy of his depiction of it, and suggest specific models among Waugh's acquaintance for subversives such as Gilpin and Cattermole.[65]

As *Unconditional Surrender* opens, Guy hears the news of Italy's defeat and comments to his father that the Pope would have done better to remain impassive in his Vatican fortress rather than dirty his hands with the series of political accommodations that began in 1860 and ended with the Lateran Treaty. (The speech recalls the account of Guy's spiritual aridity at the start of *Men at Arms*, with its evocation of 'the last pope' alone in his fastness.) Old Mr Crouchback quickly rebukes such 'nonsense': 'That isn't at all what the Church is like. It isn't what she's *for*'.

> The Mystical Body doesn't strike attitudes and stand on its dignity. It accepts suffering and injustice.... When you spoke of the Lateran Treaty did you consider how many souls may have been reconciled and have died at peace as the result of it? How many children may have been brought up in the faith who might have lived in ignorance? Quantitative judgments don't apply. If only one soul was saved, that is full compensation for any amount of loss of 'face'.
>
> (US10)

Mr Crouchback's words are recalled again and again in the narrative to follow.

Guy first recalls them at his father's funeral. In this carefully constructed scene (whose 'souped-up traditionalism' Kingsley Amis would ridicule), Guy 'makes the fundamental act of the will on which the entire action [of the novel] turns'.[66] Recognizing in the language of the Mass that his saintly father is 'mutatur, non tollitur' ('changed, not ended'), Guy prays 'to, rather than for' the 'best man, the only entirely good man, he had ever known': 'Show me what to do and help me to do it' (78–80). With this act Guy begins to kindle the active faith that will allow him once again to find a 'place', a way of participating in the world – and that will make his father's words come true in his own life, in acts of charity to his ex-wife and, in the sequence that incorporates 'Compassion', to the Jews of Begoy.

The climactic moment of Guy's spiritual regeneration (and of the novel) comes at the end, in a final penitential act, the last of the trilogy's many scenes of confession. In a speech reminiscent of Sonia Trumpington's explanation of

Alastair's enlistment in *Put Out More Flags*, the Jewish leader Mme Kanyi evokes the whole confused and culpable ethos of war:

> 'Is there any place that is free from evil? It is too simple to say that only the Nazis wanted war. These communists wanted it too. It was the only way in which they could come to power. Many of my people wanted it, to be revenged on the Germans, to hasten the creation of the national state. It seems to me that there was a will to war, a death wish, everywhere. Even good men thought their private honour would be satisfied by war. They could assert their manhood by killing and being killed. They would accept hardships in recompense for having been selfish and lazy. Danger justified privilege. I knew Italians – not very many perhaps – who felt this. Were there none in England?
> 'God forgive me', said Guy. 'I was one of them'.
>
> (US 300)

There could be no clearer confession of Guy's earlier illusions and guilt, and of Waugh's own. In the providential economy of the trilogy, this act of penitence is what causes events, as his brother-in-law sourly observes, to 'turn out very conveniently for Guy' (311).

Yet Waugh allows Guy neither the luxury of a glamorous recommitment to his faith (to match the military glamour he renounces) nor any sense that his conquest of sloth will purchase worldly advantage. From *Men at Arms* onward, Guy's few efforts at kindness to others (such as the well-meant gift of a bottle of whisky that triggered Apthorpe's death) and even his acts of loyalty have resulted in disaster. Now his agreement to resume his marriage leads Virginia to move in with Uncle Peregrine, and so to her death from a buzz-bomb. Later, when the Jews of Begoy, interned by the Partisans, also excite Guy's 'compassion' – 'less than he had felt for Virginia and her child but a similar sense that here again, in a world of hate and waste, he was being offered the chance of doing a single small act to redeem the times' (248) – his efforts to help result only in a 'frustrated act of mercy' (301). Those Jews who escape find themselves behind barbed wire in an Italian refugee camp; as a direct result of Guy's intervention, Mme Kanyi and her husband are executed by the Partisans as traitors.

But it is the task of providence to educe spiritual good from worldly disaster, usually ironically. Though he cannot heroically redeem the whole 'Modern Age in arms', Guy can care for the soul of one child; Virginia, who converts in order that Guy may adopt her child, dies 'at the one time in her life when she could be sure of heaven – eventually'.[67] Even from the political decisions 'on the highest level' that betray Yugoslavia to Tito, there emerges, 'as an unintended by-product', 'one infinitesimal positive good' (248). Twelve years earlier Waugh had explored the pattern in 'Compassion', whose agnostic hero Major Gordon, in his efforts to save a Jewish couple, accomplishes their execution. That tale ended:

> [Gordon] told the story of the Kanyis. 'Those are the real horrors of war – not just people having their legs blown off', he concluded. 'How do you explain that, padre?'

There was no immediate answer until the second-in-command said: 'You did all you could. A darn sight more than most people would have done'.

'That's your answer', said the chaplain. 'You mustn't judge actions by their apparent success. Everything you did was good in itself'.

'A fat lot of good that did the Kanyis'.

'No. But don't you think it just possible that they did you good? No suffering need ever be wasted. It is just as much a part of Charity to receive cheerfully as to give'....

'I'd like you to tell me a bit more about that', said Major Gordon.

(Compassion 98)

It is Guy's charity toward Virginia and little Trimmer that, 'in the terms Waugh would have been familiar with, gained him *actual* grace, which in turn prompts him toward further good action': his efforts for the Kanyis, and culminating act of penitence (Davis, *Writer*, 320).

Of his two acts of compassion, Guy's decision to take back Virginia when, as Waugh makes clear, he no longer loves her – in order to adopt a hairdresser's bastard as his own – constitutes the clearer embodiment of his father's words about the Mystical Body.[68] In a fine scene, Kerstie Kilbannock, 'with anger and pity and something near love in her voice', denounces what from her worldly viewpoint seems Guy's foolish chivalry: 'Can't you see how ridiculous you will look playing the knight errant? Ian thinks you are insane, literally. Can you tell me any sane reason for doing this thing?' Guy answers in a speech that recalls Sebastian's reasons for taking up with Kurt in *Brideshead*:

'Knights errant...used to go out looking for noble deeds. I don't think I've ever in my life done a single, positively unselfish action. I certainly haven't gone out of my way to find opportunities. Here was something most unwelcome, put into my hands; something which I believe the Americans describe as "beyond the call of duty"; not the normal behaviour of an officer and a gentleman; something they'll laugh about in Bellamy's'....

'My dear Guy, the world is full of unwanted children. Half the population of Europe are homeless. What is one child more or less in all the misery?'...

It was no good trying to explain, Guy thought. Had someone said: 'All differences are theological differences'? He turned once more to his father's letter: *Quantitative judgments don't apply.*[69]

Swallowing personal and family pride to pass on the Crouchback name and legacy to 'little Trimmer', Guy enacts more fully than any character since Helena Waugh's hard-won understanding of the Church's function: not to fortify the walls against barbarism, but to bring the Hoopers and the Trimmers in. (To emphasize Guy's healing humiliation, Waugh altered later editions of the novel so that when he remarries after Virginia's death, there are no legitimate children.)[70] In adopting Trimmer's child Guy fulfills (ironically) Mr Goodall's words in *Men at Arms* about another Catholic who perpetuates his family by returning to his estranged wife: 'Explain it how you will, I see the workings of Providence there' (MA 147). Taking up parental responsibility, Guy begins to fulfill the task of emulating his father – and brings to resolution the theme of broken families (and the broken selves who spring from them) that had haunted Waugh's fiction since *Decline and Fall*.[71]

By the end of *Unconditional Surrender*, Guy has succeeded in excising all those unhealthy parts of himself which in the course of the trilogy Waugh had externalized in Guy's various doppelgängers and heroes. Ritchie-Hook and the whole world of *Men at Arms* makes a final appearance in order to die again, in the appropriately ignominious tragi-comedy of a bogus raid staged by the Partisans – a raid not even on the Germans, but only a small company of fellow Yugoslavs occupying a 'little fort built more than a century earlier, part of the defensive line of Christendom against the Turk' (284). The mystique of Ivor Claire dies again in Guy's generous decision *not* to emulate 'the behaviour of an officer and a gentleman' with the pregnant Virginia. The new demon of volume three that Guy must purge is what the novel repeatedly identifies as 'The Death Wish' – not mere slothful sadness in the face of spiritual good, but full-fledged despair at the collapse of all one's deepest worldly hopes. Waugh planted the theme in *Men at Arms*, in Apthorpe's remarks on his deathbed that he has 'lost the will to live', and in *Officers and Gentlemen* in Ludovic's observation that 'Major Hound seems strangely lacking in the Death-Wish'. Memory of 'the despair in which his brother, Ivo, had starved himself to death' (and Guy's tendencies in the same direction) is kept alive throughout the trilogy. Guy begins *Unconditional Surrender* eager to fight, but with no will to win; Virginia, Ritchie-Hook and General Whale variously express their wish to escape into death.[72] Guy alone, after an explicit diagnosis – 'Crouchback has the death wish', announces a shrewd American – recognizes the error of his 'presumption', confesses it, and with the help of his father, Virginia, and Mme Kanyi, turns it to good use (219–20).

Of all the characters who shadow Guy, the most complex is Ludovic. Established in *Officers and Gentlemen* as Guy's murderous saviour, Ludovic blossoms in volume three into Waugh's last homosexual aesthete, the long-time pupil who has accepted all Sir Ralph Brompton's teaching but his Communism, and is now an accomplished author. That he is in some sense Guy's double comes clear in the novel's first scene, when Ludovic jumps the line at Westminster Abbey to see the Sword of Stalingrad, as at the start of *Men at Arms* Guy had interrupted a line of 'peccant urchins' on their way to confession (MA 7); like Guy, Ludovic has had his locust years ('His last two years had been as uneventful as Guy's (US 40).) In the middle sections of the novel, while Guy grows in charity, Ludovic buys himself a Pekinese (named 'Fido' after the officer he has murdered on Crete) 'for *love*' (134); as Guy's faith revives, Ludovic spiritually dies. (De Souza speaks more truly than he knows in calling him 'Major Dracula' and a 'zombie'.) At the end, Ludovic buys Castello Crouchback, adopting an Italian exile (with Padfield as factotum) – a debased version of the condition in which Guy began. He makes the purchase on the proceeds of an immensely successful novel, appropriately entitled *The Death Wish*.

Waugh uses Ludovic to shadow not only Guy but himself, thereby making the trilogy not only the story of Guy Crouchback but also a commentary on the career of Evelyn Waugh, Writer. As Waugh proceeded through the volumes of his *maximum opus*, he increasingly used it as the vehicle for self-conscious criticism of his earlier fiction. *Officers and Gentlemen* revised his understanding of Mrs Stitch (as individual, and as literary and social type). In a remarkable manoeuvre, *Unconditional Surrender*'s Everard Spruce identifies Virginia as the real-life version of a familiar literary type – 'the last of twenty years' succession of heroines', the 'ghosts of romance who walked between the two wars'.[73] Through the startlingly compassionate treatment she receives in his last novel, Waugh revises our understanding of the female type who had populated his prewar fiction, from Margot Metroland to Brenda Last (whom Virginia is explicitly made to recall).[74] In the same way, Ludovic's *Death Wish*, that 'melancholy, self-conscious, deliberately "artistic" work', so obviously parallel in style and plot to *Brideshead Revisited*, 'fairly declares the trilogy to be (in part) a judgment on Waugh's own earlier melancholy work' (O'Hare 300). Two years earlier, Waugh had pruned *Brideshead* for a new edition; now he engages in a more complex act of revision.

Unconditional Surrender uses not only Ludovic's novel – written at the same moment in the war at which, with an obsessional ease previously unknown to him, Waugh wrote *Brideshead* – but also Ludovic himself as a tool with which to confess and exorcise what Waugh thought his own misguided tendencies. By 1961, a succession of critics had followed Donat O'Donnell in diagnosing the author of *Brideshead* as a 'disappointed' or (in V. S. Pritchett's phrase) 'wounded romantic'.[75] (Guy's final confession to Mme Kanyi registers Waugh's qualified agreement with this judgment.) We learn of Ludovic before he writes *The Death Wish*: 'Only a preternaturally astute reader of Ludovic's aphorisms could discern that their author had once been at heart ... a romantic'. But as a result of his association with Sir Ralph and the guilty events on Crete that continue to haunt him, 'whatever romantic image of himself Ludovic had ever set up was finally defaced'. 'In this lonely condition' – at the point during the war when Waugh himself was beginning to understand writing as his vocation, and committing himself to what 'Fan-Fare' would call 'attention to style' – Ludovic finds 'solace, positive excitement, in the art of writing': 'work[ing] over his note-books, curtailing, expanding, polishing; often consulting Fowler, not disdaining Roget' (39–40). At last he produces *The Death Wish*: 'His book grew as little Trimmer grew in Virginia's womb, without her conscious volition' (207).

Like little Trimmer, then, *The Death Wish* is a child of sin. As all those in the novel who have read it agree, it is also sentimental trash. But 'there is good in a decadent world', Waugh told John Freeman in 1960. Just as providence oversees Guy's adoption of Trimmer's child so that it may be brought up in the faith, Waugh uses the many parallels between *Brideshead* and the war trilogy to insinuate not a total rejection of his earlier novel, but a correction.

Like *Brideshead*, *Sword of Honour* constantly keeps its reader aware of different orders of reality: the human world of frustration and corruption, and the transcendent, orderly reality of God. (The latter, and its often ironic distance from the former, is repeatedly signalled by the trilogy's dating of events by the liturgical calendar.) Central to both novels is the death of a father and its spiritual effects. But Guy's answered prayer at old Mr Crouchback's funeral is a much more understated miracle than the powerfully dramatic spectacle at

Lord Marchmain's deathbed that precipitates Charles Ryder's conversion. Guy is not called upon to make the heroic renunciations of a Sebastian Flyte or a Charles Ryder. Throughout, Waugh allows a gently mocking humour to play about even his best characters – even the saintly Mr Crouchback; the brutal and alien figure of Bridey is softened into old Uncle Peregrine, a pious 'bore of international repute'.

The difference makes itself felt throughout the trilogy. God's ways are not so easy of discovery as in the earlier novel; they are to be found not in moments of high drama, but in the tedium of daily life – often with difficulty, and only after the fact. *Sword of Honour* understates all the providential signs and portents given such prominence in *Brideshead*. Meanwhile, human efforts to ape providence – the Electronic Personnel Selector which turns up Guy as a candidate for posting to Italy, the elaborate web of (bogus) top-secret information assembled by Grace-Groundling-Marchpole, who hopes that once the whole world has a place in the intricate mosaic of his files, war will cease – are foolish and vain, and serve God's ends willy-nilly. (It is Grace-Groundling-Marchpole who, because he thinks Guy a bad security risk, prevents his posting to Italy and so makes possible his saving journey to Yugoslavia.)

The most important difference between the two novels, of course, is in their endings. Ryder ended 'homeless, childless, middle-aged, loveless', his sole solace the spiritual satisfactions of the novel's final paragraphs; Guy ends at his ancestral estate at Broome (albeit in the 'lesser House') with wife and family. No longer the soul apart with which *Men at Arms* began, we last see him enjoying a reunion dinner of Commandos. Where Marchmain's death spelt the earthly extinction of a family, Guy's father's death begins the process by which the Crouchback line is continued. But again Waugh does not romanticize. 'You're looking unusually cheerful today', Hooper said to Ryder; 'For a chap who's on his way home you don't seem very cheerful', Guy hears (US 305–6). Guy's reward is not joy but hard-won content, achieved through charity and resignation: 'Only Box-Bender thought the ending happy', Waugh told Nancy Mitford (L 577). Thus in a far more carefully measured way than *Brideshead*, the trilogy presents its moral of 'limited hope'. In the elections of 1951 mentioned in the novel's Epilogue, Box-Bender – an example of the sort of Conservative Waugh despised – loses his parliamentary seat; but the Communist Gilpin is elected.

VIII

On finishing *Unconditional Surrender* in April 1961, Waugh wrote to Peters to suggest a film version of the trilogy – Alec Guinness might play Guy – and to propose his long-planned stay against poverty in old age: an autobiography, to appear like Diana Cooper's in three volumes.[76] Peters had no difficulty interesting publishers in what all assumed would be a mine of society gossip and scandal. For three volumes published 'at two-yearly intervals', the *Sunday Times* would buy serial rights at £5000 per volume; confident of advances of at least £3000 per volume in England and $5000 from America, Peters predicted the project would 'bring in over £29,000 – say £5,000 a year for six years'.[77]

Waugh began writing to the friends of his youth for permission to use their names. Only two refused – his Lancing friend Hugh Molson, and Matthew Ponsonby (who did not want the story of his arrest for drunk driving revived). From an almshouse in Winchester came the reply of Dick Young: 'Publish and be damned'; 'I always flatter myself that I was the original of Capt. Grimes' – followed by a second letter requesting discretion.[78]

That summer, satisfying a longstanding desire, Waugh broadcast over the BBC a celebration of P. G. Wodehouse on his eightieth birthday, a belated rebuttal of the charges of treason made against Wodehouse by Duff Cooper's wartime Ministry of Information.[79] But amidst public success came a succession of private frustrations and disappointments. Graham Greene's *A Burnt-Out Case* (1961) gave signs of an apostasy more troubling even than Clarissa Avon's; Auberon and Teresa married outside the faith – she to the American classical scholar John D'Arms, he to Lady Teresa Onslow (both spouses eventually agreed to take instruction).

In the autumn came reviews of *Unconditional Surrender*. Waugh's efforts to write of a world in which the workings of providence are agonizingly difficult to descry succeeded only too well: few even among Catholic readers grasped the intricate economy of grace he had carefully engineered.[80] Instead, the novel became a political shuttlecock, with the most famous names lining up in opposition. Kingsley Amis, Philip Toynbee, Frank Kermode, Joseph Heller and Gore Vidal all raised the familiar complaints against Waugh's 'snobbery' and 'reactionary nostalgia'; Simon Raven produced a favourable notice, then on reconsideration wrote a long essay on the 'sheer *silliness*' that 'recur[s] so often and mar[s] so much' of the novel. In response a young Joan Didion took Waugh's part by attacking those who sought to dismiss Waugh 'as "anachronistic" and "reactionary" (an adjective employed by Gore Vidal and others to indicate their suspicion that Waugh harbours certain lingering sympathies with the central tenets of Western civilization)'. She proclaimed the trilogy 'a complex elegiac study of the breakdown of a civilization, a great work... right in every way'.[81] Less political critics joined in noting Waugh's new emphasis on charity, but mourned that this theme caused the trilogy's original promise as satire to remain unfulfilled.[82]

That winter, again unable to find a publisher willing to subsidize a trip to India, Peters arranged for Waugh to revisit Guiana. The *Daily Mail* agreed to pay £2000 for four articles retracing the journey of *Ninety-Two Days*. Taking his daughter Meg as 'secretary' and companion, Waugh sailed in November 1961 on the *Stella Polaris*, the same ship on which he and Evelyn Gardner had honeymooned thirty years before. 'What changes did I find remarkable in British Guiana? Not the new bauxite town, not the jeeps on the savannah, not the air-conditioning in Georgetown. The great change was something more typical of the modern age than any of these things. It was the increase of hate'.[83] He met the premier Cheddi Jagan, an American-trained dentist whose People's Progressive Party was then incurring the disapproval of the Kennedy administration for its public celebrations of Fidel Castro; he interviewed members of the opposition People's National Congress, a black nationalist party, also Marxist, which advocated division of the country into three racially segregated zones, black, Indian and mixed. ('Guiana must be the only place where you find a Negro advocating apartheid'.) In thirty years the country had gained 'something ugly and new' – 'political consciousness', making its difficulties 'a microcosm of universal unrest'. Its racial hatreds had been unleashed, Waugh thought, as 'the direct result of the attempt to introduce representative government on the basis of universal suffrage'.

On the voyage out he had stayed in Trinidad with Lord Hailes, governor-general of the West Indies; after his return in February 1962, irked that he had not also stopped in Jamaica, Ann Fleming passed along the gossip that the Haileses had been bored by his company. Waugh was shocked, and brooded on the decline of what had always been one of his greatest sources of pleasure: pleasing others. A month later he was still brooding:

> I must explain about boring the Hailses because it has been what the young people call 'traumatic'....I was confident they both enjoyed my visit....I talked loud & long & they laughed like anything. Now I find I bored them. Well of course everyone is a bore to someone. One recognizes that. But it is a ghastly thing if one loses the consciousness of being a bore. You do see it means I can never go out again.

> (L 584–5)

For Waugh, as he later said of his father, 'The wish to cause pleasure and the wish for affection were indistinguishable' (ALL 66); 'We cherish our friends not for their ability to amuse us but for ours to amuse them – a diminishing number in my case' (D 786).

The incident was so disturbing in part because it came amidst a mortifying wrangle with the *Mail*. After Waugh sailed for Guiana, the *Mail* changed editors. The new editor explained that what he expected from Waugh was light travel articles, not political essays; he was willing to print 'Return to Eldorado' only in a form so truncated as to make its argument sound foolish. After a long correspondence Waugh withdrew the article and agreed to fulfill his contract by writing the 'challenging' pieces desired, including 'Manners and Morals', a two-part review of the *Pan Book of Etiquette*. He took the new assignment seriously, using the occasion to compare Victorian with modern books of conduct. 'I know it is no good complaining' he wrote to Peters when the *Mail* 'gravely mutilated' even this review (HRC E1254). Peters was able to place 'Return to Eldorado' in the *Sunday Times* (and the American *National Review*), but Waugh saw only too clearly what editors wanted from him, and that the work he most cared about was becoming progressively harder to sell.

That summer Meg – Waugh's favourite and most devoted child, recipient of his most playful letters, the one always able to cheer him – announced that she too wished to marry. Waugh was scrupulously kind and polite when she brought her fiancé Giles FitzHerbert to Combe Florey in August, and in October when they married. But with his usual mixture of humour and lacerating honesty, he confessed his gloom to Diana Cooper:

It is, to me, a bitter pill and ungilded. I would forbid the marriage if I had any other cause than jealousy & snobbery. As it is, I pretend to be complaisant.... You see with Meg I have exhausted my capacity for finding objects of love. How does one exist without them?

(L 593)

'One of the marks of love is the wish to communicate', he had once written to Meg (Hastings 605). It seemed that with age, both love and the ability to communicate were drying up.

The same letter to Lady Diana, written shortly after his first meeting with Meg's fiancé, remarks: 'Do you remember books I wrote about a character called "Basil Seal"[?] ... I suddenly yesterday began a story about Basil Seal at 60. Jolly good so far'. Waugh's last, slender work of fiction, *Basil Seal Rides Again* (described in its dedication to Ann Fleming as 'a senile attempt to recapture the manner of my youth') is both a protest against the new decade of the sixties, a 'generation of beatniks and rancorous students' (EAR 617), and a fantasy of preventing Meg's marriage. Still recognizable by his 'childish mouth', Basil is now well-groomed and respectable, and enjoys with his daughter Barbara the same quasi-incestuous intimacy that informed his relations with her namesake Barbara Sothill in *Put Out More Flags*. Basil is also transparently Waugh himself: prematurely aged at sixty, fat, deaf, short of breath and stricken when Barbara announces her decision to marry a scruffy young man who has already stolen Basil's shirts, broken into his wine cellar, and worst of all, reminds him of his own younger self. Using an idea from Ivy Compton-Burnett, Waugh allows Basil to derail the marriage by persuading Barbara that her suitor is really her brother, the child of one of Basil's long-forgotten affairs.[84] In an act of self-punishing irony, Waugh agreed to defer hardcover publication of the story – in an expensive edition limited to 750 copies in Britain and 1000 in America – to coincide with his own sixtieth birthday.

The events of the 1960s that most troubled Waugh came not from publishers, his friends or family, but from Rome. Since the forties he had opposed proposals for rapprochement between Catholics and Protestants and complained of the liturgical changes wrought by Pius XII, especially the changes in Holy Week that since 1956 spoiled his annual Easter retreats at Downside.[85] He made fun of new practices such as priests saying Mass facing the congregation ('May this not be due to television?'), which until the early sixties seemed only 'fads'.[86] Now changes of much broader scope threatened.

In 1958, nearly seventy-seven years old, John XXIII was elected pope. 'I have a crush on the new Pope', Waugh told Lady Acton; 'A most trustworthy looking man and good for 25 years of placid inactivity' (L 515). Others read in the election of the man soon to be known as 'the people's pope', the first pope to leave Rome since Pius IX immured himself in the Vatican, signs of a new era in the Church.[87] Three months after his election John surprised everyone by calling a general council, which first convened in October 1962. In November, scenting danger, Waugh wrote one of his most famous essays, 'The Same Again, Please'.

> [I]n the preliminary welcome which the [Council] has enjoyed during the past three years there has been an insistent note that the 'Voice of the Laity' shall be more clearly heard, and that voice, so far as it has been audible in northern Europe and the United States, has been largely that of the minority who demand radical reform.
>
> (EAR 604)

Claiming himself 'typical' of the 'middle rank' of Catholics, Waugh worried that the 'modernists' at the Council, 'a minority who demand radical reform', would get the upper hand. There were rumours of 'startling changes' such as a vernacular Mass, a new emphasis on the lay apostolate to the detriment of the special authority and dignity of the priest, and a rush to ecumenism that seemed to imply dilution of the faith (instead of making 'manifest the true character of the Church' so that 'dissenters will be drawn to make their submission'). 'When young theologians talk, as they do, of Holy Communion as "a social meal", they find little response in the hearts or minds of their less sophisticated brothers'.

Response to the essay was immediate and long-lasting: letters of praise from conservatives in the hierarchy such as Archbishop Heenan and Bishop Dwyer of Leeds, and a heated controversy in the Catholic press. After it appeared in the *Spectator*, Waugh offered 'The Same Again' to editors abroad, regardless of fee; William F. Buckley ran it in the *National Review*, and again as a separate pamphlet. Essays appeared in response, followed by lengthy correspondence. The man who in 1954 had written in reply to Hugh-Trevor Roper, 'I have never, loudly or quietly or in the silence of my heart, claimed or aspired to represent or lead any one of my fellow Catholics' now found himself the recognized lay spokesman for the conservative ecclesiological cause.[88]

Waugh always revered John as a 'conservative', an unworldly man who 'had no idea of the Pandora's box he was opening' by calling a council.[89] (In an Apostolic Constitution published in February 1962, John in fact warned bishops to guard lest any in their care 'write against the use of Latin in the teaching of the higher sacred studies or in the liturgy'.) Waugh reserved criticism for John's predecessor Pius XII – 'Many of the innovations, which many of us find so obnoxious, were introduced by Pius XII' – and for his successor Paul VI, elected 1963, in whose reign the Council's most radical reforms, such as the vernacular Mass, were instituted.[90] In the years following Paul's election Waugh would write another essay on conciliar matters and seventeen responses to others; by 1964 he could speak of 'the arguments I have propounded with tedious frequency in recent years'. His correspondence is full of references to how 'The Vatican Council weighs heavy on my spirits'.[91] What began as apprehension turned to anger – spawning some injudicious remarks about 'cranks in authority' and 'traitors from within'[92] – and finally to desolation. 'The Vatican Council has knocked the guts out of me', he told Diana Mosley in 1966, explaining why 'I have become very old the last two years' (L 638).

To outsiders he put on a strong public face, insisting with proper submission that the decisions of the council fathers were ultimately divinely inspired, and so that any changes they instituted could go no farther than superficial matters of form. 'They are destroying all that was superficially attractive about my Church', he told Diana Cooper (DC 316); the famous 1965 preface describing the war trilogy as 'an obituary of the Roman Catholic Church in England as it had existed for many centuries' was careful to add: 'It never occurred to me, writing *Sword of Honour* that the Church was susceptible to change. I was wrong and I have seen a superficial revolution in what then seemed permanent' (SH 9). When an article in the *Times* suggested that the vernacular liturgy would 'split the Roman Catholic Church in England from top to bottom', he wrote in reply: 'The effect is more likely to be that church-going will become irksome but still a duty we shall all perform'. Privately he wrote to the *Clergy Review* to ask what was the absolute minimum obligatory attendance at Mass for a man of his age and circumstances: 'I do not ask what is best for me; merely what is the least I am obliged to do without grave sin'.[93] 'I have not yet soaked myself in petrol and gone up in flames, but I now cling to the Faith doggedly without joy. Church going is pure duty parade' (L 639).

Many of Waugh's opponents in the debates sparked by Vatican II thought him motivated merely by traditionalist aesthetic preferences and a snobbish anti-ecumenism. (Paradoxically, his very insistence on the superficial nature of the changes helped foster this impression.) But Waugh always stressed that 'the dangers threatening the Church were to be resisted on graver grounds than the merely sentimental, aesthetic, or traditional': they posed, he believed, a grave threat to piety.[94] Lurking behind this explicit argument was perhaps another fear. 'I think the heart of the matter is: do you seek uniformity or diversity in the Church?'[95] Many asked in the wake of the Council whether in sacrificing uniformity, the Church might not also endanger universality. For thirty years – in contexts from Abyssinia to Azania, Guiana to Neutralia – the Church's universality had been the cornerstone of Waugh's thought and a source of profound joy. He had argued that human freedom and diversity were possible only within a framework of accepted moral truth; that relativism frustrated individual and social growth; that an objective ethics could rest only on a religious foundation. Since 1930 he had argued that the most fundamental moral, social and political choice was between 'Christianity and Chaos'. Was his own Church now taking the first steps toward accommodation with a new brand of modernism, put forward by 'traitors from within'?[96]

IX

By the end of 1962 Waugh's life was taking on the shape described in his essay on 'Sloth': 'It is in that last undesired decade, when passion is cold, appetites feeble, curiosity dulled and experience has begotten cynicism, that *accidia* lies in wait as the final temptation to destruction. That is the time which is given a man to "make his soul"' (EAR 576). The 1964 elections, which Harold Wilson won under the Labour slogan 'MODERNITY', drew from him only the comment: 'Now it will be 1946 again with nobs on' (L 628). Like the elderly Basil Seal, he had 'scorned to order his life with a view of longevity or spurious youth' (BSRA 2). He told Ann Fleming:

28 Evelyn Waugh at sixty (Mark Gerson).

When I saw the doctor he asked about my habits. I said 'I have practically given up
drinking – only about 7 bottles of wine & 3 of spirits a week'. 'A week? Surely you
mean a month?' 'No, and I smoke 30 cigars a week & take 40 grains of sodium
amytal'. He looked graver & graver. 'Oh, yes, a bottle of paraldehyde a week'.

(L 618)

Laura too, when not outdoors overseeing her market garden, began to drink too
much. Painfully arthritic, Waugh found it difficult to walk without a stick;
holidays abroad no longer gave pleasure. In November 1963, he had to be
prodded into attending a dinner in London commemorating the fortieth anniversary of John Sutro's Railway Club, where he felt himself a ghost. An obtuse
Randolph Churchill inquired 'When are we going to have the fourth volume on
the war' (RC 12), but Waugh was in no doubt that *Unconditional Surrender* was his
'last novel' (LAF 291). His last task as a writer of fiction would be the one-
volume *Sword of Honour*, after which, Fr D'Arcy later suggested, he felt his

vocation would be completed.[97] Meanwhile he proceeded without pleasure through *A Little Learning*, the first volume of his autobiography.

'The future, dreariest of prospects!' it begins; 'Only when one has lost all curiosity about the future has one reached the age to write an autobiography'. After its highly publicized serialization in the *Sunday Times*, *A Little Learning* appeared in book form in September 1964. Many had feared its revelations, but Waugh was ostentatiously discreet: 'He keeps the lid on', noted V. S. Pritchett. ('It is unsafe to trust the elegiac tone of this volume', Pritchett added shrewdly; 'he may also be trying out his own funeral in advance'.)[98]

A Little Learning is a series of homages. The title phrase from Alexander Pope had previously been used for a memoir by Ronald Knox's sister, Winifred Peck; Waugh's long opening chapter of family history seems a 'filial tribute to the precedent set by his father's own autobiography, *One Man's Road*' (Hinchcliffe 289). Most of all the book is a tribute to memory itself and to the past, bulwarks against a drab present. At the house of his Victorian aunts, 'There was nothing worth very much, but it all belonged to another age which I instinctively, even then, recognised as superior to my own'; 'To have been born into a world of beauty, to die amid ugliness, is the common fate of all us exiles' (ALL 48, 33). 'He is liable to use words like "eschew", phrases like "the precipitancy of my dispatch", and occasionally a sentence of eighteenth-century stateliness', said William Plomer (CH 454) – who might also have cited words such as 'conurbation', 'invigilators', and 'gibbous', all of which point an implicit moral as well as aesthetic standard.

Publicly, Waugh maintained as strong a front as ever of success and sardonic strength; privately he chronicled his own deterioration. Invited in January 1965 to a Foyles luncheon on the publication of *Objections to Roman Catholicism*, he was duly reported as replying: 'I would gladly attend an *auto-da-fé* at which your guests were incinerated. But I will certainly not sit down to a social meal in their company'.[99] In the same month he had all his remaining teeth extracted, by choice without anaesthetic; the operation and a pair of ill-fitted dentures left him wholly uninterested in food. 'My snappers still uncomfortable', he told Ann Fleming a year later; 'You must literally be starving yourself to death', wrote a worried Meg. In June 1965 Waugh described himself as 'toothless, deaf, melancholic, shaky on my pins, unable to eat, full of dope, quite idle – a wreck'.[100]

That summer he revised the war trilogy; the one-volume *Sword of Honour* was published in September 1965 (1966 in the United States). He was unable to make progress on the next volume of his autobiography, to be called *A Little Hope*, after the verse from Alfred de Musset:

> La vie est brève,
> Un peu d'amour,
> Un peu de rêve,
> Et puis, Bonjour.
>
> La vie est vaine,
> Un peu d'espoir,
> Un peu de haine,
> Et puis, Bonsoir.

'After twenty-one, I've used all my more interesting experiences in one form or another in novels', he told an interviewer; at the time of his death he had completed only five pages.[101]

January 1965 had also brought news, long threatening, that monies drawn from the Save the Children Fund were indeed subject to tax. '[H]uge sums of back taxes will have to be paid', he wrote to Meg; 'In fact we may have to auction our carpets and pictures and silver'.[102] He owed fifteen years' back taxes; Peters was able to compound for six, at a cost of £5000. To make money quickly Waugh agreed to write a series of books: a work on American history; a picture-history of the Crusades; even – though he had once declared such a book impossible, since it would 'mean the history of the entire Western world & much of the Eastern for 2000 years'[103] – a history of the papacy. By early 1966, realizing that none of these books would be written, he cancelled the contracts.

'I very seldom mind people's deaths. I long for my own', Waugh wrote to Nancy Mitford as early as January 1962 (NM 476). The sentiment came often to his pen: 'All fates are worse than death' (D 787). Early in 1966 he wrote Ann Fleming:

> Those who love me tell me I am dying but professional opinion does not confirm them. Fr. Hubert van Zeller... expresses beautifully what I feel. 'Dying is just growing up. I am not unhappy. I just do not much like being alive'.
>
> (L 636)

Dom Humbert had written in his autobiography, *One Foot in the Cradle*:

> A wish for death superseded, and in intensity vastly overmatched, the wish to grow up. The attraction has remained with me ever since. I was not unhappy. There was nothing morbid about it....Earlier I had seen in growing up the means to emancipation; in 1916 I saw in death the means to a more significant emancipation. It is just that I do not much like living.

'There will be many readers quite lacking in Dom Hubert's holiness, who will dimly understand and echo these words', Waugh observed in a review, his last publication.[104] On Easter day, 10 April 1966, Waugh died at Combe Florey of heart failure after hearing a Latin Mass celebrated by Fr Caraman at a village church nearby. Laura and the children agreed that he had long prayed for death. He was buried, by special permission, outside the Anglican churchyard at Combe Florey; on 21 April friends crowded Westminster Cathedral to hear a (Latin) Requiem Mass.

Notes

Notes to the Preface

1   The most searching response to Stannard's life is Donat Gallagher's long review
'Martin Stannard's Waugh,' which examines Stannard's treatment of two crucial
events: Waugh's participation in the Battle of Crete and, later in the War, in the
British mission to Yugoslavia. Whereas on Crete, according to Stannard, 'Waugh's
hypocrisy rocketed to new heights' as he sought to justify cowardly conduct in
defiance of orders (ST2 38), Gallagher persuasively reveals a man tormented by
following orders he could not approve; where Stannard reads Waugh's concern
with Yugoslav Catholics as officious meddlesomeness, Gallagher finds honest and
consistent application of long-held principles. Like Selina Hastings, I agree with
Gallagher's analysis in both instances (see ch. 5 below).

Stannard's lack of sympathy, and consequently of understanding, for his subject is most
evident in his treatment of Waugh's politics and especially Waugh's religion ('all I am
interested in really', he once told Nancy Mitford (NM 106)). It is audible in a comment
such as '[Waugh's] ostensible political position was violent right-wing, *yet* on one occasion
he insisted that he was the only 'man in the street' among the arrogant intellectuals of
Oxford' (my italics), and, in a discussion of Sykes on Waugh's first marriage, 'As a
Catholic, Christopher Sykes is justified in his intolerance of adultery' (ST1 75, 184). In
the formative decade of the 1930s, on Stannard's showing, Waugh's socialist enemies
acted from 'commitment' and 'principle', while Waugh himself possessed only 'prejudices' and an 'aesthetic' approach to politics. Despite Waugh's extensive remarks to the
contrary, Stannard finds him treating the Abyssinian war as if it 'could be isolated from
political instability in Europe'. Refusing to entertain any view of the Spanish Civil War
but as a 'conflict between Catholic conservatism and democratic socialism', Stannard
overlooks Waugh's analysis of the conflict (based on a sense of the fundamental identity of
tyrannies, Left or Right) and finds only waffling and a refusal to face facts (ST1 396, 424).
Waugh's widely shared distaste for the postwar Labour government becomes in Stannard's account something idiosyncratic (and his unremarkable attempts to avoid
Labour's crushingly high rate of taxation peculiarly dishonest and greedy).

The cumulative result of such failure to take his subject seriously is a biography that
cannot get to the heart of Waugh's works of political travel or integrate these with the

fiction. It is of course a mistake to claim Waugh as the peculiar property of any party or sect: his literary genius and audience transcend both his political conservatism and his Roman Catholicism. But to make sense of that genius, it is surely necessary to recognize Waugh's commitments and habits of mind for what they are.

Notes to Chapter 1

1   EAR 190–2; EWN 3: 1 (1969), 2.
2   In 1920 Waugh began a novel whose self-dedication speaks of the 'difficulties' of a 'boy with literary aspirations' raised in a household 'entirely literary': ' "Another of those precocious Waughs," they will say, "one more nursery novel" ' (*Apprentice* 60–1).
3   Alec Waugh, *My Brother*, 193.
4   'The Book Unbeautiful', *Spectator*, 20 Nov. 1959, 728; L 439; L 348. Waugh nonetheless also admitted that his characters were indeed generally 'drawn from life', though only minor ones constituted simple 'portraits' (EAR 302). When *Life* magazine proposed a picture-story on the 'models' for his characters in *Brideshead*, Waugh threatened to sue (L 221) – not because too few characters were so drawn, but because too many were. Waugh's letters of advice to Nancy Mitford reveal how he constructed characters by thinking in terms of types from his own acquaintance: 'The Captain doesn't ring true to me', he told her after reading *The Blessing*; 'Ed Stanley & Boots [Cyril Connolly] don't mix' (L 346); 'you should try to make him languid & feeble – a sort of David-Cecil-Eddie-West' (L 348). When asked in 1958 by Richard Acton 'What was the most difficult thing you ever did as a novelist', he replied 'Turn a woman into a man' – i.e., transform the personality of a woman he had known into *A Handful of Dust*'s John Beaver. (Auberon Waugh guessed he meant London's 'spare woman', Baby Jungman: Acton, 'Lion,' 41).
5   'Bioscope', *Spectator*, 29 June 1962, 863.
6   'Cubism,' EAR 6–8; 'Voice from Valhalla' (1937), unpublished review (ND 276).
7   Alec Waugh, 'My Childhood', MS HRCT.
8   Carew recalled Waugh's schoolboy taste for Eliot in *The House*, 101.
9   Arthur Waugh, *One Man's Road*, 370; ALL 127.
10 Stopp, *Portrait*, 20; 'Face to Face' interview, BBC, 26 July 1960 ('I'm still an aesthete, but in middle life one doesn't have to dress up to look at architecture, you know'); ALL 44.
11 Alec Waugh, *My Brother*, 183, 185.
12 To Cruttwell's criticisms of his lack of scholarly industry, Waugh liked to reply that he planned a long work on *Great Women of the Industrial Revolution* (Greenidge 68). When in 1935 Cecil Hunt conducted a survey asking well-known novelists which works they considered their best, Waugh replied that his own favourite had not yet been written, and might take years to complete: 'It is the memorial biography of C. R. M. F. Cruttwell, some time Dean of Hertford College, Oxford, and my old history tutor. It is a labour of love to one to whom, under God, I owe everything' (Hunt 216).
13 Acton, *Memoirs*, 126; 'Anthony,' *Oxford Broom*, 1: 3 (June 1923), 14–20 (rpr. *Apprentice*, 128–31).
14 'Those were the days,' Betjeman recalled, 'when that divine baroque / Transformed our English altars and our ways' (*Bells* 83). In *Vision and Design* (1920), a book Waugh

owned and read carefully, Roger Fry called the baroque 'bad taste': 'florid', insincerely 'rhetorical', and sentimentally religiose (7). Waugh noted in 1955: 'The Baroque came to England late and left early....When it fell from favour it fell into contempt and loathing, which persisted for 200 years' (EAR 459).

15 R 36. Wilde's 'wit is ornamental, Firbank's is structural', Waugh declared in 1929; 'Wilde is rococo; Firbank is baroque' (EAR 36–7).

16 'As a rule, primitive art is good', wrote Bell, because it is 'free from descriptive qualities' (*Art* 22); in chapters on 'The Art of the Bushmen', 'Negro Sculpture', and 'Ancient American Art', Fry's *Vision and Design* celebrates 'barbaric and primitive art' (12).

17 *Oxford Magazine*, 1 Mar. 1923, 258–9; Carew, *Fragment*, 83; EAR 301.

18 Powell, *Infants*, 71; Acton, *Memoirs*, 155; Ryan 42. In the 1930s, Catholics in particular were sensitive to the political valence of the term: cf. Pius XI writing against socialism in *Quadragesimo anno* (1931): 'to the harassed workers there have come "intellectuals", as they are called' (§55).

19 L 435; ALL 191. To others Waugh said, 'I was cuckolded by [Cyril] Connolly' (Pryce-Jones, *Connolly*, 63).

20 A decade later, staying at Campion Hall in Oxford, Waugh hesitantly showed the film to a Jesuit friend, C. C. Martindale, who was delighted with it; the playful imprimatur 'Nihil Obstat Projiciatur' was duly added to its opening frames. A screenplay has been reconstructed by Charles Linck (EWN 3: 2 (1969), 2–7), whose Cow Hill Press also makes copies of the film publicly available. In the midde twenties Waugh acted in at least three other films – *The Mummers*, *666* and (in the role of a negro priest) *Cities of the Plain* – all now lost (Greenidge 168–71).

21 Acton, quoted in Sykes, 118; Carew, *Fragment*, 76.

22 'The Prince in a Treasure Hunt, Midnight Chase in London, 50 Motorcars, The Bright Young People,' *Daily Express*, 26 July 1924; ALL 216.

23 A mélange of Bergson and F. H. Bradley cast in autobiographical form reminiscent of Carlyle's *Sartor Resartus*, this pretentious, quasi-mystical work of Stokes's adolescence, pointedly omitted from the three volumes of his *Critical Writings*, attempts a complete renovation in philosophy: 'I hope to lay anew the foundations of ideas' (58). 'Analysis', says the pupil of Bergson, 'is inevitably inadequate, and makes static that which is living. Mathematical Thought is the enemy of art' and true religion (86–7). 'Meaning', not 'logic' or 'mathematical thought', is the key to what Stokes repeatedly invokes as psychic '*balance*'. Though professing himself an enemy of Christianity, with its 'resort to sentiment and pity which smacks of Golders Green' (93), Stokes defends 'mysticism', especially 'the beauty of the mysticism and the grandeur of the ceremony and its power of suggestion' to be found in 'Roman Catholicism at its best' (94–5).

24 Verschoyle, quoted in Sykes, 93–5; Hastings 135. Young later gave up schoolteaching to become a lawyer, and under the pseudonym Richard MacNaughton wrote *Preparatory School Murder* (1934), a detective novel set in a school not unlike Arnold House (see Higham).

25 Jebb 108. Cf. L 390; ALL 225. He told John Betjeman to continue teaching rather than take other jobs: 'you'll never laugh so much or enjoy yourself so much again' (WM 15).

26 The book's last sentence was yet a further afterthought, mailed to his agent on a postcard (HRC E1329, 1337). It is perhaps also relevant that when Grimes arranges a similar death by drowning in *Decline and Fall* (appropriately, at Easter), the suicide turns out a fake.

27 *Apprentice*, 182, 184. Much from 'The Balance' would soon be reused: 'Adam' and 'Imogen Quest' recur in *Vile Bodies*; *Decline and Fall* concludes with a similarly freighted scene of a hero falling asleep. Adam's final resolution of 'immediate escape from the scene upon which the bodiless harlequinade was played, into a third dimension beyond it' is echoed (ironically) in *Brideshead* when Charles Ryder leaves Brideshead Castle, resolved never to return: ' "I have left behind illusion," I said to myself. "Henceforth I lie in a world of three dimensions" ' (BR 150).

28 'The Tutor's Tale. A House of Gentlefolks', printed in Hugh Chesterman's *The New Decameron: The Fifth Day* (1927; rpn. *Apprentice*, 186–95).

29 *Thirty-Four Decorative Designs By Francis Crease* (M. R. Mowbray, 1927), printed in sixty copies; Waugh's preface rpr. EAR 22–5.

30 R 138. In the same way, Waugh writes that to appreciate Rossetti's poetry 'one has to resist the temptation of being priggishly "modern" ': 'Read [Rossetti's love poems] for yourself purely intellectually, without pronouncing the words, and the effect is lost; read them aloud and loudly, allowing the voice to fall into softness at the end of the lines, and if it does not make you feel shy, Rossetti's intention is in some way realised' (156–7).

31 Lewis, unsigned review, *Oxford Magazine*, 25 Oct. 1928, 66, 69; Murray, *Artwork*, Autumn 1928, 172, 175 (see Gallagher, 'Industria', 336).

32 R 222–3, 204. Waugh had put forward similar arguments already in *P.R.B.*, for instance that 'conscientious analysis does not reveal the existence of any such quality' as 'aesthetic emotion' (PRB 18). As R. M. Davis points out, Waugh also drew ammunition for his opposition to Bloomsbury aesthetics from his reading of I. A. Richards's *Principles of Literary Criticism* (1925). In his copy of this book Waugh marked passages arguing against the supposed irrelevance of the 'representational element' in art by citing great paintings 'in which the contribution to the whole response made through representation is not less than that made more directly through form and colour....there is no reason why representative and formal factors in an experience should conflict... The psychology of "unique aesthetic emotions" and "pure art values" upon which the contrary view relies is merely a caprice of the fancy' (Davis, *Writer*, 11–12). Richards's view that 'representation in painting corresponds to thought in poetry' informs Waugh's question at the end of *Rossetti*: 'Why of the Arts should literature alone be expected to be "impure"?' (225).

33 See 235. R contains much else that recurs in BR: references to Athanasius (source of Sebastian's phrase 'contra mundum'); a long discussion of the verse 'Quomodo sedet sola civitas', which Rossetti inscribed on the frame of *Beata Beatrix* and which BR cites at three crucial moments; and an elaborate passage, much like the closing paragraphs of BR, that begins 'Vanitas vanitatum', followed by a turn from 'despair' to 'hope' as 'humanity stretches out to some other system where compensation will be more equitable'.

34 See Davis, *Writer*, 41, and Alec Waugh, *Early Years*, 203.

35 VB 23. As Home Secretary under Baldwin (1924–9), Sir William Joyson-Hix oversaw all the cases of censorship cited (and in 1927–8 led the attack in Parliament on the new Prayer Book as too Anglo-Catholic). Waugh's opposition to censorship, voiced in his first signed newspaper article, 'Yes, Give Us a Censor' (*Daily Express*, 20 Oct. 1928; EAR 43–4) and again in 'For Adult Audiences' (1930; EAR 89–91), never waned. Though he ridiculed the 'popular heresy' that 'the arts flourish best in a liberal society' (L 499), he went on in the forties to protest censorship of Hollywood films see (see 271), and in the sixties, the Index of Prohibited Books (EAR 604–5).

36 'Poor Mr. Outrage, thought Mr Outrage.... Was Mr. Outrage an immortal soul, thought Mr. Outrage' (VB 141); 'But Ambrose, thought Ambrose, what of him?' (POMF 51); 'Who was Ludovic, Ludovic questioned' (US 109).

37 Heygate to Selina Hastings (Hastings 192).

38 Son of a ruined German farmer, Peters was raised in England and opened his agency, soon one of the most successful and respected in the new field of literary representation, in 1924 (see McNamara, *Literary Agent*).

39 EAR 518; Ralph Strauss, review of *Labels*, *Bystander* 1 Oct. 1930, 48.

40 Graham to Mark Amory (Hastings 186).

41 'Mothers': *Evening Standard*, 8 Apr. 1929, 7; 'Elders': *Daily Herald*, 19 May 1930, 8; 'War': *Spectator*, 13 April 1929 (EAR 61–3).

42 EAR 128. Waugh's first sentence recalls Adrian Stokes's maxim, 'Wrong headedness was better than no headedness' (*Ariadne* 18; cf. von Hügel: 'We talk such a lot about toleration nowadays: take care. In nine cases out of ten toleration means indifference': *Letters* 39). Use of 'tolerance' to suggest relativism – absence of all standards – recurs in RP (see 91) and is a hallmark of Waugh's fiction. 'Life teaches one to be tolerant' says Jenny Abdul-Akbar (HD 139); 'I try not to discriminate, but I am only human' says Mr. Joyboy (LO 60); Mr. Baldwin 'tolerantly' gives absinthe to the homicidal Swede (S 239); in OG, Jumbo Trotter 'tolerantly' arranges for Trimmer, whom he knows to have been cashiered from the Halberdiers, to join the Commandos (103). Only in the war trilogy's carefully framed account of old Mr. Crouchback's 'tolerance and humility' (MA 34), the fruit of profound religious alienation from modern society, does the word appear in the fiction without irony.

43 Mitford in EWN 1: 1 (Spring 1967), 1.

44 Sutro, 'Three Evocations of Evelyn Waugh', *Adam International Review*, nos 301–3 (1966), 16; Mosley 55, 57; Carew, *Fragment*, 88.

45 GP 167; MA 1–2; VB (Boston: Little Brown, 1930), 123 (the sentence appears only in American editions).

46 'To an Un-Named Listener,' BBC Radio, 28 Nov. 1932.

47 'Motor Racing,' *The Times*, 19 Aug. 1929, 6. On a rainy day like that in *Vile Bodies*, 'about half a million people watched', crowding especially for a view of the dangerous curves at 'Mill Corner' and 'Quarry Corner'; 'The crowds at the corners blessed the rain for the additional thrills that it provided'; an Italian driver named Carraciola won (cf. VB's 'Italian ace' Marino). Fascinated, Waugh telegraphed Peters from Belfast to ask about the market for a satiric article on the race (HRC E109).

48 *Daily Mail*, 8 Oct. 1929, 12.

49 Stannard, 'Mystery of the Missing Manuscript'.

50 West, *Bookman*, 71 (Mar. 1930), 84; Pritchett, CH 97.

51 Critics have often spoken as if Waugh were among the best-paid writers of the era; in fact his earnings never approached those of Somerset Maugham, Winston Churchill, or J. B. Priestley.

52 Marginalia to Cyril Connolly's *Unquiet Grave* (HRC I15); Breit 1956, 45.

53 Benson xxi, 21; von Hügel 218.

54 L 242. Alec Waugh tells the story of the army psychiatrist in *Early Years* 217–18 and *Best Wine* 213. Through the character of Potts, Waugh makes fun of modern theories of educational psychology as early as DF; in *Scoop*, a scientific psychology that elides the animal and human realms is responsible for William Boot's frightful London hotel room: 'A psychologist, hired from Cambridge, had planned the decorations – magenta and gamboge, colours which – it had been demonstrated by experiments

on poultry and mice – conduce to a mood of dignified gaiety' (S 46). Cf. the many dismissive references to 'psychology' and 'psychiatry' in ALL (1, 51, 185, etc.).

55 Letters to *New Statesman*, 10 Sept. 1949, 274; 3 Sept. 1949, 246 (cf. Waugh's complaints to Nancy Mitford on the same grounds, L 356).

56 *Bell*, 14 (July 1947), 77, replying to Conor Cruise O'Brien: cf. 262–6.

57 Alec Waugh, *Brother* 191–2; cf. Waugh's description of the 'wholly and blindly selfish' Rossetti: 'He did what he wanted to, when he wanted to, because he wanted to' (R 108). For other echoes, see 64 and 373 n27.

58 Stopp, *Portrait*, 21; Greene, *Mt. Zion*, 49, 56, 59.

59 We are meant to smile at the unconscious irony of Rex Mottram's complaint in *Brideshead*: 'If I remembered all [my instructor] told me I shouldn't have time for anything else' (BR 173).

60 See Wilson, *Belloc*, 109; Belloc, *Reformation*, 270; Dawson, quoted in Scott, 102; D'Arcy 26–7. As Keith Robbins notes, historians in the first part of this century who spoke (like Dawson) of a 'European consciousness' and of the need to 'rewrite history from a European point of view' were 'not highly regarded within the academic world and were apt to be Roman Catholics' (Robbins 33).

61 Letter to *Spectator*, 27 July 1956, 143.

62 EAR 324; Knox, *Belief*, 191; D 708. Cf. his criticism in 1955 of Belloc for mistakenly identifying the 'traditional and cultural aspect of the Church' with 'the continent of Europe' (EAR 473).

63 CH 113; Edgar Holt, *Bookman*, Nov. 1930, 140.

64 This section was also published, with Waugh's snapshots, in *Architectural Review*, June 1930, 627–39.

65 *Sunday Dispatch*, 3 Feb. 1929, 4; Balfour's notice, 'Evelyn Waugh Artist,' appeared in the *Daily Sketch*, 30 Jan. 1929, 5.

66 Waugh, preface to William Clonmore, Earl of Wicklow, *Fireside Fusilier* (Dublin: Clonmore & Reynolds, 1958), vii. Among those to compare Waugh and Byron was Rebecca West: see *Ending*, 82–3.

67 Lawrence 384; Byron 317. DF had made a polite gesture to Byron (and Roger Fry) in describing 'Byzantine mosaics', along with 'budgets and birth control', as among the 'subjects of public importance' discussed by Paul Pennyfeather and his friend Potts (159).

68 *Labels* 110–11. The competition did not soon abate. In writing novels based on previous travels Waugh scooped Byron, and so when Byron and Sykes published their travel novel *Innocence and Design* in 1935, based on a tour of Persia and India, they did so under the name 'Richard Waughburton.'

69 Stannard, 'Debunking', 105.

70 *Labels* 47, 28. There had been no butler at Underhill; Waugh's own French was intolerable. In 1948 he turned down an offer from the BBC to talk on Georges Bernanos' with a postcard reading simply '*je ne parle ni comprens la langues des grenouilles*' (Bogaards 97).

71 *Labels* 14–15, 44; Fussell, *Abroad*, 15–23, 171–202.

72 At the seventh Lambeth Conference that year, the Anglican Church reversed its previous proscription of artificial contraception, a reversal soon followed by other Protestant sects; meanwhile Pius XI forcefully reaffirmed traditional teaching in his encyclical *Casta connubii*. Waugh had glancingly raised the subject as one of 'public importance' in DF (159) and again in 'The War and the Younger Generation' (see 30); in the years after his conversion, RP – with its 'prominent feminist, devoted to the fomentation of birth-control and regional cookery in rural England,

[though] the atmosphere of Kenya had softened these severe foibles a little' (197) – and BM use contraception as a stick to beat liberal Protestantism. In LAR (1953) a bureaucrat complains of his failure to advance: 'I've been in Contraception for five years. It's a blind alley' (19).

73 One oft-cited passage that may have spurred Waugh's monitory Author's Note concerns 'the troglodytic inclinations of the Holy Family'. But the passage actually defends the rationalist Church the young Waugh so valued: 'We were shown the site of the Annunciation and Joseph's Workshop; both these were caves. A cheerful Irish monk with a red beard opened the gates for us. He was as sceptical as ourselves about the troglodytic inclinations of the Holy Family. The attitude of my fellow travellers was interesting. This sensible ecclesiastic vexed them. They had expected someone very superstitious and credulous and mediæval, whom they would be able to regard with discreet ridicule. As it was, the laugh was all on the side of the Church. It was we who had driven twenty four miles, and had popped our tribute into the offertory box, and were being gently humoured for our superstition' (65).

74 In 1929 Waugh offered Peters an article to be called ' "They do it better in France (?)" pointing out the number of superior refinements & comforts London has to offer over Paris' (L 47). His comments in *Labels* on the 'limits and circumscription of language and territorial boundary' echo Yorick's similar remarks early in Sterne's *A Sentimental Journey* (1768).

75 Preface to Eric Newby, *A Short Walk: A Preposterous Adventure* (New York: Doubleday, 1959), 12; EAR 134. 'No one but Mr. Graham Greene could have written his latest novel', Waugh wrote in a review of *The End of the Affair*, 'his unique personality is apparent on every page' (EAR 404; cf. L 238, 421, 635; NM 332; Acton, 'Lion,' 41; and in the fiction, WS 189, POMF 221, LO 69).

Notes to Chapter 2

1 See, e.g., Hubert Waley's statement of 'the aesthetic problem' in *The Revival of Aesthetics* (1926), which Waugh considered a 'brilliant essay' identifying the 'possible essence of aesthetic expression' (R 224).

2 Pius required the oath in his pontifical letter *Sacrorum antistitum*. The literature on the modernist controversy is immense; Marvin O'Connell provides a useful historical analysis, built up of biographies of the major participants, in *Critics on Trial: An Introduction to the Catholic Modernist Crisis* (1994).

3 Sabatier 227, 228, 253. In the words of one of *Pascendi*'s American interpreters, modernism reduced the Church to 'a number of individuals holding different views on every religious question' (Searle 636–7); but Christ, as Cardinal Mercier joked, 'did not leave a modifiable system of opinions to the discussion of his disciples' (Mercier 28). The term 'immanence' entered modernist discussion especially through Maurice Blondel's philosophical treatise *L'Action* (1893).

4 See McCartney, ch. 3 (Bergson's *Matter and Memory* had appeared in 1896, *Creative Evolution* in 1907). Both DF and VB call prominently on the Bergsonian terminology of the 'static' and the 'dynamic', only to celebrate (in anti-Bergsonian fashion) the former. McCartney speculates that Waugh read Wyndham Lewis's anti-Bergsonian *Time and Western Man* (1927); Waugh could as easily have learnt his new preference for the 'static' by reading in the modernist controversy, where Bergsonian terminology also figured largely.

5 Mercier 28; Ward, 'The Encyclical *Pascendi*', *Dublin Review*, Jan. 1908, 1–2; D'Arcy
   231. Ward proceeded to define modernist 'subjectivism' as 'the identification of
   religion with sentiment or emotion rather than with belief in objective truth, issuing
   in the conception of a deity immanent in man and not transcendent, and of
   dogmatic formulae as no longer the expression of facts – of the dogmatic truths of
   revelation – but as the mind's reflection on its own subjective experience'. (According to Belloc, 'the man suffering from subjectivism . . . cannot understand [faith] as
   the acceptance of the word of an Authority . . . of an objective truth': *Reformation* 269).
   It was in the spirit of anti-modernism that Fr D'Arcy praised Waugh as a catechumen come to 'learn and understand' what he already 'believed to be God's revelation', rather than to test 'how far it corresponded with his experience', with his own
   'likings and impressions' (HW 64).

6 Hulme 8–13; Eliot, 'Humanism', 420–2; EAR 439. On Eliot's debt to Maurras, see
   Asher, *T. S. Eliot and Ideology*. The first to recognize Waugh's debt to Hulme was
   George Orwell (*Essays* 3: 63).

7 Mercier 38; Benson xiii–iv, 7, 185, 145. In 1956, in an effort to rehabilitate an author
   he greatly enjoyed, Waugh produced a preface for Benson's *Richard Reynal, Solitary*
   several times as long as his usual commissioned work in the form. Brother of the
   writers E. F. and Arthur Benson (and son of an Archbishop of Canterbury), R. H.
   Benson became like Ronald Knox first an Anglican, then a Catholic priest. *Lord of the
   World* is a story of the Antichrist set in about the year 2000; its resolutely medievalizing
   Pope John XXIV is a portrait, physically as well as intellectually, of Pius X (Martindale 1: 284). Benson's 'Free Church' echoes the nineteenth-century slogan, equally
   the property of liberal Catholics such as Montalembert and anti-clericals like Cavour
   (and anathema to popes from Pius IX onward), of 'A free church in a free state'.

8 H 198. For the background of Helena's musings one need look no farther than Pius
   IX's condemnations of 'democracy', or Leo XIII's condemnation in *Diuturnum illud*
   (1881) of those who 'say that all power comes from the people; so that those who
   exercise it in the State do so not as their own, but as delegated to them by the
   people, and that, by this rule, it can be revoked by the will of the very people by
   whom it was delegated. But from these, Catholics dissent, who affirm that the right
   to rule is from God, as from a natural and necessary principle' (§5).

9 DF 188. Waugh probably had in mind Bishop Barnes and his Modern Churchman's
   Union, an Anglican organization loosely modelled on Paul Desjardins' *Union pour
   l'action morale* in France.

10 Von Hügel 165, 231, 67, 68; Gwendoline Greene 50.

11 A 'great tradition had been broken' through the Reformation, argues EC (16);
   according to RUL, Mexico 'was saturated with Spanish influence; then the European source was cut off' (66).

12 VB 51, HD 108 (my italics). Hoop's invitations ('adapt[ed] from *Blast* and Marinetti's
   Futurist Manifesto') are modelled on Brian Howard's for the 'Great Urban Dionysia'
   party of April 1929, which listed likes and dislikes under the headings 'J'accuse'
   (Intellect, Belloc, Anglo-Catholicism, Nationalism, Public Schools) and 'J'adore'
   (Love, Intuition, Lawrence, Spengler, Germany, Picasso, Stravinsky, Jazz).

13 EAR 102; Lewis, *Satire*, 46; ND 211.

14 'Fan-Fare' (1946) explains that satire is no longer possible in 'the Century of the
   Common Man where vice no longer pays lip service to virtue' (EAR 303); in a 1956
   radio broadcast for the CBC Waugh argued that satire presupposes 'as background
   what is accepted as being moral and proper', but 'no normal or proper society or
   code of behaviour' any longer exists (Lynch, 'Pinfold Years', 554).

15 Lewis, *Satire*, 46, 52–3, 45; St John Ervine, *Daily Express*, 30 Jan. 1930, 6.

16 CH 81–9. Those like Bennett who recognized satire singled out for praise the novel's 'third part dealing with the prison system' (82); those who read only a farce found that 'the fun goes off after the school part', since 'penal systems are in themselves repugnant to the idea of light treatment' (81).

17 CH 95, 106; 'saturikon': Stanley Went, *Saturday Review of Literature*, 5 Apr. 1930, 891; Macaulay 362 (cf. CH 100).

18 'Evelyn Waugh', *Commonweal*, 4 Dec. 1964, 343.

19 Bradbury 7 (developing A. E. Dyson's view that Waugh's irony has no 'centre': Dyson 74); O'Faolain 68–9; Brophy, in CH 161.

20 Newman 10; in 1925 Waugh noted that he was 'beginning to detest Elizabethan architecture' (D 220).

21 'I've eaten all your eggs', Peter Pastmaster tells Paul in *Decline and Fall*; 'I just couldn't help it' (DF 207). The symbolism is repeated in the voracious appetite of Colonel Blount in *Vile Bodies*; in Mrs. Beaver's 'gobbling' and the 'ruthless' eating of Reggie St Cloud in *A Handful of Dust* ('it was his habit, often, without noticing it, to consume things that others usually left on their plates, the heads and tails of whiting, whole mouthfuls of chicken bone, peach stones and apple cores'); the 'luncheon of Dickensian dimensions' devoured by Simon Lent in 'Excursion in Reality'; the elaborate meals of the Boot family and their servants in *Scoop*; and in *Brideshead*, in Sebastian's appetite for plover's eggs.

22 DF 5; EAR 214. Lumsden of Strathdrummond recalls the 'enormous' Lumsden of Balmedie Waugh met while visiting Scotland with the Grahams in 1926 (D 261).

23 DF 168–9. In the first printing, the homosexuals Miles Malpractice and Lord Parakeet were 'Martin Gaythorn-Brodie' and 'Kevin Saunderson', names changed because they were too close to their originals Eddie Gathorne-Hardy and Gavin Henderson. Davy Lennox, author of a modernist portrait of 'the back of Margot's head' (223) and of her hands reflected in a dish of ink, is transparently Cecil Beaton, who similarly photographed Henry Yorke, Aldous Huxley and Margot, Lady Oxford.

24 DF 85. Waugh later admitted that Alastair Graham's domineering American mother was his 'model' for Lady Circumference (ALL 192).

25 DF 2, 163; 227. On the supposed medical benefits of incandescent 'artificial sunlight' – practised for instance in the 'light baths' given at Dr. Kellogg's Battle Creek Sanitarium, and already a common satiric target (cf. Benson xxiv) – see M. Luckiesch, *Artificial Sunlight: Combining Radiation for Health with Light for Vision* (1930).

26 DF contains no character who succeeds in mediating extremes; VB contains one: Imogen Quest. Achieving 'a superb mean between those two poles of savagery Lady Circumstance and Lady Metroland', living in what Waugh describes in careful eighteenth-century diction as 'uncontrolled dignity of life', Imogen embodies the Augustan ideal of *concordia discors*: 'Her character was a lovely harmony of contending virtues – she was witty and tender-hearted; passionate and serene, sensual and temperate, impulsive and discreet'. Her only defect is that she does not exist: she is the invention of a gossip-columnist (McCartney 25–6).

27 DF 38. Grimes's credo echoes not only Browning's *Pippa Passes* but also Matthew Arnold's repeated complaints in 'Doing as One Likes' (ch. 2 of *Culture and Anarchy*) against 'our notion of its being the great right and happiness of an Englishman to do as far as possible what he likes, [whereby] we are in danger of drifting towards anarchy'. Cf. also von Hügel's and Waugh's other versions of the sentiment, quoted 38, 56.

28   DF 132–3. Delivered, in an echo of *The Waste Land*, at a Welsh 'Metropole Hotel', the pederast Grimes's agonized questions why no one warned him about women, marriage, home, and family ('Oh, why did nobody warn me?'; 'They should have warned me about Flossie, not about the fires of hell') slyly transform the stock scene from Victorian fiction in which fallen women such as Hardy's Tess ask why they have not been warned about 'men'. (Waugh would shortly produce a sour essay on Hardy's novel for a series on modern responses to the classics: see '*Tess*'.)

29   DF 234, 243. Another religious maniac appears at the car-races in VB bearing the ironically appropriate banner, 'WITHOUT SHEDDING OF BLOOD IS NO REMISSION OF SIN' (181). Like that novel's Mrs Ape, both men embody Waugh's view that 'the modern abdication of intellectual authority... calls forth the fanatic' (McCartney 24).

30   DF captures these details accurately, though even as it appeared the title 'warder' and the broad-arrow uniform (worn in Waugh's illustration by prisoners at Egdon Heath) were disappearing (Sharpe 97).

31   I borrow the phrase 'starting from zero' from Tom Wolfe's account of the parallel effort by members of the Bauhaus to create a wholly new architecture, one that owed nothing to past models (*Bauhaus*, ch. 1). In 1938, recalling his youthful enthusiasm for Bloomsbury morality, Lord Keynes provided a striking parallel to Waugh's portrayal of Sir Wilfred:

> We were living in a specious present.... We entirely repudiated a personal liability on us to obey general rules. We claimed the right to judge every individual case on its merits, and the wisdom, experience and self-control to do so successfully. This was a very important part of our faith, violently and aggressively held, and for the outer world it was our most dangerous characteristic. We repudiated entirely customary morals, conventions and traditional wisdom.... In short, we repudiated all versions of the doctrine of original sin.... We were not then aware that civilization was a thin and precarious crust erected by conventions skillfully put across and guilefully preserved.... It did not occur to us to respect the extraordinary accomplishment of our predecessors in the ordering of life (as it now seems to me to have been) or the elaborate framework which they had devised to protect this order. (Keynes 95–100, also cited by McCartney, 149).

Keynes describes such attitudes as 'Utopian' in their assumption of inevitable 'progress' ('We used to regard the Christians as the enemy, because they appeared as the representatives of tradition'), and on reflection 'rather a Russian' outlook than an 'English' one.

32   Review of *City of Tomorrow* (1929), EAR 63–5. On Le Corbusier's triumphant efforts to alter the cityscape of Moscow, see Jean-Louis Cohen, *Le Corbusier and the Mystique of the USSR* (1992). Waugh as much as signals that Otto is based on Le Corbusier in making the foolish Potts, wrong about architecture as about education, remark to Paul that Silenus has 'got right away from Corbusier': Paul replies, probably speaking for Waugh, that Corbusier is really 'pure nineteenth century, Manchester school utilitarian' (another debased Victorian holdover) (160). Tom Wolfe's *Bauhaus*, written from a viewpoint close to Waugh's, provides an excellent gloss on Otto's architecture and its politics.

33   For a brief sketch of pairings of pride and despair in literature, see my essay 'Love Deny'd'.

34 At the house-party 'Peter tossed Sir Humphrey double or quits, and won' (173). Similar moments recur in the betting scenes of VB and the paired scenes of coin-tossing that frame *Scoop*. Otto's image also parodies the doctrines of Futurism and Vorticism ('The Vorticist', according to Wyndham Lewis, 'is at his maximum point of energy when stillest'), a theme to which Waugh returns in VB's description of racing-cars such as that driven by Marino (named for the Futurist Marinetti) as existing 'solely for their own propulsion through space', 'a vortex of combining and disintegrating units' (VB 178) (see Loss).

35 The classic study of Fielding's providentialism is Aubrey Williams, 'Interpositions of Providence and the Design of Fielding's Novels', *South Atlantic Quarterly*, 70 (1971): 265–86; on the later tradition, see Thomas Vargish, *The Providential Aesthetic in Victorian Fiction* (1985).

36 DF 280. Paul now owns his own copy of 'Dean Stanley's Eastern Church', which in the Prologue he had only borrowed; he shelves it next to Fagan's study of modern heresy and barbarism, *Mother Wales* (whose title recalls Katherine Mayo's popular exposé, *Mother India* [1927]). Stanley's book – presumably the same text young Burne-Jones and Holman Hunt discuss in R ('They used to go for angry walks together every afternoon, and read this history of the Eastern Church aloud to each other in the evenings': 79) – seems to have been a favourite of Waugh's: cf. 88.

37 DF 288. Waugh later explained that Galsworthy 'was not read in England by the younger generation' of the twenties, because 'he had come to be identified with the very class and character whose deficiencies he had set himself to oppose': *The Man of Property* (New York: Heritage Press, 1964), Introduction, v.

38 VB (London: Chapman & Hall, 1965), Preface.

39 1965 Preface. 'I was introduced to the Cavendish by Mr. Alastair Graham, ... and welcomed as one of the moneyless young men whose wine was charged to the older and richer customers', Waugh wrote in a preface to his friend Daphne Fielding's biography of Rosa Lewis, *The Duchess of Jermyn Street* (1964).

40 Balfour cites his own columns on 'titled eccentrics' as the source for Adam's (*Society Racket*, 92; cf. Wheen, *Driberg*, 76–80). The *Daily Excess*'s editor Lord Monomark, with his North American slang ('Shucks, Margot. You know better than to get on a high horse with me') is Waugh's first swipe at Canadian-born Max Aitken, Lord Beaverbrook (proprietor of the *Express*).

41 Waugh adopts the fanciful etymology of *runcible* – 'about to' or 'liable to crash' – proposed by Richard Pares in 'A Disquisition on the Word "Runcible" in Edward Lear', *Cherwell*, 2 Feb. 1924, 44–6. Columnists debated whether Agatha was modelled more on Elizabeth Ponsonby or Olivia Plunket Greene: 'Now Which Is It?' *Sunday Dispatch*, 16 March 1930, 4.

42 Such inarticulateness reaches its apogee in Ginger Littlejohn, who can protest Adam's continuing affair with Nina – now Ginger's fiancée – only in the most garbled version of what Paul Pennyfeather called the 'code of ready-made honour': 'Look here, Symes', said Ginger, 'what I mean to say is, what I'm going to say may sound damned unpleasant, you know, and all that, but look here, you know, damn it, I mean *the better man won* – not that I mean I'm the *better* man.... Awful rough luck on you, I mean, and all that, but still, when you come to think of it, after all, well look here, damn it, I mean, d'you see what I mean?' (VB 216–17).

43 VB 143. In later years Waugh liked to claim (not quite accurately) that when writing VB he had as yet met no Jesuits, and so merely reproduced 'the wily Jesuit of popular fiction' (Face to Face). Readers have traced his inspiration to such characters as Fr Holt in Thackeray's *Henry Esmond* (see Isaacs); Waugh himself described

the literary type at length in an essay on Mrs Trollope's *Father Eustace: A Tale of the Jesuits* ('The Jesuit Who Was Thursday', *Tablet*, 21 Dec. 1946, 338–9).

44 VB 3. While working on VB, Waugh suggested to Peters 'an article on Superstitions pointing out how people who think themselves enlightened & free thinkers are far more superstitious than religious people' (L 47). Mrs Hoop – like Brian Howard's mother, an American – remarks after the teachings of her New York 'yogi' fail to cure her sea-sickness: 'I'm through with theosophy after this journey. Reckon I'll give the Catholics the once over' (VB 15).

45 VB 14 (in manuscript Mrs Ape cites 'two great evils': 'Communism and constipation').

46 'The Passing of Devonshire House', *Nineteenth Century and After*, July-Dec. 1926, 312.

47 VB 69, 80, 136; see 40. Waugh began to deploy this shorthand architectural symbolism (especially of neoclassical buildings, at once beautiful and flawed) in DF, where Paul and Margot first talk of love in an 'an eighteenth-century pavilion' on the grounds of King's Thursday (a structure of the sort Cyril Connolly would later celebrate in his 1962 picture-book, *Les Pavillions of the Eighteenth Century*). Later novels evoke abandoned or decayed domestic architecture by Vanbrugh (HD 60), Hawksmoor (S 4), Nash (S 9), and 'a provincial predecessor of Repton' (S 19).

48 'The Books You Read' (review of W. R. Burnett, *Iron Man*), *Graphic*, 12 July 1930, 75.

49 EAR 362. McCartney analyses filmic devices in Waugh's fiction in *Roaring*, chs. 7–8. The theme emerges again in the story 'Excursion in Reality' (1934, rpn. in MLLO), wherein all those in the film business (especially the 'continuity editor' Miss Grits) prosecute lives of breathtaking discontinuity.

50 'Old Men at the Zoo', *Spectator*, 13 Oct. 1961, 501; 'Cornucopia', *Spectator*, 23 June 1961, 928; 'Folkestone, For Shame!' (1937) (EAR 204).

Notes to Chapter 3

1 Sykes 16. To Martin Stannard, Waugh was 'a politically naïve aesthete' (ST1 435); to Selina Hastings, 'he was never seriously interested in politics, and his political understanding was and remained simplistic and immature' (Hastings 100). Stannard's characterization is meant to recall Walter Benjamin's famous critique of Fascism as an 'aestheticisation of politics' in 'The Work of Art in the Age of Mechanical Reproduction' (1936).

2 Reported in the *Sunday Times*, 14 Nov. 1937, 31.

3 EAR 449; Sheehan 213; Auberon Waugh, 'A Death', 562.

4 'We were giving a garden party, and half the guests had disappeared...into the boys' playroom upstairs, where Evelyn was delivering an impassioned address on the injustice of the male sex, and the imperative necessity of a franchise extending to women before the next General Election. His impromptu oratory was the success of the party' (Arthur Waugh, *One Man's Road*, 334).

5 Auden and Lewis vii; Michael Roberts, *New Signatures*, 19; Spender, *Destructive Element*, 222–3.

6 Day Lewis, 'Controversy', *Left Review*, 1 (Jan. 1935), 128.

7 Roughton, 'Surrealism and Communism', *Contemporary Poetry and Prose*, nos 4–5 (Aug.–Sept. 1936), 75; *Left Review*, see 146; Connolly, *Enemies*, 131.

8 D'Arcy 27; 'Scrutiny: A Manifesto' (Bentley 1).

9 VB 52; Lehmann, *Gallery*, 178.

10 'An Angelic Doctor: The Work of Mr. P. G. Wodehouse' (1939, EAR 252–5); 'Carroll and Dodgson' (1939, EAR 260–2); 'A Victorian Escapist' (1938; EAR 230–2).

11 'Gilded Youth: Evelyn Waugh Talks About Class in the Commons', *Nash's Pall Mall Magazine* (May 1937), 11.

12 Hynes, *Auden*, 111, 191.

13 Bevis Hillier, 'When Evelyn Waugh Joked with his Publisher', *The Times* (15 July 1968), 8.

14 WGG 8; Isherwood 74, 76; Orwell, *Essays* 1: 538.

15 *The Times*, 22 Dec. 1930 (EAR 119–22).

16 See Donat Gallagher's fine investigation, 'Black Majesty and Press Mischief'.

17 'Coronation Banquet in Abyssinia, 30,000 Guests (From our Special Correspondent)', *The Times* (5 Nov. 1930), 13.

18 'Ethiopia Today' (EAR 119–22); RP 101. Dudley Carew noted Waugh's 'lifelong... interest in the language of off-beat sexual deviation' (*Fragment* 8).

19 RP 99, 110. Of the Cairo taxi driver in *Labels* Waugh noted blandly, 'I liked this man' (64); of Bergebedgian, 'I became genuinely attached to this man' (RP 99); Basil Seal says to Youkoumian, 'you seem to me a good chap' (BM 134). Like Bergebedgian and Youkoumian, the Cairo taxi driver 'had no religious beliefs, he told me, no home, and no nationality.... He liked America; there were a lot of rich people there.... Did he like his present job? What else was there to do in a stinking place like the Holy Land?' (*Labels* 64; cf. Youkoumian: 'You don't know this country. Stinking place': BM 128).

20 'British Policy in Aden: A Conference of Tribal Chiefs', *The Times* (17 March 1931), 13.

21 With 'light, springing steps' Besse led Waugh on an athletically harrowing 'little walk', after which he 'had laid out for him in the car a clean white suit, a shirt of green crêpe-de-Chine, a bow tie, silk socks, buckskin shoes, ivory hairbrushes, scent spray, and hair lotion. We ate banana sandwiches and drank very rich China tea' (RP 141, 143). Like Baldwin, Besse owned a vineyard in the south of France: 'It is not a luxurious wine, but I am fond of it; it grows on a little estate of my own', he told Waugh (RP 138), as in *Scoop* Baldwin tells William Boot: 'I have a little vineyard in Bordeaux [whose wine] my friends... are kind enough to find drinkable' (S 72).

22 See H. B. Parkes's attack on 'Evelyn Waugh, Catholic and Cynic' (*Nation*, 24 Feb. 1932, 232).

23 Donaldson 52; Hance 140; Dorothy Lygon, HW 50.

24 Graves 34. It was probably from Lady Diana that Waugh gleaned much of the information for his essay 'In Quest of the Pre-War Georgian' (1935), which explains in the voice of a social insider that 'The great change in English social life began, not as is generally thought with the war, but with the season of 1914 and the new generation who came out in that spring' (EAR 167).

25 *Apprentice* 209 (written in 1932 for *John Bull*).

26 Waugh to Alfred McIntyre (president of Little, Brown), 1 Aug. 1948 (private collection). Adam's first sight of Doubting Hall in VB reuses material from 'The House of Gentlefolks'; BR's famous evocation of 'the languor of youth' develops ideas first raised in Waugh's 1920 'Fragment of a Novel': 'Youth, far from being a time of burning quests and wild, gloriously vain ideals... is essentially one of languor and repose' (*Apprentice* 67).

27 MLLO 138. On Gray's debt to Waugh, see Healey.

28 Waugh admitted to Nancy Mitford (L 593) and in ALL (204) that Basil Seal was 'a mixture' of two men he had know since Oxford days: 'satanic' Basil Murray, the drunk, unkempt, dishonest, magnetic son of Gilbert Murray, who died in Spain; and

the beautiful Peter Rodd, 'a superior con man' (Acton, *Mitford* 42) given like Basil to world travel and lecturing acquaintances on all subjects. ('No one minds [Basil's] being rude, but he's so *teaching*'; 'He either cuts me or corners me with interminable lectures about Asiatic politics': BM 97–8.) Between being sent down from Oxford for having a woman in his rooms and marrying Nancy Mitford in December 1933, Rodd was sent by his family to work at a bank in Brazil (where he learnt Russian and Portuguese, was arrested for drunkenness, and sent home as a Distressed British Subject), sacked from jobs in the City and as a journalist in Germany, and finally taken off by his diplomat father on a two-year expedition in the Sahara. As if by a process of life imitating art, Rodd spent much of World War II organizing relief efforts in Abyssinia, for a time running much of the country.

29 Pius XI had recently condemned coeducation in his encyclical *Rappresentanti in terra* (1929); the topic emerges again in *Scoop*, where Ishmaelia's rulers seek to impress foreigners by erecting 'Non-Sectarian Co-educational Technical Schools and other humane institutions' (S 104). The Esperanto movement, launched in the 1880s by the Polish physician Ludwig Zamenhof, had from the start a strong tinge of socialist ideology. The language had been condemned in tsarist Russia, but under Communist rule (at least until Stalin's shift in the mid- thirties to the doctrine of 'socialism in one country'), teaching and publication in Esperanto received strong government support. So well known were its internationalist (and Communist) associations that Hitler condemned Esperanto in *Mein Kampf* (Large 98–105).

30 The stocky General takes his name from Cyril Connolly, 'Black Bitch' from Connolly's dark-complexioned wife Jean Bakewell. Waugh would test this deep but 'always precarious friendship' (L 579) again and again, giving Connolly's name to the horrible evacuee children of POMF and to 'Connolly's Chemical Closet' (Apthorpe's thunderbox) in MA. The General's dispute with Basil over boots recalls 'Smarty-Boots', a nickname for Connolly spread by A. J. Ayer (who claimed that Virginia Woolf invented it): in correspondence with others Waugh habitually calls Connolly 'Boots'.

31 The first Latin quotation comes from Luke 1: 38, the second from the Ave Maria; since the early Middle Ages, both Marian texts have been part of the Angelus, or prayer honouring the Incarnation through the ringing of bells.

32 The endearment comes from a book that has 'been all around the compound' (63) – in fact, William Gerhardie's *The Polyglots* (1925) (Craig 601–2).

33 Stopes was a Scottish geologist famous for advocating racial purity through birth control; claiming that the 'art of contraception' had been revealed to her directly by God, she founded a chain of 'Centres for Constructive Birth Control and Racial Progress'. A decade earlier she had visited Oxford and Waugh presented her with a bouquet of flowers (Hall 238).

34 HRC C9. In 1949 Waugh wrote to Nancy Mitford: 'I must beg you with all earnestness if we are to continue friends, never use the word 'progressive' in writing to me' (L 235).

35 L 82, 84; DC 41; D 386–7. The 43 appears in HD and, ironically renamed for the Psalm, as BR's 'Old Hundredth'; Winnie perhaps served as model for Milly, the call-girl in HD who brings her daughter Winnie along to Brighton.

36 Priestley, *Evening Standard*, 6 Oct. 1932, 11; TLS, 13 Oct. 1932, 736; James Agate, *Daily Express*, 6 Oct. 1932, 6; Howard Marshall, *Daily Telegraph*, 4 Oct. 1932, 16; *Manchester Guardian*, 5 Oct. 1932, 6; Cowley, *New Republic*, 16 Nov. 1932, 22–3.

37 D 372; to Peters, 15 Feb. 1933 (HRC E208). Hastings points out (278–9) that 'The Man Who Liked Dickens' makes use of events that occurred only after Waugh left Boa Vista, concluding that it could not be the story mentioned in the letter to Peters.

But Waugh probably posted an initial version of the story (whose manuscript is lost), to which further details were added later; the articles arrived safely, and no other 'grade A story' survives from this period.

38 *Tablet*, 18. Feb. 1933, 212–15, 200–1 (partially rpn. CH 134–9).

39 A lay convert, once a Protestant preacher, as editor Oldmeadow championed his new faith by such methods as pointedly referring even to Anglican bishops as 'Mr', thus implying – in line with Leo XIII's 1896 bull on the subject, *Apostolicae curae* – the invalidity of their orders.

40 L77. Waugh's text is Swift's sentence explaining that 'a young healthy Child, well nursed, is, at a Year old, a most delicious, nourishing, and wholesome Food; whether *Stewed, Roasted, Baked*, or *Boiled*; and, I make no doubt, that it will equally serve in a *Fricasie*, or *Ragoust*'.

41 *Tablet*, 18 Feb. 1933, 213 (CH 135).

42 *Tablet*, 8 Sept. 1934, 300 (CH 150). With even greater modesty, *Scoop* marks the occasion when Kätchen at last allows William Boot to make love to her by announcing only that the next morning, a cheerful William feels as if he has 'awoke[n] in a new world' (S 197).

43 *Tablet*, 12 Oct. 1935, 451; 19 Oct. 1935, 490.

44 CH 142; Fleming, CH 143–4; 'Gathering Wisdom', *New Statesman*, 17 March 1934, 420.

45 Once again Waugh took belated revenge in his life of Knox: 'Delegation of any task to Bishop Myers notoriously meant its relegation to oblivion' (K 291).

46 Pryce-Jones, *Mitford*, 61. There seems equally little truth to the speculation that HD was a contribution to the agitation for legal reform that led in 1937 to Parliament's liberalization of the grounds for divorce. It is true that Waugh, unlike most Catholics, argued for such reform, suggesting that religious opposition to liberalization was 'a gross burden on unbelievers' and futile for 'Christians because they cannot make use of it anyhow' ('Home Life is so Dull', *Sunday Express*, 1 Dec. 1935, 4). But Tony Last's charade in Brighton results from misplaced chivalry, not legal requirements; the novel puts support for 'reform' into the mouth not of Tony but Brenda's predatory friend Veronica: 'Now I understand why they keep going on in the papers about divorce law reform. It's *too* monstrous that [Tony] should be allowed to get away with it' (i.e., refusing to sell his house to meet Brenda's demand for a settlement four times what she had originally agreed upon) (HD 237–8).

47 Yorke, quoted L 88–9. Reviewers complained as well: that 'the author has not made a clear choice between tragi-comedy and farce' (Oldmeadow, CH 151), cannot decide between 'ironic farce' and 'satiric tragedy' (Ralph Strauss, *Sunday Times*, 2 Sept. 1934, 7), and so produces an 'incongruous hodgepodge' of seriousness and 'sheer buffoonery' (Prescott 168–9).

48 Quennell, CH 155; Brigid Brophy, CH 161; Priestley, quoted in Sykes 88.

49 HD 27, 30. In a passage that looks forward to the discussions of ends and means in BR, Tony nonetheless finds the rebuilt Hetton 'good of its kind' (HD 59).

50 'Mr. Waugh's Cities' (1960), CH 283.

51 HD 96. Tendril's last sentence may owe something to Dr Johnson's self-parody in ch. 2 of *Rasselas*: 'On one part were flocks and herds feeding in the pastures, on another all the beasts of the chase frisking in the lawns; the sprightly kid was bounding on the rocks, the subtle monkey frolicking in the trees, and the solemn elephant reposing in the shade'.

52 HD 182. On the cosmopolitan Mrs Rattery, who descends on Hetton by airplane like a god from a machine, see McCartney 82–8.

53 Todd's name also recalls the sinister fox of Beatrix Potter's *Tale of Mr Tod* (1912).
54 Richards, *Science and Poetry* (New York: Norton, 1926), 95; Eliot, 'Literature, Science, and Dogma', *Dial*, March 1927, 243. In similar fashion Nietzsche attacked George Eliot (and the English in general) in *Twilight of the Gods* for failing to realize that 'when one gives up Christian belief one thereby deprives oneself of the *right* to Christian morality': 'the origin of English morality has been forgotten, so that the highly conditional nature of its right to exist is no longer felt' (Nietzsche 69–70).
55 Muir, *Listener*, 19 Sept. 1934, 506; Priestley, quoted in Sykes 202; Macaulay, CH 158.
56 Bedoyère, *Catholic Herald*, 22 Sept. 1934, 11; Quennell, CH 155. 'Insubstantial' and 'empty': James Agate, *Daily Express*, 6 Sept. 1934, 6; *America*, 20 Oct. 1934, 44; *Boston Transcript*, 17 Oct. 1934, 3.
57 'Fiasco' (EAR 144–9) was written for a collection titled *The First Time I . . .* (1935). Glen also wrote an account of the journey, to be found in his *Young Men in the Arctic: The Oxford University Expedition to Spitsbergen* (1935), ch. 12.
58 L 87; Bogaards 89–90; L 92.
59 EC2a, Preface. The first British edition in fact contained an extensive bibliography.
60 *Month*, Oct. 1935, 377–8. Other favourable reviews appeared in *Blackfriars* (Jan. 1936, 70); *Pax* (Dec. 1935, 213–14), and, by C. C. Martindale, in *G. K.'s Weekly* (19 Sept. 1935, 450).
61 Quennell, *New Statesman* (CH 163); TLS, 3 Oct. 1935, 606; *Quarterly Review*, Oct. 1935, 365. The praise that meant most to Waugh came not from these sources but in Frank Pakenham's autobiography, *Born to Believe* (1953). Waugh had by then badgered the whole family into conversion; Lord Longford wrote of what *Campion* had meant to his wife: 'The first time Elizabeth felt a really strong emotional feel from Catholicism was actually after she had been received when she read Evelyn Waugh's *Edmund Campion*. Now at last she thought of the Catholics as "we" instead of "they"' (Pakeaham 122).
62 EC 59–60, 113, 54. How far the English Reformation was a popular movement, how far an alien imposition from above on a vital Catholic tradition, continues of course to be debated, but since J. J. Scarisbrick's *The Reformation and the English People* (1984) and Eamon Duffy's *The Stripping of the Altars* (1992) something very like Waugh's position has become commonplace among historians.
63 Macaulay 369 (Pius was in fact canonized in 1712); Symons 8.

Notes to Chapter 4

1 *Daily Express*, 3 Sept. 1934, 6.
2 Letter from A. D. Peters to Waugh, 25 Jan. 1935 (HRCT).
3 See for instance Ralph Fox, *The Novel and the People* (1937): 'Shall the writer renounce his country for a religion[?] Mr Evelyn Waugh has done this, only to find that it lands him in the receptive lap of another country's nationalism. Apparently to-day Roman Catholicism implies support for Fascist Italy' (12).
4 He wrote to Diana Cooper, while learning to use a typewriter: 'I suppose if this war is worlders i mustv come home to fight' (DC 52); according to WA, 'the Socialists of Europe, in their hatred of the internal administration of Italy, nearly succeeded [in 1935] in precipitating world war in defence of an archaic African despotism' (WA 29–30).

5 The *Mail* – which in supporting the Italians in 1935 reversed what had been its policy during Waugh's first visit to Abyssinia – had just lost its star reporter, Waugh's old enemy Sir Percival Phillips, as in *Scoop* Lord Copper's *Daily Beast* has just lost the famous Sir Jocelyn Hitchcock.

6 Orwell, 'Looking Back on the Spanish War' (1942), *Essays*, 2: 256–7.

7 The government reasonably did not want news of the Emperor's route and destination to leak out. One American working for the Associated Press was able to get the information to New York in a coded cable; the Emperor's new headquarters at Dessye was bombed the next day. As a result the AP was denied further use of the cable office, but since its despatches brought in over $1000 a week this policy was soon reversed.

8 He wrote to Diana Cooper in October, 'it seems as though the wops will lose this war as i sagely said all along' (DC 54), and his parents in November: 'I believe the Italians are beaten. Not by sanctions but because they never contemplated the necessity of military conquest on any large scale' (L 101). WA elaborates his view that Mussolini had hoped through a show of force and some well-placed bribes to achieve their objective without war (45).

9 Hugh's mother, the Countess Beauchamp, had died shortly before; on that occasion, because of a warrant against him, her husband been unable return to England for the funeral. After Hugh's death – despite protests from the Duke of Westminster – the government on compassionate grounds voided its warrant against the Earl, who returned from his long absence in Venice to Madresfield. The whole chain of events contributed to Waugh's portrayal of Lord Marchmain's return from Venice in BR.

10 Lawrence Athill, *Spectator*, 13 Nov. 1936, 864.

11 Macaulay 370; Garnett (author in 1922 of *Lady into Fox*, mentioned critically at the beginning of *Labels* [15]), *New Statesman* (CH 188–90).

12 See the *Month* editorials 'Those Words "Fascist" and "Anti-Fascist"' (May–June 1942, 187–8) and 'This "Fascist" Business' (July–Aug. 1942, 262–3).

13 'Risks from Extreme Sanctions', *The Times*, 22 Oct. 1935, 22.

14 Shaw, *The Times*, 22 Oct. 1935, 12; Churchill, *Gathering Storm*, 167.

15 WGG 9. That Britain itself had driven Mussolini into the arms of Hitler remained a widespread opinion among conservative Catholics: see for instance *Tablet*, 20 Apr. 1940, 367 (on how 'the differences which forced Italy into her present diplomatic position should never have existed') and Christopher Hollis, *Italy in Africa* (1941).

16 Jerrold, *Tablet*, 6 May 1939, 584; *Georgian Adventure*, 371.

17 'Popes and Peoples', *Night and Day*, 2 Dec. 1937, 24.

18 'Where is Mr Maugham, for example, or the Sitwell family, Mr Roy Campbell, Mr Wyndham Lewis, Mr Peter Fleming, Mr Graham Greene, Mr Michael Arlen, Mr Gilbert Frankau?': Anthony Powell, 'Marginal Comment', *Spectator*, 3 Dec. 1937, 991.

19 See 'For Schoolboys Only' (1937), EAR 199, and 'Folkstone, for Shame!' (1937), EAR 202–4.

20 'Cocktail Hour', *Harper's Bazaar*, 9 Nov. 1933, 26; 'The New Countrymen', *Spectator*, 161 (8 July 1938), 54–5.

21 Christopher Hawtree provides a history of the magazine – and reproduces not only the offending notice of Shirley Temple but several of Waugh's reviews not elsewhere reprinted (including three never actually published) – in ND.

22 Gabriel Herbert, in Sykes, 210; Auberon Waugh, 'Laura Waugh', 31–2, and *Will This Do*, 27, 89, 207.

23 Hastings 530; Auberon Waugh, 'Laura Waugh', 30.

24 While wooing Laura Waugh pursued various affairs, always with non-Catholics ('According to Alec, Evelyn during this period drew back from an affair with a young actress who was much taken with him because he was afraid of endangering her soul': Hastings 331). The woman he asked to accompany him to Africa was Joyce Fagan, the friend whose flat in Canonbury Square he had rented at the time of his first marriage; now married to an American businessman, Donald Gill, she turned down the offer, but was nonetheless deeply in love with Waugh and remained so for many years. He told her 'write to me if it helps'; in February 1938, two years after his marriage to Laura, she still wrote to him: 'I think of you all the time when I am making love, until the word and Evelyn are synonymous!' 'in the darkness each night & in the greyness of each morning when I wake and remember your face' (Hastings 330).

25 In May 1930 Waugh broadcast over the BBC a celebration of the 'free entertainment' to be found not only in London salerooms but also in the country, where 'We most of us gather round when a house in our neighbourhood is being sold up' (reported in *Listener*, 2 June 1938, 1168).

26 'Books of the Year Chosen by Eminent Contemporaries', *Sunday Times*, 26 Dec. 1954, 6.

27 Eliot, 'Politics', 143; EAR 545, 527 (cf. Lecture 277: 'Before 1914, there was a world where sweetness of life could exist').

28 The author of eight books (Waugh had written nine before WA), John Boot began with a life of Rimbaud (Waugh's *Rossetti*), and is now working on '*Waste of Time*, a studiously modest description of some harrowing months among the Patagonian Indians' (*Ninety-Two Days*). 'Between novels he kept his name sweet in intellectual circles with unprofitable but modish works on history and travel'. He wants to leave England to escape his 'American girl' (as Waugh escaped his 'Dutch girl' Teresa Jungman by going to South America) and ends the novel travelling to the Antarctic (Waugh's Spitzbergen).

29 Julia Stitch's original, Diana Cooper, owned a baby Fiat and received visitors in bed; like John Boot, Waugh had asked whether her politician husband (the novel's Algy) could send him abroad 'as a spy' (S 11). The Boot family name again refers to Connolly; the 'great crested grebe' (for which in a column William's sister substitutes the badger) was a joke for the Actons, who in 1936 had pressed an unwilling Waugh to see a prized example of such a bird on their estate at Aldenham (see Acton, 'Will a lion come?').

30 Waugh reviewed Wodehouse's *Laughing Gas* in *The Tablet*, 17 Oct. 1936, 522–3. Auberon Waugh recalls the Herbert family response to parallels between Boot Magna and Pixton in *Will This Do*, 14.

31 Knightley 173. As late as 1955 – when Waugh's agent A. D. Peters negotiated the sale of film rights to *Scoop* to Alexander Korda, who planned to cast Alec Guinness as William Boot – W. A. Evill, the lawyer overseeing the family trust that by then owned the novel, insisted that Waugh indemnify him against potential libel actions from disgruntled journalists (McNamara 182–3).

32 According to one story, when Frederic Remington, working as a photographer in Cuba, cabled home 'EVERYTHING IS QUIET. THERE IS NO TROUBLE HERE. THERE WILL BE NO WAR. I WISH TO RETURN', Hearst replied, 'PLEASE REMAIN. YOU FURNISH THE PICTURES AND I'LL FURNISH THE WAR'. Wenlock Jakes is revered by his colleagues for having been sent to cover a Balkan revolution, arriving by mistake at a peaceful city, and despatching such potent reports of fighting that he thereby fomented the war he'd been sent to cover. 'They gave Jakes the Nobel Peace Prize for his harrowing descriptions of the carnage – but that was colour stuff'.

33 CH 201–2. Laku – Ishmaelite for 'I don't know', as William Boot learns from an old school friend in the British consulate (135) – recalls both the Soviet oil town of Baku, then much in the news, and 'kangaroo', supposedly named when British explorers asked natives who understood no English what the unfamiliar animal was called, only to be told 'Kangaroo' ('I don't understand').

34 'The Prime Minister is nuts on rural England', says the *Beast*'s managing editor (S 18). Baldwin's speeches often sounded like William's 'Lush Places' column, for instance in 1924, evoking 'what England means': 'the tinkle of the hammer on the anvil in the country smithy, the cornrake on a dewy morning, the sound of the scythe against the whetstone, and the sight of a plough team covering over the brow of a hill' (Baldwin, 5–6).

35 Patrick Balfour recalled at the Deutsches Haus (Waugh's Pension Dressler) not a goat but 'a couple of anti-European geese, who if you were white, flew at you as you came up the path' ('Fiasco', 59).

36 S 244. Waugh himself, though he attempted in Abyssinia to learn to type, always wrote longhand; Charles Ryder comments of the odious Samgrass in BR: 'there was something a little too brisk about his literary manners; I suspected the existence of a concealed typewriter somewhere in his panelled rooms' (98).

37 S 6, 25, 308. Reviewing Cyril Connolly's *Enemies of Promise* in 1938, Waugh wrote: 'writing is an art which exists in a time sequence; each sentence … may owe its significance to another fifty pages distant. I beg Mr Connolly to believe that even quite popular writers take great trouble sometimes in this matter' (EAR 239).

38 Lionel Mander was a socialist author and radio commentator; the 'Red' Duchess of Atholl, author of *Searchlight on Spain* (1938), raised money for the Spanish Republicans, whom Julian Huxley also supported; David Garnett savagely reviewed WA in the *New Statesman*. In 1937 Waugh attacked the pacifism of Bertrand Russell and the Peace Balloters: 'There is, thank God, no considerable party in England which attempts to glorify war. … The danger in England today is that people will come to look on it as a dirty job to be evaded at all costs', on the theory that 'no one gains anything in war. This is of course true, absolutely. War is an absolute loss, but it admits of degrees; it is very bad to fight, but it is worse to lose' (EAR 200).

39 Dawson 148, following Pius XI's formulation in *Quadragesimo anno*: 'let all remember that Liberalism is the father of this Socialism that is pervading morality and culture and that Bolshevism will be its heir' (§122).

40 Waugh to Peters, Aug. 1955 (HRC E 896).

41 *Night and Day*, 16 Dec. 1937, 26.

42 S 16, 53–3, 18. Paul Farr analyses the novel's voices and the narrator from which they diverge in 'Style as Satiric Norm'. None of H. R. Knickerbocker's many popular books, including *Fighting the Red Menace* (1931), *The German Crisis* (1932), *The Boiling Point* (1934) and *The Siege of Alcazar* (1936) corresponds to Jakes's (crudely titled) *Under the Ermine*, but all share something of its voice.

43 Waugh's use of the phrase dissents from Dawson, who had written: 'The conflict between Christianity and Marxism – between the Catholic Church and the Communist party – is the vital issue of our time. … It is not a straight fight between Communism and Catholicism or between Communism and Capitalism. It is a fight of each against all' (*Religion*, 59, 61).

44 RUL 208, 102–3, 163–4, 131, 190–2, 324–6.

45 Eliot, 'Literature of Politics', 138; RUL 306. Here as elsewhere in his work, those of Waugh's political views that most disturbed his progressive contemporaries constituted little more than restatements of what had long been the social teaching of his

Church. In *Rerum novarum*, Leo XIII propounded the fundamental importance of private property (§11); the inevitability and necessity of social inequalities ('Society cannot exist or be conceived of without them': §17); and the family as the fundamental unit of civil life ('the State must not absorb the individual or the family': §§13, 34–5). Pius XI's *Quadragesimo anno* – to which POMF also refers (137) – restates Leo's stress on the inviolability of private property, arguing that 'it is grossly unjust for a State to exhaust private wealth through the weight of imposts and taxes' (§49) and concludes a long discussion of Communism and socialism: 'Religious socialism, Christian socialism, are contradictory terms; no one can be at the same time a good Catholic and a true socialist' (§120).

46 William Gower, *Spectator*, 21 July 1939, 103; *Manchester Guardian*, 29 July 1939, 7.

47 EAR 204–5; Calder-Marshall, *Life and Letters Today*, 22 (Sept. 1939), 468–74; Fisher 178. When the *Daily Mail*'s Philip Page misread *Robbery* as an exposé of the 'fantastic riches' and 'repulsive immorality' of the Mexican Church, Waugh threatened to sue and received a printed apology (see Waugh's own account in *Tablet*, 19 Aug. 1939, 250).

48 Martin, *New York Times*, 19 Nov. 1939, 9, 19.

49 See, e.g., *Commonweal*, 24 Nov. 1939, 120; *America*, 4 Nov. 1939, 106–7.

50 D433; L132; WS1 1; L 132.

51 See Waugh's correspondence with Peters, HRC E403–5. As late as 1948 Waugh continued to argue for separate publication in America as well: 'I should very much like to have it published in book form in America', he wrote Alfred McIntyre at Little, Brown; 'I myself have a liking for short books but I think this is uncommon in America' (1 Aug. 1948, private collection). No separate American edition appeared.

52 Teichmann 243, 288; Woollcott 392–3.

53 Samuel Hynes, *Auden*, 152, 196; Orwell, *Essays*, 1: 522; Upward 48. Waugh reviewed *The Mind in Chains* under the title 'For Schoolboys Only' (EAR 198–9).

54 Orwell, *Essays*, 1: 502; Jameson, quoted in Samuel Hynes, *Auden*, 273, 355.

55 Edgell Rickword, 'Straws for the Unwary: Antecedents to Fascism', *Left Review* 1:1 (Oct. 1934), 19; Spender, *Left Review*, 1:5 (Feb. 1935), 148.

56 ND 160; EAR 257. Gide's speech is reprinted in *Left Review*, 1: 11 (Aug. 1935), 44–52.

57 Alec Brown, *Left Review*, 1:3 (Dec. 1934), 76–7; Hutt, *Left Review*, 1:4 (Jan. 1935), 130–5; Orwell, *Essays*, 1: 497.

58 Smith, *Fine Writing*, 205, 209; EAR 478.

59 Grigson, *New Verse*, 1: 1 (Jan. 1933), 1; Sykes 306–7.

60 As Stannard notes, Lucy Simmonds is a composite of all the women Waugh had loved over the decade: she recalls Diana Guinness, pregnant when Waugh was closest to her, and Diana Cooper, with whom he went house-hunting; young but socially assured, she recalls most of all the similarly named Laura, pregnant with their second child while WS was being written. Plant describes Lucy, who thinks her husband 'a great writer', as 'a critical girl', a phrase Waugh often used of Laura. (See ST1 495 and Stannard's more extended discussion in 'Waugh's Climacteric'.)

61 EC 29; EAR 196; letter to *New Statesman*, 3 July 1954, 16.

62 WS 145. Waugh later described Ronald Knox's view of his five detective novels: 'He was not seeking to write novels' (K 188).

63 Sexual attractiveness: 'Miss O'Brien has also failed in what, perhaps, is an impossibility – to create a character of her own sex who is sexually attractive' (EAR 230); love: 'To write of someone loved, of oneself loving, above all of oneself being loved – how can these things be done with propriety? How can they be done at all?' (WS 182); psychological shocks such as amnesia: 'Within the limits of a novel any solution must be inadequate' (ND 211).

Notes to Chapter 5

1   L 130; D 444; Auberon Waugh, *Will This Do*, 17; Lewis, *People's War*, 12.

2   By the end of 1941, Tom Harrisson of Mass Observation noted a rising tide of 'evacuation novels', most 'distinctly middle-class and often distinctly unsympathetic to "the masses"' ('War Books', 418).

3   Cf. MA 220: 'There was in Romance great virtue in unequal odds'. 'Thank God, we are now alone', said Air Marshal Sir Hugh Dowding after Dunkirk, and Queen Mary, 'Personally I feel happier now that we have no allies to be polite to and pamper'.

4   L 199; Auberon Waugh, 'Laura Waugh', 31.

5   Sykes 291–2. The scene is reproduced in OG when Guy has his troop, dimly aware that their 'performance was being played not solely for their own discomfort', practice pilearms beneath the window of Brigade Major Hound (160).

6   D 499, from Waugh's 'Memorandum on Layforce; July 1940–July 1941', written in December 1941 and included in his diary, a detailed eyewitness account that remains valuable to military historians, most recently Anthony Beevor in his authoritative study *Crete: The Battle and the Resistance* (1994).

7   Cf. OG 264: 'Someone's got to stay behind and cover the final withdrawal. Hookforce were last on, so I'm afraid you're the last off'.

8   To Laura, Sept. 1941 (BL); to Dorothy Lygon, 27 Nov. 1962 (Hastings 573); L 585.

9   Hastings 430. For a review of the complex details, see Beevor, *Crete*, 216–22, and 'First Casualty'; and Gallagher, 'Stannard's Waugh'.

10   From Wordsworth's 'Character of the Happy Warrior': 'Who is the happy Warrior? Who is he / That every man in arms should wish to be?'

11   Peters to Waugh, 23 Sept. 1941 (HRCT). Henry Luce, like those in the British government who approved its publication, hoped such an essay would help speed America's entry into the war, 'an object the Japanese effected more spectacularly barely three weeks later' (McNamara 120).

12   'Commando Raid on Bardia: Specially Trained British Bands Stealthily Attack Axis Strongholds in Libya at Night', *Life*, 17 Nov. 1941, 63.

13   Peters to Waugh, 1 April 1942 (HRCT). The whole incident contributed to Waugh's creation of BR's crudely vulgar Rex Mottram, widely recognized as a portrait of Bracken; to the conclusion of MA, where during the Dakar raid Guy Crouchback blots his copy-book with his superiors, through no clear fault of his own; and most of all to 'Operation Popgun' in OG, the trivial, botched commando raid that through Lord Kilbannock's journalistic skill is marketed as an extraordinary display of heroism.

14   'I went to Bognor for a night and fell out as usual with Duff. Since then he has been spreading it about that I am pro-Nazi. I told him I could see little difference between Hitler's new order and Virgil's idea of the Roman Empire' (D 525).

15   ST2 12 Waugh's soldier-servant in the Commandos Ralph Tanner, later interviewed in the hope of turning up scandalous gossip, testified that stories of Waugh's unpopularity with the other ranks were 'Absolute rubbish. He fitted in very well. He was everything you'd expect an officer to be, if you were an ordinary soldier' ('I Was Evelyn Waugh's Batman', *Punch*, 19 Nov. 1975, 960).

16   McNamara 138. Lord Lovat, author of the most acid of all portraits of Waugh as soldier (*Marching Past*, 233–5), claimed specific credit for having ended Waugh's career in the Commandos. A decade later Waugh took revenge with a reference to Ronald

Knox's failure when working as tutor to the young Lovat and his siblings: 'His delicate English humour did not easily penetrate their little Scottish skulls' (K 195).

17 Preface to revised edition (1966). Waugh persisted in supposing WS a 'major work' by comparison (L 158).

18 POMF 11. Waugh perhaps borrows his description of the Trumpingtons and their circle as a 'race of ghosts' from George Orwell's account in *The Lion and the Unicorn* (1941) of the ordinary Englishman as 'still kept under by a generation of ghosts', the upper classes (122–3).

19 In 1952 Waugh described POMF to Nancy Mitford as 'a book about' Howard (L 356), who was furious at the likeness. Like Ambrose, Brian had drifted Left since his Oxford days, gone abroad, and found a German lover Toni (Silk's Hans). 'Evelyn Waugh has made an absolutely vicious attack on me in his new novel *Put out more Flags*', he wrote to Toni; '*You* come into it, too!' (Lancaster 428). On returning from Germany Howard became an agent for M5, employed to detect Fascist sympathizers.

Acton (who had spent 1932–9 in China) probably inspired both Ambrose's interest in ancient Chinese sages and the novel's epigraphs from Lin Yutang. But Ambrose's journal *Ivory Tower*, intended to keep culture alive in wartime, is a pastiche of Cyril Connolly's *Horizon*. (In his editorial for December 1944, Connolly would write – in prose worthy of Silk – that as 'the whole world moves noisily into the Dehydra-headed Utility epoch', *Horizon* has been accused of 'aestheticism', 'escapism', 'ivory-towerism', 'bourgeois formalism', 'frivolity' and 'preferring art to life': 'it pleads on all these counts "guilty and proud of it"'.) Waugh's friends had long attacked *Horizon*'s commitment to the Left (e.g., Douglas Woodruff in the *Tablet*, 12 Apr 1941, 296); Ambrose fears for his fate should Fascism take root in England.

20 Mainwaring naively accepts the government's portrayal of Dunkirk as 'a great and tangible success' (246); Waugh himself noted at the time: 'Duff has dealt cleverly with the news and is putting out the surrender of the Channel ports as a great feat of heroism' (D 471).

21 POMF 125. In fact we last hear of Alistair being invited to join as an officer in Peter's Commando unit (255). BSRA reveals that Alastair indeed died in the war.

22 'Ambrose lived in and for conversation; he rejoiced in the whole intricate art of it, the timing and striking, the proper juxtaposition of narrative and comment, the bursts of spontaneous parody, the allusion one would recognize and one would not, the changes of alliance, the betrayals, the diplomatic revolutions, the waxing and waning of dictatorships that could happen in an hour's session about a table' (POMF 71). Waugh reflected on the shortcomings of his companions in Yugoslavia in 1944: 'Of conversation as I love it – a fantasy growing in the telling, apt repartee, argument based on accepted postulates, spontaneous reminiscences and quotation – they know nothing' (D 585; cf. L 191).

23 POMF 33–4. Cedric shares his wife's despair: 'In the case of her husband grottoes took the place of fashion'. Having married Angela for love (he 'was most romantic – genuinely'), Cedric now has only the aesthetic escape offered by his collection of grottoes ('Always the same; joys for ever, not like men and women with their loves and hates'). As he leaves to go into battle Angela says 'Take care of yourself', to which Cedric replies, simply, 'Why?' (190, 197, 200).

24 POMF 34, 140. Here and elsewhere, POMF seems a first effort to raise issues that Waugh will treat again, with more dexterity, in BR. Ambrose Silk, as is often recognized, is preparatory to Anthony Blanche; the analysis of Hans's youthful homosexuality as 'retarded adolescence' (241) looks forward to BR's more searching analysis of Charles Ryder's second 'childhood'. Having frustrated the ends of her

nature, Angela is 'thwarted' in just the way Cordelia finds of Julia and Charles (BR 271). Angela's lashing out at Basil looks forward to the scene in BR in which, for similar reasons, Julia lashes Charles Ryder with a switch; her long monologue about France (27–9) – really about Basil, who has recently failed to keep an assignation with her at Cannes – is the forerunner (especially in her meditation on the question 'What's eating you') of Julia's speech on sin.

25 POMF 189 (cf. 141, 185); 49; 72.

26 POMF 52, from W. S. Landor's 'Dying Speech of an Old Philosopher' (1849) (also published as 'On His Seventy-Fifth Birthday' and 'Finis'). The entire epigram is ironically relevant to the despairing Ambrose, who refuses to join the war and will soon 'depart' for Ireland:

> I strove with none, for none was worth my strife:
> Nature I loved, and, next to Nature, Art:
> I warm'd both hands before the fire of Life;
> It sinks; and I am ready to depart.

27 POMF 72. Waugh has in mind figures such as Gabriel Carritt, who changed his first name to the more suitably proletarian 'Bill'.

28 Immediately after a scene in which a young Communist in Poppet's circle, 'due to be called up in the near future', decides to 'plead conscientious objections', Waugh cuts to Sonia talking with Margot on the telephone: 'Peter's here and Basil. We're all feeling very gay and warlike' (51). Like the larger contrast between Sonia's circle and Poppet's, this montage insinuates Waugh's disagreement with views like those Victor Gollancz had advanced in *Guilty Men* (1940) that England's upper classes had abetted Fascism through appeasement and a continuing lack of appetite for the war.

29 Connolly, quoted in Fisher, 193; POMF 48. Waugh had addressed the same question with which Ambrose wrestles in a letter to *Horizon* in December 1941. Under the title 'Why Not War Writers?' a group of Left writers including Calder-Marshall, Connolly, Orwell and Spender had put forward the suggestion that their national service should comprise not fighting but writing, in an effort 'to interpret the war world so that cultural unity is re-established and the war effort emotionally co-ordinated' (Oct. 1941, 238). Waugh acidly replied that real artists would profit from a tour of active duty:

> What a picture of fun it makes of English writers! First, while Europe was overrun, they were 'hesitant'. Then one enemy fell out, over the division of the spoils, with his larger and wealthier partner. This welcome but not unforeseen diversion 'crystallized' our writers' 'feelings'. They are now for total war. So be it. To the less literary this reasoning seems fatuous, and, in the context, their expression 'the interest of their country' ambiguous.... But what do your chums propose doing? They would like to form an Official Group; ... they would 'co-ordinate the war-effort emotionally'. Cor, chase my Aunt Nancy round the prickly pear!

(Letter from 'Combatant', *Horizon*, Dec. 1941, 437–8. Cf. POMF 87 : 'Cor chase my Aunt Fanny round a mulberry bush, thought Ambrose, what a herd'.)

30 POMF 48. 'In 1939, after the Nazi-Soviet Pact', Kingsley Martin recalled, 'the Communists suddenly decided to oppose the war as "Imperialist aggression".' The position was put by Palme Dutt (briefly Harry Pollitt's replacement as head of

the Party) in his pamphlet *Why this War?*: 'This is an Imperialist war like the war of 1914. It is a sordid exploiters' war of rival millionaire groups, using the workers as their pawns in the struggle for world domination for markets, colonies, and profits, for the oppression of peoples. This is a war in which no worker in any country can give support' (Kingsley Martin 207–8).

31 Woodruff, 'The German-Russian Collusion', *The Tablet*, 20 Apr. 1940, 366.

32 *Month*, Jan–Feb. 1944, 5–6; cf. 'Poland the Test', *The Tablet*, 4 Jan 1941, 2. Like his creator, Guy Crouchback is a regular reader of *The Tablet* (MA 64, 178), which declared in 1945, when it was unblinkably clear that the Allies were prepared to betray Poland: 'it will be a long time before Britain regains the ground lost in the eyes of Europe by conduct which makes such contemptuous nonsense of our published war aims. This loss is the price paid for the good-will of a Power [the Soviet Union] whose Government has many times declared its intention of over-throwing the whole social fabric of the West' (3 Mar., 98).

33 MA 21–2. Cf. Ronald Knox writing shortly after VE day on 'The Responsibilities of Victory': 'There are many people in the world, a good many people even in our own country, to whom all this talk about justice sounds old-fashioned and absurd', but if the Allies fail to do 'justice', if they 'condemn a large part of mankind to slavery, or to extinction', 'we have lost the war in winning it' (*The Tablet*, 12 May 1945, 219). Though always more tolerantly aware than Waugh that 'a nation at war has difficulty keeping its hands clean' (*Atom*, 147), Knox added a year later, in a judgment with which many Catholics agreed: 'So far as justice is concerned, I hope I may be allowed to record my own impression that in these last few years the very notion of it has been largely forgotten' ('Religion and Civilisation', *The Tablet*, 3 Aug. 1946, 58).

34 Lucas, *Forgotten Holocaust*, 72–3. Documents recently released by the KGB have confirmed that the massacres were directly ordered by Stalin (see *New York Times*, 26 Apr. 1995, A10).

35 'An Unposted Letter', *The Times*, 17 June 1959, 11; RC 7; D 631.

36 Broadcasts of 21 July and 22 Sept. 1940, in Priestley, *All England Listened*, 54–5, 118. Waugh perhaps had Priestley's last-cited comment in mind in making Hooper say of Brideshead Castle, 'It doesn't seem to make any sense – one family in a place this size. What's the use of it?' (BR 303), and again in US when Guy asks the fate of a village priest, only to be told by the Communist Bakic that the Party has taken over his church: 'Too big a house for one old man' (US 293).

37 Keynes to Martin, 17 Dec. 1940, quoted in Kingsley Martin, 305; EAR 274; *The Tablet*, 22 Mar. 1941, 224. *The Tablet*'s attacks on those using the war to further 'a particular kind of egalitarian Socialist Commonwealth at home' were at first mainly satirical ('St. George today is expected to have an attractive plan for the after-care of all maidens from dragons, and a war is expected to have its prospectus, like a general election') (ibid.), though still forceful enough to draw letters of protest from readers such as Frank Pakenham (19 Apr. 1941, 316). But by 1942 the magazine began to devote long and serious columns to arguments that 'liberty is basically more valuable and more necessary than equality at home' (22 July 1942, 38) and that 'The Totalitarian Tide is running very strongly in Britain just now' (19 Sept. 1942, 135); with the publication of the Beveridge Report, nearly every issue contains extended attacks explicitly directed against the idea that 'This is a People's War', construing that phrase as the slogan of those who sought the 'Nazification' of England through programmes that 'appear to be a big further step towards dividing the country into an omnipotent bureaucracy on top and a helpless proletariat below, taught to look to its

master, the State, for everything' (21 Nov. 1941, 246; cf. 'The Beveridge Report', 5 Dec. 1942, 271–2; 'The Voice of the People', 27 Feb. 1943, 102–3).

38 Kingsley Martin 302, 296. Historians agree that ABCA discussions, which Waugh labelled 'harsh nonsense' (EAR 309), 'tended to work in a left-wing direction' and contributed to a 'radicalisation of the forces' (Addison, *War is Over*, 12, 18). William Beveridge, whose slogan was 'A People's War for a People's Peace', published the famous *Social Insurance and the Allied Services*, usually known simply as his *Report*, in December 1942; versions of it sold an astounding 635,000 copies. Often said to be Labour's blueprint for the postwar welfare state, its effects were felt long before, as its popularity led the War Cabinet to appoint a Reconstruction Committee which in turn issued a series of White Papers: *Educational Reconstruction* (1943), *A National Health Service* (1944), *Employment Policy* (1944), *Social Insurance* (1944), and *Housing Policy* (1945) – all the 'deeply depressing publications of His Majesty's Stationery Office' that LO's Dennis Barlow recalls from wartime (17).

39 BR 112. Cf. *The Tablet* on 'The "Austerity" Budget', 18 Apr. 1942: 'The main Christian tradition is to view riches as a snare and a danger, as bringing imperative moral obligations, and making it very difficult to recognize and observe those obligations. But it has not been a tradition which in either theory or practice has considered great inequalities of fortune to be morally wrong, and still less has it been a tradition to call upon the State to enforce economic equality' (192). Such sentiments of course concern only the structure of human society, not the capacities of individual souls. When Nancy Mitford accused Waugh of believing the rich to possess spiritual privileges unavailable to the poor, he exploded: 'It is not true that any Catholic thinks the poor go to a servants' hall in heaven. Read Bossuet's great sermon on the Eminent Dignity of the Poor. Also Gospels' (NM 325).

40 'Comment', *Horizon*, Dec. 1944, 367. In 1952, Connolly borrowed the phrase 'a twitch upon the thread' – surely from *Brideshead* rather than Chesterton – to describe Communist masters calling their agents back to Moscow (*Missing Diplomats*, 25).

41 *New Statesman*, 25 Sept. 1943, 202. For Catholic response to the Henshaw Report, see Robert Gorman, SJ, 'Juvenile Delinquency and Catholic Schools', *The Tablet*, 13 Nov. 1943, 234–5.

42 Waugh, *New Statesman*, 2 Oct., 217; Stopes and 'Medical Psychologist', 9 Oct., 233–4; Waugh, 16 Oct., 251.

43 Waugh 'saw the spark' on 13 October; on the 22nd he went to Pixton intending 'to stay and start writing' (D 553). The scene was still fresh in his mind sixteen years later, when he wrote to Mary Lygon: 'I believe that everyone once in his (or her) life has the moment when he is open to Divine Grace. It is there, of course, for the asking all the time, but human lives are so planned that usually there's a particular time – sometimes, like Hubert, on his death bed – when all resistance is down and Grace can come flooding in' (L 520).

44 US 128–9. The words *locum refrigerii, lucis et pacis* ('a place of refreshment, light and peace') come from the prayer *Memento etiam*, a prayer for the dead within the Canon of the Mass.

45 Gilbert 693. The phrase recurs in US when Guy expresses surprise that Bulgarians would join the Yugoslav Partisans under Tito, to be told by the Communist Frank de Souza: 'You don't follow politics any more than poor Winston does. The Bulgarians have, as our Prime Minister might have put it, "found their souls"' (US 297).

46 After the war Maclean claimed that his commission from Churchill had been simply 'to find out who was killing the most Germans and how they could be helped to kill more'; Deakin recalled Churchill's response to his briefings: 'Do you mean to make a

home in Yugoslavia after the war? Neither do I'. *Unconditional Surrender* slyly puts these remarks – along with others by Anthony Eden (for which see below, p. 219) – into the mouth of the Communist Joe Cattermole, who tells Guy: 'Now, remember, we are soldiers not politicians. Our job is simply to do all we can to hurt the enemy. Neither you nor I are going to make his home in Jugoslavia after the war. How they choose to govern themselves is entirely their business' (217).

47   *The Tablet*, 1 Jan. 1944. See among many similar essays: 'Mihailovitch and the Chetnicks' (25 Sept. 1943, 148–9); 'The Catholic Church and Tito's Army: The Background to the Communist Bid for Control of Yugoslavia' (18 Dec. 1943, 293–4); and 'Yugoslavia After Three Years' (25 Mar. 1944, 148–50).

48   Differing versions of the story are told by Birkenhead (HW 151–2, 161), Sykes (362), and Churchill himself (WM 25).

49   US 290; D 579. A descriptive passage in US subtly implies the Partisans' lack of unified support from any level of Croatian society, low, middle or high. Its key sentences are: 'Partisans obeyed orders and it was vital to them to keep the good-will of the peasants'; 'The bourgeois had all left Begoy with the retreating garrison'; 'The circle of villas in the outskirts of the town [had been] abandoned precipitately by their owners' (222–3).

50   Waugh did, however, reject the view (spread by the Partisans and popular among Tito's supporters abroad) that the Chetniks were quislings in disguise – a position that has recently been revived by Tito's apologist Vladimir Dedijer in *The Yugoslav Auschwitz and the Vatican* (1992).

51   Gallagher, 'Stannard's Waugh', 62; see also David Martin, *Ally Betrayed: The Uncensored Story of Tito and Mihailovich* (1946) and *Web of Disinformation* (1990); Nora Beloff, *Tito's Flawed Legacy* (1985, a source that makes use of Waugh's testimony); and Michael Lees, *The Rape of Serbia: The British Role in Tito's Grab for Power* (1990).

52   Speech in Brussels, Dec. 1945, reported in *The Tablet*, 5 Jan. 1946, 2.

53   Letters to *The Times*, 23 May and 5 June 1945 (EAR 282–5; the former given a favourable notice in *Month*, May–June 1945, 157); reviews rpn. EAR 307–9, 321–2.

54   Johnson 433, 436 ('The Americans could not understand', noted General Montgomery, 'that it was of little avail to win the war strategically if we lost it politically'). Cf. MA 222–3: 'Guy knew of Mr. Churchill only as a professional politician, a master of sham-Augustan prose, a Zionist, an advocate of the Popular Front in Europe, an associate of the press-lords and of Lloyd George'.

55   MA 221. After the war, Waugh and Deakin remained friends – 'Bill Deakin full of guilt about Tito', he noted approvingly after a supper together at Piers Court in 1946 (D 650). But like many others, Waugh was unconvinced by Maclean's postwar protestations that he had not really known what was going on in Yugoslavia. Waugh thought these apologies 'dishonest' (D 651) and later cast Maclean in the role of the treacherous Constantius of *Helena* (see 399 n10).

Notes to Chapter 6

1   In the 1945 edition (still the only one available in America) the novel had this two-book structure; in manuscript and the 1960 revision – the text now published by Penguin – it is divided into three books, forming a pattern Sebastian-Loss-Julia (though the divisions between books one and two fall in different places in the two cases). On Waugh's longstanding interest in the theology of deathbed repentance, see EAR 224.

2 BR 19. In 1960 Waugh made Charles's conversion explicit, adding to the paragraph quoted above about his religious upbringing: 'Later, too, I have come to accept claims which then, in 1923, I never troubled to examine, and to accept the supernatural as the real' (BR2 98).

3 BR 41, 71, 54, 71, 39. Waugh himself kept a human skull in a bowl of flowers in his rooms at Oxford (Greenidge 15). On the maxim 'I too [Death] am in Arcadia', see Panofsky, '*Et in Arcadia Ego*'.

4 BR 41, 77. Sebastian makes the second remark in the course of explaining that his being a Catholic makes him 'wickeder' than others when he transgresses, a point also made by Julia when she reflects that 'If she apostasized now, having been brought up in the Church, she would go to hell, while the Protestant girls of her acquaintance, schooled in happy ignorance, could marry eldest sons, live at peace with their world, and get to heaven before her'. The point in both cases is that sin entails *knowing* choice (of a lesser good over a greater).

5 Thomas Arnold, letter to John Taylor Coleridge, 17 Sept. 1832, quoted in Paul M. Puccio, *Brothers of the Heart*. I am grateful to Professor Puccio for allowing me to read his unpublished dissertation, from which I have derived all the material in this paragraph.

6 BR 282. The mature Ryder adds a recognition that this hope disguises a dangerous temptation, describing the estate as 'such a prospect perhaps as a high pinnacle of the temple afforded after the hungry days in the desert'.

7 Joseph Hynes, 'Two Affairs', 241.

8 BR 196–7. The whole scene of Marchmain's death calls upon familiar Christian iconography: two kneeling women pray for him, like the two Marys mourning Christ; just before dying, Marchmain – who has himself likened his final confinement to Christ's Agony in the Garden, and asked his daughter to 'watch' with him – appears to Ryder 'as I had seen him that morning, but his eyes were now shut; his hands lay, palm-upward, above the bedclothes'.

9 Lamentations 1:1 (the *Tenebrae* service was abolished in 1955: see EAR 607).

10 Dawson 81; MGM 229. We are also to understand that between Prologue and Epilogue Ryder has learnt a certain charity. In the Prologue he objects to Hooper's 'Rightyoh', snapping 'And for Christ's sake don't say "rightyoh"'; in the Epilogue he lets two uses of the same word pass unremarked. In the Prologue Ryder disclaims responsibility ('That wasn't our rubbish'), bringing trouble to his company; in the Epilogue he assumes responsibility, telling a Hooper who has once again failed in his duty, 'It's my fault for going away' and 'don't let on to anyone that *we've* made a nonsense of this morning' (350, my italics).

11 BR 17, 304. In proof the novel ended yet more explicitly:

> I quickened my pace and reached the hut which served us for our anteroom.
> 'You're looking unusually cheerful today', said the second-in command; 'have you had a good morning?'
> 'Yes, thank you', I said; 'a very good morning'.

12 BR 49, 245, 144, 83. Waugh himself described Bridey as 'an old-fashioned, unambitious, just, slightly inhuman figure – a throw-back to the Middle Ages' (MGM 228).

13 BR 250. One index of Bridey's wisdom particularly worth recalling, given *Brideshead*'s reputation for snobbery, is his refusal to take sides in the General Strike of 1926.

Charles joins in opposing the workers (as Waugh himself had volunteered as a special constable), but the Earl of Brideshead holds back, 'not satisfied with the justice of the cause' (184). Waugh had already recanted his youthful participation in the Strike (as merely an occasion when the leisured 'clubbed several unoffending citizens') in *Put Out More Flags* (54). *Brideshead* underlines the point by meting out to Charles's fellow strike-breaker, the Belgian Futurist who claims 'the right to bear arms anywhere against the lower classes', the satisfying fate of having 'a pot of ferns dropped on his head by an elderly widow in Camden Town' (177, 183).

14 As Blanche makes clear ('My dear, I should like to stick you full of barbed arrows') (31), Sebastian is named for the Roman aristocrat who gave up his position and life for the faith (and became the subject of centuries of homoerotic art). His teddy-bear Aloysius is perhaps ironically named for St Aloysius Gonzaga, patron of Catholic youth.

15 BR 34, 70, 120; 95, 120; 92; 113. In 1955 Waugh described Sebastian as 'a contemplative without the necessary grace of fortitude' (L 439). Waugh's own drinking, as well as his relations with Alastair Graham and Olivia Greene, had of course supplied him with the knowledge to realize so fully both what he called the 'gradual stages' by which Sebastian becomes 'an incurable alcoholic' (MGM 228) and, in an extraordinary sentence, the plight of Charles in loving an alcoholic:'A blow, expected, repeated, falling on a bruise, with no smart or shock of surprise, only a dull and sickening pain and the doubt whether another like it could be borne' (BR 148). Thomas Gilmore examines the symptomology of Sebastian's drinking in relation to modern therapeutic literature in *Equivocal Spirits*, ch. 2.

16 L 196, 195. Betjeman recalled Waugh's response to a critic of Lady Marchmain: '*You* may not like her. But God loves her' ('Waugh', 149).

17 BR 189; cf. Von Hügel 32, 118.

18 BR 272, 285, 298. Cf. Dawson 153: 'spiritual reality ... stands all the time looking down on our ephemeral activities like the snow mountains above the jazz and gigolos of a jerry-built hotel'.

19 BR 20, 159. Both passages echo phrases from some of Hopkins's best-known poems ('God's Grandeur', 'Pied Beauty', 'As kingfishers catch fire'). Such echoes are especially prevalent in the novel's early sections, where Ryder recalls Keats's 'Grecian Urn' (in describing the 'still unravished' grounds leading to the river Bride: (18)), and more distantly, Wordsworth's descriptions of the declension from youth to maturity in the 'Immortality' ode (56, 70).

20 See 60.

21 BR 23. For variations on 'a finger's breadth' (or 'a hair's breadth') 'above reality': NTD 64; POMF 31; OG 53.

22 BR 26. Sebastian's quotation comes from Bell, *Art*, 12–13.

23 'Insular and medieval' well describes the style of most Anglican churches Charles might have known, 'baroque' that of much Catholic church architecture in Victorian and early twentieth-century England. In his 'conversion to the baroque', Charles follows in the footsteps of such other British converts as John Henry Newman, who wrote (albeit without Waugh's firmer grasp of art-historical terminology) after a visiting a splendid baroque church in Milan in 1846: 'It is like a Jesuit Church, Grecian and Palladian – and I cannot deny that, however my reason may go with the Gothic, my heart has ever gone with the Grecian.... There is in the Italian style such ... elegance, beauty, brightness, which I suppose the word "classical" implies, that it seems to befit the notion of an Angel or a Saint' (Ward 1: 139).

24 Exodus 31: 2–5, prooftext for centuries of theological speculation about art.

25   'But Ambrose, thought Ambrose, what of him? Born after his time, in an age which made a type of him, a figure of farce' (POMF 51). (Meanwhile we hear of Julia that even her youthful efforts to dress like her contemporaries 'could not reduce her to type.')

26   BR 202. In Newman's famous maxim from the *Apologia*, 'growth' is 'the evidence of life'. Waugh recalls the maxim again in describing Virginia Troy in *Unconditional Surrender*: 'She was not a woman to repine. She accepted change, though she did not so express it to herself, as the evidence of life' (US 99).

27   To Waugh, 25 Feb. 1945 (BL).

28   To Waugh, 30 May 1945 (BL). Even Clive Bell, now a club friend, wrote to say he thought BR the best novel in either English or French since *To the Lighthouse* (ST2 157n).

29   See Aslet 250–5. Aslet includes detailed colour photographs of the Madresfield chapel.

30   Dakers, ch. 10. Waugh had written to Nancy Mitford from Yugoslavia that he thought of Ryder as 'a bad painter' (L 196), and later tried to arrange for the novel to be illustrated by John Piper, whom he had met while visiting the Sitwells at Renishaw in 1942 – 'There is an extremely charming artist called Piper staying here making a series of drawings of the house' (L 163) – and whose work he confessed 'I don't much admire' (L 207). (Focusing 'traditional elegance' on 'the maelstrom of barbarism', Ryder's Mexican paintings also reflect Waugh's changing sense of his own prewar novels, seen now as productions inferior to BR.)

31   'A Story with a Moral' (1956), EAR 511–12. Even after conversion Waugh could speak of Oscar Wilde as having 'got himself into trouble, poor old thing, by the infringement of a very silly law, which is just as culpable and just as boring as an infringement of traffic or licensing regulations' (EAR 124).

32   See 321–2. The subject does not enter Waugh's fiction again in any important way until the sixties. In the aftermath of the Burgess and Maclean spy scandal of 1956, *Unconditional Surrender* connects sexual lawlessness not only with rejection of what Grimes calls 'the impulse of family life' but with treason.

33   Macaulay 372; Yorke to Waugh, 25 Dec. 1944 (BL).

34   See Fussell, *Wartime*, ch. 15. 'I *want* my memories to be old-fashioned and extra-vagant', Sitwell began *Left Hand*. Connolly predicted soon after war was declared: 'Nostalgia will return as one of the soundest creative emotions, whether it is for the sun, or the snow, or the freedom which the democracies have had temporarily to discontinue' ('The Ivory Shelter', *New Statesman*, 7 Oct. 1939, 483).

35   One specimen from among many: 'E. Sackville-West has made pansy-high-brow-journalistic history with the phrase "I seem to feel". Surely the height of diffidence. First the statement. Then the qualification "I think"; then the qualification "I feel". And now "I seem to feel"' (L 297).

36   BR2 9. On 'Basic English', see Harold Goad, 'Basic English: Some Criticisms of the New Movement', *The Tablet*, 9 Oct. 1943, 173–4.

37   1960 Preface, 9. Cf. MGM: 'The long speech which [Julia] makes in the novel was not intended to be a verbal transcription of anything she actually said, but a half-poetic epitome of what was in her mind' (229).

38   Cf. Andrew Beck on 'The Theology of Freedom', in a passage richly revelatory of the intellectual context from which BR emerges: 'With this substituting of means for ends, this wanting to choose, but never to have made a permanent choice, we reach the stage where men have gone back to a sort of second childhood. For St Thomas and the whole Catholic tradition teach that a man is not really grown up until he has considered his last end, the purpose of his existence' (*The Tablet*, 31 March 1945, 149).

39 Hebrews 13: 14 ('For we have not here a lasting city, but we seek one that is to come').

40 'Faut-il dire beaucoup de mal de son siècle? Non ... marchez avec votre siècle, donnez à votre foi la parure de vos connaissances intellectuelles.... Il ne faut pas non plus se scandaliser de ce qui est nouveau' (Green 15).

41 D 627 (6 May 1945). The previous December in *Horizon* Connolly had spoken of the need for authors, in the face of the new Europe then emerging, to 'appeal through being uncontemporary' (368).

Notes to Chapter 7

1 Pritchett 8; cf. Elizabeth Bowen in the same volume: 'At present, we writers are the victims of a, one must hope, temporary but acute disaster – the complete *non-existence* of all our earlier written books. That is to say, they do not exist commercially: owing to the paper shortage they are out of print – the income, however modest, that we should have expected to derive from their continuous sales is lost to us. Twenty or twenty-five years of work is of prestige-value only; not worth a farthing. Oh yes, it leaves us with one asset – reputation. So we have to market that, making good our lost royalty incomes by odd-jobbing' (54).

2 Myddleton 54. When the schoolmaster Scott-King earns twelve guineas for a journal article, six go in taxes (SK 6).

3 TE 239, 240; Connolly, ST2 200.

4 As late as 1956, Rayner Heppenstall predicted that future historians would recall the writing of his time 'as a butlers' and antique-dealers' cult of gracious living and more spacious ages' ('Decade Talk', *New Statesman*, 14 Apr. 1956, 377).

5 With an introduction by Michael Sissons, TLS, 5 Mar. 1982; rpr. in *Work Suspended and Other Stories* (Penguin, 1982). Discussions of the fragment include Davis, *Forms*, ch. 11, and Meckier, 'Gaslight'.

6 SK 7, 18, 14. As such passages suggest, the gluttonous descriptions of food so often remarked upon in wartime writing survived into the era of Austerity. *Helena* lingers over lavish meals of 'oysters stewed with saffron, boiled crabs, soles fried in butter, suckling pig seethed in milk' (H 17); the hero of John Braine's *Room at the Top* (1957, begun 1952) catalogues a buffet procured through the black market: 'There was lobster, mushroom patties, anchovy rolls, chicken sandwiches, ham sandwiches, turkey sandwiches, smoked roe on rye-bread, real fruit salad flavoured with sherry, meringues, apple pie, Danish Blue and Cheshire and Gorgonzola and a dozen different kinds of cake loaded with cream and chocolate and fruit and marzipan'.

7 'A Visit to America', *The Times*, 6 Nov. 1947, 6.

8 See 'Goa: The Home of a Saint' (EAR 448–56).

9 EAR 312–16 (published in the American *Town and Country*, Sept. 1946).

10 'Palinurus in Never-Never Land: or, The *Horizon* Blue-Print of Chaos' (*The Tablet*, 27 July 1946), EAR 309–12.

11 Eliot, *Notes*, 159; EAR 389, 422.

12 Orwell, *Wigan*, 204; Hennessey 145; Hopkins 116.

13 Porter 276–7. In 'Towards the Cocktail Party', David Pryce-Jones discusses Waugh among many other writers (Christopher Fox, Warwick Deeping, Rosamund Lehmann, Howard Spring, Elizabeth Taylor, Angela Thirkell) who felt themselves a threatened middle class.

14 Lehmann, *Ample Proposition*, 37; Lambeth Conference, *1948 Encyclical Letter* (Hennessey 437); MacRae, 'Domestic Record of the Labour Government', *Political Quarterly*, 20: 1 (Oct.–Dec. 1949), 10.

15 Spender, *God*, 270, 236, 272; Priestley and Muggeridge quoted in Hewison, 12.

16 Amidst many other discussions of socialism at home, Hayek's book – with its long section 'Why I am not a Conservative' – received an unusually detailed and laudatory review in *The Tablet* (11 Mar. 1944, 123–4).

17 TE 240; EAR 311–22; Auberon Waugh, 'A Death', 563.

18 Once again, though great benefits might flow from the classes above, Waugh clearly locates himself among 'the classes of industry and scholarship', the working, professional middle class with which he also identifies himself in GP (130) and TA (19).

19 Amis 81, 78. Similar provocations include Waugh's description of Helena's 'plain fare' at home (quoted above, n.6) and the account in *Unconditional Surrender* of the 'rudimentary comforts', 'nothing sumptuous', to which Mrs Scrope-Weld hopes to return after the war: a lady's maid, butler, footman, cook and kitchen-maid, 'self-effacing housemaids to dust and tidy', a groom and two gardeners (190). Objecting to the last passage, Philip Toynbee called Waugh a 'lunatic romantic' (CH 436).

20 L 278; cf. Waugh to Peters, 28 June 1945: 'I do not see the advantage of making more than £5,000 a year under the present regime' (HRC E436). In 1950, the Treasury's Gower report outlined the difficulty of earning more than £5,000 annually (Beard 92); in 1958, Ian Fleming reported to his wife Ann that, without drawing on capital, 5,000 a year 'is as rich as one can be' (LAF 214). Waugh discusses his marginal rate of tax at L 318, L 357, DC 125, and DC 160; in 1953 he complains to Peters of regularly paying at the rate of seventy-five per cent (HRC E793).

21 In 1948, addressing the question 'Is this still a free country?', C. K. Allen complained of 'the whole demoralizing under-the-counter rigmarole, and, worst of all, the pervading atmosphere of petty corruption, direct and indirect, in cash and in kind. Not only kissing but all life goes by favour, and it becomes a maxim, grinned or groaned at, that 'you can't get anything done unless you know somebody'. One must either belong to the commissar class, or sedulously cultivate acquaintance among it' ('The Pinpricked Life', *Spectator*, 5 Nov. 1948, 584).

22 Far from hackwork, WPW required careful research into the firm's records to flesh out the engaging anecdotal history of Saccone and Speed presented in the pamphlet's first half; the second half contains Waugh's mature thoughts on the varieties of wine (including especially heavy wines like port, then going out of fashion), each considered in a larger intellectual context not as 'a mere luxury', but 'a staple of civilization' and, 'until the sinister developments of the last quarter century', 'an essential part of the Art of Life'. 'All fermented and distilled liquors have their due place in the adventure of the human soul. It is the art of civilization to multiply them and discriminate their proper uses' (WPW 11–12, 44).

23 L 235; to Francis Talbot, SJ, 17 June 1948 (EWN 19: 1 (Spring 1985), 6).

24 27 Apr. 1946 (HRCT).

25 In 1949 Waugh received what he called a 'Cripps bonus' when Britain's devaluation of the pound from $4.03 to $2.80 increased the value of his holdings in dollars by over 40 per cent.

26 'Paperbacks bring in nothing', Waugh told an interviewer in 1960; 'The royalty is a penny h'penny a copy, and some damn fool writes you a letter about it and you have to spend three pence replying' (Allsop).

27 Between 1950 and 1964, for instance, Peters earned over $25,000 for Waugh by selling the rights to *A Handful of Dust* to a succession of producers (Sam Marx paid

$17,500 in hopes of making a film to be called *The Man Who Liked Dickens*, starring David Niven and Judy Garland) (McNamara 260–2).

28 Peters to Waugh, 14 Dec. 1950 (HRCT).

29 'Evelyn Waugh's Books Transfer Rights for Children', *Daily Telegraph*, 5 Oct. 1951, 5.

30 *Tablet*, 9 June 1945, 273–74; *Spectator*, CH 237–8; *Sunday Times*, 3 June 1945, 3. Both the secular and Catholic press drew attention to the issues that had troubled Knox and Laura. The *Manchester Guardian* confessed 'a strong personal prejudice against' the novel's evocations of 'adultery, perversion, and drunkenness' (CH 233); Frank Sheed protested its 'stale smell of homosexuality' (*Books on Trial*, Feb. 1946, 141).

31 Churchill, 'Captain Evelyn Waugh', *Book of the Month Club News* (Dec. 1945), 4–5. Churchill goes on to cite a comment by Waugh himself: 'What they can't stand about *Brideshead Revisited* is that the hero has two love affairs both with women of his own class. One they might forgive, but two is a sure indication to Left-wing intellectuals of reactionary crypto-fascist ideology'.

32 Waugh wrote in the preface to SH (1965), 'When I wrote *Brideshead Revisited* I was consciously writing an obituary of the doomed English upper class' (SH 9). Introducing the revised BR2 in 1960, he admitted that his fears had been exaggerated: 'the English aristocracy has maintained its identity to a degree that then seemed impossible. The advance of Hooper has been held up at several points. Much of this book therefore is a panegyric preached over an empty coffin' (BR2 10).

33 EAR 302. The last point, his solution to the narratological problem posed in *Work Suspended*, is one Waugh would make over and over in subsequent years. In 1948 he argued that 'In the last twenty-five years the artist's interest has moved from sociology to eschatology' (EAR 360); in 1950 he praised Antonia White's 'superior vision of the nature of human life': 'She knows that man is in the world...to love and serve God, and any portrayal of him which neglects this primary function must be superficial. Sexual love, prosperity, culture may determine numberless decisions but they do not explain a purpose. The more novelists try to squeeze an explanation out of them, the more they are betraying their duty. In this sense *No Orchids for Miss Blandish* is a better book than *Howard's End*. You can show man bereft of God and therefore hopeless as Macbeth and Miss Blandish, but you must not flatter his pretensions to self-sufficiency' (EAR 389–90).

34 Kermode, 'Mr. Waugh's Cities', *Encounter*, Nov. 1960 (CH 279, 285); 'Evelyn Waugh Replies', *Encounter*, Dec. 1960, 83 (also quoted 37). Waugh replied to similar claims by John Betjeman (L 253), Hugh Trevor-Roper and Gerard Meath (see 295, 405 n20). In 1948 he replied at length to a charge that, along with the works of Graham Greene, *Brideshead* had 'done more harm to the Catholic cause than any of the objective attacks by avowed enemies of the Church' ('Mr Waugh on the Catholic Novelist', *Duckett's Register*, Mar. 1948, 3).

35 L 264, responding to John Russell's comment in the *Sunday Times* that in SK the voice of the satirist 'has often been shouted down by the voice of an irritable and self-infatuated child' (CH 293).

36 DC 150; Mitford to Waugh, 26 Apr. 1956 (Hastings 568).

37 The phrase is F. X. Connolly's in a review of MA (*America*, 1 Nov. 1952, 133).

38 SK 1–2. On science as 'stinks': EAR 359 and more generally ALL 131, 140, 173. As William Myers notes, Scott-King's 'classical scholarship is a cultural empire and a surrogate for Waugh's Catholicism' (Myers 81).

39 SK 4–5. Cf., among many other instances, Swift's account in *Gulliver's Travels* of the effects of European luxury: 'Hence it follows of Necessity, that vast Numbers of our People are compelled to seek their Livelihood by Begging, Robbing, Stealing,

Cheating, Pimping, Forswearing, Flattering, Suborning, Forging, Gaming, Lying, Fawning, Hectoring, Voting, Scribling, Stargazing, Poysoning, Whoring, Canting, Libelling, Free-thinking, and the like Occupations' (bk 4, ch. 6).

40 Reported in Foxe's *Book of Martyrs*: 'Be of good comfort, Master Ridley, and play the man; we shall this day light such a candle by God's grace in England as (I trust) shall never be put out'. Waugh echoes the passage again in OG, when Ian Kilbannock tries to inspirit the cowardly Trimmer to complete a fraudulent act of heroism being staged for publicity purposes (OG 197).

41 Breit (1956) 44. The novel repeats, among much else, the epithet 'chryselephantine' (20) from *Scoop*; like Grimes in DF, Scott-King is described in a parody of Pater on *Mona Lisa* (9); the unveiling of Bellorius's statue recalls the unveiling of Menelik's in RP.

42 To Randolph Churchill, 12 Feb. 1948 (L 268), echoing Connolly's letter to Waugh ten days earlier: 'One thing I think you will enjoy [when LO appears] will be the praise of those 'highbrow' critics who irritated you somewhat about *Brideshead*' (2 Feb. 1948: BL).

43 Davis, 'Impasse', 474–5. Breen objected specifically to *Brideshead* as 'a story of illicit sex and adultery without sufficient compensating moral values', noting that the novel did not, as the Code demanded, give 'a proportionate dramatization' of 'the punishment, reform, and repentance' of its characters.

44 *Daily Telegraph*, 30 Apr. and 1 May 1947, later joined under the first title (EAR 325–31).

45 EAR 330. In fact *The Best Years* had already been much altered to meet Hays Office specifications, not only by cutting a scene in which a dog wets the floor but more substantially in its initially explicit handling of divorce (Leff 136, 151).

46 See Davis, *Writer*, ch. 10, and Lynch, '*Art Guide*'. The novel's 'Wee Kirk o' Auld Lang Syne' ('dedicated to Robert Burns and Harry Lauder') and nearby 'Lover's Seat' are in fact Forest Lawn's Wee Kirk o' the Heather (a reproduction of Annie Laurie's church in Glencairn) and the Annie Laurie Wishing Chair, a construction of Scots granite inscribed with a pledge of fidelity even more bizarre than that intoned by Waugh's characters:

> Busk't i' oor braws, an' a' oor lane,
> We're doupit i' the wissen chair,
> Whilk spaes bien fairin tae ilka ane
> Wha gies a bridal hansel there.

47 *Life* (29 Sept. 1947), rpn. with minor changes as 'Half in Love with Easeful Death', *The Tablet*, 10 Oct. 1947 (EAR 331–7).

48 Connolly, ST2: 205. Because of its gruesomeness and superficial similarity to the novels of Nathanael West – whom Waugh had not read – Peters failed to find any American magazine willing to serialize LO: it was rejected by *Good Housekeeping*, *Town and Country*, the *Atlantic Monthly*, and most disappointingly, the *New Yorker*, a magazine Waugh never persuaded to accept his work. (*Town and Country* rejected the story, Waugh's American agent wrote, because 'Mr. Hearst doesn't like to have death mentioned': Harold Matson to A. D. Peters, 10 Dec. 1947, HRCT.)

49 LO 34, 85, 67, 44. Many years later Waugh explained that he meant the novel to satirize 'the theological vaccum, the assumption that the purpose of a funeral service is to console the bereaved not to pray for the soul of the dead' (NM 459). The Happier Hunting Ground, the novel's pets' cemetery, is a parody of Whispering

Glades (and thus a parody of a parody). It too aims to relieve its patrons of 'all responsibility' (14); its proprietor Mr Schultz complains of misers who allow faithful pets to 'get buried anyhow like they was just animals' (52). Waugh himself explained the parallel as meant to suggest a blurring of 'the distinction between animal and human life' (Ryan 42).

50 LO 26, 55. Dennis asks advice about non-sectarian ministry from a certain 'Rev. Errol Bartholomew', a conflation of Errol Flynn and Freddie Bartholomew.

51 Cf. the use of 'I' in Lord Marchmain's dying speech, quoted 233. Juanita seems a hybrid of Bebe Daniels, the early British star 'who made screen history when she had her Hittite nose Grecianized by plastic surgery in the interests of her art' (Graves 141), and Hollywood's own more elaborate makeovers; her alliterative slogan ('luscious, languid, and lustful') echoes the new kind of publicity campaign invented for Jane Russell ('mean, moody, and magnificent') in *The Outlaw.*

52 Waugh also suggested the titles for Nancy Mitford's *In Pursuit of Love* (1945) and *Voltaire in Love* (1957).

53 Greene, *Essays*, 50. In this garden Dennis meditates on Kaiser's Stoneless Peaches, a spiritually dead world's substitute for the traditional apple.

54 Letter to *New Statesman*, 20 Aug. 1949, 197; Breit 1956 (interview of March 1949), 45.

55 L 283. Waugh had as model such previous efforts as John Eppstein's 'The Church in the United States', *The Tablet*, 18 Jan 1948, 36–7, 25 Jan. 1948, 52–4.

56 Freemantle, 'Waugh in America', *Vogue*, 15 Nov. 1960, 54, 65, 66.

57 See G. A. Cavasco's memoir, 'Waugh, Dorothy Day and the Catholic Worker Movement', EWN 29: 2 (Autumn 1995), 6–8.

58 L 308. Waugh also edited for British publication Merton's *Waters of Siloe*, which was dedicated to him.

59 EAR 383–8. As Gallagher notes, Waugh altered a reference in the essay to Irish 'peasant' priests getting 'above themselves'. But he allowed to stand an even more inflammatory reference (astonishing from an Englishman) to the Irish in America as members of the 'same adroit and joyless race that broke the hearts of all who ever tried to help them' (EAR 384).

60 Waugh's use of the term recalls Leo's condemnation, which had also made clear that 'Americanism' was not in fact the position of most American Catholics. The standard study of theological 'Americanism' remains Thomas T. McAvoy, *The Great Crisis in American Catholic History, 1895–1900* (1935).

61 'The Making of an American', *Spectator*, 16 Oct. 1959, 525.

Notes to Chapter 8

1 L 276. 'Could you not have a B.W.T. (Bought When Tight) column in your ledger?' he asked Handasyde Buchanan on returning some books to the Heywood Hill shop (undated postcard, Georgetown University).

2 Orwell, *Lion*, 47–8; *Essays* 3: 317–18. In 1939, C. C. Martindale wrote of Orwell in *The Month* under the title 'Why Not Our Ally?' (Feb. 1939, 126). See also Watson, 'Orwell and Waugh', *Partisan Review*, 55: 2 (1988), 264–75 and David Gervais, *Literary Englands* (Cambridge: Cambridge Univ. Press, 1993), ch. 6.

3 In 1946 Waugh found Orwell's 'brilliant' and 'delightful' *Critical Essays* to embody such 'high moral principles' as to represent 'the new humanism' 'at its best' (EAR

304–5); Orwell in turn told friends that 'Unlike a lot of people I thought *Brideshead Revisited* was very good, in spite of its hideous faults on the surface' (*Essays* 4: 438).

4 L 302; Connolly, *Colonnade*, 346. At the time of his death, Orwell had finished only a brief outline of an essay devoted mainly to *Brideshead*, its 'snobbery' and 'departure from the humanist attitude', which was to conclude that since 'One cannot really be a Catholic & grown up', 'Waugh is abt as good a novelist as one can be (i.e. as novelists go today) while holding untenable opinions' (*Essays* 4: 511–12).

5 Correspondence with Betjeman, L 242–51. Waugh also set his proselytizing sights on Pamela Berry (L 297), Stuart Boyle (D 691), and Robert Henriques (D 642) and continued his efforts with Diana Cooper and Nancy Mitford.

6 Sykes 451; Face to Face; Phillips 97.

7 Menen, 'The Baroque and Mr. Waugh', *Month* (Apr. 1951), 226, 237; Allen, *Irish Monthly* (Feb. 1951), 96–7; D'Arcy, letter to *The Tablet*, 24 Nov. 1951, 384. Strong Catholic support also came from Julian Holroyd (*Catholic Herald*, 27 Oct. 1950, 6), Gerard Hopkins (*Time and Tide*, 14 Oct. 1950, 1025) and W. J. Igoe (*Duckett's Register*, 2 Feb. 1951, 20–1).

8 Mortimer, *Sunday Times*, 15 Oct. 1950, 3; Toynbee, *Observer*, 5 Nov. 1950, 7; Reed, *Listener*, 30 Sept. 1950, 515.

9 L 340; Sykes 451. Sykes's account is probably exaggerated. Four years earlier, recognizing its limited appeal, Waugh sought to have *Helena* printed in a limited edition by the Golden Cockerell Press: 'The profits accruing to myself are of secondary importance; my first interest is to see the work beautifully produced, for it is one on which I am taking great pains. I have written a number of novels.... This is something more ambitious and less likely to be generally popular' (Waugh to Christopher Sandford, 18 Apr. 1946) (Berg Collection, New York Public Library).

10 Waugh confessed modelling Constantius on his old enemy from Yugoslavian days, Fitzroy Maclean (DC 83), and on publishing the first sections of *Helena* in the *Tablet*, he noted that Constantius' involvement in Tetricus' betrayal of his own people was 'similar to many incidents of recent history', doubtless a reference to Allied policy in Eastern Europe generally and Yugoslavia in particular (*The Tablet*, 22 Nov. 1945, 299). Waugh perhaps adapted the phrase 'Power without Grace' from Stanley Baldwin's famous attack in 1931 on recklessly partisan press lords such as Northcliffe and Beaverbrook for exercising 'power without responsibility – the prerogative of the harlot throughout the ages' (Baldwin, *My Father*, 161). The phrase carries what Richard Rovere in the *New Yorker* (21 Oct. 1950, 116) rightly recognized as the novel's central 'polemic against democracy' and 'all forms of secular liberalism': see 55.

11 In the Penguin edition (1963), long the only version in print, both 'Homoousion' and 'Homoiousion' appear as 'Homoousion'. Waugh perhaps drew his joke from Ronald Knox, who on the occasion of the *Tablet*'s hundredth anniversary in 1940 contributed a series of imaginary letters from the journal's first editor to various famous contributors, among them:

TO MR. NEWMAN, LITTLEMORE.
MY DEAR SIR,
No one can regret more profoundly than myself the circumstances that a careless printer, in handling the letter you wrote us the other day, should have printed 'harum-scarum' for 'homoiousion' throughout. It is these harassing details which make the life of an Editor so unenviable. I am sorry, too – I had

not myself observed it – that in retracting the error we should have printed *homoousion* for *homoiousion*....

(18 May 1940, 475)

12   H 192, 203. In his 1946 encyclical *Deiparae Virginis Mariae*, Pius XII, who had a special veneration for Mary, consulted the episcopate for their views on the tradition of her Assumption; Waugh was delighted (and many liberal Catholics upset) when in his letter *Munificentissimus Deus* (1950), Pius defined the doctrine and proclaimed it a dogma of faith. (Later, toward the end of his pontificate, Waugh was disappointed when Pius declined to press further into the heady waters of theological adventurism by defining Mary as 'co-redemptress' with Christ: see Waugh's letters on the subject to the *Spectator*, 3 Aug. 1956, 178 and – joining Hugh Ross Williamson in support of the doctrine – 24 Aug. 1956, 261.)

13   Waugh claimed to have based this figure on Brian Howard (L 221), already figured as the Wandering Jew in POMF.

14   Preface. '*Helena* is even less explicit than *Brideshead*', he told interviewers; 'The whole thing is done in anagrams and cyphers; it's full of hints and allusions, and little jokes are tucked away in it' (Marshall 6).

15   H 168–74. Unable to find any modern sculptor able to craft suitable adornments for his triumphal arch, Constantine at last explodes, 'Then God damn it, go and pull the carvings off Trajan's arch and stick them on mine'. Waugh has again taken his inspiration from Gibbon: 'The triumphal arch of Constantine still remains a melancholy proof of the decline of the arts and a singular testimony to the meanest vanity. As it was not possible to find in the capital of the empire a sculptor who was capable of adorning that public monument; the arch of Trajan, without any respect either for his memory or for the rules of propriety, was stripped of its most elegant figures. The difference of times and persons, of actions and characters, was totally disregarded.... The new ornaments which it was necessary to introduce between the vacancies of ancient sculpture are executed in the rudest and most unskilful manner' (Gibbon 1: 428).

16   Gibbon 1: 405. In a similar proleptic joke, Waugh has Fausta say dismissively of Pope Sylvester: 'he's not a man of *personal* distinction, I assure you. If he's ever declared a saint they ought to commemorate him on the last day of the year' (H 149). The feast of Sylvester was in fact later set on 31 December.

17   H 188. Waugh had heard the slogan 'Zivio Tito' in Yugoslavia; in some 1950 'Notes on translating Helena' (HRC C36), he explained: 'bones' = dice; 'natural' = winning score; 'chop' = food.

18   Raymond, CH 320–1; Meath, *The Tablet*, 27 Oct. 1951, 295. For Waugh's response to Meath see *The Tablet*, 3 Nov. 1951, 324 and 17 Nov. 1951, 364; Fr D'Arcy's defence of Waugh (24 Nov., 384); and Douglas Woodruff's memoir of the incident (HW 127).

19   D'Arcy, quoted in Phillips, 97. 'Every being in existence has a special end determined by God himself' mused a young Alfred Loisy in 1884; 'this particular end is subordinated to the general end of the universe, which is the revelation and glorification of God'. In addition, 'Each person has his calling' (O'Connell 65).

20   DC 83. Before his conversion a teacher of rhetoric, Lactantius (known to later ages as 'the Christian Cicero') produced his most famous work, the *Divine Institutes* – an effort to reconcile classical literary culture with the simple, sometimes inelegantly expressed message of the Gospels – at Trèves, to which he was called by Constantine in about AD 306 to serve as tutor to the emperor's oldest son, Crispus.

21   To others he put on a front of utter certainty: 'I have not myself met the Catholics you speak of who are subject to assaults of doubt' (L 244). But he could also write

feelingly of what Ronald Knox called 'the 4 a.m. mood', 'black moments when the enthusiasm of the rally has worn off' and 'a sense of futility creeps in, a suspicion that the Christian system does not really hang together, that there are flaws in the logic' (EAR 432).

22 Pick 16; Lecture 277 (cf. Reynal xii: 'A life spent in the laborious perfection of [literary] form was to him a life of vanity').

23 Pius's encyclicals on Palestine include: *Auspicia quaedam* (May 1948), *In multiplicibus curis* (Oct. 1948), and his most urgent call to action, *Redemptoris nostri cruciatus* (April 1949).

24 Despite both Churchill's and Labour's declared intent to establish a Jewish home-land, America remained suspicious of Britain's supposed imperial intentions and offered no help in resolving the increasingly expensive problem (yet one more example, it seemed, of American ingratitude to Britain for her wartime sacrifices). In 1946, Menachem Begin's terrorist Irgun bombed the Mandatory Administration's headquarters at the King David Hotel in Jerusalem, killing over a hundred; when British forces retaliated the next April by executing two of the bombers, Irgun in turn hanged two British sergeants. Photographs of the dead sergeants appeared widely in British newspapers; what had been popular sympathy for the Jewish cause changed to a wave of anti-semitic outbreaks. Britain had by this time spent hundreds of millions of pounds trying to engineer a Palestinian peace; Anglo-British relations only worsened when there came from America responses like the open letter sent in May 1947 to the Irgun by Ben Hecht, then a Hollywood scriptwriter, saying 'We are out to raise funds for you', followed by Hecht's much-publicized remark that he heard 'a song in his heart' every time a British soldier was killed (Leitch 78). All these events help explain LO's undercurrent of anti-semitism: its references to the 'Grand Sanhedrin' that runs Hollywood's studios; Sir Ambrose's remark, 'Your five-to-two [slang for Jew] is a judge of quality'; and the ferryman's comment to Dennis, 'It's mostly the good-style Jews we get here' (which Little, Brown failed to persuade Waugh to recast as 'newly rich people') (LO 22, 7, 71).

25 He noted that December: 'Big things will happen in Palestine where the American jews have made it possible for the Red Army to reach its goal in the Mediterranean' (L 263).

26 Sir Ronald Storr in the *New Statesman*, quoted in Gallagher, 'Limited Editions'.

27 Fleming 41. Written to allay 'the alarm and despondency with which so many of my fellow-countrymen appear to contemplate the future', the novel imagines a secret, Soviet-backed plan 'of accelerating the current deterioration of the British national character' by the simple means of hiring media personalities to reconcile Britons to Labour policies. Clement Attlee figures in the story as 'Little Mr. Goodbody', the Prime Minister with a 'manner like a well-trained parlourmaid'. The novel was dedicated to Peter's younger brother Ian Fleming and according to Peter's bio-grapher, its hero, a writer of stories about the daring spy Colonel Hackforth – stories that in the dull world of Welfare are vastly successful – suggested to Ian the idea for James Bond, launched a year later in *Casino Royale* (Hart-Davis 329).

28 MA 10-1; cf. D 676 (see 298–9). Waugh commented in his life of Knox on 'R. H. Benson's vision in the *Lord of the World*, of the universal Church reduced to a fugitive Pope bearing solitary witness to the truth which all mankind else had abandoned' (K 176). In portraying Guy, he also had in mind Christopher Tietjens from *Parade's End*, who thinks of himself as spiritually akin to some reclusive seventeenth-century Anglican parson such as George Herbert. So much did Waugh discuss with friends the nature of sloth that, on the basis of such conversations, Ian Fleming picked up

the idea or use in *Live and Let Die* (1954), whose Mr Big (a parodic rendering of Waugh?) confesses: 'Mister Bond, I suffer from boredom. I am prey to what the early Christians called "accidie", the deadly lethargy that envelops those who are sated, those who have no more desires... I take pleasure now only in artistry' (Lycett 238).

29 David Malbert, 'Civil Waugh', *Evening Standard*, 19 Sept. 1976, 19. *Time* magazine reported on 27 October 1952: 'No sooner had he published the first volume – *Men at Arms* – of a trilogy than Novelist Evelyn Waugh unwittingly gave his fans a hint of the subject matter of Vol. II. A personal advertisement in the London *Times* announced: "Evelyn Waugh seeks detailed information P.O.W. routine from then junior officer taken prisoner unwounded France, 1940; hospitality, expenses and 50 offered to applicant willing to spend two days in near future under interrogation"' (47).

30 MA 139, 109–10. Kut-al-Imara was the site of Britain's most humiliating defeat in World War I, where 13,000 Englishmen and territorials surrendered to the Turks in Apr. 1916; Waugh's original for the house was a 'hideous, derelict Victorian villa without carpets, curtains or furniture' (L 134) at Kingsdown Camp, to which he was moved in January 1940 after serving first at Chatham.

31 During the attempted seduction Guy wears his late brother Gervase's religious medal – a medal that, as old Mr Crouchback has explained, though it did not protect Gervase from death in World War I, did protect him in a more important way – from sin – by helping to deter him from an illicit sexual affair.

32 MA 207–8. Waugh suggested that MA appear in a dust-jacket reminiscent of such reading, to which Jack McDougall of Chapman and Hall replied: 'I think your idea of a school-story or P. G. Wodehouse wrapper is terrible. True, a half-dozen connoisseurs wd. be amused, but it wouldn't do at all' (ST2 306). Captain Truslove was excised in the one-volume SH.

33 Norman Shrapnel, *Manchester Guardian*, 12 Sept. 1952, 4.

34 Raymond, CH 339; Muir, *Observer*, 7 Sept. 1952, 7; Frank, CH 346; Schwartz, *Partisan Review*, 3 Nov. 1952, 703–4.

35 EAR 427. In March 1952 Tito had called publicly for 'a long-term policy' of 'stamping out religious inclination' in his country (see Waugh, 'Tito and Stepinac', *New Statesman*, 28 Feb. 1953, 233).

36 'Yugoslavia: The Guest of Dishonor', *Time*, 29 Dec. 1952, 21.

37 Waugh, 'Marshall Tito's Visit', *Spectator*, 19 Dec. 1952, 846.

38 HRC E922. After Tito's visit Waugh returned to the attack only once more, in a long review of *Tito* (1953), an autobiography ghost-written by Vladimir Dedijer (EAR 435–40).

39 Susan Mary Patten (later Mrs Joseph Alsop), a new friend Waugh met in Paris through the Coopers, has left a charming account of dinner at Piers Court on coronation night: Laura (despite a recently broken leg and no help in the kitchen) appeared in 'a ball dress and a tiara', Waugh in 'white tie and decorations': Susan Mary Alsop, *To Marietta from Paris* (New York, Doubleday, 1975), 224–6.

40 The Euthanasia Centre's Director protests the death of individual initiative under Welfare: 'My father and mother hanged themselves in their own back-yard with their own clothes-line. Now no one will lift a finger to help himself. There's something wrong with the system, Plastic. There are still rivers to drown in, trains – every now and then – to put your head under; gas fires in some of the huts. The country is full of the natural resources of death' (LAR 22). His remarks recall Seneca's great oration on arranging one's own release from pain: 'Everywhere you look there is an end to your troubles. See that precipice? That is a path to freedom. See that ocean, that river, that well? Freedom sits at the bottom of it. See that tree, stunted, burned

and barren? From it hangs freedom.... Do you ask where is the road to freedom? Any vein in your body' (*Dialogues* 5.15). For other echoes, see Miles, 'Improving Culture'.

41 LAR 1. In Benson's novel as in Waugh's, physical nature proves resistant to bureaucratic manipulation: 'the experts were at present unable to exclude' thunder and an 'entirely unexpected heat-wave' leaves the 'men who professed to have taken the earth under their charge' 'humiliated' and 'baffled' (Benson 322, 303). Once the Catholic Church ('this hateful thing that had so long restrained the euthanasia movement with all its splendid mercy') is driven underground, 'ministers of euthanasia' ensure that 'Individualism [is] at least so far recognized as to secure to those weary of life the right of relinquishing it' (21, 16, 301).

42 Sykes 475; Beerbohm, *Garland*, 33–47.

43 Peter Miles's 'Improving Culture' explores Waugh's use of *The Works of Antonio Canova in Sculpture and Modelling, Engraved in Outline by Henry Moses* (1876).

44 'There may or may not be an intrinsic value in the content of traditional European education, but I do not see how a literary culture can survive at all without *some* corpus of common texts' (EAR 351). The concern arises again in *Knox* and in Waugh's 1960 interview with John Freeman. Appropriately for a work about cultural decline, LAR bears a dedication in Latin: 'Johanni McDougall, Amico qui nostri sedet in loco parentis'. (Waugh's friend Jack McDougall was his editor at Chapman & Hall, and now as the firm's director occupied the seat once held by Waugh's father.)

45 LAR 6, a reference to the now disused devotional custom of 'First Fridays' initiated by St Margaret Mary Alacoque, wherein Catholics received the Eucharist on the first Friday of nine consecutive months.

46 LAR 19–20. Cf. Waugh's description in 1950 of Malcolm Muggeridge: 'The best of our light reading nowadays comes from disgruntled middle-aged humanists. Caged, mulcted, ignored, troubled in most cases by guilt of youthful collaboration with their present enemies, these waifs of the Welfare State still have their wits about them' ('As Others See Us', *The Tablet*, 4 Feb. 1950, 91).

47 Waugh had glanced at the subject in *Brideshead*, where Hooper says of the inmates of an insane asylum: 'Hitler would have put them in a gas chamber ... I reckon we can learn a thing or two from him' (8). He wrote to Nancy Mitford in 1950: 'Gas chambers were not a Nazi invention. All "Progressives" like Lord Ponsonby believed in them and called it Euthanasia and had a Society all the Fabians belonged to simply to build gas chambers' (L 320). His reference is to the Voluntary Euthanasia Legalization Society, founded in 1935 with support from Wells, Shaw, Eleanor Rathbone and Julian Huxley. In 1936 the Society drafted a (failed) Voluntary Euthanasia Bill, introduced in the Lords by the Labour MP Arthur Ponsonby, father of Waugh's youthful friend Matthew. Revelations of Nazi eugenic techniques temporarily slowed the Society's efforts, but another bill was brought in 1950, amidst much public debate.

48 New Hall, the first, experimental open prison for adults, was established in 1936; the Criminal Justice Act of 1948 – enthusiastically supported by Frank Pakenham, now a Labour MP – abolished penal servitude and hard labour and set up in their place a system of 'reprimand centres', 'remand homes', 'detention centres' and borstals, along with new regimes of 'corrective training'. During the war many country houses had been taken over for use as detention centres; in 1949 Waugh wrote to Nancy Mitford from Piers Court: 'We have a "prison without bars" next door to us. 73 escapes in the last eighteen months. The other day an air force officer walked out

into a cottage & bludgeoned three inhabitants' (Miles Plastic has served in the Air Force); 'There are 17 murderers there.... All are convicted of crimes of violence. The countryside is terrorised and today indignant to learn that last week-end they performed *Rope* with an all-murderer cast' (L 311). A Royal Commission on capital punishment was named in 1949 and reported in 1953 (for Waugh's well-known views on this subject, see 324 and his letters to the *Spectator* in 1960: 9 Dec., 936; 16 Dec., 955).

49 LAR 20, 27. Clara's paintings represent 'the transmission of culture through the family rather than the state' (Miles 15). Originally called Pamela and given 'flame-red hair' (the correlative of Miles's acts of arson), her hair changed from red to gold at the same time the story's title changed to LAR : Browning's shepherd-hero awaits a beloved 'girl with eager eyes and yellow hair' (see Davis, 'Shaping a World'). As Waugh admitted obliquely to Daphne Fielding (L 407), she was renamed Clara after Clarissa Eden, who had betrayed her Catholic faith.

50 'It does go wrong like that every now and then' observes Dr Beamish; 'They had two or three cases at Cambridge' (LAR 24). The reference is to Jack Klugmann's activities at Cambridge recruiting spies to the CPB: see Miles, 23–5 and 409 n65.

51 LAR 40, 38 (in LO, Dennis wrote of Sir Francis's corpse as 'salmon-pink'). In another bitter irony, Waugh describes Dennis's gradual loss of love for Aime&e when she disappears fo her abortion and surgery: 'spasmodically, mechanically, the thought of Clara returned. He timed it and found that it came very 7 1/2 minutes', then 'every twenty minutes', then 'irregularly' (35) – a parodic reversal of the contractions Clara would have undergone in giving birth.

Notes to Chapter 9

1 In 1944, Waugh predicted that he would die in 1970 (L 190); in 1946, that his career would be over about 1961 (D662). The family trust set up in 1950 assumed the likelihood of his death by the time his last child came of age, in 1971 (ST2 256).

2 'Matter-of-Fact Mothers', *Evening Standard*, 8 Apr. 1929, 7; EAR 587.

3 Kenneth Allsop, 'The Living Arts 1960: Waugh Looks Forward to Poverty', *Daily Mail*, 26 Apr. 1960, 4. Cf. Waugh's judgment of Ronald Firbank in 1962: 'I enjoyed him very much when I was young. I can't read him now'; 'I think there would be something wrong with an elderly man who could enjoy Firbank' (Jebb 111).

4 After a five-minute meeting at White's, Oliver Knox (Ronald's nephew) published 'A Desperate Conversation with Evelyn Waugh' (*Cornhill*, Autumn-Winter 1968–9, 181–4); *Daily Telegraph* announced Waugh's agreement to be interviewed by John Freeman in 'Mr. Waugh Succumbs' (20 June 1960, 15); *Daily Mail* reported Teresa's plan to visit Turkey after graduating from Oxford (12 Feb. 1959, 12); readers of *Daily Express* learnt of Waugh's enjoyment of 'a new after-dinner game' in 'Waugh Tests Guests' (27 Feb. 1962).

5 EAR 441–2; 'Nancy Spain Reads a Book in Rome', *Daily Express*, 29 May 1953, 4; Shulman, 'What a Wet Squib, Mr Waugh!', *Sunday Express*, 31 May 1953, 8; Thomson, 'Why So Gloomy, Mr. Waugh?', *Evening Standard*, 3 June 1953, 10.

6 Spender, 'Movements', 68; L 375, 378, 380.

7 Pick 16. See on Wilson, EAR 420; Spark, 339; Naipaul, 'an "East" Indian Trinidadian with an exquisite mastery of the English language which should put to shame his British contemporaries', EAR 601.

8   Allsop; L 445, EAR 495. The Butler Act produced an increase of university students between 1938 and 1948 of over 50 per cent; already by 1949 emerged a 'more is worse' controversy, with conservatives such as Michael Oakeshott and T. S. Eliot - and later Kingsley Amis himself - arguing views akin to Waugh's.

9   Spender, 'Movements', 66, *Struggle*, 130.

10 Amis, quoted in Rabinovitz, 899; EAR 478.

11 On the sexual politics of the Movement, see Sinfield ch. 4. In addition to public statements such as his praise in 1952 for Angus Wilson's *Hemlock and After* (whose depiction of homosexuals shocked contemporaries) and 1956 review of Compton Mackenzie's *Thin Ice* (discussed 241–2), Waugh's new openness about homosexuality comes clear in a stream of letters full of references to 'Richard Pares, my first homosexual love' (L 435); 'I can't blame Debo for falling in love with Mr Xan [Fielding]. I am a little in love with him myself' (L 472); 'Army always queer in best regiments, hence decent appearance' (L 473); 'I thought he was the most enchanting creature of either sex I have met for twenty years... goodness I fell in love' (L 476); 'Haddington had a delightful and woebegone younger brother Charlie whom I loved' (L 538); 'I thought O'Neill much prettier when I saw him in your house' (L 563).

12 To Joseph Crowley, 11 Aug. 1958 (private collection).

13 Samuel Hynes, 'Random Events and Random Characters' (rev. of *I Like It Here*), *Commonweal*, 21 Mar. 1958, 642.

14 Amis, *New York Times Book Review*, 7 July 1957, 1, 13; Fussell, *Anti-Egoist*, 84. Amis's furious, almost loving campaign against Waugh - fully reprinted in *The Amis Collection* - began in 1955 with a review of OG ('appalling') and ended only with 'How I Lived in a Very Big House and Found God' (1981), a review of Granada Television's dramatization of BR.

15 Charles Rolo, *Atlantic*, Aug. 1955, 84; F. O'Gorman, *Best Sellers*, 15 (Aug. 1955), 79; TLS, CH 382–3 (cf. Howard Nemerov's use of *Pinfold* to demonstrate 'the basic triviality' of all Waugh's writing: *Partisan Review*, Aurunm 1957, 602–4).

16 EAR 487–8, quoting Toynbee from *Observer*, 29 Oct. 1961, 21 (CH 436–8).

17 ST2 334; in *Pinfold* the remark becomes, 'You didn't like those people much, did you papa?'

18 L 415; cf. GP 16: 'They tried to make an ass of me. I don't think they succeeded'.

19 'Frankly Speaking', BBC Home Service, 16 Nov. 1953. I am grateful to Arlene Wszalek for her transcription of this interview.

20 Their mutual dislike began in 1947, when in *Last Days of Hitler* Trevor-Roper likened Himmler to Cardinal Bellarmine. Waugh replied in an angry letter to *The Tablet* (28 June 1947, 335), citing a misquotation from Newman and other difficulties with the book. Trevor-Roper hung fire until 1953, in the course of arguing that 'the Counter-Reformation was not a compliance with Reform but a defiance of it: monastic orders, images, miracles and mumbo-jumbo were not attenuated but multiplied', he inserted the comment: 'Come unto us, say the Roman clergy, follow me, says Mr Evelyn Waugh, (for in the intellectual emptiness of modern Catholicism only the snob-appeal is left)... and join the old English recusants in their armigerous tombs' (*New Statesman*, 5 Dec. 1953, 735–6). Waugh at once wrote to protest Trevor-Roper's historical 'howlers', initiating a correspondence that lasted till the end of January 1954 (Waugh's side is reproduced in L 642–7). Three years later Trevor-Roper again attacked, this time writing of 'convert-novelists' who 'puff' traitors as simple missionaries (*New Statesman*, 25 Aug. 1956, 217–18), provoking three more letters from Waugh. Both exchanges are notable not only for the acerbity on both sides, but Waugh's ability to match

facts as well as wits with a distinguished historian. Waugh had the last word, in the form of slighting references to Regius Professors, of which Trevor-Roper became one in 1957 (see EAR 537).

21 ST2 341; Hastings 562.

22 Medical authorities disagree whether Waugh's illness resulted from the cumulative effect of drink and narcotics (Strauss's diagnosis, defended by Dr Daniel and Mary Jane Hurst in 'Bromide Poisoning in *The Ordeal of Gilbert Pinfold*', EWN 16 (1982): 1–4), or was a case of 'alcoholic auditory hallucinosis', the result of a too-sudden *reduction* in intake (the position of Dr. Paul McHugh, Director of Psychiatry at the Johns Hopkins University Medical Center, in '*The Ordeal of Gilbert Pinfold*', public lecture, Johns Hopkins University, 17 Oct. 1995).

23 Whale's office, HOO-HQ, was in reality Combined Operations Headquarters; his nickname comes from the famous George Joseph ('Brides-in-the-Bath') Smith, who early in the century drowned seven wives. Smith was often recalled in coverage of later serial killers - while Waugh worked on OG, in the Christie case (see 'She "Married" a Murderer', *Evening Standard*, 23 June 1953, 11).

24 OG 320. Tommy's maxim is also that of the wicked empress Fausta: 'Never do harm except for positive, immediate advantage. Beyond that simple rule, Fausta held, lay disaster and perhaps damnation' (H 186). When Waugh later apologized to Mrs Stitch's original for casting her in so unfavourable a light, Lady Diana replied that in the same circumstances, she would have acted just as Mrs. Stitch did.

25 Koestler, *Yogi*, 36–7. Waugh first gave this new character (and new Doppelgänger) the name 'Connolly'; 'I have Books as a Corporal of Horse in the Blues, composing palinurus during the battle of Crete', he fold Nancy Mitford (NM 354). He probably substituted 'Ludovic' not merely to spare the old friend he had so often taunted before, but as he became aware of the depth of evil he meant Ludovic to embody.

26 'Mr Waugh Makes Good with a Motto', *Sunday Express*, 15 May 1955, 4.

27 Kenneth Allsop, 'Mr Waugh Wields the Scalpel', *Daily Mail*, 18 July 1957, 4.

28 An intelligence officer with the CIA in London, Crowley asked that his anonymity be preserved and so appeared in Sheehan's 'A Weekend with Waugh' as 'Conley'. He arrived at Piers Court having read Waugh's advertisement in *The Tablet*, not expecting that Waugh himself would even be present. Later he wrote to Frances Donaldson: 'There was no Prussian helmet. The admittance signal given Auberon was not 'Vile Bodies' but Sheehan's offer of a cigarette'; 'There was no promise of scullery service'. The fellow-visitor with whom he left, called 'Davenport' by Sheehan, was in reality Anthony De Houghton (Joseph Crowley to Frances Donaldson, 6 Jan. 1973, private collection).

In the year after this first meeting, Waugh invited Crowley back to Piers Court and entertained him in White's; the two visited an exhibition at the Royal Academy. (Later Crowley invited Waugh to join him for a holiday in Spain.) In October 1954, as he later told Nancy Mitford (NM 354), Waugh sought Crowley's literary advice. Famous for his ability to reproduce colloquial conversation, Waugh had been criticized for his uncertain grasp of American slang in LO. Determined that OG should contain no such slips, he wrote Crowley: 'In the book I am writing I have introduced some American journalists. I should greatly like to have their conversation vetted. . . . Few things are more exasperating than bogus slang' (16 Oct. 1954, private collection). Crowley suggested changes such as from 'Why' to 'How come', to which Waugh replied: 'I am deeply grateful to you for all your trouble in correcting my attempts at American dialogue. . . . I will set about revising the passage and will certainly adopt your philological advice. The character 'Ian'. . . is a British liaison officer trying to be matey by adopting what he thinks is suitable jargon, so that his errors of diction are admissable. I am sure I am wrong in the other cases. I relied on a faulty ear at the cinema. The Americans I know speak as you do' (22 Nov. 1954, private collection). As further thanks, in the scene in which Ian Kilbannock introduces Trimmer to three American reporters (originally named Bum Schlum, Scab Dunz and Mick Mulligan), Waugh changed 'Mick' to 'Joe' (interview with Joseph Crowley, 18 Nov. 1995).

29 *Sunday Express*, 15 Aug. 1954, 7; Brien, 'Waugh Among the Ruins'. (Brien confessed authorship of the latter only after Waugh's death, in 'Permission to Speak'.)

30 L 446; Wodehouse to Waugh, 23 July 1955 (BL).

31 'Dr. Wodehouse and Mr. Wain', EAR 509. 'At-a-boy', Wodehouse again wrote in support, 'That's the stuff to give 'em'; 'Kingsley Amis is another to whom we might attend some day' (11 Mar. 1956, BL).

32 Waugh recounts the case (brought in May 1955, decided in October 1956) in 'Randolph's Finest Hour', *Spectator*, 22 March 1957, 369 (a review of Churchill's *What I Said About the Press*).

33 *Daily Express*, 16 Oct. 1956, 6. Hern both rearranged West's comments (on Mauriac as well as Waugh and Greene) for effect, and omitted qualifiers such as that the three writers 'would not themselves sympathize with treachery' (*Treason* 312–13).

34 West reached her conclusions about Waugh as early as 1952, before the war trilogy began to appear: in August 1952 she wrote to her friend Doreen Wallace that Waugh had 'made drunkenness cute and chic, and then took to religion, simply to have the most expensive carpet to be sick on' (Glendinning 210).

35 'Mr Evelyn Waugh's Libel Action Settled', *The Times*, 14 Dec. 1956, 15.

36 The barristers for Nancy Spain and the *Express* were Sir Hartley Shawcross (who had prosecuted William Joyce and was later one of the authors of the Defamation Statute of 1952) and H. J. P. Milmo (a specialist in libel who had also interrogated Kim Philby); Waugh was represented by Gerald Gardiner (later Lord Chancellor), the libel specialist Neville Faulkes (later a judge), and J. E. Adams.

37 *The Times*, 20 Feb. 1957, 5. Peters's testimony included figures for Waugh's total sales to date: 2,744,995 copies in Britain, 1,483,130 in the United States (McNamara 225).

38 LAF 193. For all his pleasure in success, Waugh recognized that his victory was a near thing, decided less by the merits of his case than popular dislike for Beaverbrook's papers: 'I had a fine solid jury who were out to fine the *Express* for their impertinence to the Royal Family [over the matter of Princess Margaret and Peter Townsend], irrespective of any rights and wrongs. They were not at all amused by the judge. All the 300 a day barristers rocked with laughter at his sallies. [Justice Stable had likened the case to Shakespeare's *Much Ado About Nothing*.] They glowered. That was not what they paid a judge for, they thought' (L 485).

39 See Chisolm and Davie 494; and Graham Greene, *Yours Etc. Letters to the Press* (London: Reinhardt, 1989), 76–88.

40 HRC A26; to Peters, 7 March 1957 (HRCT). Waugh's final version of the passage reads: 'Every week his press-cutting agents brought to his breakfast-table two or three rather offensive allusions. He accepted without much resentment the world's estimate of himself. It was part of the price he paid for his privacy' (GP 9–10).

41 Ryan 43. A letter to Nancy Mitford of October 1954 on plans for future books contains no hint of *Pinfold* (L 432); the idea of 'writing about my lunacy' first surfaces in a letter to Laura from Jamaica the following January (25 Jan. 1955, BL), and was first mentioned to Peters two months later still, in March 1955 (HRC E880).

42 'Mr Waugh Goes Sane', *Daily Telegraph*, 20 July 1957, 6. Like VB's Mr Chatterbox, Waugh soon received letters from fellow-sufferers asking advice or simply expressing thanks for having brought sympathetic notice to their condition.

43 Lehmann, *London Magazine*, Sept. 1957, 9, 11.

44 Sykes 482f, Donaldson ch. 4; EAR 396. In the shrewdest contemporary review, Martin Price noted that whatever Pinfold's voices represent, they never come together in any 'form that makes sense' (*Yale Review*, Autumn 1957, 150–1).

45 'My sexual passion for my ten year old daughter [Margaret] is obsessive', Waugh told Ann Fleming in 1952; 'I can't keep my hands off her' (L 380). Such remarks were partly a joke for women friends with young children of their own, partly a wise method to prevent desire from growing 'obsessive'. By 1954 he could report to Nancy Mitford, 'My unhealthy affection for my second daughter has waned' (L 423).

46 GP 118, 167, 120. The last accusation is made in French as a joke for Nancy Mitford, in the wake of the public interest she had sparked over 'U' and 'Non-U' speech and behaviour. Inspired by Alan Ross's essays on language as England's sole remaining class-marker, Mitford wrote an essay for *Encounter* on 'The English Aristocracy', to which Waugh replied in 'An Open Letter to the Honourable Mrs Peter Rodd on a Very Serious Subject' (first printed in *Encounter* in Dec. 1955, then in 1956 reprinted with pieces by Ross, Mitford, Betjeman and others in *Noblesse Oblige*). Waugh quickly recognized in Mitford's essay not merely a commentary on language but a socialist attack on private wealth: the upper classes 'are not beaten yet, comrades', he paraphrased her argument; 'Up and at them again' (EAR 502). His own essay outlines an alternative to the Marxist notion of class, which he believed had no application in Britain.

47 'Mgr Ronald Knox', *Horizon*, May 1948 (EAR 347–56); *A Selection from the Occasional Sermons of the Right Reverend Monsignor Ronald Arbuthnott Knox* (London: Dropmore Press, 1949) (Waugh's preface rpn. EAR 369–71); Knox, *Enthusiasm: A Chapter in the History of Religion* (London: Oxford Univ. Press, 1950), praised by Waugh, EAR 479.

48 HRC E1036; Peters to Little, Brown, 26 Jan. 1960 (HRCT). In his obituary of Waugh, Christopher Hollis too claimed that *Knox* 'was of all his works that by which he set the highest store' (*The Times*, 11 Apr. 1966, 10).

49 K 13; Hastings 584. Waugh says notably little about Knox's proudest literary accomplishment, the translation of the Bible, because (as he confessed in 1948) he thought it 'grimly functional', full of 'the driest periphrases' (EAR 354).

50 Barton to Waugh, 1 Oct. 1959 (BL).

51 Bourne was defended in a review by Mgr Barton in *The Month* (Dec. 1959, 365–7) and much more vigorously by Gordon Wheeler in the *Dublin Review* (Winter 1959–60, 348–9). Denis Gwyn told another story of the *Manual* in the *Irish Ecclesiastical Record* (Jan.-June 1966, 294–8).

52 Woodruff, 'Altar and Writing Table', *The Tablet*, 10 Oct. 1959, 857–8; Waugh, 'The Life of Ronald Knox', *The Tablet*, 7 Nov. 1959, 970.

53 K 75, 280, 217, 211; CH 397, 408.

54 HRC E1087. On Waugh's continuing fascination with India, see TA 5; DC 281; EAR 593; McNamara 268–9.

55 L 517–21, DC 265, L 530.

56 HRC E1145 (15 Mar. 1960), 1149 (5 Apr. 1960).

57 EAR 539–40. Cf., among countless others, *Encounter*'s editorial complaint in 1956: 'In an overcrowded country approaching the condition where the majority receive almost equal shares, there is little vivid variousness, a spreading grey of suburbs

which make up in quantity of dimness for the more concentrated intense ugliness of nineteenth-century slums. Everywhere...is sacrifice of quality' (June 1956, 2).

58 'Literary Musings', *Spectator*, 8 July 1960, 70. Mary Crozier presented a balanced account of the interview (though with inaccurate transcriptions) in 'Interviewing Mr Waugh', *The Tablet*, 2 July 1960, 623.

59 EAR 538. *A Tourist* concludes: 'The foundations of Empire are often occasions of woe; their dismemberment, always' (164).

60 L 565. In 1955 he had replied to an American whose novel of army life, also called *Officers and Gentlemen*, appeared shortly before his own: 'I am very sorry indeed to have plagiarized your title. I don't think your book has yet appeared in my country. I do hope that, if it does so, it will not suffer from prejudice raised by my little story' (Waugh to Constance Mills, 27 June 1955, private collection).

61 See Wykes, 'Waugh's Sword'. The full-throated poem celebrating the sword quoted in US indeed appeared in *The Times*, which also carried the letter to which Jumbo Trotter refers, commenting on its upside-down scabbard; *Time and Tide* ran just such a poetry contest about the sword as Ludovic enters.

62 Wykes 86, US 4. Waugh perhaps also recalled another alternative to the 'State Sword': the Sword of the Spirit, a Catholic organization founded in 1940 to influence the formulation of Britain's war aims. The organization was active throughout the war, and received influential support from Fr D'Arcy and Christopher Dawson (see, among many other reports, *The Tablet*, 5 July 1941, 14).

63 US 28, 180. Brompton is sometimes taken as a portrait of Harold Nicolson (Sykes 564; Heath 246). 'Loot' Padfield was Sgt Stuart Preston, known as 'the sergeant', an American art historian 'much lionized in London towards the end of the war' (Acton, Mitford, 82–3). Another homosexual and fellow-traveller, Padfield (recently a guest of the Stitches in Algiers) is the 'young American' mentioned by Joe Cattermole who while passing through Algiers exposes a courier carrying a gift from King Peter to Mihajlović (US 212). The gift is inconvenient in its implications for Tito's supporters; Padfield's information causes the courier to be executed by the Partisans.

64 'McCarthy' (review of Richard Rovere, *Senator Joe McCarthy*), *Spectator*, 5 Feb. 1960, 185. Despite William Buckley's efforts to persuade him otherwise, Waugh remained convinced that McCarthy was an 'insincere rascal' who 'on the whole prospered the Communist cause' by attacking, for the most part, 'well-intentioned boobies', and doing so after the Truman administration had already rooted out the most dangerous collaborators.

65 The 'Headquarters of British Mission to the Anti-Fascist Forces of National Liberation (Adriatic)' (US 197) to which Guy reports in Bari and where he meets Gilpin and Major Joe Cattermole was in reality the Special Operations Executive (Yugoslav Section), to which Waugh himself reported on his way to Topusko. Headquartered first in Cairo, then after April 1944 in Bari, SOE was run by Brigadier C. M. Keble, its Yugoslav Section by the ardent Tito supporter Major Basil Davidson, assisted by intelligence and coordination officer James Klugmann. On his way to Jugoslavia Waugh probably passed through Davidson and Klugmann's hands. In the novel Guy is briefed on Yugoslav affairs by Cattermole, after which Brigadier Cape advises him: 'remember, we are soldiers not politicians....Keep clear of politics' (US 215). In 1958, Peter Kemp would recall of his briefing at SOE in Cairo, shortly before Waugh's own at Bari:

Although it was impressed upon me from the moment of my arrival in Cairo that when I went into the field I must regard myself simply as a soldier, whose task would be the prosecution of military operations to the exclusion of politics, I could not fail to be aware of the strong political differences which divided the staff officers both in London and Cairo. Nowhere were they more evident than in the Yugoslav Section. Boughey in London [Peter Boughey, head of SOE(Y), London] had maintained that because Mihailovic was the representative of the recognized Yugoslav Government he should be given every support. Major Basil Davidson, on the other hand, the head of the Country Section in Cairo, who later distinguished himself in action with partisan forces in Yugoslavia and in Northern Italy, could not conceal his antipathy to the Cetniks. He wanted me to sign a declaration that I had been subjected in London to indoctrination on behalf of Mihailovic; I refused, but the incident warned me of the sort of feeling that was to embitter relations between British officers in the field as well as at headquarters.

(Kemp 94)

Klugmann was an ex-academic whose fluency in Serbo-Croat, appetite for work, and (for all his seeming unworldliness) intellectual zeal ensured Davidson's trust and his own early promotion to major and deputy chief of the Section. He was also an open member of the CPB; already suspected in the forties as a Soviet agent, Klugmann has seemed to historians a key figure in the systematic falsification of data about the relative strength and intentions of Yugoslavia's various factions that helped persuade Churchill to switch support from Mihajlović to Tito. Anthony Powell, with Military Intelligence in London, noted of that decision, 'largely based on dubiously reliable advice sent in by some of the British elements in the structure at work on the spot': 'I have myself read reports circulated on the situation applauding the Yugoslav Communist irregulars in a tone more suitable to an adventure story in the *Boy's Own Paper* than a sober appreciation of what was happening' (*Faces* 177); Waugh's old friend Alexander Glen (during the war a naval attaché) was one of many who confessed himself 'astounded that Klugmann was left installed in a key position in Bari' (Beloff 88). As intelligence officer at Bari, Klugmann made it his task to ensure than new men 'were "properly" oriented on the Tito-Mihailovic conflict'. (Later Klugmann would be identified not only as a spy, but the man who at Cambridge recruited Donald Maclean and, with Burgess's help, Anthony Blunt: see David Martin, *Disinformation*, 1–9, 95–100.)

Waugh had already attacked Klugmann in *Love Among the Ruins*; in September 1960, as he began to write the Yugoslav section of *Unconditional Surrender*, Davidson published his review calling *A Tourist in Africa* 'silly' and 'out of touch with reality'. In the next months Waugh seems to have called on his memories of these men in shaping Guy's experience in Yugoslavia. Like Klugmann, Cattermole is a Communist ex-don, an 'enthusiast' (and tireless worker) with the appearance of 'a Zurbaran ascetic'; like Davidson (and William Deakin), Cattermole 'did absolutely splendidly' fighting with the Partisans. 'The Jugs love him and they don't love many of us. And Joe loves the Jugs, which is something more unusual still' (US 208, 215).

66 Amis, CH 422; Myers 115. Mr Crouchback's terminology of 'quantitative judgments' is commonplace moral theology; see, e.g., Martindale 1: 82–3.

67 US 261. 'There's a special providence in the fall of a bomb', Eloise Plessington adds – not knowing that as a result of the bomb that kills Virginia, her own daughter Domenica will become Guy's second wife. Stories of soldiers returning from the front to find that it is their wives at home who have died (such as Alun Lewis's 'They Came'), and of civilians puzzling over how to pray when bombs come, were

commonplaces of wartime fiction and news reporting from the time of the Blitz. A famous story from 1940 ran: 'An East End parson, the Rev. H. A. Wilson, asked one of his parishioners if she prayed when she heard a bomb fall nearby. Oh yes, she said, she prayed "don't let it fall here." But it would be a bit rough on other people, he pointed out, if her prayer was answered and it dropped on *them*. "I can't help that", replied the devout lady, "They must say their prayers and push it off further"' (Peter Lewis, *People's War*, 60). Guy's sister instructs Eloise to pray not 'Please God let it fall on me and no one else' but 'Please God let it be a dud and not explode at all' (a prayer immediately answered).

68   The whole situation ironically reverses Guy's attempt at seduction in *Men at Arms*: Virginia's proposal that Guy take her back because she is penniless and pregnant is just as insulting to him as his earlier proposal had been to her (Hinchcliffe 308).

69   US 193–4. 'What do two more or less matter?' the commandant of the refugee camp to which the Yugoslav Jews have been consigned asks Guy (303).

70   'I am disconcerted to find I have given the general impression of a "happy ending"', Waugh wrote Anthony Powell. 'This was far from my intention. The mistake was allowing Guy legitimate offspring. They shall be deleted in any subsequent edition. I thought it more ironical that there should be real heirs of the Blessed Gervase Crouchback dispossessed by Trimmer but I plainly failed to make that clear. So no nippers for Guy and Domenica in Penguin' (L 579). After Waugh's death Laura told an interviewer that he made the change 'to reinforce the fact that Guy had married Domenica as an act of charity, to provide a home for her and for Virginia's child' (Phillips 137).

71   See Hinchcliffe. When asked by John Freeman in 1960 about the extent to which he valued 'service to others', Waugh replied: 'My service is simply to bring up one family' (Face to Face). Since Arthur Waugh died at almost exactly the same point in the war as Guy's father, it is tempting to read *Unconditional Surrender* as an act of belated reconciliation. But we have no real evidence of Waugh's need or desire for such an act of piety.

72   MA 301, 304; OG 211, 217. As bombs fall in London, General Whale asks 'Why am I taking cover when all I want to do is die?'; Virginia wonders, 'Is that the one that's coming here?' (247); Ritchie-Hook tells his batman, 'Dawkins, I wish those bastards would shoot better. I don't want to go home' (289).

73   US 258. Cyril Connolly was deeply hurt by this last satire on him and *Horizon* in the character of Everard Spruce, editor of *Survival*; looking on, Maurice Bowra commented, 'It is sad that Evelyn has such an urge to torture him. It must be a form of love' (LAF 295).

74   'Just what they said to Brenda' says Kerstie Kilbannock on hearing of Virginia's financial plight (US 51). But SH also stresses Virginia's difference from such as Brenda: her 'high, fine candour', generosity of spirit, and freedom from convention. 'You thought perhaps I might provide your third ——', she tells Uncle Peregrine, using a word of 'timeless obscenity', 'then unprintable' (US 177) - a reference to effects of the *Lady Chatterley* trial, for which in November 1960 Waugh jokingly volunteered testimony against publication (so that he might appear in the dock in opposition to such celebrators of the novel's merits as Rebecca West, Day Lewis, E. M Forster and the Bishop of Woolwich).

75   CH 257; Pritchett, 'Vanities and Servitudes', *Spectator*, 27 Oct. 1961, 603. In 1955, the *Observer* joined in diagnosing Waugh as an 'embitered romantic' (NM 367).

76   Waugh to Peters, 4 Apr. 1961 (HRC E1197). The three volumes of Lady Diana's autobiography appeared between 1958 and 1960. Guinness and Waugh had been

friends since 1955, when they met at Edith Sitwell's reception into the Church. (Waugh had stood godfather, and thereafter received letters from Sitwell, sixteen years his senior, signed 'your loving god-daughter'.) Even before 1955, Guinness had sought to act in a screenplay from Waugh, an ambition he was not to realise until 1988.

77 Peters to Waugh, 27 Apr. 1961 (BL).

78 Young to Waugh, 21 Nov. 1963 (BL).

79 'An Act of Homage and Reparation to P. G. Wodehouse', BBC Home Service, 15 July 1961; rpn. in *Sunday Times* and EAR 561–8. As early as 1953 Waugh had written to the *Daily Mail* suggesting the BBC invite 'the originator of their war-time attack to make an apology' to Wodehouse (24 Nov. 1953, 4). The core of Waugh's argument in 1961 was that, amidst the ideology of the 'people's war' and the Left's general tendency 'to identify aristocracy with treason', Wodehouse had been attacked 'on grounds not of patriotism but of class' (EAR 562–3).

80 Two remarkable exceptions were Christopher Derrick in *The Tablet* (CH 427–30) and Thomas Corbishley in *The Month* (Mar. 1962).

81 CH 419–46; Didion, *National Review*, 27 March 1962, 215–16.

82 See especially TLS, 27 Oct. 1961, 770. Along with William Ready (*Critic*, Mar. 1962, 70–1), this reviewer was among the few to recall 'Compassion' and note Waugh's use of it in US.

83 'Return to Eldorado', EAR 594–5. Waugh's account of Guianese racial politics is strikingly accurate: see Singh, ch. 2.

84 The same device occurs in Compton-Burnett's *A Heritage and Its History*, which Waugh reviewed four years earlier: 'The situation is explained to the young people and Hamish goes away' ('Op. XVI', *Spectator*, 18 Sept. 1959, 380).

85 As early as 1949, in the wake of Pius XII's calls in *Mystici corporis* (1943) for a more active lay apostolate and in *Mediator Dei* (1947) for liturgical reform, Waugh wrote: 'It may well be that Catholics of today, in their own lifetime, may have to make enormous adjustments in their conception of the temporal nature of their Church' (EAR 378); in 1957 Gilbert Pinfold complains that 'the leaders of his Church were exhorting their people ... to make their influence felt in democratic politics and to regard worship as a corporate rather than a private act' (GP 6). *Mediator Dei* helped inspire the new liturgy of Holy Week instituted in 1955, and specifically commended the dialogue Mass (§105) to which Waugh strenuously objected. 'Active participation' in worship, he argued, does not mean 'making a row in church'; 'One participates in a work of art when one studies it with reverence and understanding' (L 602, D 789).

86 'Ecclesiology' (rev. of Peter Anson, *Fashions in Church Furnishings*), *Spectator*, 22 Apr. 1960, 581.

87 Paul Johnson greeted John's election with an essay in the *New Statesman*, 'Rome Moves Left' (1 Nov. 1958, 583–4). On reading Johnson's predictions that John's pontificate would 'inaugurate an era of change' - including an increase in bishops and cardinals from 'ex-colonial regions', who would 'compel the Vatican to abandon its opposition to artificial birth control, just as the Indian bishops swung round the Lambeth Conference' - Waugh sent him a postcard: 'I see your vision of the future church: coloured cardinals distributing contraceptives to the faithful' (Johnson, *Pope John XXIII* (Boston: Little, Brown, 1974), 111).

88 L 646. See especially the series of exchanges in the progressive American Catholic magazine *Commonweal*: George Casey, 'The Same Always, Please: Evelyn Waugh's Hopes for the Council', 1 Feb. 1963, 487–9; John Cogley, 'Understanding the

Conservatives', 19 June 1964, 388–9 (response by Waugh, 7 Aug. 1964, 547–8); John Cogley, 'A Suggestion for Mr. Waugh', 23 Oct. 1964, 120–2 (response by Waugh, 4 Dec. 1964, 352–3); J. M. Cameron, 'A Post-Waugh Insight', 29 Oct. 1965 (response by Waugh, 7 Jan. 1966, 391).

89 Letter to *Commonweal*, 7 Jan. 1966, 391; to Ann Fleming (Hastings, 617).

90 EAR 629. In 1964, Waugh publicly accused Paul of finding 'Italian literature a more enjoyable pursuit than apologetics' ('Changes in the Church', *Catholic Herald*, 7 Aug. 1964, 4); in 1965 he wrote to Daphne Acton: 'It has been a sad disappointment to me that the Pope escaped from Palestine with a buffeting. I hoped for assassination' (L 617). Later he jokingly proposed hiring Ann Fleming's young son Caspar to remedy the deficiency.

91 *Commonweal*, 4 Dec. 1964, 352; DC 312.

92 'Sweetness of Temper', *The Tablet*, 14 Aug. 1965, 914; EAR 617.

93 'Using English in the Latin Mass', *The Times*, 8 Aug. 1964, 7; L 631.

94 Letter to *The Tablet*, 18 Sept. 1965, 1040.

95 *The Tablet*, 31 July 1965, 864.

96 The question everywhere informs Waugh's 'Appreciation of Pope John', commissioned by the *Saturday Evening Post* on John's death in 1963 and an essay full of praise for a man who knew from experience of 'the disastrous fragmentation of Christendom', and so of the need for authority and universality in the Church (EAR 615). Remarkably, the 'Appreciation' praises even John's rapprochement with Communist states in *Pacem in terris* (1963), interpreting the encyclical as a statement of 'the primacy of the individual and the family over the state, which is the antithesis of Communism' and – in the spirit of Guy Crouchback at the end of *Unconditional Surrender* – criticising the stoutly anti-Communist Pius XII (who in 1947 threatened Italians who voted Communist with excommunication) for leaving believers with a sense that 'any government that opposed Communists had a holy cause' (EAR 618).

97 'Father Martin D'Arcy, who will be 80 this year, talks to Quinton Hogg', *Listener*, 18 Jan. 1968, 75.

98 CH 461, 464. Only one reader wrote to complain of his treatment in the book: Dudley Carew, whose boyish love for Waugh at Lancing is depreciated: 'He was warmly confidential; I patronising and sardonic' (ALL 130–1). 'Why on earth you should deliberately spit in the eye of one who has always wished you well passes my comprehension', Carew wrote. 'I have long letters of yours over a period of years which give a very different picture . . . of our relationship' (Carew to Waugh, 4 Sept. 1964, BL). Carew's *A Fragment of a Friendship* (1974), an attempt to correct the picture of himself in ALL, succeeded only in corroborating Waugh's judgment that 'He was a natural hero-worshipper'.

99 'Book Stirs Catholics in Britain', *New York Times*, 14 Jan. 1965, 15.

100 DC 315; L 635; Margaret Waugh to Waugh, 19 Dec. 1965 (BL); Waugh to Jack McDougall, 15 June 1965 (Hastings 622).

101 'An Aged Novelist: Evelyn Waugh at 60', BBC TV 'Monitor' interview with Elizabeth Jane Howard, 16 Feb. 1964.

102 Waugh to Margaret FitzHerbert, 18 Jan. 1965 (Hastings 620).

103 Waugh to Handasyde Buchanan, 30 Mar. 1952 (Georgetown University).

104 *Downside Review*, Apr. 1966, 232

Bibliography

Major works by and about Waugh which are cited throughout the text in abbreviated form are listed in the abbreviations at the front of the book, on xiii–xv.

Acton, Harold. *Memoirs of an Aesthete*. London: Methuen, 1948.
——*More Memoirs of an Aesthete*. London: Methuen, 1970.
——*Nancy Mitford*. London: Hamish Hamilton, 1975.
Acton, Richard. ' "Will a lion come?" Memories of Evelyn Waugh'. *Spectator*, 19 Sept. 1992, 38–43.
Addison, Paul. *Now the War is Over: A Social History of Britain 1945–51*. London: Cape, 1985.
Allsop, Kenneth. 'Waugh and Peace'. *Sunday Times*, 8 Apr. 1973, 42.
Amis, Kingsley. *The Amis Collection: Selected Non-Fiction 1954–1990*. London: Hutchinson, 1990.
Annan, Noel. *Our Age: Intellectuals between the World Wars – a Group Portrait*. New York: Random House, 1990.
Asher, Kenneth. *T. S. Eliot and Ideology*. Cambridge: Cambridge University Press, 1995.
Aslet, Clive. *The Last Country Houses*. New Haven: Yale University Press, 1982.
Auden, W. H. and C. Day Lewis. *Oxford Poetry 1927*. Oxford: Basil Blackwell, 1927.
Baldwin, A. W. *My Father: The True Story*. London: Allen & Unwin, 1955.
Baldwin, Stanley. *On England and Other Addresses*. London: Philip Allan, 1933.
Balfour, Patrick (John Patrick Kinross). *Society Racket: A Survey of Modern Social Life*. London: J. Long, 1933.
——'Fiasco in Addis Ababa'. In *Abyssinia Stop Press*, ed. Ladislas Farago. London: Robert Hale, 1935, 47–80.
Beard, Madeleine. *Acres and Heirlooms: The Survival of Britain's Historic Houses*. New York: Routledge, 1989.
Beaty, Frederick L. 'Evelyn Waugh and Lance Sieveking: New Light on Waugh's Relations with the BBC'. *Papers on Language and Literature*, 25: 2 (1989), 186–200.
Beerbohm, Max. *A Christmas Garland*. 1912; New York: Dutton, 1913.
——'Lytton Strachey.' In *Mainly on the Air*. New York: Knopf, 1943, 192–212.
Beevor, Anthony. 'The First Casualty of Waugh'. *Spectator*, 6 Apr. 1991, 25–6.
——*Crete: The Battle and the Resistance*. Boulder: Westview Press, 1994.
Bell, Clive. *Art*. 1914; London: Chatto & Windus, 1928.

Belloc, Hilaire. *How the Reformation Happened.* 1928; New York: McBride, 1930.

Beloff, Nora. *Tito's Flawed Legacy: Yugoslavia and the West since 1939.* Boulder: Westview Press, 1985.

Benson, Robert Hugh. *Lord of the World.* 1907; New York: Dodd, Mead, 1908.

Bentley, Eric, ed. *The Importance of Scrutiny: Selections from* Scrutiny: A Quarterly Review, *1932–1948.* New York: George Stewart, 1948.

Betjeman, John. 'Evelyn Waugh' (1947). Rpn. in Gilbert Phelps, ed., *Living Writers: Being Critical Studies Broadcast in the B.B.C. Third Programme.* London: Sylvan Press, 1949, 137–50.

—— *Summoned by Bells.* Boston: Houghton, Mifflin, 1960.

Blayac, Alain, ed. *Evelyn Waugh: New Directions.* New York: St. Martin's, 1992.

Bogaards, Winnifred M. 'Evelyn Waugh and the BBC'. In Blayac, 85–111.

Bonham, John. *The Middle Class Vote.* London: Faber, 1954.

Bowra, C. M. *Memories 1898–1939.* London: Weidenfeld and Nicholson, 1966.

Bradbury, Malcolm. *Evelyn Waugh.* Edinburgh: Oliver and Boyd, 1964.

Breit, Harvey. 'Evelyn Waugh'. (1948 interview.) *The Writer Observed.* Cleveland: World, 1956, 43–6.

—— 'W. Somerset Maugham and Evelyn Waugh'. (1950 interview.) *The Writer Observed.* Cleveland: World, 1957, 148–9.

[Brien, Alan]. 'Evelyn Waugh Among the Ruins'. *Truth,* 8 Oct. 1954, 1242.

Brien, Alan. 'Permission to Speak, Captain?' *Spectator,* 15 Apr. 1966, 462.

Buckley, William F. 'Notes & Asides'. *National Review,* 14 Nov. 1980, 1374–7.

Byron, Robert. *Europe in the Looking-Glass: Reflections of a Motor Drive from Grimsby to Athens.* London: Routledge, 1926.

—— *The Byzantine Achievement: An Historical Perspective.* New York: Knopf, 1929.

Carens, James, ed. *Critical Essays on Evelyn Waugh.* Boston: G. K. Hall, 1987.

Carew, Dudley. *The House is Gone: A Personal Retrospect.* London: Robert Hale, 1949.

—— *A Fragment of Friendship: A Memory of Evelyn Waugh When Young.* London: Everest, 1974.

Carpenter, Humphrey. *The Brideshead Generation: Evelyn Waugh and his Generation.* London: Faber, 1990.

Chesterton, G. K. *The Resurrection of Rome.* New York: Dodd, Mead, 1930.

Chisolm, Anne and Michael Davie. *Lord Beaverbrook: A Life.* New York: Knopf, 1983.

Churchill, Winston. *The Gathering Storm.* London: Cassell, 1967.

Cockburn, Claud. 'Evelyn Waugh's Lost Rabbit'. *The Atlantic,* Dec. 1973, 53–9.

Connolly, Cyril. *Enemies of Promise.* 1938; 2nd edn., New York, 1948.

—— *The Unquiet Grave: A Word Cycle by Palinurus.* New York: Harper & Brothers, 1945.

—— *The Condemned Playground: Essays 1927–1944.* London: Routledge, 1945.

—— *The Missing Diplomats.* London: Queen Anne Press, 1952.

—— *The Evening Colonnade.* New York: Harcourt, Brace, 1975.

Corbishley, Thomas, S. J. *Ronald Knox the Priest.* 1964; bound with Robert Speaight, *Ronald Knox the Writer,* New York: Sheed & Ward, 1965.

Craig, Randall. 'Evelyn Waugh and William Gerhardie'. *Journal of Modern Literature,* 26: 4 (1990), 597–615.

D'Arcy, Martin. *The Nature of Belief.* London: Sheed and Ward, 1931.

Dakers, Caroline. *Clouds: The Biography of a Country House.* New Haven: Yale University Press, 1993.

Davis, Robert Murray. 'Shaping a World: The Textual History of *Love Among the Ruins'. Analytical & Enumerative Bibliography,* 1 (1977): 137–54.

—— *Evelyn Waugh, Writer.* Norman, OK: Pilgrim Books, 1981.

—— *Evelyn Waugh and the Forms of His Time.* Washington: Catholic University of America Press, 1989.

—— *Brideshead Revisited: The Past Redeemed.* Boston: Twayne, 1990.

—— 'Anglo-American Impasse: Catholic Novel and Catholic Censor'. *Dalhousie Review,* 72: 4 (1992–3), 467–81.

Dawson, Christopher. *Religion and the Modern State.* New York: Sheed and Ward, 1935.

Donaldson, Frances. *Evelyn Waugh: Portrait of a Country Neighbour.* 1967; New York: Chilton, 1968.

Dyson, A. E. 'Evelyn Waugh and the Mysteriously Disappearing Hero'. *Critical Quarterly,* 2: 1 (1960), 72–9.

Eagleton, Terry. *Exiles and Emigrés: Studies in Modern Literature.* New York: Shocken, 1970.

Edwards, Ruth Dudley. *Victor Gollancz: A Biography.* London: Gollancz, 1987.

Eliot, T. S. 'The Humanism of Irving Babbit' (1927) and 'Second Thoughts about Humanism' (1928). In *Selected Essays.* New York: Harcourt, Brace, 1964, 419–38.

—— *Notes Towards the Definition of Culture.* London: Faber, 1948.

—— 'The Literature of Politics.' In *To Criticize the Critic and Other Writings.* London: Faber, 1965, 136–44.

Fagg, John Edwin. *Latin America: A General History.* 3rd edn. New York: Macmillan, 1977.

Farr, D. Paul. 'The Novelist's Coup: Style as Satiric Norm in *Scoop'. Connecticut Review,* 8 (April 1975), 42–54.

Faulkner, Peter. *Modernism.* London: Methuen, 1977.

Fielding, Daphne. *The Duchess of Jermyn Street: The Life and Good Times of Rosa Lewis of the Cavendish Hotel. With a Preface by Evelyn Waugh.* Boston: Little, Brown, 1964.

Fisher, Clive. *Cyril Connolly: The Life and Times of England's Most Controversial Literary Critic.* New York: St. Martin's, 1995.

Fitzgerald, Penelope. *The Knox Brothers.* New York: Coward, McCann, 1977.

Fleming, Ann. *The Letters of Ann Fleming,* ed. Mark Amory. London: Collins Harvill, 1985.

Foot, Michael. *Aneurin Bevan: A Biography.* Vol. 2: *1945–1960.* London: Macgibbon & Kee, 1973.

Fox, Ralph. *The Novel and the People.* New York: International Publishers, 1937.

Frayn, Michael. 'Festival'. In Sissons and French, 319–38.

Fry, Roger. *Vision and Design.* 1920; London: Chatto & Windus, 1957.

Fussell, Paul. *Abroad: British Literary Traveling Between the Wars.* New York: Oxford University Press, 1980.

—— *Wartime: Understanding and Behavior in the Second World War.* New York: Oxford University Press, 1989.

—— *The Anti-Egoist: Kingsley Amis, Man of Letters.* New York: Oxford University Press, 1994.

Gallagher, Donat. 'Black Majesty and Press Mischief'. *London Magazine,* 22: 7 (1982), 25–38.

—— 'Industria Ditat – Mark III'. *Southern Review* (Australia), 15 (1982), 334–43.

—— 'Limited Editions and "Misprints Unlimited": Evelyn Waugh's *The Defence of the Holy Places'. Analytical and Enumerative Bibliography,* 8: 1 (1984), 18–31.

—— 'Evelyn Waugh and Vatican Divorce'. In Blayac, 62–84.

—— 'Martin Stannard's Waugh'. *Quadrant,* June 1993, 57–64.

Garnett, Robert R. *From Grimes to Brideshead: The Early Novels of Evelyn Waugh.* Lewisburg, PA: Bucknell University Press, 1990.

Gibbon, Edward. *The Decline and Fall of the Roman Empire,* ed. David Womersley. 3 vols. London: Allen Lane, 1994.

Gilbert, Martin. *Churchill: A Life.* New York: Henry Holt, 1991.

Gilmore, Thomas B. *Equivocal Spirits: Alcoholism and Drinking in Twentieth-Century Literature.* Chapel Hill: University of North Carolina Press, 1987.

Glendinning, Victoria. *Rebecca West: A Life.* London: Weidenfeld & Nicolson, 1957.

Gorer, Geoffrey. *The American People: A Study in National Character.* New York: Norton, 1948.

Graves, Robert and Alan Hodge. *The Long Week-End: A Social History of Great Britain, 1918–1939.* London: Faber, 1940.

Green, Martin. *Yeats's Blessings on von Hügel: Essays on Literature and Religion.* London: Longmans, Green, 1967.

Greene, Graham. *Collected Essays.* London: Bodley Head, 1969.

Greene, Gwendoline. *Mt. Zion.* London: Dent, 1929.

Greenidge, Terence. *Evelyn Waugh in Letters, by Terence Greenidge,* ed. Charles Linck. Commerce, TX: Cow Hill Press, 1994.

Guy, Donna J. *Sex and Danger in Buenos Aires: Prostitution, Family, and Nation in Argentina.* Lincoln: University of Nebraska Press, 1991.

Hall, Ruth. *Passionate Crusader: The Life of Marie Stopes.* New York: Harcourt Brace, 1977.

Hamilton, Alastair. *The Appeal of Fascism: A Study of Intellectuals and Fascism, 1919–1945.* London: Anthony Blond, 1971.

Hance, John Edward. *Riding Master.* London: Robert Hale, 1960.

Harrisson, Tom. 'War Books'. *Horizon,* Dec. 1941, 416–37.

Hart-Davis, Duff. *Peter Fleming: A Biography.* London: Jonathan Cape, 1974.

Hastings, Selina. *Evelyn Waugh: A Biography.* London: Sinclair-Stevenson, 1994.

Healey, Philip. 'Text and Context in John Gray's *Park*: Prester John's "Black Mischief"'. *English Literature in Transition,* 36: 4 (1993), 412–27.

Heath, Jeffrey. *The Picturesque Prison: Evelyn Waugh and His Writing.* Montreal: McGill-Queen's University Press, 1982.

Hennessy, Peter. *Never Again: Britain, 1945–1951.* New York: Pantheon, 1993.

Hewison, Robert. *In Anger: British Culture in the Cold War 1945–60.* New York: Oxford University Press, 1981.

Higham, T. M. 'Captain Grimes's Revenge'. *London Magazine,* 17 (Apr.–May 1977), 65–73.

Hinchcliffe, Peter. 'Fathers and Children in the Novels of Evelyn Waugh'. *University of Toronto Quarterly,* 35 (1966): 293–310.

Hollander, Paul. *Political Pilgrims: Travels of Western Intellectuals to the Soviet Union, China, and Cuba.* New York: Harper, 1983.

Hollis, Christopher. *Writers and their Work: Evelyn Waugh.* London: Longmans, 1958.

——— *Oxford in the Twenties: Recollections of Five Friends.* London: Heinemann, 1976.

Hopkins, Harry. *The New Look: A Social History of the Forties and Fifties in Britain.* Boston: Houghton, Mifflin, 1964.

Hoskins, Katherine Bail. *Today the Struggle: Literature and Politics in England During the Spanish Civil War.* Austin: University of Texas Press, 1969.

Howarth, Herbert. 'Quelling the Riot: Evelyn Waugh's Progress'. In J. Mooney and T. Staley, eds., *The Shapeless God: Essays on Modern Fiction* (Pittsburgh: University of Pittsburgh Press, 1968), 67–89.

Hügel, Fiedrich von. *Letters from Basen von Hügel to a Niece,* ed. Gwendoline Greene. London: Dent, 1928.

Hulme, T. E. *Speculations: Essays on Humanism and the Philosophy of Art.* 1924; 2nd edn. London: Routledge, 1936.

Hunt, Cecil. *Author-Biography.* London: Hutchinson, 1935.

Huxley, Aldous. *Ends and Means: An Enquiry into the Nature of Ideals and into the Methods Employed for their Realisation.* London: Chatto & Windus, 1937.

Hynes, Joseph. 'Two Affairs Revisited'. *Twentieth-Century Literature,* 33: 2 (1987): 234–53.

——— 'Varieties of Death Wish: Evelyn Waugh's Central Theme'. *Criticism,* 14: 1 (1972): 65–77.

Hynes, Samuel. *The Auden Generation: Literature and Politics in England in the 1930s*. London: Bodley Head, 1976.

Isherwood, Christopher. *Lions and Shadows: An Education in the Twenties*. London: Hogarth Press, 1938.

Jebb, Julian. Interview with Evelyn Waugh (1962). In *Writers at Work*, London: Secker & Warburg, 1968, 105–14.

Jerrold, Douglas. *Georgian Adventure*. London: William Collins, 1937.

Johnson, Paul. *Modern Times: The World from the Twenties to the Eighties*. New York: Harper & Row, 1985.

Kemp, Peter. *No Colours or Crest*. London: Cassell, 1958.

Kernan, Alvin. *The Plot of Satire*. New Haven: Yale University Press, 1965.

—— 'The Wall and the Jungle: The Early Novels of Evelyn Waugh'. In Carens, 82–91.

Keynes, John Maynard. 'My Early Beliefs'. In *Two Memoirs*, ed. David Garnett. London: Rupert Hart-Davis, 1949.

Kluckhorn, Frank L. *The Mexican Challenge*. New York: Doubleday, Doran, 1939.

Knightley, Phillip. *The First Casualty: From Crimea to Vietnam, The War Correspondent as Hero, Propagandist, and Myth Maker*. New York: Harcourt, Brace, 1975.

Knox, Ronald. *The Belief of Catholics*. London: Benn, 1927.

—— *God and the Atom*. New York: Sheed and Ward, 1945.

Koestler, Arthur. *The Yogi and the Commissar*. London: Macmillan, 1945.

—— *The Invisible Writing*. London: William Collins, 1954.

Lancaster, Marie-Jacqueline, ed. *Brian Howard: Portrait of a Failure*. London: Anthony Blond, 1968.

Large, Andrew. *The Artificial Language Movement*. Oxford: Basil Blackwell, 1985.

Lawrence, D. H. *Phoenix: The Posthumous Papers of D. H. Lawrence*, ed. Edward D. McDonald. New York: Viking, 1936.

Leff, Leonard J. and Jerold L. Simmons. *The Dame in the Kimono: Hollywood, Censorship, and the Production Code from the 1920s to the 1960s*. New York: Grove Weidenfeld, 1990.

Lehmann, John. *The Whispering Gallery: Autobiography I*. London: Longmans, Green, 1955.

—— *The Ample Proposition: Autobiography III*. London: Eyre & Spottiswoode, 1966.

Leitch, David. 'Explosion at the King David Hotel: Britain and the problem of Palestine'. In Sissons and French, 55–79.

Lewis, C. Day, ed. *The Mind in Chains*. London: Frederick Muller, 1937.

Lewis, Peter. *A People's War*. London: Thames Methuen, 1986.

Lewis, Roy and Angus Maude. *The English Middle Classes*. 1949; New York: Knopf, 1950.

Lewis, Wyndham. *The Doom of Youth*. 1932; facs. rpn. New York: Haskell House, 1973.

Lewis, Wyndham and Roy Campbell. *Satire and Fiction*. London: Arthur Press, 1930.

Linck, Charles E. 'The Public View of Waugh's Conversion'. In R. M. Davis, ed., *Evelyn Waugh*. Christian Critic Series. St Louis: Herder, n.d., 25–32.

Littlewood, Ian. *The Writings of Evelyn Waugh*. Totowa: Barnes & Noble, 1983.

Loss, Archie. '*Vile Bodies*, Vorticism, and Italian Futurism'. *Journal of Modern Literature*, 18: 1 (Winter 1992), 155–64.

Lovat, Simon Fraser, Baron. *March Past: A Memoir*. London: Widenfeld and Nicolson, 1979.

Lucas, Richard C. *The Forgotten Holocaust: The Poles Under German Occupation, 1939–44*. Lexington: University Press of Kentucky, 1986.

Lunn, Arnold. 'Evelyn Waugh Revisited'. *National Review*, 27 Feb. 1968, 189–90, 205.

Lynch, James J. '*The Loved One* and the Art Guide of Forest Lawn'. EWN 17: 3 (Winter 1983), 1–5.

—— 'Evelyn Waugh During the Pinfold Years'. *Modern Fiction Studies*, 32: 4 (Winter 1986), 543–59.

McCartney, George. *Confused Roaring: Evelyn Waugh and the Modernist Tradition.* Blooming-
ton: Indiana University Press, 1987.

McNamara, Jack Donald. *Literary Agent A. D. Peters and Evelyn Waugh 1928–1966: 'Quantitative Judgments Don't Apply'.* PhD Dissestation University of Texas (Austin), 1983.

Macaulay, Rose. 'The Best and the Worst II: Evelyn Waugh'. *Horizon,* Dec. 1946,
360–76.

Martin, David. *The Web of Disinformation: Churchill's Yugoslav Blunder.* New York: Harcourt
Brace, 1990.

Martin, Kingsley. *Editor: A Second Volume of Autobiography, 1931–45.* London: Hutchinson,
1968.

Martindale, C. C., SJ. *The Life of Monsignor Robert Hugh Benson.* 2 vols. London: Longmans,
1916.

Marshall, David and Demetrius Manousos. 'Evelyn Waugh Comments on *Helena*'. *Anno
Domini,* 1: 1 (1950), 5–9.

Meckier, Jerome. 'Why the Man Who Liked Dickens Reads Dickens Instead of Conrad:
Waugh's *A Handful of Dust*'. *Novel,* 13: 2 (1980), 171–87.

—— 'Evelyn Waugh's "Ryder by Gaslight": A Postmortem'. *Twentieth Century Literature,*
31: 4 (1985), 399–409.

Mercier, Désiré, Cardinal. *Modernism.* London: Burns & Oates, 1910.

Merton, Thomas. *The Waters of Siloe.* New York: Harcourt, Brace, 1949.

Miles, Peter. 'Improving Culture: The Politics of Illustration in Evelyn Waugh's *Love
Among the Ruins*'. *Trivium,* 18 (May 1983), 7–38.

Mitford, Nancy. *Love from Nancy: The Letters of Nancy Mitford,* ed. Charlotte Mosley. Boston:
Houghton Mifflin, 1993.

Morgan, Ted. *Maugham.* New York: Simon and Schuster, 1980.

Mosley, Diana. *Loved Ones: Pen Portraits.* London: Sidgwick & Jackson, 1985.

Myddleton, D. R. *The Power to Destroy: A Study of the British Tax System.* London: Johnson
Publications, 1969.

Myers, William. *Evelyn Waugh and the Problem of Evil.* London: Faber, 1991.

Newman, John Henry. *Sermons Bearing on Subjects of the Day.* London: Longmans, Green,
1891.

Nietzsche, Friedrich. "The Twilight of the Idols" and "The Anti-Christ", trans. R. J.
Hollingdale. Harmondsworth: Penguin, 1968.

O'Brien, Conor Cruise. *Maria Cross: Imaginative Patterns in a Group of Modern Catholic Writers.*
2nd edn. London: Burns & Oates, 1963.

O'Connell, Marvin R. *Critics on Trial: An Introduction to the Catholic Modernist Crisis.* Washington, D.C.: Catholic University Press of America, 1994.

O'Connor, Flannery. *Collected Works,* ed. Sally Fitzgerald. New York: Library of America,
1988.

O'Faolain, Sean. *The Vanishing Hero: Studies in Novelists of the Twenties.* London: Eyre &
Spottiswoode, 1956.

O'Hare, Colman. 'The Sacred and Profane Memories of Evelyn Waugh's Men at War'.
Papers on Language and Literature, 20: 3 (1984), 301–11.

Orwell, George. *The Road to Wigan Pier.* 1937; Harmondsworth: Penguin, 1962.

—— *Coming Up for Air.* 1939; New York: Harcourt, Brace, 1950.

—— *The Lion and the Unicorn.* London: Secker & Warburg, 1941.

—— *The Collected Essays, Journalism, and Letters of George Orwell.* 4 vols. New York: Harcourt,
Brace, 1968.

Pakenham, Frank, Earl of Longford. *Born to Believe: An Autobiography.* London: Jonathan
Cape, 1953.

Panofsky, Erwin. 'Et in Arcadia Ego: Poussin and the Elegiac Tradition'. In *Meaning in the Visual Arts*. New York: Doubleday, 1955, 295–320.

The Papal Encyclicals 1903–1939, ed. Claudia Ihm. Ann Arbor: Pierian Press, 1990.

Patey, Douglas Lane. '"Love Deny'd": Pope and the Allegory of Despair'. *Eighteenth-Century Studies*, 20: 1 (1986), 34–55.

Phillips, Gene D. *Evelyn Waugh's Officers, Gentlemen, and Rogues*. Chicago: Nelson-Hall, 1975.

Pick, John. 'London Letter'. *Renascence*, 9: 1 (1956), 3–25.

Porter, Bernard. *Britannia's Burden: The Political Evolution of Modern Britain 1851–1990*. London: Edward Arnold, 1994.

Powell, Anthony. *Infants of the Spring*. New York: Holt, 1977.

—— *Messengers of Day*. London: Heinemann, 1978.

—— *Faces in My Time*. London: Heinemann, 1980.

Prescott, Orville. In *My Opinion: An Inquiry into the Contemporary Novel*. 1942; Indianapolis: Bobbs-Merrill, 1952.

Priestley, J. B. *Blackout in Gretley*. New York: Sun Dial Press, 1942.

—— *All England Listened: The Wartime Broadcasts of J. B. Priestley*. New York: Chilmark Press, 1968.

Pritchett, V. S., Elizabeth Bowen and Graham Greene. *Why Do I Write?* London: Percival Marshall, 1948.

Pryce-Jones, David. 'Towards the Cocktail Party: The conservatism of post-war writing'. In Sissons and French, 209–30.

—— *Unity Mitford: An Enquiry Into Her Life and the Frivolity of Evil*. New York: Dial, 1977.

—— *Cyril Connolly: Journal and Memoir*. London: Collins, 1983.

Puccio, Paul M. *Brothers of the Heart: Friendship in Victorian and Edwardian Schoolboy Narrative*. PhD. Dissertation, University of Massachusetts (Amherst), 1995.

Rabinovitz, Rubin. 'The Reaction against Modernism: Amis, Snow, Wilson'. *Columbia History of the British Novel*, ed. John Richetti. New York: Columbia University Press, 1994, 895–917.

Ritchie, Harry. *Success Stories: Literature and the Media in England, 1950–59*. London: Faber, 1988.

Robbins, Keith. *History, Religion and Identity in Modern Britain*. London: Hambleton Press, 1993.

Roberts, Michael, ed. *New Signatures: Poems by Several Hands*. London: Hogarth Press, 1932.

Ryan, Thomas C. 'A Talk with Evelyn Waugh'. *The Sign*, Aug. 1957, 41–3.

Sabatier, Paul. *Modernism: The Jowett Lectures, 1908*. New York: Scribner's, 1908.

St John, John. *To the War With Waugh*. London: Whittington, 1973.

Scott, Christina. *A Historian and His World: A Life of Christopher Dawson 1889–1970*. London: Sheed & Ward, 1984.

Searle, George M. 'Mr. Charles Johnston on Modernism'. *Catholic World*, Feb. 1908, 636–44.

Sharpe, J. A. *Judicial Punishment in England*. London: Faber, 1990.

Sheehan, Edward R. F. 'A Weekend with Waugh'. *Cornhill Magazine*, Summer 1960, 209–25.

Sinfield, Alan. *Literature Politics and Culture in Postwar Britain*. Oxford: Basil Blackwell, 1979.

Singh, Chaitram. *Guyana: Politics in a Plantation Society*. New York: Praeger, 1988.

Sissons, Michael and Philip French, eds. *The Age of Austerity*. London: Hodder and Stoughton, 1963.

Sitwell, Osbert. *Left Hand Right Hand! An Autobiography*. Vol. 1: *The Cruel Month*. London: Macmillan, 1945.

Skinner, James M. *The Cross and the Cinema: The Legion of Decency and the National Catholic Office for Motion Pictures, 1933–1970*. Westport, CT: Praeger, 1993.

Smith, Logan Pearsall. *Fine Writing*. S.P.E. Tract No. 46. Oxford: Clarendon Press, 1936.

Spark, Muriel. *The Comforters*. Philadelphia: Lippincott, 1957.

Spender, Stephen. *The Destructive Element: A Study of Modern Writers and Beliefs*. London: Cape, 1935.

The Creative Element: A Study of Vision, Despair and Orthodoxy among some Modern Writers. London: Hamish Hamilton, 1953.

—— 'On Literary Movements'. *Encounter*, Oct. 1953, 66–8.

—— *The Struggle of the Modern*. London: Hamish Hamilton, 1963.

——, et al. *The God that Failed*. New York: Harper, 1949.

Stanley, Arthur Penrhyn. *The Eastern Church*. London: John Murray, 1861.

Stannard, Martin. '*Work Suspended*: Evelyn Waugh's Climacteric'. *Essays in Criticism*, 28: 4 (1978), 302–20.

—— 'Debunking the Jungle: The Context of Evelyn Waugh's Travel Books 1930–39'. *Prose Studies*, 5: 1 (May 1982), 105–26.

—— 'The Mystery of the Missing Manuscript'. *Times Higher Education Supplement*, 1 June 1984, 13.

Stokes, Adrian. *The Thread of Ariadne*. London: Kegan Paul, 1925.

Stopp, Frederick J. 'Grace in Reins: Reflections on Mr. Waugh's *Brideshead* and *Helena*'. *Month*, Aug. 1953, 69–84.

—— 'The Circle and the Tangent: An Interpretation of Mr. Waugh's *Men at Arms*'. *Month*, July 1954, 17–34.

—— *Evelyn Waugh: Portrait of an Artist*. Boston: Little, Brown, 1958.

Strachey, John. *The Coming Struggle for Power*. 1932; London: Gollancz, 1934.

Sykes, Christopher. *Evelyn Waugh: A Biography*. 1975; Harmondsworth: Penguin, 1977.

Symons, Julian. *The Thirties: A Dream Revolved*. London: Cresset, 1960.

Teichmann, Howard. *Smart Aleck: The Work, World and Life of Alexander Woollcott*. New York: Morrow, 1976.

Thirkell, Angela. *Peace Breaks Out*. London: Hamish Hamilton, 1946.

—— *Love Among the Ruins*. London: Hamish Hamilton, 1948.

Upward, Edward. 'Sketch for a Marxist Interpretation of Literature'. In C. Day Lewis, ed., *The Mind in Chains*, 39–55.

Van Zeller, Dom Hubert. 'An Appreciation of Evelyn Waugh'. *Downside Review*, July 1966, 285–7.

Waley, Hubert. *The Revival of Aesthetics*. London: Hogarth Press, 1926.

Wallace, Henry, et al. *Prefaces to Peace*. New York: Simon & Schuster, Doubleday, Reynal & Hitchcock, and Columbia University Press, 1943.

Ward, Wilfrid. *The Life of John Henry, Cardinal Newman, Based on his Private Journals and Correspondence*. 2 vols. London: Longmans, Green, 1912.

Wasson, Richard. '*A Handful of Dust*: Critique of Victorianism'. In Carens, *Critical Essays*, 133–43.

Watson, John. 'The Prison System'. In Leon Radzinowicz, ed., *Penal Reform in England*. London: P. S. King, 1940, 152–69.

Waugh, Alec. *The Early Years of Alec Waugh*. London: Cassell, 1962.

—— *My Brother Evelyn and Other Profiles*. London: Cassell, 1967.

—— *The Best Wine Last*. London: W. H. Allen 1978.

Waugh, Arthur. *One Man's Road: Being a Picture of Life in a Passing Generation*. London: Chapman and Hall, 1931.

Waugh, Auberon. 'A Death in the Family'. *Spectator*, 6 May 1966, 562–3.

—— 'Laura Waugh 1916–1973'. *Antigonish Review*, 54 (1984): 27–32.

—— *Will This Do? The First Fifty Years of Auberon Waugh: An Autobiography*. London: Century, 1991.

West, Rebecca. *Ending in Earnest: A Literary Log*. New York: Doubleday, Doran, 1931.

—— *The Meaning of Treason*. Revised. edn. London: Pan Books, 1956.

Wheen, Francis. *Tom Driberg: His Life and Indiscretions*. London: Chatto & Windus, 1990.

White, T. H. *The Age of Scandal: An Excursion through a Minor Period*. New York: Putnam, 1950.

Wilson, A. N. *Hilaire Belloc*. New York: Athenaeum, 1984.

Wilson, Edmund. *Travels in Two Democracies*. New York: Harcourt, Brace, 1936.

Wolfe, Tom. *From Bauhaus to Our House*. New York: Farrar Straus Giroux, 1981.

Woolf, Virginia. 'Modern Fiction'. In *The Common Reader*. New York: Harcourt, Brace, 1925, 207–18.

Woollcott, Alexander. *The Letters of Alexander Woollcott*, ed. B. Kaufman and J. Hennessey. New York: Garden City Publishing Co., 1946.

Wykes, David. 'Evelyn Waugh's Sword of Volgograd'. *Dutch Quarterly Review of Anglo-American Letters*, 7: 2 (1977), 82–99.

Index